Programming Ruby 1.9 & 2.0

The Pragmatic Programmers' Guide

Dave Thomas
with Chad Fowler
Andy Hunt

The Pragmatic Bookshelf

Dallas, Texas • Raleigh, North Carolina

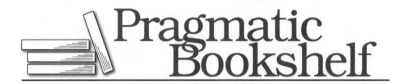

Many of the designations used by manufacturers and sellers to distinguish their products are claimed as trademarks. Where those designations appear in this book, and The Pragmatic Programmers, LLC was aware of a trademark claim, the designations have been printed in initial capital letters or in all capitals. The Pragmatic Starter Kit, The Pragmatic Programmer, Pragmatic Programming, Pragmatic Bookshelf, PragProg and the linking *g* device are trademarks of The Pragmatic Programmers, LLC.

Every precaution was taken in the preparation of this book. However, the publisher assumes no responsibility for errors or omissions, or for damages that may result from the use of information (including program listings) contained herein.

Our Pragmatic courses, workshops, and other products can help you and your team create better software and have more fun. For more information, as well as the latest Pragmatic titles, please visit us at *http://pragprog.com*.

The team that produced this book includes:

Janet Furlow (producer)
Juliet Benda (rights)
Ellie Callahan (support)

Printed in the United States of America.
ISBN-13: 978-1-93778-549-9
Printed on acid-free paper.
Book version: P1.0—June, 2013

Contents

Part II — Ruby in Its Setting

Part III — Ruby Crystallized

Part IV — Ruby Library Reference

Foreword to the Third Edition

I wrote forewords to the previous two editions of this book. For the first edition, I wrote about motivation. For the second edition, I wrote about miracles.

For this third edition, I'd like to write about courage. I always admire brave people. People around Ruby seem to be brave, like the authors of this book. They were brave to jump in to a relatively unknown language like Ruby. They were brave to try new technology. They could have happily stayed with an old technology, but they didn't. They built their own world using new bricks and mortar. They were adventurers, explorers, and pioneers. By their effort, we have a fruitful result—Ruby.

Now, I feel that I've created my own universe with help from those brave people. At first, I thought it was a miniature universe, like the one in "Fessenden's Worlds." But now it seems like a real universe. Countless brave people are now working with Ruby. They challenge new things every day, trying to make the world better and bigger. I am very glad I am part of the Ruby world.

I suppose that even the world itself could not contain the books that should be written. But now we have the first book, updated to the most recent. Enjoy.

Yukihiro Matsumoto, aka "Matz"
Japan, February 2009
まつもと ゆきひろ

Preface

This book is a new version of the PickAxe, as *Programming Ruby* is known to Ruby programmers. It is a tutorial and reference for versions 1.9 and 2.0 of the Ruby programming language.

Ruby 1.9 was a significant departure from previous versions. There are major changes in string handling, the scoping of block variables, and the threading model. It has a new virtual machine. The built-in libraries have grown, adding many hundreds of new methods and almost a dozen new classes. The language now supports scores of character encodings, making Ruby one of the only programming languages to live fully in the whole world.

Ruby 2.0 is a (fairly minor) incremental improvement on Ruby 1.9.

Why Ruby?

When Andy and I wrote the first edition, we had to explain the background and appeal of Ruby. Among other things, we wrote, "When we discovered Ruby, we realized that we'd found what we'd been looking for. More than any other language with which we have worked, Ruby *stays out of your way*. You can concentrate on solving the problem at hand, instead of struggling with compiler and language issues. That's how it can help you become a better programmer: by giving you the chance to spend your time creating solutions for your users, not for the compiler."

That belief is even stronger today. More than thirteen years later, Ruby is still my language of choice: I use it for client applications and web applications. I use it to run our publishing business (our online store, http://pragprog.com, is more than 40,000 lines of Rails code), and I use it for all those little programming jobs I do just to get things running smoothly.

In all those years, Ruby has progressed nicely. A large number of methods have been added to the built-in classes and modules, and the size of the standard library (those libraries included in the Ruby distribution) has grown tremendously. The community now has a standard documentation system (RDoc), and RubyGems has become the system of choice for packaging Ruby code for distribution. We have a best-of-breed web application framework, Ruby on Rails, with others waiting in the wings. We are leading the world when it comes to testing, with tools such as RSpec and Cucumber, and we're working through the hard problems of packaging and dependency management. We've matured nicely.

But Ruby is older than that. The first release of this book happened on Ruby's 20th birthday (it was created on February 24, 1993). The release of Ruby 2.0 is a celebration of that anniversary.

Ruby Versions

This version of the PickAxe documents both Ruby 2.0 and Ruby 1.9.3.[1]

Exactly what version of Ruby did I use to write this book? Let's ask Ruby:

```
$ ruby -v
ruby 2.0.0p0 (2013-02-24 revision 39474) [x86_64-darwin12.2.0]
```

This illustrates an important point. Most of the code samples you see in this book are actually executed each time I format the book. When you see some output from a program, that output was produced by running the code and inserting the results into the book.

Changes in the Book

New in 2.0

Throughout the book I've tried to mark differences between Ruby 1.9 and 2.0 using a small symbol, like the one here. If you're reading this as an ebook, you'll see little arrows next to this flag. Clicking those will take you to the next or previous 2.0 change. One change I didn't make: I decided to continue to use the word *we* when talking about the authors in the body of the book. Many of the words come from the first edition, and I certainly don't want to claim any credit for Andy's work on that book.

Changes in the Ruby 2.0 Printing

Compared to the major change that occurred between Ruby 1.8 and Ruby 1.9, the update to Ruby 2 is fairly gentle. This book documents all the updated builtin class changes and the new keyword arguments. It spends some time looking at lazy enumerators, and at the updates to the regular expression engine. But, in general, users of Ruby 1.9 will feel right at home, and folks still using Ruby 1.8 should consider skipping straight to Ruby 2.

Resources

Visit the Ruby website at http://www.ruby-lang.org to see what's new. Chat with other Ruby users on the newsgroup or mailing lists (see Appendix 1, *Support*, on page 829).

And I'd certainly appreciate hearing from you. Comments, suggestions, errors in the text, and problems in the examples are all welcome. Email us at rubybook@pragprog.com.

If you find errors in the book, you can add them to the errata page.[2] If you're reading the PDF version of the book, you can also report an erratum by clicking the link in the page footers.

You'll find links to the source code for almost all the book's example code at http://www.prag-prog.com/titles/ruby4.

---

1.   Ruby version numbering used to follow the same scheme used for many other open source projects. Releases with even minor version numbers—1.6, 1.8, and so on—were stable, public releases. These are the releases that are prepackaged and made available on the various Ruby websites. Development versions of the software had odd minor version numbers, such as 1.5 and 1.7. However, in 2007 Matz broke with convention and made 1.9 a stable public release of Ruby.

2.   http://www.pragprog.com/titles/ruby4/errata.html

Acknowledgments

The first International Ruby Conference had something like 32 attendees. We could all fit into the tiny hotel bar and talk the night away. Things have changed. The annual conference now sells out many hundreds of seats within hours, and an increasing number of secondary conferences have sprung up to meet the needs of folks who can't get to RubyConf.

As the community has grown, so has Ruby. The language and its libraries are now many times bigger than they were back when the first edition of this book came out.

And as the language has grown, so has this book. The PickAxe is now massive, mostly because I still want to document every single built-in class, module, and method. But a book of this size can never be a solo undertaking. This edition builds on the work from the first two editions, which included major contributions from Chad Fowler and Andy Hunt. Just as significant, all three editions have been works created by the Ruby community. On the mailing lists, in the forums, and on this book's errata pages, hundreds of people have contributed ideas, code, and corrections to make it better. As always, I owe every one of you a big "thank you!" for all you have done and for all that you do. The Ruby community is still as vibrant, interesting, and (mostly) friendly as it ever was—that's quite an achievement given the explosive growth we've enjoyed.

For the third (tenth anniversary) printing, Wayne E. Seguin was kind enough to check the section on the wonderful tool RVM, and Luis Lavena checked the section on installing under Windows, as well as the chapter on running Ruby on Windows. And I'd like to call Anthony Burns a hero for doing an amazing job of reading through the changes as I was writing them, but that would take away from the fact that he's a true hero.[3]

Getting this book into production has also been a challenge. Kim Wimpsett is the world's best copy editor—she's the only copy editor I know who finds errors in code and fixes XML markup. Any remaining errors in this book are a result of my mistyping her suggested corrections. And, as we raced to get the book to the printer in time for RubyConf X, Janet Furlow patiently kept us all on track.

Finally, I'm still deeply indebted to Yukihiro "Matz" Matsumoto, the creator of Ruby. Throughout this prolonged period of growth and change, he has remained helpful, cheery, and dedicated to polishing this gem of a language. The friendly and open spirit of the Ruby community is a direct reflection of the person at its center.

Thank you all. Domo arigato gozaimasu.

Dave Thomas
The Pragmatic Programmers
dave@pragprog.com
June 2013

3.　http://www.flickr.com/photos/pragdave/sets/72157625046498937/

Notation Conventions

Literal code examples are shown using a sans-serif font:

```
class SampleCode
  def run
    #...
  end
end
```

Within the text, Fred#do_something is a reference to an instance method (in this case the method do_something) of class Fred, Fred.new[4] is a class method, and Fred::EOF is a class constant. The decision to use a hash character to indicate instance methods was a tough one. It isn't valid Ruby syntax, but we thought that it was important to differentiate between the instance and class methods of a particular class. When you see us write File.read, you know we're talking about the class method read. When instead we write File#read, we're referring to the instance method read. This convention is now standard in most Ruby discussions and documentation.

This book contains many snippets of Ruby code. Where possible, we've tried to show what happens when they run. In simple cases, we show the value of expressions on the same line as the expression. Here's an example:

```
a = 1
b = 2
a + b       # => 3
```

Here, you can see that the result of evaluating a + b is the value 3, shown to the right of the arrow. Note that if you were to run this program, you wouldn't see the value 3 output— you'd need to use a method such as puts to write it out.

At times, we're also interested in the values of assignment statements:

```
a = 1       # => 1
a + 2       # => 3
```

If the program produces more complex output, we show it after the program code:

```
3.times { puts "Hello!" }
```

produces:

```
Hello!
Hello!
Hello!
```

In some of the library documentation, we wanted to show where spaces appear in the output. You'll see these spaces as ␣ characters.

Command-line invocations are shown with literal text in a regular font, and parameters you supply are shown in an *italic* font. Optional elements are shown in brackets.

ruby ‹ *flags* ›* *progname* ‹ *arguments* ›*

---

4.   In some other Ruby documentation, you may see class methods written as Fred::new. This is perfectly valid Ruby syntax; we just happen to think that Fred.new is less distracting to read.

Road Map

The main text of this book has four separate parts, each with its own personality and each addressing different aspects of the Ruby language.

In *Part I, Facets of Ruby*, you'll find a Ruby tutorial. It starts with some notes on getting Ruby running on your system followed by a short chapter on some of the terminology and concepts that are unique to Ruby. This chapter also includes enough basic syntax so that the other chapters will make sense. The rest of the tutorial is a top-down look at the language. There we talk about classes and objects, types, expressions, and all the other things that make up the language. We end with chapters on unit testing and digging yourself out when trouble strikes.

One of the great things about Ruby is how well it integrates with its environment. *Part II, Ruby in Its Setting*, investigates this. Here you'll find practical information on using Ruby: using the interpreter options, using irb, documenting your Ruby code, and packaging your Ruby gems so that others can enjoy them. You'll also find tutorials on some common Ruby tasks: using Ruby with the Web and using Ruby in a Microsoft Windows environment (including wonderful things such as native API calls, COM integration, and Windows Automation). We'll also touch on using Ruby to access the Internet.

Part III, Ruby Crystallized, contains more advanced material. Here you'll find all the gory details about the language, the concept of *duck typing*, the object model, metaprogramming, tainting, reflection, and marshaling. You could probably speed-read this the first time through, but we think you'll come back to it as you start to use Ruby in earnest.

The *Ruby Library Reference* is Part IV. It's big. We document more than 1,300 methods in 57 built-in classes and modules (up from 800 methods in 40 classes and modules in the previous edition). On top of that, we now document the library modules that are included in the standard Ruby distribution (98 of them).

So, how should you read this book? Well, depending on your level of expertise with programming in general and OO in particular, you may initially want to read just a few portions of the book. Here are our recommendations.

If you're a beginner, you may want to start with the tutorial material in Part I. Keep the library reference close at hand as you start to write programs. Get familiar with the basic classes such as Array, Hash, and String. As you become more comfortable in the environment, you may want to investigate some of the more advanced topics in Part III.

If you're already comfortable with Perl, Python, Java, or Smalltalk, then we suggest reading Chapter 1, *Getting Started*, on page 3, which talks about installing and running Ruby, followed by the introduction in Chapter 2, *Ruby.new*, on page 15. From there, you may want to take the slower approach and keep going with the tutorial that follows, or you can skip ahead to the gritty details starting in Part III, followed by the library reference in Part IV.

Experts, gurus, and "I-don't-need-no-stinking-tutorial" types can dive straight into the language reference in Chapter 22, *The Ruby Language*, on page 297; skim the library reference; and then use the book as a (rather attractive) coffee coaster.

Of course, nothing is wrong with just starting at the beginning and working your way through page by page.

And don't forget, if you run into a problem that you can't figure out, help is available. For more information, see Appendix 1, *Support*, on page 829.

Part I

Facets of Ruby

## CHAPTER 1

Getting Started

Before we start talking about the Ruby language, it would be useful if we helped you get Ruby running on your computer. That way, you can try sample code and experiment on your own as you read along. In fact, that's probably essential if you want to learn Ruby—get into the habit of writing code as you're reading. We will also show you some different ways to run Ruby.

1.1 The Command Prompt

(Feel free to skip to the next section if you're already comfortable at your system's command prompt.)

Although there's growing support for Ruby in IDEs, you'll probably still end up spending some time at your system's command prompt, also known as a *shell prompt* or just plain *prompt*. If you're a Linux user, you're probably already familiar with the prompt. If you don't already have a desktop icon for it, hunt around for an application called Terminal or xterm. (On Ubuntu, you can navigate to it using Applications → Accessories → Terminal.) On Windows, you'll want to run cmd.exe, accessible by typing cmd into the dialog box that appears when you select Start → Run. On OS X, run Applications → Utilities → Terminal.app.

In all three cases, a fairly empty window will pop up. It will contain a banner and a prompt. Try typing echo hello at the prompt and hitting Enter (or Return, depending on your keyboard). You should see hello echoed back, and another prompt should appear.

Directories, Folders, and Navigation

It is beyond the scope of this book to teach the commands available at the prompt, but we do need to cover the basics of finding your way around.

If you're used to a GUI tool such as Explorer on Windows or Finder on OS X for navigating to your files, then you'll be familiar with the idea of *folders*—locations on your hard drive that can hold files and other folders.

When you're at the command prompt, you have access to these same folders. But, somewhat confusingly, at the prompt these folders are called *directories* (because they contain lists of other directories and files). These directories are organized into a strict hierarchy. On Unix-based systems (including OS X), there's one top-level directory, called / (a forward slash). On Windows, there is a top-level directory for each drive on your system, so you'll find the top level for your C: drive at C:\ (that's the drive letter C, a colon, and a backslash).

The path to a file or directory is the set of directories that you have to traverse to get to it from the top-level directory, followed by the name of the file or directory itself. Each component in this name is separated by a forward slash (on Unix) or a backslash (on Windows). So, if you organized your projects in a directory called projects under the top-level directory and if the projects directory had a subdirectory for your time_planner project, the full path to the README file would be /projects/time_planner/readme.txt on Unix and C:\projects\time_planner\readme.txt on Windows.

Spaces in Directory Names and Filenames

Most operating systems now allow you to create folders with spaces in their names. This is great when you're working at the GUI level. However, from the command prompt, spaces can be a headache, because the shell that interprets what you type will treat the spaces in file and folder names as being parameter separators and not as part of the name. You can get around this, but it generally isn't worth the hassle. If you are creating new folders and files, it's easiest to avoid spaces in their names.

To navigate to a directory, use the cd command. (Because the Unix prompt varies from system to system, we'll just use a single dollar sign to represent it here.)

```
$ cd /projects/time_planner        (on Unix)
C:\> cd \projects\time_planner      (on Windows)
```

On Unix boxes, you probably don't want to be creating top-level directories. Instead, Unix gives each user their own *home directory*. So, if your username is dave, your home directory might be located in /usr/dave, /home/dave, or /Users/dave. At the shell prompt, the special character ~ (a single tilde) stands for the path to your home directory. You can always change directories to your home directory using cd ~, which can also be abbreviated to just cd.

To find out the directory you're currently in, you can type pwd (on Unix) or cd on Windows. So, for Unix users, you could type this:

```
$ cd /projects/time_planner
$ pwd
/projects/time_planner
$ cd
$ pwd
/Users/dave
```

On Windows, there's no real concept of a user's home directory:

```
C:\> cd \projects\time_planner
C:\projects\time_planner> cd \projects
C:\projects>
```

You can create a new directory under the current directory using the mkdir command:

```
$ cd /projects
$ mkdir expense_tracker
$ cd expense_tracker
$ pwd
/projects/expense_tracker
```

Notice that to change to the new directory, we could just give its name relative to the current directory—we don't have to enter the full path.

We suggest you create a directory called pickaxe to hold the code you write while reading this book:

```
$ mkdir ~/pickaxe        (on Unix)
C:\> mkdir \pickaxe      (on Windows)
```

Get into the habit of changing into that directory before you start work:

```
$ cd ~/pickaxe           (on Unix)
C:\> cd \pickaxe         (on Windows)
```

1.2 Installing Ruby

Ruby comes preinstalled on many Linux distributions, and Mac OS X includes Ruby (although the version of Ruby that comes with OS X is normally several releases behind the current Ruby version). Try typing ruby -v at a command prompt—you may be pleasantly surprised.

If you don't already have Ruby on your system or if you'd like to upgrade to a newer version (remembering that this book describes Ruby 1.9 and Ruby 2.0), you can install it pretty simply. What you do next depends on your operating system.

Installing on Windows

There are two options for installing Ruby on Windows. The first is a simple installer package—download it, and you'll have Ruby up and running in minutes. The second is slightly more complex but gives you the flexibility of easily managing multiple Ruby environments on the same computer at the same time. Whichever option you choose, you'll first need to download and install a working Ruby.

Install Ruby with RubyInstaller

The simple solution (and probably the right one to use if you're not planning on running multiple versions of Ruby at the same time) is Luis Lavena's RubyInstaller.org.

Simply navigate to http://rubyinstaller.org, click the big DOWNLOAD button, and select the Ruby version you want. Save the file to your downloads folder, and then run it once it has downloaded. Click through the Windows nanny warnings, and you'll come to a conventional installer. Accept the defaults, and when the installer finishes, you'll have an entry for Ruby in your *All Programs* menu of the Start menu:

Select *Start Command Prompt with Ruby* to open a copy of the Windows command shell with the environment set up to run Ruby.

pik: Install Multiple Ruby Environments

The pik system by Gordon Thiesfeld allows you to manage multiple Ruby interpreters on the same machine, switching between them easily. Obviously, this isn't something everyone needs, so you may want to skip to *Source Code from This Book* on page 9.

Before you start, make sure you have a working Ruby on your machine, using the instructions from the previous section to download and use RubyInstaller if necessary.

Then, install pik. Visit http://github.com/vertiginous/pik/downloads. Look near the top for the list of .msi files, and choose the latest. Double-click the filename to download and install it.

After a few seconds, the Pik Setup dialog box will appear. Accept the defaults, and pik will be installed.

At this time, you'll probably need to either log out and log back in or (possibly) restart Windows to get pik successfully integrated into your environment.

Now bring up a Ruby command prompt (*Start Command Prompt with Ruby*), and type the following at the prompt:

```
C:\Users\dave> pik add
** Adding: 193: ruby 1.9.3p0 (2011-10-30) [i386-mingw32]
```

You've now registered that Ruby interpreter with pik. At any other command prompt, you can use the pik command to list the Ruby interpreters pik knows about and to tell pik to make a particular interpreter current:

```
C:\>pik list
  193: ruby 1.9.3p0 (2011-10-30) [i386-mingw32]

C:\>pik use 193

C:\>ruby -v
ruby 1.9.3p0 (2011-10-30) [i386-mingw32]
```

Having gotten one Ruby registered with pik, let's install another. We'll play with JRuby, an implementation of Ruby written in Java. Before doing this, you'll need to download the Java runtime (Google is your friend). Once Java is installed, tell pik to install the JRuby interpreter:

```
C:\> pik install jruby
** Downloading:  http://jruby.org......downloads/1.5.2/jruby-bin-1.5.2.zip
to:  C:\Users\dave\.pik\downloads\jruby-bin-1.5.2.zip
** Extracting:  C:\Users\dave\.pik\downloads\jruby-bin-1.5.2.zip
to:  C:\Users\dave\.pik\rubies\JRuby-152
done

** Adding:  152: jruby 1.5.2 (ruby 1.8.7 patchlevel 249) (2010-08-20 1c5e29d)
(Java HotSpot(TM) Client VM 1.6.0_21) [x86-java]
Located at:  C:\Users\dave\.pik\rubies\JRuby-152\bin
```

You now have two Ruby interpreters managed by pik. You can switch between them at the command line:

```
C:\>pik list
  152: jruby 1.5.2 (ruby 1.8.7 patchlevel 249) (2010-08-20 1c5e29d) (Java H...
  193: ruby 1.9.3p0 (2011-10-30) [i386-mingw32]
```

```
C:\>pik use 152
C:\>jruby -v
jruby 1.5.2 (ruby 1.8.7 patchlevel 249) (2010-08-20 1c5e29d)
(Java HotSpot(TM)  Client VM 1.6.0_21) [x86-java]

C:\>pik use 193
C:\>ruby -v
ruby 1.9.3p0 (2011-10-30) [i386-mingw32]
```

If you plan on installing gems that have native code components (that is, they interface to existing Windows libraries using C code), you'll need a C development environment on your machine, and you'll need to download and install the Pik development kit.

Now that you're all set up, skip forward to *Source Code from This Book* on page 9.

Installing on Linux and Mac OS X

One of the interesting things about the various Unix-like systems out there is that their maintainers all have their own ideas about how to package tools such as Ruby. It is very nice that they have gone to this trouble, but it also means that if you go with the flow, you'll need to learn their way of doing things. It also often means that you'll be stuck with what you're given. So, we're going to take a different approach. We're going to use a system called the Ruby Version Manager (RVM), written by Wayne E. Seguin. RVM is a tool that lets you have multiple independent Ruby installations on the same machine. You can switch between them using a single command. This is wonderful, because you can experiment with new versions of Ruby while still keeping the old ones on your system. We use RVM to keep a Ruby environment for the examples in this book that's isolated from our daily work.[1]

Installing RVM

Although you can install RVM using RubyGems (assuming you already have a working Ruby on your system), the preferred approach is to install it directly.

Most Unix-like systems will already have all the dependencies installed.[2] The possible fly in the ointment is Ubuntu, where the curl utility is not installed by default. Add it before you start with this:

```
$ sudo apt-get update
$ sudo apt-get install curl
```

You install RVM by executing a script that you download from its repository in github.

```
$ curl -L https://get.rvm.io | bash -s stable
```

If this makes you nervous, you can always download the script first, inspect it, and then run it.

```
$ curl -L get.rvm.io >rvm-installer
$ less rvm-installer
$ bash rvm-installer
```

---

1. RVM isn't the only way of managing multiple Ruby installations. You might want to look at rbenv (https://github.com/sstephenson/rbenv/) or chruby (https://github.com/postmodern/chruby).
2. http://rvm.io/rvm/prerequisites/

Behind the scenes, either option fetches a script from the RVM git repository and executes it on your local box. The end result is that RVM is installed in a directory named .rvm beneath your home directory. At the end of the process, RVM spits out a page or so of information. You should read it.

You may need to knit RVM into your environment. To find out, have a look at the end of ~/.bashrc. If it doesn't mention RVM, add the following:

```
source $HOME/.rvm/scripts/rvm
```

Once that's done, start a new terminal window (because RVM gets loaded only when your .bashrc file executes). Type rvm help, and you should get a summary of RVM usage.[3]

Before we use RVM to install Ruby, we have to let it install a few things that it will need. To do that, we need to let RVM install various system libraries and utilities that are used when building Ruby. First, we have to give it permission to manage packages:

```
dave@ubuntu:~$ rvm autolibs packages
```

If you run into problems, Wayne has a great set of hints on the RVM installation page.[4]

Installing Ruby 2.0 Under RVM

This is where we start to see the payoff. Let's install Ruby 2.0. (Note that in the following commands we do not type sudo. One of the joys of RVM is that it does everything inside your home directory—you don't have to be privileged to install or use new Ruby versions.)

```
$ rvm install 2.0.0
```

RVM first installs the system packages it needs (if any). At this stage, you may be prompted to enter a password that gives you superuser privileges.[5]

RVM then downloads the appropriate source code and builds Ruby 2.0. It also installs a few tools (including irb, RDoc, ri, and RubyGems). Be patient—the process may take five minutes or so. Once it finishes, you'll have Ruby 2.0 installed. To use it, type the following:

```
dave@ubuntu:~$ rvm use 2.0.0
info: Using ruby 2.0.0
dave@ubuntu:~$ ruby -v
ruby 2.0.0p0 (2013-02-24 revision 39474) [i686-linux]
```

This is probably more work than you were expecting. If all you wanted to do was install a prepacked Ruby, we'd agree. But what you've really done here is given yourself an incredible amount of flexibility. Maybe in the future a project comes along that requires that you use Ruby 1.8.7. That's not a problem—just use rvm install 1.8.7 to install it, and use rvm use 1.8.7 to switch to it.

The rvm use command applies only to the current terminal session. If you want to make it apply to all your sessions, issue this command:

```
$ rvm use --default 2.0.0
```

---

3. The website, http://rvm.io/, has even more information.
4. http://rvm.io/rvm/install/
5. This is the only time you'll need these privileges. Once your system has all the tools it needs, RVM can do the rest of its work as a regular user.

The RubyGems that you install while you're using an RVM-installed Ruby will be added to that version of Ruby and not installed globally. Do not prepend the gem install command with a sudo—bad things will happen.

Why Stop with Ruby 2.0?

As well as installing stable versions of the Matz Ruby interpreter, RVM will also manage interpreters from different sources (JRuby, Rubinius, Ruby Enterprise Edition, and so on—rvm list known gives the full list). It will also install versions of Ruby directly from the developers' repository—versions that are not official releases.

The Ruby developers use Subversion (often abbreviated as SVN) as their revision control system, so you'll need a Subversion client installed on your machine. Once done, you can use RVM to install the very latest Ruby using rvm install ruby-head or the latest version of the 2.0 branch using rvm install 2.0-head.

Source Code from This Book

If a code listing is preceded by a filename in a shaded bar, the source is available for download.[6] Sometimes, the listings of code in the book correspond to a complete source file. Other times, the book shows just part of the source in a file—the program file may contain additional scaffolding to make the code run.

If you're reading this as an ebook, you can download the code for an example by clicking the heading.

1.3 Running Ruby

Now that Ruby is installed, you'd probably like to run some programs. Unlike compiled languages, you have two ways to run Ruby—you can type in code interactively, or you can create program files and run them. Typing in code interactively is a great way to experiment with the language, but for code that's more complex or that you will want to run more than once, you'll need to create program files and run them. But, before we go any further, let's test to see whether Ruby is installed. Bring up a fresh command prompt, and type this:[7]

```
$ ruby -v
ruby 2.0.0p0 (2013-02-24 revision 39474) [x86_64-darwin12.2.0]
```

If you believe that you should have Ruby installed and yet you get an error saying something like "ruby: command not found," then it is likely that the Ruby program is not in your path —the list of places that the shell searches for programs to run. If you used the Windows One-Click Installer, make sure you rebooted before trying this command. If you're on Linux or OS X and you're using RVM, make sure you type rvm use 2.0 before trying to use Ruby.

Interactive Ruby

One way to run Ruby interactively is simply to type ruby at the shell prompt. Here we typed in the single puts expression and an end-of-file character (which is Ctrl+D on our system).

---

6. http://pragprog.com/titles/ruby4/code
7. Remember, you may need to use ruby1.9 as the command name if you installed using a package management system.

This process works, but it's painful if you make a typo, and you can't really see what's going on as you type.

```
$ ruby
puts "Hello, world!"
^D
Hello, world!
```

For most folks, *irb*—Interactive Ruby—is the tool of choice for executing Ruby interactively. irb is a Ruby shell, complete with command-line history, line-editing capabilities, and job control. (In fact, it has its own chapter: Chapter 18, *Interactive Ruby Shell*, on page 253.) You run irb from the command line. Once it starts, just type in Ruby code. It will show you the value of each expression as it evaluates it. Exit an irb session by typing exit or by using the Ctrl+D.

```
$ irb
2.0.0 :001 > def sum(n1, n2)
2.0.0 :002?>     n1 + n2
2.0.0 :003?>   end
=> nil
2.0.0 :004 > sum(3,4)
=> 7
2.0.0 :005 > sum("cat", "dog")
=> "catdog"
2.0.0 :006 > exit
```

We recommend that you get familiar with irb so you can try our examples interactively.

Ruby Programs

The normal way to write Ruby programs is to put them in one or more files. You'll use a text editor (Emacs, vim, Sublime, and so on) or an IDE (such as NetBeans) to create and maintain these files. You'll then run the files either from within the editor or IDE or from the command line. I personally use both techniques, typically running from within the editor for single-file programs and from the command line for more complex ones.

Let's start by creating a simple Ruby program and running it. Open a command window, and navigate to the pickaxe directory you created earlier:

```
$ cd ~/pickaxe          (unix)
C:\> cd \pickaxe        (windows)
```

Then, using your editor of choice, create the file myprog.rb, containing the following text.

```
gettingstarted/myprog.rb
puts "Hello, Ruby Programmer"
puts "It is now #{Time.now}"
```

(Note that the second string contains the text Time.now between curly braces, not parentheses.)

You can run a Ruby program from a file as you would any other shell script, Perl program, or Python program. Simply run the Ruby interpreter, giving it the script name as an argument:

```
$ ruby myprog.rb
Hello, Ruby Programmer
It is now 2013-05-27 12:30:36 -0500
```

On Unix systems, you can use the "shebang" notation as the first line of the program file:[8]

```
#!/usr/bin/ruby
puts "Hello, Ruby Programmer"
puts "It is now #{Time.now}"
```

If you make this source file executable (using, for instance, chmod +x myprog.rb), Unix lets you run the file as a program:

```
$ ./myprog.rb
Hello, Ruby Programmer
It is now 2013-05-27 12:30:36 -0500
```

You can do something similar under Microsoft Windows using file associations, and you can run Ruby GUI applications by double-clicking their names in Windows Explorer.

1.4 Ruby Documentation: RDoc and ri

As the volume of the Ruby libraries has grown, it has become impossible to document them all in one book; the standard library that comes with Ruby now contains more than 9,000 methods. Fortunately, an alternative to paper documentation exists for these methods (and classes and modules). Many are now documented internally using a system called *RDoc*.

If a source file is documented using RDoc, its documentation can be extracted and converted into HTML and ri formats.

Several websites contain a complete set of the RDoc documentation for Ruby.[9] Browse on over, and you should be able to find at least some form of documentation for any Ruby library. The sites are adding new documentation all the time.

The ri tool is a local, command-line viewer for this same documentation. Most Ruby distributions now also install the resources used by the ri program.[10]

To find the documentation for a class, type ri *ClassName*. For example, the following is the summary information for the GC class. (To get a list of classes with ri documentation, type ri with no arguments.)

```
$ ri GC
-------------------------------------------------------------------------------
The GC module provides an interface to Ruby's garbage collection mechanism. Some of
the underlying methods are also available via the ObjectSpace module.

You may obtain information about the operation of the GC through GC::Profiler.
-------------------------------------------------------------------------------
Class methods:
  count, disable, enable, malloc_allocated_size, malloc_allocations,
  start, stat, stress, stress=

Instance methods:
  garbage_collect
```

---

8. If your system supports it, you can avoid hard-coding the path to Ruby in the "shebang" line by using #!/usr/bin/env ruby, which will search your path for *ruby* and then execute it.
9. Including http://www.ruby-doc.org and http://rubydoc.info
10. If you installed Ruby using rvm, there's one additional step to get ri documentation available. At a prompt, enter rvm docs generate.

For information on a particular method, give its name as a parameter:

```
$ ri GC::enable
-------------------------------------------------------------- GC::enable
GC.enable      => true or false
------------------------------------------------------------------------
Enables garbage collection, returning true if garbage collection was disabled.

GC.disable    #=> false
GC.enable     #=> true
GC.enable     #=> false
```

If the method you give ri occurs in more than one class or module, ri will list the alternatives.

```
$ ri assoc
Implementation from Array
------------------------------------------------------------------------
  ary.assoc(obj)   -> new_ary  or  nil
------------------------------------------------------------------------
Searches through an array whose elements are also arrays comparing obj
with the first element of each contained array using obj.==.

Returns the first contained array that matches (that is, the first associated
array), or nil if no match is found.

See also Array#rassoc

  s1 = [ "colors", "red", "blue", "green" ]
  s2 = [ "letters", "a", "b", "c" ]
  s3 = "foo"
  a  = [ s1, s2, s3 ]
  a.assoc("letters")  #=> [ "letters", "a", "b", "c" ]
  a.assoc("foo")      #=> nil

(from ruby site)
Implementation from ENV
------------------------------------------------------------------------
  ENV.assoc(name) -> Array or nil
------------------------------------------------------------------------
Returns an Array of the name and value of the environment variable with
name or nil if the name cannot be found.

(from ruby site)
Implementation from Hash
------------------------------------------------------------------------
  hash.assoc(obj)   ->  an_array  or  nil
------------------------------------------------------------------------
Searches through the hash comparing obj with the key using ==.
Returns the key-value pair (two elements array) or nil if no match is
found.  See Array#assoc.

  h = {"colors"  => ["red", "blue", "green"],
       "letters" => ["a", "b", "c" ]}
  h.assoc("letters")  #=> ["letters", ["a", "b", "c"]]
  h.assoc("foo")      #=> nil
```

For general help on using ri, type ri --help. In particular, you might want to experiment with the --format option, which tells ri how to render decorated text (such as section headings). If your terminal program supports ANSI escape sequences, using --format=ansi will generate a nice, colorful display. Once you find a set of options you like, you can set them into the RI environment variable. Using our shell (zsh), this would be done using the following:

```
$ export RI="--format ansi --width 70"
```

If a class or module isn't yet documented in RDoc format, ask the friendly folks over at suggestions@ruby-doc.org to consider adding it.

All this command-line hacking may seem a tad off-putting if you're not a regular visitor to the shell prompt. But, in reality, it isn't that difficult, and the power you get from being able to string together commands this way is often surprising. Stick with it, and you'll be well on your way to mastering both Ruby and your computer.

## CHAPTER 2

Ruby.new

Most books on programming languages look about the same. They start with chapters on basic types: integers, strings, and so on. Then they look at expressions, before moving on to if and while statements. Then, perhaps around Chapter 7 or 8, they'll start mentioning classes. We find that somewhat tedious.

Instead, when we designed this book, we had a grand plan (we were younger then). We wanted to document the language from the top down, starting with classes and objects and ending with the nitty-gritty syntax details. It seemed like a good idea at the time. After all, most everything in Ruby is an object, so it made sense to talk about objects first.

Or so we thought.

Unfortunately, it turns out to be difficult to describe a language that way. If you haven't covered strings, if statements, assignments, and other details, it's difficult to write examples of classes. Throughout our top-down description, we kept coming across low-level details we needed to cover so that the example code would make sense.

So, we came up with another grand plan (they don't call us pragmatic for nothing). We'd still describe Ruby starting at the top. But before we did that, we'd add a short chapter that described all the common language features used in the examples along with the special vocabulary used in Ruby, a kind of mini-tutorial to bootstrap us into the rest of the book. And that mini-tutorial is this chapter.

2.1 Ruby Is an Object-Oriented Language

Let's say it again. Ruby is a genuine object-oriented language. Everything you manipulate is an object, and the results of those manipulations are themselves objects. However, many languages make the same claim, and their users often have a different interpretation of what *object-oriented* means and a different terminology for the concepts they employ.

So, before we get too far into the details, let's briefly look at the terms and notation that *we'll* be using.

When you write object-oriented programs, you're normally looking to model concepts from the real world. During this modeling process you'll discover categories of things that need to be represented in code. In a jukebox, the concept of a "song" could be such a category. In Ruby, you'd define a *class* to represent each of these entities. A class is a combination of state (for example, the name of the song) and methods that use that state (perhaps a method to play the song).

Once you have these classes, you'll typically want to create a number of *instances* of each. For the jukebox system containing a class called Song, you'd have separate instances for popular hits such as "Ruby Tuesday," "Enveloped in Python," "String of Pearls," "Small Talk," and so on. The word *object* is used interchangeably with *class instance* (and being lazy typists, we'll probably be using the word *object* more frequently).

In Ruby, these objects are created by calling a *constructor*, a special method associated with a class. The standard constructor is called new.

```
song1 = Song.new("Ruby Tuesday")
song2 = Song.new("Enveloped in Python")
# and so on
```

These instances are both derived from the same class, but they have unique characteristics. First, every object has a unique *object identifier* (abbreviated as *object ID*). Second, you can define *instance variables*, variables with values that are unique to each instance. These instance variables hold an object's state. Each of our songs, for example, will probably have an instance variable that holds the song title.

Within each class, you can define *instance methods*. Each method is a chunk of functionality that may be called in the context of the class and (depending on accessibility constraints) from outside the class. These instance methods in turn have access to the object's instance variables and hence to the object's state. A Song class, for example, might define an instance method called play. If a variable referenced a particular Song instance, you'd be able to call that instance's play method and play that song.

Methods are invoked by sending a message to an object. The message contains the method's name, along with any parameters the method may need.[1] When an object receives a message, it looks into its own class for a corresponding method. If found, that method is executed. If the method *isn't* found...well, we'll get to that later.

This business of methods and messages may sound complicated, but in practice it is very natural. Let's look at some method calls. In this code, we're using puts, a standard Ruby method that writes its argument(s) to the console, adding a newline after each:

```
puts "gin joint".length
puts "Rick".index("c")
puts 42.even?
puts sam.play(song)
```

produces:

```
9
2
true
duh dum, da dum de dum ...
```

Each line shows a method being called as an argument to puts. The thing before the period is called the *receiver*, and the name after the period is the method to be invoked. The first example asks a string for its length; the second asks a different string to find the index of the letter *c*. The third line asks the number 42 if it is even (the question mark is part of the method

---

1. This idea of expressing method calls in the form of messages comes from Smalltalk.

name even?). Finally, we ask Sam to play us a song (assuming there's an existing variable called sam that references an appropriate object).

It's worth noting here a major difference between Ruby and most other languages. In (say) Java, you'd find the absolute value of some number by calling a separate function and passing in that number. You could write this:

```
num = Math.abs(num)      // Java code
```

In Ruby, the ability to determine an absolute value is built into numbers—they take care of the details internally. You simply send the message abs to a number object and let it do the work:

```
num      = -1234   # => -1234
positive = num.abs # => 1234
```

The same applies to all Ruby objects. In C you'd write strlen(name), but in Ruby it would be name.length, and so on. This is part of what we mean when we say that Ruby is a genuine object-oriented language.

2.2 Some Basic Ruby

Not many people like to read heaps of boring syntax rules when they're picking up a new language, so we're going to cheat. In this section, we'll hit some of the highlights—the stuff you'll just *need* to know if you're going to write Ruby programs. Later, in Chapter 22, *The Ruby Language,* on page 297, we'll go into all the gory details.

Let's start with a simple Ruby program. We'll write a method that returns a cheery, personalized greeting. We'll then invoke that method a couple of times:

```
def say_goodnight(name)
  result = "Good night, " + name
  return result
end

# Time for bed...
puts say_goodnight("John-Boy")
puts say_goodnight("Mary-Ellen")
```

produces:

```
Good night, John-Boy
Good night, Mary-Ellen
```

As the example shows, Ruby syntax is clean. You don't need semicolons at the ends of statements as long as you put each statement on a separate line. Ruby comments start with a # character and run to the end of the line. Code layout is pretty much up to you; indentation is not significant (but using two-character indentation will make you friends in the community if you plan on distributing your code).

Methods are defined with the keyword def, followed by the method name (in this case, the name is say_goodnight) and the method's parameters between parentheses. (In fact, the parentheses are optional, but we like to use them.) Ruby doesn't use braces to delimit the bodies of compound statements and definitions. Instead, you simply finish the body with the keyword end. Our method's body is pretty simple. The first line concatenates the literal string "Good night," and the parameter name and assigns the result to the local variable result.

The next line returns that result to the caller. Note that we didn't have to declare the variable result; it sprang into existence when we assigned to it.

Having defined the method, we invoke it twice. In both cases, we pass the result to the method puts, which simply outputs its argument followed by a newline (moving on to the next line of output):

```
Good night, John-Boy
Good night, Mary-Ellen
```

The line

```
puts say_goodnight("John-Boy")
```

contains two method calls, one to the method say_goodnight and the other to the method puts. Why does one call have its arguments in parentheses while the other doesn't? In this case, it's purely a matter of taste. The following lines are equivalent:

```
puts say_goodnight("John-Boy")
puts(say_goodnight("John-Boy"))
```

However, life isn't always that simple, and precedence rules can make it difficult to know which argument goes with which method invocation, so we recommend using parentheses in all but the simplest cases.

This example also shows some Ruby string objects. Ruby has many ways to create a string object, but probably the most common is to use *string literals*, which are sequences of characters between single or double quotation marks. The difference between the two forms is the amount of processing Ruby does on the string while constructing the literal. In the single-quoted case, Ruby does very little. With a few exceptions, what you enter in the string literal becomes the string's value.

In the double-quoted case, Ruby does more work. First, it looks for substitutions (sequences that start with a backslash character) and replaces them with some binary value. The most common of these is \n, which is replaced with a newline character. When a string containing a newline is output, that newline becomes a line break:

```
puts "And good night,\nGrandma"
```

produces:

```
And good night,
Grandma
```

The second thing that Ruby does with double-quoted strings is expression interpolation. Within the string, the sequence #{expression} is replaced by the value of *expression*. We could use this to rewrite our previous method:

```
def say_goodnight(name)
  result = "Good night, #{name}"
  return result
end
puts say_goodnight('Pa')
```

produces:

```
Good night, Pa
```

When Ruby constructs this string object, it looks at the current value of name and substitutes it into the string. Arbitrarily complex expressions are allowed in the #{...} construct. In the following example, we invoke the capitalize method, defined for all strings, to output our parameter with a leading uppercase letter:

```ruby
def say_goodnight(name)
  result = "Good night, #{name.capitalize}"
  return result
end
puts say_goodnight('uncle')
```

produces:

```
Good night, Uncle
```

For more information on strings, as well as on the other Ruby standard types, see Chapter 6, *Standard Types*, on page 83.

Finally, we could simplify this method some more. The value returned by a Ruby method is the value of the last expression evaluated, so we can get rid of the temporary variable and the return statement altogether. This is idiomatic Ruby.

```ruby
def say_goodnight(name)
  "Good night, #{name.capitalize}"
end
puts say_goodnight('ma')
```

produces:

```
Good night, Ma
```

We promised that this section would be brief. We have just one more topic to cover: Ruby names. For brevity, we'll be using some terms (such as *class variable*) that we aren't going to define here. However, by talking about the rules now, you'll be ahead of the game when we actually come to discuss class variables and the like later.

Ruby uses a convention that may seem strange at first: the first characters of a name indicate how the name is used. Local variables, method parameters, and method names should all start with a lowercase letter[2] or an underscore. Global variables are prefixed with a dollar sign ($), and instance variables begin with an "at" sign (@). Class variables start with two "at" signs (@@).[3] Finally, class names, module names, and constants must start with an uppercase letter. Samples of different names are given in Table 1, *Example variable, class, and constant names,* on page 20.

Following this initial character, a name can be any combination of letters, digits, and underscores (with the proviso that the character following an @ sign may not be a digit). However, by convention, multiword instance variables are written with underscores between the words, and multiword class names are written in MixedCase (with each word capitalized). Method names may end with the characters ?, !, and =.

---

2. If your source files use non-ASCII characters (for example, because they're written in UTF-8 encoding), all non-ASCII characters are assumed to be lowercase letters.

3. Although we talk about global and class variables here for completeness, you'll find they are rarely used in Ruby programs. There's a lot of evidence that global variables make programs harder to maintain. Class variables are not as dangerous—it's just that people tend not to use them much.

Local Variable:	name fish_and_chips x_axis thx1138 _x _26
Instance Variable:	@name @point_1 @X @_ @plan9
Class Variable:	@@total @@symtab @@N @@x_pos @@SINGLE
Global Variable:	$debug $CUSTOMER $_ $plan9 $Global
Class Name:	String ActiveRecord MyClass
Constant Name:	FEET_PER_MILE DEBUG

Table 1—Example variable, class, and constant names

2.3 Arrays and Hashes

Ruby's arrays and hashes are indexed collections. Both store collections of objects, accessible using a key. With arrays, the key is an integer, whereas hashes support any object as a key. Both arrays and hashes grow as needed to hold new elements. It's more efficient to access array elements, but hashes provide more flexibility. Any particular array or hash can hold objects of differing types; you can have an array containing an integer, a string, and a floating-point number, as we'll see in a minute.

You can create and initialize a new array object using an *array literal*—a set of elements between square brackets. Given an array object, you can access individual elements by supplying an index between square brackets, as the next example shows. Note that Ruby array indices start at zero.

```
a = [ 1, 'cat', 3.14 ]   # array with three elements
puts "The first element is #{a[0]}"
# set the third element
a[2] = nil
puts "The array is now #{a.inspect}"
```

produces:

```
The first element is 1
The array is now [1, "cat", nil]
```

You may have noticed that we used the special value nil in this example. In many languages, the concept of *nil* (or *null*) means "no object." In Ruby, that's not the case; nil is an object, just like any other, that happens to represent nothing. Anyway, let's get back to arrays and hashes.

Sometimes creating arrays of words can be a pain, what with all the quotes and commas. Fortunately, Ruby has a shortcut; %w does just what we want:

```
a = [ 'ant', 'bee', 'cat', 'dog', 'elk' ]
a[0]       # => "ant"
a[3]       # => "dog"
# this is the same:
a = %w{ ant bee cat dog elk }
a[0]       # => "ant"
a[3]       # => "dog"
```

Ruby hashes are similar to arrays. A hash literal uses braces rather than square brackets. The literal must supply two objects for every entry: one for the key, the other for the value. The key and value are normally separated by =>.

For example, you could use a hash to map musical instruments to their orchestral sections.

```
inst_section = {
  'cello'      => 'string',
  'clarinet'   => 'woodwind',
  'drum'       => 'percussion',
  'oboe'       => 'woodwind',
  'trumpet'    => 'brass',
  'violin'     => 'string'
}
```

The thing to the left of the => is the key, and the thing to the right is the corresponding value. Keys in a particular hash must be unique; you can't have two entries for "drum." The keys and values in a hash can be arbitrary objects. You can have hashes where the values are arrays, other hashes, and so on.

Hashes are indexed using the same square bracket notation as arrays. In this code, we'll use the p method to write the values to the console. This works like puts but displays values such as nil explicitly.

```
p inst_section['oboe']
p inst_section['cello']
p inst_section['bassoon']
```

produces:

```
"woodwind"
"string"
nil
```

As the previous example shows, a hash by default returns nil when indexed by a key it doesn't contain. Normally this is convenient, because nil means false when used in conditional expressions. Sometimes you'll want to change this default. For example, if you're using a hash to count the number of times each different word occurs in a file, it's convenient to have the default value be zero. Then you can use the word as the key and simply increment the corresponding hash value without worrying about whether you've seen that word before. This is easily done by specifying a default value when you create a new, empty hash. (Have a look at the full source for the word frequency counter on page 49.)

```
histogram = Hash.new(0)    # The default value is zero
histogram['ruby'] # => 0
histogram['ruby'] = histogram['ruby'] + 1
histogram['ruby'] # => 1
```

Array and hash objects have many useful methods; see the discussion on page 45, as well as the reference sections for arrays on page 421 and for hashes on page 521.

2.4 Symbols

Often, when programming, you need to create a name for something significant. For example, you might want to refer to the compass points by name, so you'd write this:

```
NORTH = 1
EAST  = 2
SOUTH = 3
WEST  = 4
```

Then, in the rest of your code, you could use the constants instead of the numbers:

```
walk(NORTH)
look(EAST)
```

Most of the time, the actual numeric values of these constants are irrelevant (as long as they are unique). All you want to do is differentiate the four directions.

Ruby offers a cleaner alternative. *Symbols* are simply constant names that you don't have to predeclare and that are guaranteed to be unique. A symbol literal starts with a colon and is normally followed by some kind of name:

```
walk(:north)
look(:east)
```

There's no need to assign some kind of value to a symbol—Ruby takes care of that for you. Ruby also guarantees that no matter where it appears in your program, a particular symbol will have the same value. That is, you can write the following:

```
def walk(direction)
  if direction == :north
    # ...
  end
end
```

Symbols are frequently used as keys in hashes. We could write our previous example as this:

```
inst_section = {
  :cello    => 'string',
  :clarinet => 'woodwind',
  :drum     => 'percussion',
  :oboe     => 'woodwind',
  :trumpet  => 'brass',
  :violin   => 'string'
}
inst_section[:oboe]    # => "woodwind"
inst_section[:cello]   # => "string"
# Note that strings aren't the same as symbols...
inst_section['cello']  # => nil
```

In fact, symbols are so frequently used as hash keys that Ruby has a shortcut syntax: you can use name: value pairs to create a hash if the keys are symbols:

```
inst_section = {
  cello:    'string',
  clarinet: 'woodwind',
  drum:     'percussion',
  oboe:     'woodwind',
  trumpet:  'brass',
  violin:   'string'
}
puts "An oboe is a #{inst_section[:oboe]} instrument"
```

produces:

```
An oboe is a woodwind instrument
```

2.5   Control Structures

Ruby has all the usual control structures, such as if statements and while loops. Java, C, and Perl programmers may well get caught by the lack of braces around the bodies of these statements. Instead, Ruby uses the keyword end to signify the end of a body of all the control structures:

```
today = Time.now

if today.saturday?
  puts "Do chores around the house"
elsif today.sunday?
  puts "Relax"
else
  puts "Go to work"
end
```

produces:

```
Go to work
```

Similarly, while statements are terminated with end:

```
num_pallets = 0
weight      = 0
while weight < 100 and num_pallets <= 5
  pallet  = next_pallet()
  weight += pallet.weight
  num_pallets += 1
end
```

Most statements in Ruby return a value, which means you can use them as conditions. For example, the kernel method gets returns the next line from the standard input stream or nil when the end of the file is reached. Because Ruby treats nil as a false value in conditions, you could write the following to process the lines in a file:

```
while line = gets
  puts line.downcase
end
```

Here, the assignment statement sets the variable line to either the next line of text or nil, and then the while statement tests the value of the assignment, terminating the loop when it is nil.

Ruby *statement modifiers* are a useful shortcut if the body of an if or while statement is just a single expression. Simply write the expression, followed by if or while and the condition. For example, here's a simple if statement:

```
if radiation > 3000
  puts "Danger, Will Robinson"
end
```

Here it is again, rewritten using a statement modifier:

```
puts "Danger, Will Robinson" if radiation > 3000
```

Similarly, this while loop:

```
square = 4
while square < 1000
 square = square*square
end
```

becomes this more concise version:

```
square = 4
square = square*square  while square < 1000
```

These statement modifiers should seem familiar to Perl programmers.

2.6 Regular Expressions

Most of Ruby's built-in types will be familiar to all programmers. A majority of languages have strings, integers, floats, arrays, and so on. However, regular expression support is typically built into only scripting languages, such as Ruby, Perl, and awk. This is a shame, because regular expressions, although cryptic, are a powerful tool for working with text. And having them built in, rather than tacked on through a library interface, makes a big difference.

Entire books have been written about regular expressions (for example, *Mastering Regular Expressions [Fri97]*), so we won't try to cover everything in this short section. Instead, we'll look at just a few examples of regular expressions in action. You'll find full coverage of regular expressions in Chapter 7, *Regular Expressions*, on page 93.

A regular expression is simply a way of specifying a *pattern* of characters to be matched in a string. In Ruby, you typically create a regular expression by writing a pattern between slash characters (*/pattern/*). And, Ruby being Ruby, regular expressions are objects and can be manipulated as such.

For example, you could write a pattern that matches a string containing the text *Perl* or the text *Python* using the following regular expression:

```
/Perl|Python/
```

The forward slashes delimit the pattern, which consists of the two things we're matching, separated by a pipe character (|). This pipe character means "either the thing on the right or the thing on the left," in this case either *Perl* or *Python*. You can use parentheses within patterns, just as you can in arithmetic expressions, so you could also have written this pattern like this:

```
/P(erl|ython)/
```

You can also specify *repetition* within patterns. /ab+c/ matches a string containing an *a* followed by one or more *b*'s, followed by a *c*. Change the plus to an asterisk, and /ab*c/ creates a regular expression that matches one *a*, zero or more *b*'s, and one *c*.

You can also match one of a group of characters within a pattern. Some common examples are *character classes* such as \s, which matches a whitespace character (space, tab, newline, and so on); \d, which matches any digit; and \w, which matches any character that may appear in a typical word. A dot (.) matches (almost) any character. A table of these character classes appears in Table 2, *Character class abbreviations*, on page 101.

We can put all this together to produce some useful regular expressions:

```
/\d\d:\d\d:\d\d/       # a time such as 12:34:56
/Perl.*Python/        # Perl, zero or more other chars, then Python
/Perl Python/         # Perl, a space, and Python
/Perl *Python/        # Perl, zero or more spaces, and Python
/Perl +Python/        # Perl, one or more spaces, and Python
/Perl\s+Python/       # Perl, whitespace characters, then Python
/Ruby (Perl|Python)/ # Ruby, a space, and either Perl or Python
```

Once you have created a pattern, it seems a shame not to use it. The match operator =~ can be used to match a string against a regular expression. If the pattern is found in the string, =~ returns its starting position; otherwise, it returns nil. This means you can use regular expressions as the condition in if and while statements. For example, the following code fragment writes a message if a string contains the text *Perl* or *Python*:

```
line = gets
if line =~ /Perl|Python/
  puts "Scripting language mentioned: #{line}"
end
```

The part of a string matched by a regular expression can be replaced with different text using one of Ruby's substitution methods:

```
line = gets
newline  = line.sub(/Perl/, 'Ruby')        # replace first 'Perl' with 'Ruby'
newerline = newline.gsub(/Python/, 'Ruby') # replace every 'Python' with 'Ruby'
```

You can replace every occurrence of *Perl* and *Python* with *Ruby* using this:

```
line = gets
newline = line.gsub(/Perl|Python/, 'Ruby')
```

We'll have a lot more to say about regular expressions as we go through the book.

2.7 Blocks and Iterators

This section briefly describes one of Ruby's particular strengths. We're about to look at *code blocks*, which are chunks of code you can associate with method invocations, almost as if they were parameters. This is an incredibly powerful feature. One of our reviewers commented at this point: "This is pretty interesting and important, so if you weren't paying attention before, you should probably start now." We'd have to agree.

You can use code blocks to implement callbacks (but they're simpler than Java's anonymous inner classes), to pass around chunks of code (but they're more flexible than C's function pointers), and to implement iterators.

Code blocks are just chunks of code between braces or between do and end. This is a code block:

```
{ puts "Hello" }
```

This is also a code block:

```
do
  club.enroll(person)
  person.socialize
end
```

Why are there two kinds of delimiter? It's partly because sometimes one feels more natural to write than another. It's partly too because they have different precedences: the braces bind more tightly than the do/end pairs. In this book, we try to follow what is becoming a Ruby standard and use braces for single-line blocks and do/end for multiline blocks.

All you can do with a block is associate it with a call to a method. You do this by putting the start of the block at the end of the source line containing the method call.

For example, in the following code, the block containing puts "Hi" is associated with the call to the method greet (which we don't show):

```
greet  { puts "Hi" }
```

If the method has parameters, they appear before the block:

```
verbose_greet("Dave", "loyal customer")  { puts "Hi" }
```

A method can then invoke an associated block one or more times using the Ruby yield statement. You can think of yield as being something like a method call that invokes the block associated with the call to the method containing the yield.

The following example shows this in action. We define a method that calls yield twice. We then call this method, putting a block on the same line, after the call (and after any arguments to the method).[4]

```
def call_block
  puts "Start of method"
  yield
  yield
  puts "End of method"
end

call_block { puts "In the block" }
```

produces:

```
Start of method
In the block
In the block
End of method
```

The code in the block (puts "In the block") is executed twice, once for each call to yield.

You can provide arguments to the call to yield, and they will be passed to the block. Within the block, you list the names of the parameters to receive these arguments between vertical bars (|params...|). The following example shows a method calling its associated block twice, passing the block two arguments each time:

---

4. Some people like to think of the association of a block with a method as a kind of argument passing. This works on one level, but it isn't really the whole story. You may be better off thinking of the block and the method as coroutines, which transfer control back and forth between themselves.

```ruby
def who_says_what
  yield("Dave", "hello")
  yield("Andy", "goodbye")
end

who_says_what {|person, phrase| puts "#{person} says #{phrase}"}
```

produces:

```
Dave says hello
Andy says goodbye
```

Code blocks are used throughout the Ruby library to implement *iterators,* which are methods that return successive elements from some kind of collection, such as an array:

```ruby
animals = %w( ant bee cat dog )     # create an array
animals.each {|animal| puts animal }   # iterate over the contents
```

produces:

```
ant
bee
cat
dog
```

Many of the looping constructs that are built into languages such as C and Java are simply method calls in Ruby, with the methods invoking the associated block zero or more times:

```ruby
[ 'cat', 'dog', 'horse' ].each {|name| print name, " " }
5.times {  print "*" }
3.upto(6) {|i|  print i }
('a'..'e').each {|char| print char }
puts
```

produces:

```
cat dog horse *****3456abcde
```

Here we ask an array to call the block once for each of its elements. Then, object 5 calls a block five times. Rather than use for loops, in Ruby we can ask the number 3 to call a block, passing in successive values until it reaches 6. Finally, the range of characters from *a* to *e* invokes a block using the method each.

2.8 Reading and 'Riting

Ruby comes with a comprehensive I/O library. However, in most of the examples in this book, we'll stick to a few simple methods. We've already come across two methods that do output: puts writes its arguments with a newline after each; print also writes its arguments but with no newline. Both can be used to write to any I/O object, but by default they write to standard output.

Another output method we use a lot is printf, which prints its arguments under the control of a format string (just like printf in C or Perl):

```ruby
printf("Number: %5.2f,\nString: %s\n", 1.23, "hello")
```

produces:

```
Number:  1.23,
String: hello
```

In this example, the format string "Number: %5.2f,\nString: %s\n" tells printf to substitute in a floating-point number (with a minimum of five characters, two after the decimal point) and a string. Notice the newlines (\n) embedded in the string; each moves the output onto the next line.

You have many ways to read input into your program. Probably the most traditional is to use the method gets, which returns the next line from your program's standard input stream:

```
line = gets
print line
```

Because gets returns nil when it reaches the end of input, you can use its return value in a loop condition. Notice that in the following code the condition to the while is an assignment: we store whatever gets returns into the variable line and then test to see whether that returned value was nil or false before continuing:

```
while line = gets
  print line
end
```

2.9 Command-Line Arguments

When you run a Ruby program from the command line, you can pass in arguments. These are accessible in two different ways.

First, the array ARGV contains each of the arguments passed to the running program. Create a file called cmd_line.rb that contains the following:

```
puts "You gave #{ARGV.size} arguments"
p ARGV
```

When we run it with arguments, we can see that they get passed in:

```
$ ruby cmd_line.rb ant bee cat dog
You gave 4 arguments
["ant", "bee", "cat", "dog"]
```

Often, the arguments to a program are the names of files that you want to process. In this case, you can use a second technique: the variable ARGF is a special kind of I/O object that acts like all the contents of all the files whose names are passed on the command line (or standard input if you don't pass any filenames). We'll look at that some more in *ARGF*, on page 213.

2.10 Onward and Upward

That's it. We've finished our lightning-fast tour of some of the basic features of Ruby. We took a look at objects, methods, strings, containers, and regular expressions; saw some simple control structures; and looked at some rather nifty iterators. We hope this chapter has given you enough ammunition to be able to attack the rest of this book.

It's time to move on and move up—up to a higher level. Next, we'll be looking at classes and objects, things that are at the same time both the highest-level constructs in Ruby and the essential underpinnings of the entire language.

## CHAPTER 3

Classes, Objects, and Variables

From the examples we've shown so far, you may be wondering about our earlier assertion that Ruby is an object-oriented language. Well, this chapter is where we justify that claim. We're going to be looking at how you create classes and objects in Ruby and at some of the ways that Ruby is more powerful than most object-oriented languages.

As we saw on page 15, everything we manipulate in Ruby is an object. And every object in Ruby was generated either directly or indirectly from a class. In this chapter, we'll look in more depth at creating and manipulating those classes.

Let's give ourselves a simple problem to solve. Let's say that we're running a secondhand bookstore. Every week, we do stock control. A gang of clerks uses portable bar-code scanners to record every book on our shelves. Each scanner generates a simple comma-separated value (CSV) file containing one row for each book scanned. The row contains (among other things) the book's ISBN and price. An extract from one of these files looks something like this:

```
tut_classes/stock_stats/data.csv
"Date","ISBN","Price"
"2013-04-12","978-1-9343561-0-4",39.45
"2013-04-13","978-1-9343561-6-6",45.67
"2013-04-14","978-1-9343560-7-4",36.95
```

Our job is to take all the CSV files and work out how many of each title we have, as well as the total list price of the books in stock.

Whenever you're designing OO systems, a good first step is to identify the *things* you're dealing with. Typically each type of thing becomes a class in your final program, and the things themselves are instances of these classes.

It seems pretty clear that we'll need something to represent each data reading captured by the scanners. Each instance of this will represent a particular row of data, and the collection of all of these objects will represent all the data we've captured.

Let's call this class BookInStock. (Remember, class names start with an uppercase letter, and method names normally start with a lowercase letter.)

```
class BookInStock
end
```

As we saw in the previous chapter, we can create new instances of this class using new:

```
a_book = BookInStock.new
another_book = BookInStock.new
```

After this code runs, we'd have two distinct objects, both of class BookInStock. But, besides that they have different identities, these two objects are otherwise the same—there's nothing to distinguish one from the other. And, what's worse, these objects actually don't hold any of the information we need them to hold.

The best way to fix this is to provide the objects with an initialize method. This lets us set the state of each object as it is constructed. We store this state in *instance variables* inside the object. (Remember instance variables? They're the ones that start with an @ sign.) Because each object in Ruby has its own distinct set of instance variables, each object can have its own unique state.

So, here's our updated class definition:

```
class BookInStock
  def initialize(isbn, price)
    @isbn  = isbn
    @price = Float(price)
  end
end
```

initialize is a special method in Ruby programs. When you call BookInStock.new to create a new object, Ruby allocates some memory to hold an uninitialized object and then calls that object's initialize method, passing in any parameters that were passed to new. This gives you a chance to write code that sets up your object's state.

For class BookInStock, the initialize method takes two parameters. These parameters act just like local variables within the method, so they follow the local variable naming convention of starting with a lowercase letter. But, as local variables, they would just evaporate once the initialize method returns, so we need to transfer them into instance variables. This is very common behavior in an initialize method—the intent is to have our object set up and usable by the time initialize returns.

This method also illustrates something that often trips up newcomers to Ruby. Notice how we say @isbn = isbn. It's easy to imagine that the two variables here, @isbn and isbn, are somehow related—it looks like they have the same name. But they don't. The former is an instance variable, and the "at" sign is actually part of its name.

Finally, this code illustrates a simple piece of validation. The Float method takes its argument and converts it to a floating-point number,[1] terminating the program with an error if that conversion fails. (Later in the book we'll see how to handle these exceptional situations.) What we're doing here is saying that we want to accept any object for the price parameter as long as that parameter can be converted to a float. We can pass in a float, an integer, and even a string containing the representation of a float, and it will work. Let's try this now. We'll create three objects, each with different initial state. The p method prints out an internal representation of an object. Using it, we can see that in each case our parameters got transferred into the object's state, ending up as instance variables:

---

1. Yes, we know. We shouldn't be holding prices in inexact old floats. Ruby has classes that hold fixed-point values exactly, but we want to look at classes, not arithmetic, in this section.

```ruby
class BookInStock
  def initialize(isbn, price)
    @isbn  = isbn
    @price = Float(price)
  end
end

b1 = BookInStock.new("isbn1", 3)
p b1

b2 = BookInStock.new("isbn2", 3.14)
p b2

b3 = BookInStock.new("isbn3", "5.67")
p b3
```

produces:

```
#<BookInStock:0x007fac4910f3e0 @isbn="isbn1", @price=3.0>
#<BookInStock:0x007fac4910f0c0 @isbn="isbn2", @price=3.14>
#<BookInStock:0x007fac4910eda0 @isbn="isbn3", @price=5.67>
```

Why did we use the p method to write out our objects, rather than puts? Well, let's repeat the code using puts:

```ruby
class BookInStock
  def initialize(isbn, price)
    @isbn  = isbn
    @price = Float(price)
  end
end

b1 = BookInStock.new("isbn1", 3)
puts b1

b2 = BookInStock.new("isbn2", 3.14)
puts b2

b3 = BookInStock.new("isbn3", "5.67")
puts b3
```

produces:

```
#<BookInStock:0x007fb424847468>
#<BookInStock:0x007fb424847238>
#<BookInStock:0x007fb424847058>
```

Remember, puts simply writes strings to your program's standard output. When you pass it an object based on a class you wrote, it doesn't really know what to do with it, so it uses a very simple expedient: it writes the name of the object's class, followed by a colon and the object's unique identifier (a hexadecimal number). It puts the whole lot inside #<...>.

Our experience tells us that during development we'll be printing out the contents of a BookInStock object many times, and the default formatting leaves something to be desired. Fortunately, Ruby has a standard message, to_s, that it sends to any object it wants to render as a string. So, when we pass one of our BookInStock objects to puts, the puts method calls to_s in that object to get its string representation. So, let's override the default implementation of to_s to give us a better rendering of our objects:

```ruby
class BookInStock
  def initialize(isbn, price)
    @isbn  = isbn
    @price = Float(price)
  end
  def to_s
    "ISBN: #{@isbn}, price: #{@price}"
  end
end

b1 = BookInStock.new("isbn1", 3)
puts b1
b2 = BookInStock.new("isbn2", 3.14)
puts b2
b3 = BookInStock.new("isbn3", "5.67")
puts b3
```

produces:

```
ISBN: isbn1, price: 3.0
ISBN: isbn2, price: 3.14
ISBN: isbn3, price: 5.67
```

There's something going on here that's both trivial and profound. See how the values we set into the instance variables @isbn and @price in the initialize method are subsequently available in the to_s method? That shows how instance variables work—they're stored with each object and available to all the instance methods of those objects.

3.1 Objects and Attributes

The BookInStock objects we've created so far have an internal state (the ISBN and price). That state is private to those objects—no other object can access an object's instance variables. In general, this is a Good Thing. It means that the object is solely responsible for maintaining its own consistency.

However, an object that is totally secretive is pretty useless—you can create it, but then you can't do anything with it. You'll normally define methods that let you access and manipulate the state of an object, allowing the outside world to interact with the object. These externally visible facets of an object are called its *attributes*.

For our BookInStock objects, the first thing we may need is the ability to find out the ISBN and price (so we can count each distinct book and perform price calculations). One way of doing that is to write accessor methods:

```ruby
class BookInStock
  def initialize(isbn, price)
    @isbn  = isbn
    @price = Float(price)
  end
  def isbn
    @isbn
  end
```

```
  def price
    @price
  end
  # ..
end
```

```
book = BookInStock.new("isbn1", 12.34)
puts "ISBN  = #{book.isbn}"
puts "Price = #{book.price}"
```

produces:

```
ISBN  = isbn1
Price = 12.34
```

Here we've defined two accessor methods to return the values of the two instance variables. The method isbn, for example, returns the value of the instance variable @isbn (because the last thing executed in the method is the expression that simply evaluates the @isbn variable).

Because writing accessor methods is such a common idiom, Ruby provides a convenient shortcut. attr_reader creates these attribute reader methods for you:

```
class BookInStock

  attr_reader :isbn, :price

  def initialize(isbn, price)
    @isbn  = isbn
    @price = Float(price)
  end

  # ..
end
```

```
book = BookInStock.new("isbn1", 12.34)
puts "ISBN  = #{book.isbn}"
puts "Price = #{book.price}"
```

produces:

```
ISBN  = isbn1
Price = 12.34
```

This is the first time we've used *symbols* in this chapter. As we discussed on page 21, symbols are just a convenient way of referencing a name. In this code, you can think of :isbn as meaning the *name* isbn and think of plain isbn as meaning the *value* of the variable. In this example, we named the accessor methods isbn and price. The corresponding instance variables are @isbn and @price. These accessor methods are identical to the ones we wrote by hand earlier.

There's a common misconception, particularly among people who come from languages such as Java and C#, that the attr_reader declaration somehow declares instance variables. It doesn't. It creates the accessor methods, but the variables themselves don't need to be declared —they just pop into existence when you use them. Ruby completely decouples instance variables and accessor methods, as we'll see in *Virtual Attributes*, on page 35.

Writable Attributes

Sometimes you need to be able to set an attribute from outside the object. For example, let's assume that we have to discount the price of some titles after reading in the raw scan data.

In languages such as C# and Java, you'd do this with *setter functions*:

```
class JavaBookInStock {                    // Java code
  private double _price;
  public double getPrice() {
    return _price;
  }
  public void setPrice(double newPrice) {
    _price = newPrice;
  }
}
b = new JavaBookInStock(....);
b.setPrice(calculate_discount(b.getPrice()));
```

In Ruby, the attributes of an object can be accessed as if they were any other variable. We saw this earlier with phrases such as book.isbn. So, it seems natural to be able to assign to these variables when you want to set the value of an attribute. You do that by creating a Ruby method whose name ends with an equals sign. These methods can be used as the target of assignments:

```
class BookInStock

  attr_reader :isbn, :price

  def initialize(isbn, price)
    @isbn  = isbn
    @price = Float(price)
  end

  def price=(new_price)
    @price = new_price
  end

  # ...
end

book = BookInStock.new("isbn1", 33.80)
puts "ISBN     = #{book.isbn}"
puts "Price    = #{book.price}"
book.price = book.price * 0.75         # discount price
puts "New price = #{book.price}"
```

produces:

```
ISBN      = isbn1
Price     = 33.8
New price = 25.349999999999998
```

The assignment book.price = book.price * 0.75 invokes the method price= in the book object, passing it the discounted price as an argument. If you create a method whose name ends with an equals sign, that name can appear on the left side of an assignment.

Again, Ruby provides a shortcut for creating these simple attribute-setting methods. If you want a write-only accessor, you can use the form attr_writer, but that's fairly rare. You're far more likely to want both a reader and a writer for a given attribute, so you'll use the handy-dandy attr_accessor method:

```ruby
class BookInStock
  attr_reader    :isbn
  attr_accessor :price

  def initialize(isbn, price)
    @isbn  = isbn
    @price = Float(price)
  end
  # ...
end

book = BookInStock.new("isbn1", 33.80)
puts "ISBN      = #{book.isbn}"
puts "Price     = #{book.price}"
book.price = book.price * 0.75        # discount price
puts "New price = #{book.price}"
```

produces:

```
ISBN      = isbn1
Price     = 33.8
New price = 25.349999999999998
```

Virtual Attributes

These attribute-accessing methods do not have to be just simple wrappers around an object's instance variables. For example, you may want to access the price as an exact number of cents, rather than as a floating-point number of dollars.[2]

```ruby
class BookInStock

  attr_reader    :isbn
  attr_accessor :price

  def initialize(isbn, price)
    @isbn  = isbn
    @price = Float(price)
  end

  def price_in_cents
    Integer(price*100 + 0.5)
  end
  # ...
end
```

---

2. We multiply the floating-point price by 100 to get the price in cents but then add 0.5 before converting to an integer. Why? Because floating-point numbers don't always have an exact internal representation. When we multiply 33.8 by 100, we get 3379.9999999999954525265. The Integer method would truncate this to 3379. Adding 0.5 before calling Integer rounds up the floating-point value, ensuring we get the best integer representation. This is a good example of why you want to use BigDecimal, not Float, in financial calculations.

```
book = BookInStock.new("isbn1", 33.80)
puts "Price          = #{book.price}"
puts "Price in cents = #{book.price_in_cents}"
```

produces:

```
Price          = 33.8
Price in cents = 3380
```

We can take this even further and allow people to assign to our virtual attribute, mapping the value to the instance variable internally:

```
class BookInStock

  attr_reader    :isbn
  attr_accessor :price

  def initialize(isbn, price)
    @isbn  = isbn
    @price = Float(price)
  end

  def price_in_cents
    Integer(price*100 + 0.5)
  end

  def price_in_cents=(cents)
    @price = cents / 100.0
  end
  # ...
end

book = BookInStock.new("isbn1", 33.80)
puts "Price          = #{book.price}"
puts "Price in cents = #{book.price_in_cents}"
book.price_in_cents = 1234
puts "Price          = #{book.price}"
puts "Price in cents = #{book.price_in_cents}"
```

produces:

```
Price          = 33.8
Price in cents = 3380
Price          = 12.34
Price in cents = 1234
```

Here we've used attribute methods to create a virtual instance variable. To the outside world, price_in_cents seems to be an attribute like any other. Internally, though, it has no corresponding instance variable.

This is more than a curiosity. In his landmark book *Object-Oriented Software Construction [Mey97]*, Bertrand Meyer calls this the *Uniform Access Principle*. By hiding the difference between instance variables and calculated values, you are shielding the rest of the world from the implementation of your class. You're free to change how things work in the future without impacting the millions of lines of code that use your class. This is a big win.

Attributes, Instance Variables, and Methods

This description of attributes may leave you thinking that they're nothing more than methods —why'd we need to invent a fancy name for them? In a way, that's absolutely right. An attribute *is* just a method. Sometimes an attribute simply returns the value of an instance variable. Sometimes an attribute returns the result of a calculation. And sometimes those funky methods with equals signs at the end of their names are used to update the state of an object. So, the question is, where do attributes stop and regular methods begin? What makes something an attribute and not just a plain old method? Ultimately, that's one of those "angels on a pinhead" questions. Here's a personal take.

When you design a class, you decide what internal state it has and also decide how that state is to appear on the outside (to users of your class). The internal state is held in instance variables. The external state is exposed through methods we're calling *attributes*. And the other actions your class can perform are just regular methods. It really isn't a crucially important distinction, but by calling the external state of an object its attributes, you're helping clue people in to how they should view the class you've written.

3.2 Classes Working with Other Classes

Our original challenge was to read in data from multiple CSV files and produce various simple reports. So far, all we have is BookInStock, a class that represents the data for one book.

During OO design, you identify external things and make them classes in your code. But there's another source of classes in your designs. There are the classes that correspond to things inside your code itself. For example, we know that the program we're writing will need to consolidate and summarize CSV data feeds. But that's a very passive statement. Let's turn it into a design by asking ourselves *what* does the summarizing and consolidating. And the answer (in our case) is a *CSV reader*. Let's make it into a class as follows:

```ruby
class CsvReader
  def initialize
    # ...
  end

  def read_in_csv_data(csv_file_name)
    # ...
  end

  def total_value_in_stock
    # ...
  end

  def number_of_each_isbn
    # ...
  end
end
```

We'd call it using something like this:

```
reader = CsvReader.new
reader.read_in_csv_data("file1.csv")
reader.read_in_csv_data("file2.csv")
      :       :          :
puts "Total value in stock = #{reader.total_value_in_stock}"
```

We need to be able to handle multiple CSV files, so our reader object needs to accumulate the values from each CSV file it is fed. We'll do that by keeping an array of values in an instance variable. And how shall we represent each book's data? Well, we just finished writing the BookInStock class, so that problem is solved. The only other question is how we parse data in a CSV file. Fortunately, Ruby comes with a good CSV library (which has a brief description on page 741). Given a CSV file with a header line, we can iterate over the remaining rows and extract values by name:

```
tut_classes/stock_stats/csv_reader.rb
class CsvReader
  def initialize
    @books_in_stock = []
  end

  def read_in_csv_data(csv_file_name)
    CSV.foreach(csv_file_name, headers: true) do |row|
      @books_in_stock << BookInStock.new(row["ISBN"], row["Price"])
    end
  end
end
```

Just because you're probably wondering what's going on, let's dissect that read_in_csv_data method. On the first line, we tell the CSV library to open the file with the given name. The headers: true option tells the library to parse the first line of the file as the names of the columns.

The library then reads the rest of the file, passing each row in turn to the block (the code between do and end).[3] Inside the block, we extract the data from the ISBN and Price columns and use that data to create a new BookInStock object. We then append that object to an instance variable called @books_in_stock. And just where does that variable come from? It's an array that we created in the initialize method.

Again, this is the pattern you want to aim for. Your initialize method sets up an environment for your object, leaving it in a usable state. Other methods then use that state.

So, let's turn this from a code fragment into a working program. We're going to organize our source into three files. The first, book_in_stock.rb, will contain the definition of the class BookInStock. The second, csv_reader.rb, is the source for the CsvReader class. Finally, a third file, stock_stats.rb, is the main driver program. We'll start with book_in_stock.rb:

---

3. If you encounter an error along the lines of "'Float': can't convert nil into Float (TypeError)" when you run this code, you likely have extra spaces at the end of the header line in your CSV data file. The CSV library is pretty strict about the formats it accepts.

tut_classes/stock_stats/book_in_stock.rb

```ruby
class BookInStock
  attr_reader :isbn, :price

  def initialize(isbn, price)
    @isbn  = isbn
    @price = Float(price)
  end
end
```

Here's the csv_reader.rb file. The CsvReader class has two external dependencies: it needs the standard CSV library, and it needs the BookInStock class that's in the file book_in_stock.rb. Ruby has a couple of helper methods that let us load external files. In this file, we use require to load in the Ruby CSV library and require_relative to load in the book_in_stock file we wrote. (We use require_relative for this because the location of the file we're loading is relative to the file we're loading it from—they're both in the same directory.)

tut_classes/stock_stats/csv_reader.rb

```ruby
require 'csv'
require_relative 'book_in_stock'

class CsvReader
  def initialize
    @books_in_stock = []
  end

  def read_in_csv_data(csv_file_name)
    CSV.foreach(csv_file_name, headers: true) do |row|
      @books_in_stock << BookInStock.new(row["ISBN"], row["Price"])
    end
  end
  def total_value_in_stock   # later we'll see how to use inject to sum a collection
    sum = 0.0
    @books_in_stock.each {|book| sum += book.price}
    sum
  end

  def number_of_each_isbn
    # ...
  end
end
```

And finally, here's our main program, in the file stock_stats.rb:

tut_classes/stock_stats/stock_stats.rb

```ruby
require_relative 'csv_reader'

reader = CsvReader.new

ARGV.each do |csv_file_name|
  STDERR.puts "Processing #{csv_file_name}"
  reader.read_in_csv_data(csv_file_name)
end

puts "Total value = #{reader.total_value_in_stock}"
```

Again, this file uses require_relative to bring in the library it needs (in this case, the csv_reader.rb file). It uses the ARGV variable to access the program's command-line arguments, loading CSV data for each file specified on the command line.

We can run this program using the simple CSV data file as we showed on page 29:

```
$ ruby stock_stats.rb data.csv
Processing data.csv
Total value = 122.07000000000001
```

Do we need three source files for this? No. In fact, most Ruby developers would probably start off by sticking all this code into a single file—it would contain both class definitions as well as the driver code. But as your programs grow (and almost all programs grow over time), you'll find that this starts to get cumbersome. You'll also find it harder to write automated tests against the code if it is in a monolithic chunk. Finally, you won't be able to reuse classes if they're all bundled into the final program.

Anyway, let's get back to our discussion of classes.

3.3 Access Control

When designing a class interface, it's important to consider just how much of your class you'll be exposing to the outside world. Allow too much access into your class, and you risk increasing the coupling in your application—users of your class will be tempted to rely on details of your class's implementation, rather than on its logical interface. The good news is that the only easy way to change an object's state in Ruby is by calling one of its methods. Control access to the methods, and you've controlled access to the object. A good rule of thumb is never to expose methods that could leave an object in an invalid state.

Ruby gives you three levels of protection:

- *Public methods* can be called by anyone—no access control is enforced. Methods are public by default (except for initialize, which is always private).

- *Protected methods* can be invoked only by objects of the defining class and its subclasses. Access is kept within the family.

- *Private methods* cannot be called with an explicit receiver—the receiver is always the current object, also known as self. This means that private methods can be called only in the context of the current object; you can't invoke another object's private methods.

The difference between "protected" and "private" is fairly subtle and is different in Ruby than in most common OO languages. If a method is protected, it may be called by *any* instance of the defining class or its subclasses. If a method is private, it may be called only within the context of the calling object—it is never possible to access another object's private methods directly, even if the object is of the same class as the caller.

Ruby differs from other OO languages in another important way. Access control is determined dynamically, as the program runs, not statically. You will get an access violation only when the code attempts to execute the restricted method.

Specifying Access Control

You specify access levels to methods within class or module definitions using one or more of the three functions public, protected, and private. You can use each function in two different ways.

If used with no arguments, the three functions set the default access control of subsequently defined methods. This is probably familiar behavior if you're a C++ or Java programmer, where you'd use keywords such as public to achieve the same effect:

```ruby
class MyClass

  def method1      # default is 'public'
    #...
  end

protected          # subsequent methods will be 'protected'
  def method2      # will be 'protected'
    #...
  end

private            # subsequent methods will be 'private'
  def method3      # will be 'private'
    #...
  end

public             # subsequent methods will be 'public'
  def method4      # so this will be 'public'
    #...
  end
end
```

Alternatively, you can set access levels of named methods by listing them as arguments to the access control functions:

```ruby
class MyClass
  def method1
  end
  def method2
  end
  # ... and so on

  public    :method1, :method4
  protected :method2
  private   :method3
end
```

It's time for some examples. Perhaps we're modeling an accounting system where every debit has a corresponding credit. Because we want to ensure that no one can break this rule, we'll make the methods that do the debits and credits private, and we'll define our external interface in terms of transactions.

```ruby
class Account
  attr_accessor :balance
  def initialize(balance)
    @balance = balance
  end
end

class Transaction

  def initialize(account_a, account_b)
    @account_a = account_a
    @account_b = account_b
  end

private

  def debit(account, amount)
    account.balance -= amount
  end
  def credit(account, amount)
    account.balance += amount
  end

public

  #...
  def transfer(amount)
    debit(@account_a, amount)
    credit(@account_b, amount)
  end
  #...
end

savings = Account.new(100)
checking = Account.new(200)

trans = Transaction.new(checking, savings)
trans.transfer(50)
```

Protected access is used when objects need to access the internal state of other objects of the same class. For example, we may want to allow individual Account objects to compare their cleared balances but to hide those balances from the rest of the world (perhaps because we present them in a different form):

```ruby
class Account
  attr_reader :cleared_balance  # accessor method 'cleared_balance'
  protected   :cleared_balance  # but make it protected

  def greater_balance_than?(other)
    @cleared_balance > other.cleared_balance
  end
end
```

Because cleared_balance is protected, it's available only within Account objects.

3.4 Variables

Now that we've gone to the trouble to create all these objects, let's make sure we don't lose them. Variables are used to keep track of objects; each variable holds a reference to an object. Let's confirm this with some code:

```
person = "Tim"
puts "The object in 'person' is a #{person.class}"
puts "The object has an id of #{person.object_id}"
puts "and a value of '#{person}'"
```

produces:

```
The object in 'person' is a String
The object has an id of 70230663692980
and a value of 'Tim'
```

On the first line, Ruby creates a new string object with the value Tim. A reference to this object is placed in the local variable person. A quick check shows that the variable has indeed taken on the personality of a string, with an object ID, a class, and a value.

So, is a variable an object? In Ruby, the answer is "no." A variable is simply a reference to an object. Objects float around in a big pool somewhere (the heap, most of the time) and are pointed to by variables. Let's make the example slightly more complicated:

```
person1 = "Tim"
person2 = person1
person1[0] = 'J'

puts "person1 is #{person1}"
puts "person2 is #{person2}"
```

produces:

```
person1 is Jim
person2 is Jim
```

What happened here? We changed the first character of person1 (Ruby strings are mutable, unlike Java), but both person1 and person2 changed from Tim to Jim.

It all comes back to the fact that variables hold references to objects, not the objects themselves. Assigning person1 to person2 doesn't create any new objects; it simply copies person1's object reference to person2 so that both person1 and person2 refer to the same object.

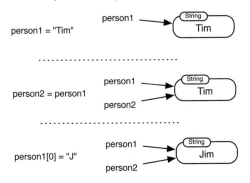

Assignment *aliases* objects, potentially giving you multiple variables that reference the same object. But can't this cause problems in your code? It can, but not as often as you'd think (objects in Java, for example, work exactly the same way). In the previous example, for instance, you could avoid aliasing by using the dup method of String, which creates a new string object with identical contents:

```
person1 = "Tim"
person2 = person1.dup
person1[0] = "J"
puts "person1 is #{person1}"
puts "person2 is #{person2}"
```

produces:

```
person1 is Jim
person2 is Tim
```

You can also prevent anyone from changing a particular object by freezing it. Attempt to alter a frozen object, and Ruby will raise a RuntimeError exception:

```
person1 = "Tim"
person2 = person1
person1.freeze          # prevent modifications to the object
person2[0] = "J"
```

produces:

```
        from prog.rb:4:in `<main>'
prog.rb:4:in `[]=': can't modify frozen String (RuntimeError)
```

There's more to say about classes and objects in Ruby. We still have to look at class methods and at concepts such as mixins and inheritance. We'll do that in Chapter 5, *Sharing Functionality: Inheritance, Modules, and Mixins*, on page 69. But, for now, know that everything you manipulate in Ruby is an object and that objects start life as instances of classes. And one of the most common things we do with objects is create collections of them. But that's the subject of our next chapter.

## CHAPTER 4

Containers, Blocks, and Iterators

Most real programs deal with collections of data: the people in a course, the songs in your playlist, the books in the store. Ruby comes with two built-in classes to handle these collections: arrays and hashes.[1] Mastery of these two classes is key to being an effective Ruby programmer. This mastery may take some time, because both classes have large interfaces.

But it isn't just these classes that give Ruby its power when dealing with collections. Ruby also has a block syntax that lets you encapsulate chunks of code. When paired with collections, these blocks become powerful iterator constructs. In this chapter, we'll look at the two collection classes as well as blocks and iterators.

4.1 Arrays

The class Array holds a collection of object references. Each object reference occupies a position in the array, identified by a non-negative integer index.

You can create arrays by using literals or by explicitly creating an Array object. A literal array is simply a list of objects between square brackets.[2]

```
a = [ 3.14159, "pie", 99 ]
a.class    # => Array
a.length   # => 3
a[0]       # => 3.14159
a[1]       # => "pie"
a[2]       # => 99
a[3]       # => nil

b = Array.new
b.class    # => Array
b.length   # => 0
b[0] = "second"
b[1] = "array"
b          # => ["second", "array"]
```

---

1. Some languages call hashes *associative arrays* or *dictionaries*.
2. In the code examples that follow, we're often going to show the value of expressions such as a[0] in a comment at the end of the line. If you simply typed this fragment of code into a file and executed it using Ruby, you'd see no output—you'd need to add something like a call to puts to have the values written to the console.

Arrays are indexed using the [ ] operator. As with most Ruby operators, this is actually a method (an instance method of class Array) and hence can be overridden in subclasses. As the example shows, array indices start at zero. Index an array with a non-negative integer, and it returns the object at that position or returns nil if nothing is there. Index an array with a negative integer, and it counts from the end.

```
a = [ 1, 3, 5, 7, 9 ]
a[-1]      # => 9
a[-2]      # => 7
a[-99]     # => nil
```

The following diagram shows this a different way.

	0	1	2	3	4	5	6
positive →	0	1	2	3	4	5	6
negative →	-7	-6	-5	-4	-3	-2	-1
a =	["ant",	"bat",	"cat",	"dog",	"elk",	"fly",	"gnu"]
a[2] →			"cat"				
a[-3] →					"elk"		
a[1..3] →		["bat",	"cat",	"dog"]			
a[1...3] →		["bat",	"cat"]				
a[-3..-1] →					["elk",	"fly",	"gnu"]
a[4..-2] →					["elk",	"fly"]	

You can also index arrays with a pair of numbers, [start,count]. This returns a new array consisting of references to count objects starting at position start:

```
a = [ 1, 3, 5, 7, 9 ]
a[1, 3]    # => [3, 5, 7]
a[3, 1]    # => [7]
a[-3, 2]   # => [5, 7]
```

Finally, you can index arrays using ranges, in which start and end positions are separated by two or three periods. The two-period form includes the end position; the three-period form does not:

```
a = [ 1, 3, 5, 7, 9 ]
a[1..3]    # => [3, 5, 7]
a[1...3]   # => [3, 5]
a[3..3]    # => [7]
a[-3..-1]  # => [5, 7, 9]
```

The [ ] operator has a corresponding [ ]= operator, which lets you set elements in the array. If used with a single integer index, the element at that position is replaced by whatever is on the right side of the assignment. Any gaps that result will be filled with nil:

```
a = [ 1, 3, 5, 7, 9 ]     #=> [1, 3, 5, 7, 9]
a[1] = 'bat'              #=> [1, "bat", 5, 7, 9]
a[-3] = 'cat'             #=> [1, "bat", "cat", 7, 9]
a[3]  = [ 9, 8 ]          #=> [1, "bat", "cat", [9, 8], 9]
a[6]  = 99                #=> [1, "bat", "cat", [9, 8], 9, nil, 99]
```

If the index to [ ]= is two numbers (a start and a length) or a range, then those elements in the original array are replaced by whatever is on the right side of the assignment. If the length is zero, the right side is inserted into the array before the start position; no elements are removed. If the right side is itself an array, its elements are used in the replacement. The array size is automatically adjusted if the index selects a different number of elements than are available on the right side of the assignment.

```
a = [ 1, 3, 5, 7, 9 ]      #=> [1, 3, 5, 7, 9]
a[2, 2] = 'cat'            #=> [1, 3, "cat", 9]
a[2, 0] = 'dog'            #=> [1, 3, "dog", "cat", 9]
a[1, 1] = [ 9, 8,  7 ]     #=> [1, 9, 8, 7, "dog", "cat", 9]
a[0..3] = []               #=> ["dog", "cat", 9]
a[5..6] = 99, 98           #=> ["dog", "cat", 9, nil, nil, 99, 98]
```

Arrays have a large number of other useful methods. Using them, you can treat arrays as stacks, sets, queues, dequeues, and FIFO queues.

For example, push and pop add and remove elements from the end of an array, so you can use the array as a stack:

```
stack = []
stack.push "red"
stack.push "green"
stack.push "blue"
stack      # => ["red", "green", "blue"]

stack.pop # => "blue"
stack.pop # => "green"
stack.pop # => "red"
stack      # => []
```

Similarly, unshift and shift add and remove elements from the head of an array. Combine shift and push, and you have a first-in first-out (FIFO) queue.

```
queue = []
queue.push "red"
queue.push "green"
queue.shift # => "red"
queue.shift # => "green"
```

The first and last methods return (but don't remove) the *n* entries at the head or end of an array.

```
array = [ 1, 2, 3, 4, 5, 6, 7 ]
array.first(4) # => [1, 2, 3, 4]
array.last(4)  # => [4, 5, 6, 7]
```

The reference section lists the methods in class Array on page 421. It is well worth firing up irb and playing with them.

4.2 Hashes

Hashes (sometimes known as *associative arrays*, *maps*, or *dictionaries*) are similar to arrays in that they are indexed collections of object references. However, while you index arrays with integers, you index a hash with objects of any type: symbols, strings, regular expressions, and so on. When you store a value in a hash, you actually supply two objects—the index, which is normally called the *key*, and the entry to be stored with that key. You can subsequently retrieve the entry by indexing the hash with the same key value that you used to store it.

The example that follows uses hash literals—a list of *key value* pairs between braces:

```
h = { 'dog' => 'canine', 'cat' => 'feline', 'donkey' => 'asinine' }
```

```
h.length   # => 3
h['dog']   # => "canine"
h['cow'] = 'bovine'
h[12]      = 'dodecine'
h['cat'] = 99
h          # => {"dog"=>"canine", "cat"=>99, "donkey"=>"asinine", "cow"=>"bovine",
           # .. 12=>"dodecine"}
```

In the previous example, the hash keys were strings, and the hash literal used => to separate the keys from the values. From Ruby 1.9, there is a new shortcut you can use if the keys are *symbols*. In that case, you can still use => to separate keys from values:

```
h = { :dog => 'canine', :cat => 'feline', :donkey => 'asinine' }
```

but you can also write the literal by moving the colon to the end of the symbol and dropping the =>:

```
h = { dog: 'canine', cat: 'feline', donkey: 'asinine' }
```

Compared with arrays, hashes have one significant advantage: they can use any object as an index. And you'll find something that might be surprising: Ruby remembers the order in which you add items to a hash. When you subsequently iterate over the entries, Ruby will return them in that order.

You'll find that hashes are one of the most commonly used data structures in Ruby. The reference section has a list of the methods implemented by class Hash on page 521.

Word Frequency: Using Hashes and Arrays

Let's round off this section with a simple program that calculates the number of times each word occurs in some text. (So, for example, in this sentence, the word *the* occurs two times.)

The problem breaks down into two parts. First, given some text as a string, return a list of words. That sounds like an array. Then, build a count for each distinct word. That sounds like a use for a hash—we can index it with the word and use the corresponding entry to keep a count.

Let's start with the method that splits a string into words:

```
tut_containers/word_freq/words_from_string.rb
def words_from_string(string)
  string.downcase.scan(/[\w']+/)
end
```

This method uses two very useful string methods: downcase returns a lowercase version of a string, and scan returns an array of substrings that match a given pattern. In this case, the pattern is [\w']+, which matches sequences containing "word characters" and single quotes.

We can play with this method. Notice how the result is an array:

```
p words_from_string("But I didn't inhale, he said (emphatically)")
```

produces:

```
["but", "i", "didn't", "inhale", "he", "said", "emphatically"]
```

Our next task is to calculate word frequencies. To do this, we'll create a hash object indexed by the words in our list. Each entry in this hash stores the number of times that word occurred. Let's say we already have read part of the list, and we have seen the word *the* already. Then we'd have a hash that contained this:

```
{ ..., "the" => 1, ... }
```

If the variable next_word contained the word *the*, then incrementing the count is as simple as this:

```
counts[next_word] += 1
```

We'd then end up with a hash containing the following:

```
{ ..., "the" => 2, ... }
```

Our only problem is what to do when we encounter a word for the first time. We'll try to increment the entry for that word, but there won't be one, so our program will fail. There are a number of solutions to this. One is to check to see whether the entry exists before doing the increment:

```
if counts.has_key?(next_word)
  counts[next_word] += 1
else
  counts[next_word] = 1
end
```

However, there's a tidier way. If we create a hash object using Hash.new(0), the parameter, 0 in this case, will be used as the hash's default value—it will be the value returned if you look up a key that isn't yet in the hash. Using that, we can write our count_frequency method:

tut_containers/word_freq/count_frequency.rb
```
def count_frequency(word_list)
  counts = Hash.new(0)
  for word in word_list
    counts[word] += 1
  end
  counts
end

p count_frequency(["sparky", "the", "cat", "sat", "on", "the", "mat"])
```

produces:

```
{"sparky"=>1, "the"=>2, "cat"=>1, "sat"=>1, "on"=>1, "mat"=>1}
```

One little job left. The hash containing the word frequencies is ordered based on the first time it sees each word. It would be better to display the results based on the frequencies of the words. We can do that using the hash's sort_by method. When you use sort_by, you give it a block that tells the sort what to use when making comparisons. In our case, we'll just use the count. The result of the sort is an array containing a set of two-element arrays, with each subarray corresponding to a key/entry pair in the original hash. This makes our whole program:

```ruby
require_relative "words_from_string.rb"
require_relative "count_frequency.rb"

raw_text = %{The problem breaks down into two parts. First, given some text
as a string, return a list of words. That sounds like an array. Then, build
a count for each distinct word. That sounds like a use for a hash---we can
index it with the word and use the corresponding entry to keep a count.}

word_list = words_from_string(raw_text)
counts    = count_frequency(word_list)
sorted    = counts.sort_by {|word, count| count}
top_five  = sorted.last(5)

for i in 0...5              # (this is ugly code--read on
  word = top_five[i][0]    #  for a better version)
  count = top_five[i][1]
  puts "#{word}:  #{count}"
end
```

produces:

```
that:   2
sounds: 2
like:   2
the:    3
a:      6
```

At this point, a quick test may be in order. To do this, we're going to use a testing framework called Test::Unit that comes with the standard Ruby distributions. We won't describe it fully yet (we do that in Chapter 13, *Unit Testing*, on page 175). For now, we'll just say that the method assert_equal checks that its two parameters are equal, complaining bitterly if they aren't. We'll use assertions to test our two methods, one method at a time. (That's one reason why we wrote them as separate methods—it makes them testable in isolation.)

Here are some tests for the word_from_string method:

```ruby
require_relative 'words_from_string'
require 'test/unit'

class TestWordsFromString < Test::Unit::TestCase

  def test_empty_string
    assert_equal([], words_from_string(""))
    assert_equal([], words_from_string("     "))
  end

  def test_single_word
    assert_equal(["cat"], words_from_string("cat"))
    assert_equal(["cat"], words_from_string("  cat   "))
  end

  def test_many_words
    assert_equal(["the", "cat", "sat", "on", "the", "mat"],
         words_from_string("the cat sat on the mat"))
  end
```

```ruby
  def test_ignores_punctuation
    assert_equal(["the", "cat's", "mat"],
        words_from_string("<the!> cat's, -mat-"))
  end
end
```

produces:

```
Run options:
# Running tests:

....
Finished tests in 0.006458s, 619.3868 tests/s, 929.0802 assertions/s.
4 tests, 6 assertions, 0 failures, 0 errors, 0 skips

ruby -v: ruby 2.0.0p0 (2013-02-24 revision 39474) [x86_64-darwin12.2.0]
```

The test starts by requiring the source file containing our words_from_string method, along with the unit test framework itself. It then defines a test class. Within that class, any methods whose names start with test are automatically run by the testing framework. The results show that four test methods ran, successfully executing six assertions.

We can also test that our count of word frequency works:

```ruby
require_relative 'count_frequency'
require 'test/unit'

class TestCountFrequency < Test::Unit::TestCase
  def test_empty_list
    assert_equal({}, count_frequency([]))
  end
  def test_single_word
    assert_equal({"cat" => 1}, count_frequency(["cat"]))
  end
  def test_two_different_words
    assert_equal({"cat" => 1, "sat" => 1}, count_frequency(["cat", "sat"]))
  end
  def test_two_words_with_adjacent_repeat
    assert_equal({"cat" => 2, "sat" => 1}, count_frequency(["cat", "cat", "sat"]))
  end
  def test_two_words_with_non_adjacent_repeat
    assert_equal({"cat" => 2, "sat" => 1}, count_frequency(["cat", "sat", "cat"]))
  end
end
```

produces:

```
Run options:
# Running tests:

.....
Finished tests in 0.006327s, 790.2639 tests/s, 790.2639 assertions/s.
5 tests, 5 assertions, 0 failures, 0 errors, 0 skips

ruby -v: ruby 2.0.0p0 (2013-02-24 revision 39474) [x86_64-darwin12.2.0]
```

4.3 Blocks and Iterators

In our program that wrote out the results of our word frequency analysis, we had the following loop:

```
for i in 0..4
  word = top_five[i][0]
  count = top_five[i][1]
  puts "#{word}:  #{count}"
end
```

This works, and it looks comfortingly familiar: a for loop iterating over an array. What could be more natural?

It turns out there *is* something more natural. In a way, our for loop is somewhat too intimate with the array; it magically knows that we're iterating over five elements, and it retrieves values in turn from the array. To do this, it has to know that the structure it is working with is an array of two-element subarrays. This is a whole lot of coupling.

Instead, we could write this code like this:

```
top_five.each do |word, count|
  puts "#{word}:  #{count}"
end
```

The method each is an *iterator*—a method that invokes a block of code repeatedly. In fact, some Ruby programmers might write this more compactly as this:

```
puts top_five.map { |word, count| "#{word}:  #{count}" }
```

Just how far you take this is a matter of taste. However you use them, iterators and code blocks are among the more interesting features of Ruby, so let's spend a while looking into them.

Blocks

A *block* is simply a chunk of code enclosed between either braces or the keywords do and end. The two forms are identical except for precedence, which we'll see in a minute. All things being equal, the current Ruby style seems to favor using braces for blocks that fit on one line and do/end when a block spans multiple lines:

```
some_array.each {|value| puts value * 3 }

sum = 0
other_array.each do |value|
  sum += value
  puts value / sum
end
```

You can think of a block as being somewhat like the body of an anonymous method. Just like a method, the block can take parameters (but, unlike a method, those parameters appear at the start of the block between vertical bars). Both the blocks in the preceding example take a single parameter, value. And, just like a method, the body of a block is not executed when Ruby first sees it. Instead, the block is saved away to be called later.

Blocks can appear in Ruby source code only immediately after the *invocation* of some method. If the method takes parameters, the block appears after these parameters. In a way, you can almost think of the block as being one extra parameter, passed to that method. Let's look at a simple example that sums the squares of the numbers in an array:

```
sum = 0
[1, 2, 3, 4].each do |value|
  square = value * value
  sum   += square
end
puts sum
```

produces:

```
30
```

The block is being called by the each method once for each element in the array. The element is passed to the block as the value parameter. But there's something subtle going on, too. Take a look at the sum variable. It's declared outside the block, updated inside the block, and then passed to puts after the each method returns.

This illustrates an important rule: if there's a variable inside a block with the same name as a variable in the same scope outside the block, the two are the same—there's only one variable sum in the preceding program. (You can override this behavior, as we'll see later.)

If, however, a variable appears only inside a block, then that variable is local to the block—in the preceding program, we couldn't have written the value of square at the end of the code, because square is not defined at that point. It is defined only inside the block itself.

Although simple, this behavior can lead to unexpected problems. For example, say our program was dealing with drawing different shapes. We might have this:

```
square = Shape.new(sides: 4) # assume Shape defined elsewhere

# .. lots of code

sum = 0

[1, 2, 3, 4].each do |value|
  square = value * value
  sum   += square
end

puts sum

square.draw    # BOOM!
```

This code would fail, because the variable square, which originally held a Shape object, will have been overwritten inside the block and will hold a number by the time the each method returns. This problem doesn't bite often, but when it does, it can be very confusing.

Fortunately, Ruby has a couple of answers.

First, parameters to a block are *always* local to a block, even if they have the same name as locals in the surrounding scope. (You'll get a warning message if you run Ruby with the -w option.)

```
value = "some shape"
[ 1, 2 ].each {|value| puts value }
puts value
```

produces:

```
1
2
some shape
```

Second, you can define block-local variables by putting them after a semicolon in the block's parameter list. So, in our sum-of-squares example, we should have indicated that the square variable was block-local by writing it as follows:

```
square = "some shape"

sum = 0
[1, 2, 3, 4].each do |value; square|
  square = value * value    # this is a different variable
  sum   += square
end
puts sum
puts square
```

produces:

```
30
some shape
```

By making square block-local, values assigned inside the block will not affect the value of the variable with the same name in the outer scope.

Implementing Iterators

A Ruby iterator is simply a method that can invoke a block of code.

We said that a block may appear only in the source adjacent to a method call and that the code in the block is not executed at the time it is encountered. Instead, Ruby remembers the context in which the block appears (the local variables, the current object, and so on) and then enters the method. This is where the magic starts.

Within the method, the block may be invoked, almost as if it were a method itself, using the yield statement. Whenever a yield is executed, it invokes the code in the block. When the block exits, control picks back up immediately after the yield.[3] Let's start with a trivial example:

```
def two_times
  yield
  yield
end
two_times { puts "Hello" }
```

produces:

```
Hello
Hello
```

---

3. Programming-language buffs will be pleased to know that the keyword yield was chosen to echo the yield function in Liskov's language CLU, a language that is more than thirty years old and yet contains features that still haven't been widely exploited by the CLU-less.

The block (the code between the braces) is associated with the call to the two_times method. Within this method, yield is called two times. Each time, it invokes the code in the block, and a cheery greeting is printed. What makes blocks interesting, however, is that you can pass parameters to them and receive values from them. For example, we could write a simple function that returns members of the Fibonacci series up to a certain value:[4]

```
def fib_up_to(max)
  i1, i2 = 1, 1        # parallel assignment (i1 = 1 and i2 = 1)
  while i1 <= max
    yield i1
    i1, i2 = i2, i1+i2
  end
end

fib_up_to(1000) {|f| print f, " " }

puts
```

produces:

```
1 1 2 3 5 8 13 21 34 55 89 144 233 377 610 987
```

In this example, the yield statement has a parameter. This value is passed to the associated block. In the definition of the block, the argument list appears between vertical bars. In this instance, the variable f receives the value passed to yield, so the block prints successive members of the series. (This example also shows parallel assignment in action. We'll come back to this later on page 130.) Although it is common to pass just one value to a block, this is not a requirement; a block may have any number of arguments.

Some iterators are common to many types of Ruby collections. Let's look at three: each, collect, and find.

each is probably the simplest iterator—all it does is yield successive elements of its collection:

```
[ 1, 3, 5, 7, 9 ].each {|i| puts i }
```

produces:

```
1
3
5
7
9
```

The each iterator has a special place in Ruby; we'll describe how it's used as the basis of the language's for loop on page 140, and we'll see on page 77 how defining an each method can add a whole lot more functionality to the classes you write–for free.

A block may also return a value to the method. The value of the last expression evaluated in the block is passed back to the method as the value of the yield. This is how the find method used by class Array works.[5] Its implementation would look something like the following:

---

4. The basic Fibonacci series is a sequence of integers, starting with two 1s, in which each subsequent term is the sum of the two preceding terms. The series is sometimes used in sorting algorithms and in analyzing natural phenomena.
5. The find method is actually defined in module Enumerable, which is mixed into class Array.

```ruby
class Array
  def find
    each do |value|
      return value if yield(value)
    end
    nil
  end
end
```

```ruby
[1, 3, 5, 7, 9].find {|v| v*v > 30 } # => 7
```

This uses each to pass successive elements of the array to the associated block. If the block returns true (that is, a value other than nil or false), the method returns the corresponding element. If no element matches, the method returns nil. The example shows the benefit of this approach to iterators. The Array class does what it does best, accessing array elements, and leaves the application code to concentrate on its particular requirement (in this case, finding an entry that meets some criteria).

Another common iterator is collect (also known as map), which takes each element from the collection and passes it to the block. The results returned by the block are used to construct a new array. The following example uses the succ method, which increments a string value:

```ruby
["H", "A", "L"].collect {|x| x.succ } # => ["I", "B", "M"]
```

Iterators are not limited to accessing existing data in arrays and hashes. As we saw in the Fibonacci example, an iterator can return derived values. This capability is used by Ruby's input and output classes, which implement an iterator interface that returns successive lines (or bytes) in an I/O stream:

```ruby
f = File.open("testfile")
f.each do |line|
  puts "The line is: #{line}"
end
f.close
```

produces:

```
The line is: This is line one
The line is: This is line two
The line is: This is line three
The line is: And so on...
```

Sometimes you want to keep track of how many times you've been through the block. The with_index method is your friend. It is added as an additional method call after an iterator, and adds a sequence number to each value returned by that iterator. The original value and that sequence number are then passed to the block:

```ruby
f = File.open("testfile")
f.each.with_index do |line, index|
  puts "Line #{index} is: #{line}"
end
f.close
```

produces:

```
Line 0 is: This is line one
Line 1 is: This is line two
```

```
Line 2 is: This is line three
Line 3 is: And so on...
```

Let's look at one more useful iterator. The (somewhat obscurely named) inject method (defined in the module Enumerable) lets you accumulate a value across the members of a collection. For example, you can sum all the elements in an array and find their product using code such as this:

```
[1,3,5,7].inject(0) {|sum, element| sum+element}       # => 16
[1,3,5,7].inject(1) {|product, element| product*element} # => 105
```

inject works like this: the first time the associated block is called, sum is set to inject's parameter, and element is set to the first element in the collection. The second and subsequent times the block is called, sum is set to the value returned by the block on the previous call. The final value of inject is the value returned by the block the last time it was called. One more thing: if inject is called with no parameter, it uses the first element of the collection as the initial value and starts the iteration with the second value. This means that we could have written the previous examples like this:

```
[1,3,5,7].inject {|sum, element| sum+element}       # => 16
[1,3,5,7].inject {|product, element| product*element} # => 105
```

And, just to add to the mystique of inject, you can also give it the name of the method you want to apply to successive elements of the collection. These examples work because, in Ruby, addition and multiplication are simply methods on numbers, and :+ is the symbol corresponding to the method +:

```
[1,3,5,7].inject(:+) # => 16
[1,3,5,7].inject(:*) # => 105
```

Enumerators—External Iterators

Let's spend a paragraph comparing Ruby's approach to iterators to that of languages such as C++ and Java. In Ruby, the basic iterator is internal to the collection—it's simply a method, identical to any other, that happens to call yield whenever it generates a new value. The thing that uses the iterator is just a block of code associated with a call to this method.

In other languages, collections don't contain their own iterators. Instead, they implement methods that generate external helper objects (for example, those based on Java's Iterator interface) that carry the iterator state. In this, as in many other ways, Ruby is a transparent language. When you write a Ruby program, you concentrate on getting the job done, not on building scaffolding to support the language itself.

It's also worth spending another paragraph looking at why Ruby's internal iterators aren't always the best solution. One area where they fall down badly is where you need to treat an iterator as an object in its own right (for example, passing the iterator into a method that needs to access each of the values returned by that iterator). It's also difficult to iterate over two collections in parallel using Ruby's internal iterator scheme.

Fortunately, Ruby comes with a built-in Enumerator class, which implements external iterators in Ruby for just such occasions.

You can create an Enumerator object by calling the to_enum method (or its synonym, enum_for) on a collection such as an array or a hash:

```
a = [ 1, 3, "cat" ]
h = { dog: "canine", fox: "vulpine" }

# Create Enumerators
enum_a = a.to_enum
enum_h = h.to_enum

enum_a.next # => 1
enum_h.next # => [:dog, "canine"]
enum_a.next # => 3
enum_h.next # => [:fox, "vulpine"]
```

Most of the internal iterator methods—the ones that normally yield successive values to a block—will also return an Enumerator object if called without a block:

```
a = [ 1, 3, "cat" ]

enum_a = a.each # create an Enumerator using an internal iterator

enum_a.next # => 1
enum_a.next # => 3
```

Ruby has a method called loop that does nothing but repeatedly invoke its block. Typically, your code in the block will break out of the loop when some condition occurs. But loop is also smart when you use an Enumerator—when an enumerator object runs out of values inside a loop, the loop will terminate cleanly. The following example shows this in action—the loop ends when the three-element enumerator runs out of values.[6]

```
short_enum = [1, 2, 3].to_enum
long_enum  = ('a'..'z').to_enum

loop do
  puts "#{short_enum.next} - #{long_enum.next}"
end
```

produces:

```
1 - a
2 - b
3 - c
```

Enumerators Are Objects

Enumerators take something that's normally executable code (the act of iterating) and turn it into an object. This means you can do things programmatically with enumerators that aren't easily done with regular loops.

For example, the Enumerable module defines each_with_index. This invokes its host class's each Method, returning successive values along with an index:

```
result = []
[ 'a', 'b', 'c' ].each_with_index {|item, index| result << [item, index] }
result    # => [["a", 0], ["b", 1], ["c", 2]]
```

---

6. You can also handle this in your own iterator methods by rescuing the StopIteration exception, but because we haven't talked about exceptions yet, we won't go into details here.

But what if you wanted to iterate and receive an index but use a different method than each to control that iteration? For example, you might want to iterate over the characters in a string. There's no method called each_char_with_index built into the String class.

Enumerators to the rescue. The each_char method of strings will return an enumerator if you don't give it a block, and you can then call each_with_index on that enumerator:

```
result = []
"cat".each_char.each_with_index {|item, index| result << [item,  index] }
result    # => [["c", 0], ["a", 1], ["t", 2]]
```

In fact, this is such a common use of enumerators that Matz has given us with_index, which makes the code read better:

```
result = []
"cat".each_char.with_index {|item, index| result << [item,  index] }
result    # => [["c", 0], ["a", 1], ["t", 2]]
```

You can also create the Enumerator object explicitly—in this case we'll create one that calls our string's each_char method. We can call to_a on that enumerator to iterate over it:

```
enum = "cat".enum_for(:each_char)
enum.to_a # => ["c", "a", "t"]
```

If the method we're using as the basis of our enumerator takes parameters, we can pass them to enum_for:

```
enum_in_threes = (1..10).enum_for(:each_slice, 3)
enum_in_threes.to_a # => [[1, 2, 3], [4, 5, 6], [7, 8, 9], [10]]
```

Enumerators Are Generators and Filters

(This is more advanced material that can be skipped on first reading.) As well as creating enumerators from existing collections, you can create an explicit enumerator, passing it a block. The code in the block will be used when the enumerator object needs to supply a fresh value to your program. However, the block isn't simply executed from top to bottom. Instead, the block is executed in parallel with the rest of your program's code. Execution starts at the top and pauses when the block yields a value to your code. When the code needs the next value, execution resumes at the statement following the yield. This lets you write enumerators that generate infinite sequences (among other things):

```
triangular_numbers = Enumerator.new do |yielder|
  number = 0
  count = 1
  loop do
    number += count
    count += 1
    yielder.yield number
  end
end

5.times { print triangular_numbers.next, " " }
puts
```

produces:

```
1 3 6 10 15
```

Enumerator objects are also enumerable (that is to say, the methods available to enumerable objects are also available to them). That means we can use Enumerable's methods (such as first) on them:

```ruby
triangular_numbers = Enumerator.new do |yielder|
  number = 0
  count = 1
  loop do
    number += count
    count  += 1
    yielder.yield number
  end
end
```

```ruby
p triangular_numbers.first(5)
```

produces:

```
[1, 3, 6, 10, 15]
```

You have to be slightly careful with enumerators that can generate infinite sequences. Some of the regular Enumerator methods such as count and select will happily try to read the whole enumeration before returning a result. If you want a version of select that works with infinite sequences, in Ruby 1.9 you'll need to write it yourself. (Ruby 2 users have a better option, which we discuss in a minute.) Here's a version that gets passed an enumerator and a block and returns a new enumerator containing values from the original for which the block returns true. We'll use it to return triangular numbers that are multiples of 10.

New in 2.0

```ruby
triangular_numbers = Enumerator.new do |yielder|
  #          ...
  # as before...
  #          ...
end
```

```ruby
def infinite_select(enum, &block)
  Enumerator.new do |yielder|
    enum.each do |value|
      yielder.yield(value) if block.call(value)
    end
  end
end
```

```ruby
p infinite_select(triangular_numbers) {|val| val % 10 == 0}.first(5)
```

produces:

```
[10, 120, 190, 210, 300]
```

Here we use the &block notation to pass the block as a parameter to the infinite_select method.

As Brian Candler pointed out in the ruby-core mailing list (message 19679), you can make this more convenient by adding filters such as infinite_select directly to the Enumerator class. Here's an example that returns the first five triangular numbers that are multiples of 10 and that have the digit 3 in them:

```
triangular_numbers = Enumerator.new do |yielder|
  # ... as before
end

class Enumerator
  def infinite_select(&block)
    Enumerator.new do |yielder|
      self.each do |value|
        yielder.yield(value) if block.call(value)
      end
    end
  end
end

p triangular_numbers
  .infinite_select {|val| val % 10 == 0}
  .infinite_select {|val| val.to_s =~ /3/ }
  .first(5)
```

produces:

```
[300, 630, 1830, 3160, 3240]
```

Lazy Enumerators in Ruby 2

As we saw in the previous section, the problem with enumerators that generate infinite sequences is that we have to write special, non-greedy, versions of methods such as select. Fortunately, if you're using Ruby 2.0, you have this support built in. New in 2.0

If you call Enumerator#lazy on any Ruby enumerator, you get back an instance of class Enumerator::Lazy. This enumerator acts just like the original, but it reimplements methods such as select and map so that they can work with infinite sequences. Putting it another way, none of the lazy versions of the methods actually consume any data from the collection until that data is requested, and then they only consume enough to satisfy that request.

To work this magic, the lazy versions of the various methods do not return arrays of data. Instead, each returns a new enumerator that includes its own special processing—the select method returns an enumerator that knows how to apply the select logic to its input collection, the map enumerator knows how to handle the map logic, and so on. The result is that if you chain a bunch of lazy enumerator methods, what you end up with is a chain of enumerators—the last one in the chain takes values from the one before it, and so on.

Let's play with this a little. To start, let's add a helper method to the Integer class that generates a stream of integers.

```
def Integer.all
  Enumerator.new do |yielder, n: 0|
    loop { yielder.yield(n += 1) }
  end.lazy
end

p Integer.all.first(10)
```

produces:

```
[1, 2, 3, 4, 5, 6, 7, 8, 9, 10]
```

There are a couple of things to note here. First, see how I used a keyword parameter on the block both to declare and initialize a local variable n.[7] Second, see how we convert the basic generator into a lazy enumerator with the call to lazy after the end of the block.

Calling the first method on this returns the numbers 1 through 10, but this doesn't exercise the method's lazy characteristics. Let's instead get the first 10 multiples of three.

```
p Integer
      .all
      .select {|i| (i % 3).zero? }
      .first(10)
```

produces:

```
[3, 6, 9, 12, 15, 18, 21, 24, 27, 30]
```

Without the lazy enumerator, the call to select would effectively never return, as select would try to read all the values from the generator. But the lazy version of select only consumes values on demand, and in this case the subsequent call to first only asks for 10 values.

Let's make this a little more complex—how about multiples of 3 whose string representations are palindromes?

```
def palindrome?(n)
  n = n.to_s
  n == n.reverse
end

p Integer
      .all
      .select { |i| (i % 3).zero? }
      .select { |i| palindrome?(i) }
      .first(10)
```

produces:

```
[3, 6, 9, 33, 66, 99, 111, 141, 171, 222]
```

Remember that our lazy filter methods simply return new Enumerator objects? That means we can split up the previous code:

```
multiple_of_three = Integer
      .all
      .select { |i| (i % 3).zero? }

p multiple_of_three.first(10)

m3_palindrome = multiple_of_three
      .select { |i| palindrome?(i) }

p m3_palindrome.first(10)
```

produces:

```
[3, 6, 9, 12, 15, 18, 21, 24, 27, 30]
[3, 6, 9, 33, 66, 99, 111, 141, 171, 222]
```

---

7.   It would be nice to be able to define a true block-local variable using the semicolon separator, but Ruby doesn't allow these variables to have initializers.

You could also code up the various predicates as free-standing procs, if you feel it aids readability or reusablility.

```
multiple_of_three = -> n { (n % 3).zero? }
palindrome        = -> n { n = n.to_s; n == n.reverse }

p Integer
  .all
  .select(&multiple_of_three)
  .select(&palindrome)
  .first(10)
```

produces:

```
[3, 6, 9, 33, 66, 99, 111, 141, 171, 222]
```

If you've ever played with ActiveRelation in Rails, you'll be familiar with this pattern—lazy enumeration methods let us build up a complex filter one piece at a time.

Blocks for Transactions

Although blocks are often used as the target of an iterator, they have other uses. Let's look at a few.

You can use blocks to define a chunk of code that must be run under some kind of transactional control. For example, you'll often open a file, do something with its contents, and then ensure that the file is closed when you finish. Although you can do this using conventional linear code, a version using blocks is simpler (and turns out to be less error prone). A naive implementation (ignoring error handling) could look something like the following:

```
class File
  def self.open_and_process(*args)
    f = File.open(*args)
    yield f
    f.close()
  end
end


File.open_and_process("testfile", "r") do |file|
  while line = file.gets
    puts line
  end
end
```

produces:

```
This is line one
This is line two
This is line three
And so on...
```

open_and_process is a *class method*—it may be called independently of any particular file object. We want it to take the same arguments as the conventional File.open method, but we don't really care what those arguments are. To do this, we specified the arguments as *args, meaning "collect the actual parameters passed to the method into an array named args." We then call File.open, passing it *args as a parameter. This expands the array back into individual parameters. The net result is that open_and_process transparently passes whatever parameters it receives to File.open.

Once the file has been opened, open_and_process calls yield, passing the open file object to the block. When the block returns, the file is closed. In this way, the responsibility for closing an open file has been shifted from the users of file objects to the file objects themselves.

The technique of having files manage their own life cycle is so useful that the class File supplied with Ruby supports it directly. If File.open has an associated block, then that block will be invoked with a file object, and the file will be closed when the block terminates. This is interesting, because it means that File.open has two different behaviors. When called with a block, it executes the block and closes the file. When called without a block, it returns the file object. This is made possible by the method block_given?, which returns true if a block is associated with the current method. Using this method, you could implement something similar to the standard File.open (again, ignoring error handling) using the following:

```
class File
  def self.my_open(*args)
    result = file = File.new(*args)
    # If there's a block, pass in the file and close the file when it returns
    if block_given?
      result = yield file
      file.close
    end
    result
  end
end
```

This has one last twist: in the previous examples of using blocks to control resources, we didn't address error handling. If we wanted to implement these methods properly, we'd need to ensure that we closed a file even if the code processing that file somehow aborted. We do this using exception handling, which we talk about later on page 145.

Blocks Can Be Objects

Blocks are like anonymous methods, but there's more to them than that. You can also convert a block into an object, store it in variables, pass it around, and then invoke its code later.

Remember we said that you can think of blocks as being like an implicit parameter that's passed to a method? Well, you can also make that parameter explicit. If the last parameter in a method definition is prefixed with an ampersand (such as &action), Ruby looks for a code block whenever that method is called. That code block is converted to an object of class Proc and assigned to the parameter. You can then treat the parameter as any other variable.

Here's an example where we create a Proc object in one instance method and store it in an instance variable. We then invoke the proc from a second instance method.

```
class ProcExample
  def pass_in_block(&action)
    @stored_proc = action
  end
  def use_proc(parameter)
    @stored_proc.call(parameter)
  end
end
```

```
eg = ProcExample.new
eg.pass_in_block { |param| puts "The parameter is #{param}" }
eg.use_proc(99)
```

produces:

```
The parameter is 99
```

See how the call method on a proc object invokes the code in the original block?

Many Ruby programs store and later call blocks in this way—it's a great way of implementing callbacks, dispatch tables, and so on. But you can go one step further. If a block can be turned into an object by adding an ampersand parameter to a method, what happens if that method then returns the Proc object to the caller?

```
def create_block_object(&block)
  block
end

bo = create_block_object { |param| puts "You called me with #{param}" }

bo.call 99
bo.call "cat"
```

produces:

```
You called me with 99
You called me with cat
```

In fact, this is so useful that Ruby provides not one but two built-in methods that convert a block to an object.[8] Both lambda and Proc.new take a block and return an object of class Proc. The objects they return differ slightly in how they behave, but we'll hold off talking about that until later on page 336.

```
bo = lambda { |param| puts "You called me with #{param}" }
bo.call 99
bo.call "cat"
```

produces:

```
You called me with 99
You called me with cat
```

Blocks Can Be Closures

Remember I said that a block can use local variables from the surrounding scope? So, let's look at a slightly different example of a block doing just that:

```
def n_times(thing)
  lambda {|n| thing * n }
end

p1 = n_times(23)
p1.call(3) # => 69
p1.call(4) # => 92
p2 = n_times("Hello ")
p2.call(3) # => "Hello Hello Hello "
```

---

8. There's actually a third, proc, but it is effectively deprecated.

The method n_times returns a Proc object that references the method's parameter, thing. Even though that parameter is out of scope by the time the block is called, the parameter remains accessible to the block. This is called a *closure*—variables in the surrounding scope that are referenced in a block remain accessible for the life of that block and the life of any Proc object created from that block.

Here's another example—a method that returns a Proc object that returns successive powers of 2 when called:

```
def power_proc_generator
  value = 1
  lambda { value += value }
end

power_proc = power_proc_generator

puts power_proc.call
puts power_proc.call
puts power_proc.call
```

produces:

```
2
4
8
```

An Alternative Notation

Ruby has another way of creating Proc objects. Rather than write this:

```
lambda { |params| ... }
```

you can now write the following:[9]

```
-> params { ... }
```

The parameters can be enclosed in optional parentheses. Here's an example:

```
proc1 = -> arg { puts "In proc1 with #{arg}" }
proc2 = -> arg1, arg2 { puts "In proc2 with #{arg1} and #{arg2}" }
proc3 = ->(arg1, arg2) { puts "In proc3 with #{arg1} and #{arg2}" }

proc1.call "ant"
proc2.call "bee", "cat"
proc3.call "dog", "elk"
```

produces:

```
In proc1 with ant
In proc2 with bee and cat
In proc3 with dog and elk
```

The -> form is more compact than using lambda and seems to be in favor when you want to pass one or more Proc objects to a method:

---

9.   Let's start by getting something out of the way. Why ->? For compatibility across all the different source file encodings, Matz is restricted to using pure 7-bit ASCII for Ruby operators, and the choice of available characters is severely limited by the ambiguities inherent in the Ruby syntax. He felt that -> was (kind of) reminiscent of a Greek lambda character λ.

```
def my_if(condition, then_clause, else_clause)
  if condition
    then_clause.call
  else
    else_clause.call
  end
end

5.times do |val|
  my_if val < 2,
        -> { puts "#{val} is small" },
        -> { puts "#{val} is big" }
end
```

produces:

```
0 is small
1 is small
2 is big
3 is big
4 is big
```

One good reason to pass blocks to methods is that you can reevaluate the code in those blocks at any time. Here's a trivial example of reimplementing a while loop using a method. Because the condition is passed as a block, it can be evaluated each time around the loop:

```
def my_while(cond, &body)
  while cond.call
    body.call
  end
end

a = 0

my_while -> { a < 3 } do
  puts a
  a += 1
end
```

produces:

```
0
1
2
```

Block Parameter Lists

Blocks written using the old syntax take their parameter lists between vertical bars. Blocks written using the -> syntax take a separate parameter list before the block body. In both cases, the parameter list looks just like the list you can give to methods. It can take default values, splat args (described later on page 120), keyword args, and a block parameter (a trailing argument starting with an ampersand). You can write blocks that are just as versatile as methods.[10] Here's a block using the original block notation:

New in 2.0

---

10. Actually, they are more versatile, because these blocks are also closures, while methods are not.

```
proc1 = lambda do |a, *b, &block|
  puts "a = #{a.inspect}"
  puts "b = #{b.inspect}"
  block.call
end

proc1.call(1, 2, 3, 4) { puts "in block1" }
```

produces:

```
a = 1
b = [2, 3, 4]
in block1
```

And here's one using the new -> notation:

```
proc2 = -> a, *b, &block do
  puts "a = #{a.inspect}"
  puts "b = #{b.inspect}"
  block.call
end

proc2.call(1, 2, 3, 4) { puts "in block2" }
```

produces:

```
a = 1
b = [2, 3, 4]
in block2
```

4.4 Containers Everywhere

Containers, blocks, and iterators are core concepts in Ruby. The more you write in Ruby, the more you'll find yourself moving away from conventional looping constructs. Instead, you'll write classes that support iteration over their contents. And you'll find that this code is compact, easy to read, and a joy to maintain. If this all seems too weird, don't worry. After a while, it'll start to come naturally. And you'll have plenty of time to practice as you use Ruby libraries and frameworks.

## CHAPTER 5

Sharing Functionality: Inheritance, Modules, and Mixins

One of the accepted principles of good design is the elimination of unnecessary duplication. We work hard to make sure that each concept in our application is expressed just once in our code.[1]

We've already seen how classes help. All the methods in a class are automatically accessible to instances of that class. But there are other, more general types of sharing that we want to do. Maybe we're dealing with an application that ships goods. Many forms of shipping are available, but all forms share some basic functionality (weight calculation, perhaps). We don't want to duplicate the code that implements this functionality across the implementation of each shipping type. Or maybe we have a more generic capability that we want to inject into a number of different classes. For example, an online store may need the ability to calculate sales tax for carts, orders, quotes, and so on. Again, we don't want to duplicate the sales tax code in each of these places.

In this chapter, we'll look at two different (but related) mechanisms for this kind of sharing in Ruby. The first, *class-level inheritance*, is common in object-oriented languages. We'll then look at *mixins*, a technique that is often preferable to inheritance. We'll wind up with a discussion of when to use each.

5.1 Inheritance and Messages

In the previous chapter, we saw that when puts needs to convert an object to a string, it calls that object's to_s method. But we've also written our own classes that don't explicitly implement to_s. Despite this, objects of these classes respond successfully when we call to_s on them. How this works has to do with inheritance, subclassing, and how Ruby determines what method to run when you send a message to an object.

Inheritance allows you to create a class that is a refinement or specialization of another class. This class is called a *subclass* of the original, and the original is a *superclass* of the subclass. People also talk of *child* and *parent* classes.

---

1. Why? Because the world changes. And when you adapt your application to each change, you want to know that you've changed exactly the code you need to change. If each real-world concept is implemented at a single point in the code, this becomes vastly easier.

The basic mechanism of subclassing is simple. The child inherits all of the capabilities of its parent class—all the parent's instance methods are available in instances of the child.

Let's look at a trivial example and then later build on it. Here's a definition of a parent class and a child class that inherits from it:

```ruby
class Parent
  def say_hello
    puts "Hello from #{self}"
  end
end

p = Parent.new
p.say_hello

# Subclass the parent...
class Child < Parent
end

c = Child.new
c.say_hello
```

produces:

```
Hello from #<Parent:0x007fb87110fd98>
Hello from #<Child:0x007fb87110fac8>
```

The parent class defines a single instance method, say_hello. We call it by creating a new instance of the class and store a reference to that instance in the variable p.

We then create a subclass using class Child < Parent. The < notation means we're creating a subclass of the thing on the right; the fact that we use less-than presumably signals that the child class is supposed to be a specialization of the parent.

Note that the child class defines no methods, but when we create an instance of it, we can call say_hello. That's because the child inherits all the methods of its parent. Note also that when we output the value of self—the current object—it shows that we're in an instance of class Child, even though the method we're running is defined in the parent.

The superclass method returns the parent of a particular class:

```ruby
class Parent
end
class Child < Parent
end
Child.superclass # => Parent
```

But what's the superclass of Parent?

```ruby
class Parent
end
Parent.superclass # => Object
```

If you don't define an explicit superclass when defining a class, Ruby automatically makes the built-in class Object that class's parent. Let's go further:

```ruby
Object.superclass # => BasicObject
```

Class BasicObject is used in certain kinds of metaprogramming, acting as a blank canvas. What's its parent?

```
BasicObject.superclass.inspect # => "nil"
```

So, we've finally reached the end. BasicObject is the root class of our hierarchy of classes. Given any class in any Ruby application, you can ask for its superclass, then the superclass of that class, and so on, and you'll eventually get back to BasicObject.

We've seen that if you call a method in an instance of class Child and that method isn't in Child's class definition, Ruby will look in the parent class. It goes deeper than that, because if the method isn't defined in the parent class, Ruby continues looking in the parent's parent, the parent's parent's parent, and so on, through the ancestors until it runs out of classes.

And this explains our original question. We can work out why to_s is available in just about every Ruby object. to_s is actually defined in class Object. Because Object is an ancestor of every Ruby class (except BasicObject), instances of every Ruby class have a to_s method defined:

```
class Person
  def initialize(name)
    @name = name
  end
end
p = Person.new("Michael")
puts p
```

produces:

```
#<Person:0x007fa08b8643f8>
```

We saw in the previous chapter that we can override the to_s method:

```
class Person
  def initialize(name)
    @name = name
  end
  def to_s
    "Person named #{@name}"
  end
end

p = Person.new("Michael")
puts p
```

produces:

```
Person named Michael
```

Armed with our knowledge of subclassing, we now know there's nothing special about this code. The puts method calls to_s on its arguments. In this case, the argument is a Person object. Because class Person defines a to_s method, that method is called. If it hadn't defined a to_s method, then Ruby looks for (and finds) to_s in Person's parent class, Object.

It is common to use subclassing to add application-specific behavior to a standard library or framework class. If you've used Ruby on Rails,[2] you'll have subclassed ActionController when writing your own controller classes. Your controllers get all the behavior of the base

---

2. http://www.rubyonrails.com

controller and add their own specific handlers to individual user actions. If you've used the FXRuby GUI framework,[3] you'll have used subclassing to add your own application-specific behavior to FX's standard GUI widgets.

Here's a more self-contained example. Ruby comes with a library called GServer that implements basic TCP server functionality. You add your own behavior to it by subclassing the GServer class. Let's use that to write some code that waits for a client to connect on a socket and then returns the last few lines of the system log file. This is an example of something that's actually quite useful in long-running applications—by building in such a server, you can access the internal state of the application while it is running (possibly even remotely).

The GServer class handles all the mechanics of interfacing to TCP sockets. When you create a GServer object, you tell it the port to listen on.[4] Then, when a client connects, the GServer object calls its serve method to handle that connection. Here's the implementation of that serve method in the GServer class:

```
def serve(io)
end
```

As you can see, it does nothing. That's where our own LogServer class comes in:

tut_modules/gserver-logger.rb
```
require 'gserver'

class LogServer < GServer

  def initialize
    super(12345)
  end

  def serve(client)
    client.puts get_end_of_log_file
  end


private

  def get_end_of_log_file
    File.open("/var/log/system.log") do |log|
      log.seek(-500, IO::SEEK_END)     # back up 500 characters from end
      log.gets                         # ignore partial line
      log.read                         # and return rest
    end
  end
end

server = LogServer.new
server.start.join
```

I don't want to focus too much on the details of running the server. Instead, let's look at how inheritance has helped us with this code. Notice that our LogServer class inherits from GServer.

---

3. http://www.fxruby.org/
4. You can tell it a lot more, as well. We chose to keep it simple here.

This means that a log server is a kind of GServer, sharing all the GServer functionality. It also means we can add our own specialized behavior.

The first such specialization is the initialize method. We want our log server to run on TCP port 12345. That's a parameter that would normally be passed to the GServer constructor. So, within the initialize method of the LogServer, we want to invoke the initialize method of GServer, our parent, passing it the port number. We do that using the Ruby keyword super. When you invoke super, Ruby sends a message to the parent of the current object, asking it to invoke a method of the same name as the method invoking super. It passes this method the parameters that were passed to super.

This is a crucial step and one often forgotten by folks new to OO. When you subclass another class, you are responsible for making sure the initialization required by that class gets run. This means that, unless you know it isn't needed, you'll need to put a call to super somewhere in your subclass's initialize method. (If your subclass doesn't need an initialize method, then there's no need to do anything, because it will be the parent class's initialize method that gets run when your objects get created.)

So, by the time our initialize method finishes, our LogServer object will be a fully fledged TCP server, all without us having to write any protocol-level code. Down at the end of our program, we start the server and then call join to wait for the server to exit.

Our server receives connections from external clients. These invoke the serve method in the server object. Remember that empty method in class GServer? Well, our LogServer class provides its own implementation. And because it gets found by Ruby first when it's looking for methods to execute, it's our code that gets run whenever GServer accepts a connection. And our code reads the last few lines of the log file and returns them to the client:[5]

```
$ telnet 127.0.0.1 12345
Trying 127.0.0.1...
Connected to localhost.
Escape character is '^]'.
Jul  9 12:22:59 doc-72-47-70-67 com.apple.mdworker.pool.0[49913]: PSSniffer error
Jul  9 12:28:55 doc-72-47-70-67 login[82588]: DEAD_PROCESS: 82588 ttys004
Connection closed by foreign host.
```

The use of the serve method shows a common idiom when using subclassing. A parent class assumes that it will be subclassed and calls a method that it expects its children to implement. This allows the parent to take on the brunt of the processing but to invoke what are effectively hook methods in subclasses to add application-level functionality. As we'll see at the end of this chapter, just because this idiom is common doesn't make it good design.

So, instead, let's look at *mixins*, a different way of sharing functionality in Ruby code. But, before we look at mixins, we'll need to get familiar with Ruby *modules*.

5.2 Modules

Modules are a way of grouping together methods, classes, and constants. Modules give you two major benefits:

- Modules provide a namespace and prevent name clashes.
- Modules support the mixin facility.

---

5. You can also access this server from a web browser by connecting to http://127.0.0.1:12345.

Namespaces

As you start to write bigger Ruby programs, you'll find yourself producing chunks of reusable code—libraries of related routines that are generally applicable. You'll want to break this code into separate files so the contents can be shared among different Ruby programs.

Often this code will be organized into classes, so you'll probably stick a class (or a set of interrelated classes) into a file. However, there are times when you want to group things together that don't naturally form a class.

An initial approach may be to put all these things into a file and simply load that file into any program that needs it. This is the way the C language works. However, this approach has a problem. Say you write a set of the trigonometry functions, sin, cos, and so on. You stuff them all into a file, trig.rb, for future generations to enjoy. Meanwhile, Sally is working on a simulation of good and evil, and she codes a set of her own useful routines, including be_good and sin, and sticks them into moral.rb. Joe, who wants to write a program to find out how many angels can dance on the head of a pin, needs to load both trig.rb and moral.rb into his program. But both define a method called sin. Bad news.

The answer is the module mechanism. Modules define a *namespace*, a sandbox in which your methods and constants can play without having to worry about being stepped on by other methods and constants. The trig functions can go into one module:

```
tut_modules/trig.rb
module Trig
  PI = 3.141592654
  def Trig.sin(x)
   # ..
  end

  def Trig.cos(x)
   # ..
  end
end
```

and the good and bad "moral" methods can go into another:

```
tut_modules/moral.rb
module Moral
  VERY_BAD = 0
  BAD      = 1
  def Moral.sin(badness)
    # ...
  end
end
```

Module constants are named just like class constants, with an initial uppercase letter.[6] The method definitions look similar, too: module methods are defined just like class methods.

If a third program wants to use these modules, it can simply load the two files (using the Ruby require statement). To reference the name sin unambiguously, our code can then qualify the name using the name of the module containing the implementation we want, followed by ::, the scope resolution operator:

---

6. But we will conventionally use all uppercase letters when writing them.

```
tut_modules/pin_head.rb
require_relative 'trig'
require_relative 'moral'
y = Trig.sin(Trig::PI/4)
wrongdoing = Moral.sin(Moral::VERY_BAD)
```

As with class methods, you call a module method by preceding its name with the module's name and a period, and you reference a constant using the module name and two colons.

5.3 Mixins

Modules have another, wonderful use. At a stroke, they pretty much eliminate the need for inheritance, providing a facility called a *mixin*.

In the previous section's examples, we defined module methods, methods whose names were prefixed by the module name. If this made you think of class methods, your next thought may well be "What happens if I define instance methods within a module?" Good question. A module can't have instances, because a module isn't a class. However, you can *include* a module within a class definition. When this happens, all the module's instance methods are suddenly available as methods in the class as well. They get *mixed in*. In fact, mixed-in modules effectively behave as superclasses.

```ruby
module Debug
  def who_am_i?
    "#{self.class.name} (id: #{self.object_id}): #{self.name}"
  end
end

class Phonograph
  include Debug
  attr_reader :name
  def initialize(name)
    @name = name
  end
  # ...
end

class EightTrack
  include Debug
  attr_reader :name
  def initialize(name)
    @name = name
  end
  # ...
end

ph = Phonograph.new("West End Blues")
et = EightTrack.new("Surrealistic Pillow")

ph.who_am_i?  # => "Phonograph (id: 70266478767560): West End Blues"
et.who_am_i?  # => "EightTrack (id: 70266478767520): Surrealistic Pillow"
```

By including the Debug module, both the Phonograph and EightTrack classes gain access to the who_am_i? instance method.

We'll make a couple of points about the include statement before we go on.

First, it has nothing to do with files. C programmers use a preprocessor directive called #include to insert the contents of one file into another during compilation. The Ruby include statement simply makes a reference to a module. If that module is in a separate file, you must use require (or its less commonly used cousin, load) to drag that file in before using include. Second, a Ruby include does not simply copy the module's instance methods into the class. Instead, it makes a reference from the class to the included module. If multiple classes include that module, they'll all point to the same thing. If you change the definition of a method within a module, even while your program is running, all classes that include that module will exhibit the new behavior.[7]

Mixins give you a wonderfully controlled way of adding functionality to classes. However, their true power comes out when the code in the mixin starts to interact with code in the class that uses it. Let's take the standard Ruby mixin Comparable as an example. The Comparable mixin adds the comparison operators (<, <=, ==, >=, and >), as well as the method between?, to a class. For this to work, Comparable assumes that any class that uses it defines the operator <=>. So, as a class writer, you define one method, <=>; include Comparable; and get six comparison functions for free.

Let's try this with a simple Person class. We'll make people comparable based on their names:

```ruby
class Person
  include Comparable
  attr_reader :name

  def initialize(name)
    @name = name
  end
  def to_s
    "#{@name}"
  end
  def <=>(other)
    self.name <=> other.name
  end
end

p1 = Person.new("Matz")
p2 = Person.new("Guido")
p3 = Person.new("Larry")


# Compare a couple of names
if p1 > p2
  puts "#{p1.name}'s name > #{p2.name}'s name"
end

# Sort an array of Person objects

puts "Sorted list:"
puts [ p1, p2, p3].sort
```

---

7.   Of course, we're speaking only of methods here. Instance variables are always per object, for example.

produces:

```
Matz's name > Guido's name
Sorted list:
Guido
Larry
Matz
```

We included Comparable in our Person class and then defined a <=> method. We were then able to perform comparisons (such as p1 > p2) and even sort an array of Person objects.

Inheritance and Mixins

Some object-oriented languages (such as C++) support multiple inheritance, where a class can have more than one immediate parent, inheriting functionality from each. Although powerful, this technique can be dangerous, because the inheritance hierarchy can become ambiguous.

Other languages, such as Java and C#, support single inheritance. Here, a class can have only one immediate parent. Although cleaner (and easier to implement), single inheritance also has drawbacks —in the real world, objects often inherit attributes from multiple sources (a ball is both a *bouncing thing* and a *spherical thing*, for example). Ruby offers an interesting and powerful compromise, giving you the simplicity of single inheritance and the power of multiple inheritance. A Ruby class has only one direct parent, so Ruby is a single-inheritance language. However, Ruby classes can include the functionality of any number of *mixins* (a mixin is like a partial class definition). This provides a controlled multiple-inheritance-like capability with none of the drawbacks.

5.4 Iterators and the Enumerable Module

The Ruby collection classes (Array, Hash, and so on) support a large number of operations that do various things with the collection: traverse it, sort it, and so on. You may be thinking, "Gee, it'd sure be nice if *my* class could support all these neat-o features, too!" (If you actually thought that, it's probably time to stop watching reruns of 1960s television shows.)

Well, your classes *can* support all these neat-o features, thanks to the magic of mixins and module Enumerable. All you have to do is write an iterator called each, which returns the elements of your collection in turn. Mix in Enumerable, and suddenly your class supports things such as map, include?, and find_all?. If the objects in your collection implement meaningful ordering semantics using the <=> method, you'll also get methods such as min, max, and sort.

5.5 Composing Modules

Enumerable is a standard mixin, implementing a bunch of methods in terms of the host class's each method. One of the methods defined by Enumerable is inject, which we saw previously on page 57. This method applies a function or operation to the first two elements in the collection and then applies the operation to the result of this computation and to the third element, and so on, until all elements in the collection have been used.

Because inject is made available by Enumerable, we can use it in any class that includes the Enumerable module and defines the method each. Many built-in classes do this.

```
[ 1, 2, 3, 4, 5 ].inject(:+)  # => 15
( 'a'..'m').inject(:+)        # => "abcdefghijklm"
```

We could also define our own class that mixes in Enumerable and hence gets inject support:

tut_modules/vowel_finder.rb

```ruby
class VowelFinder
  include Enumerable

  def initialize(string)
    @string = string
  end
  def each
    @string.scan(/[aeiou]/) do |vowel|
      yield vowel
    end
  end
end

vf = VowelFinder.new("the quick brown fox jumped")
vf.inject(:+)                     # => "euiooue"
```

Note we used the same pattern in the call to inject in these examples—we're using it to perform a summation. When applied to numbers, it returns the arithmetic sum; when applied to strings, it concatenates them. We can use a module to encapsulate this functionality too:

```ruby
module Summable
  def sum
    inject(:+)
  end
end

class Array
  include Summable
end

class Range
  include Summable
end

require_relative "vowel_finder"
class VowelFinder
  include Summable
end

[ 1, 2, 3, 4, 5 ].sum   # => 15
('a'..'m').sum          # => "abcdefghijklm"

vf = VowelFinder.new("the quick brown fox jumped")
vf.sum                  # => "euiooue"
```

Instance Variables in Mixins

People coming to Ruby from C++ often ask, "What happens to instance variables in a mixin? In C++, I have to jump through some hoops to control how variables are shared in a multiple-inheritance hierarchy. How does Ruby handle this?"

Well, for starters, it's not really a fair question. Remember how instance variables work in Ruby: the first mention of an @-prefixed variable creates the instance variable *in the current object*, self.

For a mixin, this means the module you mix into your client class (the *mixee*?) may create instance variables in the client object and may use attr_reader and friends to define accessors for these instance variables. For instance, the Observable module in the following example adds an instance variable @observer_list to any class that includes it:

tut_modules/observer_impl.rb
```ruby
module Observable
  def observers
    @observer_list ||= []
  end
  def add_observer(obj)
    observers << obj
  end
  def notify_observers
    observers.each {|o| o.update }
  end
end
```

However, this behavior exposes us to a risk. A mixin's instance variables can clash with those of the host class or with those of other mixins. The example that follows shows a class that uses our Observer module but that unluckily also uses an instance variable called @observer_list. At runtime, this program will go wrong in some hard-to-diagnose ways:

tut_modules/observer_impl_eg.rb
```ruby
require_relative 'observer_impl'

class TelescopeScheduler

  # other classes can register to get notifications
  # when the schedule changes
  include Observable

  def initialize
    @observer_list = []  # folks with telescope time
  end
  def add_viewer(viewer)
    @observer_list << viewer
  end

  # ...
end
```

For the most part, mixin modules don't use instance variables directly—they use accessors to retrieve data from the client object. But if you need to create a mixin that has to have its own state, ensure that the instance variables have unique names to distinguish them from any other mixins in the system (perhaps by using the module's name as part of the variable name). Alternatively, the module could use a module-level hash, indexed by the current object ID, to store instance-specific data without using Ruby instance variables:

```ruby
module Test
  State = {}
  def state=(value)
    State[object_id] = value
  end
```

```
  def state
    State[object_id]
  end
end

class Client
  include Test
end

c1 = Client.new
c2 = Client.new
c1.state = 'cat'
c2.state = 'dog'
c1.state  # => "cat"
c2.state  # => "dog"
```

A downside of this approach is that the data associated with a particular object will not get automatically deleted if the object is deleted. In general, a mixin that requires its own state is not a mixin—it should be written as a class.

Resolving Ambiguous Method Names

One of the other questions folks ask about mixins is, how is method lookup handled? In particular, what happens if methods with the same name are defined in a class, in that class's parent class, and in a mixin included into the class?

The answer is that Ruby looks first in the immediate class of an object, then in the mixins included into that class, and then in superclasses and their mixins. If a class has multiple modules mixed in, the last one included is searched first.

5.6 Inheritance, Mixins, and Design

Inheritance and mixins both allow you to write code in one place and effectively inject that code into multiple classes. So, when do you use each?

As with most questions of design, the answer is, well...it depends. However, over the years developers have come up with some pretty clear general guidelines to help us decide.

First let's look at subclassing. Classes in Ruby are related to the idea of types. It would be natural to say that "cat" is a string and [1,2] is an array. And that's another way of saying that the class of "cat" is String and the class of [1,2] is Array. When we create our own classes, you can think of it as adding new types to the language. And when we subclass either a built-in class or our own class, we're creating a *subtype*.

Now, a lot of research has been done on type theories. One of the more famous results is the *Liskov Substitution Principle*. Formally, this states, "Let q(x) be a property provable about objects x of type T. Then q(y) should be true for objects y of type S where S is a subtype of T." What this means is that you should be able to substitute an object of a child class wherever you use an object of the parent class—the child should honor the parent's contract. There's another way of looking at this: we should be able to say that the child object *is a* kind of the parent. We're used to saying this in English: a car *is a* vehicle, a cat *is an* animal, and so on. This means that a cat should, at the very least, be capable of doing everything we say that an animal can do.

So, when you're looking for subclassing relationships while designing your application, be on the lookout for these *is-a* relationships.

But...here's the bad news. In the real world, there really aren't that many true *is a* relationships. Instead, it's far more common to have *has a* or *uses a* relationships between things. The real world is built using composition, not strict hierarchies.

In the past, we've tended to gloss over that fact when programming. Because inheritance was the only scheme available for sharing code, we got lazy and said things like "My Person class is a subclass of my DatabaseWrapper class." (Indeed, the Rails framework makes just this mistake.) But a person object *is not* a kind of database wrapper object. A person object *uses* a database wrapper to provide persistence services.

Is this just a theoretical issue? No! Inheritance represents an incredibly tight coupling of two components. Change a parent class, and you risk breaking the child class. But, even worse, if code that uses objects of the child class relies on those objects also having methods defined in the parent, then all that code will break, too. The parent class's implementation leaks through the child classes and out into the rest of the code. With a decent-sized program, this becomes a serious inhibitor to change.

And that's why we need to move away from inheritance in our designs. Instead, we need to be using *composition* wherever we see a case of A *uses a* B, or A *has a* B. Our persisted Person object won't subclass DataWrapper. Instead, it'll construct a reference to a database wrapper object and use that object reference to save and restore itself.

But that can also make code messy. And that's where a combination of mixins and metaprogramming comes to the rescue, because we can say this:

```
class Person
  include Persistable
  # ...
end
```

instead of this:

```
class Person < DataWrapper
  # ...
end
```

If you're new to object-oriented programming, this discussion may feel remote and abstract. But as you start to code larger and larger programs, we urge you to think about the issues discussed here. Try to reserve inheritance for the times where it is justified. And try to explore all the cool ways that mixins let you write decoupled, flexible code.

## CHAPTER 6

Standard Types

So far, we've been having fun implementing programs using arrays, hashes, and procs, but we haven't really covered the other basic types in Ruby: numbers, strings, ranges, and regular expressions. Let's spend a few pages on these basic building blocks now.

6.1 Numbers

Ruby supports integers and floating-point, rational, and complex numbers. Integers can be any length (up to a maximum determined by the amount of free memory on your system). Integers within a certain range (normally $-2^{30}...2^{30}-1$ or $-2^{62}...2^{62}-1$) are held internally in binary form and are objects of class Fixnum. Integers outside this range are stored in objects of class Bignum (currently implemented as a variable-length set of short integers). This process is transparent, and Ruby automatically manages the conversion back and forth:

```
num = 10001
4.times do
  puts "#{num.class}: #{num}"
num *= num
end
```

produces:

```
Fixnum: 10001
Fixnum: 100020001
Fixnum: 10004000600040001
Bignum: 100080028005600700056002800080001
```

You write integers using an optional leading sign, an optional base indicator (0 for octal, 0d for decimal [the default], 0x for hex, or 0b for binary), followed by a string of digits in the appropriate base. Underscore characters are ignored in the digit string (some folks use them in place of commas in larger numbers).

```
123456                    =>  123456    # Fixnum
0d123456                  =>  123456    # Fixnum
123_456                   =>  123456    # Fixnum - underscore ignored
-543                      =>  -543      # Fixnum - negative number
0xaabb                    =>  43707     # Fixnum - hexadecimal
0377                      =>  255       # Fixnum - octal
-0b10_1010                =>  -42       # Fixnum - binary (negated)
123_456_789_123_456_789   =>  123456789123456789 # Bignum
```

A numeric literal with a decimal point and/or an exponent is turned into a Float object, corresponding to the native architecture's double data type. You must both precede and follow the decimal point with a digit (if you write 1.0e3 as 1.e3, Ruby will try to invoke the method e3 on the object 1).

Ruby includes support for rational and complex numbers. Rational numbers are the ratio of two integers—they are fractions—and hence have an exact representation (unlike floats). Complex numbers represent points on the complex plane. They have two components, the real and imaginary parts.

Ruby doesn't have a literal syntax for representing rational and complex numbers. Instead, you create them using explicit calls to the constructor methods Rational and Complex (although, as we'll see, you can use the mathn library to make working with rational numbers easier).

```
Rational(3, 4) * Rational(2, 3)     # => (1/2)
Rational("3/4") * Rational("2/3")   # => (1/2)

Complex(1, 2) * Complex(3, 4)       # => (-5+10i)
Complex("1+2i") * Complex("3+4i")   # => (-5+10i)
```

All numbers are objects and respond to a variety of messages (listed in full starting in the reference section at the end of this book). So, unlike (say) C++, you find the absolute value of a number by writing num.abs, not abs(num).

Finally, we'll offer a warning for Perl users. Strings that contain just digits are *not* automatically converted into numbers when used in expressions. This tends to bite most often when reading numbers from a file. For example, we may want to find the sum of the two numbers on each line for a file such as the following:

```
3 4
5 6
7 8
```

The following code doesn't work:

```
some_file.each do |line|
  v1, v2 = line.split     # split line on spaces
  print v1 + v2, " "
end
```

produces:

```
34 56 78
```

The problem is that the input was read as strings, not numbers. The plus operator concatenates strings, so that's what we see in the output. To fix this, use the Integer method to convert the strings to integers:

```
some_file.each do |line|
  v1, v2 = line.split
  print Integer(v1) + Integer(v2), " "
end
```

produces:

```
7 11 15
```

How Numbers Interact

Most of the time, numbers work the way you'd expect. If you perform some operation between two numbers of the same class, the answer will typically be a number of that same class (although, as we've seen, fixnums can become bignums, and vice versa). If the two numbers are different classes, the result will have the class of the more general one. If you mix integers and floats, the result will be a float; if you mix floats and complex numbers, the result will be complex.

```
1 + 2              # => 3
1 + 2.0            # => 3.0
1.0 + 2            # => 3.0
1.0 + Complex(1,2) # => (2.0+2i)
1 + Rational(2,3)  # => (5/3)
1.0 + Rational(2,3) # => 1.6666666666666665
```

The return-type rule still applies when it comes to division. However, this often confuses folks, because division between two integers yields an integer result:

```
1.0 / 2  # => 0.5
1 / 2.0  # => 0.5
1 / 2    # => 0
```

If you'd prefer that integer division instead return a fraction (a Rational number), require the mathn library (described in the library section on page 768). This will cause arithmetic operations to attempt to find the most *natural* representation for their results. For integer division where the result isn't an integer, a fraction will be returned.

```
22 / 7                   # => 3
Complex::I * Complex::I # => (-1+0i)

require 'mathn'
22 / 7                   # => (22/7)
Complex::I * Complex::I # => -1
```

Note that 22/7 is effectively a rational literal once mathn is loaded (albeit one that's calculated at runtime).

Looping Using Numbers

Integers also support several iterators. We've seen one already on page 83: 5.times. Others include upto and downto for iterating up and down between two integers. Class Numeric also provides the more general method step, which is more like a traditional for loop.

```
3.times        { print "X " }
1.upto(5)      {|i| print i, " " }
99.downto(95)  {|i| print i, " " }
50.step(80, 5) {|i| print i, " " }
```

produces:

```
X X X 1 2 3 4 5 99 98 97 96 95 50 55 60 65 70 75 80
```

As with other iterators, if you leave the block off, the call returns an Enumerator object:

```
10.downto(7).with_index {|num, index| puts "#{index}: #{num}"}
```

produces:

```
0: 10
1: 9
2: 8
3: 7
```

6.2 Strings

Ruby strings are simply sequences of characters.[1] They normally hold printable characters, but that is not a requirement; a string can also hold binary data. Strings are objects of class String. Strings are often created using string literals—sequences of characters between delimiters. Because binary data is otherwise difficult to represent within program source, you can place various escape sequences in a string literal. Each is replaced with the corresponding binary value as the program is compiled. The type of string delimiter determines the degree of substitution performed. Within single-quoted strings, two consecutive backslashes are replaced by a single backslash, and a backslash followed by a single quote becomes a single quote.

```
'escape using "\\"'   # => escape using "\"
'That\'s right'       # => That's right
```

Double-quoted strings support a boatload more escape sequences. The most common is probably \n, the newline character. For a complete list, see Table 11, *Substitutions in double-quoted strings*, on page 300. In addition, you can substitute the value of any Ruby code into a string using the sequence #{ *expr* }. If the code is just a global variable, a class variable, or an instance variable, you can omit the braces.

```
"Seconds/day: #{24*60*60}"    # => Seconds/day: 86400
"#{'Ho! '*3}Merry Christmas!" # => Ho! Ho! Ho! Merry Christmas!
"Safe level is #$SAFE"        # => Safe level is 0
```

The interpolated code can be one or more statements, not just an expression:

```
puts  "now is #{ def the(a)
                   'the ' + a
                 end
                 the('time')
               } for all bad coders..."
```

produces:

```
now is the time for all bad coders...
```

You have three more ways to construct string literals: %q, %Q, and *here documents*. %q and %Q start delimited single- and double-quoted strings (you can think of %q as a thin quote, as in ', and %Q as a thick quote, as in "):

```
%q/general single-quoted string/   # => general single-quoted string
%Q!general double-quoted string!   # => general double-quoted string
%Q{Seconds/day: #{24*60*60}}       # => Seconds/day: 86400
```

In fact, the Q is optional:

---

1.   Prior to Ruby 1.9, strings were sequences of 8-bit bytes.

```
%!general double-quoted string!    # => general double-quoted string
%{Seconds/day: #{24*60*60}}        # => Seconds/day: 86400
```

The character following the *q* or *Q* is the delimiter. If it is an opening bracket [, brace {, parenthesis (, or less-than sign <, the string is read until the matching close symbol is found. Otherwise, the string is read until the next occurrence of the same delimiter. The delimiter can be any nonalphanumeric or nonmultibyte character.

Finally, you can construct a string using a *here document*:

```
string = <<END_OF_STRING
    The body of the string is the input lines up to
    one starting with the same text that followed the '<<'
END_OF_STRING
```

A here document consists of lines in the source up to but not including the terminating string that you specify after the << characters. Normally, this terminator must start in column one. However, if you put a minus sign after the << characters, you can indent the terminator:

```
string = <<-END_OF_STRING
    The body of the string is the input lines up to
    one starting with the same text that followed the '<<'
    END_OF_STRING
```

You can also have multiple here documents on a single line. Each acts as a separate string. The bodies of the here documents are fetched sequentially from the source lines that follow:

```
print <<-STRING1, <<-STRING2
Concat
STRING1
      enate
      STRING2
```

produces:

```
Concat
      enate
```

Note that Ruby does not strip leading spaces off the contents of the strings in these cases.

Strings and Encodings

Every string has an associated encoding. The default encoding of a string literal depends on the encoding of the source file that contains it. With no explicit encoding, a source file (and its strings) will be US-ASCII in Ruby 1.9 and UTF-8 in Ruby 2.

New in 2.0

```
plain_string = "dog"
puts RUBY_VERSION
puts "Encoding of #{plain_string.inspect} is #{plain_string.encoding}"
```

produces:

```
2.0.0
Encoding of "dog" is UTF-8
```

If you override the encoding, you'll do that for all strings in the file:

```
#encoding: utf-8
plain_string = "dog"
puts "Encoding of #{plain_string.inspect} is #{plain_string.encoding}"
utf_string = "δog"
puts "Encoding of #{utf_string.inspect} is #{utf_string.encoding}"
```

produces:

```
Encoding of "dog" is UTF-8
Encoding of "δog" is UTF-8
```

We'll have a lot more to say about encoding in Chapter 17, *Character Encoding,* on page 239.

Character Constants

Technically, Ruby does not have a class for characters—characters are simply strings of length one. For historical reasons, character constants can be created by preceding the character (or sequence that represents a character) with a question mark:

```
?a         # => "a"       (printable character)
?\n        # => "\n"      (code for a newline (0x0a))
?\C-a      # => "\u0001"  (control a)
?\M-a      # => "\xE1"    (meta sets bit 7)
?\M-\C-a   # => "\x81"    (meta and control a)
?\C-?      # => "\u007F"  (delete character)
```

Do yourself a favor and forget this section. It's far easier to use regular octal and hex escape sequences than to remember these ones. Use "a" rather than ?a, and use "\n" rather than ?\n.

Working with Strings

String is probably the largest built-in Ruby class, with more than one hundred standard methods. We won't go through them all here; the library reference has a complete list. Instead, we'll look at some common string idioms—things that are likely to pop up during day-to-day programming.

Maybe we've been given a file containing information on a song playlist. For historical reasons (are there any other kind?), the list of songs is stored as lines in the file. Each line holds the name of the file containing the song, the song's duration, the artist, and the title, all in vertical bar–separated fields. A typical file may start like this:

```
tut_stdtypes/songdata
/jazz/j00132.mp3  | 3:45 | Fats      Waller       | Ain't Misbehavin'
/jazz/j00319.mp3  | 2:58 | Louis     Armstrong    | Wonderful World
/bgrass/bg0732.mp3| 4:09 | Strength in Numbers   | Texas Red
```

Looking at the data, it's clear that we'll be using some of class String's many methods to extract and clean up the fields before we use them. At a minimum, we'll need to

- break each line into fields,
- convert the running times from mm:ss to seconds, and
- remove those extra spaces from the artists' names.

Our first task is to split each line into fields, and String#split will do the job nicely. In this case, we'll pass split a regular expression, /\s*\|\s*/, that splits the line into tokens wherever split finds a vertical bar, optionally surrounded by spaces. And, because the line read from the file has a trailing newline, we'll use String#chomp to strip it off just before we apply the split. We'll store details of each song in a Struct that contains an attribute for each of the three fields. (A Struct is simply a data structure that contains a given set of attributes—in this case the title, name, and length. Struct is described in the reference section on page 693.)

```
Song = Struct.new(:title, :name, :length)

File.open("songdata") do |song_file|
  songs = []

  song_file.each do |line|
    file, length, name, title = line.chomp.split(/\s*\|\s*/)
    songs << Song.new(title, name, length)
  end

  puts songs[1]
end
```

produces:

```
#<struct Song title="Wonderful World", name="Louis    Armstrong", length="2:58">
```

Unfortunately, whoever created the original file entered the artists' names in columns, so some of them contain extra spaces that we'd better remove before we go much further. We have many ways of doing this, but probably the simplest is String#squeeze, which trims runs of repeated characters. We'll use the squeeze! form of the method, which alters the string in place:

```
Song = Struct.new(:title, :name, :length)

File.open("songdata") do |song_file|
  songs = []

  song_file.each do |line|
    file, length, name, title = line.chomp.split(/\s*\|\s*/)
    name.squeeze!(" ")
    songs << Song.new(title, name, length)
  end

  puts songs[1]
end
```

produces:

```
#<struct Song title="Wonderful World", name="Louis Armstrong", length="2:58">
```

Finally, we have the minor matter of the time format: the file says 2:58, and we want the number of seconds, 178. We could use split again, this time splitting the time field around the colon character:

```
"2:58".split(/:/) # => ["2", "58"]
```

Instead, we'll use a related method. String#scan is similar to split in that it breaks a string into chunks based on a pattern. However, unlike split, with scan you specify the pattern that you want the chunks to match. In this case, we want to match one or more digits for both the minutes and seconds components. The pattern for one or more digits is /\d+/:

```ruby
Song = Struct.new(:title, :name, :length)

File.open("songdata") do |song_file|
  songs = []

  song_file.each do |line|
    file, length, name, title = line.chomp.split(/\s*\|\s*/)
    name.squeeze!(" ")
    mins, secs = length.scan(/\d+/)
    songs << Song.new(title, name, mins.to_i*60 + secs.to_i)
  end

  puts songs[1]
end
```

produces:

```
#<struct Song title="Wonderful World", name="Louis Armstrong", length=178>
```

We could spend the next fifty pages looking at all the methods in class String. However, let's move on instead to look at a simpler data type: the range.

6.3 Ranges

Ranges occur everywhere: January to December, 0 to 9, rare to well done, lines 50 through 67, and so on. If Ruby is to help us model reality, it seems natural for it to support these ranges. In fact, Ruby goes one better: it actually uses ranges to implement three separate features: sequences, conditions, and intervals.

Ranges as Sequences

The first and perhaps most natural use of ranges is to express a sequence. Sequences have a start point, an end point, and a way to produce successive values in the sequence. In Ruby, these sequences are created using the .. and ... range operators. The two-dot form creates an inclusive range, and the three-dot form creates a range that excludes the specified high value:

```ruby
1..10
'a'..'z'
0..."cat".length
```

You can convert a range to an array using the to_a method and convert it to an Enumerator using to_enum:[2]

```ruby
(1..10).to_a         # => [1, 2, 3, 4, 5, 6, 7, 8, 9, 10]
('bar'..'bat').to_a # => ["bar", "bas", "bat"]
enum = ('bar'..'bat').to_enum
enum.next            # => "bar"
enum.next            # => "bas"
```

Ranges have methods that let you iterate over them and test their contents in a variety of ways:

---

2. Sometimes people worry that ranges take a lot of memory. That's not an issue: the range 1..100000 is held as a Range object containing references to two Fixnum objects. However, convert a range into an array, and all that memory will get used.

```
digits = 0..9
digits.include?(5)          # => true
digits.max                  # => 9
digits.reject {|i| i < 5 }  # => [5, 6, 7, 8, 9]
digits.inject(:+)           # => 45
```

So far we've shown ranges of numbers and strings. However, as you'd expect from an object-oriented language, Ruby ranges can be based on objects that you define. The only constraints are that the objects must respond to succ by returning the next object in sequence and the objects must be comparable using <=>. Sometimes called the *spaceship operator*, <=> compares two values, returning -1, 0, or +1 depending on whether the first is less than, equal to, or greater than the second.

In reality, this isn't something you do very often, so examples tend to be a bit contrived. Here's one—a class that presents numbers that are powers of 2. Because it defines <=> and succ, we can use objects of this class in ranges:

```
class PowerOfTwo
  attr_reader :value
  def initialize(value)
    @value = value
  end
  def <=>(other)
    @value <=> other.value
  end
  def succ
    PowerOfTwo.new(@value + @value)
  end
  def to_s
    @value.to_s
  end
end

p1 = PowerOfTwo.new(4)
p2 = PowerOfTwo.new(32)

puts (p1..p2).to_a
```

produces:

```
4
8
16
32
```

Ranges as Conditions

As well as representing sequences, ranges can also be used as conditional expressions. Here, they act as a kind of toggle switch—they turn on when the condition in the first part of the range becomes true, and they turn off when the condition in the second part becomes true. For example, the following code fragment prints sets of lines from standard input, where the first line in each set contains the word *start* and the last line contains the word *end*:

```
while line = gets
  puts line if line =~ /start/ .. line =~ /end/
end
```

Behind the scenes, the range keeps track of the state of each of the tests. We'll show some examples of this in the description of loops on page 138 and in the .language section on page 320.

Ranges as Intervals

A final use of the versatile range is as an interval test: seeing whether some value falls within the interval represented by the range. We do this using ===, the case equality operator:

```
(1..10)     === 5       # => true
(1..10)     === 15      # => false
(1..10)     === 3.14159 # => true
('a'..'j') === 'c'      # => true
('a'..'j') === 'z'      # => false
```

This is most often used in case statements:

```
car_age = gets.to_f    # let's assume it's 9.5
case car_age
when 0...1
  puts "Mmm.. new car smell"
when 1...3
  puts "Nice and new"
when 3...10
  puts "Reliable but slightly dinged"
when 10...30
  puts "Clunker"
else
  puts "Vintage gem"
end
```

produces:

```
Reliable but slightly dinged
```

Note the use of exclusive ranges in the previous example. These are normally the correct choice in case statements. If instead we had written the following, we'd get the wrong answer because 9.5 does not fall within any of the ranges, so the else clause triggers:

```
car_age = gets.to_f    # let's assume it's 9.5
case car_age
when 0..0
  puts "Mmm.. new car smell"
when 1..2
  puts "Nice and new"
when 3..9
  puts "Reliable but slightly dinged"
when 10..29
  puts "Clunker"
else
  puts "Vintage gem"
end
```

produces:

```
Vintage gem
```

## CHAPTER 7

Regular Expressions

We probably spend most of our time in Ruby working with strings, so it seems reasonable for Ruby to have some great tools for working with those strings. As we've seen, the String class itself is no slouch—it has more than 100 methods. But there are still things that the basic String class can't do. For example, we might want to see whether a string contains two or more repeated characters, or we might want to replace every word longer than fifteen characters with its first five characters and an ellipsis. This is when we turn to the power of regular expressions.

Now, before we get too far in, here's a warning: there have been whole books written on regular expressions.[1] There is complexity and subtlety here that rivals that of the rest of Ruby. So if you've never used regular expressions, don't expect to read through this whole chapter the first time. In fact, you'll find two emergency exits in what follows. If you're new to regular expressions, I strongly suggest you read through to the first and then bail out. When some regular expression question next comes up, come back here and maybe read through to the next exit. Then, later, when you're feeling comfortable with regular expressions, you can give the whole chapter a read.

7.1 What Regular Expressions Let You Do

A regular expression is a pattern that can be matched against a string. It can be a simple pattern, such as *the string must contain the sequence of letters "cat"*, or the pattern can be complex, such as *the string must start with a protocol identifier, followed by two literal forward slashes, followed by...*, and so on. This is cool in theory. But what makes regular expressions so powerful is what you can do with them in practice:

- You can test a string to see whether it matches a pattern.
- You can extract from a string the sections that match all or part of a pattern.
- You can change the string, replacing parts that match a pattern.

Ruby provides built-in support that makes pattern matching and substitution convenient and concise. In this section, we'll work through the basics of regular expression patterns and see how Ruby supports matching and replacing based on those patterns. In the sections that follow, we'll dig deeper into both the patterns and Ruby's support for them.

---

1. Such as *Mastering Regular Expressions: Powerful Techniques for Perl and Other Tools* [Fri97]

7.2 Ruby's Regular Expressions

There are many ways of creating a regular expression pattern. By far the most common is to write it between forward slashes. Thus, the pattern /cat/ is a regular expression literal in the same way that "cat" is a string literal.

/cat/ is an example of a simple, but very common, pattern. It matches any string that contains the substring cat. In fact, inside a pattern, all characters except ., |, (,), [,], {, }, +, \, ^, $, *, and ? match themselves. So, at the risk of creating something that sounds like a logic puzzle, here are some patterns and examples of strings they match and don't match:

/cat/	Matches "dog and cat" and "catch" but not "Cat" or "c.a.t."
/123/	Matches "86512312" and "abc123" but not "1.23"
/t a b/	Matches "hit a ball" but not "table"

If you want to match one of the special characters literally in a pattern, precede it with a backslash, so /*/ is a pattern that matches a single asterisk, and /\// is a pattern that matches a forward slash.

Pattern literals are like double-quoted strings. In particular, you can use #{...} expression substitutions in the pattern.

Matching Strings with Patterns

The Ruby operator =~ matches a string against a pattern. It returns the character offset into the string at which the match occurred:

```
/cat/ =~ "dog and cat" # => 8
/cat/ =~ "catch"       # => 0
/cat/ =~ "Cat"         # => nil
```

You can put the string first if you prefer:[2]

```
"dog and cat" =~ /cat/ # => 8
"catch" =~ /cat/       # => 0
"Cat" =~ /cat/         # => nil
```

Because pattern matching returns nil when it fails and because nil is equivalent to false in a boolean context, you can use the result of a pattern match as a condition in statements such as if and while.

```
str = "cat and dog"

if str =~ /cat/
  puts "There's a cat here somewhere"
end
```

produces:

```
There's a cat here somewhere
```

---

2. Some folks say this is inefficient, because the string will end up calling the regular expression code to do the match. These folks are correct in theory but wrong in practice.

The following code prints lines in testfile that have the string on in them:

```
File.foreach("testfile").with_index do |line, index|
  puts "#{index}: #{line}" if line =~ /on/
end
```

produces:

```
0: This is line one
3: And so on...
```

You can test to see whether a pattern does not match a string using !~:

```
File.foreach("testfile").with_index do |line, index|
  puts "#{index}: #{line}" if line !~ /on/
end
```

produces:

```
1: This is line two
2: This is line three
```

Changing Strings with Patterns

The sub method takes a pattern and some replacement text.[3] If it finds a match for the pattern in the string, it replaces the matched substring with the replacement text.

```
str = "Dog and Cat"
new_str = str.sub(/Cat/, "Gerbil")
puts "Let's go to the #{new_str} for a pint."
```

produces:

```
Let's go to the Dog and Gerbil for a pint.
```

The sub method changes only the first match it finds. To replace all matches, use gsub. (The *g* stands for global.)

```
str = "Dog and Cat"
new_str1 = str.sub(/a/, "*")
new_str2 = str.gsub(/a/, "*")
puts "Using sub: #{new_str1}"
puts "Using gsub: #{new_str2}"
```

produces:

```
Using sub: Dog *nd Cat
Using gsub: Dog *nd C*t
```

Both sub and gsub return a new string. (If no substitutions are made, that new string will just be a copy of the original.)

If you want to modify the original string, use the sub! and gsub! forms:

```
str = "now is the time"
str.sub!(/i/, "*")
str.gsub!(/t/, "T")
puts str
```

produces:

```
now *s The Time
```

---

3. Actually, it does more than that, but we won't get to that for a while.

Unlike sub and gsub, sub! and gsub! return the string only if the pattern was matched. If no match for the pattern is found in the string, they return nil instead. This means it can make sense (depending on your need) to use the ! forms in conditions.

So, at this point you know how to use patterns to look for text in a string and how to substitute different text for those matches. And, for many people, that's enough. So if you're itching to get on to other Ruby topics, now is a good time to move on to the next chapter. At some point, you'll likely need to do something more complex with regular expressions (for example, matching a time by looking for two digits, a colon, and two more digits). You can then come back and read the next section.

Or, you can just stay right here as we dig deeper into patterns, matches, and replacements.

7.3 Digging Deeper

Like most things in Ruby, regular expressions are just objects—they are instances of the class Regexp. This means you can assign them to variables, pass them to methods, and so on:

```
str = "dog and cat"
pattern = /nd/
pattern =~ str # => 5
str =~ pattern # => 5
```

You can also create regular expression objects by calling the Regexp class's new method or by using the %r{...} syntax. The %r syntax is particularly useful when creating patterns that contain forward slashes:

```
/mm\/dd/           # => /mm\/dd/
Regexp.new("mm/dd") # => /mm\/dd/
%r{mm/dd}          # => /mm\/dd/
```

Playing with Regular Expressions

If you're like us, you'll sometimes get confused by regular expressions. You create something that *should* work, but it just doesn't seem to match. That's when we fall back to irb. We'll cut and paste the regular expression into irb and then try to match it against strings. We'll slowly remove portions until we get it to match the target string and add stuff back until it fails. At that point, we'll know what we were doing wrong.

Regular Expression Options

A regular expression may include one or more options that modify the way the pattern matches strings. If you're using literals to create the Regexp object, then the options are one or more characters placed immediately after the terminator. If you're using Regexp.new, the options are constants used as the second parameter of the constructor.

i   *Case insensitive.* The pattern match will ignore the case of letters in the pattern and string. (The old technique of setting $= to make matches case insensitive no longer works.)

o   *Substitute once.* Any #{...} substitutions in a particular regular expression literal will be performed just once, the first time it is evaluated. Otherwise, the substitutions will be performed every time the literal generates a Regexp object.

m   *Multiline mode.* Normally, "." matches any character except a newline. With the /m option, "." matches any character.

x   *Extended mode.* Complex regular expressions can be difficult to read. The x option allows you to insert spaces and newlines in the pattern to make it more readable. You can also use # to introduce comments.

Another set of options allows you to set the language encoding of the regular expression. If none of these options is specified, the regular expression will have US-ASCII encoding if it contains only 7-bit characters. Otherwise, it will use the default encoding of the source file containing the literal: n: no encoding (ASCII), e: EUC, s: SJIS, and u: UTF-8.

Matching Against Patterns

Once you have a regular expression object, you can match it against a string using the (Regexp#match(*string*) method or the match operators =~ (positive match) and !~ (negative match). The match operators are defined for both String and Regexp objects. One operand of the match operator must be a regular expression.

```
name = "Fats Waller"
name =~ /a/                    # => 1
name =~ /z/                    # => nil
/a/ =~ name                    # => 1
/a/.match(name)                # => #<MatchData "a">
Regexp.new("all").match(name)  # => #<MatchData "all">
```

The match operators return the character position at which the match occurred, while the match method returns a MatchData object. In all forms, if the match fails, nil is returned.

After a successful match, Ruby sets a whole bunch of magic variables. For example, $& receives the part of the string that was matched by the pattern, $` receives the part of the string that preceded the match, and $' receives the string after the match. However, these particular variables are considered to be fairly ugly, so most Ruby programmers instead use the MatchData object returned from the match method, because it encapsulates all the information Ruby knows about the match. Given a MatchData object, you can call pre_match to return the part of the string before the match, post_match for the string after the match, and index using [0] to get the matched portion.

We can use these to write a show_regexp, a method that shows where a pattern matches:

```
tut_regexp/show_match.rb
def show_regexp(string, pattern)
  match = pattern.match(string)
  if match
    "#{match.pre_match}->#{match[0]}<-#{match.post_match}"
  else
    "no match"
  end
end
```

We could use this method like this:

```
show_regexp('very interesting', /t/) # => very in->t<-eresting
show_regexp('Fats Waller', /lle/)    # => Fats Wa->lle<-r
show_regexp('Fats Waller', /z/)      # => no match
```

Deeper Patterns

We said earlier that, within a pattern, all characters match themselves except . | ( ) [ ] { } + \
^ $ * and ?. Let's dig a bit deeper into this.

First, always remember that you need to escape any of these characters with a backslash if
you want them to be treated as regular characters to match:

```
show_regexp('yes | no', /\|/)       # => yes ->|<- no
show_regexp('yes (no)', /\(no\)/)   # => yes ->(no)<-
show_regexp('are you sure?', /e\?/) # => are you sur->e?<-
```

Now let's see what some of these characters mean if you use them without escaping them.

Anchors

By default, a regular expression will try to find the first match for the pattern in a string.
Match /iss/ against the string "Mississippi," and it will find the substring "iss" starting at
position 1 (the second character in the string). But what if you want to force a pattern to
match only at the start or end of a string?

The patterns ^ and $ match the beginning and end of a line, respectively. These are often
used to *anchor* a pattern match; for example, /^option/ matches the word *option* only if it
appears at the start of a line. Similarly, the sequence \A matches the beginning of a string,
and \z and \Z match the end of a string. (Actually, \Z matches the end of a string *unless* the
string ends with \n, in which case it matches just before the \n.)

```
str = "this is\nthe time"
show_regexp(str, /^the/)   # => this is\n->the<- time
show_regexp(str, /is$/)    # => this ->is<-\nthe time
show_regexp(str, /\Athis/) # => ->this<- is\nthe time
show_regexp(str, /\Athe/)  # => no match
```

Similarly, the patterns \b and \B match word boundaries and nonword boundaries, respectively. Word characters are ASCII letters, numbers, and underscores:

```
show_regexp("this is\nthe time", /\bis/) # => this ->is<-\nthe time
show_regexp("this is\nthe time", /\Bis/) # => th->is<- is\nthe time
```

Character Classes

A *character class* is a set of characters between brackets: [*characters*] matches any single character between the brackets, so [aeiou] matches a vowel, [,.:;!?] matches some punctuation, and
so on. The significance of the special regular expression characters—.|(){+^$*?—is turned
off inside the brackets. However, normal string substitution still occurs, so (for example) \b
represents a backspace character, and \n represents a newline (see Table 11, *Substitutions in
double-quoted strings*, on page 300). In addition, you can use the abbreviations shown in Table
2, *Character class abbreviations*, on page 101, so that \s matches any whitespace character, not
just a literal space:

```
show_regexp('Price $12.', /[aeiou]/) # => Pr->i<-ce $12.
show_regexp('Price $12.', /[\s]/)    # => Price-> <-$12.
show_regexp('Price $12.', /[$.]/)    # => Price ->$<-12.
```

Within the brackets, the sequence c_1-c_2 represents all the characters from c_1 to c_2 in the current encoding:

```
a = 'see [The PickAxe-page 123]'
show_regexp(a, /[A-F]/)       # => see [The Pick->A<-xe-page 123]
show_regexp(a, /[A-Fa-f]/)    # => s->e<-e [The PickAxe-page 123]
show_regexp(a, /[0-9]/)       # => see [The PickAxe-page ->1<-23]
show_regexp(a, /[0-9][0-9]/)  # => see [The PickAxe-page ->12<-3]
```

You can negate a character class by putting an up arrow (^, sometimes called a *caret*) immediately after the opening bracket:

```
show_regexp('Price $12.', /[^A-Z]/)     # => P->r<-ice $12.
show_regexp('Price $12.', /[^\w]/)      # => Price-> <-$12.
show_regexp('Price $12.', /[a-z][^a-z]/) # => Pric->e <-$12.
```

Some character classes are used so frequently that Ruby provides abbreviations for them. These abbreviations are listed in Table 2, *Character class abbreviations*, on page 101—they may be used both within brackets and in the body of a pattern.

```
show_regexp('It costs $12.', /\s/) # => It-> <-costs $12.
show_regexp('It costs $12.', /\d/) # => It costs $->1<-2.
```

If you look at the table, you'll see that some of the character classes have different interpretations depending on the character set option defined for the regular expression. Basically, these options tell the regexp engine whether (for example) word characters are just the ASCII alphanumerics, or whether they should be extended to include Unicode letters, marks, numbers, and connection punctuation. The options are set using the sequence (?option), where the option is one of d (for Ruby 1.9 behavior), a for ASCII-only support, and u for full Unicode support. If you don't specify an option, it defaults to (?d).

New in 2.0

```
show_regexp('über.', /(?a)\w+/) # => ü->ber<-.
show_regexp('über.', /(?d)\w+/) # => ü->ber<-.
show_regexp('über.', /(?u)\w+/) # => ->über<-.

show_regexp('über.', /(?d)\W+/) # => ->ü<-ber.
show_regexp('über.', /(?u)\W+/) # => über->.<-
```

The POSIX character classes, as shown in Table 3, *Posix character classes*, on page 114, correspond to the ctype(3) macros of the same names. They can also be negated by putting an up arrow (or caret) after the first colon:

```
show_regexp('Price $12.', /[aeiou]/)        # => Pr->i<-ce $12.
show_regexp('Price $12.', /[[:digit:]]/)    # => Price $->1<-2.
show_regexp('Price $12.', /[[:space:]]/)    # => Price-> <-$12.
show_regexp('Price $12.', /[[:^alpha:]]/)   # => Price-> <-$12.
show_regexp('Price $12.', /[[:punct:]aeiou]/) # => Pr->i<-ce $12.
```

If you want to include the literal characters] and - in a character class, escape them with \:

```
a = 'see [The PickAxe-page 123]'
show_regexp(a, /[\]]/)     # => see [The PickAxe-page 123->]<-
show_regexp(a, /[0-9\]]/)  # => see [The PickAxe-page ->1<-23]
show_regexp(a, /[\d\-]/)   # => see [The PickAxe->-<-page 123]
```

You can create the intersection of character classes using &&. So, to match all lowercase ASCII letters that aren't vowels, you could use this:

```
str = "now is the time"
str.gsub(/[a-z&&[^aeiou]]/, '*') # => "*o* i* **e *i*e"
```

The \p construct gives you an encoding-aware way of matching a character with a particular Unicode property (shown in Table 4, *Unicode character properties*, on page 114):

```
# encoding: utf-8
string = "∂y/∂x = 2πx"
show_regexp(string, /\p{Alnum}/) # => ∂->y<-/∂x = 2πx
show_regexp(string, /\p{Digit}/) # => ∂y/∂x = ->2<-πx
show_regexp(string, /\p{Space}/) # => ∂y/∂x-> <-= 2πx
show_regexp(string, /\p{Greek}/) # => ∂y/∂x = 2->π<-x
show_regexp(string, /\p{Graph}/) # => ->∂<-y/∂x = 2πx
```

Finally, a period (.) appearing outside brackets represents any character except a newline (though in multiline mode it matches a newline, too):

```
a = 'It costs $12.'
show_regexp(a, /c.s/) # => It ->cos<-ts $12.
show_regexp(a, /./)   # => ->I<-t costs $12.
show_regexp(a, /\./)  # => It costs $12->.<-
```

Repetition

When we specified the pattern that split the song list line, /\s*\|\s*/, we said we wanted to match a vertical bar surrounded by an arbitrary amount of whitespace. We now know that the \s sequences match a single whitespace character and \| means a literal vertical bar, so it seems likely that the asterisks somehow mean "an arbitrary amount." In fact, the asterisk is one of a number of modifiers that allow you to match multiple occurrences of a pattern.

If *r* stands for the immediately preceding regular expression within a pattern, then

*r**	Matches zero or more occurrences of *r*
r+	Matches one or more occurrences of *r*
r?	Matches zero or one occurrence of *r*
r{m,n}	Matches at least m and at most n occurrences of *r*
r{m,}	Matches at least m occurrences of *r*
r{,n}	Matches at most n occurrences of *r*
r{m}	Matches exactly m occurrences of *r*

These repetition constructs have a high precedence—they bind only to the immediately preceding matching construct in the pattern. /ab+/ matches an *a* followed by one or more *b*'s, not a sequence of *ab*'s.

These patterns are called *greedy*, because by default they will match as much of the string as they can. You can alter this behavior and have them match the minimum by adding a question mark suffix. The repetition is then called *lazy*—it stops once it has done the minimum amount of work required.

Sequence	Logical intent Characters matched
\d	Decimal digit (?a), (?d) → [0-9] (?u) → *Decimal_Number*
\D	Any character except a decimal digit
\h	Hexadecimal digit character [0-9a-fA-F]
\H	Any character except a hex digit
\R	A generic linebreak sequence. May match the two characters \r\n. (new in 2.0)
\s	Whitespace (?a), (?d) → [␣\t\r\n\f] (?a), (?d) → [0-9] (?u) → [\t\n\r\x{000B}\x{000C}\x{0085}] plus *Line_Separator, Paragraph_Separator, Space_Separator*
\S	Any character except whitespace
\w	A "word" character (really, a programming language identifier) (?a), (?d) → [a-zA-Z0-9_] (?u) → *Letter, Mark, Number ,Connector_Punctuation*
\W	Any character except a word character
\X	An extended Unicode grapheme (two or more characters that combine to form a single visual character). (new in 2.0)

Table 2—Character class abbreviations

For some of these classes, the meaning depends on the character set mode selected for the pattern. In these cases, the dfferent options are shown like this:

(?a), (?d) → [a-zA-Z0-9_]
(?u) → *Letter, Mark, Number, Connector_Punctuation*

In this case, the first line applies to ASCII and default modes, and the second to unicode. In the second part of each line, the [...] is a conventional character class. Words in italic are Unicode character classes.

```
a = "The moon is made of cheese"
show_regexp(a, /\w+/)          # => ->The<- moon is made of cheese
show_regexp(a, /\s.*\s/)       # => The-> moon is made of <-cheese
show_regexp(a, /\s.*?\s/)      # => The-> moon <-is made of cheese
show_regexp(a, /[aeiou]{2,99}/) # => The m->oo<-n is made of cheese
show_regexp(a, /mo?o/)         # => The ->moo<-n is made of cheese
# here's the lazy version
show_regexp(a, /mo??o/)        # => The ->mo<-on is made of cheese
```

(There's an additional modifier, +, that makes them greedy and also stops backtracking, but that will have to wait until the advanced section of the chapter.)

Be very careful when using the * modifier. It matches zero or more occurrences. We often forget about the zero part. In particular, a pattern that contains just a * repetition will always match, whatever string you pass it. For example, the pattern /a*/ will always match, because every string contains zero or more a's.

```
a = "The moon is made of cheese"
# both of these match an empty substring at the start of the string
show_regexp(a, /m*/) # => -><-The moon is made of cheese
show_regexp(a, /Z*/) # => -><-The moon is made of cheese
```

Alternation

We know that the vertical bar is special, because our line-splitting pattern had to escape it with a backslash. That's because an unescaped vertical bar, as in |, matches either the construct that precedes it or the construct that follows it:

```
a = "red ball blue sky"
show_regexp(a, /d|e/)                  # => r->e<-d ball blue sky
show_regexp(a, /al|lu/)                # => red b->al<-l blue sky
show_regexp(a, /red ball|angry sky/) # => ->red ball<- blue sky
```

There's a trap for the unwary here, because | has a very low precedence. The last example in the previous lines matches *red ball* or *angry sky*, not *red ball sky* or *red angry sky*. To match *red ball sky* or *red angry sky*, you'd need to override the default precedence using grouping.

Grouping

You can use parentheses to group terms within a regular expression. Everything within the group is treated as a single regular expression.

```
# This matches an 'a' followed by one or more 'n's
show_regexp('banana', /an+/)   # => b->an<-ana
# This matches the sequence 'an' one or more times
show_regexp('banana', /(an)+/) # => b->anan<-a

a = 'red ball blue sky'
show_regexp(a, /blue|red/)            # => ->red<- ball blue sky
show_regexp(a, /(blue|red) \w+/)      # => ->red ball<- blue sky
show_regexp(a, /(red|blue) \w+/)      # => ->red ball<- blue sky
show_regexp(a, /red|blue \w+/)        # => ->red<- ball blue sky
show_regexp(a, /red (ball|angry) sky/) # => no match
a = 'the red angry sky'
show_regexp(a, /red (ball|angry) sky/) # => the ->red angry sky<-
```

Parentheses also collect the results of pattern matching. Ruby counts opening parentheses and for each stores the result of the partial match between it and the corresponding closing parenthesis. You can use this partial match both within the rest of the pattern and in your Ruby program. Within the pattern, the sequence \1 refers to the match of the first group, \2 the second group, and so on. Outside the pattern, the special variables $1, $2, and so on, serve the same purpose.

```
/(\d\d):(\d\d)(..)/ =~ "12:50am"   # => 0
"Hour is #$1, minute #$2"          # => "Hour is 12, minute 50"
/((\d\d):(\d\d))(..)/ =~ "12:50am" # => 0
"Time is #$1"                      # => "Time is 12:50"
"Hour is #$2, minute #$3"          # => "Hour is 12, minute 50"
"AM/PM is #$4"                     # => "AM/PM is am"
```

If you're using the MatchData object returned by the match method, you can index into it to get the corresponding subpatterns:

```
md = /(\d\d):(\d\d)(..)/.match("12:50am")
"Hour is #{md[1]}, minute #{md[2]}" # => "Hour is 12, minute 50"
md = /((\d\d):(\d\d))(..)/.match("12:50am")
"Time is #{md[1]}"                   # => "Time is 12:50"
"Hour is #{md[2]}, minute #{md[3]}" # => "Hour is 12, minute 50"
"AM/PM is #{md[4]}"                  # => "AM/PM is am"
```

The ability to use part of the current match later in that match allows you to look for various forms of repetition:

```
# match duplicated letter
show_regexp('He said "Hello"', /(\w)\1/) # => He said "He->ll<-o"
# match duplicated substrings
show_regexp('Mississippi', /(\w+)\1/)    # => M->ississ<-ippi
```

Rather than use numbers, you can also use names to refer to previously matched content. You give a group a name by placing ?<name> immediately after the opening parenthesis. You can subsequently refer to this named group using \k<name> (or \k'name').

```
# match duplicated letter
str = 'He said "Hello"'
show_regexp(str, /(?<char>\w)\k<char>/) # => He said "He->ll<-o"

# match duplicated adjacent substrings
str = 'Mississippi'
show_regexp(str, /(?<seq>\w+)\k<seq>/)  # => M->ississ<-ippi
```

The named matches in a regular expression are also available as local variables, but only if you use a literal regexp and that literal appears on the left hand side of the =~ operator. (So you can't assign a regular expression object to a variable, match the contents of that variable against a string, and expect the local variables to be set.)

```
/(?<hour>\d\d):(?<min>\d\d)(..)/ =~ "12:50am" # => 0
"Hour is #{hour}, minute #{min}"              # => "Hour is 12, minute 50"

# You can mix named and position-based references
"Hour is #{hour}, minute #{$2}"               # => "Hour is 12, minute 50"
"Hour is #{$1}, minute #{min}"                # => "Hour is 12, minute 50"
```

Pattern-Based Substitution

We've already seen how sub and gsub replace the matched part of a string with other text. In those previous examples, the pattern was always fixed text, but the substitution methods work equally well if the pattern contains repetition, alternation, and grouping.

```
a = "quick brown fox"
a.sub(/[aeiou]/, '*') # => "q*ick brown fox"
a.gsub(/[aeiou]/, '*') # => "q**ck br*wn f*x"
a.sub(/\s\S+/, '')    # => "quick fox"
a.gsub(/\s\S+/, '')    # => "quick"
```

The substitution methods can take a string or a block. If a block is used, it is passed the matching substring, and the block's value is substituted into the original string.

```
a = "quick brown fox"
a.sub(/^./) {|match| match.upcase }        # => "Quick brown fox"
```

```ruby
a.gsub(/[aeiou]/) {|vowel| vowel.upcase } # => "qUIck brOwn fOx"
```

Maybe we want to normalize names entered by users into a web application. They may enter DAVE THOMAS, dave thomas, or dAvE tHoMas, and we'd like to store it as Dave Thomas. The following method is a simple first iteration. The pattern that matches the first character of a word is \b\w—look for a word boundary followed by a word character. Combine this with gsub, and we can hack the names:

```ruby
def mixed_case(name)
  name.downcase.gsub(/\b\w/) {|first| first.upcase }
end
mixed_case("DAVE THOMAS") # => "Dave Thomas"
mixed_case("dave thomas") # => "Dave Thomas"
mixed_case("dAvE tHoMas") # => "Dave Thomas"
```

There's an idiomatic way to write the substitution in Ruby 1.9, but we'll have to wait until *The Symbol.to_proc Trick,* on page 352 to see why it works:

```ruby
def mixed_case(name)
  name.downcase.gsub(/\b\w/, &:upcase)
end

mixed_case("dAvE tHoMas") # => "Dave Thomas"
```

You can also give sub and gsub a hash as the replacement parameter, in which case they will look up matched groups and use the corresponding values as replacement text:

```ruby
replacement = { "cat" => "feline", "dog" => "canine" }
replacement.default = "unknown"

"cat and dog".gsub(/\w+/, replacement) # => "feline unknown canine"
```

Backslash Sequences in the Substitution

Earlier we noted that the sequences \1, \2, and so on, are available in the pattern, standing for the *n*th group matched so far. The same sequences can be used in the second argument of sub and gsub.

```ruby
puts "fred:smith".sub(/(\w+):(\w+)/, '\2, \1')
puts "nercpyitno".gsub(/(.)(.)/, '\2\1')
```

produces:

```
smith, fred
encryption
```

You can also reference named groups:

```ruby
puts "fred:smith".sub(/(?<first>\w+):(?<last>\w+)/, '\k<last>, \k<first>')
puts "nercpyitno".gsub(/(?<c1>.)(?<c2>.)/, '\k<c2>\k<c1>')
```

produces:

```
smith, fred
encryption
```

Additional backslash sequences work in substitution strings: \& (last match), \+ (last matched group), \` (string prior to match), \' (string after match), and \\ (a literal backslash).

It gets confusing if you want to include a literal backslash in a substitution. The obvious thing to write is str.gsub(/\\/, '\\\\').

Clearly, this code is trying to replace each backslash in str with two. The programmer doubled up the backslashes in the replacement text, knowing that they'd be converted to \\ in syntax analysis. However, when the substitution occurs, the regular expression engine performs another pass through the string, converting \\ to \, so the net effect is to replace each single backslash with another single backslash. You need to write gsub(/\\/, '\\\\\\\\')!

```
str = 'a\b\c'                # => "a\b\c"
str.gsub(/\\/, '\\\\\\\\')   # => "a\\b\\c"
```

However, using the fact that \& is replaced by the matched string, you could also write this:

```
str = 'a\b\c'              # => "a\b\c"
str.gsub(/\\/, '\&\&')     # => "a\\b\\c"
```

If you use the block form of gsub, the string for substitution is analyzed only once (during the syntax pass), and the result is what you intended:

```
str = 'a\b\c'                   # => "a\b\c"
str.gsub(/\\/) { '\\\\' }       # => "a\\b\\c"
```

At the start of this chapter, we said that it contained two emergency exits. The first was after we discussed basic matching and substitution. This is the second: you now know as much about regular expressions as the vast majority of Ruby developers. Feel free to break away and move on to the next chapter. But if you're feeling brave....

7.4 Advanced Regular Expressions

You may never need the information in the rest of this chapter. But, at the same time, knowing some of the real power in the Ruby regular expression implementation might just dig you out of a hole.

Regular Expression Extensions

Ruby uses the Onigmo[4] regular expression library. This offers a large number of extensions over traditional Unix regular expressions. Most of these extensions are written between the characters (? and). The parentheses that bracket these extensions are groups, but they do not necessarily generate backreferences—some do not set the values of \1, $1, and so on.

New in 2.0

The sequence (?# comment) inserts a comment into the pattern. The content is ignored during pattern matching. As we'll see, commenting complex regular expressions can be as helpful as commenting complex code.

(?:re) makes *re* into a group without generating backreferences. This is often useful when you need to group a set of constructs but don't want the group to set the value of $1 or whatever. In the example that follows, both patterns match a date with either colons or slashes between the month, day, and year. The first form stores the separator character (which can be a slash or a colon) in $2 and $4, but the second pattern doesn't store the separator in an external variable.

```
date = "12/25/2010"
```

---

4. Onigmo is an extension of the Oniguruma regular expression engine.

```
date =~ %r{(\d+)(/|:)(\d+)(/|:)(\d+)}
[$1,$2,$3,$4,$5] # => ["12", "/", "25", "/", "2010"]

date =~ %r{(\d+)(?:/|:)(\d+)(?:/|:)(\d+)}
[$1,$2,$3]       # => ["12", "25", "2010"]
```

Lookahead and Lookbehind

You'll sometimes want to match a pattern only if the matched substring is preceded by or followed by some other pattern. That is, you want to set some context for your match but don't want to capture that context as part of the match.

For example, you might want to match every word in a string that is followed by a comma, but you don't want the comma to form part of the match. Here you could use the charmingly named *zero-width positive lookahead* extension. (?=re) matches *re* at this point but does not consume it—you can look forward for the context of a match without affecting $&. In this example, we'll use scan to pick out the words:

```
str = "red, white, and blue"
str.scan(/[a-z]+(?=,)/) # => ["red", "white"]
```

You can also match before the pattern using (?<=re) (*zero-width positive lookbehind*). This lets you look for characters that precede the context of a match without affecting $&. The following example matches the letters *dog* but only if they are preceded by the letters *hot*:

```
show_regexp("seadog hotdog", /(?<=hot)dog/) # => seadog hot->dog<-
```

For the lookbehind extension, *re* either must be a fixed length or consist of a set of fixed-length alternatives. That is, (?<=aa) and (?<=aa|bbb) are valid, but (?<=a+b) is not.

Both forms have negated versions, (?!re) and (?<!re), which are true if the context is not present in the target string.

New in 2.0 The \K sequence is related to backtracking. If included in a pattern, it doesn't affect the matching process. However, when Ruby comes to store the entire matched string in $& or \&, it only stores the text to the right of the \K.

```
show_regexp("thx1138", /[a-z]+\K\d+/) # => thx->1138<-
```

Controlling Backtracking

Say you're given the problem of searching a string for a sequence of *X*s not followed by an *O*. You know that a string of *X*s can be represented as X+, and you can use a lookahead to check that it isn't followed by an *O*, so you code up the pattern /(X+)(?!O)/. Let's try it:

```
re = /(X+)(?!O)/

# This one works
re =~ "test XXXY" # => 5
$1               # => "XXX"

# But, unfortunately, so does this one
re =~ "test XXXO" # => 5
$1               # => "XX"
```

Why did the second match succeed? Well, the regular expression engine saw the X+ in the pattern and happily gobbled up all the Xs in the string. It then saw the pattern (?!O), saying that it should not now be looking at an O. Unfortunately, it is looking at an O, so the match doesn't succeed. But the engine doesn't give up. No sir! Instead it says, "Maybe I was wrong to consume every single X in the string. Let's try consuming one less and see what happens." This is called *backtracking*—when a match fails, the engine goes back and tries to match a different way. In this case, by backtracking past a single character, it now finds itself looking at the last X in the string (the one before the final O). And that X is not an O, so the negative lookahead succeeds, and the pattern matches. Look carefully at the output of the previous program: there are three Xs in the first match but only two in the second.

But this wasn't the intent of our regexp. Once it finds a sequence of Xs, those Xs should be locked away. We don't want one of them being the terminator of the pattern. We can get that behavior by telling Ruby not to backtrack once it finds a string of Xs. There are a couple of ways of doing this.

The sequence (?>re) nests an independent regular expression within the first regular expression. This expression is anchored at the current match position. If it consumes characters, these will no longer be available to the higher-level regular expression. This construct therefore inhibits backtracking.

Let's try it with our previous code:

```
re = /((?>X+))(?!O)/
```

```
# This one works
re =~ "test XXXY"        # => 5
$1                       # => "XXX"


# Now this doesn't match
re =~ "test XXXO"        # => nil
$1                       # => nil


# And this finds the second string of Xs
re =~ "test XXXO XXXXY"  # => 10
$1                       # => "XXXX"
```

You can also control backtracking by using a third form of repetition. We're already seen greedy repetition, such as re+, and lazy repetition, re+?. The third form is called *possessive*. You code it using a plus sign after the repetition character. It behaves just like greedy repetition, consuming as much of the string as it can. But once consumed, that part of the string can never be reexamined by the pattern—the regular expression engine can't backtrack past a possessive qualifier. This means we could also write our code as this:

```
re = /(X++)(?!O)/
```

```
re =~ "test XXXY"        # => 5
$1                       # => "XXX"


re =~ "test XXXO"        # => nil
$1                       # => nil


re =~ "test XXXO XXXXY"  # => 10
$1                       # => "XXXX"
```

Backreferences and Named Matches

Within a pattern, the sequences \n (where n is a number), \k'n', and \k<n> all refer to the nth captured subpattern. Thus, the expression /(...)\1/ matches six characters with the first three characters being the same as the last three.

Rather than refer to matches by their number, you can give them names and then refer to those names. A subpattern is named using either of the syntaxes (?<name>...) or (?'name'...). You then refer to these named captures using either \k<name> or \k'name'.

For example, the following shows different ways of matching a time range (in the form hh:mm-hh:mm) where the hour part is the same:

```
same    = "12:15-12:45"
differ = "12:45-13:15"


# use numbered backreference
same   =~ /(\d\d):\d\d-\1:\d\d/          # => 0
differ =~ /(\d\d):\d\d-\1:\d\d/          # => nil


# use named backreference
same   =~ /(?<hour>\d\d):\d\d-\k<hour>:\d\d/ # => 0
differ =~ /(?<hour>\d\d):\d\d-\k<hour>:\d\d/ # => nil
```

Negative backreference numbers count backward from the place they're used, so they are relative, not absolute, numbers. The following pattern matches four-letter palindromes (words that read the same forward and backward).

```
"abab" =~ /(.)(.)\k<-1>\k<-2>/ # => nil
"abba" =~ /(.)(.)\k<-1>\k<-2>/ # => 0
```

You can invoke a named subpattern using \g<name> or \g<number>. Note that this reexecutes the match in the subpattern, in contrast to \k<name>, which matches whatever is matched by the subpattern:

```
re = /(?<color>red|green|blue) \w+ \g<color> \w+/


re =~ "red sun blue moon"  # => 0
re =~ "red sun white moon" # => nil
```

You can use \g recursively, invoking a pattern within itself. The following code matches a string in which braces are properly nested:

```
re = /
  \A
    (?<brace_expression>
      {
        (
          [^{}]                      # anything other than braces
          |                          # ...or...
          \g<brace_expression>       # a nested brace expression
        )*
      }
    )
  \Z
/x
```

We use the x option to allow us to write the expression with lots of space, which makes it easier to understand. We also indent it, just as we would indent Ruby code. And we can also use Ruby-style comments to document the tricky stuff. You can read this regular expression as follows: a brace expression is an open brace, then a sequence of zero or more characters or brace expressions, and then a closing brace.

Nested Groups

The ability to invoke subpatterns recursively means that backreferences can get tricky. Ruby solves this by letting you refer to a named or numbered group at a particular level of the recursion—add a +n or -n for a capture at the given level relative to the current level.

Here's an example from the Oniguruma cheat sheet. It matches palindromes:

```
/\A(?<a>|.|(?:(?<b>.)\g<a>\k<b+0>))\z/
```

That's pretty hard to read, so let's spread it out:

tut_regexp/palindrome_re.rb
```
palindrome_matcher = /
\A
  (?<palindrome>
                   # nothing, or
   | \w            # a single character, or
   | (?:           # x <palindrome> x
      (?<some_letter>\w)
      \g<palindrome>
      \k<some_letter+0>
     )
  )
\z
/x

palindrome_matcher.match "madam" # => madam
palindrome_matcher.match "m"     # => m
palindrome_matcher.match "adam"  # =>
```

A palindrome is an empty string, a string containing a single character, or a character followed by a palindrome, followed by that same character. The notation \k<some_letter+0> means that the letter matched at the end of the inner palindrome will be the same letter that was at the start of it. Inside the nesting, however, a different letter may wrap the interior palindrome.

Conditional Groups

Just because it's all been so easy so far, Onigmo adds a new twist to regular expressions—conditional subexpressions. New in 2.0

Say you were validating a list of banquet attendees:

```
Mr Jones and Sally
Mr Bond and Ms Moneypenny
Samson and Delilah
Dr Jekyll and himself
Ms Hinky Smith and Ms Jones
Dr Wood and Mrs Wood
Thelma and Louise
```

The rule is that if the first person in the list has a title, then so should the second. This means that the first and fourth lines in this list are invalid.

We can start with a pattern to match a line with an optional title and a name. We know we've reached the end of the name when we find the word *and* with spaces around it.

```
re = %r{ (?:(Mrs | Mr | Ms | Dr )\s)? (.*?) \s and \s }x
"Mr Bond and Ms Monneypenny" =~ re # => 0
[ $1, $2 ]                         # => ["Mr", "Bond"]
"Samson and Delilah" =~ re        # => 0
[ $1, $2 ]                         # => [nil, "Samson"]
```

We've defined the regexp with the x (extended) option so we can include whitespace. We also used the ?: modifier on the group that defines the optional title followed by a space. This stops that group getting captured into $1. We do however capture just the title part.

So now we need to match the second name. We can start with the same code as for the first.

```
re = %r{
   (?:(Mrs | Mr | Ms | Dr )\s)? (.*?)
   \s and \s
   (?:(Mrs | Mr | Ms | Dr )\s)? (.+)
}x
"Mr Bond and Ms Monneypenny" =~ re # => 0
[ $1, $2, $3, $4 ]                 # => ["Mr", "Bond", "Ms", "Monneypenny"]
"Samson and Delilah" =~ re        # => 0
[ $1, $2, $3, $4 ]                 # => [nil, "Samson", nil, "Delilah"]
```

Before we go any further, let's clean up the duplication using a named group:

```
re = %r{
   (?:(?<title>Mrs | Mr | Ms | Dr )\s)? (.*?)
   \s and \s
   (\g<title>\s)? (.+)
}x
re.match("Mr Bond and Ms Monneypenny") # => #<MatchData "Mr Bond and Ms
                                        # .. Monneypenny" title:"Ms">
re.match("Samson and Delilah")          # => #<MatchData "Samson and Delilah"
                                        # .. title:nil>
```

But this code also matches a line where the first name has a title and the second doesn't:

```
re = %r{
   (?:(?<title>Mrs | Mr | Ms | Dr )\s)? (.*?)
   \s and \s
   (\g<title>\s)? (.+)
}x
re.match("Mr Smith and Sally") # => #<MatchData "Mr Smith and Sally" title:"Mr">
```

We need to make the second test for a title mandatory if the first test matches. That's where the conditional subpatterns come in.

The syntax (?(n)subpattern) will apply the subpattern match only if a previous group number *n* also matched. You can also test named groups using the syntaxes (?(<name>)subpattern) or (?('name')subpattern).

In our case, we want to apply a test for the second title if the first title is present. That first title is matched by the group named title, so the condition group looks like (?<title>...):

```
re = %r{
    (?:(?<title>Mrs | Mr | Ms | Dr )\s)? (.*?)
    \s and \s
    (?(<title>)\g<title>\s) (.+)
}x
re.match("Mr Smith and Sally") # => #<MatchData "Mr Smith and Sally" title:nil>
```

This didn't work—the match succeeded when we expected it to fail. That's because the regular expression applied *backtracking*. It matched the optional first name, the *and*, and then was told to match a second title (because group 1 matched the first). There's no second title, so the match failed. But rather than stopping, the engine went back to explore alternatives.

It noticed that the first title was optional, and so it tried matching the whole pattern again, this time skipping the title. It successfully matched *Mr Smith* using the (.*?) group, and matched *Sally* with the second name group. So we want to tell it never to backtrack over the first name—once it has found a title there, it has to use it. (?>...) to the rescue:

```
re = %r{
  ^(?>
      (?:(?<title>Mrs | Mr | Ms | Dr )\s)? (.*?)
      \s and \s
    )
    (?(<title>)\g<title>\s) (.+)
}x
re.match("Mr Smith and Sally")    # => nil
re.match("Mr Smith and Ms Sally") # => #<MatchData "Mr Smith and Ms Sally"
                                   # .. title:"Ms">
```

The match failed, as we expected, but when we add a title to Sally, it succeeds.

Let's try this on our list:

```
DATA.each do |line|
  re = %r{ ^(?>
              (?:(?<title>Mrs | Mr | Ms | Dr )\s)? (.*?) \s and \s
          )
              (?(<title>)\g<title>\s) (.+)
        }x
  if line =~ re
    print "VALID:   "
  else
    print "INVALID: "
  end
  puts line
end
__END__
Mr Jones and Sally
Mr Bond and Ms Moneypenny
Samson and Delilah
Dr Jekyll and himself
Ms Hinky Smith and Ms Jones
Dr Wood and Mrs Wood
Thelma and Louise
```

produces:

```
INVALID: Mr Jones and Sally
VALID:   Mr Bond and Ms Moneypenny
VALID:   Samson and Delilah
INVALID: Dr Jekyll and himself
VALID:   Ms Hinky Smith and Ms Jones
VALID:   Dr Wood and Mrs Wood
VALID:   Thelma and Louise
```

Alternatives in Conditions

Being British, I have a national duty to emulate my compatriates on informercials and shout "But Wait! There's More!" Conditional subpatterns can also have an *else* clause.

```
(?(group_id) true-pattern | fail-pattern )
```

If the identified group was previously matched, the true pattern is applied. If it failed, the fail pattern is applied.

Here's a regular expression that deals with red or blue balls or buckets. The deal is that the colors of the ball and bucket must be different.

```
re = %r{(?:(red)|blue) ball and (?(1)blue|red) bucket}

re.match("red ball and blue bucket")  # => #<MatchData "red ball and blue bucket"
                                       # .. 1:"red">
re.match("blue ball and red bucket")  # => #<MatchData "blue ball and red bucket"
                                       # .. 1:nil>
re.match("blue ball and blue bucket") # => nil
```

If the first group, the red alternative, matched, then the conditional subpattern is blue, otherwise it is red.

Named Subroutines

There's a trick that allows us to write subroutines inside regular expressions. Recall that we can invoke a named group using \g<name>, and we define the group using (?<name>...). Normally, the definition of the group is itself matched as part of executing the pattern. However, if you add the suffix {0} to the group, it means "zero matches of this group," so the group is not executed when first encountered:

```
sentence = %r{
  (?<subject>    cat   | dog    | gerbil   ){0}
  (?<verb>       eats  | drinks | generates ){0}
  (?<object>     water | bones  | PDFs     ){0}
  (?<adjective>  big   | small  | smelly   ){0}
  (?<opt_adj>    (\g<adjective>\s)?         ){0}

  The\s\g<opt_adj>\g<subject>\s\g<verb>\s\g<opt_adj>\g<object>
}x

md = sentence.match("The cat drinks water")
puts "The subject is #{md[:subject]} and the verb is #{md[:verb]}"

md = sentence.match("The big dog eats smelly bones")
puts "The last adjective in the second sentence is #{md[:adjective]}"
```

```
sentence =~ "The gerbil generates big PDFs"
puts "And the object in the last sentence is #{$~[:object]}"
```

produces:

```
The subject is cat and the verb is drinks
The last adjective in the second sentence is smelly
And the object in the last sentence is PDFs
```

Setting Options

We saw earlier that you can control the characters matched by \b, \d, \s, and \w (along with their negations). To do that, we embedded a sequence such as (?u) in our pattern. That sequence sets an option inside the regular expression engine.

New in 2.0

We also saw at the start of this chapter that you can add one or more of the options i (case insensitive), m (multiline), and x (allow spaces) to the end of a regular expression literal. You can also set these options within the pattern itself. As you'd expect, they are set using (?i), (?m), and (?x). You can also put a minus sign in front of these three options to disable them.

(?adimux)	Turns on the corresponding option. If used inside a group, the effect is limited to that group.
(?-imx)	Turns off the i, m, or x option.
(?adimux:re)	Turns on the option for *re*.
(?-imx:re)	Turns off the option for *re*.

7.5 \z

So, that's it. If you've made it this far, consider yourself a regular expression ninja. Get out there and match some strings.

POSIX Character Classes (Unicode)	
Text in parentheses indicates the Unicode classes. These apply if the regular expression's encoding is one of the Unicode encodings.	
[:alnum:]	Alphanumeric (*Letter* | *Mark* | *Decimal_Number*)
[:alpha:]	Uppercase or lowercase letter (*Letter* | *Mark*)
[:ascii:]	7-bit character including nonprinting
[:blank:]	Blank and tab (+ *Space_Separator*)
[:cntrl:]	Control characters—at least 0x00–0x1f, 0x7f (*Control* | *Format* | *Unassigned* | *Private_Use* | *Surrogate*)
[:digit:]	Digit (*Decimal_Number*)
[:graph:]	Printable character excluding space (Unicode also excludes *Control*, *Unassigned*, and *Surrogate*)
[:lower:]	Lowercase letter (*Lowercase_Letter*)
[:print:]	Any printable character (including space)
[:punct:]	Printable character excluding space and alphanumeric (*Connector_Punctuation* | *Dash_Punctuation* | *Close_Punctuation* | *Final_Punctuation* | *Initial_Punctuation* | *Other_Punctuation* | *Open_Punctuation*)
[:space:]	Whitespace (same as \s)
[:upper:]	Uppercase letter (*Uppercase_Letter*)
[:xdigit:]	Hex digit (0–9, a–f, A–F)
[:word:]	Alphanumeric, underscore, and multibyte (*Letter* | *Mark* | *Decimal_Number* | *Connector_Punctuation*)

Table 3—Posix character classes

Character Properties	
\p{name}	Matches character with named property
\p{^name}	Matches any character except named property
\P{name}	Matches any character except named property

Property names.

Spaces, underscores, and case are ignored in property names.

All encodings	Alnum, Alpha, Blank, Cntrl, Digit, Graph, Lower, Print, Punct, Space, Upper, XDigit, Word, ASCII
EUC and SJIS	Hiragana, Katakana
UTF-n	Any, Assigned, C, Cc, Cf, Cn, Co, Cs, L, Ll, Lm, Lo, Lt, Lu, M, Mc, Me, Mn, N, Nd, Nl, No, P, Pc, Pd, Pe, Pf, Pi, Po, Ps, S, Sc, Sk, Sm, So, Z, Zl, Zp, Zs, Arabic, Armenian, Bengali, Bopomofo, Braille, Buginese, Buhid, Canadian_Aboriginal, Cherokee, Common, Coptic, Cypriot, Cyrillic, Deseret, Devanagari, Ethiopic, Georgian, Glagolitic, Gothic, Greek, Gujarati, Gurmukhi, Han, Hangul, Hanunoo, Hebrew, Hiragana, Inherited, Kannada, Katakana, Kharoshthi, Khmer, Lao, Latin, Limbu, Linear_B, Malayalam, Mongolian, Myanmar, New_Tai_Lue, Ogham, Old_Italic, Old_Persian, Oriya, Osmanya, Runic, Shavian, Sinhala, Syloti_Nagri, Syriac, Tagalog, Tagbanwa, Tai_Le, Tamil, Telugu, Thaana, Thai, Tibetan, Tifinagh, Ugaritic, Yi

Table 4—Unicode character properties

## CHAPTER 8

More About Methods

So far in this book, we've been defining and using methods without much thought. Now it's time to get into the details.

8.1 Defining a Method

As we've seen, a method is defined using the keyword def. Method names should begin with a lowercase letter or underscore,[1] followed by letters, digits, and underscores.

A method name may end with one of ?, !, or =. Methods that return a boolean result (so-called predicate methods) are often named with a trailing ?:

```
1.even?                 # => false
2.even?                 # => true
1.instance_of?(Fixnum)  # => true
```

Methods that are "dangerous," or that modify their receiver, may be named with a trailing exclamation mark, !. These are sometimes called *bang methods*. For instance, class String provides both chop and chop! methods. The first returns a modified string; the second modifies the receiver in place.

Methods that can appear on the left side of an assignment (a feature we discussed back in the chapter on classes on page 34) end with an equal sign (=).

?, !, and = are the only "weird" characters allowed as method name suffixes.

Now that we've specified a name for our new method, we may need to declare some parameters. These are simply a list of local variable names in parentheses. (The parentheses around a method's arguments are optional; our convention is to use them when a method has arguments and omit them when it doesn't.)

```
def my_new_method(arg1, arg2, arg3)    # 3 arguments
  # Code for the method would go here
end
```

---

1. You won't get an immediate error if you start a method name with an uppercase letter, but when Ruby sees you calling the method, it might guess that it is a constant, not a method invocation, and as a result it may parse the call incorrectly. By convention, methods names starting with an uppercase letter are used for type conversion. The Integer method, for example, converts its parameter to an integer.

```
def my_other_new_method                    # No arguments
  # Code for the method would go here
end
```

Ruby lets you specify default values for a method's arguments—values that will be used if the caller doesn't pass them explicitly. You do this using an equal sign (=) followed by a Ruby expression. That expression can include references to previous arguments in the list:

```
def cool_dude(arg1="Miles", arg2="Coltrane", arg3="Roach")
  "#{arg1}, #{arg2}, #{arg3}."
end
```

```
cool_dude                              # => "Miles, Coltrane, Roach."
cool_dude("Bart")                      # => "Bart, Coltrane, Roach."
cool_dude("Bart", "Elwood")            # => "Bart, Elwood, Roach."
cool_dude("Bart", "Elwood", "Linus")   # => "Bart, Elwood, Linus."
```

Here's an example where the default argument references a previous argument:

```
def surround(word, pad_width=word.length/2)
  "[" * pad_width  + word +   "]" * pad_width
end
```

```
surround("elephant") # => "[[[[elephant]]]]"
surround("fox")      # => "[fox]"
surround("fox", 10)  # => "[[[[[[[[[[fox]]]]]]]]]]"
```

The body of a method contains normal Ruby expressions. The return value of a method is the value of the last expression executed or the argument of an explicit return expression.

Variable-Length Argument Lists

But what if you want to pass in a variable number of arguments or want to capture multiple arguments into a single parameter? Placing an asterisk before the name of the parameter after the "normal" parameters lets you do just that. This is sometimes called *splatting an argument* (presumably because the asterisk looks somewhat like a bug after hitting the windscreen of a fast-moving car).

```
def varargs(arg1, *rest)
  "arg1=#{arg1}.  rest=#{rest.inspect}"
end
```

```
varargs("one")                  # => arg1=one.  rest=[]
varargs("one", "two")           # => arg1=one.  rest=["two"]
varargs "one", "two", "three"   # => arg1=one.  rest=["two", "three"]
```

In this example, the first argument is assigned to the first method parameter as usual. However, the next parameter is prefixed with an asterisk, so all the remaining arguments are bundled into a new Array, which is then assigned to that parameter.

Folks sometimes use a splat to specify arguments that are not used by the method but that are perhaps used by the corresponding method in a superclass. (Note that in this example we call super with no parameters. This is a special case that means "invoke this method in the superclass, passing it all the parameters that were given to the original method.")

```
class Child < Parent
  def do_something(*not_used)
    # our processing
    super
  end
end
```

In this case, you can also leave off the name of the parameter and just write an asterisk:

```
class Child < Parent
  def do_something(*)
    # our processing
    super
  end
end
```

You can put the splat argument anywhere in a method's parameter list, allowing you to write this:

```
def split_apart(first, *splat, last)
  puts "First: #{first.inspect}, splat: #{splat.inspect}, " +
       "last: #{last.inspect}"
end
```

```
split_apart(1,2)
split_apart(1,2,3)
split_apart(1,2,3,4)
```

produces:

```
First: 1, splat: [], last: 2
First: 1, splat: [2], last: 3
First: 1, splat: [2, 3], last: 4
```

If you cared only about the first and last parameters, you could define this method using this:

```
def split_apart(first, *, last)
```

You can have only one splat argument in a method—if you had two, it would be ambiguous. You also can't put arguments with default values after the splat argument. In all cases, the splat argument receives the values left over after assigning to the regular arguments.

Methods and Blocks

As we discussed in the section on blocks and iterators on page 52, when a method is called it may be associated with a block. Normally, you call the block from within the method using yield:

```
def double(p1)
  yield(p1*2)
end
```

```
double(3) {|val| "I got #{val}" }         # => "I got 6"
double("tom") {|val| "Then I got #{val}" } # => "Then I got tomtom"
```

However, if the last parameter in a method definition is prefixed with an ampersand, any associated block is converted to a Proc object, and that object is assigned to the parameter. This allows you to store the block for use later.

```ruby
class TaxCalculator
  def initialize(name, &block)
    @name, @block = name, block
  end
  def get_tax(amount)
    "#@name on #{amount} = #{ @block.call(amount) }"
  end
end


tc = TaxCalculator.new("Sales tax") {|amt| amt * 0.075 }

tc.get_tax(100) # => "Sales tax on 100 = 7.5"
tc.get_tax(250) # => "Sales tax on 250 = 18.75"
```

8.2 Calling a Method

You call a method by optionally specifying a receiver, giving the name of the method, and optionally passing some parameters and an optional block. Here's a code fragment that shows us calling a method with a receiver, a parameter, and a block:

```ruby
connection.download_mp3("jitterbug") {|p| show_progress(p) }
```

In this example, the object connection is the receiver, download_mp3 is the name of the method, the string "jitterbug" is the parameter, and the stuff between the braces is the associated block. During this method call, Ruby first sets self to the receiver and then invokes the method in that object. For class and module methods, the receiver will be the class or module name.

```ruby
File.size("testfile") # => 66
Math.sin(Math::PI/4)  # => 0.7071067811865475
```

If you omit the receiver, it defaults to self, the current object.

```ruby
class InvoiceWriter
  def initialize(order)
    @order = order
  end
  def write_on(output)
    write_header_on(output)   # called on current object.
    write_body_on(output)     # self is not changed, as
    write_totals_on(output)   # there is no receiver
  end
  def write_header_on(output)
    # ...
  end
  def write_body_on(output)
    # ...
  end
  def write_totals_on(output)
    # ...
  end
end
```

This defaulting mechanism is how Ruby implements private methods. Private methods may *not* be called with a receiver, so they must be methods available in the current object. In the previous example, we'd probably want to make the helper methods private, because they shouldn't be called from outside the InvoiceWriter class:

```ruby
class InvoiceWriter
  def initialize(order)
    @order = order
  end
  def write_on(output)
    write_header_on(output)
    write_body_on(output)
    write_totals_on(output)
  end

private

  def write_header_on(output)
    # ...
  end
  def write_body_on(output)
    # ...
  end
  def write_totals_on(output)
    # ...
  end
end
```

Passing Parameters to a Method

Any parameters follow the method name. If no ambiguity exists, you can omit the parentheses around the argument list when calling a method.[2] However, except in the simplest cases we don't recommend this—some subtle problems can trip you up.[3] Our rule is simple: if you have any doubt, use parentheses.

```ruby
# for some suitable value in obj:
a = obj.hash     # Same as
a = obj.hash()   # this.

obj.some_method "Arg1", arg2, arg3    # Same thing as
obj.some_method("Arg1", arg2, arg3)   # with parentheses.
```

Older Ruby versions compounded the problem by allowing you to put spaces between the method name and the opening parenthesis. This made it hard to parse: is the parenthesis the start of the parameters or the start of an expression? As of Ruby 1.8, you get a warning if you put a space between a method name and an open parenthesis.

Method Return Values

Every method you call returns a value (although there's no rule that says you have to use that value). The value of a method is the value of the last statement executed by the method:

---

2. Other Ruby documentation sometimes calls these method calls without parentheses *commands*.
3. In particular, you *must* use parentheses on a method call that is itself a parameter to another method call (unless it is the last parameter).

```
def meth_one
  "one"
end
meth_one       # => "one"

def meth_two(arg)
  case
  when arg > 0  then "positive"
  when arg < 0  then "negative"
  else               "zero"
  end
end
meth_two(23) # => "positive"
meth_two(0)  # => "zero"
```

Ruby has a return statement, which exits from the currently executing method. The value of a return is the value of its argument(s). It is idiomatic Ruby to omit the return if it isn't needed, as shown by the previous two examples.

This next example uses return to exit from a loop inside the method:

```
def meth_three
  100.times do |num|
    square = num*num
    return num, square if square > 1000
  end
end
meth_three # => [32, 1024]
```

As the last case illustrates, if you give return multiple parameters, the method returns them in an array. You can use parallel assignment to collect this return value:

```
num, square = meth_three
num      # => 32
square   # => 1024
```

Splat! Expanding Collections in Method Calls

We've seen that if you prefix the name of a parameter with an asterisk, multiple arguments in the call to the method will be passed as an array. Well, the same thing works in reverse.

When you call a method, you can convert any collection or enumerable object into its constituent elements and pass those elements as individual parameters to the method. Do this by prefixing array arguments with an asterisk:

```
def five(a, b, c, d, e)
  "I was passed #{a} #{b} #{c} #{d} #{e}"
end

five(1, 2, 3, 4, 5 )        # => "I was passed 1 2 3 4 5"
five(1, 2, 3, *['a', 'b']) # => "I was passed 1 2 3 a b"
five(*['a', 'b'], 1, 2, 3) # => "I was passed a b 1 2 3"
five(*(10..14))            # => "I was passed 10 11 12 13 14"
five(*[1,2], 3, *(4..5))   # => "I was passed 1 2 3 4 5"
```

As of Ruby 1.9, splat arguments can appear anywhere in the parameter list, and you can intermix splat and regular arguments.

Making Blocks More Dynamic

We've already seen how to associate a block with a method call:

```
collection.each do |member|
  # ...
end
```

Normally, this is perfectly good enough—you associate a fixed block of code with a method in the same way you'd have a chunk of code after an if or while statement. But sometimes you'd like to be more flexible. Maybe we're teaching math skills. The student could ask for an *n*-plus table or an *n*-times table. If the student asked for a 2-times table, we'd output 2, 4, 6, 8, and so on. (This code does not check its inputs for errors.)

```
print "(t)imes or (p)lus: "
operator = gets
print "number: "
number = Integer(gets)

if operator =~ /^t/
  puts((1..10).collect {|n| n*number }.join(", "))
else
  puts((1..10).collect {|n| n+number }.join(", "))
end
```

produces:

```
(t)imes or (p)lus: t
number: 2
2, 4, 6, 8, 10, 12, 14, 16, 18, 20
```

This works, but it's ugly, with virtually identical code on each branch of the if statement. It would be nice if we could factor out the block that does the calculation:

```
print "(t)imes or (p)lus: "
operator = gets
print "number: "
number = Integer(gets)
if operator =~ /^t/
  calc = lambda {|n| n*number }
else
  calc = lambda {|n| n+number }
end
puts((1..10).collect(&calc).join(", "))
```

produces:

```
(t)imes or (p)lus: t
number: 2
2, 4, 6, 8, 10, 12, 14, 16, 18, 20
```

If the last argument to a method is preceded by an ampersand, Ruby assumes that it is a Proc object. It removes it from the parameter list, converts the Proc object into a block, and associates it with the method.

Hash and Keyword Arguments

People commonly use hashes as a way of passing optional named arguments to a method. For example, we could consider adding a search facility to an MP3 playlist:

```ruby
class SongList
  def search(field, params)
    # ...
  end
end
```

```ruby
list = SongList.new
list.search(:titles, { genre: "jazz", duration_less_than: 270 })
```

The first parameter tells the search what to return. The second parameter is a hash literal of search parameters. (Note how we used symbols as the keys for this options hash. This has become idiomatic in Ruby libraries and frameworks.) The use of a hash means we can simulate keywords: look for songs with a genre of "jazz" and a duration less than 4.5 minutes.

However, this approach is slightly clunky, and that set of braces could easily be mistaken for a block associated with the method. So, Ruby has a shortcut. You can place key => value pairs in an argument list, as long as they follow any normal arguments and precede any splat and block arguments. All these pairs will be collected into a single hash and passed as one argument to the method. No braces are needed.

```ruby
list.search(:titles, genre: "jazz", duration_less_than: 270)
```

Keyword Argument Lists

New in 2.0   Let's look inside our search method. It gets passed a field name and an options hash. Maybe we want to default the duration to 120 seconds, and validate that no invalid options are passed. Pre Ruby 2.0, the code would look something like:

```ruby
def search(field, options)
  options = { duration: 120 }.merge(options)
  if options.has_key?(:duration)
    duration = options[:duration]
    options.delete(:duration)
  end
  if options.has_key?(:genre)
    genre = options[:genre]
    options.delete(:genre)
  end
  fail "Invalid options: #{options.keys.join(', ')}" unless options.empty?
  # rest of method
end
```

Do this enough times, and you end up writting a helper function to validate and extract hash parameters to methods.

Ruby 2 to the rescue. You can now define keyword arguments to your methods. You still pass in the hash, but Ruby now matches the hash contents to your keyword argument list. It also validates that you don't pass in any unknown arguments.

```ruby
def search(field, genre: nil, duration: 120)
  p [field, genre, duration ]
end
```

```
search(:title)
search(:title, duration: 432)
search(:title, duration: 432, genre: "jazz")
```

produces:

```
[:title, nil, 120]
[:title, nil, 432]
[:title, "jazz", 432]
```

Pass in an invalid option, and Ruby complains:

```
def search(field, genre: nil, duration: 120)
  p [field, genre, duration ]
end
```

```
search(:title, duraton: 432)
```

produces:

```
prog.rb:5:in `<main>': unknown keyword: duraton (ArgumentError)
```

You can collect these extra hash arguments as a hash parameter—just prefix one element of your argument list with two asterisks (a *double splat*).

```
def search(field, genre: nil, duration: 120, **rest)
  p [field, genre, duration, rest ]
end
```

```
search(:title, duration: 432, stars: 3, genre: "jazz", tempo: "slow")
```

produces:

```
[:title, "jazz", 432, {:stars=>3, :tempo=>"slow"}]
```

And, just to prove that all we're passing in is a hash, here's the same calling sequence:

```
def search(field, genre: nil, duration: 120, **rest)
  p [field, genre, duration, rest ]
end
```

```
options = { duration: 432, stars: 3, genre: "jazz", tempo: "slow" }
search(:title, options)
```

produces:

```
[:title, "jazz", 432, {:stars=>3, :tempo=>"slow"}]
```

A well-written Ruby program will typically contain many methods, each quite small, so it's worth getting familiar with the options available when defining and using them. At some point you'll probably want to read *Method Arguments*, on page 324 to see exactly how arguments in a method call get mapped to the method's formal parameters when you have combinations of default parameters and splat parameters.

## CHAPTER 9

Expressions

So far, we've been fairly cavalier in our use of expressions in Ruby. After all, a = b + c is pretty standard stuff. You could write a whole heap of Ruby code without reading any of this chapter.

But it wouldn't be as much fun ;-).

One of the first differences with Ruby is that anything that can reasonably return a value does: just about everything is an expression. What does this mean in practice?

Some obvious things include the ability to chain statements together:

```
a = b = c = 0               # => 0
[ 3, 1, 7, 0 ].sort.reverse # => [7, 3, 1, 0]
```

Perhaps less obvious, things that are normally statements in C or Java are expressions in Ruby. For example, the if and case statements both return the value of the last expression executed:

```
song_type = if song.mp3_type == MP3::Jazz
              if song.written < Date.new(1935, 1, 1)
                  Song::TradJazz
              else
                  Song::Jazz
              end
            else
                Song::Other
            end

rating = case votes_cast
         when 0...10    then Rating::SkipThisOne
         when 10...50   then Rating::CouldDoBetter
         else                Rating::Rave
         end
```

We'll talk more about if and case later on page 135.

9.1 Operator Expressions

Ruby has the basic set of operators (+, -, *, /, and so on) as well as a few surprises. A complete list of the operators, and their precedences, is given in Table 13, *Ruby operators (high to low precedence)*, on page 318.

In Ruby, many operators are implemented as method calls. For example, when you write a*b+c, you're actually asking the object referenced by a to execute the method *, passing in the parameter b. You then ask the object that results from that calculation to execute the + method, passing c as a parameter. This is the same as writing the following (perfectly valid) Ruby:

```ruby
a, b, c = 1, 2, 3
a * b + c       # => 5
(a.*(b)).+(c) # => 5
```

Because everything is an object and because you can redefine instance methods, you can always redefine basic arithmetic if you don't like the answers you're getting:

```ruby
class Fixnum
  alias old_plus +   # We can reference the original '+' as 'old_plus'

  def +(other)        # Redefine addition of Fixnums. This is a BAD IDEA!
    old_plus(other).succ
  end
end


1 + 2      # => 4
a = 3
a += 4     # => 8
a + a + a # => 26
```

More useful is that classes you write can participate in operator expressions just as if they were built-in objects. For example, the left shift operator, <<, is often used to mean *append to receiver*. Arrays support this:

```ruby
a = [ 1, 2, 3 ]
a << 4     # => [1, 2, 3, 4]
```

You can add similar support to your classes:

```ruby
class ScoreKeeper
  def initialize
    @total_score = @count = 0
  end
  def <<(score)
    @total_score += score
    @count += 1
    self
  end
  def average
    fail "No scores" if @count.zero?
    Float(@total_score) / @count
  end
end
```

```
scores = ScoreKeeper.new
scores << 10 << 20 << 40
puts "Average = #{scores.average}"
```

produces:

```
Average = 23.333333333333332
```

Note that there's a subtlety in this code—the << method explicitly returns self. It does this to allow the method chaining in the line scores << 10 << 20 << 40. Because each call to << returns the scores object, you can then call << again, passing in a new score.

As well as the obvious operators, such as +, *, and <<, indexing using square brackets is also implemented as a method call. When you write this:

```
some_obj[1,2,3]
```

you're actually calling a method named [] on some_obj, passing it three parameters. You'd define this method using this:

```
class SomeClass
  def [](p1, p2, p3)
    # ...
  end
end
```

Similarly, assignment to an element is implemented using the []= method. This method receives each object passed as an index as its first *n* parameters and the value of the assignment as its last parameter:

```
class SomeClass
  def []=(*params)
    value = params.pop
    puts "Indexed with #{params.join(', ')}"
    puts "value = #{value.inspect}"
  end
end

s = SomeClass.new
s[1] = 2
s['cat', 'dog'] = 'enemies'
```

produces:

```
Indexed with 1
value = 2
Indexed with cat, dog
value = "enemies"
```

9.2 Miscellaneous Expressions

As well as the obvious operator expressions and method calls and the (perhaps) less obvious statement expressions (such as if and case), Ruby has a few more things that you can use in expressions.

Command Expansion

If you enclose a string in backquotes (sometimes called *backticks*) or use the delimited form prefixed by %x, it will (by default) be executed as a command by your underlying operating system. The value of the expression is the standard output of that command. Newlines will not be stripped, so it is likely that the value you get back will have a trailing return or linefeed character.

```
`date`                   # => "Mon May 27 12:30:56 CDT 2013\n"
`ls`.split[34]           # => "newfile"
%x{echo "hello there"}   # => "hello there\n"
```

You can use expression expansion and all the usual escape sequences in the command string:

```
for i in 0..3
  status = `dbmanager status id=#{i}`
  # ...
end
```

The exit status of the command is available in the global variable $?.

Redefining Backquotes

In the description of the command output expression, we said that the string in backquotes would "by default" be executed as a command. In fact, the string is passed to the method called Object#` (a single backquote). If you want, you can override this. This example uses $?, which contains the status of the last external process run:

```
alias old_backquote `
def `(cmd)
  result = old_backquote(cmd)
  if $? != 0
    puts "*** Command #{cmd} failed: status = #{$?.exitstatus}"
  end
  result
end
print `ls -l /etc/passwd`
print `ls -l /etc/wibble`
```

produces:

```
-rw-r--r--  1 root  wheel  5086 Jul 20  2011 /etc/passwd
ls: /etc/wibble: No such file or directory
*** Command ls -l /etc/wibble failed: status = 1
```

9.3 Assignment

Just about every example we've given so far in this book has featured assignment. Perhaps it's about time we said something about it.

An assignment statement sets the variable or attribute on its left side (the *lvalue*) to refer to the value on the right (the *rvalue*). It then returns that rvalue as the result of the assignment expression. This means you can chain assignments, and you can perform assignments in some unexpected places:

```
a = b = 1 + 2 + 3
a           # => 6
b           # => 6
a = (b = 1 + 2) + 3
a           # => 6
b           # => 3

File.open(name = gets.chomp)
```

Ruby has two basic forms of assignment. The first assigns an object reference to a variable or constant. This form of assignment is hardwired into the language:

```
instrument = "piano"
MIDDLE_A   = 440
```

The second form of assignment involves having an object attribute or element reference on the left side. These forms are special, because they are implemented by calling methods in the lvalues, which means you can override them.

We've already seen how to define a writable object attribute. Simply define a method name ending in an equals sign. This method receives as its parameter the assignment's rvalue. We've also seen that you can define [] as a method:

```
class ProjectList
  def initialize
    @projects = []
  end
  def projects=(list)
    @projects = list.map(&:upcase)  # store list of names in uppercase
  end
  def [](offset)
    @projects[offset]
  end
end

list = ProjectList.new
list.projects = %w{ strip sand prime sand paint sand paint rub paint }
list[3]    # => "SAND"
list[4]    # => "PAINT"
```

As this example shows, these attribute-setting methods don't have to correspond with internal instance variables, and you don't need an attribute reader for every attribute writer (or vice versa).

In older Rubys, the result of the assignment was the value returned by the attribute-setting method. As of Ruby 1.8, the value of the assignment is *always* the value of the parameter; the return value of the method is discarded. In the code that follows, older versions of Ruby would set result to 99. Now result will be set to 2.

```
class Test
  def val=(val)
    @val = val
    return 99
  end
end
```

```
t = Test.new
result = (t.val = 2)
result    # => 2
```

Parallel Assignment

During your first week in a programming course (or the second semester if it was a party school), you may have had to write code to swap the values in two variables:

```
int a = 1;    # C, or Java, or ...
int b = 2;
int temp;

temp = a;
a = b;
b = temp;
```

You can do this much more cleanly in Ruby:

```
a, b = 1, 2    # a=1,  b=2
a, b = b, a    # b=2,  a=1
```

Ruby lets you have a comma-separated list of rvalues (the things on the right of the assignment). Once Ruby sees more than one rvalue in an assignment, the rules of parallel assignment come into play. What follows is a description at the logical level: what happens inside the interpreter is somewhat hairier. Users of older versions of Ruby should note that these rules have changed in Ruby 1.9.

First, all the rvalues are evaluated, left to right, and collected into an array (unless they are already an array). This array will be the eventual value returned by the overall assignment.

Next, the left side (lhs) is inspected. If it contains a single element, the array is assigned to that element.

```
a = 1, 2, 3, 4    # a=[1, 2, 3, 4]
b = [1, 2, 3, 4]   # b=[1, 2, 3, 4]
```

If the lhs contains a comma, Ruby matches values on the rhs against successive elements on the lhs. Excess elements are discarded.

```
a, b = 1, 2, 3, 4    # a=1, b=2
c, = 1, 2, 3, 4      # c=1
```

Splats and Assignment

If Ruby sees any splats on the right side of an assignment (that is, rvalues preceded by an asterisk), each will be expanded inline into its constituent values during the evaluation of the rvalues and before the assignment to lvalues starts:

```
a, b, c, d, e = *(1..2), 3, *[4, 5]    # a=1, b=2, c=3, d=4, e=5
```

Exactly one lvalue may be a splat. This makes it greedy—it will end up being an array, and that array will contain as many of the corresponding rvalues as possible. So, if the splat is the last lvalue, it will soak up any rvalues that are left after assigning to previous lvalues:

```
a, *b = 1, 2, 3     # a=1, b=[2, 3]
a, *b = 1           # a=1, b=[]
```

If the splat is not the last lvalue, then Ruby ensures that the lvalues that follow it will all receive values from rvalues at the end of the right side of the assignment—the splat lvalue will soak up only enough rvalues to leave one for each of the remaining lvalues.

```
*a, b = 1, 2, 3, 4       # a=[1, 2, 3], b=4
c, *d, e = 1, 2, 3, 4    # c=1, d=[2, 3], e=4
f, *g, h, i, j = 1, 2, 3, 4   # f=1, g=[], h=2, i=3, j=4
```

As with method parameters, you can use a raw asterisk to ignore some rvalues:

```
first, *, last = 1,2,3,4,5,6    # first=1, last=6
```

Nested Assignments

The left side of an assignment may contain a parenthesized list of terms. Ruby treats these terms as if they were a nested assignment statement. It extracts the corresponding rvalue, assigning it to the parenthesized terms, before continuing with the higher-level assignment.

```
a, (b, c), d = 1,2,3,4       # a=1, b=2, c=nil, d=3
a, (b, c), d = [1,2,3,4]     # a=1, b=2, c=nil, d=3
a, (b, c), d = 1,[2,3],4     # a=1, b=2, c=3, d=4
a, (b, c), d = 1,[2,3,4],5   # a=1, b=2, c=3, d=5
a, (b,*c), d = 1,[2,3,4],5   # a=1, b=2, c=[3, 4], d=5
```

Other Forms of Assignment

In common with other languages, Ruby has a syntactic shortcut: a = a + 2 may be written as a += 2. The second form is converted internally to the first. This means that operators you have defined as methods in your own classes work as you'd expect:

```
class Bowdlerize
  def initialize(string)
    @value = string.gsub(/[aeiou]/, '*')
  end
  def +(other)
    Bowdlerize.new(self.to_s + other.to_s)
  end
  def to_s
    @value
  end
end

a = Bowdlerize.new("damn ")   # => d*mn
a += "shame"                  # => d*mn sh*m*
```

Something you won't find in Ruby are the autoincrement (++) and autodecrement (–) operators of C and Java. Use the += and -= forms instead.

9.4 Conditional Execution

Ruby has several different mechanisms for conditional execution of code; most of them should feel familiar, and many have some neat twists. Before we get into them, though, we need to spend a short time looking at boolean expressions.

Boolean Expressions

Ruby has a simple definition of truth. Any value that is not nil or the constant false is true— "cat", 99, 0, and :a_song are all considered true.

In this book, when we want to talk about a general true or false value, we use regular Roman type: true and false. When we want to refer to the actual constants, we write true and false.

The fact that nil is considered to be false is convenient. For example, IO#gets, which returns the next line from a file, returns nil at the end of file, enabling you to write loops such as this:

```
while line = gets
  # process line
end
```

However, C, C++, and Perl programmers sometimes fall into a trap. The number zero is *not* interpreted as a false value. Neither is a zero-length string. This can be a tough habit to break.

And, Or, and Not

Ruby supports all the standard boolean operators. Both the keyword and and the operator && return their first argument if it is false. Otherwise, they evaluate and return their second argument (this is sometimes known as *shortcircuit* evaluation). The only difference in the two forms is precedence (and binds lower than &&).

```
nil   && 99 # => nil
false && 99 # => false
"cat" && 99 # => 99
```

Thus, && and and both return a true value only if both of their arguments are true, as expected.

Similarly, both or and || return their first argument unless it is false, in which case they evaluate and return their second argument.

```
nil   || 99 # => 99
false || 99 # => 99
"cat" || 99 # => "cat"
```

As with and, the only difference between or and || is their precedence. To make life interesting, and and or have the same precedence, but && has a higher precedence than ||.

A common idiom is to use ||= to assign a value to a variable only if that variable isn't already set:

```
var ||= "default value"
```

This is almost, but not quite, the same as var = var || "default value". It differs in that no assignment is made at all if the variable is already set. In pseudocode, this might be written as var = "default value" unless var or as var || var = "default value".

not and ! return the opposite of their operand (false if the operand is true and true if the operand is false). And, yes, not and ! differ only in precedence.

All these precedence rules are summarized in Table 13, *Ruby operators (high to low precedence)*, on page 318.

defined?

The defined? operator returns nil if its argument (which can be an arbitrary expression) is not defined; otherwise, it returns a description of that argument. If the argument is yield, defined? returns the string "yield" if a code block is associated with the current context.

```ruby
defined? 1         # => "expression"
defined? dummy     # => nil
defined? printf    # => "method"
defined? String    # => "constant"
defined? $_        # => "global-variable"
defined? Math::PI  # => "constant"
defined? a = 1     # => "assignment"
defined? 42.abs    # => "method"
defined? nil       # => "nil"
```

Comparing Objects

In addition to the boolean operators, Ruby objects support comparison using the methods ==, ===, <=>, =~, eql?, and equal? (see Table 5, *Common comparison operators*, on page 134). All but <=> are defined in class Object but are often overridden by descendants to provide appropriate semantics. For example, class Array redefines == so that two array objects are equal if they have the same number of elements and the corresponding elements are equal.

Both == and =~ have negated forms, != and !~. Ruby first looks for methods called != or !~, calling them if found. If not, it will then invoke either == or =~, negating the result.

In the following example, Ruby calls the == method to perform both comparisons:

```ruby
class T
  def ==(other)
    puts "Comparing self == #{other}"
    other == "value"
  end
end

t = T.new
p(t == "value")
p(t != "value")
```

produces:

```
Comparing self == value
true
Comparing self == value
false
```

Operator	Meaning
==	Test for equal value.
===	Used to compare each of the items with the target in the when clause of a case statement.
<=>	General comparison operator. Returns -1, 0, or +1, depending on whether its receiver is less than, equal to, or greater than its argument.
<, <=, >=, >	Comparison operators for less than, less than or equal, greater than or equal, and greater than.
=~	Regular expression pattern match.
eql?	True if the receiver and argument have both the same type and equal values. 1 == 1.0 returns true, but 1.eql?(1.0) is false.
equal?	True if the receiver and argument have the same object ID.

Table 5—Common comparison operators

If instead we explicitly define !=, Ruby calls it:

```
class T
  def ==(other)
    puts "Comparing self == #{other}"
    other == "value"
  end
  def !=(other)
    puts "Comparing self != #{other}"
    other != "value"
  end
end

t = T.new
p(t == "value")
p(t != "value")
```

produces:

```
Comparing self == value
true
Comparing self != value
false
```

You can use a Ruby range as a boolean expression. A range such as exp1..exp2 will evaluate as false until exp1 becomes true. The range will then evaluate as true until exp2 becomes true. Once this happens, the range resets, ready to fire again. We show some examples of this later on page 138.

Prior to Ruby 1.8, you could use a bare regular expression as a boolean expression. This is now deprecated. You can still use the ~ operator (described in the reference section on page 661) to match $_ against a pattern, but this will probably also disappear in the future.

if and unless Expressions

An if expression in Ruby is pretty similar to if statements in other languages:

```ruby
if artist == "Gillespie" then
  handle = "Dizzy"
elsif artist == "Parker" then
  handle = "Bird"
else
  handle = "unknown"
end
```

The then keyword is optional if you lay out your statements on multiple lines:

```ruby
if artist == "Gillespie"
  handle = "Dizzy"
elsif artist == "Parker"
  handle = "Bird"
else
  handle = "unknown"
end
```

However, if you want to lay out your code more tightly, you must separate the boolean expression from the following statements with the then keyword:[1]

```ruby
if artist == "Gillespie" then  handle = "Dizzy"
elsif artist == "Parker" then  handle = "Bird"
else  handle = "unknown"
end
```

You can have zero or more elsif clauses and an optional else clause. And notice that there's no e in the middle of elsif.

As we've said before, an if statement is an expression—it returns a value. You don't have to use the value of an if statement, but it can come in handy:

```ruby
handle = if artist == "Gillespie"
           "Dizzy"
         elsif artist == "Parker"
           "Bird"
         else
           "unknown"
         end
```

Ruby also has a negated form of the if statement:

```ruby
unless duration > 180
  listen_intently
end
```

The unless statement does support else, but most people seem to agree that it's clearer to switch to an if statement in these cases.

---

1.   Ruby 1.8 allowed you to use a colon character in place of the then keyword. This is no longer supported.

Finally, for the C fans out there, Ruby also supports the C-style conditional expression:

```
cost = duration > 180 ? 0.35 : 0.25
```

A conditional expression returns the value of the expression either before or after the colon, depending on whether the boolean expression before the question mark is true or false. In the previous example, if the duration is greater than three minutes, the expression returns 0.35. For shorter durations, it returns 0.25. The result is then assigned to cost.

if and unless Modifiers

Ruby shares a neat feature with Perl. Statement modifiers let you tack conditional statements onto the end of a normal statement:

```
mon, day, year = $1, $2, $3 if date =~ /(\d\d)-(\d\d)-(\d\d)/
puts "a = #{a}" if $DEBUG
print total unless total.zero?
```

For an if modifier, the preceding expression will be evaluated only if the condition is true. unless works the other way around:

```
File.foreach("/etc/passwd") do |line|
  next if line =~ /^#/           # Skip comments
  parse(line) unless line =~ /^$/   # Don't parse empty lines
end
```

Because if itself is an expression, you can get really obscure with statements such as this:

```
if artist == "John Coltrane"
  artist = "'Trane"
end unless use_nicknames == "no"
```

This path leads to the gates of madness.

9.5   case Expressions

The Ruby case expression is a powerful beast: a multiway if on steroids. And just to make it even more powerful, it comes in two flavors.

The first form is fairly close to a series of if statements; it lets you list a series of conditions and execute a statement corresponding to the first one that's true:

```
case
when song.name == "Misty"
  puts "Not again!"
when song.duration > 120
  puts "Too long!"
when Time.now.hour > 21
  puts "It's too late"
else
  song.play
end
```

The second form of the case statement is probably more common. You specify a target at the top of the case statement, and each when clause lists one or more comparisons to be tested against that target:

```
case command
when "debug"
  dump_debug_info
  dump_symbols
when /p\s+(\w+)/
  dump_variable($1)
when "quit", "exit"
  exit
else
  print "Illegal command: #{command}"
end
```

As with if, case returns the value of the last expression executed, and you can use a then keyword if the expression is on the same line as the condition:[2]

```
kind = case year
       when 1850..1889 then "Blues"
       when 1890..1909 then "Ragtime"
       when 1910..1929 then "New Orleans Jazz"
       when 1930..1939 then "Swing"
       else                "Jazz"
       end
```

case operates by comparing the target (the expression after the keyword case) with each of the comparison expressions after the when keywords. This test is done using comparison === target. As long as a class defines meaningful semantics for === (and all the built-in classes do), objects of that class can be used in case expressions.

For example, regular expressions define === as a simple pattern match:

```
case line
when /title=(.*)/
  puts "Title is #$1"
when /track=(.*)/
  puts "Track is #$1"
end
```

Ruby classes are instances of class Class. The === operator is defined in Class to test whether the argument is an instance of the receiver or one of its superclasses. So (abandoning the benefits of polymorphism and bringing the gods of refactoring down around your ears), you can test the class of objects:

```
case shape
when Square, Rectangle
  # ...
when Circle
  # ...
when Triangle
  # ...
else
  # ...
end
```

---

2.   Ruby 1.8 lets you use a colon in place of the then keyword. Ruby 1.9 does not support this.

9.6 Loops

Don't tell anyone, but Ruby has pretty primitive built-in looping constructs.

The while loop executes its body zero or more times as long as its condition is true. For example, this common idiom reads until the input is exhausted:

```
while line = gets
  # ...
end
```

The until loop is the opposite; it executes the body *until* the condition becomes true:

```
until play_list.duration > 60
  play_list.add(song_list.pop)
end
```

As with if and unless, you can use both of the loops as statement modifiers:

```
a = 1
a *= 2  while a < 100
a          # => 128
a -= 10 until a < 100
a          # => 98
```

Back in the section on boolean expressions on page 134, we said that a range can be used as a kind of flip-flop, returning true when some event happens and then staying true until a second event occurs. This facility is normally used within loops. In the example that follows, we read a text file containing the first ten ordinal numbers ("first," "second," and so on) but print only the lines starting with the one that matches "third" and ending with the one that matches "fifth":

```
file = File.open("ordinal")
while line = file.gets
  puts(line)  if line =~ /third/ .. line =~ /fifth/
end
```

produces:

```
third
fourth
fifth
```

You may find folks who come from Perl writing the previous example slightly differently:

```
file = File.open("ordinal")
while file.gets
  print  if ~/third/ .. ~/fifth/
end
```

produces:

```
third
fourth
fifth
```

This uses some behind-the-scenes magic behavior: gets assigns the last line read to the global variable $_, the ~ operator does a regular expression match against $_, and print with no arguments prints $_. This kind of code is falling out of fashion in the Ruby community and may end up being removed from the language.

The start and end of a range used in a boolean expression can themselves be expressions. These are evaluated each time the overall boolean expression is evaluated. For example, the following code uses the fact that the variable $. contains the current input line number to display line numbers 1 through 3 as well as those between a match of /eig/ and /nin/:

```
File.foreach("ordinal") do |line|
  if (($. == 1) || line =~ /eig/) .. (($. == 3) || line =~ /nin/)
    print line
  end
end
```

produces:

```
first
second
third
eighth
ninth
```

You'll come across a wrinkle when you use while and until as statement modifiers. If the statement they are modifying is a begin...end block, the code in the block will always execute at least one time, regardless of the value of the boolean expression:

```
print "Hello\n" while false
begin
  print "Goodbye\n"
end while false
```

produces:

```
Goodbye
```

Iterators

If you read the beginning of the previous section, you may have been discouraged. "Ruby has pretty primitive built-in looping constructs," it said. Don't despair, gentle reader, for we have good news. Ruby doesn't need any sophisticated built-in loops, because all the fun stuff is implemented using Ruby iterators.

For example, Ruby doesn't have a for loop—at least not the kind that iterates over a range of numbers. Instead, Ruby uses methods defined in various built-in classes to provide equivalent, but less error-prone, functionality.

Let's look at some examples:

```
3.times do
  print "Ho! "
end
```

produces:

```
Ho! Ho! Ho!
```

It's easy to avoid fence-post and off-by-one errors; this loop will execute three times, period. In addition to times, integers can loop over specific ranges by calling downto and upto, and all numbers can loop using step. For instance, a traditional "for" loop that runs from 0 to 9 (something like for(i=0; i < 10; i++)) is written as follows:

```
0.upto(9) do |x|
  print x, " "
end
```

produces:

```
0 1 2 3 4 5 6 7 8 9
```

A loop from 0 to 12 by 3 can be written as follows:

```
0.step(12, 3) {|x| print x, " " }
```

produces:

```
0 3 6 9 12
```

Similarly, iterating over arrays and other containers is easy if you use their each method:

```
[ 1, 1, 2, 3, 5 ].each {|val| print val, " " }
```

produces:

```
1 1 2 3 5
```

And once a class supports each, the additional methods in the Enumerable module become available. (We talked about this back in the Modules chapter on page 77, and we document it fully in *Enumerable*, on page 466.) For example, the File class provides an each method, which returns each line of a file in turn. Using the grep method in Enumerable, we could iterate over only those lines that end with a d:

```
File.open("ordinal").grep(/d$/) do |line|
  puts line
end
```

produces:

```
second
third
```

Last, and probably least, is the most basic loop of all. Ruby provides a built-in iterator called loop:

```
loop do
  # block ...
end
```

The loop iterator calls the associated block forever (or at least until you break out of the loop, but you'll have to read ahead to find out how to do that).

for ... in

Earlier we said that the only built-in Ruby looping primitives were while and until. What's this for thing, then? Well, for is almost a lump of syntactic sugar.

When you write this:

```
for song in playlist
  song.play
end
```

Ruby translates it into something like this:

```
playlist.each do |song|
  song.play
end
```

The only difference between the for loop and the each form is the scope of local variables that are defined in the body. This is discussed in Section 9.7, *Variable Scope, Loops, and Blocks*, on page 142.

You can use for to iterate over any object that responds to the method each, such as an Array or a Range:

```
for i in ['fee', 'fi', 'fo', 'fum']
  print i, " "
end
for i in 1..3
  print i, " "
end
for i in File.open("ordinal").find_all {|line| line =~ /d$/}
  print i.chomp, " "
end
```

produces:

```
fee fi fo fum 1 2 3 second third
```

As long as your class defines a sensible each method, you can use a for loop to traverse its objects:

```
class Periods
  def each
    yield "Classical"
    yield "Jazz"
    yield "Rock"
  end
end

periods = Periods.new
for genre in periods
  print genre, " "
end
```

produces:

```
Classical Jazz Rock
```

break, redo, and next

The loop control constructs break, redo, and next let you alter the normal flow through a loop or iterator.[3]

break terminates the immediately enclosing loop; control resumes at the statement following the block. redo repeats the current iteration of the loop from the start but without reevaluating the condition or fetching the next element (in an iterator). next skips to the end of the loop, effectively starting the next iteration:

---

3. Ruby 1.8 and earlier also supported the retry keyword as a looping mechanism. This has been removed in Ruby 1.9.

```
while line = gets
  next  if line =~ /^\s*#/  # skip comments
  break if line =~ /^END/   # stop at end

  # substitute stuff in backticks and try again
  redo if line.gsub!(/`(.*?)`/) { eval($1) }

  # process line ...
end
```

These keywords can also be used within blocks. Although you can use them with any block, they typically make the most sense when the block is being used for iteration:

```
i=0
loop do
  i += 1
  next if i < 3
  print i
  break if i > 4
end
```

produces:

345

A value may be passed to break and next. When used in conventional loops, it probably makes sense only to do this with break, where it sets the value returned by the loop. (Any value given to next is effectively lost.) If a conventional loop doesn't execute a break, its value is nil.

```
result = while line = gets
           break(line) if line =~ /answer/
         end

process_answer(result) if result
```

If you want the nitty-gritty details of how break and next work with blocks and procs, take a look at the reference description on page 338. If you are looking for a way of exiting from nested blocks or loops, take a look at Object#catch on page 341.

9.7 Variable Scope, Loops, and Blocks

The while, until, and for loops are built into the language and do not introduce new scope; previously existing locals can be used in the loop, and any new locals created will be available afterward.

The scoping rules for blocks (such as those used by loop and each) are different. Normally, the local variables created in these blocks are not accessible outside the block:

```
[ 1, 2, 3 ].each do |x|
  y = x + 1
end
[ x, y ]
```

produces:

```
prog.rb:4:in `<main>': undefined local variable or method `x' for main:Object
(NameError)
```

However, if at the time the block executes a local variable already exists with the same name as that of a variable in the block, the existing local variable will be used in the block. Its value will therefore be available after the block finishes. As the following example shows, this applies to normal variables in the block but not to the block's parameters:

```
x = "initial value"
y = "another value"
[ 1, 2, 3 ].each do |x|
  y = x + 1
end
[ x, y ]  # => ["initial value", 4]
```

Note that the assignment to the variable doesn't have to be executed; the Ruby interpreter just needs to have seen that the variable exists on the left side of an assignment:

```
a = "never used" if false
[99].each  do |i|
  a = i              # this  sets the variable in the outer scope
end
a          # => 99
```

You can list *block-local variables* in the block's parameter list, preceded by a semicolon. Contrast this code, which does not use block-locals:

```
square = "yes"
total = 0

[ 1, 2, 3 ].each do |val|
  square = val * val
  total += square
end

puts "Total = #{total}, square = #{square}"
```

produces:

```
Total = 14, square = 9
```

with the following code, which uses a block-local variable, so square in the outer scope is not affected by a variable of the same name within the block:

```
square = "yes"
total = 0

[ 1, 2, 3 ].each do |val; square|
  square = val * val
  total += square
end

puts "Total = #{total}, square = #{square}"
```

produces:

```
Total = 14, square = yes
```

If you are concerned about the scoping of variables with blocks, turn on Ruby warnings, and declare your block-local variables explicitly.

## CHAPTER 10

Exceptions, catch, and throw

So far, we've been developing code in Pleasantville, a wonderful place where nothing ever, ever goes wrong. Every library call succeeds, users never enter incorrect data, and resources are plentiful and cheap. Well, that's about to change. Welcome to the real world!

In the real world, errors happen. Good programs (and programmers) anticipate them and arrange to handle them gracefully. This isn't always as easy as it may sound. Often the code that detects an error does not have the context to know what to do about it. For example, attempting to open a file that doesn't exist is acceptable in some circumstances and is a fatal error at other times. What's your file-handling module to do?

The traditional approach is to use return codes. The open method could return some specific value to say it failed. This value is then propagated back through the layers of calling routines until someone wants to take responsibility for it. The problem with this approach is that managing all these error codes can be a pain. If a function calls open, then read, and finally close and if each can return an error indication, how can the function distinguish these error codes in the value it returns to *its* caller?

To a large extent, *exceptions* solve this problem. Exceptions let you package information about an error into an object. That exception object is then propagated back up the calling stack automatically until the runtime system finds code that explicitly declares that it knows how to handle that type of exception.

10.1 The Exception Class

Information about an exception is encapsulated in an object of class Exception or one of class Exception's children. Ruby predefines a tidy hierarchy of exceptions, shown in Figure 1, *Standard exception hierarchy*, on page 146. As we'll see later, this hierarchy makes handling exceptions considerably easier.

When you need to raise an exception, you can use one of the built-in Exception classes, or you can create one of your own. Make your own exceptions subclasses of StandardError or one of its children. If you don't, your exceptions won't be caught by default.

Every Exception has associated with it a message string and a stack backtrace. If you define your own exceptions, you can add extra information.

```
Exception
    NoMemoryError
    ScriptError
        LoadError
            Gem::LoadError
        NotImplementedError
        SyntaxError
    SecurityError
    SignalException
        Interrupt
    StandardError
        ArgumentError
            Gem::Requirement::BadRequirementError
        EncodingError
            Encoding::CompatibilityError
            Encoding::ConverterNotFoundError
            Encoding::InvalidByteSequenceError
            Encoding::UndefinedConversionError
        FiberError
        IndexError
            KeyError
            StopIteration
        IOError
            EOFError
        LocalJumpError
        Math::DomainError
        NameError
            NoMethodError
        RangeError
            FloatDomainError
        RegexpError
        RuntimeError
            Gem::Exception
        SystemCallError
        ThreadError
        TypeError
        ZeroDivisionError
    SystemExit
        Gem::SystemExitException
    SystemStackError
```

Figure 1—Standard exception hierarchy

10.2 Handling Exceptions

Here's some simple code that uses the open-uri library to download the contents of a web page and write it to a file, line by line:

tut_exceptions/fetch_web_page/fetch1.rb
```
require 'open-uri'
web_page = open("http://pragprog.com/podcasts")
output = File.open("podcasts.html", "w")
while line = web_page.gets
```

```
    output.puts line
end
output.close
```

What happens if we get a fatal error halfway through? We certainly don't want to store an incomplete page to the output file.

Let's add some exception-handling code and see how it helps. To do exception handling, we enclose the code that could raise an exception in a begin/end block and use one or more rescue clauses to tell Ruby the types of exceptions we want to handle. Because we specified Exception in the rescue line, we'll handle exceptions of class Exception and all of its subclasses (which covers all Ruby exceptions). In the error-handling block, we report the error, close and delete the output file, and then reraise the exception:

```
tut_exceptions/fetch_web_page/fetch2.rb
require 'open-uri'
page = "podcasts"
file_name = "#{page}.html"
web_page = open("http://pragprog.com/#{page}")
output = File.open(file_name, "w")
begin
  while line = web_page.gets
    output.puts line
  end
  output.close
rescue Exception
  STDERR.puts "Failed to download #{page}: #{$!}"
  output.close
  File.delete(file_name)
  raise
end
```

When an exception is raised and independent of any subsequent exception handling, Ruby places a reference to the associated exception object into the global variable $! (the exclamation point presumably mirroring our surprise that any of *our* code could cause errors). In the previous example, we used the $! variable to format our error message.

After closing and deleting the file, we call raise with no parameters, which reraises the exception in $!. This is a useful technique, because it allows you to write code that filters exceptions, passing on those you can't handle to higher levels. It's almost like implementing an inheritance hierarchy for error processing.

You can have multiple rescue clauses in a begin block, and each rescue clause can specify multiple exceptions to catch. At the end of each rescue clause, you can give Ruby the name of a local variable to receive the matched exception. Most people find this more readable than using $! all over the place:

```
begin
  eval string
rescue SyntaxError, NameError => boom
  print "String doesn't compile: " + boom
rescue StandardError => bang
  print "Error running script: " + bang
end
```

How does Ruby decide which rescue clause to execute? It turns out that the processing is pretty similar to that used by the case statement. For each rescue clause in the begin block, Ruby compares the raised exception against each of the parameters in turn. If the raised exception matches a parameter, Ruby executes the body of the rescue and stops looking. The match is made using parameter===$!. For most exceptions, this means that the match will succeed if the exception named in the rescue clause is the same as the type of the currently thrown exception or is a superclass of that exception.[1] If you write a rescue clause with no parameter list, the parameter defaults to StandardError.

If no rescue clause matches or if an exception is raised outside a begin/end block, Ruby moves up the stack and looks for an exception handler in the caller, then in the caller's caller, and so on.

Although the parameters to the rescue clause are typically the names of exception classes, they can be arbitrary expressions (including method calls) that return an Exception class.

System Errors

System errors are raised when a call to the operating system returns an error code. On POSIX systems, these errors have names such as EAGAIN and EPERM. (If you're on a Unix box, you could type man errno to get a list of these errors.)

Ruby takes these errors and wraps them each in a specific exception object. Each is a subclass of SystemCallError, and each is defined in a module called Errno. This means you'll find exceptions with class names such as Errno::EAGAIN, Errno::EIO, and Errno::EPERM. If you want to get to the underlying system error code, Errno exception objects each have a class constant called (somewhat confusingly) Errno that contains the value.

```
Errno::EAGAIN::Errno        # => 35
Errno::EPERM::Errno         # => 1
Errno::EWOULDBLOCK::Errno   # => 35
```

Note that EWOULDBLOCK and EAGAIN have the same error number. This is a feature of the operating system of the computer used to produce this book—the two constants map to the same error number. To deal with this, Ruby arranges things so that Errno::EAGAIN and Errno::EWOULDBLOCK are treated identically in a rescue clause. If you ask to rescue one, you'll rescue either. It does this by redefining SystemCallError#=== so that if two subclasses of SystemCallError are compared, the comparison is done on their error number and not on their position in the hierarchy.

Tidying Up

Sometimes you need to guarantee that some processing is done at the end of a block of code, regardless of whether an exception was raised. For example, you may have a file open on entry to the block, and you need to make sure it gets closed as the block exits.

The ensure clause does just this. ensure goes after the last rescue clause and contains a chunk of code that will always be executed as the block terminates. It doesn't matter if the block exits normally, if it raises and rescues an exception, or if it is terminated by an uncaught exception—the ensure block will get run:

---

1. This comparison happens because exceptions are classes, and classes in turn are kinds of Module. The === method is defined for modules, returning true if the class of the operand is the same as or is a descendant of the receiver.

```
f = File.open("testfile")
begin
  # .. process
rescue
  # .. handle error
ensure
  f.close
end
```

Beginners commonly make the mistake of putting the File.open inside the begin block. In this case, that would be incorrect, because open can itself raise an exception. If that were to happen, you wouldn't want to run the code in the ensure block, because there'd be no file to close.

The else clause is a similar, although less useful, construct. If present, it goes after the rescue clauses and before any ensure. The body of an else clause is executed only if no exceptions are raised by the main body of code.

```
f = File.open("testfile")
begin
  # .. process
rescue
  # .. handle error
else
  puts "Congratulations-- no errors!"
ensure
  f.close
end
```

Play It Again

Sometimes you may be able to correct the cause of an exception. In those cases, you can use the retry statement within a rescue clause to repeat the entire begin/end block. Clearly, tremendous scope exists for infinite loops here, so this is a feature to use with caution (and with a finger resting lightly on the interrupt key).

As an example of code that retries on exceptions, take a look at the following, adapted from Minero Aoki's net/smtp.rb library:

```
@esmtp = true

begin
  # First try an extended login. If it fails, fall back to a normal login
  if @esmtp then @command.ehlo(helodom)
            else @command.helo(helodom)
  end

rescue ProtocolError
  if @esmtp then
    @esmtp = false
    retry
  else
    raise
  end
end
```

This code tries first to connect to an SMTP server using the EHLO command, which is not universally supported. If the connection attempt fails, the code sets the @esmtp variable to false and retries the connection. If this fails a second time, the exception is raised up to the caller.

10.3 Raising Exceptions

So far, we've been on the defensive, handling exceptions raised by others. It's time to turn the tables and go on the offensive. (Some say your gentle authors are always offensive, but that's a different book.)

You can raise exceptions in your code with the Object#raise method (or its somewhat judgmental synonym, Object#fail):

```
raise
raise "bad mp3 encoding"
raise InterfaceException, "Keyboard failure", caller
```

The first form simply reraises the current exception (or a RuntimeError if there is no current exception). This is used in exception handlers that intercept an exception before passing it on.

The second form creates a new RuntimeError exception, setting its message to the given string. This exception is then raised up the call stack.

The third form uses the first argument to create an exception and then sets the associated message to the second argument and the stack trace to the third argument. Typically the first argument will be either the name of a class in the Exception hierarchy or a reference to an instance of one of these classes.[2] The stack trace is normally produced using the Object#caller method.

Here are some typical examples of raise in action:

```
raise

raise "Missing name" if name.nil?

if i >= names.size
  raise IndexError, "#{i} >= size (#{names.size})"
end

raise ArgumentError, "Name too big", caller
```

In the last example, we remove the current routine from the stack backtrace, which is often useful in library modules. We do this using the caller method, which returns the current stack trace. We can take this further; the following code removes two routines from the backtrace by passing only a subset of the call stack to the new exception:

```
raise ArgumentError, "Name too big", caller[1..-1]
```

---

2. Technically, this argument can be any object that responds to the message exception by returning an object such that object.kind_of?(Exception) is true.

Adding Information to Exceptions

You can define your own exceptions to hold any information that you need to pass out from the site of an error. For example, certain types of network errors may be transient depending on the circumstances. If such an error occurs and the circumstances are right, you could set a flag in the exception to tell the handler that it may be worth retrying the operation:

```
tut_exceptions/retry_exception.rb
class RetryException < RuntimeError
  attr :ok_to_retry
  def initialize(ok_to_retry)
    @ok_to_retry = ok_to_retry
  end
end
```

Somewhere down in the depths of the code, a transient error occurs:

```
tut_exceptions/read_data.rb
def read_data(socket)
  data = socket.read(512)
  if data.nil?
    raise RetryException.new(true), "transient read error"
  end
  # .. normal processing
end
```

Higher up the call stack, we handle the exception:

```
begin
  stuff = read_data(socket)
  # .. process stuff
rescue RetryException => detail
  retry if detail.ok_to_retry
  raise
end
```

10.4 catch and throw

Although the exception mechanism of raise and rescue is great for abandoning execution when things go wrong, it's sometimes nice to be able to jump out of some deeply nested construct during normal processing. This is where catch and throw come in handy. Here's a trivial example—this code reads a list of words one at a time and adds them to an array. When done, it prints the array in reverse order. However, if any of the lines in the file doesn't contain a valid word, we want to abandon the whole process.

```
word_list = File.open("wordlist")
catch (:done)  do
  result = []
  while line = word_list.gets
    word = line.chomp
    throw :done unless word =~ /^\w+$/
    result << word
  end
  puts result.reverse
end
```

catch defines a block that is labeled with the given name (which may be a Symbol or a String). The block is executed normally until a throw is encountered.

When Ruby encounters a throw, it zips back up the call stack looking for a catch block with a matching symbol. When it finds it, Ruby unwinds the stack to that point and terminates the block. So, in the previous example, if the input does not contain correctly formatted lines, the throw will skip to the end of the corresponding catch, not only terminating the while loop but also skipping the code that writes the reversed list. If the throw is called with the optional second parameter, that value is returned as the value of the catch. In this example, our word list incorrectly contains the line "*wow*." Without the second parameter to throw, the corresponding catch returns nil.

```ruby
word_list = File.open("wordlist")
word_in_error = catch(:done) do
  result = []
  while line = word_list.gets
    word = line.chomp
    throw(:done, word) unless word =~ /^\w+$/
    result << word
  end
  puts result.reverse
end
if word_in_error
  puts "Failed: '#{word_in_error}' found, but a word was expected"
end
```

produces:

```
Failed: '*wow*' found, but a word was expected
```

The following example uses a throw to terminate interaction with the user if ! is typed in response to any prompt:

tut_exceptions/catchthrow.rb
```ruby
def prompt_and_get(prompt)
  print prompt
  res = readline.chomp
  throw :quit_requested if res == "!"
  res
end

catch :quit_requested do
  name = prompt_and_get("Name: ")
  age  = prompt_and_get("Age:  ")
  sex  = prompt_and_get("Sex:  ")
  # ..
  # process information
end
```

As this example illustrates, the throw does not have to appear within the static scope of the catch.

## CHAPTER 11

Basic Input and Output

Ruby provides what at first sight looks like two separate sets of I/O routines. The first is the simple interface—we've been using it pretty much exclusively so far:

```
print "Enter your name: "
name = gets
```

A whole set of I/O-related methods is implemented in the Kernel module—gets, open, print, printf, putc, puts, readline, readlines, and test—that makes it simple and convenient to write straightforward Ruby programs. These methods typically do I/O to standard input and standard output, which makes them useful for writing filters. You'll find them documented under class Object on page 599.

The second way, which gives you a lot more control, is to use IO objects.

11.1 What Is an IO Object?

Ruby defines a single base class, IO, to handle input and output. This base class is subclassed by classes File and BasicSocket to provide more specialized behavior, but the principles are the same. An IO object is a bidirectional channel between a Ruby program and some external resource.[1] An IO object may have more to it than meets the eye, but in the end you still simply write to it and read from it.

In this chapter, we'll be concentrating on class IO and its most commonly used subclass, class File. For more details on using the socket classes for networking, see the library description on page 807.

11.2 Opening and Closing Files

As you may expect, you can create a new file object using File.new:

```
file = File.new("testfile", "r")
# ... process the file
file.close
```

---

1. For those who just have to know the implementation details, this means that a single IO object can sometimes be managing more than one operating system file descriptor. For example, if you open a pair of pipes, a single IO object contains both a read pipe and a write pipe.

The first parameter is the filename. The second is the mode string, which lets you open the file for reading, writing, or both. (Here we opened testfile for reading with an "r". We could also have used "w" for write or "r+" for read-write. The full list of allowed modes appears in the reference section on page 494.) You can also optionally specify file permissions when creating a file; see the description of File.new on page 494 for details. After opening the file, we can work with it, writing and/or reading data as needed. Finally, as responsible software citizens, we close the file, ensuring that all buffered data is written and that all related resources are freed.

But here Ruby can make life a little bit easier for you. The method File.open also opens a file. In regular use, it behaves just like File.new. However, if you associate a block with the call, open behaves differently. Instead of returning a new File object, it invokes the block, passing the newly opened File as a parameter. When the block exits, the file is automatically closed.

```
File.open("testfile", "r") do |file|
  # ... process the file
end      # <- file automatically closed here
```

This second approach has an added benefit. In the earlier case, if an exception is raised while processing the file, the call to file.close may not happen. Once the file variable goes out of scope, then garbage collection will eventually close it, but this may not happen for a while. Meanwhile, resources are being held open.

This doesn't happen with the block form of File.open. If an exception is raised inside the block, the file is closed before the exception is propagated on to the caller. It's as if the open method looks like the following:

```
class File
  def File.open(*args)
    result = f = File.new(*args)
    if block_given?
      begin
        result = yield f
      ensure
        f.close
      end
    end

    result
  end
end
```

11.3 Reading and Writing Files

The same methods that we've been using for "simple" I/O are available for all file objects. So, gets reads a line from standard input (or from any files specified on the command line when the script was invoked), and file.gets reads a line from the file object *file*.

For example, we could create a program called copy.rb:

```
tut_io/copy.rb
while line = gets
  puts line
end
```

If we run this program with no arguments, it will read lines from the console and copy them back to the console. Note that each line is echoed once the Return key is pressed. (In this and later examples, we show user input in a bold font.) The ^D is the end-of-file character on Unix systems.

```
$ ruby copy.rb
These are lines
These are lines
that I am typing
that I am typing
^D
```

We can also pass in one or more filenames on the command line, in which case gets will read from each in turn:

```
$ ruby copy.rb testfile
This is line one
This is line two
This is line three
And so on...
```

Finally, we can explicitly open the file and read from it:

```
File.open("testfile") do |file|
  while line = file.gets
    puts line
  end
end
```

produces:

```
This is line one
This is line two
This is line three
And so on...
```

As well as gets, I/O objects enjoy an additional set of access methods, all intended to make our lives easier.

Iterators for Reading

As well as using the usual loops to read data from an IO stream, you can also use various Ruby iterators. IO#each_byte invokes a block with the next 8-bit byte from the IO object (in this case, an object of type File). The chr method converts an integer to the corresponding ASCII character:

```
File.open("testfile") do |file|
  file.each_byte.with_index do |ch, index|
    print "#{ch.chr}:#{ch} "
    break if index > 10
  end
end
```

produces:

```
T:84 h:104 i:105 s:115  :32 i:105 s:115  :32 l:108 i:105 n:110 e:101
```

IO#each_line calls the block with each line from the file. In the next example, we'll make the original newlines visible using String#dump so you can see that we're not cheating:

```
File.open("testfile") do |file|
  file.each_line {|line| puts "Got #{line.dump}" }
end
```

produces:

```
Got "This is line one\n"
Got "This is line two\n"
Got "This is line three\n"
Got "And so on...\n"
```

You can pass each_line any sequence of characters as a line separator, and it will break up the input accordingly, returning the line ending at the end of each line of data. That's why you see the \n characters in the output of the previous example. In the next example, we'll use the character e as the line separator:

```
File.open("testfile") do |file|
  file.each_line("e") {|line|  puts "Got #{ line.dump }" }
end
```

produces:

```
Got "This is line"
Got " one"
Got "\nThis is line"
Got " two\nThis is line"
Got " thre"
Got "e"
Got "\nAnd so on...\n"
```

If you combine the idea of an iterator with the autoclosing block feature, you get IO.foreach. This method takes the name of an I/O source, opens it for reading, calls the iterator once for every line in the file, and then closes the file automatically:

```
IO.foreach("testfile") {|line| puts line }
```

produces:

```
This is line one
This is line two
This is line three
And so on...
```

Or, if you prefer, you can retrieve an entire file into a string or into an array of lines:

```
# read into string
str = IO.read("testfile")
str.length # => 66
str[0, 30] # => "This is line one\nThis is line "

# read into an array
arr = IO.readlines("testfile")
arr.length # => 4
arr[0]     # => "This is line one\n"
```

Don't forget that I/O is never certain in an uncertain world—exceptions will be raised on most errors, and you should be ready to rescue them and take appropriate action.

Writing to Files

So far, we've been merrily calling puts and print, passing in any old object and trusting that Ruby will do the right thing (which, of course, it does). But what exactly *is* it doing?

The answer is pretty simple. With a couple of exceptions, every object you pass to puts and print is converted to a string by calling that object's to_s method. If for some reason the to_s method doesn't return a valid string, a string is created containing the object's class name and ID, something like #<ClassName:0x123456>:

```
# Note the "w", which opens the file for writing
File.open("output.txt", "w") do |file|
  file.puts "Hello"
  file.puts "1 + 2 = #{1+2}"
end

# Now read the file in and print its contents to STDOUT
puts File.read("output.txt")
```

produces:

```
Hello
1 + 2 = 3
```

The exceptions are simple, too. The nil object will print as the empty string, and an array passed to puts will be written as if each of its elements in turn were passed separately to puts.

What if you want to write binary data and don't want Ruby messing with it? Well, normally you can simply use IO#print and pass in a string containing the bytes to be written. However, you can get at the low-level input and output routines if you really want—look at the documentation for IO#sysread and IO#syswrite on page 554.

And how do you get the binary data into a string in the first place? The three common ways are to use a literal, poke it in byte by byte, or use Array#pack:[2]

```
str1 = "\001\002\003"   # => "\u0001\u0002\u0003"
str2 = ""
str2 << 1 << 2 << 3     # => "\u0001\u0002\u0003"
[ 1, 2, 3 ].pack("c*")  # => "\x01\x02\x03"
```

But I Miss My C++ iostream

Sometimes there's just no accounting for taste. However, just as you can append an object to an Array using the << operator, you can also append an object to an output IO stream:

```
endl = "\n"
STDOUT << 99 << " red balloons" << endl
```

produces:

```
99 red balloons
```

Again, the << method uses to_s to convert its arguments to strings before printing them.

Although we started off disparaging the poor << operator, there are actually some good reasons for using it. Because other classes (such as String and Array) also implement a <<

---

2.   The pack method takes an array of data and packs it into a string. See the description in the reference section on page 432.

operator with similar semantics, you can quite often write code that appends to something using << without caring whether it is added to an array, a file, or a string. This kind of flexibility also makes unit testing easy. We discuss this idea in greater detail in the chapter on duck typing on page 343.

Doing I/O with Strings

There are often times where you need to work with code that assumes it's reading from or writing to one or more files. But you have a problem: the data isn't in files. Perhaps it's available instead via a SOAP service, or it has been passed to you as command-line parameters. Or maybe you're running unit tests, and you don't want to alter the real file system.

Enter StringIO objects. They behave just like other I/O objects, but they read and write strings, not files. If you open a StringIO object for reading, you supply it with a string. All read operations on the StringIO object then read from this string. Similarly, when you want to write to a StringIO object, you pass it a string to be filled.

```ruby
require 'stringio'

ip = StringIO.new("now is\nthe time\nto learn\nRuby!")
op = StringIO.new("", "w")

ip.each_line do |line|
  op.puts line.reverse
end
op.string # => "\nsi won\n\nemit eht\n\nnrael ot\n!ybuR\n"
```

11.4 Talking to Networks

Ruby is fluent in most of the Internet's protocols, both low-level and high-level.

For those who enjoy groveling around at the network level, Ruby comes with a set of classes in the socket library (described briefly in this book on page 807 and in detail on the web page of the previous edition of this book at http://pragprog.com/book/ruby3/programming-ruby-1-9?tab=tab-contents). These give you access to TCP, UDP, SOCKS, and Unix domain sockets, as well as any additional socket types supported on your architecture. The library also provides helper classes to make writing servers easier. Here's a simple program that gets information about our user website on a local web server using the HTTP OPTIONS request:

```ruby
require 'socket'

client = TCPSocket.open('127.0.0.1', 'www')
client.send("OPTIONS /~dave/ HTTP/1.0\n\n", 0)    # 0 means standard packet
puts client.readlines
client.close
```

produces:

```
HTTP/1.1 200 OK
Date: Mon, 27 May 2013 17:31:00 GMT
Server: Apache/2.2.22 (Unix) DAV/2 PHP/5.3.15 with Suhosin-Patch mod_ssl/2.2.22
OpenSSL/0.9.8r
Allow: GET,HEAD,POST,OPTIONS
Content-Length: 0
Connection: close
Content-Type: text/html
```

At a higher level, the lib/net set of library modules provides handlers for a set of application-level protocols (currently FTP, HTTP, POP, SMTP, and telnet). These are documented in the library section on page 772. For example, the following program lists the images that are displayed on this book's home page. (To save space, we show only the first three):

```
require 'net/http'

http = Net::HTTP.new('pragprog.com', 80)
response = http.get('/book/ruby3/programming-ruby-1-9')

if response.message == "OK"
  puts response.body.scan(/<img alt=".*?" src="(.*?)"/m).uniq[0,3]
end
```

produces:

```
http://pragprog.com/assets/logo-c5c7f9c2f950df63a71871ba2f6bb115.gif
http://pragprog.com/assets/drm-free80-9120ffac998173dc0ba7e5875d082f18.png
http://imagery.pragprog.com/products/99/ruby3_xlargecover.jpg?1349967653
```

Although attractively simple, this example could be improved significantly. In particular, it doesn't do much in the way of error handling. It should really report "Not Found" errors (the infamous 404) and should handle redirects (which happen when a web server gives the client an alternative address for the requested page).

We can take this to a higher level still. By bringing the open-uri library into a program, the Object#open method suddenly recognizes http:// and ftp:// URLs in the filename. Not just that —it also handles redirects automatically.

```
require 'open-uri'

open('http://pragprog.com') do |f|
  puts f.read.scan(/<img alt=".*?" src="(.*?)"/m).uniq[0,3]
end
```

produces:

```
http://pragprog.com/assets/logo-c5c7f9c2f950df63a71871ba2f6bb115.gif
http://pragprog.com/assets/drm-free80-9120ffac998173dc0ba7e5875d082f18.png
http://imagery.pragprog.com/products/353/jvrails2_xlargebeta.jpg?1368826914
```

11.5 Parsing HTML

Having read HTML from a website, you might want to parse information out of it. Often, simple regular expressions do the job. In the example that follows, we're using the %r{...} regular expression literal, because the match contains a forward slash character, and regular expressions are complex enough without having to add extra backslashes.

```
require 'open-uri'
page = open('http://pragprog.com/titles/ruby3/programming-ruby-1-9').read
if page =~ %r{<title>(.*?)</title>}m
  puts "Title is #{$1.inspect}"
end
```

produces:

```
Title is "The Pragmatic Bookshelf | Programming Ruby 1.9"
```

But regular expressions won't always work. For example, if someone had an extra space in the <title> tag, the match would have failed. For real-world use, you probably want to use a library that can parse HTML (and XML) properly. Although not part of Ruby, the Nokogiri library is very popular.[3] It's a very rich library—we'll only scratch the surface here. Documentation is available inside the gem.

```
require 'open-uri'
require 'nokogiri'

doc = Nokogiri::HTML(open("http://pragprog.com/"))

puts "Page title is " + doc.xpath("//title").inner_html

# Output the first paragraph in the div with an id="copyright"
# (nokogiri supports both xpath and css-like selectors)
puts doc.css('div#copyright p')

# Output the second hyperlink in the site-links div using xpath and css
puts "\nSecond hyperlink is"
puts doc.xpath('id("site-links")//a[2]')
puts doc.css('#site-links a:nth-of-type(2)')
```

produces:

```
Page title is The Pragmatic Bookshelf
<p>
    The <em>Pragmatic Bookshelf™</em> is an imprint of
        <a href="http://pragprog.com/">The Pragmatic Programmers, LLC</a>.
    <br>
    Copyright © 1999–2013 The Pragmatic Programmers, LLC.
    All Rights Reserved.
  </p>

Second hyperlink is
<a href="http://pragprog.com/about">About Us</a>
<a href="http://pragprog.com/about">About Us</a>
```

Nokogiri can also update and create HTML and XML.

---

3.   Install it using gem install nokogiri.

## CHAPTER 12

Fibers, Threads, and Processes

Ruby gives you two basic ways to organize your program so that you can run different parts of it apparently "at the same time." Fibers let you suspend execution of one part of your program and run some other part. For more decoupled execution, you can split up cooperating tasks *within* the program, using multiple threads, or you can split up tasks between different programs, using multiple processes. Let's look at each in turn.

12.1 Fibers

Ruby 1.9 introduced *fibers*. Although the name suggests some kind of lightweight thread, Ruby's fibers are really just a very simple coroutine mechanism. They let you write programs that look like you are using threads without incurring any of the complexity inherent in threading. Let's look at a simple example. We'd like to analyze a text file, counting the occurrence of each word. We could do this (without using fibers) in a simple loop:

```
counts = Hash.new(0)
File.foreach("testfile") do |line|
  line.scan(/\w+/) do |word|
    word = word.downcase
    counts[word] += 1
  end
end
counts.keys.sort.each {|k| print "#{k}:#{counts[k]} "}
```

produces:

```
and:1 is:3 line:3 on:1 one:1 so:1 this:3 three:1 two:1
```

However, this code is messy—it mixes word finding with word counting. We could fix this by writing a method that reads the file and yields each successive word. But fibers give us a simpler solution:

```
words = Fiber.new do
  File.foreach("testfile") do |line|
    line.scan(/\w+/) do |word|
      Fiber.yield word.downcase
    end
  end
  nil
end
```

```
counts = Hash.new(0)
while word = words.resume
  counts[word] += 1
end
counts.keys.sort.each {|k| print "#{k}:#{counts[k]} "}
```

produces:

```
and:1 is:3 line:3 on:1 one:1 so:1 this:3 three:1 two:1
```

The constructor for the Fiber class takes a block and returns a fiber object. For now, the code in the block is not executed.

Subsequently, we can call resume on the fiber object. This causes the block to start execution. The file is opened, and the scan method starts extracting individual words. However, at this point, Fiber.yield is invoked. This suspends execution of the block—the resume method that we called to run the block returns any value given to Fiber.yield.

Our main program enters the body of the loop and increments the count for the first word returned by the fiber. It then loops back up to the top of the while loop, which again calls words.resume while evaluating the condition. The resume call goes back into the block, continuing just after it left off (at the line after the Fiber.yield call).

When the fiber runs out of words in the file, the foreach block exits, and the code in the fiber terminates. Just as with a method, the return value of the fiber will be the value of the last expression evaluated (in this case the nil).[1] The next time resume is called, it returns this value nil. You'll get a FiberError if you attempt to call resume again after this.

Fibers are often used to generate values from infinite sequences on demand. Here's a fiber that returns successive integers divisible by 2 and not divisible by 3:

```
twos = Fiber.new do
  num = 2
  loop do
    Fiber.yield(num) unless num % 3 == 0
    num += 2
  end
end
10.times { print twos.resume, " " }
```

produces:

```
2 4 8 10 14 16 20 22 26 28
```

Because fibers are just objects, you can pass them around, store them in variables, and so on. Fibers can be resumed only in the thread that created them.

New in 2.0 Ruby 2.0 adds a new twist to this—you can now use lazy enumerators to gracefully handle infinite lists. These are described *Lazy Enumerators in Ruby 2*, on page 61.

Fibers, Coroutines, and Continuations

The basic fiber support in Ruby is limited—fibers can yield control only back to the code that resumed them. However, Ruby comes with two standard libraries that extend this behavior. The fiber library (described in the library section on page 755) adds full coroutine

---

1. In fact, the nil is not strictly needed, as foreach will return nil when it terminates. The nil just makes it explicit.

support. Once it is loaded, fibers gain a transfer method, allowing them to transfer control to arbitrary other fibers.

A related but more general mechanism is the *continuation*. A continuation is a way of recording the state of your running program (where it is, the current binding, and so on) and then resuming from that state at some point in the future. You can use continuations to implement coroutines (and other new control structures). Continuations have also been used to store the state of a running web application between requests—a continuation is created when the application sends a response to the browser; then, when the next request arrives from that browser, the continuation is invoked, and the application continues from where it left off. You enable continuations in Ruby by requiring the continuation library, described in the library section on page 739.

12.2 Multithreading

Often the simplest way to do two things at once is to use *Ruby threads*. Prior to Ruby 1.9, these were implemented as green threads—threads were switched within the interpreter. In Ruby 1.9, threading is now performed by the operating system. This is an improvement, but not quite as big an improvement as you might want. Although threads can now take advantage of multiple processors (and multiple cores in a single processor), there's a major catch. Many Ruby extension libraries are not thread safe (because they were written for the old threading model). So, Ruby compromises: it uses native operating system threads but operates only a single thread at a time. You'll never see two threads in the same application running Ruby code truly concurrently. (You will, however, see threads busy doing, say, I/O while another thread executes Ruby code. That's part of the point.)

Creating Ruby Threads

Creating a new thread is pretty straightforward. The code that follows is a simple example. It downloads a set of web pages in parallel. For each URL that it is asked to download, the code creates a separate thread that handles the HTTP transaction.

```
require 'net/http'

pages = %w( www.rubycentral.org  slashdot.org  www.google.com )

threads = pages.map do |page_to_fetch|
  Thread.new(page_to_fetch) do |url|
    http = Net::HTTP.new(url, 80)
    print "Fetching: #{url}\n"
    resp = http.get('/')
    print "Got #{url}:  #{resp.message}\n"
  end
end
threads.each {|thr|  thr.join }
```

produces:

```
Fetching: www.rubycentral.org
Fetching: slashdot.org
Fetching: www.google.com
Got www.google.com:  OK
Got slashdot.org:  OK
Got www.rubycentral.org:  OK
```

Let's look at this code in more detail, because a few subtle things are happening.

New threads are created with the Thread.new call. It is given a block that contains the code to be run in a new thread. In our case, the block uses the net/http library to fetch the top page from each of our nominated sites. Our tracing clearly shows that these fetches are going on in parallel.

When we create the thread, we pass the required URL as a parameter. This parameter is passed to the block as url. Why do we do this, rather than simply using the value of the variable page_to_fetch within the block?

A thread shares all global, instance, and local variables that are in existence at the time the thread starts. As anyone with a kid brother can tell you, sharing isn't always a good thing. In this case, all three threads would share the variable page_to_fetch. The first thread gets started, and page_to_fetch is set to "www.rubycentral.org". In the meantime, the loop creating the threads is still running. The second time around, page_to_fetch gets set to "slashdot.org". If the first thread has not yet finished using the page_to_fetch variable, it will suddenly start using this new value. These kinds of bugs are difficult to track down.

However, local variables created within a thread's block are truly local to that thread—each thread will have its own copy of these variables. In our case, the variable url will be set at the time the thread is created, and each thread will have its own copy of the page address. You can pass any number of arguments into the block via Thread.new.

This code also illustrates a gotcha. Inside the loop, the threads use print to write out the messages, rather than puts. Why? Well, behind the scenes, puts splits its work into two chunks: it writes its argument, and then it writes a newline. Between these two, a thread could get scheduled, and the output would be interleaved. Calling print with a single string that already contains the newline gets around the problem.

Manipulating Threads

Another subtlety occurs on the last line in our download program. Why do we call join on each of the threads we created?

When a Ruby program terminates, all threads are killed, regardless of their states. However, you can wait for a particular thread to finish by calling that thread's Thread#join method. The calling thread will block until the given thread is finished. By calling join on each of the requester threads, you can make sure that all three requests have completed before you terminate the main program. If you don't want to block forever, you can give join a timeout parameter—if the timeout expires before the thread terminates, the join call returns nil. Another variant of join, the method Thread#value, returns the value of the last statement executed by the thread.

In addition to join, a few other handy routines are used to manipulate threads. The current thread is always accessible using Thread.current. You can obtain a list of all threads using Thread.list, which returns a list of all Thread objects that are runnable or stopped. To determine the status of a particular thread, you can use Thread#status and Thread#alive?.

You can adjust the priority of a thread using Thread#priority=. Higher-priority threads will run before lower-priority threads. We'll talk more about thread scheduling, and stopping and starting threads, in just a bit.

Thread Variables

A thread can normally access any variables that are in scope when the thread is created. Variables local to the block containing the thread code are local to the thread and are not shared. But what if you need per-thread variables that can be accessed by other threads— including the main thread? Class Thread has a facility that allows thread-local variables to be created and accessed by name. You simply treat the thread object as if it were a Hash, writing to elements using []= and reading them back using []. In the example that follows, each thread records the current value of the variable count in a thread-local variable with the key mycount. To do this, the code uses the symbol :mycount when indexing thread objects. (A *race condition*[2] exists in this code, but we haven't talked about synchronization yet, so we'll just quietly ignore it for now.)

```
count = 0
threads = 10.times.map do |i|
  Thread.new do
    sleep(rand(0.1))
    Thread.current[:mycount] = count
    count += 1
  end
end

threads.each {|t| t.join; print t[:mycount], ", " }
puts "count = #{count}"
```

produces:

```
7, 0, 6, 8, 4, 5, 1, 9, 2, 3, count = 10
```

The main thread waits for the subthreads to finish and then prints that thread's value of count. Just to make it interesting, each thread waits a random time before recording the value.

Threads and Exceptions

What happens if a thread raises an unhandled exception depends on the setting of the abort_on_exception flag (documented in the reference on page 702) and on the setting of the interpreter's $DEBUG flag (described in the Ruby options section on page 210).

If abort_on_exception is false and the debug flag is not enabled (the default condition), an unhandled exception simply kills the current thread—all the rest continue to run. In fact, you don't even hear about the exception until you issue a join on the thread that raised it. In the following example, thread 1 blows up and fails to produce any output. However, you can still see the trace from the other threads.

---

2.   A race condition occurs when two or more pieces of code (or hardware) both try to access some shared resource, and the outcome changes depending on the order in which they do so. In the example here, it is possible for one thread to set the value of its mycount variable to count, but before it gets a chance to increment count, the thread gets descheduled and another thread reuses the same value of count. These issues are fixed by synchronizing the access to shared resources (such as the count variable).

```
threads = 4.times.map do |number|
  Thread.new(number) do |i|
    raise "Boom!" if i == 1
    print "#{i}\n"
  end
end
puts "Waiting"
sleep 0.1
puts "Done"
```

produces:

```
0
2
Waiting
3
Done
```

You normally don't sleep waiting for threads to terminate—you'd use join. If you join to a thread that has raised an exception, then that exception will be raised in the thread that does the joining:

```
threads = 4.times.map do |number|
  Thread.new(number) do |i|
    raise "Boom!" if i == 1
    print "#{i}\n"
  end
end

puts "Waiting"
threads.each do |t|
  begin
    t.join
  rescue RuntimeError => e
    puts "Failed: #{e.message}"
  end
end
puts "Done"
```

produces:

```
0
Waiting
2
3
Failed: Boom!
Done
```

However, set abort_on_exception to true or use -d to turn on the debug flag, and an unhandled exception kills the main thread, so the message Done never appears. (This is different from Ruby 1.8, where the exception killed all running threads.)

```
Thread.abort_on_exception = true
threads = 4.times.map do |number|
  Thread.new(number) do |i|
    raise "Boom!" if i == 1
    print "#{i}\n"
```

```
    end
end
puts "Waiting"
threads.each {|t| t.join }
puts "Done"
```

produces:

```
0
2
prog.rb:4:in `block (2 levels) in <main>': Boom! (RuntimeError)
```

12.3 Controlling the Thread Scheduler

In a well-designed application, you'll normally just let threads do their thing; building timing dependencies into a multithreaded application is generally considered to be bad form, because it makes the code far more complex and also prevents the thread scheduler from optimizing the execution of your program.

The Thread class provides a number of methods that control the scheduler. Invoking Thread.stop stops the current thread, and invoking Thread#run arranges for a particular thread to be run. Thread.pass deschedules the current thread, allowing others to run, and Thread#join and #value suspend the calling thread until a given thread finishes. These last two are the only low-level thread control methods that the average program should use. In fact, we now consider most of the other low-level thread control methods too dangerous to use correctly in programs we write.[3] Fortunately, Ruby has support for higher-level thread synchronization.

12.4 Mutual Exclusion

Let's start by looking at a simple example of a race condition—multiple threads updating a shared variable:

```
sum = 0
threads = 10.times.map do
  Thread.new do
    100_000.times do
      new_value = sum + 1
      print "#{new_value}    " if new_value % 250_000 == 0
      sum = new_value
    end
  end
end
threads.each(&:join)
puts "\nsum = #{sum}"
```

produces:

```
250000   250000   250000   250000   250000   500000   500000
sum = 599999
```

We create 10 threads, and each increments the shared sum variable 100,000 times. And yet, when the threads all finish, the final value in sum is considerably less than 1,000,000. Clearly we have a race condition. The reason is the print call that sits between the code that calculates the new value and the code that stores it back into sum. In one thread, the updated value

---

3.   And, worse, some of these primitives are unsafe in use. Charles Nutter of JRuby fame has a blog post that illustrates one problem: http://blog.headius.com/2008/02/rubys-threadraise-threadkill-timeoutrb.html.

gets calculated—let's say that the value of sum is 99,999, so new_value will be 100,000. Before storing the new value back into sum, we call print, and that causes another thread to be scheduled (because we're waiting for the I/O to complete). So a second thread also fetches the value of 99,999 and increments it. It stores 100,000 into sum, then loops around again and stores 100,001, and 100,002, and so on. Eventually the original thread continues running because it finished writing its message. It immediate stores it's value of 100,000 into the sum, overwriting (and losing) all the values stored by the other thread(s). We lost data.

Fortunately, that's easy to fix. We use the built-in class Mutex to create synchronized regions —areas of code that only one thread may enter at a time.

Some grade schools coordinate students' access to the bathrooms during class time using a system of bathroom passes. Each room has two passes, one for girls and one for boys. To visit the bathroom, you have to take the appropriate pass with you. If someone else already has that pass, you have to cross your legs and wait for them to return. The bathroom pass controls access to the critical resource—you have to own the pass to use the resource, and only one person can own it at a time.

A mutex is like that bathroom pass. You create a mutex to control access to a resource and then lock it when you want to use that resource. If no one else has it locked, your thread continues to run. If someone else has already locked that particular mutex, your thread suspends (crossing its legs) until they unlock it.

Here's a version of our counting code that uses a mutex to ensure that only one thread updates the count at a time:

```
sum = 0
mutex = Mutex.new
threads = 10.times.map do
  Thread.new do
    100_000.times do
      mutex.lock                    ####    one at a time, please
      new_value = sum + 1            #
      print "#{new_value}  " if new_value % 250_000 == 0
      sum = new_value                #
      mutex.unlock                  ####
    end
  end
end

threads.each(&:join)
puts "\nsum = #{sum}"
```

produces:

```
250000  500000  750000  1000000
sum = 1000000
```

This pattern is so common that the Mutex class provides Mutex#synchronize, which locks the mutex, runs the code in a block, and then unlocks the mutex. This also ensures that the mutex will get unlocked even if an exception is thrown while it is locked.

```
sum = 0
mutex = Mutex.new
threads = 10.times.map do
  Thread.new do
    100_000.times do
      mutex.synchronize do        ####
        new_value = sum + 1         #
        print "#{new_value}  " if new_value % 250_000 == 0
        sum = new_value             #
      end                         ####
    end
  end
end

threads.each(&:join)
puts "\nsum = #{sum}"
```

produces:

```
250000  500000  750000  1000000
sum = 1000000
```

Sometimes you want to claim a lock if a mutex is currently unlocked, but you don't want to suspend the current thread if it isn't. The Mutex#try_lock method takes the lock if it can, but returns false if the lock is already taken. The following code illustrates a hypothetical currency converter. The ExchangeRates class caches rates from an online feed, and a background thread updates that cache once an hour. This update takes a minute or so. In the main thread, we interact with our user. However, rather than just go dead if we can't claim the mutex that protects the rate object, we use try_lock and print a status message if the update is in process.

```
rate_mutex = Mutex.new
exchange_rates = ExchangeRates.new
exchange_rates.update_from_online_feed

Thread.new do
  loop do
    sleep 3600
    rate_mutex.synchronize do
      exchange_rates.update_from_online_feed
    end
  end
end

loop do
  print "Enter currency code and amount: "
  line = gets
  if rate_mutex.try_lock
    puts(exchange_rates.convert(line)) ensure rate_mutex.unlock
  else
    puts "Sorry, rates being updated. Try again in a minute"
  end
end
```

If you are holding the lock on a mutex and you want to temporarily unlock it, allowing others to use it, you can call Mutex#sleep. We could use this to rewrite the previous example:

```
rate_mutex = Mutex.new
exchange_rates = ExchangeRates.new
exchange_rates.update_from_online_feed

Thread.new do
  rate_mutex.lock
  loop do
    rate_mutex.sleep 3600
    exchange_rates.update_from_online_feed
  end
end

loop do
  print "Enter currency code and amount: "
  line = gets
  if rate_mutex.try_lock
    puts(exchange_rates.convert(line)) ensure rate_mutex.unlock
  else
    puts "Sorry, rates being updated. Try again in a minute"
  end
end
```

Queues and Condition Variables

Most of the examples in this chapter use the Mutex class for synchronization. However, Ruby comes with another library that is particularly useful when you need to synchronize work between producers and consumers. The Queue class, located in the thread library, implements a thread-safe queuing mechanism. Multiple threads can add and remove objects from each queue, and each addition and removal is guaranteed to be atomic. For an example, see the description of the thread library on page 813.

A condition variable is a controlled way of communicating an event (or a condition) between two threads. One thread can wait on the condition, and the other can signal it. The thread library extends threads with condition variables. Again, see the Monitor library for an example.

12.5 Running Multiple Processes

Sometimes you may want to split a task into several process-sized chunks—maybe to take advantage of all those cores in your shiny new processor. Or perhaps you need to run a separate process that was not written in Ruby. Not a problem: Ruby has a number of methods by which you may spawn and manage separate processes.

Spawning New Processes

You have several ways to spawn a separate process; the easiest is to run some command and wait for it to complete. You may find yourself doing this to run some separate command or retrieve data from the host system. Ruby does this for you with the system and backquote (or backtick) methods:

```
system("tar xzf test.tgz") # => true
`date`                     # => "Mon May 27 12:31:17 CDT 2013\n"
```

The method Object#system executes the given command in a subprocess; it returns true if the command was found and executed properly. It raises an exception if the command cannot be found. It returns false if the command ran but returned an error. In case of failure, you'll find the subprocess's exit code in the global variable $?.

One problem with system is that the command's output will simply go to the same destination as your program's output, which may not be what you want. To capture the standard output of a subprocess, you can use the backquote characters, as with `date` in the previous example. Remember that you may need to use String#chomp to remove the line-ending characters from the result.

OK, this is fine for simple cases—we can run some other process and get the return status. But many times we need a bit more control than that. We'd like to carry on a conversation with the subprocess, possibly sending it data and possibly getting some back. The method IO.popen does just this. The popen method runs a command as a subprocess and connects that subprocess's standard input and standard output to a Ruby IO object. Write to the IO object, and the subprocess can read it on standard input. Whatever the subprocess writes is available in the Ruby program by reading from the IO object.

For example, on our systems one of the more useful utilities is pig, a program that reads words from standard input and prints them in pig latin (or igpay atinlay). We can use this when our Ruby programs need to send us output that our five-year-olds shouldn't be able to understand:

```
pig = IO.popen("local/util/pig", "w+")
pig.puts "ice cream after they go to bed"
pig.close_write
puts pig.gets
```

produces:
```
iceway eamcray afterway eythay ogay otay edbay
```

This example illustrates both the apparent simplicity and the more subtle real-world complexities involved in driving subprocesses through pipes. The code certainly looks simple enough: open the pipe, write a phrase, and read back the response. But it turns out that the pig program doesn't flush the output it writes. Our original attempt at this example, which had a pig.puts followed by a pig.gets, hung forever. The pig program processed our input, but its response was never written to the pipe. We had to insert the pig.close_write line. This sends an end-of-file to pig's standard input, and the output we're looking for gets flushed as pig terminates.

popen has one more twist. If the command you pass it is a single minus sign (-), popen will fork a new Ruby interpreter. Both this and the original interpreter will continue running by returning from the popen. The original process will receive an IO object back, and the child will receive nil. This works only on operating systems that support the fork(2) call (and for now this excludes Windows).

```
pipe = IO.popen("-","w+")
if pipe
  pipe.puts "Get a job!"
  STDERR.puts "Child says '#{pipe.gets.chomp}'"
else
  STDERR.puts "Dad says '#{gets.chomp}'"
  puts "OK"
end
```

produces:

```
Dad says 'Get a job!'
Child says 'OK'
```

As well as the popen method, some platforms support Object#fork, Object#exec, and IO.pipe. The filenaming convention of many IO methods and Object#open will also spawn subprocesses if you put a | as the first character of the filename (see the introduction to class IO on page 536 for details). Note that you *cannot* create pipes using File.new; it's just for files.

Independent Children

Sometimes we don't need to be quite so hands-on; we'd like to give the subprocess its assignment and then go on about our business. Later, we'll check to see whether it has finished. For instance, we may want to kick off a long-running external sort:

```
exec("sort testfile > output.txt") if fork.nil?
# The sort is now running in a child process
# carry on processing in the main program

# ... dum di dum ...

# then wait for the sort to finish
Process.wait
```

The call to Object#fork returns a process ID in the parent and returns nil in the child, so the child process will perform the Object#exec call and run sort. Later, we issue a Process.wait call, which waits for the sort to complete (and returns its process ID).

If you'd rather be notified when a child exits (instead of just waiting around), you can set up a signal handler using Object#trap (described in the reference on page 630). Here we set up a trap on SIGCLD, which is the signal sent on "death of child process":

```
trap("CLD") do
  pid = Process.wait
  puts "Child pid #{pid}: terminated"
end

fork { exec("sort testfile > output.txt") }

# Do other stuff...
```

produces:

```
Child pid 22026: terminated
```

For more information on using and controlling external processes, see the documentation for Object#open and IO.popen, as well as the section on the Process module on page 637.

Blocks and Subprocesses

IO.popen works with a block in pretty much the same way as File.open does. If you pass it a command, such as date, the block will be passed an IO object as a parameter:

```
IO.popen("date") {|f| puts "Date is #{f.gets}" }
```

produces:

```
Date is Mon May 27 12:31:17 CDT 2013
```

The IO object will be closed automatically when the code block exits, just as it is with File.open.

If you associate a block with fork, the code in the block will be run in a Ruby subprocess, and the parent will continue after the block:

```
fork do
  puts "In child, pid = #$$"
  exit 99
end
pid = Process.wait
puts "Child terminated, pid = #{pid}, status = #{$?.exitstatus}"
```

produces:

```
In child, pid = 22033
Child terminated, pid = 22033, status = 99
```

$? is a global variable that contains information on the termination of a subprocess. See the section on Process::Status on page 644 for more information.

## CHAPTER 13

Unit Testing

Unit testing is testing that focuses on small chunks (units) of code, typically individual methods or lines within methods. This is in contrast to most other forms of testing, which consider the system as a whole.

Why focus in so tightly? It's because ultimately all software is constructed in layers; code in one layer relies on the correct operation of the code in the layers below. If this underlying code turns out to contain bugs, then all higher layers are potentially affected. This is a big problem. Fred may write some code with a bug one week, and then you may end up calling it, indirectly, two months later. When your code generates incorrect results, it will take you a while to track down the problem in Fred's method. And when you ask Fred why he wrote it that way, the likely answer will be "I don't remember. That was months ago."

If instead Fred had unit tested his code when he wrote it, two things would have happened. First, he'd have found the bug while the code was still fresh in his mind. Second, because the unit test was only looking at the code he'd just written, when the bug *did* appear, he'd only have to look through a handful of lines of code to find it, rather than doing archaeology on the rest of the code base.

Unit testing helps developers write better code. It helps before the code is actually written, because thinking about testing leads you naturally to create better, more decoupled designs. It helps as you're writing the code, because it gives you instant feedback on how accurate your code is. And it helps after you've written code, both because it gives you the ability to check that the code still works and because it helps others understand how to use your code.

Unit testing is a Good Thing.

But why have a chapter on unit testing in the middle of a book on Ruby? Well, it's because unit testing and languages such as Ruby seem to go hand in hand. The flexibility of Ruby makes writing tests easy, and the tests make it easier to verify that your code is working. Once you get into the swing of it, you'll find yourself writing a little code, writing a test or two, verifying that everything is copacetic, and then writing some more code.

Unit testing is also pretty trivial—run a program that calls part of your application's code, get back some results, and then check the results are what you expected.

Let's say we're testing a Roman number class. So far, the code is pretty simple: it just lets us create an object representing a certain number and display that object in Roman numerals:

```
unittesting/romanbug.rb
# This code has bugs
class Roman
  MAX_ROMAN = 4999

  def initialize(value)
    if value <= 0 || value > MAX_ROMAN
      fail "Roman values must be > 0 and <= #{MAX_ROMAN}"
    end
    @value = value
  end

  FACTORS = [["m", 1000], ["cm", 900], ["d",  500], ["cd", 400],
             ["c",  100], ["xc",  90], ["l",   50], ["xl",  40],
             ["x",   10], ["ix",   9], ["v",    5], ["iv",   4],
             ["i",    1]]

  def to_s
    value = @value
    roman = ""
    for code, factor in FACTORS
      count, value = value.divmod(factor)
      roman << code unless count.zero?
    end
    roman
  end
end
```

We could test this code by writing another program, like this:

```
require_relative 'romanbug'

r = Roman.new(1)
fail "'i' expected" unless r.to_s == "i"

r = Roman.new(9)
fail "'ix' expected" unless r.to_s == "ix"
```

However, as the number of tests in a project grows, this kind of ad hoc approach can start to get complicated to manage. Over the years, various unit testing frameworks have emerged to help structure the testing process. Ruby comes with Ryan Davis' MiniTest.[1]

MiniTest is largely compatible with Test::Unit but without a lot of bells and whistles (test-case runners, GUI support, and so on). However, because there are areas where it is different and because there are tens of thousands of tests out there that assume the Test::Unit API, Ryan has also added a compatibility layer to MiniTest. For a little bit more information on the differences between the two, see *MiniTest::Unit vs. Test::Unit*, on page 177. In this chapter, we'll be using the Test::Unit wrapper, because it automatically runs tests for us. But we'll also be using some of the new assertions available in MiniTest.

---

1. In Ruby 1.8, this was Nathaniel Talbott's Test::Unit framework. MiniTest is a rewrite of this.

MiniTest::Unit vs. Test::Unit

Folks have been using Test::Unit with Ruby for a good number of years now. However, the core team decided to replace the testing framework that comes as standard with Ruby with something a little leaner. Ryan Davis and Eric Hodel wrote MiniTest::Unit as a partial drop-in replacement for Test::Unit.

Most of the assertions in MiniTest mirror those in Test::Unit::TestCase. The major differences are the absence of assert_not_raises and assert_not_throws and the renaming of all the negative assertions. In Test::Unit you'd say assert_not_nil(x) and assert_not(x); in MiniTest you'd use refute_nil(x) and refute(x).

MiniTest also drops most of the little-used features of Test::Unit, including test cases, GUI runners, and some assertions.

And, probably most significantly, MiniTest does not automatically invoke the test cases when you execute a file that contains them.

So, you have three basic options with this style of unit testing:

- require "minitest/unit", and use the MiniTest functionality.
- require "test/unit", and use MiniTest with the Test::Unit compatibility layer. This adds in the assertions in *Additional Test::Unit assertions*, on page 194, and enables the autorun functionality.
- You can install the test-unit gem and get all the original Test::Unit functionality back, along with a bunch of new assertions.

13.1 The Testing Framework

The Ruby testing framework is basically three facilities wrapped into a neat package:

- It gives you a way of expressing individual tests.
- It provides a framework for structuring the tests.
- It gives you flexible ways of invoking the tests.

Assertions == Expected Results

Rather than have you write series of individual if statements in your tests, the testing framework provides a set of assertions that achieve the same thing. Although a number of different styles of assertion exist, they all follow basically the same pattern. Each gives you a way of specifying a desired result and a way of passing in the actual outcome. If the actual doesn't equal the expected, the assertion outputs a nice message and records the failure.

For example, we could rewrite our previous test of the Roman class using the testing framework. For now, ignore the scaffolding code at the start and end, and just look at the assert_equal methods:

```ruby
require_relative 'romanbug'
require 'test/unit'
class TestRoman < Test::Unit::TestCase

  def test_simple
    assert_equal("i",  Roman.new(1).to_s)
    assert_equal("ix", Roman.new(9).to_s)
  end

end
```

produces:

```
Run options:
# Running tests:

.
Finished tests in 0.006937s, 144.1545 tests/s, 288.3091 assertions/s.
1 tests, 2 assertions, 0 failures, 0 errors, 0 skips

ruby -v: ruby 2.0.0p0 (2013-02-24 revision 39474) [x86_64-darwin12.2.0]
```

The first assertion says that we're expecting the Roman number string representation of 1 to be "i," and the second test says we expect 9 to be "ix." Luckily for us, both expectations are met, and the tracing reports that our tests pass. Let's add a few more tests:

```
require_relative 'romanbug'
require 'test/unit'
class TestRoman < Test::Unit::TestCase
  def test_simple
    assert_equal("i",    Roman.new(1).to_s)
    assert_equal("ii",   Roman.new(2).to_s)
    assert_equal("iii",  Roman.new(3).to_s)
    assert_equal("iv",   Roman.new(4).to_s)
    assert_equal("ix",   Roman.new(9).to_s)
  end
end
```

produces:

```
Run options:
# Running tests:
F
Finished tests in 0.006579s, 151.9988 tests/s, 303.9976 assertions/s.
  1) Failure:
test_simple(TestRoman) [prog.rb:6]:
<"ii"> expected but was
<"i">.

1 tests, 2 assertions, 1 failures, 0 errors, 0 skips

ruby -v: ruby 2.0.0p0 (2013-02-24 revision 39474) [x86_64-darwin12.2.0]
```

Uh-oh! The second assertion failed. See how the error message uses the fact that the assert knows both the expected and actual values: it expected to get "ii" but instead got "i." Looking at our code, you can see a clear bug in to_s. If the count after dividing by the factor is greater than zero, then we should output that many Roman digits. The existing code outputs just one. The fix is easy:

```
def to_s
  value = @value
  roman = ""
  for code, factor in FACTORS
    count, value = value.divmod(factor)
    roman << (code * count)
  end
  roman
end
```

Now let's run our tests again:

```
require_relative 'roman3'
require 'test/unit'
class TestRoman < Test::Unit::TestCase
  def test_simple
    assert_equal("i",   Roman.new(1).to_s)
    assert_equal("ii",  Roman.new(2).to_s)
    assert_equal("iii", Roman.new(3).to_s)
    assert_equal("iv",  Roman.new(4).to_s)
    assert_equal("ix",  Roman.new(9).to_s)
  end
end
```

produces:

```
Run options:
# Running tests:

.
Finished tests in 0.006027s, 165.9200 tests/s, 829.6001 assertions/s.
1 tests, 5 assertions, 0 failures, 0 errors, 0 skips

ruby -v: ruby 2.0.0p0 (2013-02-24 revision 39474) [x86_64-darwin12.2.0]
```

Looking good. We can now go a step further and remove some of that duplication:

```
require_relative 'roman3'
require 'test/unit'

class TestRoman < Test::Unit::TestCase

  NUMBERS = { 1 => "i", 2 => "ii", 3 => "iii", 4 => "iv", 5 => "v", 9 => "ix" }

  def test_simple
    NUMBERS.each do |arabic, roman|
      r = Roman.new(arabic)
      assert_equal(roman, r.to_s)
    end
  end
end
```

produces:

```
Run options:
# Running tests:

.
Finished tests in 0.006280s, 159.2357 tests/s, 955.4140 assertions/s.
1 tests, 6 assertions, 0 failures, 0 errors, 0 skips

ruby -v: ruby 2.0.0p0 (2013-02-24 revision 39474) [x86_64-darwin12.2.0]
```

What else can we test? Well, the constructor checks that the number we pass in can be represented as a Roman number, throwing an exception if it can't. Let's test the exception:

```ruby
require_relative 'roman3'
require 'test/unit'

class TestRoman < Test::Unit::TestCase

  NUMBERS = { 1 => "i", 2 => "ii", 3 => "iii", 4 => "iv", 5 => "v", 9 => "ix" }

  def test_simple
    NUMBERS.each do |arabic, roman|
      r = Roman.new(arabic)
      assert_equal(roman, r.to_s)
    end
  end

  def test_range
    # no exception for these two...
    Roman.new(1)
    Roman.new(4999)
    # but an exception for these
    assert_raises(RuntimeError) { Roman.new(0) }
    assert_raises(RuntimeError) { Roman.new(5000) }
  end
end
```

produces:

```
Run options:
# Running tests:

..
Finished tests in 0.006736s, 296.9121 tests/s, 1187.6485 assertions/s.
2 tests, 8 assertions, 0 failures, 0 errors, 0 skips

ruby -v: ruby 2.0.0p0 (2013-02-24 revision 39474) [x86_64-darwin12.2.0]
```

We could do a lot more testing on our Roman class, but let's move on to bigger and better things. Before we go, though, we should say that we've only scratched the surface of the set of assertions available inside the testing framework. For example, for every positive assertion, such as assert_equal, there's a negative refutation (in this case refute_equal). The additional assertions you get if you load the Test::Unit shim (which we do in this chapter) are listed in *Additional Test::Unit assertions*, on page 194, and a full list of the MiniTest assertions is given in Section 13.5, *Test::Unit assertions*, on page 193.

The final parameter to every assertion is a message that will be output before any failure message. This normally isn't needed, because the failure messages are normally pretty reasonable. The one exception is the test refute_nil (or assert_not_nil in Test::Unit), where the message "Expected nil to not be nil" doesn't help much. In that case, you may want to add some annotation of your own. (This code assumes the existence of some kind of User class.)

```ruby
require 'test/unit'
class ATestThatFails < Test::Unit::TestCase
  def test_user_created
    user = User.find(1)
    refute_nil(user, "User with ID=1 should exist")
  end
end
```

produces:

```
Run options:
# Running tests:
F
Finished tests in 0.007598s, 131.6136 tests/s, 131.6136 assertions/s.
  1) Failure:
test_user_created(ATestThatFails) [prog.rb:11]:
User with ID=1 should exist.
Expected nil to not be nil.

1 tests, 1 assertions, 1 failures, 0 errors, 0 skips

ruby -v: ruby 2.0.0p0 (2013-02-24 revision 39474) [x86_64-darwin12.2.0]
```

13.2 Structuring Tests

Earlier we asked you to ignore the scaffolding around our tests. Now it's time to look at it.

You include the testing framework facilities in your unit test either with this:

```
require 'test/unit'
```

or, for raw MiniTest, with this:

```
require 'minitest/unit'
```

Unit tests seem to fall quite naturally into high-level groupings, called *test cases*, and lower-level groupings, which are the test methods themselves. The test cases generally contain all the tests relating to a particular facility or feature. Our Roman number class is fairly simple, so all the tests for it will probably be in a single test case. Within the test case, you'll probably want to organize your assertions into a number of test methods, where each method contains the assertions for one type of test; one method could check regular number conversions, another could test error handling, and so on.

The classes that represent test cases must be subclasses of Test::Unit::TestCase. The methods that hold the assertions must have names that start with test. This is important: the testing framework uses reflection to find tests to run, and only methods whose names start with test are eligible.

Quite often you'll find all the test methods within a test case start by setting up a particular scenario. Each test method then probes some aspect of that scenario. Finally, each method may then tidy up after itself. For example, we could be testing a class that extracts jukebox playlists from a database. (We're using the low-level DBI library to access the database.)

```
require 'test/unit'
require_relative 'playlist_builder'

class TestPlaylistBuilder < Test::Unit::TestCase

  def test_empty_playlist
    db = DBI.connect('DBI:mysql:playlists')
    pb = PlaylistBuilder.new(db)
    assert_empty(pb.playlist)
    db.disconnect
  end
```

```ruby
  def test_artist_playlist
    db = DBI.connect('DBI:mysql:playlists')
    pb = PlaylistBuilder.new(db)
    pb.include_artist("krauss")
    refute_empty(pb.playlist, "Playlist shouldn't be empty")
    pb.playlist.each do |entry|
      assert_match(/krauss/i, entry.artist)
    end
    db.disconnect
  end

  def test_title_playlist
    db = DBI.connect('DBI:mysql:playlists')
    pb = PlaylistBuilder.new(db)
    pb.include_title("midnight")
    refute_empty(pb.playlist, "Playlist shouldn't be empty")
    pb.playlist.each do |entry|
      assert_match(/midnight/i, entry.title)
    end
    db.disconnect
  end

  # ...
end
```

produces:

```
Run options:
# Running tests:
...
Finished tests in 0.008272s, 362.6692 tests/s, 5560.9284 assertions/s.
3 tests, 46 assertions, 0 failures, 0 errors, 0 skips

ruby -v: ruby 2.0.0p0 (2013-02-24 revision 39474) [x86_64-darwin12.2.0]
```

Each test starts by connecting to the database and creating a new playlist builder. Each test ends by disconnecting from the database. (The idea of using a real database in unit tests is questionable, because unit tests are supposed to be fast running, context independent, and easy to set up, but it illustrates a point.)

We can extract all this common code into *setup* and *teardown* methods. Within a TestCase class, a method called setup will be run before each and every test method, and a method called teardown will be run after each test method finishes. Let's emphasize that: the setup and teardown methods bracket each test, rather than being run once per test case. This is shown in the code that follows.

```ruby
require 'test/unit'
require_relative 'playlist_builder'

class TestPlaylistBuilder < Test::Unit::TestCase

  def setup
    @db = DBI.connect('DBI:mysql:playlists')
    @pb = PlaylistBuilder.new(@db)
  end
```

```
    def teardown
      @db.disconnect
    end

    def test_empty_playlist
      assert_empty(@pb.playlist)
    end

    def test_artist_playlist
      @pb.include_artist("krauss")
      refute_empty(@pb.playlist, "Playlist shouldn't be empty")
      @pb.playlist.each do |entry|
        assert_match(/krauss/i, entry.artist)
      end
    end

    def test_title_playlist
      @pb.include_title("midnight")
      refute_empty(@pb.playlist, "Playlist shouldn't be empty")
      @pb.playlist.each do |entry|
        assert_match(/midnight/i, entry.title)
      end
    end

    # ...
  end
```

produces:

```
Run options:
# Running tests:
...
Finished tests in 0.007683s, 390.4725 tests/s, 5987.2446 assertions/s.
3 tests, 46 assertions, 0 failures, 0 errors, 0 skips

ruby -v: ruby 2.0.0p0 (2013-02-24 revision 39474) [x86_64-darwin12.2.0]
```

Inside the teardown method, you can detect whether the preceding test succeeded with the passed? method.

13.3 Organizing and Running Tests

The test cases we've shown so far are all runnable Test::Unit programs. If, for example, the test case for the Roman class was in a file called test_roman.rb, we could run the tests from the command line using this:

```
$ ruby test_roman.rb
Run options:
# Running tests:
..
Finished tests in 0.004540s, 440.5286 tests/s, 1762.1145 assertions/s.
2 tests, 8 assertions, 0 failures, 0 errors, 0 skips
ruby -v: ruby 2.0.0p0 (2013-02-24 revision 39474) [x86_64-darwin12.2.0]
```

Test::Unit is clever enough to run the tests even though there's no main program. It collects all the test case classes and runs each in turn.

If we want, we can ask it to run just a particular test method:

```
$ ruby test_roman.rb -n test_range
Run options: -n test_range
# Running tests:
.
Finished tests in 0.004481s, 223.1645 tests/s, 446.3289 assertions/s.
1 tests, 2 assertions, 0 failures, 0 errors, 0 skips
ruby -v: ruby 2.0.0p0 (2013-02-24 revision 39474) [x86_64-darwin12.2.0]
```

or tests whose names match a regular expression:

```
$ ruby test_roman.rb -n /range/
Run options: -n /range/
# Running tests:
.
Finished tests in 0.005042s, 198.3340 tests/s, 396.6680 assertions/s.
1 tests, 2 assertions, 0 failures, 0 errors, 0 skips
ruby -v: ruby 2.0.0p0 (2013-02-24 revision 39474) [x86_64-darwin12.2.0]
```

This last capability is a great way of grouping your tests. Use meaningful names, and you'll be able to run (for example) all the shopping-cart-related tests by simply running tests with names matching /cart/.

Where to Put Tests

Once you get into unit testing, you may well find yourself generating almost as much test code as production code. All of those tests have to live somewhere. The problem is that if you put them alongside your regular production code source files, your directories start to get bloated—effectively you end up with two files for every production source file.

A common solution is to have a test/ directory where you place all your test source files. This directory is then placed parallel to the directory containing the code you're developing. For example, for our Roman numeral class, we may have this:

```
roman/
    lib/
        roman.rb
        other files...

    test/
        test_roman.rb
        other tests...

    other stuff...
```

This works well as a way of organizing files but leaves you with a small problem: how do you tell Ruby where to find the library files to test? For example, if our TestRoman test code was in a test/ subdirectory, how does Ruby know where to find the roman.rb source file, the thing we're trying to test?

An option that *doesn't* work reliably is to build the path into require statements in the test code and run the tests from the test/ subdirectory:

```
require 'test/unit'
require '../lib/roman'

class TestRoman < Test::Unit::TestCase
  # ...
end
```

Why doesn't it work? It's because our roman.rb file may itself require other source files in the library we're writing. It'll load them using require (without the leading ../lib/), and because they aren't in Ruby's $LOAD_PATH, they won't be found. Our test just won't run. A second, less immediate problem is that we won't be able to use these same tests to test our classes once installed on a target system, because then they'll be referenced simply using require 'roman'.

A better solution is to assume that your Ruby program is packaged according to the conventions we'll be discussing in Section 16.2, *Organizing Your Source*, on page 226. In this arrangement, the top-level lib directory of your application is assumed to be in Ruby's load path by all other components of the application. Your test code would then be as follows:

```
require 'test/unit'
require 'roman'

class TestRoman < Test::Unit::TestCase
  # ...
end
```

And you'd run it using this:

```
$ ruby -I path/to/app/lib path/to/app/test/test_roman.rb
```

The normal case, where you're already in the application's directory, would be as follows:

```
$ ruby -I lib test/test_roman.rb
```

This would be a good time to investigate using Rake to automate your testing.

Test Suites

After a while, you'll grow a decent collection of test cases for your application. You may well find that these tend to cluster: one group of cases tests a particular set of functions, and another group tests a different set of functions. If so, you can group those test cases together into *test suites*, letting you run them all as a group.

This is easy to do—just create a Ruby file that requires test/unit and then requires each of the files holding the test cases you want to group. This way, you build yourself a hierarchy of test material.

- You can run individual tests by name.
- You can run all the tests in a file by running that file.
- You can group a number of files into a test suite and run them as a unit.
- You can group test suites into other test suites.

This gives you the ability to run your unit tests at a level of granularity that you control, testing just one method or testing the entire application.

At this point, it's worthwhile to think about naming conventions. Nathaniel Talbott, the author of Test::Unit, uses the convention that test cases are in files named tc_xxx and test suites are in files named ts_xxx. Most people seem to use test_ as the test-case filename prefix:

```
# file ts_dbaccess.rb
require_relative 'test/unit'
require_relative 'test_connect'
require_relative 'test_query'
require_relative 'test_update'
require_relative 'test_delete'
```

Now, if you run Ruby on the file ts_dbaccess.rb, you execute the test cases in the four files you've required.

13.4 RSpec and Shoulda

The built-in testing framework has a lot going for it. It is simple, and it is compatible in style with frameworks from other languages (such as JUnit for Java and NUnit for C#).

However, there's a growing movement in the Ruby community to use a different style of testing. So-called behavior-driven development encourages people to write tests in terms of your expectations of the program's behavior in a given set of circumstances. In many ways, this is like testing according to the content of *user stories*, a common requirements-gathering technique in agile methodologies. With these testing frameworks, the focus is not on assertions. Instead, you write expectations.

Although both RSpec and Shoulda allow this style of testing, they focus on different things. RSpec is very much concerned with driving the design side of things. You can write and execute specs with RSpec well before you've written a line of application code. These specs, when run, will output the user stories that describe your application. Then, as you fill in the code, the specs mutate into tests that validate that your code meets your expectations.

Shoulda, on the other hand, is really more focused on the testing side. Whereas RSpec is a complete framework, Shoulda works inside a testing framework, Test::Unit or RSpec. You can even mix Shoulda tests with regular Test::Unit and RSpec test methods.

Let's start with a simple example of RSpec in action.

Starting to Score Tennis Matches

The scoring system used in lawn tennis originated in the Middle Ages. As players win successive points, their scores are shown as 15, 30, and 40. The next point is a win unless your opponent also has 40. If you're both tied at 40, then different rules apply—the first player with a clear two-point advantage is the winner.[2]

We have to write a class that handles this scoring system. Let's use RSpec specifications to drive the process. We install RSpec with gem install rspec. We'll then create our first specification file:

---

2. Some say the 0, 15, 30, 40 system is a corruption of the fact that scoring used to be done using the quarters of a clock face. Us, we just think those medieval folks enjoyed a good joke.

```
unittesting/bdd/1/ts_spec.rb
```
```ruby
describe "TennisScorer", "basic scoring" do
  it "should start with a score of 0-0"
  it "should be 15-0 if the server wins a point"
  it "should be 0-15 if the receiver wins a point"
  it "should be 15-15 after they both win a point"
  # ...
end
```

This file contains nothing more than a description of an aspect of the tennis scoring class (that we haven't yet written, by the way). It contains a description of the basic scoring system. Inside the description are a set of four expectations (it *"should start..."* and so on). We can run this specification using the rspec command:[3]

```
$ rspec ts_spec.rb
****
Pending:
  TennisScorer basic scoring should start with a score of 0-0
    # Not yet implemented
    # ./ts_spec.rb:2
  TennisScorer basic scoring should be 15-0 if the server wins a point
    # Not yet implemented
    # ./ts_spec.rb:3
  TennisScorer basic scoring should be 0-15 if the receiver wins a point
    # Not yet implemented
    # ./ts_spec.rb:4
  TennisScorer basic scoring should be 15-15 after they both win a point
    # Not yet implemented
    # ./ts_spec.rb:5
Finished in 0.00039 seconds
4 examples, 0 failures, 4 pending
```

That's pretty cool. Executing the tests echoes our expectations back at us, telling us that each has yet to be implemented. Coding, like life, is full of these disappointments. However, unlike life, fixing things is just a few keystrokes away. Let's start by meeting the first expectation—when a game starts, the score should be 0 to 0. We'll start by fleshing out the test:

```
unittesting/bdd/2/ts_spec.rb
```
```ruby
require_relative "tennis_scorer"

describe TennisScorer, "basic scoring" do
  it "should start with a score of 0-0" do
    ts = TennisScorer.new
    ts.score.should == "0-0"
  end

  it "should be 15-0 if the server wins a point"
  it "should be 0-15 if the receiver wins a point"
  it "should be 15-15 after they both win a point"
end
```

---

3. We're running these examples with RSpec2. This will probably be the default version by the time you read this, but I had to use gem install rspec --pre because it was prerelease when I was writing this chapter.

Note that we've assumed we have a class TennisScorer in a file called tennis_scorer.rb. Our first expectation now has a code block associated with it. Inside that block, we create a TennisScorer and then use a funky RSpec syntax to validate that the score starts out at 0 to 0. This particular aspect of RSpec probably generates the most controversy—some people love it, others find it awkward. Either way, ts.score.should == "0-0" is basically the same as an assertion in Test::Unit.

We'll beef up our TennisScorer class, but only enough to let it satisfy this assertion:

unittesting/bdd/2/tennis_scorer.rb
```ruby
class TennisScorer
  def score
    "0-0"
  end
end
```

We'll run our spec again:

```
$ rspec ts_spec.rb
.***
Pending:
  TennisScorer basic scoring should be 15-0 if the server wins a point
    # Not yet implemented
    # ./ts_spec.rb:9
  TennisScorer basic scoring should be 0-15 if the receiver wins a point
    # Not yet implemented
    # ./ts_spec.rb:10
  TennisScorer basic scoring should be 15-15 after they both win a point
    # Not yet implemented
    # ./ts_spec.rb:11
Finished in 0.00054 seconds
4 examples, 0 failures, 3 pending
```

Note that we now have three pending expectations; the first one has been satisfied.

Let's write the next expectation:

unittesting/bdd/3/ts_spec.rb
```ruby
require_relative "tennis_scorer"

describe TennisScorer, "basic scoring" do
  it "should start with a score of 0-0" do
    ts = TennisScorer.new
    ts.score.should == "0-0"
  end

  it "should be 15-0 if the server wins a point" do
    ts = TennisScorer.new
    ts.give_point_to(:server)
    ts.score.should == "15-0"
  end

  it "should be 0-15 if the receiver wins a point"
  it "should be 15-15 after they both win a point"
end
```

This won't run, because our TennisScorer class doesn't implement a give_point_to method. Let's rectify that. Our code isn't finished, but it lets the test pass:

```
unittesting/bdd/3/tennis_scorer.rb
class TennisScorer

  OPPOSITE_SIDE_OF_NET = { :server => :receiver, :receiver => :server }

  def initialize
    @score = { :server => 0, :receiver => 0 }
  end

  def score
    "#{@score[:server]*15}-#{@score[:receiver]*15}"
  end

  def give_point_to(player)
    other = OPPOSITE_SIDE_OF_NET[player]
    fail "Unknown player #{player}" unless other
    @score[player] += 1
  end
end
```

Again, we'll run the specification:

```
$ rspec ts_spec.rb
..**
Pending:
  TennisScorer basic scoring should be 0-15 if the receiver wins a point
    # Not yet implemented
    # ./ts_spec.rb:15
  TennisScorer basic scoring should be 15-15 after they both win a point
    # Not yet implemented
    # ./ts_spec.rb:16
Finished in 0.00067 seconds
4 examples, 0 failures, 2 pending
```

We're now meeting two of the four initial expectations. But, before we move on, note there's a bit of duplication in the specification: both our expectations create a new TennisScorer object. We can fix that by using a before stanza in the specification. This works a bit like the setup method in Test::Unit, allowing us to run code before expectations are executed. Let's use this feature and, at the same time, build out the last two expectations:

```
unittesting/bdd/4/ts_spec.rb
require_relative "tennis_scorer"

describe TennisScorer, "basic scoring" do
  before(:each) do
    @ts = TennisScorer.new
  end

  it "should start with a score of 0-0" do
    @ts.score.should == "0-0"
  end
```

```ruby
  it "should be 15-0 if the server wins a point" do
    @ts.give_point_to(:server)
    @ts.score.should == "15-0"
  end

  it "should be 0-15 if the receiver wins a point" do
    @ts.give_point_to(:receiver)
    @ts.score.should == "0-15"
  end

  it "should be 15-15 after they both win a point" do
    @ts.give_point_to(:receiver)
    @ts.give_point_to(:server)
    @ts.score.should == "15-15"
  end
end
```

Let's run it:

```
$ rspec ts_spec.rb
....
Finished in 0.00088 seconds
4 examples, 0 failures
```

Finally, RSpec gives us an alternative way of setting up conditions for our tests. The let method creates what looks like a variable (it's actually a dynamically defined method) whose value is given by evaluating a block. This lets us write the following:

unittesting/bdd/5/ts_spec.rb
```ruby
require_relative "tennis_scorer"

describe TennisScorer, "basic scoring" do

  let(:ts) { TennisScorer.new}

  it "should start with a score of 0-0" do
    ts.score.should == "0-0"
  end

  it "should be 15-0 if the server wins a point" do
    ts.give_point_to(:server)
    ts.score.should == "15-0"
  end

  it "should be 0-15 if the receiver wins a point" do
    ts.give_point_to(:receiver)
    ts.score.should == "0-15"
  end

  it "should be 15-15 after they both win a point" do
    ts.give_point_to(:receiver)
    ts.give_point_to(:server)
    ts.score.should == "15-15"
  end
end
```

We're going to stop here, but I suggest that you might want to take this code and continue to develop it. Write expectations such as these:

```
it "should be 40-0 after the server wins three points"
it "should be W-L after the server wins four points"
it "should be L-W after the receiver wins four points"
it "should be Deuce after each wins three points"
it "should be A-server after each wins three points and the server gets one more"
```

RSpec has a lot more depth than just the description of expectations. In particular, you can use it with Cucumber, an entire language for describing and running complete user stories. But that's beyond the scope of this book.

Anyone for Shoulda?

RSpec is testing with attitude. On the other hand, Shoulda takes many of the ideas from RSpec and humbly offers them to you for integration into your regular unit tests. For many developers, particularly those with existing Test::Unit tests, this is a good compromise. You get much of the descriptive power of RSpec-style expectations without having to commit to the full framework.

Install Shoulda using gem install shoulda. Then, unlike RSpec, write a regular Test::Unit test case. Inside it, though, you can use the Shoulda mini-language to describe your tests.

Let's recast our final RSpec tennis scoring tests using Shoulda:

```
unittesting/bdd/4/ts_shoulda.rb
require 'test/unit'
require 'shoulda'
require_relative 'tennis_scorer.rb'

class TennisScorerTest < Test::Unit::TestCase

  def assert_score(target)
    assert_equal(target, @ts.score)
  end

  context "Tennis scores" do
    setup do
      @ts = TennisScorer.new
    end

    should "start with a score of 0-0" do
      assert_score("0-0")
    end

    should "be 15-0 if the server wins a point" do
      @ts.give_point_to(:server)
      assert_score("15-0")
    end

    should "be 0-15 if the receiver wins a point" do
      @ts.give_point_to(:receiver)
      assert_score("0-15")
    end
```

```
    should "be 15-15 after they both win a point" do
      @ts.give_point_to(:receiver)
      @ts.give_point_to(:server)
      assert_score("15-15")
    end
  end
end
```

```
$ ruby ts_shoulda.rb
Run options:
# Running tests:
....
Finished tests in 0.008528s, 469.0432 tests/s, 469.0432 assertions/s.
4 tests, 4 assertions, 0 failures, 0 errors, 0 skips
ruby -v: ruby 2.0.0p0 (2013-02-24 revision 39474) [x86_64-darwin12.2.0]
```

Behind the scenes, Shoulda is creating Test::Unit test methods for each should block in your tests. This is why we can use regular Test::Unit assertions in Shoulda code. But Shoulda also works hard to maintain the right context for our tests. For example, we can nest contexts and their setup blocks, allowing us to have some initialization that's common to all tests and some that's common to just a subset. We can apply this to our tennis example. We'll write nested contexts and put setup blocks at each level. When Shoulda executes our tests, it runs all the appropriate setup blocks for the should blocks.

`unittesting/bdd/4/ts_shoulda_1.rb`
```ruby
require 'test/unit'
require 'shoulda'
require_relative 'tennis_scorer.rb'

class TennisScorerTest < Test::Unit::TestCase
  def assert_score(target)
    assert_equal(target, @ts.score)
  end
  context "Tennis scores" do
    setup do
      @ts = TennisScorer.new
    end
    should "start with a score of 0-0" do
      assert_score("0-0")
    end
    context "where the server wins a point" do
      setup do
        @ts.give_point_to(:server)
      end
      should "be 15-0" do
        assert_score("15-0")
      end
      context "and the oponent wins a point" do
        setup do
          @ts.give_point_to(:receiver)
        end
        should "be 15-15" do
          assert_score("15-15")
        end
```

```
      end
    end
    should "be 0-15 if the receiver wins a point" do
      @ts.give_point_to(:receiver)
      assert_score("0-15")
    end
  end
end
```

Let's run it:

```
$ ruby ts_shoulda_1.rb
Run options:
# Running tests:

....
Finished tests in 0.008962s, 446.3289 tests/s, 446.3289 assertions/s.
4 tests, 4 assertions, 0 failures, 0 errors, 0 skips
ruby -v: ruby 2.0.0p0 (2013-02-24 revision 39474) [x86_64-darwin12.2.0]
```

Would we use these nested contexts for this tennis scoring example? We probably wouldn't as it stands, because the linear form is easier to read. But we use them all the time when we have tests where we want to run through a complex scenario that builds from test to test. This nesting lets us set up an environment, run some tests, then change the environment, run more tests, change it again, run even more tests, and so on. It ends up making tests far more compact and removes a lot of duplication.

13.5 Test::Unit assertions

assert | refute(boolean, ‹*message*›)
> Fails if *boolean* is (is not) false or nil.

assert_block { block }
> Expects the block to return true.

assert_ | refute_ empty(collection, ‹*message*›)
> Expects empty? on *collection* to return true (false).

assert_ | refute_ equal(expected, actual, ‹*message*›)
> Expects *actual* to equal/not equal *expected,* using ==.

assert_ | refute_in_delta(expected_float, actual_float, delta, ‹*message*›)
> Expects that the actual floating-point value is (is not) within *delta* of the expected value.

assert_ | refute_ in_epsilon(expected_float, actual_float, epsilon=0.001, ‹*message*›)
> Calculates a delta value as *epsilon * min(expected, actual)* and then calls the _in_delta test.

assert_ | refute_ includes(collection, obj, ‹*message*›)
> Expects include?(obj) on *collection* to return true (false).

assert_ | refute_ instance_of(klass, obj, message)
> Expects *obj* to be (not to be) a instance of *klass*.

assert_ | refute_ kind_of(klass, obj, ‹*message*›)
> Expects *obj* to be (not to be) a kind of *klass*.

assert_ | refute_ match(regexp, string, ‹*message*›)
    Expects *string* to (not) match *regexp*.

assert_ | refute_ nil(obj, ‹*message*›)
    Expects *obj* to be (not) nil.

assert_ | refute_ operator(obj1, operator, obj2, ‹*message*›)
    Expects the result of sending the message *operator* to *obj1* with parameter *obj2* to be (not to be) true.

assert_raises(Exception, ...) { block }
    Expects the block to raise one of the listed exceptions.

assert_ | refute_ respond_to(obj, message, ‹*message*›)
    Expects *obj* to respond to (not respond to) *message* (a symbol).

assert_ | refute_ same(expected, actual, ‹*message*›)
    Expects expected.equal?(actual).

assert_send(send_array, ‹*message*›)
    Sends the message in *send_array[1]* to the receiver in *send_array[0]*, passing the rest of *send_array* as arguments. Expects the return value to be true.

assert_throws(expected_symbol, ‹*message*›) { block }
    Expects the block to throw the given symbol.

flunk(message="Epic Fail!")
    Always fails.

skip(message)
    Indicates that a test is deliberately not run.

pass
    Always passes.

Additional Test::Unit assertions

assert_not_equal(expected, actual, ‹*message*›)
    Expects *actual* not to equal *expected,* using ==. Like refute_equal.

assert_not_match(regexp, string, ‹*message*›)
    Expects *string* not to match *regexp*. Like refute_match.

assert_not_nil(obj, ‹*message*›)
    Expects *obj* not to be nil. Like refute_nil.

assert_not_same(expected, actual, ‹*message*›)
    Expects !expected.equal?(actual). Like refute_same.

assert_nothing_raised(Exception, ...) { block }
    Expects the block not to raise one of the listed exceptions.

assert_nothing_thrown(expected_symbol, ‹*message*›) { block }
    Expects the block not to throw the given symbol.

assert_raise(Exception, ...) { block }
    Synonym for assert_raises.

CHAPTER 14

When Trouble Strikes!

It's sad to say, but it is possible to write buggy programs using Ruby. Sorry about that. But not to worry! Ruby has several features that will help debug your programs. We'll look at these features, and then we'll show some common mistakes you can make in Ruby and how to fix them.

14.1 Ruby Debugger

Ruby comes with a debugger, which is conveniently built into the base system. You can run the debugger by invoking the interpreter with the -r debug option, along with any other Ruby options and the name of your script:

ruby -r debug ‹ *debug-options* › ‹ *programfile* › ‹ *program-arguments* ›

The debugger supports the usual range of features you'd expect, including the ability to set breakpoints, to step into and step over method calls, and to display stack frames and variables. It can also list the instance methods defined for a particular object or class, and it allows you to list and control separate threads within Ruby. All the commands that are available under the debugger are listed in Table 6, *Debugger commands*, on page 205.

If your Ruby installation has readline support enabled, you can use cursor keys to move back and forth in command history and use line-editing commands to amend previous input.

To give you an idea of what the Ruby debugger is like, here's a sample session:

```
$ ruby -r debug t.rb
Debug.rb
Emacs support available.
t.rb:1:def fact(n)
(rdb:1) list 1-9
[1, 9] in t.rb
=> 1  def fact(n)
   2    if n <= 0
   3      1
   4    else
   5      n * fact(n-1)
   6    end
   7  end
   8
   9  p fact(5)
```

```
(rdb:1) b 2
Set breakpoint 1 at t.rb:2
(rdb:1) c
breakpoint 1, fact at t.rb:2
t.rb:2:  if n <= 0
(rdb:1) disp n
1: n = 5
(rdb:1) del 1
(rdb:1) watch n==1
Set watchpoint 2
(rdb:1) c
watchpoint 2, fact at t.rb:fact
t.rb:1:def fact(n)
1: n = 1
(rdb:1) where
--> #1  t.rb:1:in `fact'
    #2  t.rb:5:in `fact'
    #3  t.rb:5:in `fact'
    #4  t.rb:5:in `fact'
    #5  t.rb:5:in `fact'
    #6  t.rb:9
(rdb:1) del 2
(rdb:1) c
120
```

14.2 Interactive Ruby

If you want to play with Ruby, we recommend Interactive Ruby—irb, for short. irb is essentially a Ruby "shell" similar in concept to an operating system shell (complete with job control). It provides an environment where you can "play around" with the language in real time. You launch irb at the command prompt:

irb ‹*irb-options*› ‹*ruby_script*› ‹*program-arguments*›

irb displays the value of each expression as you complete it. For instance:

```
irb(main):001:0> a = 1 +
irb(main):002:0* 2 * 3 /
irb(main):003:0* 4 % 5
=> 2
irb(main):004:0> 2+2
=> 4
irb(main):005:0> def test
irb(main):006:1>   puts "Hello, world!"
irb(main):007:1>   end
=> nil
irb(main):008:0> test
Hello, world!
=> nil
irb(main):009:0>
```

irb also allows you to create subsessions, each one of which may have its own context. For example, you can create a subsession with the same (top-level) context as the original session or create a subsession in the context of a particular class or instance. The sample session that follows is a bit longer but shows how you can create subsessions and switch between them.

```
$ irb
irb(main):001:0> irb
irb#1(main):001:0> jobs
#0->irb on main (#<Thread:0x401bd654>: stop)
#1->irb#1 on main (#<Thread:0x401d5a28>: running)
irb#1(main):002:0> fg 0
#<IRB::Irb:@scanner=#<RubyLex:0x401ca7>,@signal_status=:IN_EVAL,
    @context=#<IRB::Context:0x401ca86c>>
irb(main):002:0> class VolumeKnob
irb(main):003:1> end
=> nil
irb(main):004:0> irb VolumeKnob
irb#2(VolumeKnob):001:0> def initialize
irb#2(VolumeKnob):002:1> @vol=50
irb#2(VolumeKnob):003:1> end
=> nil
irb#2(VolumeKnob):004:0> def up
irb#2(VolumeKnob):005:1> @vol += 10
irb#2(VolumeKnob):006:1> end
=> nil
irb#2(VolumeKnob):007:0> fg 0
#<IRB::Irb:@scanner=#<RubyLex:0x401ca7>,@signal_status=:IN_EVAL,
    @context=#<IRB::Context:0x401ca86c>>
irb(main):005:0> jobs
#0->irb on main (#<Thread:0x401bd654>: running)
#1->irb#1 on main (#<Thread:0x401d5a28>: stop)
#2->irb#2 on VolumeKnob (#<Thread:0x401c400c>: stop)
irb(main):006:0> VolumeKnob.instance_methods
=> ["up"]
irb(main):007:0> v = VolumeKnob.new
#<VolumeKnob: @vol=50>
irb(main):008:0> irb v
irb#3(#<VolumeKnob:0x401e7d40>):001:0> up
=> 60
irb#3(#<VolumeKnob:0x401e7d40>):002:0> up
=> 70
irb#3(#<VolumeKnob:0x401e7d40>):003:0> up
=> 80
irb#3(VolumeKnob):004:0> fg 0
#<IRB::Irb:@scanner=#<RubyLex:0x401ca7>,@signal_status=:IN_EVAL,
    @context=#<IRB::Context:0x401ca86c>>
irb(main):009:0> kill 1,2,3
=> [1, 2, 3]
irb(main):010:0> jobs
#0->irb on main (#<Thread:0x401bd654>: running)
irb(main):011:0> exit
```

In this same irb session, we'll create a new subsession in the context of class VolumeKnob

We can use fg 0 to switch back to the main session, take a look at all current jobs, and see what instance methods VolumeKnob defines

Make a new VolumeKnob object, and create a new subsession with that object as the context

Switch back to the main session, kill the subsessions, and exit

For a full description of all the commands that irb supports, see Chapter 18, *Interactive Ruby Shell*, on page 253.

As with the debugger, if your version of Ruby was built with GNU readline support, you can use Emacs- or vi-style key bindings to edit individual lines or to go back and reexecute or edit a previous line—just like a command shell.

irb is a great learning tool. It's very handy if you want to try an idea quickly and see whether it works.

14.3 Editor Support

The Ruby interpreter is designed to read a program in one pass; this means you can pipe an entire program to the interpreter's standard input, and it will work just fine.

We can take advantage of this feature to run Ruby code from inside an editor. In Emacs, for instance, you can select a region of Ruby text and use the command Meta-| to execute Ruby. The Ruby interpreter will use the selected region as standard input, and output will go to a buffer named *Shell Command Output*. This feature has come in quite handy for us while writing this book—just select a few lines of Ruby in the middle of a paragraph, and try it!

You can do something similar in the vi editor using :%!ruby, which *replaces* the program text with its output, or :w␣!ruby, which displays the output without affecting the buffer. Other editors have similar features.[1]

Some Ruby developers look for IDE support. Several decent alternatives are available. Arachno RubyAptana, RubyMine, NetBeans, Ruby in Steel, Idea, and so on, all have their devotees. It's a rapidly changing field, so we recommend a quick web search rather than rely on the advice here.

While we are on the subject, this would probably be a good place to mention that a Ruby mode for Emacs is included in the Ruby source distribution as ruby-mode.el in the misc/ subdirectory. Many other editors now include support for Ruby; check your documentation for details.

14.4 But It Doesn't Work!

So, you've read through enough of the book, you start to write your very own Ruby program, and it doesn't work. Here's a list of common gotchas and other tips:

- First and foremost, run your scripts with warnings enabled (the -w command-line option).

- If you happen to forget a comma (,) in an argument list—especially to print—you can produce some very odd error messages.

- An attribute setter is not being called. Within a class definition, Ruby will parse setter= as an assignment to a local variable, not as a method call. Use the form self.setter= to indicate the method call:

```ruby
class Incorrect
  attr_accessor :one, :two
  def initialize
    one = 1          # incorrect - sets local variable
    self.two = 2
  end
end

obj = Incorrect.new
obj.one    # => nil
obj.two    # => 2
```

- Objects that don't appear to be properly set up may have been victims of an incorrectly spelled initialize method:

```ruby
class Incorrect
  attr_reader :answer
  def initialise       # <-- spelling error
    @answer = 42
  end
end
```

---

1. Many developers use Sublime Text (http://www.sublimetext.com/), a cross-platform editor chock full of features, including Ruby code execution.

```
ultimate = Incorrect.new
ultimate.answer # => nil
```

The same kind of thing can happen if you misspell the instance variable name:

```ruby
class Incorrect
  attr_reader :answer
  def initialize
    @anwser = 42        #<-- spelling error
  end
end


ultimate = Incorrect.new
ultimate.answer # => nil
```

• A parse error at the last line of the source often indicates a missing end keyword, sometimes quite a bit earlier.

• This ugly message—syntax error, unexpected $end, expecting keyword_end—means that you have an end missing somewhere in your code. (The $end in the message means end-of-file, so the message simply means that Ruby hit the end of your code before finding all the end keywords it was expecting.) Try running with -w, which will warn when it finds ends that aren't aligned with their opening if/while/class.

• As of Ruby 1.9, block parameters are no longer in the same scope as local variables. This may be incompatibile with older code. Run with the -w flag to spot these issues:

```ruby
entry = "wibble"
[1, 2, 3].each do |entry|
  # do something with entry
end
puts "Last entry = #{entry}"
```

produces:

```
prog.rb:2: warning: shadowing outer local variable - entry
Last entry = wibble
```

• Watch out for precedence issues, especially when using {...} instead of do...end:

```ruby
def one(arg)
  if block_given?
    "block given to 'one' returns #{yield}"
  else
    arg
  end
end

def two
  if block_given?
    "block given to 'two' returns #{yield}"
  end
end

result1 = one two {
  "three"
}
```

```
result2 = one two do
  "three"
end

puts "With braces, result = #{result1}"
puts "With do/end, result = #{result2}"
```

produces:

```
With braces, result = block given to 'two' returns three
With do/end, result = block given to 'one' returns three
```

- Output written to a terminal may be buffered. This means you may not see a message you write immediately. In addition, if you write messages to both STDOUT and STDERR, the output may not appear in the order you were expecting. Always use nonbuffered I/O (set sync=true) for debug messages.

- If numbers don't come out right, perhaps they're strings. Text read from a file will be a String and will not be automatically converted to a number by Ruby. A call to Integer will work wonders (and will throw an exception if the input isn't a well-formed integer). The following is a common mistake Perl programmers make:

```
while line = gets
  num1, num2 = line.split(/,/)
  # ...
end
```

You can rewrite this as follows:

```
while line = gets
  num1, num2 = line.split(/,/)
  num1 = Integer(num1)
  num2 = Integer(num2)
  # ...
end
```

Or, you could convert all the strings using map:

```
while line = gets
  num1, num2 = line.split(/,/).map {|val| Integer(val) }
  # ...
end
```

- Unintended aliasing—if you are using an object as the key of a hash, make sure it doesn't change its hash value (or arrange to call Hash#rehash if it does):

```
arr = [1, 2]
hash = { arr => "value" }
hash[arr]    # => "value"
arr[0] = 99
hash[arr]    # => nil
hash.rehash # => {[99, 2]=>"value"}
hash[arr]    # => "value"
```

- Make sure the class of the object you are using is what you think it is. If in doubt, use puts my_obj.class.

- Make sure your method names start with a lowercase letter and class and constant names start with an uppercase letter.

- If method calls aren't doing what you'd expect, make sure you've put parentheses around the arguments.

- Make sure the open parenthesis of a method's parameter list butts up against the end of the method name with no intervening spaces.

- Use irb and the debugger.

- Use Object#freeze. If you suspect that some unknown portion of code is setting a variable to a bogus value, try freezing the variable. The culprit will then be caught during the attempt to modify the variable.

One major technique makes writing Ruby code both easier and more fun. *Develop your applications incrementally.* Write a few lines of code, and then write tests (perhaps using Test::Unit). Write a few more lines of code, and then exercise them. One of the major benefits of a dynamically typed language is that things don't have to be complete before you use them.

14.5 But It's Too Slow!

Ruby is an interpreted, high-level language, and as such it may not perform as fast as a lower-level language such as C. In the following sections, we'll list some basic things you can do to improve performance; also take a look in the index under *Performance* for other pointers.

Typically, slow-running programs have one or two performance graveyards, places where execution time goes to die. Find and improve them, and suddenly your whole program springs back to life. The trick is finding them. The Benchmark module and the Ruby profilers can help.

Benchmark

You can use the Benchmark module, also described in the library section on page 733, to time sections of code. For example, we may wonder what the overhead of method invocation is. You can use Benchmark to find out.

```
require 'benchmark'
include Benchmark

LOOP_COUNT = 1_000_000

bmbm(12) do |test|
  test.report("inline:")    do
    LOOP_COUNT.times do |x|
      # nothing
    end
  end
  test.report("method:") do
    def method
      # nothing
    end
```

```
    LOOP_COUNT.times do |x|
      method
    end
  end
end
```

produces:

```
Rehearsal -------------------------------------------------
inline:      0.100000   0.000000   0.100000 (  0.102194)
method:      0.140000   0.000000   0.140000 (  0.145651)
---------------------------------------- total: 0.240000sec

                  user     system      total       real
inline:      0.090000   0.000000   0.090000 (  0.098364)
method:      0.140000   0.000000   0.140000 (  0.146260)
```

You have to be careful when benchmarking, because oftentimes Ruby programs can run slowly because of the overhead of garbage collection. Because this garbage collection can happen any time during your program's execution, you may find that benchmarking gives misleading results, showing a section of code running slowly when in fact the slowdown was caused because garbage collection happened to trigger while that code was executing. The Benchmark module has the bmbm method that runs the tests twice, once as a rehearsal and once to measure performance, in an attempt to minimize the distortion introduced by garbage collection. The benchmarking process itself is relatively well mannered—it doesn't slow down your program much.

The Profiler

Ruby comes with a code profiler (documented in the library section on page 791). The profiler shows you the number of times each method in the program is called and the average and cumulative time that Ruby spends in those methods.

You can add profiling to your code using the command-line option -r profile or from within the code using require "profile". Here's an example:

trouble/profileeg.rb
```ruby
count = 0
words = File.open("/usr/share/dict/words")

while word = words.gets
  word = word.chomp!
  if word.length == 12
    count += 1
  end
end

puts "#{count} twelve-character words"
```

The first time we ran this (without profiling) against a dictionary of almost 235,000 words, it took a noticeable time to complete. Wondering if we could improve on this, we added the command-line option -r profile and tried again. Eventually we saw output that looked like the following:

```
20460 twelve-character words
  %   cumulative   self              self     total
 time   seconds   seconds   calls  ms/call  ms/call  name
 9.03     1.21      1.21   234936    0.01     0.01   String#chomp!
 8.88     2.40      1.19   234937    0.01     0.01   IO#gets
 7.61     3.42      1.02   234936    0.00     0.00   String#length
 6.94     4.35      0.93   234936    0.00     0.00   Fixnum#==
 0.82     4.46      0.11    20460    0.01     0.01   Fixnum#+
 0.00     4.46      0.00        2    0.00     0.00   IO#set_encoding
 0.00     4.46      0.00        1    0.00     0.00   IO#open
 . . . .
```

The first thing to notice is that the timings shown are a lot slower than when the program runs without the profiler. Profiling has a serious overhead, but the assumption is that it applies across the board, and therefore the relative numbers are still meaningful. This particular program clearly spends a lot of time in the loop, which executes almost 235,000 times. Each time, it invokes both gets and chomp!. We could probably improve performance if we could either make the stuff in the loop less expensive or eliminate the loop altogether. One way of doing the latter is to read the word list into one long string and then use a pattern to match and extract all twelve character words:

trouble/profileeg1.rb
```ruby
words = File.read("/usr/share/dict/words")
count = words.scan(/^............\n/).size

puts "#{count} twelve-character words"
```

Our profile numbers are now a lot better (and the program runs more than five times faster when we take the profiling back out):

```
% ruby -r profile code/trouble/profileeg1.rb
20462 twelve-character words
  %   cumulative   self              self     total
 time   seconds   seconds   calls  ms/call  ms/call  name
100.00    0.26      0.26        1  260.00   260.00   String#scan
 0.00     0.26      0.00        1    0.00     0.00   Fixnum#to_s
 0.00     0.26      0.00        1    0.00     0.00   IO.read
 0.00     0.26      0.00        1    0.00     0.00   TracePoint#enable
 0.00     0.26      0.00        1    0.00     0.00   Array#size
 0.00     0.26      0.00        2    0.00     0.00   IO#set_encoding
 0.00     0.26      0.00        2    0.00     0.00   IO#write
 0.00     0.26      0.00        1    0.00     0.00   IO#puts
 0.00     0.26      0.00        1    0.00     0.00   Kernel#puts
 0.00     0.26      0.00        1    0.00     0.00   TracePoint#disable
 0.00     0.26      0.00        1    0.00   260.00   #toplevel
```

Remember to check the code without the profiler afterward, though—sometimes the slow-down the profiler introduces can mask other problems.

Ruby is a wonderfully transparent and expressive language, but it does not relieve the programmer of the need to apply common sense: creating unnecessary objects, performing unneeded work, and creating bloated code will slow down your programs regardless of the language.

Code Execution Coverage

Ruby 1.9.2 comes with low-level code coverage built in to the interpreter (see the Coverage module on page 740). It tracks which lines of code were executed in your code.

People are starting to build libraries that wrap this low-level functionality with filters, HTML output, and the like. Two examples are Mark Bates' CoverMe and Christoph Olszowka's simplecov.

Both are installed as gems, and both come with comprehensive instructions on how to integrate them into your test environment.

For our simple tennis scoring example, the summary, written as an HTML file, is fairly straightforward:

Click the name of a file, and you'll get a display of which lines were executed:

empty	A null command repeats the last command.
b[reak] [file|class:]line	Sets breakpoint at given line in *file* (default current file) or *class*.
b[reak] [file|class:]name	Sets breakpoint at *method* in *file* or *class*.
b[reak]	Displays breakpoints and watchpoints.
cat[ch] exception	Stops when *exception* is raised.
cat[ch]	Lists current catches.
c[ont]	Continues execution.
del[ete] [nnn]	Deletes breakpoint *nnn* (default all).
disp[lay] expr	Displays value of *nnn* every time debugger gets control.
disp[lay]	Shows current displays.
down nnn=1	Moves down *nnn* levels in the call stack.
f[rame]	Synonym for where.
fin[ish]	Finishes execution of the current function.
h[elp]	Shows summary of commands.
l[ist] [start–end]	Lists source lines from start to end.
m[ethod] i[nstance] *obj*	Displays instance methods of *obj*.
m[ethod] Name	Displays instance methods of the class or module name.
n[ext] nnn=1	Executes next *nnn* lines, stepping over methods.
[p] expr	Evaluates *expr* in the current context. *expr* may include assignment to variables and method invocations.
q[uit]	Exits the debugger.
s[tep] nnn=1	Executes next *nnn* lines, stepping into methods.
th[read] l[ist]	Lists all threads.
th[read] [c[ur[rent]]]	Displays status of current thread.
th[read] [c[ur[rent]]] nnn	Makes thread *nnn* current and stops it.
th[read] stop nnn	Makes thread *nnn* current and stops it.
th[read] resume nnn	Resumes thread *nnn*.
th[read] [sw[itch]] nnn	Switches thread context to nnn.
tr[ace] (on|off) [all]	Toggles execution trace of current or all threads.
undisp[lay] [nnn]	Removes display (default all).
up nnn=1	Moves up *nnn* levels in the call stack.
v[ar] c[onst] Name	Displays constants in class or module name.
v[ar] g[lobal]	Displays global variables.
v[ar] l[ocal]	Displays local variables.
v[ar] i[stance] *obj*	Displays instance variables of *obj*.
wat[ch] expr	Breaks when expression becomes true.
w[here]	Displays current call stack.

Table 6—Debugger commands

Part II

Ruby in Its Setting

## CHAPTER 15

Ruby and Its World

It's an unfortunate fact of life that our applications have to deal with the big, bad world. In this chapter, we'll look at how Ruby interacts with its environment. Microsoft Windows users will probably also want to look at the platform-specific information on page 289.

15.1 Command-Line Arguments

"In the beginning was the command line."[1] Regardless of the system in which Ruby is deployed, whether it be a super-high-end scientific graphics workstation or an embedded PDA device, you have to start the Ruby interpreter somehow, and that gives us the opportunity to pass in command-line arguments.

A Ruby command line consists of three parts: options to the Ruby interpreter, optionally the name of a program to run, and optionally a set of arguments for that program:

ruby ‹ *options* › ‹ – › ‹ *programfile* › ‹ *arguments* ›*

The Ruby options are terminated by the first word on the command line that doesn't start with a hyphen or by the special flag -- (two hyphens).

If no filename is present on the command line or if the filename is a single hyphen, Ruby reads the program source from standard input.

Arguments for the program itself follow the program name. For example, the following:

```
$ ruby -w - "Hello World"
```

will enable warnings, read a program from standard input, and pass it the string "Hello World" as an argument.

---

1. This is the title of a marvelous essay by Neal Stephenson (available online via http://www.cryptonomicon.com/beginning.html).

Command-Line Options

-0[octal]

The 0 flag (the digit zero) specifies the record separator character (\0, if no digit follows). -00 indicates paragraph mode: records are separated by two successive default record separator characters. \0777 reads the entire file at once (because it is an illegal character). Sets $/.

-a

Autosplit mode when used with -n or -p; equivalent to executing $F = $_.split at the top of each loop iteration.

-C directory

Changes working directory to directory before executing.

-c

Checks syntax only; does not execute the program.

--copyright

Prints the copyright notice and exits.

-d, --debug

Sets $DEBUG and $VERBOSE to true. This can be used by your programs to enable additional tracing.

--disable-all

New in 2.0   Disable the rubygems and RUBYOPT options (see the following descriptions).

--disable-gems

Stops Ruby from automatically loading RubyGems from require. There is a corresponding --enable-gems option.

--disable-rubyopt

New in 2.0   Prevents Ruby from examining the RUBYOPT environment variable. You should probably set this in an environment you want to secure. There is a corresponding --enable-rubyopt option.

--dump option...

Tells Ruby to dump various items of internal state. options... is a comma or space separated list containing one or more of copyright, insns, parsetree, parsetree_with_comment, syntax, usage, version, and yydebug. This is intended for Ruby core developers.

--enable-all

New in 2.0   Enable the rubygems and RUBYOPT options (see the following descriptions).

--enable-gems

Allows Ruby to automatically load RubyGems from require. There is a corresponding --disable-gems option.

--enable-rubyopt

New in 2.0   Allows Ruby to use the RUBYOPT environment variable. (This is the default.) You should probably disable this option in an environment you want to secure.

-E encoding, --encoding encoding, --encoding=encoding

> Specifies the default character encoding for data read from and written to the outside world. This can be used to set both the external encoding (the encoding to be assumed for file contents) and optionally the default internal encoding (the file contents are transcoded to this when read and transcoded from this when written). The format of the *encoding* parameter is -E external, -E external:internal, or -E :internal. See Chapter 17, *Character Encoding*, on page 239 for details. See also -U.

-e 'command'

> Executes *command* as one line of Ruby source. Several -e's are allowed, and the commands are treated as multiple lines in the same program. If *programfile* is omitted when -e is present, execution stops after the -e commands have been run. Programs run using -e have access to the old behavior of ranges and regular expressions in conditions—ranges of integers compare against the current input line number, and regular expressions match against $_.

--external-encoding=encoding

> Specifies the default external coding for the program.

New in 2.0

-F pattern

> Specifies the input field separator ($;) used as the default for split (affects the -a option).

-h, --help

> Displays a short help screen.

-I directories

> Specifies directories to be prepended to $LOAD_PATH ($:). Multiple -I options may be present. Multiple directories may appear following each -I, separated by a colon on Unix-like systems and by a semicolon on DOS/Windows systems.

-i [extension]

> Edits ARGV files in place. For each file named in ARGV, anything you write to standard output will be saved back as the contents of that file. A backup copy of the file will be made if *extension* is supplied.

```
$ ruby -pi.bak -e "gsub(/Perl/, 'Ruby')" *.txt
```

--internal-encoding=encoding

> Specifies the default internal coding for the program.

New in 2.0

-l

> Enables automatic line-ending processing; sets $\ to the value of $/ and chops every input line automatically.

-n

> Assumes a while gets; ...; end loop around your program. For example, a simple grep command could be implemented as follows:

```
$ ruby -n -e "print if /wombat/"  *.txt
```

-p

> Places your program code within the loop while gets; ...; print; end.

```
$ ruby -p -e "$_.downcase!" *.txt
```

-r library

> Requires the named library or gem before executing.

-S

> Looks for the program file using the RUBYPATH or PATH environment variable.

-s

> Any command-line switches found after the program filename, but before any filename arguments or before a --, are removed from ARGV and set to a global variable named for the switch. In the following example, the effect of this would be to set the variable $opt to "electric":

```
$ ruby -s prog -opt=electric ./mydata
```

-Tlevel

> Sets the safe level, which among other things enables tainting and untrusted checks (see Chapter 26, *Locking Ruby in the Safe*, on page 409). Sets $SAFE.

-U

> Sets the default internal encoding to UTF-8. See Chapter 17, *Character Encoding*, on page 239 for details. See also -E.

-v, --verbose

> Sets $VERBOSE to true, which enables verbose mode. Also prints the version number. In verbose mode, compilation warnings are printed. If no program filename appears on the command line, Ruby exits.

--version

> Displays the Ruby version number and exits.

-w

> Enables verbose mode. Unlike -v, reads program from standard input if no program files are present on the command line. We recommend running your Ruby programs with -w.

-W level

> Sets the level of warnings issued. With a *level* of two (or with no level specified), equivalent to -w—additional warnings are given. If *level* is 1, runs at the standard (default) warning level. With -W0, absolutely no warnings are given (including those issued using Object#warn).

-X directory

> Changes working directory to *directory* before executing. This is the same as -C directory.

-x [directory]

> Strips off text before #!ruby line and changes working directory to *directory* if given.

-y, --yydebug

> Enables yacc debugging in the parser (*waaay too much information*).

Argument Processing: ARGV and ARGF

Any command-line arguments after the program filename are available to your Ruby program in the global array ARGV. For instance, assume test.rb contains the following program:

```
ARGV.each {|arg| p arg }
```

Invoke it with the following command line:

```
$ ruby -w test.rb "Hello World" a1 1.6180
```

It'll generate the following output:

```
"Hello World"
"a1"
"1.6180"
```

There's a gotcha here for all you C programmers—ARGV[0] is the first argument to the program, not the program name. The name of the current program is available in the global variable $0, which is aliased to $PROGRAM_NAME. Notice that all the values in ARGV are strings.

If your program reads from standard input (or uses the special object ARGF, described in the next section), the arguments in ARGV will be taken to be filenames, and Ruby will read from these files. If your program takes a mixture of arguments and filenames, make sure you empty the nonfilename arguments from the ARGV array before reading from the files.

ARGF

It is common for a command line program to take a list of zero or more file names to process. It will then read through these files in turn, doing whatever it does.

Ruby provides a convenience object, referenced by the name ARGF, that handles access to these files. When your program starts, ARGF is initialized with a reference ARGV. Because this is a reference, changes to make to ARGV (for example when you remove options as you process them) are seen by ARGF.

If you read from ARGF (for example by calling ARGF.gets) or from standard input (for example by calling plain gets), Ruby will open the file whose name is the first element of ARGV and perform the I/O on it. If, as you continue to read, you reach the end of that file, Ruby closes it, shifts it out of the ARGV array, and then opens the next file in the list. At some point, when you finishing reading from the last file, ARGV will return an end-of-file condition (so gets will return nil, for example). If ARGV is initially empty, ARGF will read from standard input.

You can get to the name of the file currently being read from using ARGF.filename, and you can get the current File object as ARGF.file. ARGF keeps track of the total number of lines read in ARGF.lineno—if you need the line number in the current file, use ARGV.file.lineno. Here's a program that uses this information:

```
while line = gets
  printf "%d: %10s[%d] %s", ARGF.lineno, ARGF.filename, ARGF.file.lineno, line
end
```

If we run it, passing a couple of file names, it will copy the contents of those files.

```
$ ruby copy.rb testfile otherfile
1:    testfile[1] This is line one
2:    testfile[2] This is line two
3:    testfile[3] This is line three
4:    testfile[4] And so on...
5:   otherfile[1] ANOTHER LINE ONE
6:   otherfile[2] AND ANOTHER LINE TWO
7:   otherfile[3] AND FINALLY THE LAST LINE
```

In-place Editing

In-place editing is a hack inherited from Perl. It allows you to alter the contents of files passed in on the command line, retaining a backup copy of the original contents.

To turn on in-place editing, give Ruby the file extension to use for the backup file, either with the -i [ext] command line option, or by calling ARGF.inplace_mode=ext in your code.

Now, as your code reads through each file given on the command line, Ruby will rename the original file by appending the backup extension. It will then create a new file with the original name, and open it for writing on standard output. This all means that if you code a program such as this:

```
while line = gets
  puts line.chomp.reverse
end
```

and you invoked it using

```
$ ruby -i.bak reverse.rb testfile otherfile
```

You'd find that testfile and otherfile would now have reversed lines, and that the original files would be available in testfile.bak and otherfile.bak.

For finer control over the I/O to these files, you can use the methods provided by ARGF. They're rarely used, so rather than document them here, we'll refer you to ri or the online documentation.

15.2 Program Termination

The method Object#exit terminates your program, returning a status value to the operating system. However, unlike some languages, exit doesn't terminate the program immediately—exit first raises a SystemExit exception, which you may catch, and then performs a number of cleanup actions, including running any registered at_exit methods and object finalizers. See the reference for Object#at_exit on page 612.

15.3 Environment Variables

You can access operating system environment variables using the predefined variable ENV. It responds to the same methods as Hash.[2]

```
ENV['SHELL']
ENV['HOME']
ENV['USER']
ENV.keys.size
ENV.keys[0, 4]
```

The values of some environment variables are read by Ruby when it first starts. These variables modify the behavior of the interpreter.

The environment variables used by Ruby are listed in the following table.

---

2.   ENV is not actually a hash, but if you need to, you can convert it into a Hash using ENV#to_hash.

Variable Name	Description
DLN_LIBRARY_PATH	Specifies the search path for dynamically loaded modules.
HOME	Points to user's home directory. This is used when expanding ~ in file and directory names.
LOGDIR	Specifies the fallback pointer to the user's home directory if $HOME is not set. This is used only by Dir.chdir.
OPENSSL_CONF	Specifies the location of OpenSSL configuration file.
RUBYLIB	Specifies an additional search path for Ruby programs ($SAFE must be 0).
RUBYLIB_PREFIX	(Windows only) Mangles the RUBYLIB search path by adding this prefix to each component.
RUBYOPT	Specifies additional command-line options to Ruby; examined after real command-line options are parsed ($SAFE must be 0).
RUBYPATH	With -S option, specifies the search path for Ruby programs (defaults to PATH).
RUBYSHELL	Specifies shell to use when spawning a process under Windows; if not set, will also check SHELL or COMSPEC.
RUBY_TCL_DLL	Overrides default name for Tcl shared library or DLL.
RUBY_TK_DLL	Overrides default name for Tk shared library or DLL. Both this and RUBY_TCL_DLL must be set for either to be used.

Other environment variables affect the memory allocated by the Ruby virtual machine for various tasks.[3]

New in 2.0

Variable Name	Description
RUBY_THREAD_VM_STACK_SIZE	The VM stack size used at thread creation: 128KB (32 bit CPU) or 256KB (64 bit CPU).
RUBY_THREAD_MACHINE_STACK_SIZE	The machine stack size used at thread creation: 512KB (32 bit CPU) or 1024KB (64 bit CPU).
RUBY_FIBER_VM_STACK_SIZE	VM stack size used at fiber creation: 64KB or 128KB.
RUBY_FIBER_MACHINE_STACK_SIZE	The machine stack size used at fiber creation: 256KB or 256KB.

The current value of these variables can be read using RubyVM::DEFAULT_PARAMS.

Writing to Environment Variables

A Ruby program may write to the ENV object. On most systems, this changes the values of the corresponding environment variables. However, this change is local to the process that makes it and to any subsequently spawned child processes. This inheritance of environment variables is illustrated in the code that follows. A subprocess changes an environment variable, and this change is inherited by a process that it then starts. However, the change is not visible to the original parent. (This just goes to prove that parents never really know what their children are doing.)

---

3. This applies to MRI only.

```
puts "In parent, term = #{ENV['TERM']}"
fork do
  puts "Start of child 1, term = #{ENV['TERM']}"
  ENV['TERM'] = "ansi"
  fork do
    puts "Start of child 2, term = #{ENV['TERM']}"
  end
  Process.wait
  puts "End of child 1, term = #{ENV['TERM']}"
end
Process.wait
puts "Back in parent, term = #{ENV['TERM']}"
```

produces:

```
In parent, term = xterm-256color
Start of child 1, term = xterm-256color
Start of child 2, term = ansi
End of child 1, term = ansi
Back in parent, term = xterm-256color
```

Setting an environment variable's value to nil removes the variable from the environment.

15.4 Where Ruby Finds Its Libraries

You use require or load to bring a library into your Ruby program. Some of these libraries are supplied with Ruby, some you may have installed from the Ruby Application Archive, some may have been packaged as RubyGems (of which more later), and some you may have written yourself. How does Ruby find them?

Let's start with the basics. When Ruby is built for your particular machine, it predefines a set of standard directories to hold library stuff. Where these are depends on the machine in question. You can determine this from the command line with something like this:

```
$ ruby -e 'puts $:'
```

On our OS X box, with RVM installed, this produces the following list:

```
/Users/dave/.rvm/rubies/ruby-2.0.0-p0/lib/ruby/site_ruby/2.0.0
/Users/dave/.rvm/rubies/ruby-2.0.0-p0/lib/ruby/site_ruby/2.0.0/x86_64-darwin12.2.0
...
```

The site_ruby directories are intended to hold modules and extensions that you've added. The architecture-dependent directories (x86_64-darwin... in this case) hold executables and other things specific to this particular machine. All these directories are automatically included in Ruby's search for libraries.

Sometimes this isn't enough. Perhaps you're working on a large project written in Ruby and you and your colleagues have built a substantial library of Ruby code. You want everyone on the team to have access to all this code. You have a couple of options to accomplish this. If your program runs at a safe level of zero (see Chapter 26, *Locking Ruby in the Safe*, on page 409), you can set the environment variable RUBYLIB to a list of one or more directories to be searched.[4] If your program is not setuid, you can use the command-line parameter -I to do the same thing.

---

4. The separator between entries is a semicolon on Windows; for Unix, it's a colon.

The Ruby variable $: is an array of places to search for loaded files. As we've seen, this variable is initialized to the list of standard directories, plus any additional ones you specified using RUBYLIB and -I. You can always add directories to this array from within your running program. Prior to Ruby 1.9, this used to be a common idiom:

```
$: << File.dirname(__FILE__)
require 'other_file'
```

This added the directory of the running file to the search path, so other_file.rb could be found there by the subsequent require. Now we use require_relative instead.

```
require_relative 'other_file'
```

15.5 RubyGems Integration

This section is based on the start of the chapter on RubyGems written by Chad Fowler for the second edition of this book.

RubyGems is a standardized packaging and installation framework for Ruby libraries and applications. RubyGems makes it easy to locate, install, upgrade, and uninstall Ruby packages.

Before RubyGems came along, installing a new library involved searching the Web, downloading a package, and attempting to install it—only to find that its dependencies hadn't been met. If the library you want is packaged using RubyGems, however, you can now simply ask RubyGems to install it (and all its dependencies). Everything is done for you.

In the RubyGems world, developers bundle their applications and libraries into single files called *gems*. These files conform to a standardized format and typically are stored in repositories on the Internet (but you can also create your own repositories if you want).

The RubyGems system provides a command-line tool, appropriately named gem, for manipulating these gem files. It also provides integration into Ruby so that your programs can access gems as libraries.

Prior to Ruby 1.9, it was your responsibility to install the RubyGems software on your computer. Now, however, Ruby comes with RubyGems baked right in.

Installing Gems on Your Machine

Your latest project calls for a lot of XML generation. You could just hard-code it, but you've heard about Jim Weirich's Builder library, which constructs XML directly from Ruby code.

Let's start by seeing whether Builder is available as a gem:

```
$ gem query --details --remote --name-matches builder
AntBuilder (0.4.3)
    Author: JRuby-extras
    Homepage: http://jruby-extras.rubyforge.org/
    AntBuilder: Use ant from JRuby. Only usable within JRuby
builder (2.1.2)
    Author: Jim Weirich
    Homepage: http://onestepback.org
    Builders for MarkUp.
```

The --details option displays the descriptions of any gems it finds. The --remote option searches the remote repository. And the --name-matches option says to search the central gem repository for any gem whose name matches the regular expression /builder/. (We could have used the short-form options -d, -r, and -n.) The result shows a number of gems have *builder* in their name; the one we want is just plain *builder*.

The number after the name shows the latest version. You can see a list of all available versions using the --all option. We'll also use the list command, as it lets us match on an exact name:

```
$ gem list --details --remote --all builder
*** REMOTE GEMS ***

builder (2.1.2, 2.1.1, 2.0.0, 1.2.4, 1.2.3, 1.2.2, 1.2.1, 1.2.0, 1.1.0, 0.1.1)
    Author: Jim Weirich
    Homepage: http://onestepback.org
    Builders for MarkUp.
```

Because we want to install the most recent one, we don't have to state an explicit version on the install command; the latest is downloaded by default:

```
$ gem install builder
Successfully installed builder-2.1.2
1 gem installed
Installing ri documentation for builder-2.1.2...
Installing RDoc documentation for builder-2.1.2...
```

Several things happened here. First, we see that the latest version of the Builder gem (2.1.2) has been installed. Next we see that RubyGems has determined that Jim has created documentation for his gem, so it sets about extracting it using RDoc.

If you're running gem install on a Unix platform and you aren't using rvm, you'll need to prefix the command with sudo, because by default the local gems are installed into shared system directories.

During installation, you can add the -t option to the install command, causing RubyGems to run the gem's test suite (if one has been created). If the tests fail, the installer will prompt you to either keep or discard the gem. This is a good way to gain a little more confidence that the gem you've just downloaded works on your system the way the author intended.

Let's see what gems we now have installed on our local box:

```
$ gem list
*** LOCAL GEMS ***
builder (2.1.2)
```

Reading the Gem Documentation

Being that this is your first time using Builder, you're not exactly sure how to use it. Fortunately, RubyGems installed the documentation for Builder on your machine. We just have to find it.

As with most things in RubyGems, the documentation for each gem is stored in a central, protected, RubyGems-specific place. This will vary by system and by where you may explicitly choose to install your gems. The most reliable way to find the documents is to ask the gem command where your RubyGems main directory is located:

```
$ gem environment gemdir
/usr/local/lib/ruby/gems/1.9.3
```

RubyGems stores generated documentation beneath the doc/ subdirectory of this directory.

The easiest way to view gems' RDoc documentation is to use RubyGems' included gem server utility. To start gem server, simply type this:

```
$ gem server
Server started at http://[::ffff:0.0.0.0]:8808
Server started at http://0.0.0.0:8808
```

gem server starts a web server running on whatever computer you run it on. By default, it will start on port 8808 and will serve gems and their documentation from the default RubyGems installation directory. Both the port and the gem directory are overridable via command-line options, using the -p and -d options, respectively.

Once you've started the gem server, if you are running it on your local computer, you can access the documentation for your installed gems by pointing your web browser to http://localhost:8808. There, you will see a list of the gems you have installed with their descriptions and links to their RDoc documentation. Click the rdoc link for Builder—the result will look something like the following.

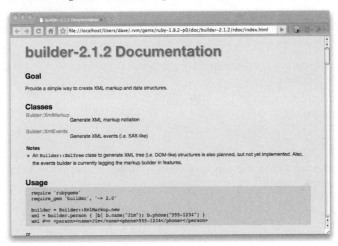

Using a Gem

Once a gem is installed, you use require to load it into your program:[5]

```ruby
require 'builder'

xml = Builder::XmlMarkup.new(target: STDOUT, indent: 2)
xml.person(type: "programmer") do
  xml.name do
    xml.first "Dave"
  end
  xml.location "Texas"
  xml.preference("ruby")
end
```

---

5. Prior to Ruby 1.9, before you could use a gem in your code, you first had to load a support library called rubygems. Ruby now integrates that support directly, so this step is no longer needed.

produces:

```
<person type="programmer">
  <name>
    <first>Dave</first>
  </name>
  <location>Texas</location>
  <preference>ruby</preference>
</person>
```

Gems and Versions

Maybe you first started using Builder a few years ago. Back then the interface was a little bit different—with versions prior to Build 1.0, you could say this:

```
xml = Builder::XmlMarkup.new(STDOUT, 2)
xml.person do
  name("Dave Thomas")
end
```

Note that the constructor takes positional parameters. Also, in the do block, we can say just name(...), whereas the current Builder requires xml.name(...). We could go through our old code and update it all to work with the new-style Builder—that's probably the best long-term solution. But we can also let RubyGems handle the issue for us.

When we asked for a listing of the Builder gems in the repository, we saw that multiple versions were available:[6]

```
$ gem list --details --remote --all builder
*** REMOTE GEMS ***
builder (2.1.2, 2.1.1, 2.0.0, 1.2.4, 1.2.3, 1.2.2, 1.2.1, 1.2.0, 1.1.0, 0.1.1)
```

When we installed Builder previously, we didn't specify a version, so RubyGems automatically installed the latest. But we can also get it to install a specific version or a version meeting some given criteria. Let's install the most recent release of Builder with a version number less than 1:

```
$ gem install builder --version '< 1'
Successfully installed builder-0.1.1
1 gem installed
Installing ri documentation for builder-0.1.1...
Installing RDoc documentation for builder-0.1.1...
```

Have we just overwritten the 2.1.2 release of Builder that we'd previously installed? Let's find out by listing our locally installed gems:

```
$ gem list builder
*** LOCAL GEMS ***
builder (2.1.2, 0.1.1)
```

Now that we have both versions installed locally, how do we tell our legacy code to use the old one while still having our new code use the latest version? It turns out that require automatically loads the latest version of a gem, so the earlier code on page 219 will work fine. If we want to specify a version number when we load a gem, we have to do a little bit more work, making it explicit that we're using RubyGems:

---

6.   By the time this book reaches you, the list of available versions will likely have changed.

```
gem 'builder', '< 1.0'
require 'builder'

xml = Builder::XmlMarkup.new(STDOUT, 2)
xml.person do
  name("Dave Thomas")
  location("Texas")
end
```

The magic is the gem line, which says, "When looking for the Builder gem, consider only those versions less than 1.0." The subsequent require honors this, so the code loads the correct version of Builder and runs. The "< 1.0" part of the gem line is a version predicate. The numbers that follow are of the form major.minor.patch_level. The various predicates that RubyGems supports are:

Operator	Description
=	Exact version match. Major, minor, and patch level must be identical.
!=	Any version that is not the one specified.
>	Any version that is greater (even at the patch level) than the one specified.
<	Any version that is less than the one specified.
>=	Any version greater than or equal to the specified version.
<=	Any version less than or equal to the specified version.
~>	"Boxed" version operator. Version must be greater than or equal to the specified version and less than the specified version after having its minor version number increased by 1. This is to avoid API incompatibilities between minor version releases.

Table 7—Version operators

You can specify multiple version predicates, so the following is valid:

```
gem 'builder', '> 0.1', '< 0.1.5'
```

Unfortunately, after all this work, there's a problem. Older versions of Builder don't run under 1.9 anyway. You can still run this code in Ruby 1.8, but you'd have to update your code to use the new-style Builder if you want to use Ruby 1.9.

Gems Can Be More Than Libraries

As well as installing libraries that can be used inside your application code, RubyGems can also install utility programs that you can invoke from the command line. Often these utilities are wrappers around the libraries included in the gem. For example, Marcel Molina's AWS:S3 gem is a library that gives you programmatic access to Amazon's S3 storage facility. As well as the library itself, Marcel provided a command-line utility, s3sh, which lets you interact with your S3 assets. When you install the gem, s3sh is automatically loaded into the same bin/ directory that holds the Ruby interpreter.

There's a small problem with these installed utilities. Although gems supports versioning of libraries, it does not version command-line utilities. With these, it's "last one in wins."

15.6 The Rake Build Tool

As well as the Builder gem, Jim Weirich wrote an incredibly useful utility program called Rake. Prior to Ruby 1.9, you had to install Rake as a separate gem, but it is now included in the base Ruby installation.

Rake was initially implemented as a Ruby version of Make, the common build utility. However, calling Rake a build utility is to miss its true power. Really, Rake is an automation tool—it's a way of putting all those tasks that you perform in a project into one neat and tidy place.

Let's start with a trivial example. As you edit files, you often accumulate backup files in your working directories. On Unix systems, these files often have the same name as the original files, but with a tilde character appended. On Windows boxes, the files often have a .bak extension.

We could write a trivial Ruby program that deletes these files. For a Unix box, it might look something like this:

```ruby
require 'fileutils'
files = Dir['*~']
FileUtils::rm files, verbose: true
```

The FileUtils module defines methods for manipulating files and directories (see the description in the library section on page 757). Our code uses its rm method. We use the Dir class to return a list of filenames matching the given pattern and pass that list to rm.

Let's package this code as a Rake *task*—a chunk of code that Rake can execute for us.

By default, Rake searches the current directory (and its parents) for a file called Rakefile. This file contains definitions for the tasks that Rake can run.

So, put the following code into a file called Rakefile:

```ruby
desc "Remove files whose names end with a tilde"
task :delete_unix_backups do
  files = Dir['*~']
  rm(files, verbose: true) unless files.empty?
end
```

Although it doesn't have an .rb extension, this is actually just a file of Ruby code. Rake defines an environment containing methods such as desc and task and then executes the Rakefile.

The desc method provides a single line of documentation for the task that follows it. The task method defines a Rake task that can be executed from the command line. The parameter is the name of the task (a symbol), and the block that follows is the code to be executed. Here we can just use rm—all the methods in FileUtils are automatically available inside Rake files.

We can invoke this task from the command line:

```
$ rake delete_unix_backups
(in /Users/dave/BS2/titles/ruby4/Book/code/rake)
rm entry~
```

The first line shows us the name of the directory where Rake found the Rakefile (remember that this might be in a directory above our current working directory). The next line is the output of the rm method, in this case showing it deleted the single file entry~.

OK, now let's write a second task in the same Rakefile. This one deletes Windows backup files.

```ruby
desc "Remove files with a .bak extension"
task :delete_windows_backups do
  files = Dir['*.bak']
  rm(files, verbose: true) unless files.empty?
end
```

We can run this with rake delete_windows_backups.

But let's say that our application could be used on both platforms, and we wanted to let our users delete backup files on either. We *could* write a combined task, but Rake gives us a better way—it lets us *compose* tasks. Here, for example, is a new task:

```ruby
desc "Remove Unix and Windows backup files"
task :delete_backups => [ :delete_unix_backups, :delete_windows_backups ] do
  puts "All backups deleted"
end
```

The task's name is delete_backups, and it depends on two other tasks. This isn't some special Rake syntax: we're simply passing the task method a Ruby hash containing a single entry whose key is the task name and whose value is the list of antecedent tasks. This causes Rake to execute the two platform-specific tasks before executing the delete_backups task:

```
$ rake delete_backups
rm entry~
rm index.bak list.bak
All backups deleted
```

Our current Rakefile contains some duplication between the Unix and Windows deletion tasks. As it is just Ruby code, we can simply define a Ruby method to eliminate this:

```ruby
def delete(pattern)
  files = Dir[pattern]
  rm(files, verbose: true) unless files.empty?
end

desc "Remove files whose names end with a tilde"
task :delete_unix_backups do
  delete "*~"
end

desc "Remove files with a .bak extension"
task :delete_windows_backups do
  delete "*.bak"
end

desc "Remove Unix and Windows backup files"
task :delete_backups => [ :delete_unix_backups, :delete_windows_backups ] do
  puts "All backups deleted"
end
```

If a Rake task is named default, it will be executed if you invoke Rake with no parameters.

You can find the tasks implemented by a Rakefile (or, more accurately, the tasks for which there is a description) using this:

```
$ rake -T
(in /Users/dave/BS2/titles/ruby4/Book/code/rake)
rake delete_backups          # Remove Unix and Windows backup files
rake delete_unix_backups     # Remove files whose names end with a tilde
rake delete_windows_backups  # Remove files with a .bak extension
```

This section only touches on the full power of Rake. It can handle dependencies between files (for example, rebuilding an executable file if one of the source files has changed), it knows about running tests and generating documentation, and it can even package gems for you. Martin Fowler has written a good overview of Rake if you're interested in digging deeper.[7] You might also want to investigate Sake,[8] a tool that makes Rake tasks available no matter what directory you're in, or Thor,[9] a tool that makes it easy to write Ruby command-line tools.

15.7 Build Environment

When Ruby is compiled for a particular architecture, all the relevant settings used to build it (including the architecture of the machine on which it was compiled, compiler options, source code directory, and so on) are written to the module RbConfig within the library file rbconfig.rb. After installation, any Ruby program can use this module to get details on how Ruby was compiled:

```
require 'rbconfig'
include RbConfig
CONFIG["host"]   # => "x86_64-apple-darwin12.2.0"
CONFIG["libdir"] # => "/Users/dave/.rvm/rubies/ruby-2.0.0-p0/lib"
```

Extension libraries use this configuration file in order to compile and link properly on any given architecture. If you visit the online page for the previous edition of this book at http://pragprog.com/titles/ruby3 and select the *Contents/Extracts* tab, you can download a free chapter on writing extension libraries.

---

7. http://martinfowler.com/articles/rake.html
8. http://errtheblog.com/posts/60-sake-bomb
9. http://github.com/wycats/thor

## CHAPTER 16

Namespaces, Source Files, and Distribution

As your programs grow (and they all seem to grow over time), you'll find that you'll need to start organizing your code—simply putting everything into a single huge file becomes unworkable (and makes it hard to reuse chunks of code in other projects). So, we need to find a way to split our project into multiple files and then to knit those files together as our program runs.

There are two major aspects to this organization. The first is internal to your code: how do you prevent different things with the same name from clashing? The second area is related: how do you conveniently organize the source files in your project?

16.1 Namespaces

We've already encountered a way that Ruby helps you manage the names of things in your programs. If you define methods or constants in a class, Ruby ensures that their names can be used only in the context of that class (or its objects, in the case of instance methods):

```ruby
class Triangle
  SIDES = 3
  def area
    # ..
  end
end

class Square
  SIDES = 4
  def initialize(side_length)
    @side_length = side_length
  end
  def area
    @side_length * @side_length
  end
end

puts "A triangle has #{Triangle::SIDES} sides"

sq = Square.new(3)
puts "Area of square = #{sq.area}"
```

produces:

```
A triangle has 3 sides
Area of square = 9
```

Both classes define a constant called SIDES and an instance method area, but these things don't get confused. You access the instance method via objects created from the class, and you access the constant by prefixing it with the name of the class followed by a double colon. The double colon (::) is Ruby's namespace resolution operator. The thing to the left must be a class or module, and the thing to the right is a constant defined in that class or module.[1]

So, putting code inside a module or class is a good way of separating it from other code. Ruby's Math module is a good example—it defines constants such as Math::PI and Math::E and methods such as Math.sin and Math.cos. You can access these constants and methods via the Math module object:

```
Math::E              # => 2.718281828459045
Math.sin(Math::PI/6.0) # => 0.49999999999999994
```

(Modules have another significant use—they implement Ruby's *mixin* functionality, which we discussed Section 5.3, *Mixins*, on page 75.)

Ruby has an interesting little secret. The names of classes and modules are themselves just constants.[2] And that means that if you define classes or modules inside other classes and modules, the names of those inner classes are just contants that follow the same namespacing rules as other constants:

```
module Formatters
  class Html
    # ...
  end
  class Pdf
    # ...
  end
end

html_writer = Formatters::Html.new
```

You can nest classes and modules inside other classes and modules to any depth you want (although it's rare to see them more than three deep).

So, now we know that we can use classes and modules to partition the names used by our programs. The second question to answer is, what do we do with the source code?

16.2 Organizing Your Source

This section covers two related issues: how do we split our source code into separate files, and where in the file system do we put those files?

Some languages, such as Java, make this easy. They dictate that each outer-level class should be in its own file and that file should be named according to the name of the class. Other

---

1. The thing to the right of the :: can also be a class or module method, but this use is falling out of favor —using a period makes it clearer that it's just a regular old method call.
2. Remember that we said that most everything in Ruby is an object. Well, classes and modules are, too. The name that you use for a class, such as String, is really just a Ruby constant containing the object representing that class.

languages, such as Ruby, have no rules relating source files and their content. In Ruby, you're free to organize your code as you like.

But, in the real world, you'll find that some kind of consistency really helps. It will make it easier for you to navigate your own projects, and it will also help when you read (or incorporate) other people's code.

So, the Ruby community is gradually adopting a kind of de facto standard. In many ways, it follows the spirit of the Java model, but without some of the inconveniences suffered by our Java brethren. Let's start with the basics.

Small Programs

Small, self-contained scripts can be in a single file. However, if you do this, you won't easily be able to write automated tests for your program, because the test code won't be able to load the file containing your source without the program itself running. So, if you want to write a small program that also has automated tests, split that program into a trivial driver that provides the external interface (the command-line part of the code) and one or more files containing the rest. Your tests can then exercise these separate files without actually running the main body of your program.

Let's try this for real. Here's a simple program that finds anagrams in a dictionary. Feed it one or more words, and it gives you the anagrams of each. Here's an example:

```
$  ruby anagram.rb teaching code
Anagrams of teaching: cheating, teaching
Anagrams of code: code, coed
```

If we were typing in this program for casual use, we might just enter it into a single file (perhaps anagram.rb). It would look something like this:[3]

packaging/anagram.rb
```
#!/usr/bin/env ruby

require 'optparse'

dictionary = "/usr/share/dict/words"

OptionParser.new do |opts|

  opts.banner = "Usage:  anagram [ options ]  word..."

  opts.on("-d", "--dict path", String, "Path to dictionary") do |dict|
    dictionary = dict
  end

  opts.on("-h", "--help", "Show this message") do
    puts opts
    exit
  end
```

---

3. You might be wondering about the line word.unpack("c*").sort.pack("c*"). This uses the function unpack to break a string into an array of characters, which are then sorted and packed back into a string.

```
  begin
    ARGV << "-h" if ARGV.empty?
    opts.parse!(ARGV)
  rescue OptionParser::ParseError => e
    STDERR.puts e.message, "\n", opts
    exit(-1)
  end
end

# convert "wombat" into "abmotw". All anagrams share a signature
def signature_of(word)
  word.unpack("c*").sort.pack("c*")
end

signatures = Hash.new

File.foreach(dictionary) do |line|
  word = line.chomp
  signature = signature_of(word)
  (signatures[signature] ||= []) << word
end

ARGV.each do |word|
  signature = signature_of(word)
  if signatures[signature]
    puts "Anagrams of #{word}: #{signatures[signature].join(', ')}"
  else
    puts "No anagrams of #{word} in #{dictionary}"
  end
end
```

Then someone asks us for a copy, and we start to feel embarrassed. It has no tests, and it isn't particularly well packaged.

Looking at the code, there are clearly three sections. The first twenty-five or so lines do option parsing, the next ten or so lines read and convert the dictionary, and the last few lines look up each command-line argument and report the result. Let's split our file into four parts:

- An option parser
- A class to hold the lookup table for anagrams
- A class that looks up words given on the command line
- A trivial command-line interface

The first three of these are effectively library files, used by the fourth.

Where do we put all these files? The answer is driven by some strong Ruby conventions, first seen in Minero Aoki's setup.rb and later enshrined in the RubyGems system. We'll create a directory for our project containing (for now) three subdirectories:

```
anagram/        <- top-level
    bin/        <- command-line interface goes here
    lib/        <- three library files go here
    test/       <- test files go here
```

Now let's look at the library files. We know we're going to be defining (at least) three classes. Right now, these classes will be used only inside our command-line program, but it's conceivable that other people might want to include one or more of our libraries in their own code. This means that we should be polite and not pollute the top-level Ruby namespace with the names of all our classes and so on. We'll create just one top-level module, Anagram, and then place all our classes inside this module. This means that the full name of (say) our options-parsing class will be Anagram::Options.

This choice informs our decision on where to put the corresponding source files. Because class Options is inside the module Anagram, it makes sense to put the corresponding file, options.rb, inside a directory named anagram/ in the lib/ directory. This helps people who read your code in the future; when they see a name like A::B::C, they know to look for c.rb in the b/ directory in the a/ directory of your library. So, we can now flesh out our directory structure with some files:

```
anagram/
    bin/
        anagram        <- command-line interface
    lib/
        anagram/
            finder.rb
            options.rb
            runner.rb
    test/
        ... various test files
```

Let's start with the option parser. Its job is to take an array of command-line options and return to us the path to the dictionary file and the list of words to look up as anagrams. The source, in lib/anagram/options.rb, looks like this: Notice how we define the Options class inside a top-level Anagram module.

packaging/anagram/lib/anagram/options.rb
```ruby
require 'optparse'

module Anagram
  class Options
    DEFAULT_DICTIONARY = "/usr/share/dict/words"
    attr_reader :dictionary, :words_to_find

    def initialize(argv)
      @dictionary = DEFAULT_DICTIONARY
      parse(argv)
      @words_to_find = argv
    end

  private

    def parse(argv)
      OptionParser.new do |opts|
        opts.banner = "Usage:  anagram [ options ]  word..."

        opts.on("-d", "--dict path", String, "Path to dictionary") do |dict|
          @dictionary = dict
        end
```

```
        opts.on("-h", "--help", "Show this message") do
          puts opts
          exit
        end

        begin
          argv = ["-h"] if argv.empty?
          opts.parse!(argv)
        rescue OptionParser::ParseError => e
          STDERR.puts e.message, "\n", opts
          exit(-1)
        end
      end
    end
  end
end
```

Let's write some unit tests. This should be fairly easy, because options.rb is self-contained—the only dependency is to the standard Ruby OptionParser. We'll use the Test::Unit framework, extended with the Shoulda gem.[4] We'll put the source of this test in the file test/test_options.rb:

packaging/anagram/test/test_options.rb

```
require 'test/unit'
require 'shoulda'
require_relative '../lib/anagram/options'

class TestOptions < Test::Unit::TestCase

  context "specifying no dictionary" do
    should "return default" do
      opts = Anagram::Options.new(["someword"])
      assert_equal Anagram::Options::DEFAULT_DICTIONARY, opts.dictionary
    end
  end

  context "specifying a dictionary" do
    should "return it" do
      opts = Anagram::Options.new(["-d", "mydict", "someword"])
      assert_equal "mydict", opts.dictionary
    end
  end

  context "specifying words and no dictionary" do
    should "return the words" do
      opts = Anagram::Options.new(["word1", "word2"])
      assert_equal ["word1", "word2"], opts.words_to_find
    end
  end

  context "specifying words and a dictionary" do
    should "return the words" do
      opts = Anagram::Options.new(["-d", "mydict", "word1", "word2"])
```

---

4.   We talk about Shoulda in the Unit Testing chapter on page 186.

```
    assert_equal ["word1", "word2"], opts.words_to_find
  end
 end
end
```

The line to note in this file is as follows:

```
require_relative '../lib/anagram/options'
```

This is where we load the source of the Options class we just wrote. We use require_relative, as it always loads from a path relative to the directory of the file that invokes it.

```
$ ruby test/test_options.rb
Run options:
# Running tests:
....
Finished tests in 0.010588s, 377.7862 tests/s, 377.7862 assertions/s.
4 tests, 4 assertions, 0 failures, 0 errors, 0 skips
ruby -v: ruby 2.0.0p0 (2013-02-24 revision 39474) [x86_64-darwin12.2.0]
```

The finder code (in lib/anagram/finder.rb) is modified slightly from the original version. To make it easier to test, we'll have the default constructor take a list of words, rather than a filename. We'll then provide an additional factory method, from_file, that takes a filename and constructs a new Finder from that file's contents:

packaging/anagram/lib/anagram/finder.rb

```ruby
module Anagram
  class Finder

    def self.from_file(file_name)
      new(File.readlines(file_name))
    end

    def initialize(dictionary_words)
      @signatures = Hash.new
      dictionary_words.each do |line|
        word = line.chomp
        signature = Finder.signature_of(word)
        (@signatures[signature] ||= []) << word
      end
    end

    def lookup(word)
      signature = Finder.signature_of(word)
      @signatures[signature]
    end

    def self.signature_of(word)
      word.unpack("c*").sort.pack("c*")
    end
  end
end
```

Again, we embed the Finder class inside the top-level Anagram module. And, again, this code is self-contained, allowing us to write some simple unit tests:

packaging/anagram/test/test_finder.rb

```ruby
require 'test/unit'
require 'shoulda'
require_relative '../lib/anagram/finder'

class TestFinder < Test::Unit::TestCase

  context "signature" do
    { "cat" => "act", "act" => "act", "wombat" => "abmotw" }.each do
      |word, signature|
        should "be #{signature} for #{word}" do
          assert_equal signature, Anagram::Finder.signature_of(word)
      end
    end
  end

  context "lookup" do
    setup do
      @finder = Anagram::Finder.new(["cat", "wombat"])
    end

    should "return word if word given" do
      assert_equal ["cat"], @finder.lookup("cat")
    end

    should "return word if anagram given" do
      assert_equal ["cat"], @finder.lookup("act")
      assert_equal ["cat"], @finder.lookup("tca")
    end

    should "return nil if no word matches anagram" do
      assert_nil @finder.lookup("wibble")
    end
  end

end
```

These go in test/test_finder.rb:

```
$ ruby test/test_finder.rb
Run options:
# Running tests:
......
Finished tests in 0.009453s, 634.7191 tests/s, 740.5057 assertions/s.
6 tests, 7 assertions, 0 failures, 0 errors, 0 skips
ruby -v: ruby 2.0.0p0 (2013-02-24 revision 39474) [x86_64-darwin12.2.0]
```

We now have all the support code in place. We just need to run it. We'll make the command-line interface—the thing the end user actually executes—really thin. It's in the bin/ directory in a file called anagram (no .rb extension, because that would be unusual in a command).[5]

---

5. If you're on Windows, you might want to wrap the invocation of this in a .cmd file.

packaging/anagram/bin/anagram

```
#! /usr/local/rubybook/bin/ruby
require 'anagram/runner'

runner = Anagram::Runner.new(ARGV)
runner.run
```

The code that this script invokes (lib/anagram/runner.rb) knits our other libraries together:

packaging/anagram/lib/anagram/runner.rb

```
require_relative 'finder'
require_relative 'options'

module Anagram
  class Runner
    def initialize(argv)
      @options = Options.new(argv)
    end

    def run
      finder = Finder.from_file(@options.dictionary)
      @options.words_to_find.each do |word|
        anagrams = finder.lookup(word)
        if anagrams
          puts "Anagrams of #{word}: #{anagrams.join(', ')}"
        else
          puts "No anagrams of #{word} in #{@options.dictionary}"
        end
      end
    end
  end
end
```

In this case, the two libraries finder and options are in the same directory as the runner, so require_relative finds them perfectly.

Now that all our files are in place, we can run our program from the command line:

```
$ ruby -I lib bin/anagram teaching code
Anagrams of teaching: cheating, teaching
Anagrams of code: code, coed
```

There's nothing like a cheating coed teaching code.

16.3 Distributing and Installing Your Code

Now that we have our code a little tidier, it would be nice to be able to distribute it to others. We could just zip or tar it up and send them our files, but then they'd have to run the code the way we do, remembering to add the correct -I lib options and so on. They'd also have some problems if they wanted to reuse one of our library files—it would be sitting in some random directory on their hard drive, not in a standard location used by Ruby. Instead, we're looking for a way to take our little application and *install* it in a standard way.

Now, Ruby already has a standard installation structure on your computer. When Ruby is installed, it puts its commands (ruby, ri, irb, and so on) into a directory of binary files. It puts its libraries into another directory tree and documentation somewhere else. So, one option would be to write an installation script that you distribute with your code that copies components of your application to the appropriate directories on the system that's installing it.

Being a Good Packaging Citizen

So, I've ignored some stuff that you'd want to do before distributing your code to the world. Your distributed directory tree really should have a README file, outlining what it does and probably containing a copyright statement; an INSTALL file, giving installation instructions; and a LICENSE file, giving the license it is distributed under.

You'll probably want to distribute some documentation, too. This would go in a directory called doc/, parallel with the bin and lib directories.

You might also want to distribute native C-language extensions with your library. These extensions would go into your project's ext/ directory.

Using RubyGems

The RubyGems package management system (which is also just called *Gems*) has become the standard for distributing and managing Ruby code packages. As of Ruby 1.9, it comes bundled with Ruby itself.[6]

RubyGems is also a great way to package your own code. If you want to make your code available to the world, RubyGems is the way to go. Even if you're just sending code to a few friends or within your company, RubyGems gives you dependency and installation management—one day you'll be grateful for that.

RubyGems needs to know information about your project that isn't contained in the directory structure. Instead, you have to write a short RubyGems specification: a GemSpec. Create this in a separate file named project-name.gemspec in the top-level directory of your application (in our case, the file is anagram.gemspec):

packaging/anagram/anagram.gemspec
```
Gem::Specification.new do |s|
  s.name        = "anagram"
  s.summary     = "Find anagrams of words supplied on the command line"
  s.description = File.read(File.join(File.dirname(__FILE__), 'README'))
  s.requirements =
      [ 'An installed dictionary (most Unix systems have one)' ]
  s.version     = "0.0.1"
  s.author      = "Dave Thomas"
  s.email       = "dave@pragprog.com"
  s.homepage    = "http://pragdave.pragprog.com"
  s.platform    = Gem::Platform::RUBY
  s.required_ruby_version = '>=1.9'
  s.files       = Dir['**/**']
  s.executables = [ 'anagram' ]
  s.test_files  = Dir["test/test*.rb"]
  s.has_rdoc    = false
end
```

---

6. Prior to RubyGems, folks often distributed a tool called setup.rb with their libraries. This would install the library into the standard Ruby directory structure on a user's machine.

The first line of the spec gives our gem a name. This is important—it will be used as part of the package name, and it will appear as the name of the gem when installed. Although it can be mixed case, we find that confusing, so do our poor brains a favor and use lowercase for gem names.

The version string is significant, because RubyGems will use it both for package naming and for dependency management. Stick to the *x.y.z* format.[7]

The platform field tells RubyGems that (in this case) our gem is pure Ruby code. It's also possible to package (for example) Windows .exe files inside a gem, in which case you'd use Gem::Platform::Win32.

The next line is also important (and oft-forgotten by package developers). Because we use require_relative, our gem will run only with Ruby 1.9 and newer.

We then tell RubyGems which files to include when creating the gem package. Here we've been lazy and included everything. You can be more specific.

The s.executables line tells RubyGems to install the anagram command-line script when the gem gets installed on a user's machine.

To save space, we haven't added RDoc documentation comments to our source files (RDoc is described in Chapter 19, *Documenting Ruby*, on page 263). The last line of the spec tells RubyGems not to try to extract documentation when the gem is installed.

Obviously I've skipped a lot of details here. A full description of GemSpecs is available online,[8] along with other documents on RubyGems.[9]

Packaging Your RubyGem

Once the gem specification is complete, you'll want to create the packaged .gem file for distribution. This is as easy as navigating to the top level of your project and typing this:

```
$ gem build anagram.gemspec
WARNING:  no rubyforge_project specified
  Successfully built RubyGem
  Name: anagram
  Version: 0.0.1
  File: anagram-0.0.1.gem
```

You'll find you now have a file called anagram-0.0.1.gem.

```
$ ls *gem
anagram-0.0.1.gem
```

You can install it:

```
$ sudo gem install pkg/anagram-0.0.1.gem
Successfully installed anagram-0.0.1
1 gem installed
```

---

7. And read http://www.rubygems.org/read/chapter/7 for information on what the numbers mean.
8. http://www.rubygems.org/read/book/4
9. http://www.rubygems.org/

And check to see that it is there:

```
$ gem list anagram -d
*** LOCAL GEMS ***
anagram (0.0.1)
    Author: Dave Thomas
    Homepage: http://pragdave.pragprog.com
    Installed at: /usr/local/lib/ruby/gems/1.9.0

    Find anagrams of words supplied on the command line
```

Now you can send your .gem file to friends and colleagues or share it from a server. Or, you could go one better and share it from a RubyGems server.

If you have RubyGems installed on your local box, you can share them over the network to others. Simply run this:

```
$ gem server
Server started at http://[::ffff:0.0.0.0]:8808
Server started at http://0.0.0.0:8808
```

This starts a server (by default on port 8808, but the --port option overrides that). Other people can connect to your server to list and retrieve RubyGems:

```
$ gem list --remote --source http://dave.local:8808
*** REMOTE GEMS ***
anagram (0.0.1)
builder (2.1.2, 0.1.1)
..
```

This is particularly useful in a corporate environment.

You can speed up the serving of gems by creating a static index—see the help for gem generate_index for details.

Serving Public RubyGems

RubyGems.org (http://rubygems.org) has become the main repository for public Ruby libraries and projects. And, if you create a RubyGems.org account, you can push your .gem file to their public servers.

```
$ gem push anagram-0.0.1.gem
Enter your RubyGems.org credentials.
Email:   dave@pragprog.com
Password:
Pushing gem to RubyGems.org...
Successfully registered gem: anagram (0.0.1)
```

And, at that point, any Ruby user in the world can do this:

```
$ gem search -r anagram
*** REMOTE GEMS ***
anagram (0.0.1)
```

and, even better, can do this:

```
$ gem install anagram
```

Adding Even More Automation

The Jeweler library[10] can create a new project skeleton that follows the layout guidelines in this chapter. It also provides a set of Rake tasks that will help create and manage your project as a gem.

If you're a Rails user, you'll have come across bundler, a utility that manages the gems used by your application. Bundler is more general than this: it can be used to manage the gems used by any piece of Ruby code.

Some folks like the extra features of these utilities, while others prefer the leaner "roll-your-own" approach. Whatever route you take, taking the time to package your applications and libraries will pay you back many times over.

See You on GitHub

Finally, if you're developing a Ruby application or library that you'll be sharing, you'll probably want to store it on GitHub.[11] Although it started as a public Git repository, GitHub is now a community in its own right. It's a home away from home for many in the Ruby community.

---

10. http://github.com/technicalpickles/jeweler
11. http://github.com

## CHAPTER 17

Character Encoding

Prior to Ruby 1.9, Ruby programs were basically written using the ASCII character encoding. You could always override this with the -K command-line option, but this led to inconsistencies when manipulating strings and doing file I/O.

Ruby 1.9 changed all this. Ruby now supports the idea of character encodings. And, what's more, these encodings can be applied relatively independently to your program source files, to objects in your running programs, and to the interpretation of I/O streams.

Before delving into the details, let's spend a few minutes thinking about why we need to separate the encodings of source files, variables, and I/O streams. Let's imagine Yui is a developer in Japan who wants to code in her native language. Her editor lets her write code using Shift JIS (SJIS), a Japanese character encoding, so she writes her variable names using katakana and kanji characters. But, by default, Ruby assumes that source files are written in ASCII, and the SJIS characters would not be recognized as such. However, by setting the encoding to be used when compiling the source file, Ruby can now parse her program.

She converts her program into a gem, and users around the world try it. Dan, in the United States, doesn't read Japanese, so the content of her source files makes no sense to him. However, because the source files carry their encoding around with them, there's no problem; his Ruby happily compiles her code. But Dan wants to test her code against a file that contains regular old ASCII characters. That's no problem, because the file encoding is determined by Dan's locale, not by the encoding of the Ruby source. Similarly, Sophie in Paris uses the same gem, but her data is encoded in ISO-8859-1 (which is basically ASCII plus a useful subset of accented European characters in character positions above 127). Again, no problem.

Back in Japan, Yui has a new feature to add to her library. Users want to create short PDF summaries of the data she reads, but the PDF-writing library she's using supports only ISO-8859-1 characters. So, regardless of the encoding of the source code of her program and the files she reads, she needs to be able to create 8859-1 strings at runtime. Again, we need to be able to decouple the encoding of individual objects from the encoding of everything else.

If this sounds complex, well...it is. But the good news is that the Ruby team spent a long time thinking up ways to make it all relatively easy to use when you're writing code. In this section, we'll look at how to work with the various encodings, and I'll try to list some conventions that will make your code work in the brave new multinational world.

17.1 Encodings

At the heart of the Ruby encoding system is the new Encoding class.[1] Objects of class Encoding each represent a different character encoding. The Encoding.list method returns a list of the built-in encodings, and the Encoding.aliases method returns a hash where the keys are aliases and the values are the corresponding base encoding. We can use these two methods to build a table of known encoding names:

```
encoding/list_encodings.rb
encodings = Encoding
            .list
            .each.with_object({}) do |enc, full_list|
                full_list[enc.name] = [enc.name]
            end

Encoding.aliases.each do |alias_name, base_name|
  fail "#{base_name} #{alias_name}" unless encodings[base_name]
  encodings[base_name] << alias_name
end

puts(encodings
       .values
       .sort_by {|base_name, *| base_name.downcase}
       .map do |base_name, *rest|
         if rest.empty?
           base_name
         else
           "#{base_name} (#{rest.join(', ')})"
         end
       end)
```

Table 8, *Encodings and their aliases,* on page 241 shows the output, wrapped into columns.

However, that's not the full story. Encodings in Ruby can be dynamically loaded—Ruby actually comes with more encodings than those shown in the output from this code.

Strings, regular expressions, symbols, I/O streams, and program source files are all associated with one of these encoding objects.

Encodings commonly used in Ruby programs include ASCII (7-bit characters), ASCII-8BIT,[2] UTF-8, and Shift JIS.

17.2 Source Files

First and foremost, there's a simple rule: if you only ever use 7-bit ASCII characters in your source, then the source file encoding is irrelevant. So, the simplest way to write Ruby source files that just work everywhere is to stick to boring old ASCII.

---

1. For a nice, easy read on encodings, charcter sets, and Unicode, you could take a look at Joel Spolsky's 2003 article on the Web at http://www.joelonsoftware.com/articles/Unicode.html.
2. There isn't actually a character encoding called ASCII-8BIT. It's a Ruby fantasy but a useful one. We'll talk about it shortly.

ASCII-8BIT (BINARY)	Big5	Big5-HKSCS (Big5-HKSCS:2008)
Big5-UAO	CP50220	CP50221
CP51932	CP850 (IBM850)	CP852
CP855	CP949	CP950
CP951	Emacs-Mule	EUC-JP (eucJP)
EUC-JP-2004 (EUC-JISX0213)	EUC-KR (eucKR)	EUC-TW (eucTW)
eucJP-ms (euc-jp-ms)	GB12345	GB18030
GB1988	GB2312 (EUC-CN, eucCN)	GBK (CP936)
IBM437 (CP437)	IBM737 (CP737)	IBM775 (CP775)
IBM852	IBM855	IBM857 (CP857)
IBM860 (CP860)	IBM861 (CP861)	IBM862 (CP862)
IBM863 (CP863)	IBM864 (CP864)	IBM865 (CP865)
IBM866 (CP866)	IBM869 (CP869)	ISO-2022-JP (ISO2022-JP)
ISO-2022-JP-2 (ISO2022-JP2)	ISO-2022-JP-KDDI	ISO-8859-1 (ISO8859-1)
ISO-8859-10 (ISO8859-10)	ISO-8859-11 (ISO8859-11)	ISO-8859-13 (ISO8859-13)
ISO-8859-14 (ISO8859-14)	ISO-8859-15 (ISO8859-15)	ISO-8859-16 (ISO8859-16)
ISO-8859-2 (ISO8859-2)	ISO-8859-3 (ISO8859-3)	ISO-8859-4 (ISO8859-4)
ISO-8859-5 (ISO8859-5)	ISO-8859-6 (ISO8859-6)	ISO-8859-7 (ISO8859-7)
ISO-8859-8 (ISO8859-8)	ISO-8859-9 (ISO8859-9)	KOI8-R (CP878)
KOI8-U	macCentEuro	macCroatian
macCyrillic	macGreek	macIceland
MacJapanese (MacJapan)	macRoman	macRomania
macThai	macTurkish	macUkraine
Shift_JIS	SJIS-DoCoMo	SJIS-KDDI
SJIS-SoftBank	stateless-ISO-2022-JP	stateless-ISO-2022-JP-KDDI
TIS-620	US-ASCII (ASCII, ANSI_X3.4-1968, 646)	UTF-16
UTF-16BE (UCS-2BE)	UTF-16LE	UTF-32
UTF-32BE (UCS-4BE)	UTF-32LE (UCS-4LE)	UTF-7 (CP65000)
UTF-8 (CP65001)	UTF8-DoCoMo	UTF8-KDDI
UTF8-MAC (UTF-8-MAC, UTF-8-HFS)	UTF8-SoftBank	Windows-1250 (CP1250)
Windows-1251 (CP1251)	Windows-1252 (CP1252)	Windows-1253 (CP1253)
Windows-1254 (CP1254)	Windows-1255 (CP1255)	Windows-1256 (CP1256)
Windows-1257 (CP1257)	Windows-1258 (CP1258)	Windows-31J (CP932, csWindows31J, SJIS, PCK)
Windows-874 (CP874)		

Table 8—Encodings and their aliases

However, once a source file contains a byte whose top bit is set, you've just left the comfortable world of ASCII and entered the wild and wacky nightmare of character encodings. Here's how it works.

If your source files are not written using 7-bit ASCII, you probably want to tell Ruby about it. Because the encoding is an attribute of the source file, and not anything to do with the environment where the file is used, Ruby has a way of setting the encoding on a file-by-file basis using a new *magic comment*. If the first line of a file[3] is a comment (or the second line if the first line is a #! shebang line), Ruby scans it looking for the string coding:. If it finds it, Ruby then skips any spaces and looks for the (case-insensitive) name of an encoding. Thus, to specify that a source file is in UTF-8 encoding, you can write this:

```
# coding: utf-8
```

As Ruby is just scanning for coding:, you could also write the following.

---

3.   Or a string passed to eval

```
# encoding: ascii
```

Emacs users might like the fact that this also works:

```
# -*- encoding: shift_jis -*-
```

(Your favorite editor may also support some kind of flag comment to set a file's encoding.)

If there's a shebang line, the encoding comment must be the second line of the file:

```
#!/usr/local/rubybook/bin/ruby
# encoding: utf-8
```

Additionally, Ruby detects any files that start with a UTF-8 byte order mark (BOM). If Ruby sees the byte sequence \xEF\xBB\xBF at the start of a source file, it assumes that file is UTF-8 encoded.

The special constant __ENCODING__ returns the encoding of the current source file.

Ruby 1.9 vs. Ruby 2.0

New in 2.0

In Ruby 1.9, the default source file encoding is US-ASCII. If your source files contain any characters with byte value greater than 127, you'll need to tell Ruby the encoding of the file, or Ruby will report an error, probably saying something like "invalid multibyte char." Here's an example where we typed some UTF-8 characters into a Ruby program:

```
π = 3.14159
puts "π = #{π}"
```

With Ruby 1.9, you'll get an error unless you add the encoding: utf-8 comment at the top.

In Ruby 2.0, however, the default source file encoding is UTF-8, and the previous program will run as it stands.

We can verify that Ruby correctly interprets π as a single character.

```
# encoding: utf-8
PI = "π"
puts "The size of a string containing π is #{PI.size}"
```

produces:

```
The size of a string containing π is 1
```

Now, let's get perverse. The two-byte sequence \xcf\x80 represents π in UTF-8 but is not a valid byte sequence in the SJIS encoding. Let's see what happens if we tell Ruby that this same source file is SJIS encoded. (Remember, when we do this, we're not changing the actual bytes in the string—we're just telling Ruby to interpret them with a different set of encoding rules.)

```
# encoding: sjis
PI = "π"
puts "The size of a string containing π is #{PI.size}"
```

produces:

```
puts "The size of a string containing π is #{PI.size}"
         ^
prog.rb:2: invalid multibyte char (Windows-31J)
prog.rb:3: syntax error, unexpected tCONSTANT, expecting end-of-input
```

This time, Ruby complains because the file contains byte sequences that are illegal in the given encoding. And, to make matters even more confusing, the parser swallowed up the double quote after the π character, presumably while trying to build a valid SJIS character. This led to the second error message, because the word The is now interpreted as program text.

Source Elements That Have Encodings

String literals are always encoded using the encoding of the source file that contains them, regardless of the content of the string:

```
# encoding: utf-8
def show_encoding(str)
  puts "'#{str}' (size #{str.size}) is #{str.encoding.name}"
end
show_encoding "cat"     # latin 'c', 'a', 't'
show_encoding "∂og"     # greek delta, latin 'o', 'g'
```

produces:

```
'cat' (size 3) is UTF-8
'∂og' (size 3) is UTF-8
```

Symbols and regular expression literals that contain only 7-bit characters are encoded using US-ASCII. Otherwise, they will have the encoding of the file that contains them.

```
# encoding: utf-8
def show_encoding(str)
  puts "#{str.inspect} is #{str.encoding.name}"
end
show_encoding :cat
show_encoding :∂og

show_encoding /cat/
show_encoding /∂og/
```

produces:

```
:cat is US-ASCII
:∂og is UTF-8
/cat/ is US-ASCII
/∂og/ is UTF-8
```

You can create arbitrary Unicode characters in strings and regular expressions using the \u escape. This has two forms: \uxxxx lets you encode a character using four hex digits, and the delimited form \u{x... x... x...} lets you specify a variable number of characters, each with a variable number of hex digits:

```
# encoding: utf-8
"Greek pi: \u03c0"           # => "Greek pi: π"
"Greek pi: \u{3c0}"          # => "Greek pi: π"
"Greek \u{70 69 3a 20 3c0}"  # => "Greek pi: π"
```

Literals containing a \u sequence will always be encoded UTF-8, regardless of the source file encoding.

The String#bytes method is a convenient way to inspect the bytes in a string object. Notice that in the following code, the 16-bit codepoint is converted to a two-byte UTF-8 encoding:

```
# encoding: utf-8
"pi: \u03c0".bytes  # => [112, 105, 58, 32, 207, 128]
```

Eight-Bit Clean Encodings

Ruby supports a virtual encoding called ASCII-8BIT. Despite the *ASCII* in the name, this is really intended to be used on data streams that contain binary data (which is why it has an alias of BINARY}). However, you can also use this as an encoding for source files. If you do, Ruby interprets all characters with codes below 128 as regular ASCII and all other characters as valid constituents of variable names. This is basically a neat hack, because it allows you to compile a file written in an encoding you don't know—the characters with the high-order bit set will be assumed to be printable.

```
# encoding: ascii-8bit
π = 3.14159
puts "π = #{π}"
puts "Size of 'π' = #{'π'.size}"
```

produces:

```
π = 3.14159
Size of 'π' = 2
```

The last line of output illustrates why ASCII-8BIT is a dangerous encoding for source files. Because it doesn't know to use UTF-8 encoding, the π character looks to Ruby like two separate characters.

Source Encoding Is Per-File

Clearly, a large application will be built from many source files. Some of these files may come from other people (possibly as libraries or gems). In these cases, you may not have control over the encoding used in a file.

Ruby supports this by allowing different encodings in the files that make up a project. Each file starts with the default encoding of US-ASCII. The file's encoding may then be set with either a coding: comment or a UTF-8 BOM.

Here's a file called iso-8859-1.rb. Notice the explicit encoding.

encoding/iso-8859-1.rb
```
# -*- encoding: iso-8859-1 -*-

STRING_ISO = "ol\351"    #  \x6f \x6c \xe9
```

And here's its UTF-8 counterpart:

encoding/utf.rb
```
# file: utf.rb, encoding: utf-8

STRING_U = "∂og"    #  \xe2\x88\x82\x6f\x67
```

Now let's require both of these files into a third file. Just for the heck of it, let's declare the third file to have SJIS encoding:

```
# encoding: sjis

require_relative 'iso-8859-1'
require_relative 'utf'
```

```
def show_encoding(str)
  puts "'#{str.bytes.to_a}' (#{str.size} chars, #{str.bytesize} bytes) " +
       "has encoding #{str.encoding.name}"
end

show_encoding(STRING_ISO)
show_encoding(STRING_U)
show_encoding("cat")
```

produces:

```
'[111, 108, 233]' (3 chars, 3 bytes) has encoding ISO-8859-1
'[226, 136, 130, 111, 103]' (3 chars, 5 bytes) has encoding UTF-8
'[99, 97, 116]' (3 chars, 3 bytes) has encoding Windows-31J
```

Each file has an independent encoding, and string literals in each retain their own encoding, even when used in a different file. All the encoding directive does is tell Ruby how to interpret the characters in the file and what encoding to use on literal strings and regular expressions. Ruby will never change the actual bytes in a source file when reading them in.

17.3 Transcoding

As we've already seen, strings, symbols, and regular expressions are now labeled with their encoding. You can convert a string from one encoding to another using the String#encode method. For example, we can convert the word *olé* from UTF-8 to ISO-8859-1:

```
# encoding: utf-8
ole_in_utf = "olé"
ole_in_utf.encoding     # => #<Encoding:UTF-8>
ole_in_utf.bytes.to_a   # => [111, 108, 195, 169]

ole_in_8859 = ole_in_utf.encode("iso-8859-1")
ole_in_8859.encoding    # => #<Encoding:ISO-8859-1>
ole_in_8859.bytes.to_a  # => [111, 108, 233]
```

You have to be careful when using encode—if the target encoding doesn't contain characters that appear in your source string, Ruby will throw an exception. For example, the π character is available in UTF-8 but not in ISO-8859-1:

```
# encoding: utf-8
pi = "pi = π"
pi.encode("iso-8859-1")
```

produces:

```
        from prog.rb:3:in `<main>'
prog.rb:3:in `encode': U+03C0 from UTF-8 to ISO-8859-1
(Encoding::UndefinedConversionError)
```

You can, however, override this behavior, for example supplying a placeholder character to use when no direct translation is possible. (See the description of String#encode in the reference section on page 675 for more details.)

```
# encoding: utf-8
pi = "pi = π"
puts pi.encode("iso-8859-1", :undef => :replace, :replace => "??")
```

produces:

```
pi = ??
```

Sometimes you'll have a string containing binary data and you want that data to be interpreted as if it had a particular encoding. You can't use the encode method for this, because you don't want to change the byte contents of the string—you're just changing the encoding associated with those bytes. Use the String#force_encoding method to do this:

```
# encoding: ascii-8bit
str = "\xc3\xa9"        # e-acute in UTF-8
str.encoding    # => #<Encoding:ASCII-8BIT>
str.force_encoding("utf-8")
str.bytes.to_a # => [195, 169]
str.encoding    # => #<Encoding:UTF-8>
```

Finally, you can use encode (with two parameters) to convert between two encodings if your source string is ASCII-8BIT. This might happen if, for example, you're reading data in binary mode from a file and choose not to encode it at the time you read it. Here we fake that out by creating an ASCII-8BIT string that contains an ISO-8859-1 sequence (our old friend *olé*). We then convert the string to UTF-8. To do this, we have to tell encode the actual encoding of the bytes by passing it a second parameter:

```
# encoding: ascii-8bit
original = "ol\xe9"      # e-acute in ISO-8859-1
original.bytes.to_a # => [111, 108, 233]
original.encoding    # => #<Encoding:ASCII-8BIT>
new = original.encode("utf-8", "iso-8859-1")
new.bytes.to_a       # => [111, 108, 195, 169]
new.encoding         # => #<Encoding:UTF-8>
```

If you're writing programs that will support multiple encodings, you probably want to read Section 17.5, *Default External Encoding*, on page 248—it will greatly simplify your life.

17.4 Input and Output Encoding

Playing around with encodings within a program is all very well, but in most code we'll want to read data from and write data to external files. And, often, that data will be in a particular encoding.

Ruby's I/O objects support both encoding and transcoding of data. What does this mean?

Every I/O object has an associated external encoding. This is the encoding of the data being read from or written to the outside world. Through a piece of magic I'll describe later on page 248, all Ruby programs run with the concept of a default external encoding. This is the external encoding that will be used by I/O objects unless you override it when you create the object (for example, by opening a file).

Now, your program may want to operate internally in a different encoding. For example, some of my files may be encoded with ISO-8859-1, but we want our Ruby program to work internally using UTF-8. Ruby I/O objects manage this by having an optional associated *internal encoding*. If set, then input will be transcoded from the external to the internal encodings on read operations, and output will be transcoded from internal to external encoding on write operations.

Let's start with the simple cases. On our OS X box, the default external encoding is UTF-8. If we don't override it, all our file I/O will therefore also be in UTF-8. We can query the external encoding of an I/O object using the IO#external_encoding method:

```
f = File.open("/etc/passwd")
puts "File encoding is #{f.external_encoding}"
line = f.gets
puts "Data encoding is #{line.encoding}"
```

produces:

```
File encoding is UTF-8
Data encoding is UTF-8
```

Notice that the data is tagged with a UTF-8 encoding even though it (presumably) contains just 7-bit ASCII characters. Only literals in your Ruby source files have the "change encoding if they contain 8-bit data" rule.

You can force the external encoding associated with an I/O object when you open it—simply add the name of the encoding, preceded by a colon, to the mode string. Note that this in no way changes the data that's read; it simply tags it with the encoding you specify:

```
f = File.open("/etc/passwd", "r:ascii")
puts "File encoding is #{f.external_encoding}"
line = f.gets
puts "Data encoding is #{line.encoding}"
```

produces:

```
File encoding is US-ASCII
Data encoding is US-ASCII
```

You can force Ruby to transcode—change the encoding—of data it reads and writes by putting two encoding names in the mode string, again with a colon before each. For example, the file iso-8859-1.txt contains the word *olé* in ISO-8859-1 encoding, so the e-acute (é) character is encoded by the single byte \xe9. I can view this file's contents in hex using the od command-line tool. (Windows users can use the d command in debug to do the same.)

```
0000000    6f  6c  e9  0a
0000004
```

If we try to read it with our default external encoding of UTF-8, we'll encounter a problem:

```
f = File.open("iso-8859-1.txt")
puts f.external_encoding.name
line = f.gets
puts line.encoding
puts line
```

produces:

```
UTF-8
UTF-8
ol?
```

The problem is that the binary sequence for the e-acute isn't the same in ISO-8859-1 and UTF-8. Ruby just assumed the file contained UTF-8 characters, tagging the string it read accordingly.

We can tell the program that the file contains ISO-8859-1:

```
f = File.open("iso-8859-1.txt", "r:iso-8859-1")
puts f.external_encoding.name
line = f.gets
puts line.encoding
puts line
```

produces:

```
ISO-8859-1
ISO-8859-1
ol?
```

This doesn't help us much. The string is now tagged with the correct encoding, but our operating system is still expecting UTF-8 output.

The solution is to map the ISO-8859-1 to UTF-8 on input:

```
f = File.open("iso-8859-1.txt", "r:iso-8859-1:utf-8")
puts f.external_encoding.name
line = f.gets
puts line.encoding
puts line
```

produces:

```
ISO-8859-1
UTF-8
olé
```

If you specify two encoding names when opening an I/O object, the first is the external encoding, and the second is the internal encoding. Data is transcoded from the former to the latter on reading and the opposite way on writing.

Binary Files

In the old days, we Unix users used to make little snide comments about the way that Windows users had to open binary files using a special binary mode. Well, now the Windows folks can get their own back. If you want to open a file containing binary data in Ruby, you must now specify the binary flag, which will automatically select the 8-bit clean ASCII-8BIT encoding. To make things explicit, you can use "binary" as an alias for the encoding:

```
f = File.open("iso-8859-1.txt", "rb")
puts "Implicit encoding is #{f.external_encoding.name}"
f = File.open("iso-8859-1.txt", "rb:binary")
puts "Explicit encoding is #{f.external_encoding.name}"
line = f.gets
puts "String encoding is #{line.encoding.name}"
```

produces:

```
Implicit encoding is ASCII-8BIT
Explicit encoding is ASCII-8BIT
String encoding is ASCII-8BIT
```

17.5 Default External Encoding

If you look at the text files on your computer, the chances are that they'll all use the same encoding. In the United States, that'll probably be UTF-8 or ASCII. In Europe, it might be UTF-8 or ISO-8859-x. If you use a Windows box, you may be using a different set of encodings (use the console chcp command to find your current code page). But whatever encoding you use, the chances are good that you'll stick with it for the majority of your work.

On Unix-like boxes, you'll probably find you have the LANG environment variable set. On one of our OS X boxes, it has the value en_US.UTF-8

This says that we're using the English language in the U.S. territory and the default code set is UTF-8. On startup, Ruby looks for this environment variable and, if present, sets the default external encoding from the code set component. Thus, on this box, Ruby 1.9 programs run with a default external encoding of UTF-8. If instead we were in Japan and the LANG variable were set to ja_JP.sjis, the encoding would be set to Shift JIS. We can look at the default external encoding by querying the Encoding class. While we're at it, we'll experiment with different values in the LANG environment variable:

```
$ echo $LANG
en_US.UTF-8
$ ruby -e 'p Encoding.default_external.name'
"UTF-8"
$ LANG=ja_JP.sjis ruby -e 'p Encoding.default_external.name'
"Shift_JIS"
$ LANG= ruby -e 'p Encoding.default_external.name'
"US-ASCII"
```

The encoding set from the environment *does not* affect the encoding Ruby uses for source files—it affects only the encoding of data read and written by your programs.

Finally, you can use the -E command-line option (or the long-form --encoding) to set the default external encoding of your I/O objects, as shown in the following commands.

```
$ ruby -E utf-8 -e 'p Encoding.default_external.name'
"UTF-8"
$ ruby -E sjis -e 'p Encoding.default_external.name'
"Shift_JIS"
$ ruby -E sjis:iso-8859-1 -e 'p Encoding.default_internal.name'
"ISO-8859-1"
```

17.6 Encoding Compatibility

Before Ruby performs operations involving strings or regular expressions, it first has to check that the operation makes sense. For example, it is valid to perform an equality test between two strings with different encodings, but it is not valid to append one to the other. The basic steps in this checking are as follows:

1. If the two objects have the same encoding, the operation is valid.
2. If the two objects each contain only 7-bit characters, the operation is permitted regardless of the encodings.
3. If the encodings in the two objects are compatible (which we'll discuss next), the operation is permitted.
4. Otherwise, an exception is raised.

Let's say you have a set of text files containing markup. In some of the files, authors used the sequence … to represent an ellipsis. In other files, which have UTF-8 encoding, authors used an actual ellipsis character (\u2026). We want to convert both forms to three periods.

We can start off with a simplistic solution:

```
# encoding: utf-8
while line = gets
  result = line.gsub(/&hellip;/, "...")
                .gsub(/\u2026/, "...") # unicode ellipsis
  puts result
end
```

In my environment, the content of files is by default assumed to be UTF-8. Feed our code ASCII files and UTF-encoded files, and it works just fine. But what happens when we feed it a file that contains ISO-8859-1 characters?

```
dots.rb:4:in `gsub': broken UTF-8 string (ArgumentError)
```

Ruby tried to interpret the input text, which is ISO-8859-1 encoded, as UTF-8. Because the byte sequences in the file aren't valid UTF, it failed.

There are three solutions to this problem. The first is to say that it makes no sense to feed files with both ISO-8859 and UTF-8 encoding to the same program without somehow differentiating them. That's perfectly true. This approach means we'll need some command-line options, liberal use of force_encoding, and probably some kind of code to delegate the pattern matching to different sets of patterns depending on the encoding of each file.

A second hack is to simply treat both the data and the program as ASCII-8BIT and perform all the comparisons based on the underlying bytes. This isn't particularly reliable, but it might work in some circumstances.

The third solution is to choose a master encoding and to transcode strings into it before doing the matches. Ruby provides built-in support for this with the default_internal encoding mechanism.

17.7 Default Internal Encoding

By default, Ruby performs no automatic transcoding when reading and writing data. However, two command-line options allow you to change this.

We've already seen the -E option, which sets the default encoding applied to the content of external files. When you say -E xxx, the default external encoding is set to xxx. However, -E takes a second option. In the same way that you can give File#open both external and internal encodings, you can also set a default internal encoding using the option -E external:internal.

Thus, if all your files are written with ISO-8859-1 encoding but you want your program to have to deal with their content as if it were UTF-8, you can use this:

```
$ ruby -E iso-8859-1:utf-8
```

You can specify just an internal encoding by omitting the external option but leaving the colon:

```
$ ruby -E :utf-8
```

Indeed, because UTF-8 is probably the best of the available transcoding targets, Ruby has the -U command-line option, which sets the internal encoding to UTF-8.

You can query the default internal encoding in your code with the Encoding.default_internal method. This returns nil if no default internal encoding has been set.

One last note before we leave this section: if you compare two strings with different encodings, Ruby does not normalize them. Thus, "é" tagged with a UTF-8 encoding will not compare equal to "é" tagged with ISO-8859-1, because the underlying bytes are different.

17.8 Fun with Unicode

As Daniel Berger pointed out,[4] we can now do fun things with method and variable names:

```
# encoding: utf-8
def ∑(*args)
  args.inject(:+)
end

puts ∑ 1, 3, 5, 9
```

produces:

```
18
```

Of course, this way can lead to some pretty obscure and hard-to-use code. (For example, is the summation character in the previous code a real summation, \u2211, or a Greek sigma, \u03a3?) Just because we *can* do something doesn't mean we necessarily *should*....

---

4.   http://www.oreillynet.com/ruby/blog/2007/10/fun_with_unicode_1.html

## CHAPTER 18

Interactive Ruby Shell

Back in Section 14.2, *Interactive Ruby*, on page 196 we introduced irb, a Ruby module that lets you enter Ruby programs interactively and see the results immediately. This chapter goes into more detail on using and customizing irb.

18.1 Command Line

irb is run from the command line:

irb ‹*irb-options*› ‹*ruby_script*› ‹*program arguments*›

The command-line options for irb are listed in Table 9, *irb Command-line options*, on page 255. Typically, you'll run irb with no options, but if you want to run a script and watch the blow-by-blow description as it runs, you can provide the name of the Ruby script and any options for that script.

Once started, irb displays a prompt and waits for you to type Ruby code. irb understands Ruby, so it knows when statements are incomplete. When this happens, the cursor will be indented on the next line. (In the examples that follow, we'll use irb's default prompt.)

```
ruby 2.0 > 1 + 2
=> 3
ruby 2.0 > 3 +
ruby 2.0 >    4
=> 7
```

You can leave irb by typing exit or quit or by entering an end-of-file character (unless IGNORE_EOF mode is set).

During an irb session, the work you do is accumulated in irb's workspace. Variables you set, methods you define, and classes you create are all remembered and may be used subsequently in that session.

```
ruby 2.0 > def fib_up_to(n)
ruby 2.0 ?>   f1, f2 = 1, 1
ruby 2.0 ?>   while f1 <= n
ruby 2.0 ?>     puts f1
ruby 2.0 ?>       f1, f2 = f2, f1+f2
ruby 2.0 ?>     end
ruby 2.0 ?> end
=> nil
```

```
ruby 2.0 > fib_up_to(4)
1
1
2
3
=> nil
```

Notice the nil return values. These are the results of defining the method and then running it—our method printed the Fibonacci numbers but then returned nil.

A great use of irb is experimenting with code you've already written. Perhaps you want to track down a bug, or maybe you just want to play. If you load your program into irb, you can then create instances of the classes it defines and invoke its methods. For example, the file code/irb/fibonacci_sequence.rb contains the following method definition:

irb/fibonacci_sequence.rb
```
def fibonacci_sequence
  Enumerator.new do |generator|
    i1, i2 = 1, 1
    loop do
      generator.yield i1
      i1, i2 = i2, i1+i2
    end
  end
end
```

We can load this into irb and play with the method:

```
ruby 2.0 > load 'code/irb/fibonacci_sequence.rb'
=> True
ruby 2.0 > fibonacci_sequence.first(10)
=> [1, 1, 2, 3, 5, 8, 13, 21, 34, 55]
```

In this example, we use load, rather than require, to include the file in our session. We do this as a matter of practice: load allows us to load the same file multiple times, so if we find a bug and edit the file, we could reload it into our irb session.

Tab Completion

If your Ruby installation has readline support, then you can use irb's completion facility. Once loaded (and we'll get to how to load it shortly), completion changes the meaning of the `Tab` key when typing expressions at the irb prompt. When you press `Tab` partway through a word, irb will look for possible completions that make sense at that point. If there is only one, irb will fill it in automatically. If there's more than one valid option, irb initially does nothing. However, if you hit `Tab` again, it will display the list of valid completions at that point.

For example, the following snippet shows the middle of an irb session, where you just assigned a string object to the variable a.

```
ruby 2.0 > a = "cat"
=> "cat"
```

You now want to try the method String#reverse on this object. You start by typing a.re and hitting `Tab` twice.

Option	Description
--back-trace-limit n	Displays backtrace information using the top *n* and last *n* entries. The default value is 16.
--context-mode n	:CONTEXT_MODE is describd later on page 259.
-d	Sets $DEBUG to true (same as ruby -d).
-E enc	Same as Ruby's -E option.
-f	Suppresses reading >~/.irbrc.
-h, --help	Displays usage information.
-I directories	Same as Ruby's -I option.
--inf-ruby-mode	Sets up irb to run in inf-ruby-mode under Emacs. Same as --prompt inf-ruby --noreadline.
--inspect, --noinspect	Uses/doesn't use Object#inspect to format output (--inspect is the default, unless in math mode).
--irb_debug n	Sets internal debug level to *n* (useful only for irb development).
-m	Math mode (fraction and matrix support is available).
--noprompt	Does not display a prompt. Same as --prompt null.
--prompt prompt-mode	Switches prompt. Predefined prompt modes are null, default, classic, simple, xmp, and inf-ruby.
--prompt-mode prompt-mode	Same as --prompt.
-r module	Requires *module*. Same as ruby -r.
--readline, --noreadline	Uses/doesn't use readline extension module.
--sample-book-mode	Same as --prompt simple.
--simple-prompt	Same as --prompt simple.
--single-irb	Nested irb sessions will all share the same context.
--tracer	Displays trace for execution of commands.
-U	Same as Ruby's -U option.
-v, --version	Prints the version of irb.

Table 9—irb Command-line options

```
ruby 2.0 > a.re«Tab»«Tab»
a.replace  a.respond_to?  a.reverse  a.reverse!  a.respond_to_missing?
```

irb lists all the methods supported by the object in a whose names start with *re*. We see the one we want, reverse, and enter the next character of its name, *v*, followed by the Tab key:

```
ruby 2.0 > a.rev«TAB»
ruby 2.0 > a.reverse
=> "tac"
```

irb responds to the Tab key by expanding the name as far as it can go, in this case completing the word reverse. If we keyed Tab twice at this point, it would show us the current options, reverse and reverse!. However, because reverse is the one we want, we instead hit Enter, and the line of code is executed.

Tab completion isn't limited to built-in names. If we define a class in irb, then tab completion works when we try to invoke one of its methods:

```
ruby 2.0 > class Test
ruby 2.0 ?>   def my_method
ruby 2.0 ?>     end
ruby 2.0 ?>   end
=> nil
ruby 2.0 > t = Test.new
=> #<Test:0x000001009fc8c8>
ruby 2.0 > t.my«TAB»
ruby 2.0 > t.my_method
=> nil
```

Tab completion is implemented as an extension library. On some systems this is loaded by default. On others you'll need to load it when you invoke irb from the command line:

```
$ irb -r irb/completion
```

You can also load the completion library when irb is running:

```
ruby 2.0 > require 'irb/completion'
```

If you use tab completion all the time and if it doesn't load by default, it's probably most convenient to put the require command into your .irbrc file:

Subsessions

irb supports multiple, concurrent sessions. One is always current; the others lie dormant until activated. Entering the command irb within irb creates a subsession, entering the jobs command lists all sessions, and entering fg activates a particular dormant session. This example also illustrates the -r command-line option, which loads in the given file before irb starts:

```
dave[ruby4/Book 13:44:16] irb -r ./code/irb/fibonacci_sequence.rb
ruby 2.0 > result = fibonacci_sequence.first(5)
 => [1, 1, 2, 3, 5]
ruby 2.0 > # Created nested irb session
ruby 2.0 >   irb
ruby 2.0 > result = %w{ cat dog elk }
 => ["cat", "dog", "elk"]
ruby 2.0 > result.map(&:upcase)
 => ["CAT", "DOG", "ELK"]
ruby 2.0 > jobs
 => #0->irb on main (#<Thread:0x00000100887678>: stop)
#1->irb#1 on main (#<Thread:0x00000100952710>: running)
ruby 2.0 > fg 0
 => #<IRB::Irb: @context=#<IRB::Context:0x000001008ea6d8>, ...
ruby 2.0 > result
 => [1, 1, 2, 3, 5]
ruby 2.0 > fg 1
 => #<IRB::Irb: @context=#<IRB::Context:0x00000100952670>, ...
ruby 2.0 > result
 => ["cat", "dog", "elk"]
ruby 2.0 >
```

Subsessions and Bindings

If you specify an object when you create a subsession, that object becomes the value of *self* in that binding. This is a convenient way to experiment with objects. In the following example, we create a subsession with the string "wombat" as the default object. Methods with no receiver will be executed by that object.

```
ruby 2.0 > self
 => main
ruby 2.0 > irb "wombat"
ruby 2.0 > self
 => "wombat"
ruby 2.0 > upcase
 => "WOMBAT"
ruby 2.0 > size
 => 6
ruby 2.0 > gsub(/[aeiou]/, '*')
 => "w*mb*t"
ruby 2.0 > irb_exit
 => #<IRB::Irb: @context=#<IRB::Context:0x000001009dc4d8>, ...
ruby 2.0 > self
 => main
ruby 2.0 > upcase
NameError: undefined local variable or method `upcase' for main:Object
        from (irb):4
        from /Users/dave/.rvm/rubies/ruby 2.0/bin/irb:17:in `<main>'
```

irb is remarkably configurable. You can set configuration options with command-line options from within an initialization file and while you're inside irb itself.

Initialization File

irb uses an initialization file in which you can set commonly used options or execute any required Ruby statements. When irb is run, it will try to load an initialization file from one of the following sources in order: ~/.irbrc, .irbrc, irb.rc, _irbrc, and $irbrc.

Within the initialization file, you may run any arbitrary Ruby code. You can also set configuration values. The list of configuration variables is given in *irb Configuration Options*, on page 259—the values that can be used in an initialization file are the symbols (starting with a colon). You use these symbols to set values into the IRB.conf hash. For example, to make SIMPLE the default prompt mode for all your irb sessions, you could have the following in your initialization file:

```
IRB.conf[:PROMPT_MODE] = :SIMPLE
```

As an interesting twist on configuring irb, you can set IRB.conf[:IRB_RC] to a Proc object. This proc will be invoked whenever the irb context is changed and will receive the configuration for that context as a parameter. You can use this facility to change the configuration dynamically based on the context. For example, the following .irbrc file sets the prompt so that only the main prompt shows the irb level, but continuation prompts and the result still line up:

```
IRB.conf[:IRB_RC] = lambda do |conf|
  leader = " " * conf.irb_name.length
  conf.prompt_i = "#{conf.irb_name} --> "
  conf.prompt_s = leader + ' |-" '
  conf.prompt_c = leader + ' |-+ '
  conf.return_format  = leader + " ==> %s\n\n"
  puts "Welcome!"
end
```

An irb session using this .irbrc file looks like the following:

```
$ irb
Welcome!
irb --> 1 + 2
    ==> 3

irb --> 2 +
    \-+   6
    ==> 8
```

Extending irb

Because the things you type into irb are interpreted as Ruby code, you can effectively extend irb by defining new top-level methods. For example, you may want to time how long certain things take. You can use the measure method in the Benchmark library to do this, but it's more convenient to wrap this in a helper method.

Add the following to your .irbrc file:

```
def time(&block)
  require 'benchmark'
  result = nil
  timing = Benchmark.measure do
    result = block.()
  end
  puts "It took: #{timing}"
  result
end
```

The next time you start irb, you'll be able to use this method to get timings:

```
ruby 2.0 > time { 1_000_000.times { "cat".upcase } }
It took:   0.320000   0.000000   0.320000 (  0.323104)
=> 1000000
```

Interactive Configuration

Most configuration values are also available while you're running irb. The list in *irb Configuration Options*, on page 259 shows these values as conf.xxx. For example, to change your prompt back to SIMPLE, you could use the following:

```
ruby 2.0 > 1 +
ruby 2.0 >   2
 => 3
ruby 2.0 > conf.prompt_mode = :SIMPLE
=> :SIMPLE
```

```
>> 1 +
?> 2
=> 3
```

irb Configuration Options

In the descriptions that follow, a label of the form :XXX signifies a key used in the IRB.conf hash in an initialization file, and conf.xxx signifies a value that can be set interactively. The value in square brackets at the end of the description is the option's default.

:AUTO_INDENT / auto_indent_mode
> If true, irb will indent nested structures as you type them. [true]

:BACK_TRACE_LIMIT / back_trace_limit
> Displays n initial and n final lines of backtrace. [16]

:CONTEXT_MODE
> Specifies what binding to use for new workspaces: 0→proc at the top level, 1→binding in a loaded, anonymous file, 2→per thread binding in a loaded file, 3→binding in a top-level function. [3]

:DEBUG_LEVEL / debug_level
> Sets the internal debug level to n. This is useful if you're debugging irb's lexer. [0]

:IGNORE_EOF / ignore_eof
> Specifies the behavior of an end of file received on input. If true, it will be ignored; otherwise, irb will quit. [false]

:IGNORE_SIGINT / ignore_sigint
> If false, ^C (Ctrl+c) will quit irb. If true, ^C during input will cancel input and return to the top level; during execution, ^C will abort the current operation. [true]

:INSPECT_MODE / inspect_mode
> Specifies how values will be displayed: true means use inspect, false uses to_s, and nil uses inspect in nonmath mode and to_s in math mode. [nil]

:IRB_RC
> Can be set to a proc object that will be called when an irb session (or subsession) is started. [nil]

last_value
> The last value output by irb. [...]

:LOAD_MODULES / load_modules
> A list of modules loaded via the -r command-line option. [[]]

:MATH_MODE / math_mode
> If true, irb runs with the mathn library loaded (described in the library section on page 768) and does not use inspect to display values. [false]

prompt_c
> The prompt for a continuing statement (for example, immediately after an if). [depends]

prompt_i
> The standard, top-level prompt. [depends]

:PROMPT_MODE / prompt_mode
> The style of prompt to display. [:DEFAULT]

prompt_s
>   The prompt for a continuing string. [depends]

:PROMPT
>   See *Configuring the Prompt*, on page 261. [...]

:RC / rc
>   If false, do not load an initialization file. [true]

return_format
>   The format used to display the results of expressions entered interactively. [depends]

:SAVE_HISTORY / save_history
>   The number of commands to save between irb sessions. [nil]

:SINGLE_IRB
>   If true, nested irb sessions will all share the same binding; otherwise, a new binding will be created according to the value of :CONTEXT_MODE. [nil]

thread
>   A read-only reference to the currently executing Thread object. [current thread]

:USE_LOADER / use_loader
>   Specifies whether irb's own file reader method is used with load/require. [false]

:USE_READLINE / use_readline
>   irb will use the readline library (described in the library section on page 795) if available, unless this option is set to false, in which case readline will never be used, or nil, in which case readline will not be used in inf-ruby-mode. [depends]

:USE_TRACER / use_tracer
>   If true, traces the execution of statements. [false]

:VERBOSE / verbose
>   In theory, switches on additional tracing when true; in practice, almost no extra tracing results. [true]

18.2 Commands

At the irb prompt, you can enter any valid Ruby expression and see the results. You can also use any of the following commands to control the irb session:[1]

help ClassName, string, or symbol
>   Displays the ri help for the given thing.

```
irb(main):001:0> help "String.encoding"
------------------------------------------------- String#encoding
obj.encoding    => encoding
------------------------------------------------------------------
Returns the Encoding object that represents the encoding of obj.
```

exit, quit, irb_exit, irb_quit
>   Quits this irb session or subsession. If you've used cb to change bindings (detailed in a moment), exits from this binding mode.

---

1.   For some inexplicable reason, many of these commands have up to nine different aliases. We don't bother to show all of them.

conf, context, irb_context

> Displays current configuration. Modifying the configuration is achieved by invoking methods of conf. The list in *irb Configuration Options,* on page 259 shows the available conf settings.

> For example, to set the default prompt to something subservient, you could use this:

```
irb(main):001:0> conf.prompt_i = "Yes, Master? "
=> "Yes, Master? "
Yes, Master? 1 + 2
```

cb, irb_change_binding ‹*obj*›

> Creates and enters a new binding (sometimes called a *workspace*) that has its own scope for local variables. If *obj* is given, it will be used as self in the new binding.

pushb obj, popb

> Pushes and pops the current binding.

bindings

> Lists the current bindings.

irb_cwws

> Prints the object that's the binding of the current workspace.

irb ‹*obj*›

> Starts an irb subsession. If *obj* is given, it will be used as self.

jobs, irb_jobs

> Lists irb subsessions.

fg n, irb_fg n

> Switches into the specified irb subsession. *n* may be any of the following: an irb subsession number, a thread ID, an irb object, or the object that was the value of *self* when a subsession was launched.

kill n, irb_kill n

> Kills an irb subsession. *n* may be any of the values as described for irb_fg.

source filename

> Loads and executes the given file, displaying the source lines.

Configuring the Prompt

You have a lot of flexibility in configuring the prompts that irb uses. Sets of prompts are stored in the prompt hash, IRB.conf[:PROMPT].

For example, to establish a new prompt mode called MY_PROMPT, you could enter the following (either directly at an irb prompt or in the .irbrc file):

```
IRB.conf[:PROMPT][:MY_PROMPT] = {  # name of prompt mode
  :PROMPT_I => '-->',              # normal prompt
  :PROMPT_S => '--"',              # prompt for continuing strings
  :PROMPT_C => '--+',              # prompt for continuing statement
  :RETURN => "    ==>%s\n"         # format to return value
}
```

Once you've defined a prompt, you have to tell irb to use it. From the command line, you can use the --prompt option. (Notice how the name of the prompt on the command line is automatically converted to uppercase, with hyphens changing to underscores.)

```
$ irb --prompt my-prompt
```

If you want to use this prompt in all your future irb sessions, you can set it as a configuration value in your .irbrc file:

```
IRB.conf[:PROMPT_MODE] = :MY_PROMPT
```

The symbols :PROMPT_I, :PROMPT_S, and :PROMPT_C specify the format for each of the prompt strings. In a format string, certain % sequences are expanded:

Flag	Description
%N	Current command.
%m	to_s of the main object (self).
%M	inspect of the main object (self).
%l	Delimiter type. In strings that are continued across a line break, %l will display the type of delimiter used to begin the string, so you'll know how to end it. The delimiter will be one of ", ', /,], or `.
%ni	Indent level. The optional number n is used as a width specification to printf, as printf("%nd").
%nn	Current line number (n used as with the indent level).
%%	A literal percent sign.

Table 10—irb prompt string substitutions

For instance, the default prompt mode is defined as follows:

```
IRB.conf[:PROMPT][:DEFAULT] = {
  :PROMPT_I => "%N(%m):%03n:%i> ",
  :PROMPT_S => "%N(%m):%03n:%i%l ",
  :PROMPT_C => "%N(%m):%03n:%i* ",
  :RETURN   => "=> %s\n"
}
```

Saving Your Session History

If you have readline support in irb (that is, you can hit the up arrow key and irb recalls the previous command you entered), then you can also configure irb to remember the commands you enter between sessions. Simply add the following to your .irbrc file:

```
IRB.conf[:SAVE_HISTORY] = 50     # save last 50 commands
```

## CHAPTER 19

Documenting Ruby

Ruby comes bundled with RDoc, a tool that extracts and formats documentation that's embedded in Ruby source code files. This tool is used to document the built-in Ruby classes and modules. An increasing number of libraries and extensions are also documented this way.[1]

RDoc does two jobs. First, it analyzes Ruby and C source files, along with some other formats such as Markdown, looking for information to document.[2] Second, it takes this information and converts it into something readable. The following image shows some RDoc output in a browser window. The overlaid box shows the source program from which this output was generated.

New in 2.0

Even though the source contains no internal documentation, RDoc still manages to extract interesting information from it. We have three panes at the top of the screen showing the files, classes, and methods for which we have documentation. For class Counter, RDoc shows us the attributes and methods (including the method signatures). And if we clicked a method signature, RDoc would pop up a window containing the source code for the corresponding method.

---

1. RDoc isn't the only Ruby documentation tool. Those who like a more formal, tag-based scheme might want to look at Yard at http://yardoc.org.
2. RDoc can also document Fortran 77 programs.

If our source code contains comments, RDoc can use them to spice up the documentation it produces.

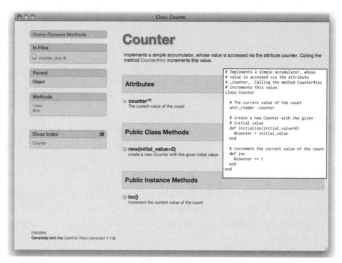

Notice how the comments before each element now appear in the RDoc output, reformatted into HTML. Less obvious is that RDoc has detected hyperlink opportunities in our comments: in the class-level comment, the reference to Counter#inc is a hyperlink to the method description, and in the comment for the new method, the reference to class Counter hyperlinks back to the class documentation. This is a key feature of RDoc: it is designed to be unintrusive in the Ruby source files and to make up for this by trying to be clever when producing output.

RDoc can also be used to produce documentation that can be read by the ri command-line utility. For example, if we ask RDoc to document the code in the previous example into ri format, we can access the documentation from the command line:

```
$ ri Counter
--------------------------------------- Class: Counter
     Implements a simple accumulator, whose value is
     accessed via the attribute counter. Calling the
     method Counter#inc increments this value.
---------------------------------------------------


Class methods:
     new
Instance methods:
     inc
Attributes:
     counter
------------------------------------------------------------- Counter#inc
     inc()
-------------------------------------------------------------------
     increment the current value of the count
```

Ruby distributions have the built-in classes and modules (and some libraries) documented this way.[3] Here's what you see if you type ri Proc:

```
$ ri Proc
Proc < Object
(from ruby core)
-----------------------------------------------------------------------
Proc objects are blocks of code that have been bound to a set of local
variables. Once bound, the code may be called in different contexts and still
access those variables.

  def gen_times(factor)
    return Proc.new {|n| n*factor }
  end

  times3 = gen_times(3)
  times5 = gen_times(5)

  times3.call(12)              #=> 36
  times5.call(5)               #=> 25
  times3.call(times5.call(4))  #=> 60
-----------------------------------------------------------------------
Class methods:
  new
Instance methods:
  ===, [], arity, binding, call, curry, hash, inspect, lambda?, parameters,
  source_location, to_proc, to_s, yield    ==
```

Many projects include README files, files containing usage notes, Changelogs, and so on. RDoc automatically finds and formats these. It calls the result a *page*. You access the list of available pages from ri using the name of the project and a colon:

New in 2.0

```
$ ri ruby:
Pages in ruby core

ChangeLog
NEWS
README
README.EXT
:    :
```

To read a particular page, add its name after the colon:

```
$ ri ruby:NEWS
NEWS for Ruby 2.0.0

This document is a list of user visible feature changes made between releases
except for bug fixes.
```

---

3. If you're using rvm, you'll need to run rvm docs generate.

19.1 Adding RDoc to Ruby Code

RDoc parses Ruby source files to extract the major elements (such as classes, modules, methods, attributes, and so on). You can choose to associate additional documentation with these by simply adding a comment block before the element in the file.

One of the design goals of RDoc was to leave the source code looking totally natural. In most cases, there is no need for any special markup in your code to get RDoc to produce decent looking documentation. For example, comment blocks can be written fairly naturally:

```
# Calculate the minimal-cost path though the graph using Debrinkski's algorithm,
# with optimized inverse pruning of isolated leaf nodes.
def calculate_path
  . . .
end
```

You can also use Ruby's block-comments by including the documentation in a =begin...=end block. If you use this (which is not generally done), the =begin line must be flagged with an rdoc tag to distinguish the block from other styles of documentation.

```
=begin rdoc
Calculate the minimal-cost path though the graph using Debrinkski's algorithm,
with optimized inverse pruning of isolated leaf nodes.
=end
def calculate_path
  . . .
end
```

Within a documentation comment, paragraphs are lines that share the left margin. Text indented past this margin is formatted verbatim.

Nonverbatim text can be marked up. To set individual words in italic, bold, or typewriter fonts, you can use _word_, *word*, and +word+, respectively. If you want to do this to multiple words or text containing nonword characters, you can use multiple words, more words, and <tt>yet more words</tt>. Putting a backslash before inline markup stops it from being interpreted.

RDoc stops processing comments if it finds a comment line starting with #--. This can be used to separate external from internal comments or to stop a comment from being associated with a method, class, attribute, or module. Documenting can be turned back on by starting a line with the comment #++:

```
# Extract the age and calculate the
# date of birth.
#--
# FIXME: fails if the birthday falls on February 29th, or if the person
# was born before epoch and the installed Ruby doesn't support negative time_t
#++
# The DOB is returned as a Time object.
#--
# But should probably change to use Date.

def get_dob(person)
  ...
end
```

Hyperlinks

Names of classes, source files, and any method names containing an underscore or preceded by a hash character are automatically hyperlinked from comment text to their description.

In addition, hyperlinks starting with http:, mailto:, ftp:, and www: are recognized. An HTTP URL that references an external image file is converted into an inline <img> tag. Hyperlinks starting with link: are assumed to refer to local files whose paths are relative to the --op directory, where output files are stored.

Hyperlinks can also be of the form label[url], where the label is used in the displayed text and url is used as the target. If the label contains multiple words, surround it in braces: {two words}[url].

Lists

Lists are typed as indented paragraphs with the following:

- As asterisk (*) or hyphen (-) for bullet lists
- A digit followed by a period for numbered lists
- An uppercase or lowercase letter followed by a period for alpha lists

For example, you could produce something like the previous text with this:

```
# Lists are typed as indented paragraphs with
# * a * or - (for bullet lists),
# * a digit followed by a period for
#   numbered lists,
# * an uppercase or lowercase letter followed
#   by a period for alpha lists.
```

Note how subsequent lines in a list item are indented to line up with the text in the element's first line.

Labeled lists (sometimes called *description lists*) are typed using square brackets for the label:

```
# [cat]    Small domestic animal
# [+cat+]  Command to copy standard input
#          to standard output
```

Labeled lists may also be produced by putting a double colon after the label. This sets the result in tabular form so the descriptions all line up in the output.

```
# cat::    Small domestic animal
# +cat+:: Command to copy standard input
#          to standard output
```

For both kinds of labeled lists, if the body text starts on the same line as the label, then the start of that text determines the block indent for the rest of the body. The text may also start on the line following the label, indented from the start of the label. This is often preferable if the label is long. Both of the following are valid labeled list entries:

```
# <tt>--output</tt> <i>name [, name]</i>::
#      specify the name of one or more output files. If multiple
#      files are present, the first is used as the index.
#
```

```
#  <tt>--quiet:</tt>::  do not output the names, sizes, byte counts,
#                       index areas, or bit ratios of units as
#                       they are processed.
```

Headings

Headings are entered on lines starting with equals signs. The more equals signs, the higher the level of heading:

```
#  = Level One Heading
#  == Level Two Heading
#  and so on...
```

Rules (horizontal lines) are entered using three or more hyphens:

```
#  and so it goes...
#  ----
#  The next section...
```

Documentation Modifiers

Method parameter lists are extracted and displayed with the method description. If a method calls yield, then the parameters passed to yield will also be displayed. For example:

```
def fred
  # ...
  yield line, address
```

This will be documented as follows:

```
fred() {|line, address| ... }
```

You can override this using a comment containing :yields: ... on the same line as the method definition:

```
def fred      # :yields: index, position
  # ...
  yield line, address
```

which will be documented as follows:

```
fred() {|index, position| ... }
```

:yields: is an example of a documentation modifier. These appear immediately after the start of the document element they are modifying. Other modifiers include the following:

:nodoc: ‹ *all* ›

> Don't include this element in the documentation. For classes and modules, the methods, aliases, constants, and attributes directly within the affected class or module will also be omitted from the documentation. By default, though, modules and classes within that class or module will be documented. This is turned off by adding the *all* modifier. For example, in the following code, only class SM::Input will be documented:
>
> ```
> module SM  #:nodoc:
>   class Input
>   end
> end
> ```

```
module Markup #:nodoc: all
  class Output
  end
end
```

:doc:

> This forces a method or attribute to be documented even if it wouldn't otherwise be. This is useful if, for example, you want to include documentation of a particular private method.

:notnew:

> (Applicable only to the initialize instance method.) Normally RDoc assumes that the documentation and parameters for #initialize are actually for the corresponding class's new method and so fakes out a new method for the class. The :notnew: modifier stops this. Remember that #initialize is protected, so you won't see the documentation unless you use the -a command-line option.

Other Directives

Comment blocks can contain other directives:

:call-seq: lines...

> Text up to the next blank comment line is used as the calling sequence when generating documentation (overriding the parsing of the method parameter list). A line is considered blank even if it starts with #. For this one directive, the leading colon is optional.

:include: filename

> This includes the contents of the named file at this point. The file will be searched for in the directories listed by the --include option or in the current directory by default. The contents of the file will be shifted to have the same indentation as the : at the start of the :include: directive.

:title: text

> This sets the title for the document. It's equivalent to the --title command-line parameter. (The command-line parameter overrides any :title: directive in the source.)

:main: name

> This is equivalent to the --main command-line parameter, setting the initial page displayed for this documentation.

:stopdoc: / :startdoc:

> This stops and starts adding new documentation elements to the current container. For example, if a class has a number of constants that you don't want to document, put a :stopdoc: before the first and a :startdoc: after the last. If you don't specify a :startdoc: by the end of the container, this disables documentation for the entire class or module.

:enddoc:

> This documents nothing further at the current lexical level.

A larger example of a file documented using RDoc is shown in Section 19.4, *Ruby source file documented with RDoc*, on page 272.

19.2 Adding RDoc to C Extensions

RDoc understands many of the conventions used when writing extensions to Ruby in C.

If RDoc sees a C function named Init_Classname, it treats it as a class definition—any C comment before the Init_ function will be used as the class's documentation.

The Init_ function is normally used to associate C functions with Ruby method names. For example, a Cipher extension may define a Ruby method salt=, implemented by the C function salt_set using a call such as this:

```
rb_define_method(cCipher, "salt=", salt_set, 1);
```

RDoc parses this call, adding the salt= method to the class documentation. RDoc then searches the C source for the C function salt_set. If this function is preceded by a comment block, RDoc uses this for the method's documentation.

This basic scheme works with no effort on your part beyond writing the normal documentation in the comments for functions. However, RDoc cannot discern the calling sequence for the corresponding Ruby method. In this example, the RDoc output will show a single argument with the (somewhat meaningless) name "arg1." You can override this using the call-seq directive in the function's comment. The lines following call-seq (up to a blank line) are used to document the calling sequence of the method:

```
/*
 * call-seq:
 *   cipher.salt = number
 *   cipher.salt = "string"
 *
 * Sets the salt of this cipher to either a binary +number+ or
 * bits in +string+.
 */

static VALUE
salt_set(cipher, salt)
...
```

If a method returns a meaningful value, it should be documented in the call-seq following the characters ->:

```
/*
 * call-seq:
 *   cipher.keylen    -> Fixnum or nil
 */
```

Although RDoc heuristics work well for finding the class and method comments for simple extensions, they don't always work for more complex implementations. In these cases, you can use the directives Document-class: and Document-method: to indicate that a C comment relates to a given class or method, respectively. The modifiers take the name of the Ruby class or method that's being documented:

```
/*
 * Document-method: reset
 *
 * Clear the current buffer and prepare to add new
 * cipher text. Any accumulated output cipher text
 * is also cleared.
 */
```

Finally, it is possible in the Init_xxx function to associate a Ruby method with a C function in a different C source file. RDoc would not find this function without your help: you add a reference to the file containing the function definition by adding a special comment to the rb_define_method call. The following example tells RDoc to look in the file md5.c for the function (and related comment) corresponding to the md5 method:

```
rb_define_method(cCipher, "md5", gen_md5, -1); /* in md5.c */
```

A C source file documented using RDoc is shown in Section 19.5, *C source file documented with RDoc*, on page 274. Note that the bodies of several internal methods have been elided to save space.

19.3 Running RDoc

You run RDoc from the command line:

```
$ rdoc ‹options›* ‹filenames...›*
```

Type rdoc --help for an up-to-date option summary.

Files are parsed, and the information they contain collected, before any output is produced. This allows cross-references between all files to be resolved. If a name is a directory, it is traversed. If no names are specified, all Ruby files in the current directory (and subdirectories) are processed.

A typical use may be to generate documentation for a package of Ruby source (such as RDoc itself):

```
$ rdoc
```

This command generates HTML documentation for the files in and below the current directory. These will be stored in a documentation tree starting in the subdirectory doc/.

RDoc uses file extensions to determine how to process each file. Filenames ending with .rb and .rbw are assumed to be Ruby source. Filenames ending .c are parsed as C files. .rdoc files are formatted as RDoc, and .md and .markdown as Markdown. All other files are assumed to contain just markup (with or without leading # comment markers). If directory names are passed to RDoc, they are scanned recursively for source files only. To include nonsource files such as READMEs in the documentation process, their names must be given explicitly on the command line.

New in 2.0

When writing a Ruby library, you often have some source files that implement the public interface, but the majority are internal and of no interest to the readers of your documentation. In these cases, construct a .document file in each of your project's directories. If RDoc enters a directory containing a .document file, it will process only the files in that directory whose names match one of the lines in that file. Each line in the file can be a filename, a directory name, or a wildcard (a file system "glob" pattern). For example, to include all Ruby files whose names start with main, along with the file constants.rb, you could use a .document file containing this:

```
main*.rb
constants.rb
```

Some project standards ask for documentation in a top-level README file. You may find it convenient to write this file in RDoc format and then use the :include: directive to incorporate the README into the documentation for the main class.

Create Documentation for ri

RDoc is also used to create documentation that will be later displayed using ri.

When you run ri, it by default looks for documentation in three places:[4]

- The *system* documentation directory, which holds the documentation distributed with Ruby and which is created by the Ruby install process

- The *site* directory, which contains sitewide documentation added locally

- The *user* documentation directory, stored under the user's own home directory

You can find these three directories using ri --list-doc-dirs.

```
$ ri --list-doc-dirs
/Users/dave/.rvm/rubies/ruby-2.0.0-p0/share/ri/2.0.0/system
/Users/dave/.rvm/rubies/ruby-2.0.0-p0/share/ri/2.0.0/site
/Users/dave/.rdoc
```

To add documentation to ri, you need to tell RDoc which output directory to use. For your own use, it's easiest to use the --ri option, which installs the documentation into ~/.rdoc:

```
$ rdoc --ri file1.rb file2.rb
```

If you want to install sitewide documentation, use the --ri-site option:

```
$ rdoc --ri-site file1.rb file2.rb
```

The --ri-system option is normally used only to install documentation for Ruby's built-in classes and standard libraries. You can regenerate this documentation from the Ruby source distribution (not from the installed libraries themselves):

```
$ cd ruby source base/lib
$ rdoc --ri-system
```

19.4 Ruby source file documented with RDoc

```
# This module encapsulates functionality related to the
# generation of Fibonacci sequences.
#--
# Copyright (c) 2004 Dave Thomas, The Pragmatic Programmers, LLC.
# Licensed under the same terms as Ruby. No warranty is provided.
module Fibonacci

  # Calculate the first _count_ Fibonacci numbers, starting with 1,1.
  #
  # :call-seq:
  #    Fibonacci.sequence(count)                    -> array
  #    Fibonacci.sequence(count) {|val| ... }    -> nil
```

---

4. You can override the directory location using the --op option to RDoc and subsequently using the --doc-dir option with ri.

```ruby
  #
  # If a block is given, supply successive values to the block and
  # return +nil+, otherwise return all values as an array.
  def Fibonacci.sequence(count, &block)
    result, block = setup_optional_block(block)
    generate do |val|
      break if count <= 0
      count -= 1
      block[val]
    end
    result
  end

  # Calculate the Fibonacci numbers up to and including _max_.
  #
  # :call-seq:
  #   Fibonacci.upto(max)              -> array
  #   Fibonacci.upto(max) {|val| ... }    -> nil
  #
  # If a block is given, supply successive values to the
  # block and return +nil+, otherwise return all values as an array.
  def Fibonacci.upto(max, &block)
    result, block = setup_optional_block(block)
    generate do |val|
      break if val > max
      block[val]
    end
    result
  end

  private

  # Yield a sequence of Fibonacci numbers to a block.
  def Fibonacci.generate
    f1, f2 = 1, 1
    loop do
      yield f1
      f1, f2 = f2, f1+f2
    end
  end

  # If a block parameter is given, use it, otherwise accumulate into an
  # array. Return the result value and the block to use.
  def Fibonacci.setup_optional_block(block)
    if block.nil?
      [ result = [], lambda {|val| result << val } ]
    else
      [ nil, block ]
    end
  end
end
```

19.5 C source file documented with RDoc

```c
#include "ruby.h"
#include "cdjukebox.h"

static VALUE cCDPlayer;
static void cd_free(void *p) { ... }
static VALUE cd_alloc(VALUE klass) { ... }
static void progress(CDJukebox *rec, int percent) { ... }

/* call-seq:
 *    CDPlayer.new(unit)  -> new_cd_player
 *
 * Assign the newly created CDPlayer to a particular unit
 */
static VALUE cd_initialize(VALUE self, VALUE unit) {
  int unit_id;
  CDJukebox *jb;

  Data_Get_Struct(self, CDJukebox, jb);
  unit_id = NUM2INT(unit);
  assign_jukebox(jb, unit_id);
  return self;
}

/* call-seq:
 *   player.seek(int_disc, int_track)  -> nil
 *   player.seek(int_disc, int_track) {|percent| } -> nil
 *
 * Seek to a given part of the track, invoking the block
 * with the percent complete as we go.
 */
static VALUE
cd_seek(VALUE self, VALUE disc, VALUE track) {
  CDJukebox *jb;
  Data_Get_Struct(self, CDJukebox, jb);
  jukebox_seek(jb, NUM2INT(disc), NUM2INT(track), progress);
  return Qnil;
}

/* call-seq:
 *    player.seek_time -> Float
 *
 * Return the average seek time for this unit (in seconds)
 */
static VALUE
cd_seek_time(VALUE self)
{
  double tm;
  CDJukebox *jb;
  Data_Get_Struct(self, CDJukebox, jb);
  tm = get_avg_seek_time(jb);
  return rb_float_new(tm);
}
```

```c
/* Interface to the Spinzalot[http://spinzalot.cd]
 * CD Player library.
 */
void Init_CDPlayer() {
  cCDPlayer = rb_define_class("CDPlayer", rb_cObject);
  rb_define_alloc_func(cCDPlayer, cd_alloc);
  rb_define_method(cCDPlayer, "initialize", cd_initialize, 1);
  rb_define_method(cCDPlayer, "seek", cd_seek, 2);
  rb_define_method(cCDPlayer, "seek_time", cd_seek_time, 0);
}
```

## CHAPTER 20

Ruby and the Web

Ruby is no stranger to the Internet. Not only can you write your own SMTP server, FTP daemon, or web server in Ruby, but you can also use Ruby for more usual tasks such as CGI programming or as a replacement for PHP.

Many options are available for using Ruby to implement web applications, and a single chapter can't do them all justice. Instead, we'll try to touch some of the highlights and point you toward libraries and resources that can help.

Let's start with some simple stuff: running Ruby programs as Common Gateway Interface (CGI) programs.

20.1 Writing CGI Scripts

You can use Ruby to write CGI scripts quite easily. To have a Ruby script generate HTML output, all you need is something like this:

```
#!/usr/bin/ruby
print "Content-type: text/html\r\n\r\n"
print "<html><body>Hello World! It's #{Time.now}</body></html>\r\n"
```

Put this script in a CGI directory, mark it as executable, and you'll be able to access it via your browser. (If your web server doesn't automatically add headers, you'll need to add the response header yourself, as shown in the following code.)

```
#!/usr/bin/ruby
print "HTTP/1.0 200 OK\r\n"
print "Content-type: text/html\r\n\r\n"
print "<html><body>Hello World! It's #{Time.now}</body></html>\r\n"
```

However, that's hacking around at a pretty low level. You'd need to write your own request parsing, session management, cookie manipulation, output escaping, and so on. Fortunately, options are available to make this easier.

20.2 Using cgi.rb

Class CGI provides support for writing CGI scripts. With it, you can manipulate forms, cookies, and the environment; maintain stateful sessions; and so on. It's a fairly large class, but we'll take a quick look at its capabilities here.

Quoting

When dealing with URLs and HTML code, you must be careful to quote certain characters. For instance, a slash character (/) has special meaning in a URL, so it must be "escaped" if it's not part of the path name. That is, any / in the query portion of the URL will be translated to the string %2F and must be translated back to a / for you to use it. Space and ampersand are also special characters. To handle this, CGI provides the routines CGI.escape and CGI.unescape:

```
require 'cgi'
puts CGI.escape("Nicholas Payton/Trumpet & Flugel Horn")
```

produces:

```
Nicholas+Payton%2FTrumpet+%26+Flugel+Horn
```

More frequently, you may want to escape HTML special characters:

```
require 'cgi'
puts CGI.escapeHTML("a < 100 && b > 200")
```

produces:

```
a &lt; 100 &amp;&amp; b &gt; 200
```

To get really fancy, you can decide to escape only certain HTML elements within a string:

```
require 'cgi'
puts CGI.escapeElement('<hr><a href="/mp3">Click Here</a><br>','A')
```

produces:

```
<hr>&lt;a href=&quot;/mp3&quot;&gt;Click Here&lt;/a&gt;<br>
```

Here only the <a...> element is escaped; other elements are left alone. Each of these methods has an un- version to restore the original string:

```
require 'cgi'
puts CGI.unescapeHTML("a &lt; 100 &amp;&amp; b &gt; 200")
```

produces:

```
a < 100 && b > 200
```

Query Parameters

HTTP requests from the browser to your application may contain parameters, either passed as part of the URL or passed as data embedded in the body of the request.

Processing of these parameters is complicated by the fact that a value with a given name may be returned multiple times in the same request. For example, say we're writing a survey to find out why folks like Ruby. The HTML for our form looks like the following.

```
<html>
  <head>
    <title>Test Form</title>
  </head>

  <body>
    <p>
      I like Ruby because:
    </p>
```

```
<form action="cgi-bin/survey.rb">
  <p>
    <input type="checkbox" name="reason" value="flexible" />
    It's flexible
  </p>
  <p>
    <input type="checkbox" name="reason" value="transparent" />
    It's transparent
  </p>
  <p>
    <input type="checkbox" name="reason" value="perlish" />
    It's like Perl
  </p>
  <p>
    <input type="checkbox" name="reason" value="fun" />
    It's fun
  </p>
  <p>
    Your name: <input type="text" name="name"/>
  </p>
  <input type="submit"/>
</form>
</body>
</html>
```

When someone fills in this form, they might check multiple reasons for liking Ruby (as shown in the following screenshot):

In this case, the form data corresponding to the name reason will have three values, corresponding to the three checked boxes.

Class CGI gives you access to form data in a couple of ways. First, we can just treat the CGI object as a hash, indexing it with field names and getting back field values.

```
require 'cgi'
cgi = CGI.new
cgi['name']   # => "Dave Thomas"
cgi['reason'] # => "flexible"
```

However, this doesn't work well with the reason field, because we see only one of the three values. We can ask to see them all by using the CGI#params method. The value returned by params acts like a hash containing the request parameters. You can both read and write this hash (the latter allows you to modify the data associated with a request). Note that each of the values in the hash is actually an array.

```
cgi = CGI.new
cgi.params           # => {"name"=>["Dave Thomas"], "reason"=>["flexible",
                     # .. "transparent", "fun"]}
cgi.params['name']   # => ["Dave Thomas"]
cgi.params['reason'] # => ["flexible", "transparent", "fun"]
```

You can determine whether a particular parameter is present in a request using CGI#has_key?:

```
require 'cgi'
cgi = CGI.new
cgi.has_key?('name') # => true
cgi.has_key?('age')  # => false
```

Generating HTML with CGI.rb

CGI contains a huge number of methods that can be used to create HTML—one method per element. To enable these methods, you must create a CGI object by calling CGI.new, passing in the required version of HTML. In these examples, we'll use html4.

To make element nesting easier, these methods take their content as code blocks. The code blocks should return a String, which will be used as the content for the element.

```
require 'cgi'
cgi = CGI.new("html4")  # add HTML generation methods
cgi.out do
  cgi.html do
    cgi.head { cgi.title { "This Is a Test"} } +
    cgi.body do
      cgi.form do
        cgi.hr +
        cgi.h1 { "A Form: " } +
        cgi.textarea("get_text") +
        cgi.br +
        cgi.submit
      end
    end
  end
end
```

Although vaguely interesting, this method of generating HTML is fairly laborious and probably isn't used much in practice. Most people seem to write the HTML directly, use a templating system, or use an application framework, such as Rails. Unfortunately, we don't have space here to discuss Rails—take a look at the online documentation at http://rubyonrails.org —but we can look at templating (including erb, the templating engine used by Rails).

20.3 Templating Systems

Templating systems let you separate the presentation and logic of your application. It seems that just about everyone who writes a web application using Ruby at some point also writes a templating system; a quick review page written in 2008 by Vidar Hokstad[1] lists nineteen. For now, let's just look at two: Haml and erb/eruby. Also, remember to look at Builder if you need to generate XHTML or XML.

---

1.   http://www.hokstad.com/mini-reviews-of-19-ruby-template-engines.html

Haml

Haml is a library that generates HTML documents from a template.[2] Unlike many other templating systems, Haml uses indentation to indicate nesting (yup, just like Python). For example, you can represent a <ul> in Haml using this:

```
%ul
  %li item one
  %li item two
```

Install Haml using this:

```
$ gem install haml
```

The Haml input syntax is rich and powerful, and the example that follows touches on only a subset of the features. Lines starting with % get converted to HTML tags, nested in the output according to their indentation in the input. An equals sign means "substitute in the value of the Ruby code that follows." A minus sign executes Ruby code but doesn't substitute the value in—our example uses that to look over the reasons when constructing the table.

There are many ways of getting values passed in to the template. In this example, we chose to pass in a hash as the second parameter to render. This results in local variables getting set as the template is expanded, one variable for each key in the hash:

```
require 'haml'
engine = Haml::Engine.new(%{
%body
  #welcome-box
    %p= greeting
  %p
    As of
    = Time.now
    the reasons you gave were:
  %table
    %tr
      %th Reason
      %th Rank
    - for reason in reasons
      %tr
        %td= reason[:reason_name]
        %td= reason[:rank]
})

data = {
  greeting: 'Hello, Dave Thomas',
  reasons: [
    { reason_name: 'flexible',    rank: '87' },
    { reason_name: 'transparent', rank: '76' },
    { reason_name: 'fun',         rank: '94' },
  ]
}

puts engine.render(nil, data)
```

---

2.   http://haml-lang.com/

produces:

```
<body>
  <div id='welcome-box'>
    <p>Hello, Dave Thomas</p>
  </div>
  <p>
    As of
    2013-05-27 12:31:30 -0500
    the reasons you gave were:
  </p>
  <table>
    <tr>
      <th>Reason</th>
      <th>Rank</th>
    </tr>
    <tr>
      <td>flexible</td>
      <td>87</td>
    </tr>
    <tr>
      <td>transparent</td>
      <td>76</td>
    </tr>
    <tr>
      <td>fun</td>
      <td>94</td>
    </tr>
  </table>
</body>
```

erb and eruby

So far we've looked at using Ruby to create HTML output, but we can turn the problem inside out; we can actually embed Ruby in an HTML document.

A number of packages allow you to embed Ruby statements in an HTML document–generically, this markup is known as "eRuby." There are several different implementations of eRuby , including erubis and erb. erubis is available as a gem, while erb is written in pure Ruby and is included with the standard distribution. We'll look at erb here.

Embedding Ruby in HTML is a very powerful concept—it basically gives us the equivalent of a tool such as ASP, JSP, or PHP, but with the full power of Ruby.

Using erb

erb is a filter. Input text is passed through untouched, with the following exceptions:

Expression	Description
<% *ruby code* %>	This executes the Ruby code between the delimiters.
<%= *ruby expression* %>	This evaluates the Ruby expression and replaces the sequence with the expression's value.
<%# *ruby code* %>	The Ruby code between the delimiters is ignored (useful for testing).

Expression	Description
% *line of ruby code*	A line that starts with a percent is assumed to contain just Ruby code.

You can run erb from the command line:

erb ‹*options*› ‹*document*›

If the *document* is omitted, erb will read from standard input. The command-line options for erb are:

Option	Description
-d	Sets $DEBUG to true
-E ext[:int]	Sets the default external/internal encodings
-n	Displays resulting Ruby script (with line numbers)
-r library	Loads the named library
-P	Doesn't do erb processing on lines starting %
-S level	Sets the *safe level*
-T mode	Sets the *trim mode*
-U	Sets default encoding to UTF-8
-v	Enables verbose mode
-x	Displays resulting Ruby script

Let's look at some simple examples. We'll run the erb executable on the following input:

```
web/f1.erb
% 99.downto(96) do |number|
<%= number %> bottles of beer...
% end
```

The lines starting with the percent sign simply execute the given Ruby. In this case, it's a loop that iterates the line between them. The sequence <%= number %> in the middle line substitutes in the value of number into the output.

```
$ erb f1.erb
99 bottles of beer...
98 bottles of beer...
97 bottles of beer...
96 bottles of beer...
```

erb works by rewriting its input as a Ruby script and then executing that script. You can see the Ruby that erb generates using the -n or -x option:

```
$ erb -x f1.erb
#coding:ASCII-8BIT
_erbout = '';  99.downto(96) do |number|
_erbout.concat(( number ).to_s); _erbout.concat " bottles of beer...\n"
;  end
_erbout.force_encoding(__ENCODING__)
```

Notice how erb builds a string, _erbout, containing both the static strings from the template and the results of executing expressions (in this case the value of number).

Embedding erb in Your Code

So far we've shown erb running as a command-line filter. However, the most common use is to use it as a library in your own code. (This is what Rails does with its .erb templates.)

```
require 'erb'

SOURCE =
%{<% for number in min..max %>
The number is <%= number %>
<% end %>
}

erb = ERB.new(SOURCE)

min = 4
max = 6
puts erb.result(binding)
```

produces:

```
The number is 4

The number is 5

The number is 6
```

Notice how we can use local variables within the erb template. This works because we pass the current *binding* to the result method. erb can use this binding to make it look as if the template is being evaluated in the context of the calling code.

erb comes with excellent documentation: use ri to read it. One thing that Rails users should know is that in the standard version of erb, you can't use the -%> trick to suppress blank lines. (In the previous example, that's why we have the extra blank lines in the output.) Take a look at the description of trim modes in the documentation of ERB.new for alternatives.

20.4 Cookies

Cookies are a way of letting web applications store their state on the user's machine. Frowned upon by some, cookies are still a convenient (if unreliable) way of remembering session information.

The Ruby CGI class handles the loading and saving of cookies for you. You can access the cookies associated with the current request using the CGI#cookies method, and you can set cookies back into the browser by setting the cookie parameter of CGI#out to reference either a single cookie or an array of cookies:

web/cookies.rb
```
#!/usr/bin/ruby
require 'cgi'

COOKIE_NAME = 'chocolate chip'

cgi = CGI.new
values = cgi.cookies[COOKIE_NAME]
```

```
if values.empty?
  msg = "It looks as if you haven't visited recently"
else
  msg = "You last visited #{values[0]}"
end

cookie = CGI::Cookie.new(COOKIE_NAME, Time.now.to_s)
cookie.expires = Time.now + 30*24*3600 # 30 days
cgi.out("cookie" => cookie ) { msg }
```

Sessions

Cookies by themselves still need a bit of work to be useful. We really want *sessions:* information that persists between requests from a particular web browser. Sessions are handled by class CGI::Session, which uses cookies but provides a higher-level abstraction.

As with cookies, sessions emulate a hashlike behavior, letting you associate values with keys. Unlike cookies, sessions store the majority of their data on the server, using the browser-resident cookie simply as a way of uniquely identifying the server-side data. Sessions also give you a choice of storage techniques for this data: it can be held in regular files, in a PStore (see the description on page 793), in memory, or even in your own customized store.

Sessions should be closed after use, because this ensures that their data is written out to the store. When you've permanently finished with a session, you should delete it.

```
web/session.rb
require 'cgi'
require 'cgi/session'

cgi = CGI.new("html4")
sess = CGI::Session.new(cgi, "session_key" => "rubyweb",
                             "prefix"      => "web-session.")

if sess['lastaccess']
  msg = "<p>You were last here #{sess['lastaccess']}.</p>"
else
  msg = "<p>Looks like you haven't been here for a while</p>"
end

count = (sess["accesscount"] || 0).to_i
count += 1

msg << "<p>Number of visits: #{count}</p>"

sess["accesscount"] = count
sess["lastaccess"]  = Time.now.to_s
sess.close

cgi.out {
  cgi.html {
    cgi.body {
      msg
    }
  }
}
```

The code in the previous example used the default storage mechanism for sessions: persistent data was stored in files in your default temporary directory (see Dir.tmpdir). The filenames will all start with web-session. and will end with a hashed version of the session number. See the documentation for CGI::Session for more information.

20.5 Choice of Web Servers

So far, we've been running Ruby scripts under the Apache web server. However, Ruby comes bundled with WEBrick, a flexible, pure-Ruby HTTP server toolkit. WEBrick is an extensible plug-in–based framework that lets you write servers to handle HTTP requests and responses. The following is a basic HTTP server that serves documents and directory indexes:

web/webrick1.rb
```ruby
#!/usr/bin/ruby
require 'webrick'
include WEBrick

s = HTTPServer.new(Port: 2000,DocumentRoot: File.join(Dir.pwd, "/html"))

trap("INT") { s.shutdown }
s.start
```

The HTTPServer constructor creates a new web server on port 2000. The code sets the document root to be the html/ subdirectory of the current directory. It then uses Object#trap to arrange to shut down tidily on interrupts before starting the server running. If you point your browser at http://localhost:2000, you should see a listing of your html subdirectory.

WEBrick can do far more than serve static content. You can use it just like a Java servlet container. The following code mounts a simple servlet at the location /hello. As requests arrive, the do_GET method is invoked. It uses the response object to display the user agent information and parameters from the request.

web/webrick2.rb
```ruby
#!/usr/bin/ruby

require 'webrick'
include WEBrick

s = HTTPServer.new(Port: 2000)

class HelloServlet < HTTPServlet::AbstractServlet
  def do_GET(req, res)
    res['Content-Type'] = "text/html"
    res.body = %{
      <html><body>
        <p>Hello. You're calling from a #{req['User-Agent']}</p>
        <p>I see parameters: #{req.query.keys.join(', ')}</p>
      </body></html>}
  end
end

s.mount("/hello", HelloServlet)
trap("INT"){ s.shutdown }
s.start
```

20.6 Frameworks

In reality, almost no one uses CGI to write web-based Ruby applications any more. Most of the real action these days is with frameworks. Frameworks abstract away all this low-level detail and also help you structure your code into something that is both easy to write and (probably more importantly) easy to maintain.

At the time of writing, Ruby on Rails[3] is the leading web framework for Ruby. It has an incredibly active community and a vast set of plug-ins, so the chances are good you'll find a lot of preexisting code to help you kick-start your application. Other alternatives include Camping, Padrino, Sinatra, and Ramaze.[4] By the time you read this, the list will have grown. And, if you fancy writing your own framework, consider making it independent of the underlying web server by building it on top of Rack.[5]

---

3. http://www.rubyonrails.org
4. http://camping.rubyforge.org/files/README.html, http://padrinorb.com, http://www.sinatrarb.com/, and http://ramaze.net/
5. http://rack.rubyforge.org/

## CHAPTER 21

Ruby and Microsoft Windows

Ruby runs in a number of environments. Some of these are Unix-based, and others are based on the various flavors of Microsoft Windows. Ruby came from people who were Unix-centric, but over the years it has developed a whole lot of useful features in the Windows world, too. In this chapter, we'll look at these features and share some secrets that let you use Ruby effectively under Windows.

21.1 Running Ruby Under Windows

You'll find two versions of the Ruby interpreter in the RubyInstaller distribution.

The ruby is meant to be used at a command prompt (a DOS shell), just as in the Unix version. For applications that read and write to the standard input and output, this is fine. But this also means that any time you run ruby, you'll get a DOS shell even if you don't want one—Windows will create a new command prompt window and display it while Ruby is running. This may not be appropriate behavior if, for example, you double-click a Ruby script that uses a graphical interface (such as Tk) or if you are running a Ruby script as a background task or from inside another program.

In these cases, you will want to use rubyw. It is the same as ruby except that it does not provide standard in, standard out, or standard error and does not launch a DOS shell when run.

You can set up file associations using the assoc and ftype commands so that Ruby will automatically run Ruby when you double-click the name of a Ruby script:

```
C:\> assoc .rb=RubyScript
C:\> ftype RubyScript="C:\ruby1.9\bin\ruby.exe" %1 %*
```

You may have to run the command prompt with elevated privileges to make this work. To do this, right-click it in the Start menu, and select *Run As Administrator*.

If you don't want to have to type the .rb, you can add Ruby scripts to your PATHEXT:

```
C:\> set PATHEXT=.rb;%PATHEXT%
```

21.2 Win32API

If you plan on doing Ruby programming that needs to access some Windows 32 API functions directly or that needs to use the entry points in some other DLLs, we have good news for you—the Win32API library.

As an example, here's some code that's part of a larger Windows application used by our book fulfillment system to download and print invoices and receipts. A web application generates a PDF file, which the Ruby script running on Windows downloads into a local file. The script then uses the print shell command under Windows to print this file.

```
arg   = "ids=#{resp.intl_orders.join(",")}"
fname = "/temp/invoices.pdf"

site = Net::HTTP.new(HOST, PORT)
site.use_ssl = true
http_resp, = site.get2("/ship/receipt?" + arg,
                       'Authorization' => 'Basic ' +
                       ["name:passwd"].pack('m').strip )

File.open(fname, "wb") {|f| f.puts(http_resp.body) }

shell = Win32API.new("shell32","ShellExecute",
                     ['L','P','P','P','P','L'], 'L' )
shell.Call(0, "print", fname, 0,0, SW_SHOWNORMAL)
```

You create a Win32API object that represents a call to a particular DLL entry point by specifying the name of the function, the name of the DLL that contains the function, and the function signature (argument types and return type). In the previous example, the variable shell wraps the Windows function ShellExecute in the shell32 DLL. The second parameter is an array of characters describing the types of the parameters the method takes: n and l represent numbers, i represent integers, p represents pointers to data stored in a string, and v represents a void type (used for export parameters only). These strings are case insensitive. So, our method takes a number, four string pointers, and a number. The last parameter says that the method returns a number. The resulting object is a proxy to the underlying ShellExecute function and can be used to make the call to print the file that we downloaded.

Many of the arguments to DLL functions are binary structures of some form. Win32API handles this by using Ruby String objects to pass the binary data back and forth. You will need to pack and unpack these strings as necessary.

21.3 Windows Automation

If groveling around in the low-level Windows API doesn't interest you, Windows Automation may—you can use Ruby as a client for Windows Automation thanks to Masaki Suketa's Ruby extension called WIN32OLE. Win32OLE is part of the standard Ruby distribution.

Windows Automation allows an automation controller (a client) to issue commands and queries against an automation server, such as Microsoft Excel, Word, and so on.

You can execute an automation server's method by calling a method of the same name from a WIN32OLE object. For instance, you can create a new WIN32OLE client that launches a fresh copy of Internet Explorer and commands it to visit its home page:

win32/gohome.rb
```
require 'win32ole'
ie = WIN32OLE.new('InternetExplorer.Application')
ie.visible = true
ie.gohome
```

You could also make it navigate to a particular page:

```
win32/navigate.rb
require 'win32ole'
ie = WIN32OLE.new('InternetExplorer.Application')
ie.visible = true
ie.navigate("http://www.pragprog.com")
```

Methods that aren't known to WIN32OLE (such as visible, gohome, or navigate) are passed on to the WIN32OLE#invoke method, which sends the proper commands to the server.

Getting and Setting Properties

An automation server's properties are automatically set up as attributes of the WIN32OLE object. This means you can set a property by assigning to an object attribute. For example, to get and then set the Height property of Explorer, you could write this:

```
win32/get_set_height.rb
require 'win32ole'
ie = WIN32OLE.new('InternetExplorer.Application')
ie.visible = true
puts "Height = #{ie.Height}"
ie.Height = 300
```

The following example uses the automation interface built into the OpenOffice suite to create a spreadsheet and populate some cells:[1]

```
win32/open_office.rb
require 'win32ole'

class OOSpreadsheet
  def initialize
    mgr  = WIN32OLE.new('com.sun.star.ServiceManager')
    desktop = mgr.createInstance("com.sun.star.frame.Desktop")
    @doc = desktop.LoadComponentFromUrl("private:factory/scalc", "_blank", 0, [])
    @sheet = @doc.sheets[0]
  end

  def get_cell(row, col)
    @sheet.getCellByPosition(col, row, 0)
  end

  # tl: top_left, br: bottom_right
  def get_cell_range(tl_row, tl_col, br_row, br_col)
    @sheet.getCellRangeByPosition(tl_row, tl_col, br_row, br_col, 0)
  end
end

spreadsheet = OOSpreadsheet.new
cell = spreadsheet.get_cell(1, 0)
cell.Value = 1234

cells = spreadsheet.get_cell_range(1, 2, 5, 3)
```

---

1. See http://udk.openoffice.org/common/man/tutorial/office_automation.html for links to resources on automating OpenOffice.

```
cols = cells.Columns.count
rows = cells.Rows.count

cols.times do |col_no|
  rows.times do |row_no|
    cell = cells.getCellByPosition(col_no, row_no)
    cell.Value = (col_no + 1)*(row_no+1)
  end
end
```

Named Arguments

Other automation client languages such as Visual Basic have the concept of *named arguments*. Suppose you had a Visual Basic routine with the following signature:

```
Song(artist, title, length):      rem Visual Basic
```

Instead of calling it with all three arguments in the order specified, you could use named arguments:

```
Song title := 'Get It On':      rem Visual Basic
```

This is equivalent to the call Song(nil, "Get It On", nil).

In Ruby, you can use this feature by passing a hash with the named arguments:

```
Song.new('title' => 'Get It On')
```

for each

Where Visual Basic has a for each statement to iterate over a collection of items in a server, a WIN32OLE object has an each method (which takes a block) to accomplish the same thing:

win32/win32each.rb
```
require 'win32ole'

excel = WIN32OLE.new("excel.application")

excel.Workbooks.Add
excel.Range("a1").Value = 10
excel.Range("a2").Value = 20
excel.Range("a3").Value = "=a1+a2"

excel.Range("a1:a3").each do |cell|
  p cell.Value
end
```

Events

Your automation client written in Ruby can register itself to receive events from other programs. This is done using the WIN32OLE_EVENT class.

This example (based on code from the Win32OLE 0.1.1 distribution) shows the use of an event sink that logs the URLs that a user browses to when using Internet Explorer:

win32/record_navigation.rb

```
require 'win32ole'

urls_visited = []
running = true

def default_handler(event, *args)
  case event
  when "BeforeNavigate"
    puts "Now Navigating to #{args[0]}..."
  end
end

ie = WIN32OLE.new('InternetExplorer.Application')
ie.visible = TRUE
ie.gohome
ev = WIN32OLE_EVENT.new(ie, 'DWebBrowserEvents')

ev.on_event {|*args| default_handler(*args)}
ev.on_event("NavigateComplete") {|url| urls_visited << url }
ev.on_event("Quit") do |*args|
  puts "IE has quit"
  puts "You Navigated to the following URLs: "
  urls_visited.each_with_index do |url, i|
    puts "(#{i+1}) #{url}"
  end
  running = false
end

# hang around processing messages
WIN32OLE_EVENT.message_loop while running
```

Optimizing

As with most (if not all) high-level languages, it can be all too easy to churn out code that is unbearably slow, but that can be easily fixed with a little thought.

With WIN32OLE, you need to be careful with unnecessary dynamic lookups. Where possible, it is better to assign a WIN32OLE object to a variable and then reference elements from it, rather than creating a long chain of "." expressions.

For example, instead of writing this:

```
workbook.Worksheets(1).Range("A1").value = 1
workbook.Worksheets(1).Range("A2").value = 2
workbook.Worksheets(1).Range("A3").value = 4
workbook.Worksheets(1).Range("A4").value = 8
```

we can eliminate the common subexpressions by saving the first part of the expression to a temporary variable and then make calls from that variable:

```
worksheet = workbook.Worksheets(1)

worksheet.Range("A1").value = 1
worksheet.Range("A2").value = 2
worksheet.Range("A3").value = 4
worksheet.Range("A4").value = 8
```

You can also create Ruby stubs for a particular Windows type library. These stubs wrap the OLE object in a Ruby class with one method per entry point. Internally, the stub uses the entry point's number, not name, which speeds access.

Generate the wrapper class using the olegen.rb script, available in the Ruby source repository.[2] Give it the name of type library to reflect on:

```
C:\> ruby olegen.rb 'Microsoft TAPI 3.0 Type Library' >tapi.rb
```

The external methods and events of the type library are written as Ruby methods to the given file. You can then include it in your programs and call the methods directly.

More Help

If you need to interface Ruby to Windows NT, 2000, or XP, you may want to take a look at Daniel Berger's Win32Utils project (http://rubyforge.org/projects/win32utils/). There you'll find modules for interfacing to the Windows clipboard, event log, scheduler, and so on.

Also, the Fiddle library (described briefly in the library section on page 756) allows Ruby programs to invoke methods in dynamically loaded shared objects. This means your Ruby code can load and invoke entry points in a Windows DLL. For example, the following code pops up a message box on a Windows machine and determines which button the user clicked.

```
win32/dl.rb
require 'fiddle'

user32  = DL.dlopen("user32.dll")
msgbox  = Fiddle::Function.new(user32['MessageBoxA'],
                         [TYPE_LONG, TYPE_VOIDP, TYPE_VOIDP, TYPE_INT],
                         TYPE_INT)
MB_OKCANCEL = 1
msgbox.call(0, "OK?", "Please Confirm", MB_OKCANCEL)
```

This code wraps User32 DLL, creating a Ruby method that is a proxy to the underlying MessageBoxA method. It also specifies the return and parameter types so that Ruby can correctly marshal them between its objects and the underlying operating system types.

The wrapper object is then used to call the message box entry point in the DLL. The return values are the result (in this case, the identifier of the button pressed by the user) and an array of the parameters passed in (which we ignore).

---

2.   http://svn.ruby-lang.org/repos/ruby/trunk/ext/win32ole/sample/olegen.rb

Part III

Ruby Crystallized

## CHAPTER 22

The Ruby Language

This chapter is a bottom-up look at the Ruby language. Most of what appears here is the syntax and semantics of the language itself—we mostly ignore the built-in classes and modules (these are covered in depth in the reference material on page 417). However, Ruby sometimes implements features in its libraries that in most languages would be part of the basic syntax. Where it makes sense, we've included some of these methods here.

The contents of this chapter may look familiar—with good reason, as we've covered most of this earlier. This chapter is a self-contained reference for the Ruby language.

22.1 Source File Encoding

Ruby 1.9 programs are by default written in 7-bit ASCII, also called US-ASCII. If a code set other than 7-bit ASCII is to be used, place a comment containing coding: followed by the name of an encoding on the first line of each source file containing non-ASCII characters. The coding: comment can be on the second line of the file if the first line is a shebang comment. Ruby skips characters in the comment before the word coding:. Ruby 2 assumes the source is written in UTF-8. This assumption can be overridden using the same style coding: comment.   New in 2.0

```
# coding: utf-8     # -*- encoding: iso-8859-1 -*-     #!/usr/bin/ruby
                                                        # fileencoding: us-ascii

UTF-8 source...    ISO-8859-1 source...                ASCII source...
```

22.2 Source Layout

Ruby is a line-oriented language. Ruby expressions and statements are terminated at the end of a line unless the parser can determine that the statement is incomplete, such as if the last token on a line is an operator or comma. A semicolon can be used to separate multiple expressions on a line. You can also put a backslash at the end of a line to continue it onto the next. Comments start with # and run to the end of the physical line. Comments are ignored during syntax analysis.

```
a = 1
b = 2; c = 3
d = 4 + 5 +
    6 + 7          # no '\' needed
e = 8 + 9   \
    + 10           # '\' needed
```

Physical lines between a line starting with =begin and a line starting with =end are ignored by Ruby and may be used to comment out sections of code or to embed documentation.

You can pipe programs to the Ruby interpreter's standard input stream:

```
$ echo 'puts "Hello"' | ruby
```

If Ruby comes across a line anywhere in the source containing just __END__, with no leading or trailing whitespace, it treats that line as the end of the program—any subsequent lines will not be treated as program code. However, these lines can be read into the running program using the global IO object DATA, described in the section about constants on page 315.

BEGIN and END Blocks

Every Ruby source file can declare blocks of code to be run as the file is being loaded (the BEGIN blocks) and after the program has finished executing (the END blocks):

```
BEGIN {
   begin code
}

END {
   end code
}
```

A program may include multiple BEGIN and END blocks. BEGIN blocks are executed in the order they are encountered. END blocks are executed in reverse order.

General Delimited Input

As well as the normal quoting mechanism, alternative forms of literal strings, arrays of strings and symbols, regular expressions, and shell commands are specified using a generalized delimited syntax. All these literals start with a percent character, followed by a single character that identifies the literal's type. These characters are summarized in the following table; the actual literals are described in the corresponding sections later in this chapter.

New in 2.0

Type	Meaning	Example
%q	Single-quoted string	%q{\a and #{1+2} are literal}
%Q, %	Double-quoted string	%Q{\a and #{1+2} are expanded}
%w, %W	Array of strings	%w[one two three]
%i, %I (new in 2.0)	Array of symbols	%i[one two three]
%r	Regular expression pattern	%r{cat|dog}
%s	A symbol	%s!a symbol!
%x	Shell command	%x(df -h)

Unlike their lowercase counterparts, %I, %Q, and %W will preform interpolation:

```
%i{  one digit#{1+1} three } # => [:one, :"digit\#{1+1}", :three]
%I{  one digit#{1+1} three } # => [:one, :digit2, :three]
%q{  one digit#{1+1} three } # => "  one digit\#{1+1} three "
%Q{  one digit#{1+1} three } # => "  one digit2 three "
%w{  one digit#{1+1} three } # => ["one", "digit\#{1+1}", "three"]
%W{  one digit#{1+1} three } # => ["one", "digit2", "three"]
```

Following the type character is a delimiter, which can be any nonalphanumericic or non-multibyte character. If the delimiter is one of the characters (, [, {, or <, the literal consists of the characters up to the matching closing delimiter, taking account of nested delimiter pairs. For all other delimiters, the literal comprises the characters up to the next occurrence of the delimiter character.

```
%q/this is a string/
%q-string-
%q(a (nested) string)
```

Delimited strings may continue over multiple lines; the line endings and all spaces at the start of continuation lines will be included in the string:

```
meth = %q{def fred(a)
          a.each {|i| puts i }
        end}
```

22.3 The Basic Types

The basic types in Ruby are numbers, strings, arrays, hashes, ranges, symbols, and regular expressions.

Integer and Floating-Point Numbers

Ruby integers are objects of class Fixnum or Bignum. Fixnum objects hold integers that fit within the native machine word minus 1 bit. Whenever a Fixnum exceeds this range, it is automatically converted to a Bignum object, whose range is effectively limited only by available memory. If an operation with a Bignum result has a final value that will fit in a Fixnum, the result will be returned as a Fixnum.

Integers are written using an optional leading sign and an optional base indicator (0 or 0o for octal, 0d for decimal, 0x for hex, or 0b for binary), followed by a string of digits in the appropriate base. Underscore characters are ignored in the digit string.

```
123456                      => 123456      # Fixnum
0d123456                    => 123456      # Fixnum
123_456                     => 123456      # Fixnum - underscore ignored
-543                        => -543        # Fixnum - negative number
0xaabb                      => 43707       # Fixnum - hexadecimal
0377                        => 255         # Fixnum - octal
0o377                       => 255         # Fixnum - octal
-0b10_1010                  => -42         # Fixnum - binary (negated)
123_456_789_123_456_789     => 123456789123456789 # Bignum
```

A numeric literal with a decimal point and/or an exponent is turned into a Float object, corresponding to the native architecture's double data type. You must follow the decimal point with a digit; if you write 1.e3, Ruby tries to invoke the method e3 on the Fixnum 1. You must place at least one digit before the decimal point.

```
12.34      # => 12.34
-0.1234e2 # => -12.34
1234e-2    # => 12.34
```

Rational and Complex Numbers

Classes that support rational numbers (ratios of integers) and complex numbers are built into the Ruby interpreter. However, Ruby provides no language-level support for these numeric types—there are no rational or complex literals, for example. See the descriptions of Complex on page 451 and Rational on page 656 for more information.

Strings

Ruby provides a number of mechanisms for creating literal strings. Each generates objects of type String. The different mechanisms vary in terms of how a string is delimited and how much substitution is done on the literal's content. Literal strings are encoded using the source encoding of the file that contains them.

Single-quoted string literals ('stuff' and %q/stuff/) undergo the least substitution. Both convert the sequence \\ into a single backslash, and a backslash can be used to escape the single quote or the string delimiter. All other backslashes appear literally in the string.

```
'hello'                     # => hello
'a backslash \'\\\''        # => a backslash '\'
%q/simple string/           # => simple string
%q(nesting (really) works)  # => nesting (really) works
%q(escape a\) with backslash) # => escape a) with backslash
%q no_blanks_here ;         # => no_blanks_here
```

Double-quoted strings ("stuff", %Q/stuff/,} and %/stuff/) undergo additional substitutions; see the following table.

\#{code}	Value of *code*	\b	Backspace (0x08)	\t	Tab (0x09)
\nnn	Octal *nnn*	\cx	Control-*x*	\uxxxx	Unicode character
\x	*x*	\e	Escape (0x1b)	\u{xx xx xx}	Unicode characters
\C-x	Control-*x*	\f	Formfeed (0x0c)	\v	Vertical tab (0x0b)
\M-x	Meta-*x*	\n	Newline (0x0a)	\xnn	Hex *nn*
\M-\C-x	Meta-control-*x*	\r	Return (0x0d)		
\a	Bell/alert (0x07)	\s	Space (0x20)		

Table 11—Substitutions in double-quoted strings

Here are some examples:

```
a   = 123
"\123mile"                  # => Smile
"Greek pi: \u03c0"          # => Greek pi: π
"Greek \u{70 69 3a 20 3c0}" # => Greek pi: π
"Say \"Hello\""             # => Say "Hello"
%Q!"I said 'nuts'\!," I said! # => "I said 'nuts'!," I said
%Q{Try #{a + 1}, not #{a - 1}} # => Try 124, not 122
%<Try #{a + 1}, not #{a - 1}> # => Try 124, not 122
"Try #{a + 1}, not #{a - 1}" # => Try 124, not 122
%{ #{ a = 1; b = 2; a + b } } # =>  3
```

Last, and probably least (in terms of usage), you can get the string corresponding to an ASCII character by preceding that character with a question mark.

?a	"a"	ASCII character
?\n	"\n"	newline (0x0a)
?\C-a	"\u0001"	control a (0x65 & 0x9f) == 0x01
?\M-a	"\xE1"	meta sets bit 7
?\M-\C-a	"\x81"	meta and control a
?\C-?	"\u007F"	delete character

Strings can continue across multiple input lines, in which case they will contain newline characters. You can use *here documents* to express long string literals. When Ruby parses the sequence <<identifier or <<quoted string, it replaces it with a string literal built from successive logical input lines. It stops building the string when it finds a line that starts with *identifier* or *quoted string*. You can put a minus sign immediately after the << characters, in which case the terminator can be indented from the margin. If a quoted string was used to specify the terminator, its quoting rules are applied to the here document; otherwise, double-quoting rules apply.

```
print <<HERE
Double quoted \
here document.
It is #{Time.now}
HERE

print <<-'THERE'
    This is single quoted.
    The above used #{Time.now}
    THERE
```

produces:

```
Double quoted here document.
It is 2013-05-27 12:31:31 -0500
    This is single quoted.
    The above used #{Time.now}
```

In the previous example the backslash after Double quoted caused the logical line to be continued with the contents of the next line.

Adjacent single- and double-quoted strings are concatenated to form a single String object:

```
'Con' "cat" 'en' "ate" # => "Concatenate"
```

A new String object is created every time a string literal is assigned or passed as a parameter.

```
3.times do
  print 'hello'.object_id, " "
end
```

produces:

```
70214897722200 70214897722080 70214897721960
```

There's more information in the documentation for class String on page 666.

Ranges

Outside the context of a conditional expression, expr..expr and expr...expr construct Range objects. The two-dot form is an inclusive range; the one with three dots is a range that excludes its last element. See the description of class Range on page 650 for details. Also see the description of conditional expressions on page 320 for other uses of ranges.

Arrays

Literals of class Array are created by placing a comma-separated series of object references between square brackets. A trailing comma is ignored.

```
arr = [ fred, 10, 3.14, "This is a string", barney("pebbles"), ]
```

Arrays of strings can be constructed using the shortcut notations %w and %W. The lowercase form extracts space-separated tokens into successive elements of the array. No substitution is performed on the individual strings. The uppercase version also converts the words to an array but performs all the normal double-quoted string substitutions on each individual word. A space between words can be escaped with a backslash. This is a form of general delimited input, described earlier on page 298.

```
arr = %w( fred wilma barney betty great\ gazoo )
arr        # => ["fred", "wilma", "barney", "betty", "great gazoo"]
arr = %w( Hey!\tIt is now -#{Time.now}- )
arr        # => ["Hey!\tIt", "is", "now", "-#{Time.now}-"]
arr = %W( Hey!\tIt is now -#{Time.now}- )
arr        # => ["Hey!   It", "is", "now", "-2013-05-27 12:31:31 -0500-"]
```

Hashes

A literal Ruby Hash is created by placing a list of key/value pairs between braces. Keys and values can be separated by the sequence =>.[1]

```
colors = { "red" => 0xf00, "green" => 0x0f0, "blue" => 0x00f }
```

If the keys are symbols, you can use this alternative notation:

```
colors = { red: 0xf00, green: 0x0f0, blue: 0x00f }
```

The keys and/or values in a particular hash need not have the same type.

Requirements for a Hash Key

Hash keys must respond to the message hash by returning a hash code, and the hash code for a given key must not change. The keys used in hashes must also be comparable using eql?. If eql? returns true for two keys, then those keys must also have the same hash code. This means that certain classes (such as Array and Hash) can't conveniently be used as keys, because their hash values can change based on their contents.

If you keep an external reference to an object that is used as a key and use that reference to alter the object, thus changing its hash code, the hash lookup based on that key may not work. You can force the hash to be reindexed by calling its rehash method.

---

1. As of Ruby 1.9, a comma may no longer be used to separate keys and values in hash literals. A comma still appears between each key/value pair.

```
arr = [1, 2, 3]
hash = { arr => 'value' }
hash[arr] # => "value"
arr[1] = 99
hash      # => {[1, 99, 3]=>"value"}
hash[arr] # => nil
hash.rehash
hash[arr] # => "value"
```

Because strings are the most frequently used keys and because string contents are often changed, Ruby treats string keys specially. If you use a String object as a hash key, the hash will duplicate the string internally and will use that copy as its key. The copy will be frozen. Any changes made to the original string will not affect the hash.

If you write your own classes and use instances of them as hash keys, you need to make sure that either (a) the hashes of the key objects don't change once the objects have been created or (b) you remember to call the Hash#rehash method to reindex the hash whenever a key hash is changed.

Symbols

A Ruby symbol is an identifier corresponding to a string of characters, often a name. You construct the symbol for a name by preceding the name with a colon, and you can construct the symbol for an arbitrary string by preceding a string literal with a colon. Substitution occurs in double-quoted strings. A particular name or string will always generate the same symbol, regardless of how that name is used within the program. You can also use the %s delimited notation to create a symbol.

```
:Object
:my_variable
:"Ruby rules"
a = "cat"
:'catsup'  # => :catsup
:"#{a}sup" # => :catsup
:'#{a}sup' # => :"\#{a}sup"
```

Other languages call this process *interning* and call symbols *atoms*.

Regular Expressions

Ruby 1.9 uses the Oniguruma regular expression engine. Ruby 2.0 uses an extension of this engine called *Onigmo*. We show these extensions with the Ruby 2.0 flag. **New in 2.0**

See Chapter 7, *Regular Expressions*, on page 93 for a detailed description of regular expressions.

Regular expression literals are objects of type Regexp. They are created explicitly by calling Regexp.new or implicitly by using the literal forms, /pattern/ and %r{pattern}. The %r construct is a form of general delimited input (described earlier on page 298).

```
/pattern/
/pattern/options
%r{pattern}
%r{pattern}options
Regexp.new( 'pattern' ‹, options› )
```

options is one or more of i (case insensitive), o (substitute once), m (. matches newline), and x (allow spaces and comments). You can additionally override the default encoding of the pattern with n (no encoding-ASCII), e (EUC), s (Shift_JIS), or u (UTF-8).

Regular Expression Patterns

New in 2.0 (This section contains minor differences from previous versions of this book. Ruby 1.9 uses the Oniguruma regular expression engine.)[2]

New in 2.0 An asterisk at the end of an entry in the following list means that the match is extended beyond ASCII characters if Unicode option is set.

characters
: All except . | ( ) [\ ^ { + $ * and ? match themselves. To match one of these characters, precede it with a backslash.

\a \c*x* \e \f \r \t \u*nnnn* \v \x*nn* *nnn* \C-\M-*x* \C-*x* \M-*x*
: Match the character derived according to Table 11, *Substitutions in double-quoted strings*, on page 300.

^, $ Match the beginning/end of a line.

\A, \z, \Z
: Match the beginning/end of the string. \Z ignores trailing \n.

\d, \h Match any decimal digit or hexadecimal digit ([0-9a-fA-F]).[*]

\s Matches any whitespace character: tab, newline, vertical tab, formfeed, return, and space.[*]

\w Matches any word character: alphanumerics and underscores.[*]

\D, \H, \S, \W
: The negated forms of \d, \h, \s, and \w, matching characters that are not digits, hexadecimal digits, whitespace, or word characters.[*]

\b, \B Match word/nonword boundaries.

\G The position where a previous repetitive search completed.

\K Discards the portion of the match to the left of the \K.

New in 2.0
\R A generic end-of-line sequence.[*]

New in 2.0
\X A Unicode grapheme.[*]

New in 2.0
\p{property}, \P{property}, \p{!property}
: Match a character that is in/not in the given property (see Table 4, *Unicode character properties*, on page 114).

. (period)
: Appearing outside brackets, matches any character except a newline. (With the /m option, it matches newline, too).

[characters]
: Matches a single character from the specified set. See *Character Classes*, on page 98.

---

2. Some of the information here is based on http://www.geocities.jp/kosako3/oniguruma/doc/RE.txt.

re* Matches zero or more occurrences of *re*.

re+ Matches one or more occurrences of *re*.

re{m,n} Matches at least *m* and at most *n* occurrences of *re*.

re{m,} Matches at least *m* occurrences of *re*.

re{,n} Matches at most *n* occurrences of *re*.

re{m} Matches exactly *m* occurrences of *re*.

re? Matches zero or one occurrence of *re*.

> The ?, *, +, and {m,n} modifiers are greedy by default. Append a question mark to make them minimal, and append a plus sign to make them possessive (that is, they are greedy and will not backtrack).

re1 | re2
> Matches either *re1* or *re2*.

(...) Parentheses group regular expressions and introduce extensions.

#{...} Substitutes expression in the pattern, as with strings. By default, the substitution is performed each time a regular expression literal is evaluated. With the /o option, it is performed just the first time.

\1, \2, ... \n
> Match the value matched by the *n*th grouped subexpression.

(?# comment)
> Inserts a comment into the pattern.

(?:re) Makes *re* into a group without generating backreferences.

(?=re), (?!re)
> Matches if *re* is/is not at this point but does not consume it.

(?<=re), (?<!re)
> Matches if *re* is/is not before this point but does not consume it.

(?>re)
> Matches *re* but inhibits subsequent backtracking.

(?adimux), (?-imx)
> Turn on/off the corresponding a, d, i, m, u, or x option. If used inside a group, the effect is limited to that group.

New in 2.0

(?adimux:re), (?-imx:re)
> Turn on/off the i, m, or x option for *re*.

\n, \k'n', and \k<n>
> The nth captured subpattern.

(?<name>...) or (?'name'...)
> Name the string captured by the group.

\k<name> or \k'name'
> The contents of the named group.

\k<name>+/-n or \k'name'+/-n
> The contents of the named group at the given relative nesting level.

\g<name> or \g<number>
> Invokes the named or numbered group.

22.4 Names

Ruby names are used to refer to constants, variables, methods, classes, and modules. The first character of a name helps Ruby distinguish its intended use. Certain names, listed in the following table, are reserved words and should not be used as variable, method, class, or module names.

__ENCODING__		__FILE__	__LINE__	BEGIN	END	alias	and	begin
break	case	class	def	defined?	do	else	elsif	end
ensure	false	for	if	in	module	next	nil	not
or	redo	rescue	retry	return	self	super	then	true
undef	unless	until	when	while	yield			

Table 12—Reserved words

Method names are described later on page 323.

In these descriptions, *uppercase letter* means *A* through *Z*, and *digit* means *0* through *9*. *Lowercase letter* means the characters *a* through *z*, as well as the underscore (_). In addition, any non-7-bit characters that are valid in the current encoding are considered to be lowercase.[3]

A *name* is an uppercase letter, a lowercase letter, or an underscore, followed by *name characters*: any combination of upper- and lowercase letters, underscores, and digits.

A *local variable name* consists of a lowercase letter followed by name characters. It is conventional to use underscores rather than camelCase to write multiword names, but the interpreter does not enforce this.

```
fred  anObject  _x  three_two_one
```

If the source file encoding is UTF-8, ∂elta and été are both valid local variable names.

An *instance variable name* starts with an "at" sign (@) followed by name characters. It is generally a good idea to use a lowercase letter after the @. The @ sign forms part of the instance variable name.

```
@name  @_  @size
```

A *class variable name* starts with two "at" signs (@@) followed by name characters.

```
@@name  @@_  @@Size
```

A *constant name* starts with an uppercase letter followed by name characters. Class names and module names are constants and follow the constant naming conventions.

By convention, constant object references are normally spelled using uppercase letters and underscores throughout, while class and module names are MixedCase:

---

3.   Such names will not be usable from other source files with different encoding.

```ruby
module Math
  ALMOST_PI = 22.0/7.0
end
class BigBlob
end
```

Global variables, and some special system variables, start with a dollar sign ($) followed by name characters. In addition, Ruby defines a set of two-character global variable names in which the second character is a punctuation character. These predefined variables are listed *Predefined Variables*, on page 311. Finally, a global variable name can be formed using $- followed by a single letter or underscore. These latter variables typically mirror the setting of the corresponding command-line option (see *Execution Environment Variables*, on page 313 for details):

```ruby
$params  $PROGRAM  $!  $_  $-a  $-K
```

Variable/Method Ambiguity

When Ruby sees a name such as a in an expression, it needs to determine whether it is a local variable reference or a call to a method with no parameters. To decide which is the case, Ruby uses a heuristic. As Ruby parses a source file, it keeps track of symbols that have been assigned to. It assumes that these symbols are variables. When it subsequently comes across a symbol that could be a variable or a method call, it checks to see whether it has seen a prior assignment to that symbol. If so, it treats the symbol as a variable; otherwise, it treats it as a method call. As a somewhat pathological case of this, consider the following code fragment, submitted by Clemens Hintze:

```ruby
def a
  puts "Function 'a' called"
  99
end

for i in 1..2
  if i == 2
    puts "i==2, a=#{a}"
  else
    a = 1
    puts "i==1, a=#{a}"
  end
end
```

produces:

```
i==1, a=1
Function 'a' called
i==2, a=99
```

During the parse, Ruby sees the use of a in the first puts statement and, because it hasn't yet seen any assignment to a, assumes that it is a method call. By the time it gets to the second puts statement, though, it *has* seen an assignment and so treats a as a variable.

Note that the assignment does not have to be executed—Ruby just has to have seen it. This program does not raise an error.

```ruby
a = 1 if false; a # => nil
```

22.5 Variables and Constants

Ruby variables and constants hold references to objects. Variables themselves do not have an intrinsic type. Instead, the type of a variable is defined solely by the messages to which the object referenced by the variable responds. (When we say that a variable is not typed, we mean that any given variable can at different times hold references to objects of many different types.)

A Ruby *constant* is also a reference to an object. Constants are created when they are first assigned to (normally in a class or module definition). Ruby, unlike less flexible languages, lets you alter the value of a constant, although this will generate a warning message:

```
MY_CONST = 1
puts "First MY_CONST = #{MY_CONST}"

MY_CONST = 2   # generates a warning but sets MY_CONST to 2
puts "Then MY_CONST = #{MY_CONST}"
```

produces:

```
prog.rb:4: warning: already initialized constant MY_CONST
prog.rb:1: warning: previous definition of MY_CONST was here
First MY_CONST = 1
Then MY_CONST = 2
```

Note that although constants should not be changed, you can alter the internal states of the objects they reference (you can freeze objects to prevent this). This is because assignment potentially *aliases* objects, creating two references to the same object.

```
MY_CONST = "Tim"
MY_CONST[0] = "J"   # alter string referenced by constant
MY_CONST  # => "Jim"
```

Scope of Constants and Variables

Constants defined within a class or module may be accessed unadorned anywhere within the class or module. Outside the class or module, they may be accessed using the *scope operator*, ::, prefixed by an expression that returns the appropriate class or module object. Constants defined outside any class or module may be accessed unadorned or by using the scope operator with no prefix. Constants may not be defined in methods. Constants may be added to existing classes and modules from the outside by using the class or module name and the scope operator before the constant name.

```
OUTER_CONST = 99
class Const
  def get_const
    CONST
  end
  CONST = OUTER_CONST + 1
end
Const.new.get_const # => 100
Const::CONST        # => 100
::OUTER_CONST       # => 99
Const::NEW_CONST = 123
```

Global variables are available throughout a program. Every reference to a particular global name returns the same object. Referencing an uninitialized global variable returns nil.

Class variables are available throughout a class or module body. Class variables must be initialized before use. A class variable is shared among all instances of a class and is available within the class itself.

```ruby
class Song
  @@count = 0

  def initialize
    @@count += 1
  end

  def Song.get_count
    @@count
  end
end
```

Class variables belong to the innermost enclosing class or module. Class variables used at the top level are defined in Object and behave like global variables. In Ruby 1.9, class variables are supposed to be private to the defining class, although as the following example shows, there seems to be some leakage.

```ruby
class Holder # => prog.rb:13: warning: class variable access from toplevel
  @@var = 99

  def Holder.var=(val)
    @@var = val
  end

  def var
    @@var
  end
end

@@var = "top level variable"

a = Holder.new
a.var           # => "top level variable"
Holder.var = 123
a.var           # => 123
```

Class variables are inherited by children but propagate upward if first defined in a child:

```ruby
class Top
  @@A = "top A"
  @@B = "top B"
  def dump
    puts values
  end
  def values
    "#{self.class.name}: @@A = #@@A, @@B = #@@B"
  end
end
```

```
class MiddleOne < Top
  @@B = "One B"
  @@C = "One C"
  def values
    super + ", C = #@@C"
  end
end
class MiddleTwo < Top
  @@B = "Two B"
  @@C = "Two C"
  def values
    super + ", C = #@@C"
  end
end
class BottomOne < MiddleOne; end
class BottomTwo < MiddleTwo; end

Top.new.dump
MiddleOne.new.dump
MiddleTwo.new.dump
BottomOne.new.dump
BottomTwo.new.dump
```

produces:

```
Top: @@A = top A, @@B = Two B
MiddleOne: @@A = top A, @@B = Two B, C = One C
MiddleTwo: @@A = top A, @@B = Two B, C = Two C
BottomOne: @@A = top A, @@B = Two B, C = One C
BottomTwo: @@A = top A, @@B = Two B, C = Two C
```

I recommend against using class variables for these reasons.

Instance variables are available within instance methods throughout a class body. Referencing an uninitialized instance variable returns nil. Each object (instance of a class) has a unique set of instance variables.

Local variables are unique in that their scopes are statically determined but their existence is established dynamically.

A local variable is created dynamically when it is first assigned a value during program execution. However, the scope of a local variable is statically determined to be the immediately enclosing block, method definition, class definition, module definition, or top-level program. Local variables with the same name are different variables if they appear in disjoint scopes.

Method parameters are considered to be variables local to that method.

Block parameters are assigned values when the block is invoked.

If a local variable is first assigned in a block, it is local to the block.

If a block uses a variable that is previously defined in the scope containing the block's definition, then the block will share that variable with the scope. There are two exceptions to this. Block parameters are always local to the block. In addition, variables listed after a semicolon at the end of the block parameter list are also always local to the block.

```
a = 1
b = 2
c = 3

some_method { |b; c| a = b + 1; c = a + 1; d = c + 1 }
```

In this previous example, the variable a inside the block is shared with the surrounding scope. The variables b and c are not shared, because they are listed in the block's parameter list, and the variable d is not shared because it occurs only inside the block.

A block takes on the set of local variables in existence at the time that it is created. This forms part of its binding. Note that although the binding of the variables is fixed at this point, the block will have access to the *current* values of these variables when it executes. The binding preserves these variables even if the original enclosing scope is destroyed.

The bodies of while, until, and for loops are part of the scope that contains them; previously existing locals can be used in the loop, and any new locals created will be available outside the bodies afterward.

Predefined Variables

The following variables are predefined in the Ruby interpreter. In these descriptions, the notation [r/o] indicates that the variables are read-only; an error will be raised if a program attempts to modify a read-only variable. After all, you probably don't want to change the meaning of true halfway through your program (except perhaps if you're a politician). Entries marked [thread] are thread local.

Many global variables look something like Snoopy swearing: $_, $!, $&, and so on. This is for "historical" reasons—most of these variable names come from Perl. If you find memorizing all this punctuation difficult, you may want to take a look at the English library on page 749, which gives the commonly used global variables more descriptive names.

In the tables of variables and constants that follow, we show the variable name, the type of the referenced object, and a description.

Exception Information

$! → Exception
   The exception object passed to raise. [thread]

$@ → Array
   The stack backtrace generated by the last exception. See the description of Object#caller on page 613 for details. [thread]

Pattern Matching Variables

These variables (except $=) are set to nil after an unsuccessful pattern match.

$& → String
   The string matched (following a successful pattern match). This variable is local to the current scope. [r/o, thread]

$+ → String

> The contents of the highest-numbered group matched following a successful pattern match. Thus, in "cat" =~ /(c|a)(t|z)/, $+ will be set to "t." This variable is local to the current scope. [r/o, thread]

$` → String

> The string preceding the match in a successful pattern match. This variable is local to the current scope. [r/o, thread]

$' → String

> The string following the match in a successful pattern match. This variable is local to the current scope. [r/o, thread]

$1...$n → String

> The contents of successive groups matched in a pattern match. In "cat" =~ /(c|a)(t|z)/, $1 will be set to "a" and $2 to "t." This variable is local to the current scope. [r/o, thread]

$~ → MatchData

> An object that encapsulates the results of a successful pattern match. The variables $&, $`, $', and $1 to $9 are all derived from $~. Assigning to $~ changes the values of these derived variables. This variable is local to the current scope. [thread]

The variable $=, has been removed from Ruby 1.9.

Input/Output Variables

$/ → String

> The input record separator (newline by default). This is the value that routines such as Object#gets use to determine record boundaries. If set to nil, gets will read the entire file.

$-0 → String

> Synonym for $/.

$\ → String

> The string appended to the output of every call to methods such as Object#print and IO#write. The default value is nil.

$, → String

> The separator string output between the parameters to methods such as Object#print and Array#join. Defaults to nil, which adds no text.

$. → Fixnum

> The number of the last line read from the current input file.

$; → String

> The default separator pattern used by String#split. May be set using the -F command-line option.

$< → ARGF.class

> Synonym for ARGF. See *ARGF*, on page 213.

$> → IO

> The destination stream for Object#print and Object#printf. The default value is STDOUT.

$_ → String

The last line read by Object#gets or Object#readline. Many string-related functions in the Kernel module operate on $_ by default. The variable is local to the current scope. [thread]

$-F → String

Synonym for $;.

$stderr, $stdout, $stdin, → IO

The current standard error, standard output, and standard input streams.

The variables $defout and $deferr have been removed from Ruby 1.9.

Execution Environment Variables

$0 → String

The name of the top-level Ruby program being executed. Typically this will be the program's filename. On some operating systems, assigning to this variable will change the name of the process reported (for example) by the ps(1) command.

$* → Array

An array of strings containing the command-line options from the invocation of the program. Options used by the Ruby interpreter will have been removed. [r/o]

$" → Array

An array containing the filenames of modules loaded by require. [r/o]

$$ → Fixnum

The process number of the program being executed. [r/o]

$? → Process::Status

The exit status of the last child process to terminate. [r/o, thread]

$: → Array

An array of strings, where each string specifies a directory to be searched for Ruby scripts and binary extensions used by the load and require methods. The initial value is the value of the arguments passed via the -I command-line option, followed by an installation-defined standard library location. As of Ruby 1.9.2, the current directory is no longer added to $:. This variable may be updated from within a program to alter the default search path; typically, programs use $: << dir to append dir to the path. [r/o]

$-a → Object

True if the -a option is specified on the command line. [r/o]

__callee__ → Symbol

The name of the lexically enclosing method.

$-d → Object

Synonym for $DEBUG.

$DEBUG → Object

Set to true if the -d command-line option is specified.

__ENCODING__ → String

The encoding of the current source file. [r/o]

__FILE__ → String
> The name of the current source file. [r/o]

$F → Array
> The array that receives the split input line if the -a command-line option is used.

$FILENAME → String
> The name of the current input file. Equivalent to $<.filename. [r/o]

$-i → String
> If in-place edit mode is enabled (perhaps using the -i command-line option), $-i holds the extension used when creating the backup file. If you set a value into $-i, enables in-place edit mode, as described in the options descriptions on page 211.

$-I → Array
> Synonym for $:. [r/o]

$-l → Object
> Set to true if the -l option (which enables line-end processing) is present on the command line. See the options description on page 211. [r/o]

__LINE__ → String
> The current line number in the source file. [r/o]

$LOAD_PATH → Array
> A synonym for $:. [r/o]

$LOADED_FEATURES → Array
> Synonym for $". [r/o]

__method__ → Symbol
> The name of the lexically enclosing method.

$PROGRAM_NAME → String
> Alias for $0.

$-p → Object
> Set to true if the -p option (which puts an implicit while gets...end loop around your program) is present on the command line. See the options description on page 211. [r/o]

$SAFE → Fixnum
> The current safe level (see Section 26.1, *Safe Levels*, on page 410). This variable's value may never be reduced by assignment. [thread]

$VERBOSE → Object
> Set to true if the -v, --version, -W, or -w option is specified on the command line. Set to false if no option, or -W1 is given. Set to nil if -W0 was specified. Setting this option to true causes the interpreter and some library routines to report additional information. Setting to nil suppresses all warnings (including the output of Object#warn).

$-v, $-w → Object
> Synonyms for $VERBOSE.

$-W → Object
> Return the value set by the -W command-line option.

Standard Objects

ARGF → Object

Provides access to a list of files. Used by command line processing. See *ARGF*, on page 213.

ARGV → Array

A synonym for $*.

ENV → Object

A hash-like object containing the program's environment variables. An instance of class Object, ENV implements the full set of Hash methods. Used to query and set the value of an environment variable, as in ENV["PATH"] and ENV["term"]="ansi".

false → FalseClass

Singleton instance of class FalseClass. [r/o]

nil → NilClass

The singleton instance of class NilClass. The value of uninitialized instance and global variables. [r/o]

self → Object

The receiver (object) of the current method. [r/o]

true → TrueClass

Singleton instance of class TrueClass. [r/o]

Global Constants

DATA → IO

If the main program file contains the directive __END__, then the constant DATA will be initialized so that reading from it will return lines following __END__ from the source file.

FALSE → FalseClass

Constant containing reference to false.

NIL → NilClass

Constant containing reference to nil.

RUBY_COPYRIGHT → String

The interpreter copyright.

RUBY_DESCRIPTION → String

Version number and architecture of the interpreter.

RUBY_ENGINE → String

The name of the Ruby interpreter. Returns "ruby" for Matz's version. Other interpreters include macruby, ironruby, jruby, and rubinius.

RUBY_PATCHLEVEL → String

The patch level of the interpreter.

RUBY_PLATFORM → String

The identifier of the platform running this program. This string is in the same form as the platform identifier used by the GNU configure utility (which is not a coincidence).

RUBY_RELEASE_DATE → String

The date of this release.

RUBY_REVISION → String

The revision of the interpreter.

RUBY_VERSION → String

The version number of the interpreter.

STDERR → IO

The actual standard error stream for the program. The initial value of $stderr.

STDIN → IO

The actual standard input stream for the program. The initial value of $stdin.

STDOUT → IO

The actual standard output stream for the program. The initial value of $stdout.

SCRIPT_LINES__ → Hash

If a constant SCRIPT_LINES__ is defined and references a Hash, Ruby will store an entry containing the contents of each file it parses, with the file's name as the key and an array of strings as the value. See Object#require on page 623 for an example.

TOPLEVEL_BINDING → Binding

A Binding object representing the binding at Ruby's top level—the level where programs are initially executed.

TRUE → TrueClass

A reference to the object true.

The constant __FILE__ and the variable $0 are often used together to run code only if it appears in the file run directly by the user. For example, library writers often use this to include tests in their libraries that will be run if the library source is run directly, but not if the source is required into another program.

```ruby
# library code ...

if __FILE__ == $0
  # tests...
end
```

22.6 Expressions, Conditionals, and Loops

Single terms in an expression may be any of the following:

- *Literal*. Ruby literals are numbers, strings, arrays, hashes, ranges, symbols, and regular expressions. These are described in Section 22.3, *The Basic Types*, on page 299.

- *Shell command*. A shell command is a string enclosed in backquotes or in a general delimited string starting with %x. The string is executed using the host operating system's standard shell, and the resulting standard output stream is returned as the value of the expression. The execution also sets the $? variable with the command's exit status.

```ruby
filter = "*.c"
files = `ls #{filter}`
files = %x{ls #{filter}}
```

- *Variable reference* or *constant reference*. A variable is referenced by citing its name. Depending on scope (see *Scope of Constants and Variables,* on page 308), you reference a constant either by citing its name or by qualifying the name, using the name of the class or module containing the constant and the scope operator (::).

```
barney    # variable reference
APP_NAMR  # constant reference
Math::PI  # qualified constant reference
```

- *Method invocation*. The various ways of invoking a method are described in Section 22.8, *Invoking a Method,* on page 327.

Operator Expressions

Expressions may be combined using operators. The Ruby operators in precedence order are listed in Table 13, *Ruby operators (high to low precedence),* on page 318. The operators with a ✓ in the Method column are implemented as methods and may be overridden.

More on Assignment

The assignment operator assigns one or more *rvalues* (the *r* stands for "right," because rvalues tend to appear on the right side of assignments) to one or more *lvalues* ("left" values). What is meant by assignment depends on each individual lvalue.

As the following shows, if an lvalue is a variable or constant name, that variable or constant receives a reference to the corresponding rvalue.

```
a = /regexp/
b, c, d = 1, "cat", [ 3, 4, 5 ]
```

If the lvalue is an object attribute, the corresponding attribute-setting method will be called in the receiver, passing as a parameter the rvalue:

```
class A
  attr_writer :value
end
obj = A.new
obj.value = "hello"   # equivalent to obj.value=("hello")
```

If the lvalue is an array element reference, Ruby calls the element assignment operator ([]=) in the receiver, passing as parameters any indices that appear between the brackets followed by the rvalue. This is illustrated in the following table.

Element Reference	Actual Method Call
var[] = "one"	var.[ ]=("one")
var[1] = "two"	var.[ ]=(1, "two")
var["a", /^cat/] = "three"	var.[ ]=("a", /^cat/, "three")

If you are writing an [ ]= method that accepts a variable number of indices, it might be convenient to define it using this:

```
def []=(*indices, value)
  # ...
end
```

Method	Operator	Description
✓	[ ] [ ]=	Element reference, element set
✓	**	Exponentiation
✓	! ~ + -	Not, complement, unary plus and minus (method names for the last two are +@ and -@)
✓	* / %	Multiply, divide, and modulo
✓	+ -	Plus and minus
✓	>> <<	Right and left shift (<< is also used as the append operator)
✓	&	"And" (bitwise for integers)
✓	^		Exclusive "or" and regular "or" (bitwise for integers)
✓	<= < > >=	Comparison operators
✓	<=> == === != =~ !~	Equality and pattern match operators
	&&	Logical "and"
	||	Logical "or"
	.. ...	Range (inclusive and exclusive)
	? :	Ternary if-then-else
	= %= /= -= += |= &= >>= <<= *= &&= ||= **= ^=	Assignment
	not	Logical negation
	or and	Logical composition
	if unless while until	Expression modifiers
	begin/end	Block expression

Table 13—Ruby operators (high to low precedence)

The value of an assignment expression is its rvalue. This is true even if the assignment is to an attribute method that returns something different.

Parallel Assignment

An assignment expression may have one or more lvalues and one or more rvalues. This section explains how Ruby handles assignment with different combinations of arguments:

- If any rvalue is prefixed with an asterisk and implements to_a, the rvalue is replaced with the elements returned by to_a, with each element forming its own rvalue.

- If the assignment contains one lvalue and multiple rvalues, the rvalues are converted to an array and assigned to that lvalue.

- If the assignment contains multiple lvalues and one rvalue, the rvalue is expanded if possible into an array of rvalues as described in (1).

- Successive rvalues are assigned to the lvalues. This assignment effectively happens in parallel so that (for example) a,b=b,a swaps the values in a and b.

- If there are more lvalues than rvalues, the excess will have nil assigned to them.

- If there are more rvalues than lvalues, the excess will be ignored.

- At most one lvalue can be prefixed by an asterisk. This lvalue will end up being an array and will contain as many rvalues as possible. If there are lvalues to the right of the starred lvalue, these will be assigned from the trailing rvalues, and whatever rvalues are left will be assigned to the splat lvalue.

- If an lvalue contains a parenthesized list, the list is treated as a nested assignment statement, and then it is assigned from the corresponding rvalue as described by these rules.

See *Parallel Assignment*, on page 130 for examples of parallel assignment. The value of a parallel assignment is its array of rvalues.

Block Expressions

```
begin
    body
end
```

Expressions may be grouped between begin and end. The value of the block expression is the value of the last expression executed.

Block expressions also play a role in exception handling—see Section 22.14, *Exceptions*, on page 339.

Boolean Expressions

Ruby predefines the constants false and nil. Both of these values are treated as being false in a boolean context. All other values are treated as being true. The constant true is available for when you need an explicit "true" value.

And, Or, Not

The and and && operators evaluate their first operand. If false, the expression returns the value of the first operand; otherwise, the expression returns the value of the second operand:

```
expr1 and expr2
expr1 && expr2
```

The or and || operators evaluate their first operand. If true, the expression returns the value of their first operand; otherwise, the expression returns the value of the second operand:

```
expr1 or expr2
expr1 || expr2
```

The not and ! operators evaluate their operand. If true, the expression returns false. If false, the expression returns true.

The word forms of these operators (and, or, and not) have a lower precedence than the corresponding symbol forms (&&, ||, and !). For details, see Table 13, *Ruby operators (high to low precedence)*, on page 318.

defined?

The defined? keyword returns nil if its argument, which can be an arbitrary expression, is not defined. Otherwise, it returns a description of that argument. For examples, check out the tutorial on page 133.

Comparison Operators

The Ruby syntax defines the comparison operators ==, ===, <=>, <, <=, >, >=, and =~. All these operators are implemented as methods. By convention, the language also uses the standard methods eql? and equal? (see Table 5, *Common comparison operators*, on page 134). Although the operators have intuitive meaning, it is up to the classes that implement them to produce meaningful comparison semantics. The library reference on page 417 starting describes the comparison semantics for the built-in classes. The module Comparable provides support for implementing the operators ==, <, <=, >, and >=, as well as the method between? in terms of <=>. The operator === is used in case expressions, described in *case Expressions*, on page 321.

Both == and =~ have negated forms, != and !~. If an object defines these methods, Ruby will call them. Otherwise, a != b is mapped to !(a == b), and a !~ b is mapped to !(a =~ b).

Ranges in Boolean Expressions

if *expr1* .. *expr2*
while *expr1* .. *expr2*

A range used in a boolean expression acts as a flip-flop. It has two states, set and unset, and is initially unset.

1. For the three-dot form of a range, if the flip-flop is unset and expr1 is true, the flip-flop becomes set and the the flip-flop returns true.

2. If the flip-flop is set, it will return true. However, if expr2 is not true, the flip-flop becomes unset.

3. If the flip-flop is unset, it returns false.

The first step differs for the two-dot form of a range. If the flip-flop is unset and expr1 is true, then Ruby only sets the flip-flop if expr2 is not also true.

The difference is illustrated by the following code:

```
a = (11..20).collect {|i| (i%4 == 0)..(i%3 == 0) ? i : nil}
a           # => [nil, 12, nil, nil, nil, 16, 17, 18, nil, 20]

a = (11..20).collect {|i| (i%4 == 0)...(i%3 == 0) ? i : nil}
a           # => [nil, 12, 13, 14, 15, 16, 17, 18, nil, 20]
```

Regular Expressions in Boolean Expressions

In versions of Ruby prior to 1.8, a single regular expression in boolean expression was matched against the current value of the variable $_. This behavior is now supported only if the condition appears in a command-line -e parameter:

```
$ ruby -ne 'print if /one/' testfile
This is line one
```

In regular code, the use of implicit operands and $_ is being slowly phased out, so it is better to use an explicit match against a variable.

if and unless Expressions

```
if boolean-expression ‹then›        unless boolean-expression ‹then›
    body                                body
‹elsif boolean-expression ‹then›    ‹else
    body ›*                              body ›
‹ else                              end
    body ›
end
```

The then keyword separates the body from the condition.[4] It is not required if the body starts on a new line. The value of an if or unless expression is the value of the last expression evaluated in whichever body is executed.

if and unless Modifiers

```
expression if boolean-expression
expression unless boolean-expression
```

This evaluates *expression* only if *boolean-expression* is true (for if) or false (for unless).

Ternary Operator

```
boolean-expression ? expr1 : expr2
```

This returns *expr1* if *boolean expression* is true and *expr2* otherwise.

case Expressions

Ruby has two forms of case statement. The first allows a series of conditions to be evaluated, executing code corresponding to the first condition that is true:

```
case
when ‹boolean-expression›+ ‹then›
    body
when ‹boolean-expression›+ ‹then›
    body
...
‹else
    body ›
end
```

The second form of a case expression takes a target expression following the case keyword. It searches for a match starting at the first (top left) comparison, using comparison === target:

```
case target
when ‹comparison›+ ‹then›
    body
when ‹comparison›+ ‹then›
    body
...
‹else
    body ›
end
```

---

4.   Prior to Ruby 1.9, you could use a colon instead of then. This is no longer supported.

A comparison can be an array reference preceded by an asterisk, in which case it is expanded into that array's elements before the tests are performed on each. When a comparison returns true, the search stops, and the body associated with the comparison is executed (no break is required). case then returns the value of the last expression executed. If no comparison matches, this happens: if an else clause is present, its body will be executed; otherwise, case silently returns nil.

The then keyword separates the when comparisons from the bodies and is not needed if the body starts on a new line.

As an optimization in Matz's Ruby 1.9 and later, comparisons between literal strings and between numbers do not use ===.

Loops

```
while boolean-expression ‹do›
  body
end
```

This executes *body* zero or more times as long as *boolean-expression* is true.

```
until boolean-expression ‹do›
  body
end
```

This executes *body* zero or more times as long as *boolean-expression* is false.

In both forms, the do separates *boolean-expression* from the *body* and can be omitted when the body starts on a new line:

```
for ‹name›+ in expression ‹do›
  body
end
```

The for loop is executed as if it were the following each loop, except that local variables defined in the body of the for loop will be available outside the loop, and those defined within an iterator block will not.

```
expression.each do | ‹name›+ |
  body
end
```

loop, which iterates its associated block, is not a language construct—it is a method in module Kernel.

```
loop do
  print "Input: "
  break unless line = gets
  process(line)
end
```

while and until Modifiers

expression while *boolean-expression*
expression until *boolean-expression*

If *expression* is anything other than a begin/end block, executes *expression* zero or more times while *boolean-expression* is true (for while) or false (for until).

If *expression* is a begin/end block, the block will always be executed at least one time.

break, redo, and next

break, redo, and next alter the normal flow through a while, until, for, or iterator-controlled loop.[5]

break terminates the immediately enclosing loop—control resumes at the statement following the block. redo repeats the loop from the start but without reevaluating the condition or fetching the next element (in an iterator). The next keyword skips to the end of the loop, effectively starting the next iteration.

break and next may optionally take one or more arguments. If used within a block, the given argument(s) are returned as the value of the yield. If used within a while, until, or for loop, the value given to break is returned as the value of the statement. If break is never called or if it is called with no value, the loop returns nil.

```
match = for line in ARGF.readlines
          next if line =~ /^#/
          break line if line =~ /ruby/
        end
```

22.7 Method Definition

def *defname* ‹ (‹ , *arg* ›*) ›
  body
end

defname ← *methodname* | *expr.methodname*

defname is both the name of the method and optionally the context in which it is valid.

A *methodname* is either a redefinable operator (see Table 13, *Ruby operators (high to low precedence)*, on page 318) or a name. If *methodname* is a name, it should start with a lowercase letter (or underscore) optionally followed by uppercase and lowercase letters, underscores, and digits. A *methodname* may optionally end with a question mark (?), exclamation point (!), or equal sign (=). The question mark and exclamation point are simply part of the name. The equal sign is also part of the name but additionally signals that this method may be used as an lvalue (see the description of writeable attributes on page 34).

A method definition using an unadorned method name within a class or module definition creates an instance method. An instance method may be invoked only by sending its name to a receiver that is an instance of the class that defined it (or one of that class's subclasses).

---

5.   The retry keyword is no longer permitted in a loop context.

Outside a class or module definition, a definition with an unadorned method name is added as a private method to class Object. It may be called in any context without an explicit receiver.

A definition using a method name of the form *expr.methodname* creates a method associated with the object that is the value of the expression; the method will be callable only by supplying the object referenced by the expression as a receiver. This style of definition creates per-object or *singleton methods*. You'll find it most often inside class or module definitions, where the *expr* is either self or the name of the class/module. This effectively creates a class or module method (as opposed to an instance method).

```ruby
class MyClass
  def MyClass.method      # definition
  end
end


MyClass.method            # call

obj = Object.new
def obj.method            # definition
end


obj.method                # call

def (1.class).fred        # receiver may be an expression
end


Fixnum.fred               # call
```

Method definitions may not contain class or module definitions. They may contain nested instance or singleton method definitions. The internal method is defined when the enclosing method is executed. The internal method does not act as a closure in the context of the nested method—it is self-contained.

```ruby
def toggle
  def toggle
    "subsequent times"
  end
  "first time"
end


toggle      # => "first time"
toggle      # => "subsequent times"
toggle      # => "subsequent times"
```

The body of a method acts as if it were a begin/end block, in that it may contain exception-handling statements (rescue, else, and ensure).

Method Arguments

New in 2.0

A method definition may have zero or more regular arguments, zero or more keyword arguments, a optional splat argument, an optional double splat argument, and an optional block argument. Arguments are separated by commas, and the argument list may be enclosed in parentheses.

A regular argument is a local variable name, optionally followed by an equals sign and an expression giving a default value. The expression is evaluated at the time the method is called. The expressions are evaluated from left to right. An expression may reference a parameter that precedes it in the argument list.

```ruby
def options(a=99, b=a+1)
  [ a, b ]
end
options         # => [99, 100]
options(1)      # => [1, 2]
options(2, 4)   # => [2, 4]
```

Arguments without default values may appear after arguments with defaults. When such a method is called, Ruby will use the default values only if fewer parameters are passed to the method call than the total number of arguments.

```ruby
def mixed(a, b=50, c=b+10, d)
  [ a, b, c, d ]
end
mixed(1, 2)       # => [1, 50, 60, 2]
mixed(1, 2, 3)    # => [1, 2, 12, 3]
mixed(1, 2, 3, 4) # => [1, 2, 3, 4]
```

As with parallel assignment, one of the arguments may start with an asterisk. If the method call specifies any parameters in excess of the regular argument count, all these extra parameters will be collected into this newly created array.

```ruby
def varargs(a, *b)
  [ a, b ]
end
varargs(1)        # => [1, []]
varargs(1, 2)     # => [1, [2]]
varargs(1, 2, 3)  # => [1, [2, 3]]
```

This argument need not be the last in the argument list. See the description of parallel assignment to see how values are assigned to this parameter.

```ruby
def splat(first, *middle, last)
  [ first, middle, last ]
end
splat(1, 2)        # => [1, [], 2]
splat(1, 2, 3)     # => [1, [2], 3]
splat(1, 2, 3, 4)  # => [1, [2, 3], 4]
```

If an array argument follows arguments with default values, parameters will first be used to override the defaults. The remainder will then be used to populate the array.

```ruby
def mixed(a, b=99, *c)
  [ a, b, c]
end
mixed(1)          # => [1, 99, []]
mixed(1, 2)       # => [1, 2, []]
mixed(1, 2, 3)    # => [1, 2, [3]]
mixed(1, 2, 3, 4) # => [1, 2, [3, 4]]
```

Keyword Arguments

New in 2.0

Ruby 2 methods may declare keyword arguments using the syntax name: default_value for each. These arguments must follow any regular arguments in the list.

```ruby
def header(name, level: 1, upper: false)
  name = name.upcase if upper
  "<h#{level}>#{name}</h#{level}>"
end
```

```ruby
header("Introduction")                # => "<h1>Introduction</h1>"
header("Getting started", level:2)    # => "<h2>Getting started</h2>"
header("Conclusion", upper: true)     # => "<h1>CONCLUSION</h1>"
```

If you call a method that has keyword arguments and do not provide corresponding values in the method call's parameter list, the default values will be used. If you pass keyword parameters that are not defined as arguments, an error will be raised unless you also define a double splat argument, **arg. The double splat argument will be set up as a hash containing any uncollected keyword parameters passed to the method.

```ruby
def header(name, level: 1, upper: false, **attrs)
  name = name.upcase if upper
  attr_string = attrs.map {|k,v| %{#{k}="#{v}"}}.join(' ')
  "<h#{level} #{attr_string}>#{name}</h#{level}>"
end
```

```ruby
header("TOC", class: "nav", level:2, id: 123)
```

Block Argument

The optional block argument must be the last in the list. Whenever the method is called, Ruby checks for an associated block. If a block is present, it is converted to an object of class Proc and assigned to the block argument. If no block is present, the argument is set to nil.

```ruby
def example(&block)
puts block.inspect
end
```

```ruby
example
example { "a block" }
```

produces:

```
nil
#<Proc:0x007fb2230004d8@prog.rb:6>
```

Undefining a Method

The keyword undef allows you to undefine a method.

undef *name* | *symbol* ...

An undefined method still exists; it is simply marked as being undefined. If you undefine a method in a child class and then call that method on an instance of that child class, Ruby will immediately raise a NoMethodError—it will not look for the method in the child's parents.

22.8 Invoking a Method

⟨*receiver.*⟩*name*⟨ *parameters* ⟩⟨ *{block}* ⟩
⟨*receiver::*⟩*name*⟨ *parameters* ⟩⟨ *{block}* ⟩

parameters ← (⟨*param*⟩* ⟨, *hashlist*⟩ ⟨*array*⟩ ⟨*&a_proc*⟩)

block ← { *blockbody* } or do *blockbody* end

The parentheses around the parameters may be omitted if it is otherwise unambiguous.

Initial parameters are assigned to the actual arguments of the method. Following these parameters may be a list of key => value or key: value pairs. These pairs are collected into a single new Hash object and passed as a single parameter.

Any parameter may be a prefixed with an asterisk. If a starred parameter supports the to_a method, that method is called, and the resulting array is expanded inline to provide parameters to the method call. If a starred argument does not support to_a, it is simply passed through unaltered.

```ruby
def regular(a, b, *c)
  "a=#{a}, b=#{b}, c=#{c}"
end
regular 1, 2, 3, 4                   # => a=1, b=2, c=[3, 4]
regular(1, 2, 3, 4)                  # => a=1, b=2, c=[3, 4]
regular(1, *[2, 3, 4])               # => a=1, b=2, c=[3, 4]
regular(1, *[2, 3], 4)               # => a=1, b=2, c=[3, 4]
regular(1, *[2, 3], *4)              # => a=1, b=2, c=[3, 4]
regular(*[], 1, *[], *[2, 3], *[], 4) # => a=1, b=2, c=[3, 4]
```

Any parameter may be prefixed with two asterisks (a double splat). Such parameters are treated as hashes, and their key-value pairs are added as additional parameters to the method call. New in 2.0

```ruby
def regular(a, b)
  "a=#{a}, b=#{b}"
end
regular(99, a: 1, b: 2)              # => a=99, b={:a=>1, :b=>2}

others = { c: 3, d: 4 }
regular(99, a: 1, b: 2, **others)    # => a=99, b={:a=>1, :b=>2, :c=>3,
                                     # .. :d=>4}
regular(99, **others, a: 1, b: 2)    # => a=99, b={:c=>3, :d=>4, :a=>1,
                                     # .. :b=>2}

rest = { e: 5 }

regular(99, **others, a: 1, b: 2)    # => a=99, b={:c=>3, :d=>4, :a=>1,
                                     # .. :b=>2}
regular(99, **others, a: 1, b: 2, **rest) # => a=99, b={:c=>3, :d=>4, :a=>1,
                                     # .. :b=>2, :e=>5}
```

When a method defined with keyword arguments is called, Ruby matches the keys in the passed hash with each argument, assigning values when it finds a match.

```ruby
def keywords(a, b: 2, c: 3)
  "a=#{a}, b=#{b}, c=#{c}"
end

keywords(99)                          # => a=99, b=2, c=3
keywords(99, c:98)                    # => a=99, b=2, c=98

args = { b: 22, c: 33}
keywords(99, **args)                  # => "a=99, b=22, c=33"
keywords(99, **args, b: 'override')   # => "a=99, b=override, c=33"
```

If the passed hash contains any keys not defined as arguments, Ruby raises a runtime error unlesss the method also declares a double splat argument. In that case, the double splat receives the excess key-value pairs from the passed hash.

```ruby
def keywords1(a, b: 2, c: 3)
  "a=#{a}, b=#{b}, c=#{c}"
end

keywords1(99, d: 22, e: 33)
```

produces:

```
prog.rb:5:in `<main>': unknown keywords: d, e (ArgumentError)
```

```ruby
def keywords2(a, b: 2, c: 3, **rest)
  "a=#{a}, b=#{b}, c=#{c}, rest=#{rest}"
end

keywords2(99, d: 22, e: 33)    # => a=99, b=2, c=3, rest={:d=>22, :e=>33}
```

A block may be associated with a method call using either a literal block (which must start on the same source line as the last line of the method call) or a parameter containing a reference to a Proc or Method object prefixed with an ampersand character.

```ruby
def some_method
  yield
end

some_method { }
some_method do
end

a_proc = lambda { 99 }
some_method(&a_proc)
```

Ruby arranges for the value of Object#block_given? to reflect the availability of a block associated with the call, regardless of the presence of a block argument. A block argument will be set to nil if no block is specified on the call to a method.

```ruby
def other_method(&block)
  puts "block_given = #{block_given?}, block = #{block.inspect}"
end
other_method { }
other_method
```

produces:

```
block_given = true, block = #<Proc:0x007fafc305c3d0@prog.rb:4>
block_given = false, block = nil
```

A method is called by passing its name to a receiver. If no receiver is specified, self is assumed. The receiver checks for the method definition in its own class and then sequentially in its ancestor classes. The instance methods of included modules act as if they were in anonymous superclasses of the class that includes them. If the method is not found, Ruby invokes the method method_missing in the receiver. The default behavior defined in Object#method_missing is to report an error and terminate the program.

When a receiver is explicitly specified in a method invocation, it may be separated from the method name using either a period (.) or two colons (::). The only difference between these two forms occurs if the method name starts with an uppercase letter. In this case, Ruby will assume that receiver::Thing is actually an attempt to access a constant called Thing in the receiver *unless* the method invocation has a parameter list between parentheses. Using :: to indicate a method call is mildly deprecated.

```
Foo.Bar()       #  method call
Foo.Bar         #  method call
Foo::Bar()      #  method call
Foo::Bar        #  constant access
```

The return value of a method is the value of the last expression executed. The method in the following example returns the value of the if statement it contains, and that if statement returns the value of one of its branches.

```
def odd_or_even(val)
  if val.odd?
    "odd"
  else
    "even"
  end
end
odd_or_even(26) # => "even"
odd_or_even(27) # => "odd"
```

A return expression immediately exits a method.

return ‹ *expr* ›*

The value of a return is nil if it is called with no parameters, the value of its parameter if it is called with one parameter, or an array containing all of its parameters if it is called with more than one parameter.

super

super ‹ (‹ , *param* ›* ‹ , **array* ›) › ‹ *block* ›

Within the body of a method, a call to super acts like a call to the original method, except that the search for a method body starts in the superclass of the object that contained the original method. If no parameters (and no parentheses) are passed to super, the original method's parameters will be passed; otherwise, the parameters to super will be passed.

Operator Methods

expr operator
operator expr
expr1 operator expr2

If the operator in an operator expression corresponds to a redefinable method (see Table 13, *Ruby operators (high to low precedence)*, on page 318), Ruby will execute the operator expression as if it had been written like this:

(expr1).operator() or
(expr1).operator(expr2)

Attribute Assignment

receiver.attrname = rvalue

When the form *receiver.attrname* appears as an lvalue, Ruby invokes a method named attrname= in the receiver, passing *rvalue* as a single parameter. The value returned by this assignment is always *rvalue*—the return value of the method is discarded. If you want to access the return value (in the unlikely event that it isn't the *rvalue*), send an explicit message to the method.

```ruby
class Demo
  attr_reader :attr
  def attr=(val)
    @attr = val
    "return value"
  end
end

d = Demo.new

# In all these cases, @attr is set to 99
d.attr = 99         # => 99
d.attr=(99)         # => 99
d.send(:attr=, 99) # => "return value"
d.attr              # => 99
```

Element Reference Operator

receiver[‹expr›+]
receiver[‹expr›+] = rvalue

When used as an rvalue, element reference invokes the method [] in the receiver, passing as parameters the expressions between the brackets.

When used as an lvalue, element reference invokes the method []= in the receiver, passing as parameters the expressions between the brackets, followed by the *rvalue* being assigned.

22.9 Aliasing

alias *new_name old_name*

This creates a new name that refers to an existing method, operator, global variable, or regular expression backreference ($&, $`, $', and $+). Local variables, instance variables, class variables, and constants may not be aliased. The parameters to alias may be names or symbols.

```
class Fixnum
  alias plus +
end
1.plus(3)        # => 4

alias $prematch $`
"string" =~ /i/ # => 3
$prematch        # => "str"

alias :cmd :`
cmd "date"       # => "Mon May 27 12:31:34 CDT 2013\n"
```

When a method is aliased, the new name refers to a copy of the original method's body. If the original method is subsequently redefined, the aliased name will still invoke the original implementation.

```
def meth
  "original method"
end
alias original meth
def meth
  "new and improved"
end
meth      # => "new and improved"
original  # => "original method"
```

22.10 Class Definition

```
class ‹scope::› classname ‹< superexpr›
  body
end

class << obj
  body
end
```

A Ruby class definition creates or extends an object of class Class by executing the code in *body*. In the first form, a named class is created or extended. The resulting Class object is assigned to a constant named *classname* (keep reading for scoping rules). This name should start with an uppercase letter. In the second form, an anonymous (singleton) class is associated with the specific object.

If present, *superexpr* should be an expression that evaluates to a Class object that will be the superclass of the class being defined. If omitted, it defaults to class Object.

Within *body*, most Ruby expressions are executed as the definition is read. However:

- Method definitions will register the methods in a table in the class object.

- Nested class and module definitions will be stored in constants within the class, not as global constants. These nested classes and modules can be accessed from outside the defining class using :: to qualify their names.

```
module NameSpace
  class Example
    CONST = 123
```

```
     end
   end
   obj = NameSpace::Example.new
   a = NameSpace::Example::CONST
```

- The Module#include method will add the named modules as anonymous superclasses of the class being defined.

The *classname* in a class definition may be prefixed by the names of existing classes or modules using the scope operator (::). This syntax inserts the new definition into the namespace of the prefixing module(s) and/or class(es) but does not interpret the definition in the scope of these outer classes. A *classname* with a leading scope operator places that class or module in the top-level scope.

In the following example, class C is inserted into module A's namespace but is not interpreted in the context of A. As a result, the reference to CONST resolves to the top-level constant of that name, not A's version. We also have to fully qualify the singleton method name, because C on its own is not a known constant in the context of A::C.

```
CONST = "outer"

module A
  CONST = "inner"   # This is A::CONST
end

module A
  class B
    def B.get_const
      CONST
    end
  end
end

A::B.get_const # => "inner"

class A::C
  def (A::C).get_const
    CONST
  end
end

A::C.get_const # => "outer"
```

Remember that a class definition is executable code. Many of the directives used in class definitions (such as attr and include) are actually simply private instance methods of class Module (documented in the reference section on page 579). The value of a class definition is the value of the last executed statement.

Chapter 24, *Metaprogramming,* on page 357 describes in more detail how Class objects interact with the rest of the environment.

Creating Objects from Classes

obj = classexpr.new ‹ (‹ , *args* ›*) ›

Class Class defines the instance method Class#new, which creates an instance of the class of its receiver (*classexpr*). This is done by calling the method *classexpr*.allocate. You can override this method, but your implementation must return an object of the correct class. It then invokes initialize in the newly created object and passes it any arguments originally passed to new.

If a class definition overrides the class method new without calling super, no objects of that class can be created, and calls to new will silently return nil.

Like any other method, initialize should call super if it wants to ensure that parent classes have been properly initialized. This is not necessary when the parent is Object, because class Object does no instance-specific initialization.

Class Attribute Declarations

Class attribute declarations are not part of the Ruby syntax; they are simply methods defined in class Module that create accessor methods automatically.

```
class name
  attr attribute ‹, writable›
  attr_reader ‹attribute›+
  attr_writer ‹attribute›+
  attr_accessor ‹attribute›+
end
```

22.11 Module Definitions

```
module name
  body
end
```

A module is basically a class that cannot be instantiated. Like a class, its body is executed during definition, and the resulting Module object is stored in a constant. A module may contain class and instance methods and may define constants and class variables. As with classes, a module's class methods (sometimes called *module methods*) are invoked using the Module object as a receiver, and constants are accessed using the :: scope resolution operator. The name in a module definition may optionally be preceded by the names of enclosing class(es) and/or module(s).

```
CONST = "outer"
module Mod
  CONST = 1
  def Mod.method1      # module method
    CONST + 1
  end
end
module Mod::Inner
  def (Mod::Inner).method2
    CONST + " scope"
  end
end
Mod::CONST          # => 1
Mod.method1         # => 2
Mod::Inner::method2 # => "outer scope"
```

Mixins: Including Modules

```
class|module name
  include expr
end
```

A module may be included within the definition of another module or class using the include method. The module or class definition containing the include gains access to the constants, class variables, and instance methods of the module it includes.

If a module is included within a class definition, the module's constants, class variables, and instance methods are made available via an anonymous (and inaccessible) superclass for that class. Objects of the class will respond to messages sent to the module's instance methods. Calls to methods not defined in the class will be passed to the module(s) mixed into the class before being passed to any parent class. A module may define an initialize method, which will be called upon the creation of an object of a class that mixes in the module if either the class does not define its own initialize method or the class's initialize method invokes super.

A module may also be included at the top level, in which case the module's constants, class variables, and instance methods become available at the top level.

Module Functions

Instance methods defined in modules can be mixed-in to a class using include. But what if you want to call the instance methods in a module directly?

```
module Math
  def sin(x)
    #
  end
end
include Math     # The only way to access Math.sin
sin(1)
```

The method Module#module_function solves this problem by taking module instance methods and copying their definitions into corresponding module methods.

```
module Math
  def sin(x)
    #
  end
  module_function :sin
end
Math.sin(1)
include Math
sin(1)
```

The instance method and module method are two different methods: the method definition is copied by module_function, not aliased.

You can also use module_function with no parameters, in which case all subsequent methods will be module methods.

22.12 Access Control

```
private ⟨ symbol ⟩*
protected ⟨ symbol ⟩*
public ⟨ symbol ⟩*
```

Ruby defines three levels of protection for module and class constants and methods:

- *Public.* Accessible to anyone.

- *Protected.* Can be invoked only by objects of the defining class and its subclasses.

- *Private.* Can be called only in functional form (that is, with an implicit receiver of self). Private methods therefore can be called in the defining class and by that class's descendents and ancestors, but only within the same object. See Section 3.3, *Access Control*, on page 40 for examples.

Each function can be used in two different ways:

- If used with no arguments, the three functions set the default access control of subsequently defined methods.
- With arguments, the functions set the access control of the named methods and constants.

Access control is enforced when a method is invoked.

22.13 Blocks, Closures, and Proc Objects

A code block is a set of Ruby statements and expressions between braces or a do/end pair. The block may start with an argument list between vertical bars. A code block may appear only immediately after a method invocation. The start of the block (the brace or the do) must be on the same logical source line as the end of the invocation.

```
invocation do | a1, a2, ... |
end

invocation { | a1, a2, ... |
}
```

Braces have a high precedence; do has a low precedence. If the method invocation has parameters that are not enclosed in parentheses, the brace form of a block will bind to the last parameter, not to the overall invocation. The do form will bind to the invocation.

Within the body of the invoked method, the code block may be called using the yield keyword. Parameters passed to yield will be assigned to arguments in the block. A warning will be generated if yield passes multiple parameters to a block that takes just one. The return value of the yield is the value of the last expression evaluated in the block or the value passed to a next statement executed in the block.

A block is a *closure*; it remembers the context in which it was defined, and it uses that context whenever it is called. The context includes the value of *self*, the constants, the class variables, the local variables, and any captured block.

```
class BlockExample
  CONST = 0
  @@a = 3
  def return_closure
```

```ruby
    a = 1
    @a = 2
    lambda { [ CONST, a, @a, @@a, yield ] }
  end
  def change_values
    @a += 1
    @@a += 1
  end
end

eg = BlockExample.new
block = eg.return_closure { "original" }

block.call # => [0, 1, 2, 3, "original"]
eg.change_values
block.call # => [0, 1, 3, 4, "original"]
```

Here, the return_closure method returns a lambda that encapsulates access to the local variable a, instance variable @a, class variable @@a, and constant CONST. We call the block outside the scope of the object that contains these values, but they are still available via the closure. If we then call the object to change some values, the values accessed via the closure also change.

Block Arguments

Block argument lists are very similar to method argument lists:

- You can specify default values.
- You can specify splat (starred) arguments.
- The last argument can be prefixed with an ampersand, in which case it will collect any block passed when the original block is called.
- Block-local variables are declared by placing them after a semicolon in the argument list.

These changes make it possible to use Module#define_method to create methods based on blocks that have similar capabilities to methods created using def.

Proc Objects

Ruby's blocks are chunks of code attached to a method. Blocks are not objects, but they can be converted into objects of class Proc. There are four ways of converting a block into a Proc object.

- By passing a block to a method whose last parameter is prefixed with an ampersand. That parameter will receive the block as a Proc object.

  ```ruby
  def meth1(p1, p2, &block)
    puts block.inspect
  end
  meth1(1,2) { "a block" }
  meth1(3,4)
  ```

  produces:

  ```
  #<Proc:0x007f97cb12c400@prog.rb:4>
  nil
  ```

- By calling Proc.new, again associating it with a block.[6]

```
block = Proc.new { "a block" }
block       # => #<Proc:0x007fd4a4064638@prog.rb:1>
```

- By calling the method Object#lambda, associating a block with the call.

```
block = lambda { "a block" }
block       # => #<Proc:0x007f9d4c12c5c8@prog.rb:1 (lambda)>
```

- Using the -> syntax.

```
lam = ->(p1, p2) { p1 + p2 }
lam.call(4, 3) # => 7
```

Note that there cannot be a space between -> and the opening parenthesis.

The first two styles of Proc object are identical in use. We'll call these objects *raw procs*. The third and fourth styles, generated by lambda and ->, add some functionality to the Proc object, as we'll see in a minute. We'll call these objects *lambdas*.

Here's the big thing to remember: raw procs are basically designed to work as the bodies of control structures such as loops. Lambdas are intended to act like methods. So, lambdas are stricter when checking the parameters passed to them, and a return in a lambda exits much as it would from a method.

Calling a Proc

You call a proc by invoking its methods call, yield, or []. The three forms are identical. Each takes arguments that are passed to the proc, just as if it were a regular method. If the proc is a lambda, Ruby will check that the number of supplied arguments match the expected parameters. You can also invoke a proc using the syntax name.(args...). This is mapped internally into name.call(args...).

Procs, break, and next

Within both raw procs and lambdas, executing next causes the block to exit back to the caller of the block. The return value is the value (or values) passed to next, or nil if no values are passed.

```
def ten_times
  10.times do |i|
    if yield(i)
      puts "Caller likes #{i}"
    end
  end
end

ten_times do |number|
  next(true) if number ==7
end
```

produces:

```
Caller likes 7
```

---

6. There's also a built-in Object#proc method. In Ruby 1.8, this was equivalent to lambda. In Ruby 1.9 and later, it is the same as Proc.new. Don't use proc in new code.

Within a raw proc, a break terminates the method that invoked the block. The return value of the method is any parameters passed to the break.

Return and Blocks

A return from inside a *raw block* that's still in scope acts as a return from that scope. A return from a block whose original context is no longer valid raises an exception (LocalJumpError or ThreadError depending on the context). The following example illustrates the first case:

```ruby
def meth1
  (1..10).each do |val|
    return val          # returns from meth1
  end
end
meth1       # => 1
```

The following example shows a return failing because the context of its block no longer exists:

```ruby
def meth2(&b)
  b
end


res = meth2 { return }
res.call
```

produces:

```
        from prog.rb:6:in `call'
        from prog.rb:6:in `<main>'
prog.rb:5:in `block in <main>': unexpected return (LocalJumpError)
```

And here's a return failing because the block is created in one thread and called in another:

```ruby
def meth3
  yield
end

t = Thread.new do
  meth3 { return }
end

t.join
```

produces:

```
        from prog.rb:2:in `meth3'
        from prog.rb:6:in `block in <main>'
prog.rb:6:in `block (2 levels) in <main>': unexpected return (LocalJumpError)
```

This is also true if you create the raw proc using Proc.new.

```ruby
def meth4
  p = Proc.new { return 99 }
  p.call
  puts "Never get here"
end

meth4       # => 99
```

A lambda behaves more like a free-standing method body: a return simply returns from the block to the caller of the block:

```
def meth5
  p = lambda { return 99 }
  res = p.call
  "The block returned #{res}"
end

meth5     # => "The block returned 99"
```

Because of this, if you use Module#define_method, you'll probably want to pass it a proc created using lambda, not Proc.new, because return will work as expected in the former and will generate a LocalJumpError in the latter.

22.14 Exceptions

Ruby exceptions are objects of class Exception and its descendents (a full list of the built-in exceptions is given in Figure 1, *Standard exception hierarchy*, on page 146).

Raising Exceptions

The Object#raise method raises an exception:

```
raise
raise string
raise thing ‹, string ‹, stack trace››
```

The first form reraises the exception in $! or a new RuntimeError if $! is nil. The second form creates a new RuntimeError exception, setting its message to the given string. The third form creates an exception object by invoking the method exception on its first argument, setting this exception's message and backtrace to its second and third arguments. Class Exception and objects of class Exception contain a factory method called exception, so an exception class name or instance can be used as the first parameter to raise.

When an exception is raised, Ruby places a reference to the Exception object in the global variable $!.

Handling Exceptions

Exceptions may be handled in the following ways:

- Within the scope of a begin/end block:

```
begin
  code...
  code...
‹rescue ‹, parm›* ‹, => var› ‹, then›
  error handling code... ›*
‹else
  no exception code... ›
‹ensure
  always executed code... ›
  end
```

- Within the body of a method:

```
def method name and args
   code...
   code...
‹rescue ‹, parm›* ‹, => var› ‹, then›
    error handling code... ›*
‹else
    no exception code...›
‹ensure
    always executed code...›
end
```

- After the execution of a single statement:

  statement ‹rescue statement›*

A block or method may have multiple rescue clauses, and each rescue clause may specify zero or more exception parameters. A rescue clause with no parameter is treated as if it had a parameter of StandardError. This means that some lower-level exceptions will not be caught by a parameterless rescue class. If you want to rescue every exception, use this:

```
rescue Exception => e
```

When an exception is raised, Ruby scans the call stack until it finds an enclosing begin/end block, method body, or statement with a rescue modifier. For each rescue clause in that block, Ruby compares the raised exception against each of the rescue clause's parameters in turn; each parameter is tested using parameter===$!. If the raised exception matches a rescue parameter, Ruby executes the body of the rescue and stops looking. If a matching rescue clause ends with => and a variable name, the variable is set to $!.

Although the parameters to the rescue clause are typically the names of exception classes, they can be arbitrary expressions (including method calls) that return an appropriate class.

If no rescue clause matches the raised exception, Ruby moves up the stack looking for a higher-level begin/end block that matches. If an exception propagates to the top level of the main thread without being rescued, the program terminates with a message.

If an else clause is present, its body is executed if no exceptions were raised in *code*. Exceptions raised during the execution of the else clause are not captured by rescue clauses in the same block as the else.

If an ensure clause is present, its body is always executed as the block is exited (even if an uncaught exception is in the process of being propagated).

Within a rescue clause, raise with no parameters will reraise the exception in $!.

Rescue Statement Modifier

A statement may have an optional rescue modifier followed by another statement (and by extension another rescue modifier, and so on). The rescue modifier takes no exception parameter and rescues StandardError and its children.

If an exception is raised to the left of a rescue modifier, the statement on the left is abandoned, and the value of the overall line is the value of the statement on the right:

```
values = [ "1", "2.3", /pattern/ ]
result = values.map {|v| Integer(v) rescue Float(v) rescue String(v) }
result    # => [1, 2.3, "(?-mix:pattern)"]
```

Retrying a Block

The retry statement can be used within a rescue clause to restart the enclosing begin/end block from the beginning.

22.15 catch and throw

The method Object#catch executes its associated block:

```
catch ( object ) do
  code...
end
```

The method Object#throw interrupts the normal processing of statements:

```
throw( object ‹, obj› )
```

When a throw is executed, Ruby searches up the call stack for the first catch block with a matching *object*. If it is found, the search stops, and execution resumes past the end of the catch's block. If the throw is passed a second parameter, that value is returned as the value of the catch. Ruby honors the ensure clauses of any block expressions it traverses while looking for a corresponding catch.

If no catch block matches the throw, Ruby raises an ArgumentError exception at the location of the throw.

## CHAPTER 23

Duck Typing

You'll have noticed that in Ruby we don't declare the types of variables or methods—everything is just some kind of object.

Now, it seems like folks react to this in two ways. Some like this kind of flexibility and feel comfortable writing code with dynamically typed variables and methods. If you're one of those people, you might want to skip to Section 23.1, *Classes Aren't Types*, on page 344. Some, though, get nervous when they think about all those objects floating around unconstrained. If you've come to Ruby from a language such as C# or Java, where you're used to giving all your variables and methods a type, you may feel that Ruby is just too sloppy to use to write "real" applications.

It isn't.

We'd like to spend a couple of paragraphs trying to convince you that the lack of static typing is not a problem when it comes to writing reliable applications. We're not trying to criticize other languages here. Instead, we'd just like to contrast approaches.

The reality is that the static type systems in most mainstream languages don't really help that much in terms of program security. If Java's type system were reliable, for example, it wouldn't need to implement ClassCastException. The exception is necessary, though, because there is runtime type uncertainty in Java (as there is in C++, C#, and others). Static typing can be good for optimizing code, and it can help IDEs do clever things with tooltip help, but we haven't seen much evidence that it promotes more reliable code.

On the other hand, once you use Ruby for a while, you realize that dynamically typed variables actually add to your productivity in many ways. You'll also be surprised to discover that your fears about the type chaos were unfounded. Large, long-running Ruby programs run significant applications and just don't throw any type-related errors. Why is this?

Partly, it's a question of common sense. If you coded in Java (pre–Java 1.5), all your containers were effectively untyped: everything in a container was just an Object, and you cast it to the required type when you extracted an element. And yet you probably never saw a ClassCast-Exception when you ran these programs. The structure of the code just didn't permit it. You put Person objects in, and you later took Person objects out. You just don't write programs that would work in another way.

Well, it's the same in Ruby. If you use a variable for some purpose, chances are very good that you'll be using it for the same purpose when you access it again three lines later. The kind of chaos that *could* happen just doesn't happen.

On top of that, folks who code Ruby a lot tend to adopt a certain style of coding. They write lots of short methods and tend to test as they go along. The short methods mean that the scope of most variables is limited; there just isn't that much time for things to go wrong with their type. And the testing catches the silly errors when they happen; typos and the like just don't get a chance to propagate through the code.

The upshot is that the "safety" in "type safety" is often illusory and that coding in a more dynamic language such as Ruby is both safe and productive. So, if you're nervous about the lack of static typing in Ruby, we suggest you try to put those concerns on the back burner for a little while and give Ruby a try. We think you'll be surprised how rarely you see errors because of type issues and how much more productive you feel once you start to exploit the power of dynamic typing.

23.1 Classes Aren't Types

The issue of types is actually somewhat deeper than an ongoing debate between strong typing advocates and the hippie-freak dynamic typing crowd. The real issue is the question, what is a type in the first place?

If you've been coding in conventional typed languages, you've probably been taught that the *type* of an object is its *class*—all objects are instances of some class, and that class is the object's type. The class defines the operations (methods) the object can support, along with the state (instance variables) on which those methods operate. Let's look at some Java code:

```
Customer  c;
c = database.findCustomer("dave");    /* Java */
```

This fragment declares the variable c to be of type Customer and sets it to reference the customer object for Dave that we've created from some database record. So, the type of the object in c is Customer, right?

Maybe. However, even in Java, the issue is slightly deeper. Java supports the concept of *interfaces*, which are a kind of emasculated abstract base class. A Java class can be declared as implementing multiple interfaces. Using this facility, you may have defined your classes as follows:

```
public interface Customer {
  long  getID();
  Calendar getDateOfLastContact();
  // ...
}

public class Person
implements Customer {

  public long getID() { ... }
  public Calendar getDateOfLastContact() { ... }
  // ...
}
```

So, even in Java, the class is not always the type—sometimes the type is a subset of the class, and sometimes objects implement multiple types.

In Ruby, the class is never (OK, almost never) the type. Instead, the type of an object is defined more by what that object can do. In Ruby, we call this *duck typing*. If an object walks like a duck and talks like a duck, then the interpreter is happy to treat it as if it were a duck.

Let's look at an example. Perhaps we've written a method to write our customer's name to the end of an open file:

ducktyping/addcust.rb
```ruby
class Customer
  def initialize(first_name, last_name)
    @first_name = first_name
    @last_name  = last_name
  end
  def append_name_to_file(file)
    file << @first_name << " " << @last_name
  end
end
```

Being good programmers, we'll write a unit test for this. Be warned, though—it's messy (and we'll improve on it shortly):

```ruby
require 'test/unit'
require_relative 'addcust'

class TestAddCustomer < Test::Unit::TestCase
  def test_add
    c = Customer.new("Ima", "Customer")
    f = File.open("tmpfile", "w") do |f|
      c.append_name_to_file(f)
    end
    f = File.open("tmpfile") do |f|
      assert_equal("Ima Customer", f.gets)
    end
  ensure
    File.delete("tmpfile") if File.exist?("tmpfile")
  end
end
```

produces:
```
Run options:
# Running tests:

.
Finished tests in 0.007193s, 139.0241 tests/s, 139.0241 assertions/s.
1 tests, 1 assertions, 0 failures, 0 errors, 0 skips

ruby -v: ruby 2.0.0p0 (2013-02-24 revision 39474) [x86_64-darwin12.2.0]
```

We have to do all that work to create a file to write to, then reopen it, and read in the contents to verify the correct string was written. We also have to delete the file when we've finished (but only if it exists).

Instead, though, we could rely on duck typing. All we need is something that walks like a file and talks like a file that we can pass in to the method under test. And all that means *in this circumstance* is that we need an object that responds to the << method by appending something. Do we have something that does this? How about a humble String?

```
require 'test/unit'
require_relative 'addcust'

class TestAddCustomer < Test::Unit::TestCase
  def test_add
    c = Customer.new("Ima", "Customer")
    f = ""
    c.append_name_to_file(f)
    assert_equal("Ima Customer", f)
  end
end
```

produces:

```
Run options:
# Running tests:

.
Finished tests in 0.006737s, 148.4340 tests/s, 148.4340 assertions/s.
1 tests, 1 assertions, 0 failures, 0 errors, 0 skips

ruby -v: ruby 2.0.0p0 (2013-02-24 revision 39474) [x86_64-darwin12.2.0]
```

The method under test thinks it's writing to a file, but instead it's just appending to a string. At the end, we can then just test that the content is correct.

We didn't have to use a string; an array would work just as well for the purposes of the test:

```
require 'test/unit'
require_relative 'addcust'

class TestAddCustomer < Test::Unit::TestCase
  def test_add
    c = Customer.new("Ima", "Customer")
    f = []
    c.append_name_to_file(f)
    assert_equal(["Ima", " ", "Customer"], f)
  end
end
```

produces:

```
Run options:
# Running tests:

.
Finished tests in 0.006641s, 150.5797 tests/s, 150.5797 assertions/s.
1 tests, 1 assertions, 0 failures, 0 errors, 0 skips

ruby -v: ruby 2.0.0p0 (2013-02-24 revision 39474) [x86_64-darwin12.2.0]
```

Indeed, this form may be more convenient if we wanted to check that the correct individual things were inserted.

So, duck typing is convenient for testing, but what about in the body of applications themselves? Well, it turns out that the same thing that made the tests easy in the previous example also makes it easy to write flexible application code.

In fact, Dave had an interesting experience where duck typing dug him (and a client) out of a hole. He'd written a large Ruby-based web application that (among other things) kept a database table full of details of participants in a competition. The system provided a comma-separated value (CSV) download capability so administrators could import this information into their local spreadsheets.

Just before competition time, the phone starts ringing. The download, which had been working fine up to this point, was now taking so long that requests were timing out. The pressure was intense, because the administrators had to use this information to build schedules and send out mailings.

A little experimentation showed that the problem was in the routine that took the results of the database query and generated the CSV download. The code looked something like this:

```ruby
def csv_from_row(op, row)
  res = ""
  until row.empty?
    entry = row.shift.to_s
    if /[,"]/ =~ entry
      entry = entry.gsub(/"/, '""')
      res << '"' << entry << '"'
    else
      res << entry
    end
    res << "," unless row.empty?
  end
  op << res << CRLF
end


result = ""
query.each_row {|row|  csv_from_row(result, row)}

http.write result
```

When this code ran against moderate-size data sets, it performed fine. But at a certain input size, it suddenly slowed right down. The culprit? Garbage collection. The approach was generating thousands of intermediate strings and building one big result string, one line at a time. As the big string grew, it needed more space, and garbage collection was invoked, which necessitated scanning and removing all the intermediate strings.

The answer was simple and surprisingly effective. Rather than build the result string as it went along, the code was changed to store each CSV row as an element in an array. This meant that the intermediate lines were still referenced and hence were no longer garbage. It also meant that we were no longer building an ever-growing string that forced garbage collection. Thanks to duck typing, the change was trivial:

```ruby
def csv_from_row(op, row)
  # as before
end


result = []
query.each_row {|row|  csv_from_row(result, row)}

http.write result.join
```

All that changed is that we passed an array into the csv_from_row method. Because it (implicitly) used duck typing, the method itself was not modified; it continued to append the data it generated to its parameter, not caring what type that parameter was. After the method returned its result, we joined all those individual lines into one big string. This one change reduced the time to run from more than three minutes to a few seconds.

23.2 Coding like a Duck

If you want to write your programs using the duck typing philosophy, you really need to remember only one thing: an object's type is determined by what it can do, not by its class. (In fact, older versions of Ruby had a method Object#type that returned the class of an object.)

What does this mean in practice? At one level, it simply means that there's often little value testing the class of an object.

For example, you may be writing a routine to add song information to a string. If you come from a C# or Java background, you may be tempted to write this:

```ruby
def append_song(result, song)
  # test we're given the right parameters
  unless result.kind_of?(String)
    fail TypeError.new("String expected")
  end
  unless song.kind_of?(Song)
    fail TypeError.new("Song expected")
  end

  result << song.title << " (" << song.artist << ")"
end

result = ""
append_song(result, song)
```

Embrace Ruby's duck typing, and you'd write something far simpler:

```ruby
def append_song(result, song)
  result << song.title << " (" << song.artist << ")"
end

result = ""
append_song(result, song)
```

You don't need to check the type of the arguments. If they support << (in the case of *result*) or title and artist (in the case of *song*), everything will just work. If they don't, your method will throw an exception anyway (just as it would have done if you'd checked the types). But without the check, your method is suddenly a lot more flexible. You could pass it an array, a string, a file, or any other object that appends using <<, and it would just work.

Now sometimes you may want more than this style of *laissez-faire* programming. You may have good reasons to check that a parameter can do what you need. Will you get thrown out of the duck typing club if you check the parameter against a class? No, you won't.[1] But you may want to consider checking based on the object's capabilities, rather than its class:

---

1. The duck typing club doesn't check to see whether you're a member anyway....

```ruby
def append_song(result, song)
  # test we're given the right parameters
  unless result.respond_to?(:<<)
    fail TypeError.new("'result' needs `<<' capability")
  end
  unless song.respond_to?(:artist) && song.respond_to?(:title)
    fail TypeError.new("'song' needs 'artist' and 'title'")
  end

  result << song.title << " (" << song.artist << ")"
end

result = ""
append_song(result, song)
```

However, before going down this path, make sure you're getting a real benefit—it's a lot of extra code to write and to maintain.

23.3 Standard Protocols and Coercions

Although not technically part of the language, the interpreter and standard library use various protocols to handle issues that other languages would deal with using types.

Some objects have more than one natural representation. For example, you may be writing a class to represent Roman numbers (I, II, III, IV, V, and so on). This class is not necessarily a subclass of Integer, because its objects are representations of numbers, not numbers in their own right. At the same time, they do have an integer-like quality. It would be nice to be able to use objects of our Roman number class wherever Ruby was expecting to see an integer.

To do this, Ruby has the concept of *conversion protocols*—an object may elect to have itself converted to an object of another class. Ruby has three standard ways of doing this.

We've already come across the first. Methods such as to_s and to_i convert their receiver into strings and integers. These conversion methods are not particularly strict. If an object has some kind of decent representation as a string, for example, it will probably have a to_s method. Our Roman class would probably implement to_s in order to return the string representation of a number (VII, for instance).

The second form of conversion function uses methods with names such as to_str and to_int. These are strict conversion functions. You implement them only if your object can naturally be used every place a string or an integer could be used. For example, our Roman number objects have a clear representation as an integer and so should implement to_int. When it comes to stringiness, however, we have to think a bit harder.

Roman numbers clearly have a string representation, but are they strings? Should we be able to use them wherever we can use a string itself? No, probably not. Logically, they're a representation of a number. You can represent them as strings, but they aren't plug-compatible with strings. For this reason, a Roman number won't implement to_str—it isn't really a string. Just to drive this home, Roman numerals can be converted to strings using to_s, but they aren't inherently strings, so they don't implement to_str.

To see how this works in practice, let's look at opening a file. The first parameter to File.new can be either an existing file descriptor (represented by an integer) or a filename to open. However, Ruby doesn't simply look at the first parameter and check whether its type is

Fixnum or String. Instead, it gives the object passed in the opportunity to represent itself as a number or a string. If it were written in Ruby, it may look something like this:

```ruby
class File
  def self.new(file, *args)
    if file.respond_to?(:to_int)
      IO.new(file.to_int, *args)
    else
      name = file.to_str
      # call operating system to open file 'name'
    end
  end
end
```

So, let's see what happens if we want to pass a file descriptor integer stored as a Roman number into File.new. Because our class implements to_int, the first respond_to? test will succeed. We'll pass an integer representation of our number to IO.open, and the file descriptor will be returned, all wrapped up in a new IO object.

A small number of strict conversion functions are built into the standard library.

to_ary → Array

This is used when interpreter needs a parameter to a method to be an array and when expanding parameters and assignments containing the *xyz syntax.

```ruby
class OneTwo
  def to_ary
    [ 1, 2 ]
  end
end

ot = OneTwo.new
puts ot
```

produces:

```
1
2
```

to_a → Array

This is used when interpreter needs to convert an object into an array for parameter passing or multiple assignment.

```ruby
class OneTwo
  def to_a
    [ 1, 2 ]
  end
end

ot = OneTwo.new
a, b = *ot
puts "a = #{a}, b = #{b}"
printf("%d -- %d\n", *ot)
```

produces:

```
a = 1, b = 2
1 -- 2
```

to_enum → Enumerator

> This converts an object (presumably a collection) to an enumerator. It's never called internally by the interpreter.

to_hash → Hash

> This is used when the interpreter expects to see Hash.

to_int → Integer

> This is used when the interpreter expects to see an integer value (such as a file descriptor or as a parameter to Object#Integer).

to_io → IO

> Used when the interpreter is expecting I/O objects (for example, as parameters to the methods IO#reopen or IO.select).

to_open → IO

> Called (if defined) on the first parameter to IO.open.

to_path → String

> Called by the interpreter when it is looking for a filename (for example, by File#open).

to_proc → Proc

> Used to convert an object prefixed with an ampersand in a method call.

```ruby
class OneTwo
  def to_proc
    proc { "one-two" }
  end
end
def silly
  yield
end

ot = OneTwo.new
silly(&ot) # => "one-two"
```

to_regexp → Regexp

> Invoked by Regexp#try_convert to convert its argument to a regular expression.

to_str → String

> Used pretty much any place the interpreter is looking for a String value.

```ruby
class OneTwo
  def to_str
    "one-two"
  end
end

ot = OneTwo.new
puts("count: " + ot)
File.open(ot) rescue puts $!.message
```

produces:

```
count: one-two
No such file or directory - one-two
```

to_sym → Symbol

> Expresses the receiver as a symbol. This is used by the interpreter when compiling instruction sequences, but it's probably not useful in user code.

Note that classes such as Integer and Fixnum implement the to_int method, and String implements to_str. That way, you can call the strict conversion functions polymorphically:

```
# it doesn't matter if obj is a Fixnum or a
# Roman number, the conversion still succeeds
num = obj.to_int
```

The Symbol.to_proc Trick

Ruby implements the to_proc for objects of class symbol. Say you want to convert an array of strings to uppercase. You could write this:

```
names = %w{ant bee cat}
result = names.map {|name| name.upcase}
```

That's fairly concise, right? Return a new array where each element is the corresponding element in the original, converted to uppercase. But you can instead write this:

```
names = %w{ant bee cat}
result = names.map(&:upcase)
```

Now that's concise: apply the upcase method to each element of names.

So, how does it work? It relies on Ruby's type coercions. Let's start at the top.

When you say names.map(&xxx), you're telling Ruby to pass the Proc object in xxx to the map method as a block. If xxx isn't already a Proc object, Ruby tries to coerce it into one by sending it a to_proc message.

Now :upcase isn't a Proc object—it's a symbol. So when Ruby sees names.map(&:upcase), the first thing it does is try to convert the symbol :upcase into a Proc by calling to_proc. And, by an incredible coincidence, Ruby implements just such a method. If it was written in Ruby, it would look something like this:

```
def to_proc
  proc { |obj, *args| obj.send(self, *args) }
end
```

This method creates a Proc, which, when called on an object, sends that object the symbol itself. So, when names.map(&:upcase) starts to iterate over the strings in names, it'll call the block, passing in the first name and invoking its upcase method.

It's an incredibly elegant use of coercion and of closures. However, it comes at a price. The use of dynamic method invocations mean that the version of our code that uses &:upcase is about half as fast as the more explicitly coded block. This doesn't worry me personally unless I happen to be in a performance-critical section of my code.

Numeric Coercion

We previously said there were three types of conversion performed by the interpreter. We covered loose and strict conversion. The third is numeric coercion.

Here's the problem. When you write 1+2, Ruby knows to call the + on the object 1 (a Fixnum), passing it the Fixnum 2 as a parameter. However, when you write 1+2.3, the same + method now receives a Float parameter. How can it know what to do (particularly because checking the classes of your parameters is against the spirit of duck typing)?

The answer lies in Ruby's coercion protocol, based on the method coerce. The basic operation of coerce is simple. It takes two numbers (its receiver and its parameter). It returns a two-element array containing representations of these two numbers (but with the parameter first, followed by the receiver). The coerce method guarantees that these two objects will have the same class and therefore that they can be added (or multiplied, compared, or whatever).

```
1.coerce(2)       # => [2, 1]
1.coerce(2.3)     # => [2.3, 1.0]
(4.5).coerce(2.3) # => [2.3, 4.5]
(4.5).coerce(2)   # => [2.0, 4.5]
```

The trick is that the receiver calls the coerce method of its parameter to generate this array. This technique, called *double dispatch*, allows a method to change its behavior based not only on its class but also on the class of its parameter. In this case, we're letting the parameter decide exactly *what* classes of objects should get added (or multiplied, divided, and so on).

Let's say that we're writing a new class that's intended to take part in arithmetic. To participate in coercion, we need to implement a coerce method. This takes some other kind of number as a parameter and returns an array containing two objects of the same class, whose values are equivalent to its parameter and itself.

For our Roman number class, it's fairly easy. Internally, each Roman number object holds its real value as a Fixnum in an instance variable, @value. The coerce method checks to see whether the class of its parameter is also an Integer. If so, it returns its parameter and its internal value. If not, it first converts both to floating point.

```ruby
class Roman
  def initialize(value)
    @value = value
  end
  def coerce(other)
    if  Integer === other
      [ other, @value ]
    else
      [ Float(other), Float(@value) ]
    end
  end
  # .. other Roman stuff
end

iv = Roman.new(4)
xi = Roman.new(11)

3 * iv    # => 12
1.2 * xi  # => 13.2
```

Of course, class Roman as implemented doesn't know how to do addition. You couldn't have written xi+3 in the previous example, because Roman doesn't have a + method. And that's probably as it should be. But let's go wild and implement addition for Roman numbers:

```ruby
class Roman
  MAX_ROMAN = 4999

  attr_reader :value
  protected :value

  def initialize(value)
    if value <= 0 || value > MAX_ROMAN
      fail "Roman values must be > 0 and <= #{MAX_ROMAN}"
    end
    @value = value
  end

  def coerce(other)
    if  Integer === other
      [ other, @value ]
    else
      [ Float(other), Float(@value) ]
    end
  end

  def +(other)
    if Roman === other
      other = other.value
    end
    if Fixnum === other && (other + @value) < MAX_ROMAN
      Roman.new(@value + other)
    else
      x, y = other.coerce(@value)
      x + y
    end
  end

  FACTORS = [["m", 1000], ["cm", 900], ["d",  500], ["cd", 400],
            ["c",  100], ["xc",  90], ["l",   50], ["xl",  40],
            ["x",   10], ["ix",   9], ["v",    5], ["iv",   4],
            ["i",    1]]

  def to_s
    value = @value
    roman = ""
    for code, factor in FACTORS
      count, value = value.divmod(factor)
      roman << (code * count)
    end
    roman
  end
end

iv = Roman.new(4)
xi = Roman.new(11)

iv + 3          # => vii
iv + 3 + 4      # => xi
```

```
iv + 3.14159    # => 7.14159
xi + 4900       # => mmmmcmxi
xi + 4990       # => 5001
```

Finally, be careful with coerce—try always to coerce into a more general type, or you may end up generating coercion loops. This is a situation where A tries to coerce to B and when B tries to coerce back to A.

23.4 Walk the Walk, Talk the Talk

Duck typing can generate controversy. Every now and then a thread flares on the mailing lists or someone blogs for or against the concept. Many of the contributors to these discussions have some fairly extreme positions.

Ultimately, though, duck typing isn't a set of rules; it's just a style of programming. Design your programs to balance paranoia and flexibility. If you feel the need to constrain the types of objects that the users of a method pass in, ask yourself why. Try to determine what could go wrong if you were expecting a String and instead get an Array. Sometimes, the difference is crucially important. Often, though, it isn't. Try erring on the more permissive side for a while, and see whether bad things happen. If not, perhaps duck typing isn't just for the birds.

## CHAPTER 24

Metaprogramming

The Jacquard loom, invented more than 200 years ago, was the first device controlled using punched cards—rows of holes in each card were used to control the pattern woven into the cloth. But imagine if instead of churning out fabric, the loom could punch more cards, and those cards could be fed back into the mechanism. The machine could be used to create new programming that it could then execute. And that would be metaprogramming—writing code that writes code.

Programming is all about building layers of abstractions. As you solve problems, you're building bridges from the unrelenting and mechanical world of silicon to the more ambiguous and fluid world we inhabit. Some programming languages—such as C—are close to the machine. The distance from C code to the application domain can be large. Other languages—Ruby, perhaps—provide higher-level abstractions and hence let you start coding closer to the target domain. For this reason, most people consider a higher-level language to be a better starting place for application development (although they'll argue about the choice of language).

But when you metaprogram, you are no longer limited to the set of abstractions built in to your programming language. Instead, you create new abstractions that are integrated into the host language. In effect, you're creating a new, domain-specific programming language —one that lets you express the concepts you need to solve your particular problem.

Ruby makes metaprogramming easy. As a result, most advanced Ruby programmers will use metaprogramming techniques to simplify their code. This chapter shows how they do it. It isn't intended to be an exhaustive survey of metaprogramming techniques. Instead, we'll look at the underlying Ruby principles that make metaprogramming possible. From there you'll be able to invent your own metaprogramming idioms.

24.1 Objects and Classes

Classes and objects are obviously central to Ruby, but at first sight they can be a little confusing. It seems like there are a lot of concepts: classes, objects, class objects, instance methods, class methods, singleton classes, and virtual classes. In reality, however, Ruby has just a single underlying class and object structure.

A Ruby object has three components: a set of flags, some instance variables, and an associated class. A Ruby class is itself an object of class Class. It contains all the things an object has plus a set of method definitions and a reference to a superclass (which is itself another class).

And, basically, that's it. From here, you could work out the details of metaprogramming for yourself. But, as always, the devil lurks in the details, so let's dig a little deeper.

self and Method Calling

Ruby has the concept of the *current object*. This current object is referenced by the built-in, read-only variable self. self has two significant roles in a running Ruby program.

First, self controls how Ruby finds instance variables. We already said that every object carries around a set of instance variables. When you access an instance variable, Ruby looks for it in the object referenced by self.

Second, self plays a vital role in method calling. In Ruby, each method call is made on some object. This object is called the *receiver* of the call. When you make a call such as items.size, the object referenced by the variable items is the receiver and size is the method to invoke.

If you make a method call such as puts "hi", there's no explicit receiver. In this case, Ruby uses the current object, self, as the receiver. It goes to self's class and looks up the method (in this case, puts). If it can't find the method in the class, it looks in the class's superclass and then in that class's superclass, stopping when it runs out of superclasses (which will happen after it has looked in BasicObject).[1]

When you make a method call with an explicit receiver (for example, invoking items.size), the process is surprisingly similar. The only change—but it's a vitally important one—is the fact that self is changed for the duration of the call. Before starting the method lookup process, Ruby sets self to the receiver (the object referenced by items in this case). Then, after the call returns, Ruby restores the value that self had before the call.

Let's see how this works in practice. Here's a simple program:

```ruby
class Test
  def one
    @var = 99
    two
  end
  def two
    puts @var
  end
end

t = Test.new
t.one
```

produces:

99

The call to Test.new on the second-to-last line creates a new object of class Test, assigning that object to the variable t. Then, on the next line, we call the method t.one. To execute this call, Ruby sets self to t and then looks in t's class for the method one. Ruby finds the method defined on line 2 and calls it.

---

1. If it can't find the method in the object's class hierarchy, Ruby looks for a method called method_missing on the original receiver, starting back at the class of self and then looking up the superclass chain.

Inside the method, we set the instance variable @var to 99. This instance variable will be associated with the current object. What is that object? Well, the call to t.one set self to t, so within the one method, self will be that particular instance of class Test.

On the next line, one calls two. Because there's no explicit receiver, self is not changed. When Ruby looks for the method two, it looks in Test, the class of t.

The method two references an instance variable @var. Again, Ruby looks for this variable in the current object and finds the same variable that was set by the method one.

The call to puts at the end of two works the same way. Again, because there's no explicit receiver, self will be unchanged. Ruby looks for the puts method in the class of the current object but can't find it. It then looks in Test's superclass, class Object. Again, it doesn't find puts. However, Object mixes in the module Kernel. We'll talk more about this later; for now we can say that mixed-in modules act as if they were superclasses. The Kernel module *does* define puts, so the method is found and executed.

After two and one return, Ruby resets self to the value it had before the original call to t.one.

This explanation may seem labored, but understanding it is vital to mastering metaprogramming in Ruby.

self and Class Definitions

We've seen that calling a method with an explicit receiver changes self. Perhaps surprisingly, self is also changed by a class definition. This is a consequence of the fact that class definitions are actually executable code in Ruby—if we can execute code, we need to have a current object. A simple test shows what this object is:

```ruby
class Test
  puts "In the definition of class Test"
  puts "self = #{self}"
  puts "Class of self = #{self.class}"
end
```

produces:

```
In the definition of class Test
self = Test
Class of self = Class
```

Inside a class definition, self is set to the class object of the class being defined. This means that instance variables set in a class definition will be available to class methods (because self will be the same when the variables are defined and when the methods execute):

```ruby
class Test
  @var = 99
  def self.value_of_var
    @var
  end
end

Test.value_of_var # => 99
```

The fact that self is set to the class during a class definition turns out to be a dramatically elegant decision, but to see why, we'll first need to have a look at singletons.

24.2 Singletons

Ruby lets you define methods that are specific to a particular object. These are called *singleton methods*. Let's start with a simple string object:

```
animal = "cat"
puts animal.upcase
```

produces:

```
CAT
```

This results in the following object structure.

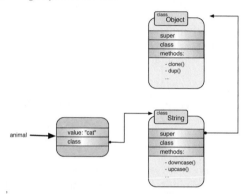

The animal variable points to an object containing (among other things) the value of the string ("cat") and a pointer to the object's class, String.

When we call animal.upcase, Ruby goes to the object referenced by the animal variable and then looks up the method upcase in the class object referenced from the animal object. Our animal is a string and so has the methods of class String available.

Now let's make it more interesting. We'll define a singleton method on the string referenced by animal:

```
animal = "cat"
def animal.speak
  puts "The #{self} says miaow"
end

animal.speak
puts animal.upcase
```

produces:

```
The cat says miaow
CAT
```

We've already seen how the call to animal.speak works when we looked at how methods are invoked. Ruby sets self to the string object "cat" referenced by animal and then looks for a method speak in that object's class. Surprisingly, it finds it. It's initially surprising because the class of "cat" is String, and String doesn't have a speak method. So, does Ruby have some kind of special-case magic for these methods that are defined on individual objects?

Thankfully, the answer is "no." Ruby's object model is remarkably consistent. When we defined the singleton method for the "cat" object, Ruby created a new anonymous class and defined the speak method in that class. This anonymous class is sometimes called a *singleton class* and other times an *eigenclass*. I prefer the former, because it ties in to the idea of singleton methods.

Ruby makes this singleton class the class of the "cat" object and makes String (which was the original class of "cat") the superclass of the singleton class. The picture looks like this:

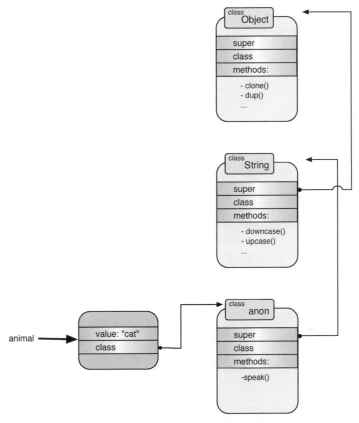

Now let's follow the call to animal.speak. Ruby goes to the object referenced by animal and then looks in its class for the method speak. The class of the animal object is the newly created singleton class, and it contains the method we need.

What happens if we instead call animal.upcase? The processing starts the same way: Ruby looks for the method upcase in the singleton class but fails to find it there. It then follows the normal processing rules and starts looking up the chain of superclasses. The superclass of the singleton is String, and Ruby finds the upcase method there. Notice that there is no special-case processing here—Ruby method calls always work the same way.

Singletons and Classes

Earlier, we said that inside a class definition, self is set to the class object being defined. It turns out that this is the basis for one of the more elegant aspects of Ruby's object model.

Recall that we can define class methods in Ruby using either of the forms def self.xxx or def ClassName.xxx:

```
class Dave
  def self.class_method_one
    puts "Class method one"
  end
  def Dave.class_method_two
    puts "Class method two"
  end
end

Dave.class_method_one
Dave.class_method_two
```

produces:

```
Class method one
Class method two
```

Now we know why the two forms are identical: inside the class definition, self is set to Dave.

But now that we've looked at singleton methods, we also know that, in reality, there is no such thing as class methods in Ruby. Both of the previous definitions define singleton methods on the class object. As with all other singleton methods, we can then call them via the object (in this case, the class Dave).

Before we created the two singleton methods in class Dave, the class pointer in the class object pointed to class Class. (That's a confusing sentence. Another way of saying it is "Dave is a class, so the class of Dave is class Class," but that's pretty confusing, too.) The situation looks like this:

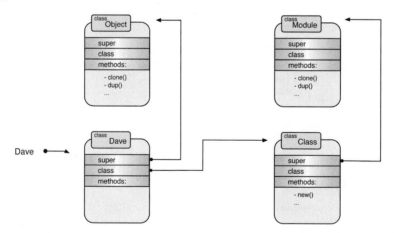

The object diagram for class Dave after the methods are defined looks like this:

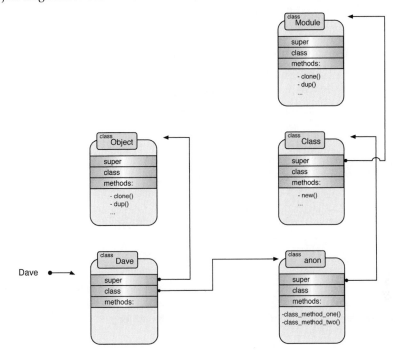

Do you see how the singleton class is created, just as it was for the animal example? The class is inserted as the class of Dave, and the original class of Dave is made this new class's parent.

We can now tie together the two uses of self, the current object. We talked about how instance variables are looked up in self, and we talked about how singleton methods defined on self become class methods. Let's use these facts to access instance variables for class objects:

```ruby
class Test
  @var = 99
  def self.var
    @var
  end
  def self.var=(value)
    @var = value
  end
end

puts "Original value = #{Test.var}"
Test.var = "cat"
puts "New value = #{Test.var}"
```

produces:

```
Original value = 99
New value = cat
```

Newcomers to Ruby commonly make the mistake of setting instance variables inline in the class definition (as we did with @var in the previous code) and then attempting to access these variables from instance methods. As the code illustrates, this won't work, because instance variables defined in the class body are associated with the class object, not with instances of the class.

Another Way to Access the Singleton Class

We've seen how you can create methods in an object's singleton class by adding the object reference to the method definition using something like def animal.speak.

You can do the same using Ruby's class << an_object notation:

```ruby
animal = "dog"
class << animal
  def speak
    puts "The #{self} says WOOF!"
  end
end


animal.speak
```

produces:

```
The dog says WOOF!
```

Inside this kind of class definition, self is set to the singleton class for the given object (animal in this case). Because class definitions return the value of the last statement executed in the class body, we can use this fact to get the singleton class object:

```ruby
animal = "dog"
def animal.speak
  puts "The #{self} says WOOF!"
end

singleton = class << animal
  def lie
    puts "The #{self} lies down"
  end
  self      # << return singleton class object
end

animal.speak
animal.lie
puts "Singleton class object is #{singleton}"
puts "It defines methods #{singleton.instance_methods - 'cat'.methods}"
```

produces:

```
The dog says WOOF!
The dog lies down
Singleton class object is #<Class:#<String:0x007fa6910471f0>>
It defines methods [:speak, :lie]
```

Note the notation that Ruby uses to denote a singleton class: #<Class:#<String:...>>.

Ruby goes to some trouble to stop you from using singleton classes outside the context of their original object. For example, you can't create a new instance of a singleton class:

```ruby
singleton = class << "cat"; self; end
singleton.new
```

produces:

```
        from prog.rb:2:in `<main>'
prog.rb:2:in `new': can't create instance of singleton class (TypeError)
```

Let's tie together what we know about instance variables, self, and singleton classes. We wrote class-level accessor methods on page 363 to let us get and set the value of an instance variable defined in a class object. But Ruby already has attr_accessor, which defines getter and setter methods. Normally, though, these are defined as instance methods and hence will access values stored in instances of a class. To make them work with class-level instance variables, we have to invoke attr_accessor in the singleton class:

```ruby
class Test
  @var = 99
  class << self
    attr_accessor :var
  end
end

puts "Original value = #{Test.var}"
Test.var = "cat"
puts "New value = #{Test.var}"
```

produces:

```
Original value = 99
New value = cat
```

24.3 Inheritance and Visibility

There's a wrinkle to when it comes to method definition and class inheritance, but it's fairly obscure. Within a class definition, you can change the visibility of a method in an ancestor class. For example, you can do something like this:

```ruby
class Base
  def a_method
    puts "Got here"
  end
  private :a_method
end

class Derived1 < Base
  public :a_method
end

class Derived2 < Base
end
```

In this example, you would be able to invoke a_method in instances of class Derived1 but not via instances of Base or Derived2.

So, how does Ruby pull off this feat of having one method with two different visibilities? Simply put, it cheats.

If a subclass changes the visibility of a method in a parent, Ruby effectively inserts a hidden proxy method in the subclass that invokes the original method using super. It then sets the visibility of that proxy to whatever you requested. This means that the following code:

```ruby
class Derived1 < Base
  public :a_method
end
```

is effectively the same as this:

```ruby
class Derived1 < Base
  def a_method(*)
    super
  end
  public :a_method
end
```

The call to super can access the parent's method regardless of its visibility, so the rewrite allows the subclass to override its parent's visibility rules. Pretty scary, eh?

24.4 Modules and Mixins

You know that when you include a module into a Ruby class, the instance methods in that module become available as instance methods of the class.

```ruby
module Logger
  def log(msg)
    STDERR.puts Time.now.strftime("%H:%M:%S: ") + "#{self} (#{msg})"
  end
end

class Song
  include Logger
end

s = Song.new
s.log("created")
```

produces:

```
12:31:37: #<Song:0x007f952b0478c0> (created)
```

Ruby implements include very simply: the module that you include is effectively added as a superclass of the class being defined. It's as if the module is the parent of the class that it is mixed in to. And that would be the end of the description except for one small wrinkle. Because the module is injected into the chain of superclasses, it must itself hold a link to the original parent class. If it didn't, there'd be no way of traversing the superclass chain to look up methods. However, you can mix the same module into many different classes, and those classes could potentially have totally different superclass chains. If there were just one module object that we mixed in to all these classes, there'd be no way of keeping track of the different superclasses for each.

To get around this, Ruby uses a clever trick. When you include a module in class Example, Ruby constructs a new class object, makes it the superclass of Example, and then sets the superclass of the new class to be the original superclass of Example. It then references the module's methods from this new class object in such a way that when you look a method up in this class, it actually looks it up in the module:

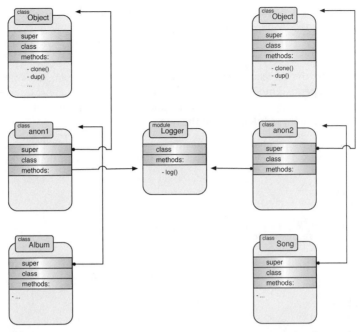

A nice side effect of this arrangement is that if you change a module after including it in a class, those changes are reflected in the class (and the class's objects). In this way, modules behave just like classes.

```ruby
module Mod
  def greeting
    "Hello"
  end
end
class Example
  include Mod
end

ex = Example.new
puts "Before change, greeting is #{ex.greeting}"

module Mod
  def greeting
    "Hi"
  end
end

puts "After change, greeting is #{ex.greeting}"
```

produces:

```
Before change, greeting is Hello
After change, greeting is Hi
```

If a module itself includes other modules, a chain of proxy classes will be added to any class that includes that module, one proxy for each module that is directly or indirectly included.

Finally, Ruby will include a module only once in an inheritance chain—including a module that is already included by one of your superclasses has no effect.

prepend

Ruby 2 introduced the prepend method. Logically, this behaves just like include, but the methods in the prepended module take precedence over those in the host class. Ruby pulls off this magic by inserting a dummy class in place of the original host class[2] and then inserting the prepended module between the two.

If a method inside a prepended module has the same name as one in the original class, it will be invoked instead of the original. The prepended method can then call the original using super.

```ruby
module VanityPuts
  def puts(*args)
    args.each do |arg|
      super("Dave says: #{arg}")
    end
  end
end

class Object
  prepend VanityPuts
end

puts "Hello and", "goodbye"
```

produces:

```
Dave says: Hello and
Dave says: goodbye
```

However, there is a problem with this—the change we just made to class Object is global. We'll see how to fix that shortly when we look at refinements.

extend

The include method effectively adds a module as a superclass of self. It is used inside a class definition to make the instance methods in the module available to instances of the class.

However, it is sometimes useful to add the instance methods to a particular object. You do this using Object#extend. Here's an example:

```ruby
module Humor
  def tickle
    "#{self} says hee, hee!"
  end
end

obj = "Grouchy"
obj.extend Humor
obj.tickle # => "Grouchy says hee, hee!"
```

---

2.   Actually, it inserts the dummy class above the original class, and then moves the methods from the original to the copy.

Stop for a second to think about how this might be implemented.

When Ruby executes obj.tickle in this code example, it does the usual trick of looking in the class of obj for a method called tickle. For extend to work, it has to add the instance methods in the Humor module into the superclass chain for the class of obj. So, just as with singleton method definitions, Ruby creates a singleton class for obj and then includes the module Humor in that class. In fact, just to prove that this is all that happens, here's the C implementation of extend in the current Ruby 1.9 interpreter:

```
void rb_extend_object(VALUE obj, VALUE module) {
    rb_include_module(rb_singleton_class(obj), module);
}
```

There is an interesting trick with extend. If you use it within a class definition, the module's methods become class methods. This is because calling extend is equivalent to self.extend, so the methods are added to self, which in a class definition is the class itself.

Here's an example of adding a module's methods at the class level:

```
module Humor
  def tickle
    "#{self} says hee, hee!"
  end
end
class Grouchy
  extend  Humor
end

Grouchy.tickle # => "Grouchy says hee, hee!"
```

Later on page 375, we'll see how to use extend to add macro-style methods to a class.

Refinements

We previously looked at applying a change to a builtin class by defining the altered version New in 2.0 of a method in a module, and then prepending that module in the class. When we subsequently call the method on instances of the class, it finds the version in the module first.

This technique is time-honored—frameworks such as Ruby on Rails rely on it. But it comes with a price—any changes we make like this are global. They apply not just to the code we wrote for our application, but also to the code in all the libraries and gems we use, too. It is possible that a change that made our code easier to write breaks someone else's library code that we rely on.[3]

Ruby 2.0 is experimenting with a new way of dealing with this problem. The technique is called *refinements*.

Now, before going any further, here is the mandatory warning. Refinements are not yet completely worked out. In fact, a fair amount of refinement functionality was removed just a few weeks before Ruby 2.0 was released. So what we're documenting here may well become

---

3. This is clearly a problem in theory. Does it happen in practice? Actually, surprisingly little. But you can never be sure that things will quite work as you expect. Even if you don't override these classes, it is possible you're using two separate libraries whose patches to third-party classes clash.

outdated as new releases of Ruby change the spec. If you are writing code that uses refinements, you'll want to keep track of these changes.

A refinement is a way of packaging a set of changes to one or more classes. These refinements are defined within a module.

If a Ruby source file then elects to use this module of refinements, the change will apply to the source in that module past the point where the refinement is used. However code outside this file is not affected.

Let's make this concrete. Here's our vanity version of puts rewritten using refinements.

```ruby
module VanityPuts
  refine Object do
    private
    def puts(*args)
      args.each do |arg|
        Kernel::puts("Dave says: #{arg}")
      end
    end
  end
end


using VanityPuts

puts "Hello", "world"
```

produces:

```
prog.rb:2: warning: Refinements are experimental, and the behavior may change in
future versions of Ruby!
Dave says: Hello
Dave says: world
```

The refinement is contained in the module VanityPuts. The refine block takes a class and a block. Within the block are the methods that you would like to update in that class. At this point, no change is made—you have defined a method, but haven't yet told Ruby to use it.

That's what the using clause does. You give it a module containing one or more refinements, and it marks the refined objects to say "for the rest of this source file, when you make a call to an instance of Object, first check to see if the method can be found in the refinement. If so, invoke it, otherwise invoke the original.

Let's step it up a notch. We'll define three source files. Here's one that contains a refinement definition:

metaprogramming/ref1/vanity_refinement.rb
```ruby
module VanityPuts
  refine Object do
    private
    def puts(*args)
      args.each do |arg|
        Kernel::puts("Dave says: #{arg}")
      end
    end
  end
end
```

And here's a file that uses this refinement.

metaprogramming/ref1/file_using_refinement.rb
```
using VanityPuts

puts "I'm in #{File::basename(__FILE__)}"

def shout(msg)
  puts(msg.upcase)
end
```

Finally, let's run them from a third file:

```
require_relative 'vanity_refinement'

puts "About to require file using refinement"
require_relative 'file_using_refinement'
puts "Back from require"

shout("finished")
```

produces:
```
prog.rb:2: warning: Refinements are experimental, and the behavior may change in
future versions of Ruby!
About to require file using refinement
Dave says: I'm in file_using_refinement.rb
Back from require
Dave says: FINISHED
```

Notice how the puts calls in the main program are unadorned, but the calls in the file that uses the refinement has the vanity prefix.

Refinements—use and scoping

You can define refinements in any module. A refinement may only refer to a class (not a module).

The using call that activates a refinement module can only occur at the top-level scope or in a string that is evaluated. using may not be called inside a class or module definition.[4]

The basic scoping rule is simple. A refinement is activated in a source file by calling using. For the rest of that source file, the methods that are defined in that refinement are active.

Designing with Refinements

Refinements are too new for the community to have come to any kind of consensus on the best way to use them. However, it seems likey that there are at least two basic use cases.

The first is the case where a developer wants to make changes to a third party class for their own use. For example, a tool such as Rake, which issues a lot of calls to run external programs using the system method might want to modify the built-in version of system so that it logs errors differently. However, it does not want that logging to apply to other calls to system that are not part of Rake. In this case, the code will use the refinement locally within its own source files. It will be an implementation detail, hidden from users of the code.

---

4.   This is the area where we're likely to see changes in the future.

The second use case is where a library writer offers the refinement as part of their external interface. For example, the Rails Active Support code defines methods such as hours, minutes, and ago on numbers, allowing you to write 3.days.ago. Right now, those changes to numbers are global. But, using refinements, the Rails team could code the new methods, but not add them in to any system classes. Instead, their API would document how to add them for yourself into just those source files that uses them. They might tell you to to write

```
using Rails::Extensions::Durations
```

in any source file that needs to use them.

Obviously there are many more use cases. And the two we've mentioned are not mutually exclusive—the Rails framework, for example, is likely to want to use these duration-related methods itself, as well as making them available via a documented refinement. So this is an interesting time to work with Ruby—as a community we'll be discussing how best to use refinements for many years.

24.5 Metaprogramming Class-Level Macros

If you've used Ruby for any time at all, you're likely to have used attr_accessor, the method that defines reader and writer methods for instance variables:

```ruby
class Song
  attr_accessor :duration
end
```

If you've written a Ruby on Rails application, you've probably used has_many:

```ruby
class Album < ActiveRecord::Base
  has_many :tracks
end
```

These are both examples of class-level methods that generate code behind the scenes. Because of the way they expand into something bigger, folks sometimes call these kinds of methods *macros*.

Let's create a trivial example and then build it up into something realistic. We'll start by implementing a simple method that adds logging capabilities to instances of a class. We previously did this using a module—this time we'll do it using a class-level method. Here's the first iteration:

```ruby
class Example
  def self.add_logging
    def log(msg)
      STDERR.puts Time.now.strftime("%H:%M:%S: ") + "#{self} (#{msg})"
    end
  end

  add_logging
end

ex = Example.new
ex.log("hello")
```

produces:

```
12:31:38: #<Example:0x007fc14310fa20> (hello)
```

Clearly, this is a silly piece of code. But bear with me—it'll get better. And we can still learn some stuff from it. First, notice that add_logging is a class method—it is defined in the class object's singleton class. That means we can call it later in the class definition without an explicit receiver, because self is set to the class object inside a class definition.

Then, notice that the add_logging method contains a nested method definition. This inner definition will get executed only when we call the add_logging method. The result is that log will be defined as an instance method of class Example.

Let's take one more step. We can define the add_logging method in one class and then use it in a subclass. This works because the singleton class hierarchy parallels the regular class hierarchy. As a result, class methods in a parent class are also available in the child class, as the following example shows.

```
class Logger
  def self.add_logging
    def log(msg)
      STDERR.puts Time.now.strftime("%H:%M:%S: ") + "#{self} (#{msg})"
    end
  end
end

class Example < Logger
  add_logging
end

ex = Example.new
ex.log("hello")
```

produces:

```
12:31:38: #<Example:0x007fcc5c0473d0> (hello)
```

Think back to the two examples at the start of this section. Both work this way. attr_accessor is an instance method defined in class Module and so is available in all module and class definitions. has_many is a class method defined in the Base class within the Rails ActiveRecord module and so is available to all classes that subclass ActiveRecord::Base.

This example is still not particularly compelling; it would still be easier to add the log method directly as an instance method of our Logger class. But what happens if we want to construct a different version of the log method for each class that uses it? For example, let's add the capability to add a short class-specific identifying string to the start of each log message. We want to be able to say something like this:

```
class Song < Logger
  add_logging "Song"
end

class Album < Logger
  add_logging "CD"
end
```

To do this, let's define the log method on the fly. We can no longer use a straightforward def...end-style definition. Instead, we'll use one of the cornerstones of metaprogramming, define_method. This takes the name of a method and a block, defining a method with the given name and with the block as the method body. Any arguments in the block definition become parameters to the method being defined.

```
class Logger
  def self.add_logging(id_string)
    define_method(:log) do |msg|
      now = Time.now.strftime("%H:%M:%S")
      STDERR.puts "#{now}-#{id_string}: #{self} (#{msg})"
    end
  end
end

class Song < Logger
  add_logging "Tune"
end

class Album < Logger
  add_logging "CD"
end

song = Song.new
song.log("rock on")
```

produces:

```
12:31:38-Tune: #<Song:0x007f9afb90e1b8> (rock on)
```

There's an important subtlety in this code. The body of the log method contains this line:

```
STDERR.puts "#{now}-#{id_string}: #{self} (#{msg})"
```

The value now is a local variable, and msg is the parameter to the block. But id_string is the parameter to the enclosing add_logging method. It's accessible inside the block because block definitions create closures, allowing the context in which the block is defined to be carried forward and used when the block is used. In this case, we're taking a value from a class-level method and using it in an instance method we're defining. This is a common pattern when creating these kinds of class-level macros.

As well as passing parameters from the class method into the body of the method being defined, we can also use the parameter to determine the name of the method or methods to create. Here's an example that creates a new kind of attr_accessor that logs all assignments to a given instance variable:

```
class AttrLogger
  def self.attr_logger(name)
    attr_reader name
    define_method("#{name}=") do |val|
      puts "Assigning #{val.inspect} to #{name}"
      instance_variable_set("@#{name}", val)
    end
  end
end

class Example < AttrLogger
  attr_logger :value
end
```

```
ex = Example.new
ex.value = 123
puts "Value is #{ex.value}"
ex.value = "cat"
puts "Value is now #{ex.value}"
```

produces:

```
Assigning 123 to value
Value is 123
Assigning "cat" to value
Value is now cat
```

Again, we use the fact that the block defining the method body is a closure, accessing the name of the attribute in the log message string. Notice we also make use of the fact that attr_reader is simply a class method—we can call it inside our class method to define the reader method for our attribute. Note another common bit of metaprogramming—we use instance_variable_set to set the value of an instance variable (duh). There's a corresponding _get method that fetches the value of a named instance variable.

Class Methods and Modules

You can define class methods in one class and then use them in subclasses of that class. But it is often inappropriate to use subclassing, either because we already have to subclass some other class or because our design aesthetic rebels against making Song a subclass of Logger.

In these cases, you can use a module to hold your metaprogramming implementation. As we've seen, using extend inside a class definition will add the methods in a module as class methods to the class being defined:

```
module AttrLogger
  def attr_logger(name)
    attr_reader name
    define_method("#{name}=") do |val|
      puts "Assigning #{val.inspect} to #{name}"
      instance_variable_set("@#{name}", val)
    end
  end
end
class Example
  extend AttrLogger
  attr_logger :value
end

ex = Example.new
ex.value = 123
puts "Value is #{ex.value}"
ex.value = "cat"
puts "Value is now #{ex.value}"
```

produces:

```
Assigning 123 to value
Value is 123
Assigning "cat" to value
Value is now cat
```

Things get a little trickier if you want to add both class methods and instance methods into the class being defined. Here's one technique, used extensively in the implementation of Rails. It makes use of a Ruby hook method, included, which is called automatically by Ruby when you include a module into a class. It is passed the class object of the class being defined.

```ruby
module GeneralLogger
  # Instance method to be added to any class that includes us
  def log(msg)
    puts Time.now.strftime("%H:%M: ") + msg
  end

  # module containing class methods to be added
  module ClassMethods
    def attr_logger(name)
      attr_reader name
      define_method("#{name}=") do |val|
        log "Assigning #{val.inspect} to #{name}"
        instance_variable_set("@#{name}", val)
      end
    end
  end

  # extend host class with class methods when we're included
  def self.included(host_class)
    host_class.extend(ClassMethods)
  end
end

class Example
  include GeneralLogger

  attr_logger :value
end

ex = Example.new
ex.log("New example created")
ex.value = 123
puts "Value is #{ex.value}"
ex.value = "cat"
puts "Value is #{ex.value}"
```

produces:

```
12:31: New example created
12:31: Assigning 123 to value
Value is 123
12:31: Assigning "cat" to value
Value is cat
```

Notice how the included callback is used to extend the host class with the methods defined in the inner module ClassMethods.

Now, as an exercise, try executing the previous example in your head. For each line of code, work out the value of self. Master this, and you've pretty much mastered this style of metaprogramming in Ruby.

24.6 Two Other Forms of Class Definition

Just in case you thought we'd exhausted the ways of defining Ruby classes, let's look at two other options.

Subclassing Expressions

The first form is really nothing new—it's simply a generalization of the regular class definition syntax. You know that you can write this:

```
class Parent
  ...
end
class Child < Parent
  ...
end
```

What you might not know is that the thing to the right of the < needn't be just a class name; it can be any expression that returns a class object. In this code example, we have the constant Parent. A constant is a simple form of expression, and in this case the constant Parent holds the class object of the first class we defined.

Ruby comes with a class called Struct, which allows you to define classes that contain just data attributes. For example, you could write this:

```
Person = Struct.new(:name, :address, :likes)

dave = Person.new('Dave', 'TX')
dave.likes = "Programming Languages"
puts dave
```

produces:

```
#<struct Person name="Dave", address="TX", likes="Programming Languages">
```

The return value from Struct.new(...) is a class object. By assigning it to the constant Person, we can thereafter use Person as if it were any other class.

But say we wanted to change the to_s method of our structure.

We could do it by opening up the class and writing the following method.

```
Person = Struct.new(:name, :address, :likes)
class Person
  def to_s
    "#{self.name} lives in #{self.address} and likes #{self.likes}"
  end
end
```

However, we can do this more elegantly (although at the cost of an additional class object) by writing this:

```
class Person < Struct.new(:name, :address, :likes)
  def to_s
    "#{self.name} lives in #{self.address} and likes #{self.likes}"
  end
end
```

```
dave = Person.new('Dave', 'Texas')
dave.likes = "Programming Languages"
puts dave
```

produces:

```
Dave lives in Texas and likes Programming Languages
```

Creating Singleton Classes

Let's look at some Ruby code:

```
class Example
end
ex = Example.new
```

When we call Example.new, we're invoking the method new on the class object Example. This is a regular method call—Ruby looks for the method new in the class of the object (and the class of Example is Class) and invokes it. So we can also invoke Class#new directly:

```
some_class = Class.new
puts some_class.class
```

produces:

```
Class
```

If you pass Class.new a block, that block is used as the body of the class:

```
some_class = Class.new do
  def self.class_method
    puts "In class method"
  end
  def instance_method
    puts "In instance method"
  end
end
```

```
some_class.class_method
obj = some_class.new
obj.instance_method
```

produces:

```
In class method
In instance method
```

By default, these classes will be direct descendents of Object. You can give them a different parent by passing the parent's class as a parameter:

```
some_class = Class.new(String) do
  def vowel_movement
    tr 'aeiou', '*'
  end
end
```

```
obj = some_class.new("now is the time")
puts obj.vowel_movement
```

produces:

```
n*w *s th* t*m*
```

How Classes Get Their Names

You may have noticed that the classes created by Class.new have no name. However, if you assign the class object for a class with no name to a constant, Ruby automatically names the class after the constant:

```
some_class = Class.new
obj = some_class.new
puts "Initial name is #{some_class.name}"
SomeClass = some_class
puts "Then the name is #{some_class.name}"
puts "also works via the object: #{obj.class.name}"
```

produces:

```
Initial name is
Then the name is SomeClass
also works via the object: SomeClass
```

We can use these dynamically constructed classes to extend Ruby in interesting ways. For example, here's a simple reimplementation of the Ruby Struct class:

```ruby
def MyStruct(*keys)
  Class.new do
    attr_accessor *keys
    def initialize(hash)
      hash.each do |key, value|
        instance_variable_set("@#{key}", value)
      end
    end
  end
end

Person = MyStruct :name, :address, :likes
dave = Person.new(name: "dave", address: "TX", likes: "Stilton")
chad = Person.new(name: "chad", likes: "Jazz")
chad.address = "CO"

puts "Dave's name is #{dave.name}"
puts "Chad lives in #{chad.address}"
```

produces:

```
Dave's name is dave
Chad lives in CO
```

24.7 instance_eval and class_eval

The methods Object#instance_eval, Module#class_eval, and Module#module_eval let you set self to be some arbitrary object, evaluate the code in a block with, and then reset self:

```ruby
"cat".instance_eval do
  puts "Upper case = #{upcase}"
  puts "Length is #{self.length}"
end
```

produces:

```
Upper case = CAT
Length is 3
```

Both forms also take a string, but this is considered a little dangerous.

First, it is slow—calling eval effectively compiles the code in the string before executing it. But, even worse, eval can be dangerous. If there's any chance that external data—stuff that comes from outside your application—can wind up inside the parameter to eval, then you have a security hole, because that external data may end up containing arbitrary code that your application will blindly execute.

That said, here's an example using a string parameter:

```
"cat".instance_eval('puts "Upper=#{upcase}, length=#{self.length}"')
```

produces:

```
Upper=CAT, length=3
```

class_eval and instance_eval both set self for the duration of the block. However, they differ in the way they set up the environment for method definition. class_eval sets things up as if you were in the body of a class definition, so method definitions will define instance methods:

```
class MyClass
end

MyClass.class_eval do
  def instance_method
    puts "In an instance method"
  end
end

obj = MyClass.new
obj.instance_method
```

produces:

```
In an instance method
```

In contrast, calling instance_eval on a class acts as if you were working inside the singleton class of self. Therefore, any methods you define will become class methods.

```
class MyClass
end

MyClass.instance_eval do
  def class_method
    puts "In a class method"
  end
end
MyClass.class_method
```

produces:

```
In a class method
```

It might be helpful to remember that, when defining methods, class_eval and instance_eval have precisely the wrong names: class_eval defines instance methods, and instance_eval defines class methods. Go figure.

Ruby has variants of these methods. Object#instance_exec, Module#class_exec, and Module#module_exec behave identically to their _eval counterparts but take only a block (that is, they do not take a string). Any arguments given to the methods are passed in as block parameters.

This is an important feature. Previously it was impossible to pass an instance variable into a block given to one of the _eval methods—because self is changed by the call, these variables go out of scope. With the _exec form, you can now pass them in:

```
@animal = "cat"
"dog".instance_exec(@animal) do |other|
  puts "#{other} and #{self}"
end
```

produces:

```
cat and dog
```

instance_eval and Constants

Ruby 1.9 changed the way Ruby looks up constants when executing a block using instance_eval and class_eval. Ruby 1.9.2 then reverted the change. In Ruby 1.8 and Ruby 1.9.2, constants are looked up in the lexical scope in which they were referenced. In Ruby 1.9.0, they are looked up in the scope in which instance_eval is called. This (artificial) example shows the behavior at the time I last built this book—it may well have changed again by the time you run it....

```
module One
  CONST = "Defined in One"
  def self.eval_block(&block)
    instance_eval(&block)
  end
end

module Two
  CONST = "Defined in Two"
  def self.call_eval_block
    One.eval_block do
      CONST
    end
  end
end

Two.call_eval_block    # => "Defined in Two"
```

In Ruby 1.9.0, this same code would evaluate to "Defined in One".

instance_eval and Domain-Specific Languages

It turns out that instance_eval has a pivotal role to play in a certain type of domain-specific language (DSL). For example, we might be writing a simple DSL for turtle graphics.[5] To draw a set of three 5x5 squares, we might write the following:[6]

---

5. In turtle graphics systems, you imagine you have a turtle you can command to move forward n squares, turn left, and turn right. You can also make the turtle raise and lower a pen. If the pen is lowered, a line will be drawn tracing the turtle's subsequent movements. Very few of these turtles exist in the wild, so we tend to simulate them inside computers.
6. Yes, the forward(4) is correct in this code. The initial point is always drawn.

```
3.times do
  forward(8)
  pen_down
  4.times do
    forward(4)
    left
  end
  pen_up
end
```

Clearly, pen_down, forward, left, and pen_up can be implemented as Ruby methods. However, to call them without a receiver like this, either we have to be within a class that defines them (or is a child of such a class) or we have to make the methods global. instance_eval to the rescue. We can define a class Turtle that defines the various methods we need as instance methods. We'll also define a walk method, which will execute our turtle DSL, and a draw method to draw the resulting picture:

```
class Turtle
  def left; ... end
  def right; ... end
  def forward(n); ... end
  def pen_up; .. end
  def pen_down; ... end
  def walk(...); end
  def draw; ... end
end
```

If we implement walk correctly, we can then write this:

```
turtle = Turtle.new
turtle.walk do
  3.times do
    forward(8)
    pen_down
    4.times do
      forward(4)
      left
    end
    pen_up
  end
end
turtle.draw
```

So, what is the correct implementation of walk? Well, we clearly have to use instance_eval, because we want the DSL commands in the block to call the methods in the turtle object. We also have to arrange to pass the block given to the walk method to be evaluated by that instance_eval call. Our implementation looks like this:

```
def walk(&block)
  instance_eval(&block)
end
```

Notice how we captured the block into a variable and then expanded that variable back into a block in the call to instance_eval.

See Section 24.11, *The Turtle Graphics Program*, on page 391 for a complete listing of the turtle program.

Is this a good use of instance_eval? It depends on the circumstances. The benefit is that the code inside the block looks simple—you don't have to make the receiver explicit:

```
4.times do
  turtle.forward(4)
  turtle.left
end
```

There's a drawback, though. Inside the block, scope isn't what you think it is, so this code wouldn't work:

```
@size = 4
turtle.walk do
  4.times do
    turtle.forward(@size)
    turtle.left
  end
end
```

Instance variables are looked up in self, and self in the block isn't the same as self in the code that sets the instance variable @size. Because of this, most people are moving away from this style of instance_evaled block.

24.8 Hook Methods

In *Class Methods and Modules*, on page 375, we defined a method called included in our General-Logger module. When this module was included in a class, Ruby automatically invoked this included method, allowing our module to add class methods to the host class.

included is an example of a *hook method* (sometimes called a *callback*). A hook method is a method that you write but that Ruby calls from within the interpreter when some particular event occurs. The interpreter looks for these methods by name—if you define a method in the right context with an appropriate name, Ruby will call it when the corresponding event happens.

The methods that can be invoked from within the interpreter are:

Method-related hooks
method_added, method_missing, method_removed, method_undefined, singleton_method_added, singleton_method_removed, singleton_method_undefined

Class and module-related hooks
append_features, const_missing, extend_object, extended, included, inherited, initialize_clone, initialize_copy, initialize_dup

Object marshaling hooks
marshal_dump, marshal_load

Coercion hooks
coerce, induced_from, to_xxx

We won't discuss all of them in this chapter—instead, we'll show just a few examples of use. The reference section of this book describes the individual methods, and Chapter 23, *Duck Typing*, on page 343 discusses the coercion methods in more detail.

The inherited Hook

If a class defines a class method called inherited, Ruby will call it whenever that class is subclassed (that is, whenever any class inherits from the original).

This hook is often used in situations where a base class needs to keep track of its children. For example, an online store might offer a variety of shipping options. Each might be represented by a separate class, and each of these classes could be a subclass of a single Shipping class. This parent class could keep track of all the various shipping options by recording every class that subclasses it. When it comes time to display the shipping options to the user, the application could call the base class, asking it for a list of its children:

```ruby
class Shipping        # Base class
  @children = []   # this variable is in the class, not instances

  def self.inherited(child)
    @children << child
  end

  def self.shipping_options(weight, international)
    @children.select {|child| child.can_ship(weight, international)}
  end
end

class MediaMail < Shipping
  def self.can_ship(weight, international)
    !international
  end
end

class FlatRatePriorityEnvelope < Shipping
  def self.can_ship(weight, international)
    weight < 64 && !international
  end
end

class InternationalFlatRateBox < Shipping
  def self.can_ship(weight, international)
    weight < 9*16 && international
  end
end

puts "Shipping 16oz domestic"
puts Shipping.shipping_options(16, false)

puts "\nShipping 90oz domestic"
puts Shipping.shipping_options(90, false)

puts "\nShipping 16oz international"
puts Shipping.shipping_options(16, true)
```

produces:

```
Shipping 16oz domestic
MediaMail
FlatRatePriorityEnvelope

Shipping 90oz domestic
MediaMail

Shipping 16oz international
InternationalFlatRateBox
```

Command interpreters often use this pattern: the base class keeps a track of available commands, each of which is implemented in a subclass.

The method_missing Hook

Earlier, we saw how Ruby executes a method call by looking for the method, first in the object's class, then in its superclass, then in that class's superclass, and so on. If the method call has an explicit receiver, then private methods are skipped in this search. If the method is not found by the time we run out of superclasses (because BasicObject has no superclass), then Ruby tries to invoke the hook method method_missing on the original object. Again, the same process is followed—Ruby first looks in the object's class, then in its superclass, and so on. However, Ruby predefines its own version of method_missing in class BasicObject, so typically the search stops there. The built-in method_missing basically raises an exception (either a NoMethodError or a NameError depending on the circumstances).

The key here is that method_missing is simply a Ruby method. We can override it in our own classes to handle calls to otherwise undefined methods in an application-specific way.

method_missing has a simple signature, but many people get it wrong:

```
def method_missing(name, *args, &block)  # ...
```

The name argument receives the name of the method that couldn't be found. It is passed as a symbol. The args argument is an array of the arguments that were passed in the original call. And the oft-forgotten block argument will receive any block passed to the original method.

```
def method_missing(name, *args, &block)
  puts "Called #{name} with #{args.inspect} and #{block}"
end

wibble
wobble 1, 2
wurble(3, 4) { stuff }
```

produces:

```
Called wibble with [] and
Called wobble with [1, 2] and
Called wurble with [3, 4] and #<Proc:0x007fd7d910fb18@prog.rb:7>
```

Before we get too deep into the details, I'll offer a tip about etiquette. There are two main ways that people use method_missing. The first intercepts every use of an undefined method and handles it. The second is more subtle; it intercepts all calls but handles only some of them. In the latter case, it is important to forward on the call to a superclass if you decide not to handle it in your method_missing implementation:

```
class MyClass < OtherClass
  def method_missing(name, *args, &block)
    if <some condition>
      # handle call
    else
      super    # otherwise pass it on
    end
  end
end
```

If you fail to pass on calls that you don't handle, your application will silently ignore calls to unknown methods in your class.

Let's show a couple of uses of method_missing.

method_missing to Simulate Accessors

The OpenStruct class is distributed with Ruby. It allows you to write objects with attributes that are created dynamically by assignment. (We describe it in more detail in the library documentation on page 786.) For example, you could write this:

```
require 'ostruct'
obj = OpenStruct.new(name: "Dave")
obj.address = "Texas"
obj.likes   = "Programming"

puts "#{obj.name} lives in #{obj.address} and likes #{obj.likes}"
```

produces:

```
Dave lives in Texas and likes Programming
```

Let's use method_missing to write our own version of OpenStruct:

```
class MyOpenStruct < BasicObject
  def initialize(initial_values = {})
    @values = initial_values
  end
  def _singleton_class
    class << self
      self
    end
  end
  def method_missing(name, *args, &block)
    if name[-1] == "="
      base_name = name[0..-2].intern
      _singleton_class.instance_exec(name) do |name|
        define_method(name) do |value|
          @values[base_name] = value
        end
      end
      @values[base_name] = args[0]
    else
      _singleton_class.instance_exec(name) do |name|
```

```
        define_method(name) do
          @values[name]
        end
      end
      @values[name]
    end
  end
end

obj = MyOpenStruct.new(name: "Dave")
obj.address = "Texas"
obj.likes   = "Programming"

puts "#{obj.name} lives in #{obj.address} and likes #{obj.likes}"
```

produces:

```
Dave lives in Texas and likes Programming
```

Notice how we base our class on BasicObject, a class introduced in Ruby 1.9. BasicObject is the root of Ruby's object hierarchy and contains only a minimal number of methods:

```
p BasicObject.instance_methods
```

produces:

```
[:==, :equal?, :!, :!=, :instance_eval, :instance_exec, :__send__, :__id__]
```

This is good, because it means that our MyOpenStruct class will be able to have attributes such as display or class. If instead we'd based MyOpenStruct on class Object, then these names, along with forty-nine others, would have been predefined and hence wouldn't trigger method_missing.

Notice also another common pattern inside method_missing. The first time we reference or assign to an attribute of our object, we access or update the @values hash appropriately. But we also define the method that the caller was trying to access. This means that the next time this attribute is used, it will use the method and not invoke method_missing. This may or may not be worth the trouble, depending on the access patterns to your object.

Also notice how we had to jump through some hoops to define the method. We want to define the method only for the current object. This means we have to put the method into the object's singleton class. We can do that using instance_exec and define_method. But that means we have to use the class << self trick to get the object's singleton class. Through an interesting implementation subtlety, define_method will always define an instance method, independent of whether it is invoked via instance_exec or class_exec.

However, this code reveals a dark underbelly of using method_missing and BasicObject:

```
obj = MyOpenStruct.new(name: "Dave")
obj.address = "Texas"

o1 = obj.dup
o1.name = "Mike"
o1.address = "Colorado"
```

produces:

```
prog.rb:37:in `<main>': undefined method `name=' for nil:NilClass
(NoMethodError)
```

The dup method is not defined by BasicObject; it appears in class Object. So when we called dup, it was picked up by our method_missing handler, and we just returned nil (because we don't have yet have an attribute called dup). We could fix this so that it at least reports an error:

```
def method_missing(name, *args, &block)
  if name[-1] == "="
    # as before...
  else
    super unless @values.has_key? name
    # as before...
  end
end
```

This class now reports an error if we call dup (or any other method) on it. However, we still can't dup or clone it (or inspect, convert to a string, and so on). Although BasicObject seems like a natural fit for method_missing, you may find it to be more trouble than it's worth.

method_missing as a Filter

As the previous example showed, method_missing has some drawbacks if you use it to intercept all calls. It is probably better to use it to recognize certain patterns of call, passing on those it doesn't recognize to its parent class to handle.

An example of this is the dynamic finder facility in the Ruby on Rails ActiveRecord module. ActiveRecord is the object-relational library in Rails—it allows you to access relational databases as if they were object stores. One particular feature allows you to find rows that match the criteria of having given values in certain columns. For example, if an Active Record class called Book were mapping a relational table called books and the books table included columns called title and author, you could write this:

```
pickaxe = Book.find_by_title("Programming Ruby")
daves_books = Book.find_all_by_author("Dave Thomas")
```

Active Record does not predefine all these potential finder methods. Instead, it uses our old friend method_missing. Inside that method, it looks for calls to undefined methods that match the pattern /^find_(all_)?by_(.*)/.[7] If the method being invoked does not match this pattern or if the fields in the method name don't correspond to columns in the database table, Active Record calls super so that a genuine method_missing report will be generated.

24.9 One Last Example

Let's bring together all the metaprogramming topics we've discussed in a final example by writing a module that allows us to trace the execution of methods in any class that mixes the module in. This would let us write the following:

---

7.   It also looks for /^find_or_(initialize|create)_by_(.*)/.

```
require_relative  'trace_calls'
class Example
  def one(arg)
    puts "One called with #{arg}"
  end
end

ex1 = Example.new
ex1.one("Hello")      # no tracing from this call

class Example
  include TraceCalls
  def two(arg1, arg2)
    arg1 + arg2
  end
end

ex1.one("Goodbye")    # but we see tracing from these two
puts ex1.two(4, 5)
```

produces:

```
One called with Hello
==> calling one with ["Goodbye"]
One called with Goodbye
<== one returned nil
==> calling two with [4, 5]
<== two returned 9
9
```

We can see immediately that there's a subtlety here. When we mix the TraceCalls module into a class, it has to add tracing to any existing instance methods in that class. It also has to arrange to add tracing to any methods we subsequently add.

Let's start with the full listing of the TraceCalls module:

metaprogramming/trace_calls.rb
```
module TraceCalls
  def self.included(klass)
    klass.instance_methods(false).each do |existing_method|
      wrap(klass, existing_method)
    end
    def klass.method_added(method)  # note: nested definition
      unless @trace_calls_internal
        @trace_calls_internal = true
        TraceCalls.wrap(self, method)
        @trace_calls_internal = false
      end
    end
  end
  def self.wrap(klass, method)
    klass.instance_eval do
      method_object = instance_method(method)

      define_method(method) do |*args, &block|
        puts "==> calling #{method} with #{args.inspect}"
```

```
            result = method_object.bind(self).call(*args, &block)
            puts "<== #{method} returned #{result.inspect}"
            result
        end
      end
    end
end
```

When we include this module in a class, the included hook method gets invoked. It first uses the instance_methods reflection method to find all the existing instance methods in the host class (the false parameter limits the list to methods in the class itself, and not in its superclasses). For each existing method, the module calls a helper method, wrap, to add some tracing code to it. We'll talk about wrap shortly.

Next, the included method uses another hook, method_added. This is called by Ruby whenever a method is defined in the receiver. Note that we define this method in the class passed to the included method. This means that the method will be called when methods are added to this host class and not to the module. This is what allows us to include TraceCalls at the top of a class and then add methods to that class—all those method definitions will be handled by method_added.

Now look at the code inside the method_added method. We have to deal with a potential problem here. As you'll see when we look at the wrap method, we add tracing to a method by creating a new version of the method that calls the old. Inside method_added, we call the wrap function to add this tracing. But inside wrap, we'll define a new method to handle this wrapping, and that definition will invoke method_added again, and then we'd call wrap again, and so on, until the stack gets exhausted. To prevent this, we use an instance variable and do the wrapping only if we're not already doing it.

The wrap method takes a class object and the name of a method to wrap. It finds the original definition of that method (using instance_method) and saves it. It then redefines this method. This new method outputs some tracing and then calls the original, passing in the parameters and block from the wrapper.[8] Note how we call the method by binding the method object to the current instance and then invoking that bound method.

The key to understanding this code, and most metaprogramming code, is to follow the basic principles we worked out at the start of this chapter—how self changes as methods are called and classes are defined and how methods are called by looking for them in the class of the receiver. If you get stuck, do what we do and draw little boxes and arrows. We find it useful to stick with the convention used in this chapter: class links go to the right, and superclass links go up. Given an object, a method call is then a question of finding the receiver object, going right once, and then following the superclass chain up as far as you need to go.

24.10 Top-Level Execution Environment

Finally, there's one small detail we have to cover to complete the metaprogramming environment. Many times in this book we've claimed that everything in Ruby is an object. However, we've used one thing time and time again that appears to contradict this—the top-level Ruby execution environment:

```
puts "Hello, World"
```

---

8. The ability of a block to take a block parameter was added in Ruby 1.9.

Not an object in sight. We may as well be writing some variant of Fortran or Basic. But dig deeper, and you'll come across objects and classes lurking in even the simplest code.

We know that the literal "Hello, World" generates a Ruby String, so that's one object. We also know that the bare method call to puts is effectively the same as self.puts. But what is self?

```
self.class # => Object
```

At the top level, we're executing code in the context of some predefined object. When we define methods, we're actually creating (private) instance methods for class Object. This is fairly subtle; as they are in class Object, these methods are available everywhere. And because we're in the context of Object, we can use all of Object's methods (including those mixed in from Kernel) in function form. This explains why we can call Kernel methods such as puts at the top level (and indeed throughout Ruby); it's because these methods are part of every object. Top-level instance variables also belong to this top-level object.

Metaprogramming is one of Ruby's sharpest tools. Don't be afraid to use it to raise up the level at which you program. But, at the same time, use it only when necessary—overly metaprogrammed applications can become pretty obscure pretty quickly.

24.11 The Turtle Graphics Program

```ruby
class Turtle
  # directions: 0 = E, 1 = S, 2 = W, 3 = N
  # axis: 0 = x, 1 = y
  def initialize
    @board = Hash.new(" ")
    @x = @y = 0
    @direction = 0
    pen_up
  end

  def pen_up
    @pen_down = false
  end

  def pen_down
    @pen_down = true
    mark_current_location
  end

  def forward(n=1)
    n.times { move }
  end

  def left
    @direction -= 1
    @direction = 3 if @direction < 0
  end

  def right
    @direction += 1
    @direction = 0 if @direction > 3
  end
```

```ruby
  def walk(&block)
    instance_eval(&block)
  end

  def draw
    min_x, max_x = @board.keys.map{|x,y| x}.minmax
    min_y, max_y = @board.keys.map{|x,y| y}.minmax
    min_y.upto(max_y) do |y|
      min_x.upto(max_x) do |x|
        print @board[[x,y]]
      end
      puts
    end
  end
  private

  def move
    increment = @direction > 1 ? -1 : 1
    if @direction.even?
      @x += increment
    else
      @y += increment
    end
    mark_current_location
  end

  def mark_current_location
    @board[[@x,@y]] = "#" if @pen_down
  end
end

turtle = Turtle.new
turtle.walk do
  3.times do
    forward(8)
    pen_down
    4.times do
      forward(4)
      left
    end
    pen_up
  end
end
turtle.draw
```

produces:

```
#####   #####   #####
#   #   #   #   #   #
#   #   #   #   #   #
#   #   #   #   #   #
#####   #####   #####
```

## CHAPTER 25

Reflection, ObjectSpace, and Distributed Ruby

One of the advantages of dynamic languages such as Ruby is the ability to *introspect*—to examine aspects of a program from within the program itself. This is also called *reflection*.

When people introspect, we think about our thoughts and feelings. This is interesting, because we're using thought to analyze thought. It's the same when programs use introspection—a program can discover the following information about itself:

- What objects it contains
- Its class hierarchy
- The attributes and methods of objects
- Information on methods

Armed with this information, we can look at particular objects and decide which of their methods to call at runtime—even if the class of the object didn't exist when we first wrote the code. We can also start doing clever things, perhaps modifying the program while it's running. Later in this chapter we'll look at distributed Ruby and marshaling, two reflection-based technologies that let us send objects around the world and through time.

25.1 Looking at Objects

Have you ever craved the ability to traverse all the living objects in your program? We have! Ruby lets you perform this trick with ObjectSpace.each_object. We can use it to do all sorts of neat tricks.

For example, to iterate over all objects of type Complex, you'd write the following:

```
a = Complex(1, 2)
b = Complex(99, -100)
ObjectSpace.each_object(Complex) {|x| puts x }
```

produces:

```
0+1i
99-100i
1+2i
```

Where did that extra number, (0+1i), come from? We didn't define it in our program. Well, the Complex class defines a constant for *I*, the square root of -1. Since we are examining all living objects in the system, these turn up as well.

Let's try the same example with different values. This time, they're objects of type Fixnum:

```
a = 102
b = 95
ObjectSpace.each_object(Fixnum) {|x| p x }
```

(Produces no output.)

Neither of the Fixnum objects we created showed up. That's because ObjectSpace doesn't know about objects with immediate values: Fixnum, Symbol, true, false, nil, and (on 64-bit platforms) most Floats.

New in 2.0

Looking Inside Objects

Once you've found an interesting object, you may be tempted to find out just what it can do. Unlike static languages, where a variable's type determines its class, and hence the methods it supports, Ruby supports liberated objects. You really cannot tell exactly what an object can do until you look under its hood.[1] We talk about this in Chapter 23, *Duck Typing*, on page 343.

For instance, we can get a list of all the methods to which an object will respond (these include methods in an object's class and that class's ancestors):

```
r = 1..10 # Create a Range object
list = r.methods
list.length # => 111
list[0..3]  # => [:==, :===, :eql?, :hash]
```

We can check to see whether an object responds to a particular method:

```
r = 1..10
r.respond_to?("frozen?") # => true
r.respond_to?(:has_key?) # => false
"me".respond_to?("==")   # => true
```

We can ask for an object's class and unique object ID and test its relationship to other classes:

```
num = 1
num.object_id           # => 3
num.class               # => Fixnum
num.kind_of? Fixnum     # => true
num.kind_of? Numeric    # => true
num.instance_of? Fixnum # => true
num.instance_of? Numeric # => false
```

25.2 Looking at Classes

Knowing about objects is one part of reflection, but to get the whole picture, you also need to be able to look at classes—the methods and constants that they contain.

---

1.   Or under its bonnet, for objects created to the east of the Atlantic

Looking at the class hierarchy is easy. You can get the parent of any particular class using Class#superclass. For classes *and* modules, the Module#ancestors method lists both superclasses and mixed-in modules:

```
klass = Fixnum
begin
  print klass
  klass = klass.superclass
  print " < " if klass
end while klass
puts
p Fixnum.ancestors
```

produces:

```
Fixnum < Integer < Numeric < Object < BasicObject
[Fixnum, Integer, Numeric, Comparable, Object, Kernel, BasicObject]
```

If you want to build a complete class hierarchy, just run that code for every class in the system. We can use ObjectSpace to iterate over all Class objects:

```
ObjectSpace.each_object(Class) do |klass|
    # ...
end
```

Looking Inside Classes

We can find out a bit more about the methods and constants in a particular object. We can ask for methods by access level, and we can ask for just singleton methods. We can also take a look at the object's constants, local, and instance variables:

```
class Demo
  @@var = 99
  CONST = 1.23
private
  def private_method
  end
protected
  def protected_method
  end
public
  def public_method
    @inst = 1
    i = 1
    j = 2
    local_variables
  end
  def Demo.class_method
  end
end

Demo.private_instance_methods(false)    # => [:private_method]
Demo.protected_instance_methods(false)  # => [:protected_method]
Demo.public_instance_methods(false)     # => [:public_method]
Demo.singleton_methods(false)           # => [:class_method]
Demo.class_variables                    # => [:@@var]
Demo.constants(false)                   # => [:CONST]
```

```
demo = Demo.new
demo.instance_variables              # => []
# Get 'public_method' to return its local variables
# and set an instance variable
demo.public_method                   # => [:i, :j]
demo.instance_variables              # => [:@inst]
```

You may be wondering what all the false parameters were in the previous code. As of Ruby 1.8, these reflection methods will by default recurse into parent classes, their parents, and so on, up the ancestor chain. Passing in false stops this kind of prying.

Given a list of method names, we may now be tempted to try calling them. Fortunately, that's easy with Ruby.

25.3 Calling Methods Dynamically

The Object#send method lets you tell any object to invoke a method by name.

```
"John Coltrane".send(:length)          # => 13
"Miles Davis".send("sub", /iles/, '.') # => "M. Davis"
```

Another way of invoking methods dynamically uses Method objects. A Method object is like a Proc object: it represents a chunk of code and a context in which it executes. In this case, the code is the body of the method, and the context is the object that created the method. Once we have our Method object, we can execute it sometime later by sending it the message call:

```
trane = "John Coltrane".method(:length)
miles = "Miles Davis".method("sub")

trane.call                # => 13
miles.call(/iles/, '.') # => "M. Davis"
```

You can pass the Method object around as you would any other object, and when you invoke Method#call, the method is run just as if you had invoked it on the original object. It's like having a C-style function pointer but in a fully object-oriented style.

You can use Method objects where you could use proc objects. For example, they work with iterators:

```
def double(a)
  2*a
end

method_object = method(:double)

[ 1, 3, 5, 7 ].map(&method_object) # => [2, 6, 10, 14]
```

Method objects are bound to one particular object. You can create *unbound* methods (of class UnboundMethod) and then subsequently bind them to one or more objects. The binding creates a new Method object. As with aliases, unbound methods are references to the definition of the method at the time they are created:

```
unbound_length = String.instance_method(:length)
class String
  def length
    99
  end
end
str = "cat"
str.length          # => 99
bound_length = unbound_length.bind(str)
bound_length.call # => 3
```

Because good things come in threes, here's yet another way to invoke methods dynamically. The eval method (and its variations such as class_eval, module_eval, and instance_eval) will parse and execute an arbitrary string of legal Ruby source code.

```
trane = %q{"John Coltrane".length}
miles = %q{"Miles Davis".sub(/iles/, '.')}

eval trane # => 13
eval miles # => "M. Davis"
```

When using eval, it can be helpful to state explicitly the context in which the expression should be evaluated, rather than using the current context. You obtain a context using Object#binding at the desired point:

```
def get_a_binding
  val = 123
  binding
end

val = "cat"

the_binding = get_a_binding
eval("val", the_binding) # => 123
eval("val")              # => "cat"
```

The first eval evaluates val in the context of the binding *as it was* when the method get_a_binding was executing. In this binding, the variable val had a value of 123. The second eval evaluates eval in the top-level binding, where it has the value "cat".

Performance Considerations

As we've seen in this section, Ruby gives us several ways to invoke an arbitrary method of some object: Object#send, Method#call, and the various flavors of eval.

You may prefer to use any one of these techniques depending on your needs, but be aware that, as the following benchmark shows, eval is significantly slower than the others (or, for optimistic readers, send and call are significantly faster than eval).

```
require 'benchmark'
include Benchmark

test = "Stormy Weather"
m = test.method(:length)
n = 100000
```

```
bm(12) do |x|
  x.report("call") { n.times { m.call } }
  x.report("send") { n.times { test.send(:length) } }
  x.report("eval") { n.times { eval "test.length" } }
end
```

produces:

```
                 user      system      total         real
call          0.020000    0.000000    0.020000 (   0.022150)
send          0.020000    0.000000    0.020000 (   0.019678)
eval          1.230000    0.000000    1.230000 (   1.237393)
```

25.4 System Hooks

A *hook* is a technique that lets you trap some Ruby event, such as object creation. Let's take a look at some common Ruby hook techniques.

Hooking Method Calls

The simplest hook technique in Ruby is to intercept calls to methods in system classes. Perhaps you want to log all the operating system commands your program executes. Simply rename the method Kernel.system, and substitute it with one of your own that both logs the command and calls the original Kernel method:

```
class Object
  alias_method :old_system, :system
  def system(*args)
    old_system(*args).tap do |result|
      puts "system(#{args.join(', ')}) returned #{result.inspect}"
    end
  end
end

system("date")
system("kangaroo", "-hop 10", "skippy")
```

produces:

```
Mon May 27 12:31:42 CDT 2013
system(date) returned true
system(kangaroo, -hop 10, skippy) returned nil
```

The problem with this technique is that you're relying on there not being an existing method called old_system. A better alternative is to make use of method objects, which are effectively anonymous:

```
class Object
  old_system_method = instance_method(:system)
  define_method(:system) do |*args|
    old_system_method.bind(self).call(*args).tap do |result|
      puts "system(#{args.join(', ')}) returned #{result.inspect}"
    end
  end
end
```

```
system("date")
system("kangaroo", "-hop 10", "skippy")
```

produces:

```
Mon May 27 12:31:43 CDT 2013
system(date) returned true
system(kangaroo, -hop 10, skippy) returned nil
```

Ruby 2.0 gives us a new way of doing this. Modules can be used to include new instance methods in some other module or class. Until now, these methods were added behind the host module or class's own methods—if the module defined a method with the same name as one in the host, the host method would be called. Ruby 2 adds the prepend method on page 585 to modules. This lets you insert the module's methods *before* the host's. Within the module's methods, calling super calls the host's method of the same name. This gives us:

New in 2.0

```
module SystemHook
  private
  def system(*args)
    super.tap do |result|
      puts "system(#{args.join(', ')}) returned #{result.inspect}"
    end
  end
end

class Object
  prepend SystemHook
end

system("date")
system("kangaroo", "-hop 10", "skippy")
```

produces:

```
Mon May 27 12:31:43 CDT 2013
system(date) returned true
system(kangaroo, -hop 10, skippy) returned nil
```

Object Creation Hooks

Ruby lets you get involved when objects are created. If you can be present when every object is born, you can do all sorts of interesting things: you can wrap them, add methods to them, remove methods from them, and add them to containers to implement persistence—you name it. We'll show a simple example here. We'll add a timestamp to every object as it's created. First, we'll add a timestamp attribute to every object in the system. We can do this by hacking class Object itself:

```
class Object
  attr_accessor :timestamp
end
```

Then, we need to hook object creation to add this timestamp. One way to do this is to do our method-renaming trick on Class#new, the method that's called to allocate space for a new object. The technique isn't perfect—some built-in objects, such as literal strings, are constructed without calling new—but it'll work just fine for objects we write.

```
class Class
  old_new = instance_method :new
  define_method :new do |*args, &block|
    result = old_new.bind(self).call(*args, &block)
    result.timestamp = Time.now
    result
  end
end
```

Finally, we can run a test. We'll create a couple of objects a few milliseconds apart and check their timestamps:

```
class Test
end

obj1 = Test.new
sleep(0.002)
obj2 = Test.new
obj1.timestamp.to_f # => 1369675903.251721
obj2.timestamp.to_f # => 1369675903.2541282
```

25.5 Tracing Your Program's Execution

While we're having fun reflecting on all the objects and classes in our programs, let's not forget about the humble statements that make our code actually do things. It turns out that Ruby lets us look at these statements, too.

First, you can watch the interpreter as it executes code. In older Rubies, you use set_trace_func, while in Ruby 2 you use the TracePoint class. Both are used to execute a proc with all sorts of juicy debugging information whenever a new source line is executed, methods are called, objects are created, and so on.

New in 2.0

The reference section contains full descriptions of set_trace_func on page 624 and TracePoint on page 722, but here's a taste:

```
class Test
  def test
    a = 1
  end
end

TracePoint.trace do |tp|
  p tp
end
t = Test.new
t.test
```

produces:

```
#<TracePoint:c_return `trace'@prog.rb:7>
#<TracePoint:line@prog.rb:10>
#<TracePoint:c_call `new'@prog.rb:10>
#<TracePoint:c_call `initialize'@prog.rb:10>
#<TracePoint:c_return `initialize'@prog.rb:10>
#<TracePoint:c_return `new'@prog.rb:10>
#<TracePoint:line@prog.rb:11>
```

```
#<TracePoint:call `test'@prog.rb:2>
#<TracePoint:line@prog.rb:3 in `test'>
#<TracePoint:return `test'@prog.rb:4>
```

The method trace_var (described in the reference section on page 630) lets you add a hook to a global variable; whenever an assignment is made to the global, your proc is invoked.

How Did We Get Here?

That's a fair question...one we ask ourselves regularly. Mental lapses aside, in Ruby you can find out "how you got there" using the method caller, which returns an array of strings representing the current call stack:

```
def cat_a
  puts caller
end
def cat_b
  cat_a
end
def cat_c
  cat_b
end
cat_c
```

produces:

```
prog.rb:5:in `cat_b'
prog.rb:8:in `cat_c'
prog.rb:10:in `<main>'
```

Ruby 1.9 also introduces __callee__, which returns the name of the current method.

Source Code

Ruby executes programs from plain old files. You can look at these files to examine the source code that makes up your program using one of a number of techniques.

The special variable __FILE__ contains the name of the current source file. This leads to a fairly short (if cheating) Quine—a program that outputs its own source code:

```
print File.read(__FILE__)
```

produces:

```
print File.read(__FILE__)
```

As we saw in the previous section, the method Object#caller returns the call stack as a list. Each entry in this list starts off with a filename, a colon, and a line number in that file. You can parse this information to display source. In the following example, we have a main program, main.rb, that calls a method in a separate file, sub.rb. That method in turns invokes a block, where we traverse the call stack and write out the source lines involved. Notice the use of a hash of file contents, indexed by the filename.

Here's the code that dumps out the call stack, including source information:

ospace/caller/stack_dumper.rb
```ruby
def dump_call_stack
  file_contents = {}
  puts "File              Line  Source Line"
  puts "---------------+----+-----------"
  caller.each do |position|
    next unless position =~ /\A(.*?):(\d+)/
    file = $1
    line = Integer($2)
    file_contents[file] ||= File.readlines(file)
    printf("%-15s:%3d - %s", File.basename(file), line,
            file_contents[file][line-1].lstrip)
  end
end
```

The (trivial) file sub.rb contains a single method:

ospace/caller/sub.rb
```ruby
def sub_method(v1, v2)
  main_method(v1*3, v2*6)
end
```

The following is the main program, which invokes the stack dumper after being called back by the submethod.

```ruby
require_relative 'sub'
require_relative 'stack_dumper'

def main_method(arg1, arg2)
  dump_call_stack
end

sub_method(123, "cat")
```

produces:

```
File              Line  Source Line
---------------+----+-----------
prog.rb          :  5 - dump_call_stack
sub.rb           :  2 - main_method(v1*3, v2*6)
prog.rb          :  8 - sub_method(123, "cat")
```

The SCRIPT_LINES__ constant is closely related to this technique. If a program initializes a constant called SCRIPT_LINES__ with a hash, that hash will receive a new entry for every file subsequently loaded into the interpreter using require or load. The entry's key is the name of the file, and the value is the source of the file as an array of strings.

25.6 Behind the Curtain: The Ruby VM

Ruby 1.9 comes with a new virtual machine, called YARV. As well as being faster than the old interpreter, YARV exposes some of its state via Ruby classes.

If you'd like to know what Ruby is doing with all that code you're writing, you can ask YARV to show you the intermediate code that it is executing. You can ask it to compile the

Ruby code in a string or in a file and then disassemble it and even run it.[2] Here's a trivial example:

```
code = RubyVM::InstructionSequence.compile('a = 1; puts 1 + a')
puts code.disassemble
```

produces:

```
== disasm: <RubyVM::InstructionSequence:<compiled>@<compiled>>==========
local table (size: 2, argc: 0 [opts: 0, rest: -1, post: 0, block: -1] s1)
[ 2] a
0000 trace            1                                                (   1)
0002 putobject_OP_INT2FIX_0_1_C_
0003 setlocal_OP__WC__0 2
0005 trace            1
0007 putself
0008 putobject_OP_INT2FIX_0_1_C_
0009 getlocal_OP__WC__0 2
0011 opt_plus         <callinfo!mid:+, argc:1, ARGS_SKIP>
0013 opt_send_simple  <callinfo!mid:puts, argc:1, FCALL|ARGS_SKIP>
0015 leave
```

Maybe you want to know how Ruby handles #{...} substitutions in strings. Ask the VM.

```
code = RubyVM::InstructionSequence.compile('a = 1; puts "a = #{a}."')
puts code.disassemble
```

produces:

```
== disasm: <RubyVM::InstructionSequence:<compiled>@<compiled>>==========
local table (size: 2, argc: 0 [opts: 0, rest: -1, post: 0, block: -1] s1)
[ 2] a
0000 trace            1                                                (   1)
0002 putobject_OP_INT2FIX_0_1_C_
0003 setlocal_OP__WC__0 2
0005 trace            1
0007 putself
0008 putobject        "a = "
0010 getlocal_OP__WC__0 2
0012 tostring
0013 putobject        "."
0015 concatstrings    3
0017 opt_send_simple  <callinfo!mid:puts, argc:1, FCALL|ARGS_SKIP>
0019 leave
```

For a full list of the opcodes, print out RubyVM::INSTRUCTION_NAMES.

25.7 Marshaling and Distributed Ruby

Ruby features the ability to *serialize* objects, letting you store them somewhere and reconstitute them when needed. You can use this facility, for instance, to save a tree of objects that represent some portion of application state—a document, a CAD drawing, a piece of music, and so on.

---

2. People often ask whether they can dump the opcodes out and later reload them. The answer is no—the interpreter has the code to do this, but it is disabled because there is not yet an intermediate code verifier for YARV.

Ruby calls this kind of serialization *marshaling* (think of railroad marshaling yards where individual cars are assembled in sequence into a complete train, which is then dispatched somewhere). Saving an object and some or all of its components is done using the method Marshal.dump. Typically, you will dump an entire object tree starting with some given object. Later, you can reconstitute the object using Marshal.load.

Here's a short example. We have a class Chord that holds a collection of musical notes. We'd like to save away a particularly wonderful chord so we can e-mail it to a couple hundred of our closest friends so they can load it into their copy of Ruby and savor it too. Let's start with the classes for Note and Chord:

ospace/chord.rb
```ruby
Note = Struct.new(:value) do
  def to_s
    value.to_s
  end
end

class Chord
  def initialize(arr)
    @arr = arr
  end

  def play
    @arr.join('-')
  end
end
```

Now we'll create our masterpiece and use Marshal.dump to save a serialized version to disk:

ospace/chord.rb
```ruby
c = Chord.new( [ Note.new("G"),
                 Note.new("Bb"),
                 Note.new("Db"),
                 Note.new("E") ] )

File.open("posterity", "w+") do |f|
  Marshal.dump(c, f)
end
```

Finally, our grandchildren read it in and are transported by our creation's beauty:

```ruby
chord =   Marshal.load(File.open("posterity"))
chord.play                  # => "G-Bb-Db-E"
```

Custom Serialization Strategy

Not all objects can be dumped: bindings, procedure objects, instances of class IO, and singleton objects cannot be saved outside the running Ruby environment (a TypeError will be raised if you try). Even if your object doesn't contain one of these problematic objects, you may want to take control of object serialization yourself.

Marshal provides the hooks you need. In the objects that require custom serialization, simply implement two instance methods: one called marshal_dump, which writes the object out to a string, and one called marshal_load, which reads a string that you had previously created and uses it to initialize a newly allocated object. (In earlier Ruby versions you'd use methods called _dump and _load, but the new versions play better with Ruby's object allocation scheme.) The instance method marshal_dump should return an object representing the state to be dumped. When the object is subsequently reconstituted using Marshal.load, the method marshal_load will be called with this object and will use it to set the state of its receiver—it will be run in the context of an allocated but not initialized object of the class being loaded.

For instance, here is a sample class that defines its own serialization. For whatever reasons, Special doesn't want to save one of its internal data members, @volatile. The author has decided to serialize the two other instance variables in an array.

```ruby
class Special
  def initialize(valuable, volatile, precious)
    @valuable = valuable
    @volatile = volatile
    @precious = precious
  end

  def marshal_dump
    [ @valuable, @precious ]
  end

  def marshal_load(variables)
    @valuable = variables[0]
    @precious = variables[1]
    @volatile = "unknown"
  end

  def to_s
    "#@valuable #@volatile #@precious"
  end
end

obj = Special.new("Hello", "there", "World")
puts "Before: obj = #{obj}"
data = Marshal.dump(obj)

obj = Marshal.load(data)
puts "After: obj = #{obj}"
```

produces:

```
Before: obj = Hello there World
After: obj = Hello unknown World
```

For more details, see the reference section on page 557.

YAML for Marshaling

The Marshal module is built into the interpreter and uses a binary format to store objects externally. Although fast, this binary format has one major disadvantage: if the interpreter changes significantly, the marshal binary format may also change, and old dumped files may no longer be loadable.

An alternative is to use a less fussy external format, preferably one using text rather than binary files. One option, supplied as a standard library, is YAML.[3]

We can adapt our previous marshal example to use YAML. Rather than implement specific loading and dumping methods to control the marshal process, we simply define the method to_yaml_properties, which returns a list of instance variables to be saved:

ospace/yaml.rb
```ruby
require 'yaml'

class Special
  def initialize(valuable, volatile, precious)
    @valuable = valuable
    @volatile = volatile
    @precious = precious
  end

  def to_yaml_properties
    %w{ @precious @valuable }
  end

  def to_s
    "#@valuable #@volatile #@precious"
  end
end

obj = Special.new("Hello", "there", "World")

puts "Before: obj = #{obj}"
data = YAML.dump(obj)
obj  = YAML.load(data)
puts "After: obj = #{obj}"
```
produces:
```
Before: obj = Hello there World
After: obj = Hello  World
```

We can take a look at what YAML creates as the serialized form of the object—it's pretty simple:

```ruby
obj = Special.new("Hello", "there", "World")
puts YAML.dump(obj)
```
produces:
```
--- !ruby/object:Special
precious: World
valuable: Hello
```

Distributed Ruby

Since we can serialize an object or a set of objects into a form suitable for out-of-process storage, we can transmit objects from one process to another. Couple this capability with the power of networking, and *voilà*—you have a distributed object system. To save you the

---

3.   http://www.yaml.org. YAML stands for YAML Ain't Markup Language, but that hardly seems important.

trouble of having to write the code, we suggest using Masatoshi Seki's Distributed Ruby library (drb), which is now available as a standard Ruby library.

Using drb, a Ruby process may act as a server, as a client, or as both. A drb server acts as a source of objects, while a client is a user of those objects. To the client, it appears that the objects are local, but in reality the code is still being executed remotely.

A server starts a service by associating an object with a given port. Threads are created internally to handle incoming requests on that port, so remember to join the drb thread before exiting your program:

```
require 'drb'

class TestServer
  def add(*args)
    args.inject {|n,v| n + v}
  end
end

server = TestServer.new
DRb.start_service('druby://localhost:9000', server)
DRb.thread.join   # Don't exit just yet!
```

A simple drb client simply creates a local drb object and associates it with the object on the remote server; the local object is a proxy:

```
ospace/drb/drb_client.rb
require 'drb'
DRb.start_service()
obj = DRbObject.new(nil, 'druby://localhost:9000')
# Now use obj
puts "Sum is: #{obj.add(1, 2, 3)}"
```

The client connects to the server and calls the method add, which uses the magic of inject to sum its arguments. It returns the result, which the client prints out:

```
Sum is: 6
```

The initial nil argument to DRbObject indicates that we want to attach to a new distributed object. We could also use an existing object.

Ho hum, you say. This sounds like Java's RMI or CORBA or whatever. Yes, it is a functional distributed object mechanism—but it is written in just a few hundred lines of Ruby code. No C, nothing fancy, just plain old Ruby code. Of course, it has no naming service, trader service, or anything like you'd see in CORBA, but it is simple and reasonably fast. On a 2.5GHz Power Mac system, this sample code runs at about 1,300 remote message calls per second. And if you do need naming services, DRb has a ring server that might fit the bill.

And, if you like the look of Sun's JavaSpaces, the basis of the JINI architecture, you'll be interested to know that drb is distributed with a short module that does the same kind of thing. JavaSpaces is based on a technology called Linda. To prove that its Japanese author has a sense of humor, Ruby's version of Linda is known as Rinda.

25.8 Compile Time? Runtime? Anytime!

The important thing to remember about Ruby is that there isn't a big difference between "compile time" and "runtime." It's all the same. You can add code to a running process. You can redefine methods on the fly, change their scope from public to private, and so on. You can even alter basic types, such as Class and Object.

Once you get used to this flexibility, it is hard to go back to a static language such as C++ or even to a half-static language such as Java.

But then, why would you want to do that?

## CHAPTER 26

Locking Ruby in the Safe

Walter Webcoder has a great idea for a portal site: the Web Arithmetic Page. Surrounded by all sorts of cool mathematical links and banner ads that will make him rich is a simple web form containing a text field and a button. Users type an arithmetic expression into the field, click the button, and the answer is displayed. All the world's calculators become obsolete overnight; Walter cashes in and retires to devote his life to his collection of car license plate numbers.

Implementing the calculator is easy, thinks Walter. He accesses the contents of the form field using Ruby's CGI library and uses the eval method to evaluate the string as an expression:

```
require 'cgi'

cgi = CGI.new("html4")

expr = cgi["expression"].to_s        # Fetch the value of the form field "expression"

begin
  result = eval(expr)
rescue Exception => detail
  # handle bad expressions
end

# display result back to user...
```

Roughly seven seconds after Walter puts the application online, a twelve-year-old from Waxahachie with glandular problems and no real life types system("rm *") into the form, and like his computer's files, Walter's dreams come tumbling down.

Walter learned an important lesson. *All external data is dangerous. Don't let it close to interfaces that can modify your system.* In this case, the content of the form field was the external data, and the call to eval was the security breach, allowing arbitrary code to be executed on Walter's server.

Fortunately, Ruby provides support for reducing this risk. All information from the outside world can be marked as *tainted*. When running in a safe mode, potentially dangerous methods will raise a SecurityError if passed a tainted object.

26.1 Safe Levels

The variable $SAFE determines Ruby's level of paranoia.

$SAFE	Constraints
0	No checking of the use of externally supplied (tainted) data is performed. This is Ruby's default mode.
≥ 1	Ruby disallows the use of tainted data by potentially dangerous operations.
≥ 2	Ruby prohibits the loading of program files from globally writable locations.
≥ 3	All newly created objects are considered tainted and untrusted.
≥ 4	Ruby effectively partitions the running program in two. Nontrusted objects may not be modified.

(For more details of the checks performed at each safe level, refer to Section 26.4, *Definition of the safe levels,* on page 412.)

The default value of $SAFE is zero under most circumstances. However, if a Ruby script is run setuid or setgid[1] or if it run under mod_ruby, its safe level is automatically set to 1. The safe level may also be set by using the -T command-line option and by assigning to $SAFE within the program. It is not possible to lower the value of $SAFE by assignment.

The current value of $SAFE is inherited when new threads are created. However, within each thread, the value of $SAFE may be changed without affecting the value in other threads. This facility may be used to implement secure "sandboxes," areas where external code may run safely without risk to the rest of your application or system. Do this by wrapping code that you load from a file in its own, anonymous module. This will protect your program's namespace from any unintended alteration.

```
File.open(filename,"w") do |f|
  f.print ...   # write untrusted program into file.
end
Thread.start do
  $SAFE = 4
  load(filename, true)
end
```

With a $SAFE level of 4, you can load *only* wrapped files. See the description of Object#load on page 619 for details.

The safe level in effect when a Proc object is created is stored with that object. The safe level may be set during the execution of a proc object without affecting the safe level of the code that invoked that proc. A proc may not be passed to a method if it is tainted and the current safe level is greater than that in effect when the block was created.

26.2 Tainted Objects

Any Ruby object derived from some external source (for example, a string read from a file or an environment variable) is automatically marked as being tainted. If your program uses a tainted object to derive a new object, then that new object will also be tainted, as shown in

---

1. A Unix script may be flagged to be run under a different user or group ID than the person running it. This allows the script to have privileges that the user does not have; the script can access resources that the user would otherwise be prohibited from using. These scripts are called *setuid* or *setgid.*

the following code. Any object with external data somewhere in its past will be tainted. This tainting process is performed regardless of the current safe level. You can see whether an object is tainted using Object#tainted?.

```
# internal data

x1 = "a string"
x1.tainted?      # => false

x2 = x1[2, 4]
x2.tainted?      # => false

x1 =~ /([a-z])/ # => 0
$1.tainted?      # => false

# external data

y1 = ENV["HOME"]
y1.tainted?      # => true

y2 = y1[2, 4]
y2.tainted?      # => true

y1 =~ /([a-z])/ # => 2
$1.tainted?      # => true
```

You can taint any object by invoking its taint method. If the safe level is less than 3, you can remove the taint from an object by invoking untaint.[2] This is not something to do lightly.

26.3 Trusted Objects

Ruby 1.9 adds *trust*, a new dimension to the concept of safety. All objects are marked as being *trusted* or *untrusted*. In addition, running code can be trusted or not. And, when you're running untrusted code, objects that you create are untrusted, and the only objects that you can modify are those that are marked untrusted. What this in effect means is that you can create a sandbox to execute untrusted code, and code in that sandbox cannot affect objects outside that sandbox.

Let's get more specific. Objects created while Ruby's safe level is less than 3 are trusted. However, objects created while the safe level is 3 or 4 will be untrusted. Code running at safe levels 3 and 4 is also considered to be untrusted. Because untrusted code can modify only untrusted objects, code at safe levels 3 and 4 will not be able to modify objects created at a lower safe level.

---

2.   You can also use some devious tricks to do this without using untaint. We'll leave it up to your darker side to find them.

```
dog = "dog is trusted"
cat = lambda { $SAFE = 3; "cat is untrusted" }.call

puts "dog.untrusted? =  #{dog.untrusted?}"
puts "cat.untrusted? =  #{cat.untrusted?}"

# running at safe level 1, these operations will succeed
puts dog.upcase!
puts cat.upcase!

# running at safe level 4, we can modify the cat
lambda { $SAFE = 4; cat.downcase! }.call
puts "cat is now '#{cat}'"

# but we can't modify the dog
lambda { $SAFE = 4; dog.downcase! }.call
puts "so we never get here"
```

produces:

```
        from prog.rb:16:in `block in <main>'
        from prog.rb:16:in `call'
        from prog.rb:16:in `<main>'
dog.untrusted? =  false
cat.untrusted? =  true
DOG IS TRUSTED
CAT IS UNTRUSTED
cat is now 'cat is untrusted'
prog.rb:16:in `downcase!': Insecure: can't modify string (SecurityError)
```

You can set and unset the trusted status of an object using Object#untrust and Object#trust (but you have to be at below safe level 4 to call untrust and below safe level 3 to call trust). The method Object#untrusted? returns true if an object is untrusted.

26.4 Definition of the safe levels

$SAFE ≥ 1

- The environment variables RUBYLIB and RUBYOPT are not processed, and the current directory is not added to the path.
- The command-line options -e, -i, -l, -r, -s, -S, and -x are not allowed.
- Can't start processes from $PATH if any directory in it is world-writable.
- Can't manipulate or chroot to a directory whose name is a tainted string.
- Can't glob tainted strings.
- Can't eval tainted strings.
- Can't load or require a file whose name is a tainted string (unless the load is wrapped).
- Can't manipulate or query the status of a file or pipe whose name is a tainted string.
- Can't execute a system command or exec a program from a tainted string.
- Can't pass trap a tainted string.

$SAFE ≥ 2

- Can't change, make, or remove directories, or use chroot.
- Can't load a file from a world-writable directory.
- Can't load a file from a tainted filename starting with ~.

- Can't use File#chmod, File#chown, File#lstat, File.stat, File#truncate, File.umask, File#flock, IO#ioctl, IO#stat, Object#fork, Object#syscall, Object#trap. Process.setpgid, Process.setsid, Process.setpriority, or Process.egid=.
- Can't handle signals using trap.

$SAFE ≥ 3

- All objects are tainted when they are created.
- Can't untaint objects.
- Can't add trust to an object.
- Objects are created untrusted.

$SAFE ≥ 4

- Can't modify a nontainted array, hash, or string.
- Can't modify a global variable.
- Can't access instance variables of nontainted objects.
- Can't change an environment variable.
- Can't close or reopen nontainted files.
- Can't freeze nontainted objects.
- Can't change visibility of methods (private/public/protected).
- Can't make an alias in a nontainted class or module.
- Can't get metainformation (such as method or variable lists).
- Can't define, redefine, remove, or undef a method in a nontainted class or module.
- Can't modify Object.
- Can't remove instance variables or constants from nontainted objects.
- Can't manipulate threads, terminate a thread other than the current thread, or set abort_on_exception.
- Can't have thread-local variables.
- Can't raise an exception in a thread with a lower $SAFE value.
- Can't move threads between ThreadGroups.
- Can't invoke exit, exit!, or abort.
- Can load only wrapped files and can't include modules in untainted classes and modules.
- Can't convert symbol identifiers to object references.
- Can't write to files or pipes.
- Can't use autoload.
- Can't taint objects.
- Can't untrust an object.

Part IV

Ruby Library Reference

## CHAPTER 27

Built-in Classes and Modules

This chapter documents the classes and modules built into the standard Ruby language. They are available to every Ruby program automatically; no require is required. This section does not contain the various predefined variables and constants; they are listed in *Predefined Variables*, on page 311.

In the descriptions that follow, we show sample invocations for each method.

---

new String.new(*val*) → *str*

This description shows a class method that is called as String.new. The italic parameter indicates that a single string is passed in, and the arrow indicates that another string is returned from the method. Because this return value has a different name than that of the parameter, it represents a different object.

When we illustrate instance methods, we show a sample call with a dummy object name in italics as the receiver.

---

lines *str*.lines(*sep*=$/) { | line | ... } → *str*

The parameter to String#lines is shown to have a default value; call lines with no parameter, and the value of $/ will be used. This method is an iterator, so the call is followed by a block. String#lines returns its receiver, so the receiver's name (*str* in this case) appears again after the arrow.

Some methods have optional parameters. We show these parameters between angle brackets, ‹ *xxx* ›. We use the notation ‹ *xxx* ›* to indicate zero or more occurrences of *xxx*, and we use ‹ *xxx* ›+ to indicate one or more occurrences of *xxx*.

---

index *str*.index(*string* ‹, *offset* ›) → *int* or nil

Finally, for methods that can be called in several different forms, we list each form on a separate line.

27.1 Alphabetical Listing

Standard classes are listed alphabetically, followed by the standard modules. Within each, we list the class (or module) methods, followed by the instance methods.

Array (page 421): Class [], new, try_convert Instance &, *, +, -, <<, <=>, ==, [], []=, |, assoc, at, bsearch, combination, collect!, compact, compact!, concat, count, cycle, delete, delete_at, delete_if, each, each_index, empty?, eql?, fetch, fill, find_index, flatten, flatten!, frozen?, index, insert, join, keep_if, last, length, map!, pack, permutation, pop, product, push, rassoc, reject!, repeated_combination, repeated_permutation, replace, reverse, reverse!, reverse_each, rindex, rotate, rotate!, sample, select!, shift, shuffle, shuffle!, size, slice, slice!, sort!, sort_by!, to_a, to_ary, to_s, transpose, uniq, uniq!, unshift, values_at

BasicObject (page 439): Instance !, ==, !=, __id__, equal?, instance_eval, instance_exec, __send__ Private method_missing, singleton_method_added, singleton_method_removed, singleton_method_undefined

Bignum (page 444): Instance Arithmeticoperations, Bitoperations, <=>, ==, [], abs, div, divmod, eql?, fdiv, magnitude, modulo, remainder, size, to_f, to_s

Binding (page 447): Instance eval

Class (page 448): Class new Instance allocate, new, superclass Private inherited

Complex (page 451): Class polar, rect, rectangular Instance Arithmeticoperations, ==, abs, abs2, angle, arg, conj, conjugate, denominator, eql?, fdiv, imag, imaginary, magnitude, numerator, phase, polar, quo, rationalize, rect, rectangular, real, real?, to _f, to_i, to_r

Dir (page 456): Class [], chdir, chroot, delete, entries, exist?, exists?, foreach, getwd, glob, home, mkdir, new, open, pwd, rmdir, unlink Instance close, each, path, pos, pos=, read, rewind, seek, tell, to_path

Encoding (page 462): Class aliases, compatible?, default_external, default_external=, default_internal, default_internal=, find, list, locale_charmap, name_list Instance ascii_compatible?, dummy?, name, names, replicate

Enumerator (page 477): Class new Instance each, each_with_index, each_with_object, feed, next, next_values, peek, peek _values, rewind, size, with_index, with_object

Exception (page 483): Class exception, new Instance ==, backtrace, exception, message, set_backtrace, status, success?, to _s

FalseClass (page 486): Instance &, ^, |

Fiber (page 487): Class new, yield Instance resume

File (page 488): Class absolute_path, atime, basename, blockdev?, chardev?, chmod, chown, ctime, delete, directory?, dirname, executable?, executable_real?, exist?, exists?, expand_path, extname, file?, fnmatch, fnmatch?, ftype, grpowned?, identical?, join, lchmod, lchown, link, lstat, mtime, new, owned?, path, pipe?, readable?, readable_real?, readlink, realdirpath, realpath, rename, setgid?, setuid?, size, size?, socket?, split, stat, sticky?, symlink, symlink?, truncate, umask, unlink, utime, world_readable?, world_writable?, writable?, writable_real?, zero? Instance atime, chmod, chown, ctime, flock, lstat, mtime, path, size, to_path, truncate

File::Stat (page 503): Instance <=>, atime, blksize, blockdev?, blocks, chardev?, ctime, dev, dev_major, dev_minor, directory?, executable?, executable_real?, file?, ftype, gid, grpowned?, ino, mode, mtime, nlink, owned?, pipe?, rdev, rdev_major, rdev_ minor, readable?, readable_real?, setgid?, setuid?, size, size?, socket?, sticky?, symlink?, uid, world_readable?, world_writable?, writable?, writable_real?, zero?

Fixnum (page 510): Instance Arithmeticoperations, Bitoperations, Comparisons, <=>, [], abs, div, even?, divmod, fdiv, magnitude, modulo, odd?, size, succ, to_f, to_s, zero?

Float (page 513): Instance Arithmeticoperations, Comparisons, <=>, ==, abs, ceil, divmod, eql?, fdiv, finite?, floor, infinite?, magnitude, modulo, nan?, quo, rationalize, round, to_f, to_i, to_int, to_r, to_s, truncate, zero?

Hash (page 521): Class [], new, try_convert Instance ==, [], []=, assoc, clear, compare_by_identity, compare_by_identity?, default, default=, default_proc, default_proc=, delete, delete_if, each, each_key, each_pair, each_value, empty?, fetch, flatten, has_key?, has_value?, include?, index, invert, keep_if, key, key?, keys, length, member?, merge, merge!, rassoc, rehash, reject, reject!, replace, select, select!, shift, size, sort, store, to_a, to_h, to_hash, to_s, update, value?, values, values_at

Integer (page 532): Instance ceil, chr, denominator, downto, even?, floor, gcd, gcdlcm, integer?, lcm, next, numerator, odd?, ord, pred, rationalize, round, succ, times, to_i, to_int, to_r, truncate, upto

IO (page 536): Class binread, binwrite, copy_stream, for_fd, foreach, new, open, pipe, popen, read, readlines, select, sysopen, try_convert, write Instance <<, advise, autoclose=, autoclose?, binmode, binmode?, bytes, chars, close, close_on_exec?, close _on_exec=, close_read, close_write, closed?, codepoints, each, each_byte, each_char, each_codepoint, each_line, eof, eof?, external_encoding, fcntl, fdatasync, fileno, flush, fsync, getbyte, getc, gets, internal_encoding, ioctl, isatty, lineno, lineno=, lines, pid, pos, pos=, print, printf, putc, puts, read, readbyte, readchar, readline, readlines, readpartial, read_nonblock, reopen, rewind, seek, set_encoding, stat, sync, sync=, sysread, sysseek, syswrite, tell, to_i, to_io, tty?, ungetbyte, ungetc, write, write_nonblock

MatchData (page 559): Instance [], begin, captures, end, length, names, offset, post_match, pre_match, regexp, size, string, to_a, to_s, values_at

Method (page 565): Instance [], ==, arity, call, eql?, name, owner, parameters, receiver, source_location, to_proc, unbind

Module (page 568): Class constants, nesting, new Instance <,<=,==,>,>=, <=>, ===, ancestors, autoload, autoload?, class_eval, class_exec, class_variable_defined?, class_variable_get, class_variable_set, class_variables, const_defined?, const_get, const_missing, const_set, constants, include?, included_modules, instance_method, instance_methods, method_defined?, module_eval, module_exec, name, private_class_method, private_constant, private_instance_methods, private_method_defined?, protected_instance_methods, protected_method_defined?, public_class_method, public_constant, public_instance_method, public_instance_methods, public_method_defined?, remove_class_variable Private alias_method, append_features, attr, attr_accessor, attr_reader, attr_writer, define_method, extend_object, extended, include, included, method_added, method_removed, method_undefined, module_function, prepend, private, protected, public, refine, remove_const, remove_method, undef_method

Mutex (page 588): Instance lock, locked?, owned?, sleep, synchronize, try_lock, unlock

NilClass (page 589): Instance &, ^, |, nil?, rationalize, to_a, to_c, to_f, to_h, to_i, to_r, to_s

Numeric (page 591): Instance +@, -@, <=>, %, abs, abs2, angle, arg, ceil, coerce, conj, conjugate, denominator, div, divmod, eql?, fdiv, floor, i, imag, imaginary, integer?, magnitude, modulo, nonzero?, numerator, phase, polar, quo, real, real?, rect, rectangular, remainder, round, step, to_c, to_int, truncate, zero?

Object (page 599): Instance ===, <=>, =~, !~, class, clone, define_singleton_method, display, dup, enum_for, eql?, extend, freeze, frozen?, hash, initialize_clone, initialize_copy, initialize_dup, inspect, instance_of?, instance_variable_defined?, instance_variable_get, instance_variable_set, instance_variables, is_a?, kind_of?, method, methods, nil?, object_id, private_methods, protected_methods, public_method, public_methods, public_send, respond_to?, respond_to_missing?, send, singleton_class, singleton_methods, taint, tainted?, tap, to_enum, to_s, trust, untaint, untrust, untrusted? Private __callee__, __dir__, __method__, `(backquote), Array, Complex, Float, Hash, Integer, Rational, String, abort, at_exit, autoload, autoload?, binding, block_given?, caller, caller_locations, catch, chomp, chop, define_method, eval, exec, exit, exit!, fail, fork, format, gem, gem_original_require, gets, global_variables, gsub, initialize, iterator?, lambda, load, local_variables, loop, open, p, print, printf, proc, putc, puts, raise, rand, readline, readlines, remove_instance_variable, require, require_relative, select, set_trace_func, sleep, spawn, sprintf, srand, sub, syscall, system, test, throw, trace_var, trap, untrace_var, using, warn

Proc (page 633): Class new Instance [], ==, ===, arity, binding, call, curry, lambda?, parameters, source_location, to_proc, to_s, yield

Process::Status (page 644): Instance ==, &, >>, coredump?, exited?, exitstatus, pid, signaled?, stopped?, success?, stopsig, termsig, to_i, to_s

Random (page 655): Class new, new_seed, rand, srand Instance bytes, rand, seed

Range (page 650): Class new Instance ==, ===, begin, bsearch, cover?, each, end, eql?, exclude_end?, first, include?, last, max, member?, min, size, step

Rational (page 656): Instance Arithmeticoperations, Comparisons, <=>, ==, ceil, denominator, fdiv, floor, numerator, quo, rationalize, round, to_f, to_i, to_r, truncate

Regexp (page 659): Class compile, escape, last_match, new, quote, try_convert, union Instance ==, ===, =~, ~, casefold?, encoding, fixed_encoding?, match, named_captures, names, options, source, to_s

String (page 666): Class new, try_convert Instance %, *, +, <<, <=>, ==, =~, [], []=, ascii_only?, b, bytes, bytesize, byteslice, capitalize, capitalize!, casecmp, center, chars, chr, clear, chomp, chomp!, chop, chop!, codepoints, concat, count, crypt, delete, delete!, downcase, downcase!, dump, each_byte, each_char, each_codepoint, each_line, empty?, encode, encode!, encoding, end_with?, eql?, force_encoding, getbyte, gsub, gsub!, hex, include?, index, insert, intern, length, lines, ljust, lstrip, lstrip!, match, next, next!, oct, ord, partition, prepend, replace, reverse, reverse!, rindex, rjust, rpartition, rstrip, rstrip!, scan, setbyte, size, slice, slice!, split, squeeze, squeeze!, start_with?, strip, strip!, sub, sub!, succ, succ!, sum, swapcase, swapcase!, to_c, to_f, to_i, to_r, to_s, to_str, to_sym, tr, tr!, tr_s, tr_s!, unpack, upcase, upcase!, upto, valid_encoding?

Struct (page 693): Class new, new, [], members Instance ==, [], []=, each, each_pair, length, members, size, to_a, to_h, values, values_at

Struct::Tms (page 697):

Symbol (page 698): Class all_symbols Instance <=>, ==, =~, [], capitalize, casecmp, downcase, empty?, encoding, id2name, inspect, intern, length, match, next, size, slice, succ, swapcase, to_proc, to_s, to_sym, upcase

Thread (page 702): Class abort_on_exception, abort_on_exception=, current, exclusive, exit, fork, kill, list, main, new, pass, start, stop Instance [], []=, abort_on_exception, abort_on_exception=, add_trace_func, alive?, backtrace, backtrace_locations, exit, group, join, keys, key?, kill, priority, priority=, raise, run, safe_level, set_trace_func, status, stop?, terminate, thread_variable?, thread_variables, thread_variable_get, thread_variable_set, value, wakeup

ThreadGroup (page 710): Class new Instance add, enclose, enclosed?, list

Time (page 712): Class at, gm, local, mktime, new, now, utc Instance +, -, <=>, day-name?, asctime, ctime, day, dst?, getgm, getlocal, getutc, gmt?, gmtime, gmt_offset, gmtoff, hour, isdst, localtime, mday, min, mon, month, nsec, round, sec, strftime, subsec, succ, to_a, to_f, to_i, to_r, to_s, tv_nsec, tv_sec, tv_usec, usec, utc, utc?, utc_offset, wday, yday, year, zone

TracePoint (page 722): Class new, trace Instance binding, defined_class, disable, enable, enabled?, event, lineno, method_id, path, raised_exception, return_value, self

TrueClass (page 725): Instance &, ^, |

UnboundMethod (page 726): Instance arity, bind, name, owner, parameters, source_location

Built-in Modules

Comparable (page 450): Instance Comparisons, between?

Enumerable (page 466): Instance all?, any?, chunk, collect, collect_concat, count, cycle, detect, drop, drop_while, each_cons, each_entry, each_slice, each_with_index, each_with_object, entries, find, find_all, find_index, first, flat_map, grep, group_by, include?, inject, lazy, map, max, max_by, member?, min, min_by, minmax, minmax_by, none?, one?, partition, reduce, reject, reverse_each, select, slice_before, sort, sort_by, take, take_while, to_a, zip

Errno (page 482):

FileTest (page 509):

GC (page 517): Class count, disable, enable, start, stat, stress, stress= Instance garbage_collect

GC::Profiler (page 519): Class clear, disable, enable, enabled?, raw_data, report, result, total_time

Kernel (page 556):

Marshal (page 557): Class dump, load, restore

Math (page 562): Class acos, acosh, asin, asinh, atan, atanh, atan2, cbrt, cos, cosh, erf, erfc, exp, frexp, gamma, hypot, ldexp, lgamma, log, log10, log2, sin, sinh, sqrt, tan, tanh

ObjectSpace (page 631): Class _id2ref, count_objects, define_finalizer, each_object, garbage_collect, undefine_finalizer

Process (page 637): Class abort, daemon, detach, egid, egid=, euid, euid=, exec, exit, exit!, fork, getpgid, getpgrp, getpriority, getrlimit, getsid, gid, gid=, groups, groups=, initgroups, kill, maxgroups, maxgroups=, pid, ppid, setpgid, setpgrp, setpriority, setrlimit, setsid, spawn, times, uid, uid=, wait, waitall, wait2, waitpid, waitpid2

Process::GID (page 643): Class change_privilege, eid, eid=, grant_privilege, re_exchange, re_exchangeable?, rid, sid_available?, switch

Process::Sys (page 647): Class getegid, geteuid, getgid, getuid, issetugid, setegid, seteuid, setgid, setregid, setresgid, setresuid, setreuid, setrgid, setruid, setuid

Process::UID (page 648): Class change_privilege, eid, eid=, grant_privilege, re_exchange, re_exchangeable?, rid, sid_available?, switch

Signal (page 664): Class list, signame, trap

Array

Arrays are ordered, integer-indexed collections of any object. Array indexes start at 0, as in C or Java. A negative index is relative to the end of the array; that is, an index of -1 indicates the last element of the array, -2 is the next-to-last element in the array, and so on.

Mixes In

Enumerable: all?, any?, chunk, collect, collect_concat, count, cycle, detect, drop, drop_while, each_cons, each_entry, each_slice, each_with_index, each_with_object, entries, find, find_all, find_index, first, flat_map, grep, group_by, include?, inject, lazy, map, max, max_by, member?, min, min_by, minmax, minmax_by, none?, one?, partition, reduce, reject, reverse_each, select, slice_before, sort, sort_by, take, take_while, to_a, zip

Class Methods

[ ]

Array[⟨obj⟩*] → *an_array*

Returns a new array populated with the given objects. Equivalent to the operator form Array.[...].

```
Array.[]( 1, 'a', /^A/ ) # => [1, "a", /^A/]
Array[ 1, 'a', /^A/ ]    # => [1, "a", /^A/]
[ 1, 'a', /^A/ ]         # => [1, "a", /^A/]
```

new

Array.new → *an_array*
Array.new (*size=0, obj=nil*) → *an_array*
Array.new(*array*) → *an_array*
Array.new(*size*) { |i| ... } → *an_array*

Returns a new array. In the first form, the new array is empty. In the second, it is created with *size* copies of *obj* (that is, *size* references to the same *obj*). The third form creates a copy of the array passed as a parameter (the array is generated by calling to_ary on the parameter). In the last form, an array of the given size is created. Each element in this array is calculated by passing the element's index to the given block and storing the return value.

```
Array.new          # => []
Array.new(2)       # => [nil, nil]
Array.new(5, "A")  # => ["A", "A", "A", "A", "A"]

# only one instance of the default object is created
a = Array.new(2, Hash.new)
a[0]['cat'] = 'feline'
a          # => [{"cat"=>"feline"}, {"cat"=>"feline"}]
a[1]['cat'] = 'Felix'
a          # => [{"cat"=>"Felix"}, {"cat"=>"Felix"}]

a = Array.new(2) { Hash.new }  # Multiple instances
a[0]['cat'] = 'feline'
a          # => [{"cat"=>"feline"}, {}]

squares = Array.new(5) {|i| i*i}
squares    # => [0, 1, 4, 9, 16]
```

```
copy = Array.new(squares)      # initialized by copying
squares[5] = 25
squares    # => [0, 1, 4, 9, 16, 25]
copy       # => [0, 1, 4, 9, 16]
```

---

try_convert   Array.try_convert(*obj*) → *an_array* or nil

If *obj* is not already an array, attempts to convert it to one by calling its to_ary method. Returns nil if no conversion could be made.

```
class Stooges
  def to_ary
    [ "Larry", "Curly", "Moe" ]
  end
end
Array.try_convert(Stooges.new) # => ["Larry", "Curly", "Moe"]
Array.try_convert("Shemp")     # => nil
```

Instance Methods

&   *arr* & *other_array* → *an_array*

Set Intersection—Returns a new array containing elements common to the two arrays, with no duplicates. The rules for comparing elements are the same as for hash keys. If you need setlike behavior, see the library class .Set on page 804.

```
[ 1, 1, 3, 5 ] & [ 1, 2, 3 ] # => [1, 3]
```

---

*   *arr* * *int* → *an_array*
                                                   arr * *str* → *a_string*

Repetition—With an argument that responds to to_str, equivalent to arr.join(str). Otherwise, returns a new array built by concatenating *int* copies of *arr*.

```
[ 1, 2, 3 ] * 3   # => [1, 2, 3, 1, 2, 3, 1, 2, 3]
[ 1, 2, 3 ] * "--" # => "1--2--3"
```

+   *arr* + *other_array* → *an_array*

Concatenation—Returns a new array built by concatenating the two arrays together to produce a third array.

```
[ 1, 2, 3 ] + [ 4, 5 ] # => [1, 2, 3, 4, 5]
```

-   *arr* - *other_array* → *an_array*

Array Difference—Returns a new array that is a copy of the original array, removing any items that also appear in *other_array*. If you need setlike behavior, see the library class Set on page 804.

```
[ 1, 1, 2, 2, 3, 3, 4, 5 ] - [ 1, 2, 4 ] # => [3, 3, 5]
```

<<   *arr << obj→ arr*

Append—Pushes the given object on to the end of this array. This expression returns the array itself, so several appends may be chained together. See also Array#push.

```
[ 1, 2 ] << "c" << "d" << [ 3, 4 ] # => [1, 2, "c", "d", [3, 4]]
```

<=>   *arr <=> other_array → -1, 0, +1, or nil*

Comparison—Returns an integer -1, 0, or +1 if this array is less than, equal to, or greater than *other_array*. Successive objects in each array are compared using <=>. If any pair are not equal, then that inequality is the return value. If all pair are equal, then the longer array is considered greater. Thus, two arrays are "equal" according to Array#<=> if and only if they have the same length and the values of each corresponding element are equal. nil is returned if the argument is not comparable to *arr*.

```
[ "a", "a", "c" ]    <=> [ "a", "b", "c" ]  # => -1
[ 1, 2, 3, 4, 5, 6 ] <=> [ 1, 2 ]           # => 1
[ 1, 2, 3, 4, 5, 6 ] <=> "wombat"           # => nil
```

==   *arr == obj → true* or *false*

Equality—Two arrays are equal if they contain the same number of elements and if each element is equal to (according to Object#==) the corresponding element in the other array. If *obj* is not an array, attempt to convert it using to_ary and return *obj==arr*.

```
[ "a", "c" ]    == [ "a", "c", 7 ]  # => false
[ "a", "c", 7 ] == [ "a", "c", 7 ]  # => true
[ "a", "c", 7 ] == [ "a", "d", "f" ] # => false
```

[ ]   *arr[int] → obj* or nil
                                                      arr[start, length] → an_array or nil
                                                            arr[range] → an_array or nil

---

Element Reference—Returns the element at index *int*; returns a *length* element subarray starting at index *start*; or returns a subarray specified by *range*. Negative indices count backward from the end of the array (-1 is the last element). Returns nil if the index of the first element selected is greater than the array size. If the start index equals the array size and a *length* or *range* parameter is given, an empty array is returned. Equivalent to Array#slice.

```
a = [ "a", "b", "c", "d", "e" ]
a[2] +  a[0] + a[1] # => "cab"
a[6]                # => nil
a[1, 2]             # => ["b", "c"]
a[1..3]             # => ["b", "c", "d"]
a[4..7]             # => ["e"]
a[6..10]            # => nil
a[-3, 3]            # => ["c", "d", "e"]
# special cases
a[5]                # => nil
a[5, 1]             # => []
a[5..10]            # => []
```

[ ]=
$$arr[int] = obj \rightarrow obj$$
$$arr[start, length] = obj \rightarrow obj\}$$
$$arr[range] = obj \rightarrow obj$$

Element Assignment—Sets the element at index *int*, replaces a subarray starting at index *start* and continuing for *length* elements, or replaces a subarray specified by *range*. If *int* is greater than the size of the array, the array grows automatically. A negative *int* counts backward from the end of the array. Inserts elements if *length* is zero. If *obj* is an array, the form with the single index inserts that array into *arr*, and the forms with a length or with a range replace the given elements in *arr* with the array contents. An IndexError is raised if a negative index points past the beginning of the array. (Prior to Ruby 1.9, assigning nil with the second and third forms of element assignment deleted the corresponding array elements; it now assigns nil to them.) See also Array#push and Array#unshift.

```
a = Array.new            # => []
a[4] = "4";              a # => [nil, nil, nil, nil, "4"]
a[0] = [ 1, 2, 3 ];      a # => [[1, 2, 3], nil, nil, nil, "4"]
a[0, 3] = [ 'a', 'b', 'c' ]; a # => ["a", "b", "c", nil, "4"]
a[1..2] = [ 1, 2 ];      a # => ["a", 1, 2, nil, "4"]
a[0, 2] = "?";           a # => ["?", 2, nil, "4"]
a[0..2] = "A", "B", "C"; a # => ["A", "B", "C", "4"]
a[-1]  = "Z";            a # => ["A", "B", "C", "Z"]
a[1..-1] = nil;          a # => ["A", nil]
```

|
$$arr \mid other\_array \rightarrow an\_array$$

Set Union—Returns a new array by joining this array with *other_array*, removing duplicates. The rules for comparing elements are the same as for hash keys. If you need setlike behavior, see the library class Set on page 804.

```
[ "a", "b", "c" ] | [ "c", "d", "a" ] # => ["a", "b", "c", "d"]
```

assoc
$$arr.assoc(\ obj\ ) \rightarrow an\_array \text{ or nil}$$

Searches through an array whose elements are also arrays comparing *obj* with the first element of each contained array using *obj*.==. Returns the first contained array that matches (that is, the first *assoc*iated array) or nil if no match is found. See also Array#rassoc.

```
s1 = [ "colors", "red", "blue", "green" ]
s2 = [ "letters", "a", "b", "c" ]
s3 = "foo"
a  = [ s1, s2, s3 ]
a.assoc("letters") # => ["letters", "a", "b", "c"]
a.assoc("foo")     # => nil
```

at
$$arr.at(\ int\ ) \rightarrow obj \text{ or nil}$$

Returns the element at index *int*. A negative index counts from the end of *arr*. Returns nil if the index is out of range. See also Array#[].

```
a = [ "a", "b", "c", "d", "e" ]
a.at(0)   # => "a"
a.at(-1)  # => "e"
```

bsearch

arr.bsearch { | val | ... } → *obj* or nil

New in 2.0

Assuming *arr* is sorted in ascending order, performs a binary search in $O(log\ n)$ time. The method operates in two modes depending on the values returned by the block:

To find the minimum value in *arr* greater than or equal to the required value, have the block return false if its argument is less than that value, true otherwise.

```
arr = %w{ ant bee cat dog elk fox gnu }
arr.bsearch {|val| val >= "c" }   # => "cat"
arr.bsearch {|val| val >= "cod" } # => "dog"
arr.bsearch {|val| val >= "kea" } # => nil
```

To find a value in the array that lies between two limits, write the block to return a positive number if the argument is less than the lower bound, a negative number if it is greater than the upper bound, or zero if it is inclusively between the bounds.

```
arr = [ 1, 1, 2, 3, 5, 8, 13, 21, 34 ]
res = arr.bsearch do |val|
  case
  when val < 19 then +1
  when val > 23 then -1
  else 0
  end
end
res       # => 21
```

combination

arr.combination(*size*) → *enumerator*
arr.combination(*size*) { | array | ... } → *arr*

Constructs all combinations of the elements of *arr* of length *size*. If called with a block, passes each combination to that block; otherwise, returns an enumerator object. An empty result is generated if no combinations of the given length exist. See also Array#permutation.

```
a = [ "a", "b", "c" ]
a.combination(1).to_a # => [["a"], ["b"], ["c"]]
a.combination(2).to_a # => [["a", "b"], ["a", "c"], ["b", "c"]]
a.combination(3).to_a # => [["a", "b", "c"]]
a.combination(4).to_a # => []
```

collect!

arr.collect! { | obj | ... } → *arr*

Invokes *block* once for each element of *arr*, replacing the element with the value returned by *block*. See also Enumerable#collect.

```
a = [ "a", "b", "c", "d" ]
a.collect! {|x| x + "!" } # => ["a!", "b!", "c!", "d!"]
a                         # => ["a!", "b!", "c!", "d!"]
```

---

compact

arr.compact → *an_array*

Returns a copy of *arr* with all nil elements removed.

```
[ "a", nil, "b", nil, "c", nil ].compact # => ["a", "b", "c"]
```

---

compact!

arr.compact! → *arr* or nil

Removes nil elements from *arr*. Returns nil if no changes were made.

```
[ "a", nil, "b", nil, "c" ].compact! # => ["a", "b", "c"]
[ "a", "b", "c" ].compact!           # => nil
```

---

concat

arr.concat(*other_array*) → *arr*

Appends the elements in *other_array* to *arr*.

```
[ "a", "b" ].concat( ["c", "d"] ) # => ["a", "b", "c", "d"]
```

---

count

arr.count(*obj*) → *int*
arr.count { | obj | ... } → *int*

Returns the count of objects in *arr* that equal *obj* or for which the block returns a true value. Shadows the corresponding method in Enumerable.

```
[1, 2, 3, 4].count(3)             # => 1
[1, 2, 3, 4].count {|obj| obj > 2 } # => 2
```

---

cycle

arr.cycle { | obj | ... } → nil or *enumerator*
arr.cycle(*times*) { | obj | ... } → nil or *enumerator*

Returns nil if *arr* has no elements; otherwise, passes the elements, one at a time to the block. When it reaches the end, it repeats. The number of times it repeats is set by the parameter. If the parameter is missing, cycles forever. Returns an Enumerator object if no block is given.

```
[1,2,3].cycle(3)      # => #<Enumerator: [1, 2, 3]:cycle(3)>
[1,2,3].cycle(3).to_a # => [1, 2, 3, 1, 2, 3, 1, 2, 3]

columns = [ 1, 2, 3 ]
data    = %w{ a b c d e f g h }

columns.cycle do |column_number|
  print column_number, ":", data.shift, "\t"
  puts   if column_number == columns.last
  break if data.empty?
end
```

produces:

```
1:a    2:b    3:c
1:d    2:e    3:f
1:g    2:h
```

delete

arr.delete(obj) → obj or nil
arr.delete(obj) { ... } → obj or nil

Deletes items from *arr* that are equal to *obj*. If the item is not found, returns nil. If the optional code block is given, returns the result of *block* if the item is not found.

```
a = [ "a", "b", "b", "b", "c" ]
a.delete("b")                   # => "b"
a                               # => ["a", "c"]
a.delete("z")                   # => nil
a.delete("z") { "not found" }   # => "not found"
```

delete_at

arr.delete_at(index) → obj or nil

Deletes the element at the specified index, returning that element or nil if the index is out of range. See also Array#slice!.

```
a = %w( ant bat cat dog )
a.delete_at(2)  # => "cat"
a               # => ["ant", "bat", "dog"]
a.delete_at(99) # => nil
```

delete_if

arr.delete_if { | item | ... } → arr

Deletes every element of *arr* for which *block* evaluates to true.

```
a = [ "a", "b", "c" ]
a.delete_if {|x| x >= "b" } # => ["a"]
```

each

arr.each { | item | ... } → arr

Calls *block* once for each element in *arr*, passing that element as a parameter.

```
a = [ "a", "b", "c" ]
a.each {|x| print x, " -- " }
```

produces:

```
a -- b -- c --
```

each_index

arr.each_index { | index | ... } → arr

Same as Array#each but passes the index of the element instead of the element itself.

```
a = [ "a", "b", "c" ]
a.each_index {|x| print x, " -- " }
```

produces:

```
0 -- 1 -- 2 --
```

---

empty?

Returns true if *arr* array contains no elements.

```
[].empty?          # => true
[ 1, 2, 3 ].empty? # => false
```

---

eql?

Returns true if *arr* and *other* are the same object or if *other* is an object of class Array with the same length and content as *arr*. Elements in the arrays are compared using Object#eql?. See also Array#<=>.

```
[ "a", "b", "c" ].eql?(["a", "b", "c"]) # => true
[ "a", "b", "c" ].eql?(["a", "b"])      # => false
[ "a", "b", "c" ].eql?(["b", "c", "d"]) # => false
```

---

fetch

arr.fetch(*index*) → *obj*
arr.fetch(*index*, *default*) → *obj*
arr.fetch(*index*) { |i| ... } → *obj*

Tries to return the element at position *index*. If the index lies outside the array, the first form throws an IndexError exception, the second form returns *default*, and the third form returns the value of invoking the block, passing in the index. Negative values of *index* count from the end of the array.

```
a = [ 11, 22, 33, 44 ]
a.fetch(1)          # => 22
a.fetch(-1)         # => 44
a.fetch(-1, 'cat')  # => 44
a.fetch(4, 'cat')   # => "cat"
a.fetch(4) {|i| i*i } # => 16
```

---

fill

arr.fill(*obj*) → *arr*
arr.fill(*obj*, *start* ‹, *length*›) → *arr*
arr.fill(*obj*, *range*) → *arr*
arr.fill { |i| ... } → *arr*
arr.fill(*start* ‹, *length*›) { |i| ... } → *arr*
arr.fill(*range*) { |i| ... } → *arr*

The first three forms set the selected elements of *arr* (which may be the entire array) to *obj*. A *start* of nil is equivalent to zero. A *length* of nil is equivalent to *arr*.length. The last three forms fill the array with the value of the block. The block is passed the absolute index of each element to be filled.

```
a = [ "a", "b", "c", "d" ]
a.fill("x")         # => ["x", "x", "x", "x"]
a.fill("z", 2, 2)   # => ["x", "x", "z", "z"]
a.fill("y", 0..1)   # => ["y", "y", "z", "z"]
a.fill {|i| i*i}    # => [0, 1, 4, 9]
a.fill(-3) {|i| i+100} # => [0, 101, 102, 103]
```

find_index

arr.find_index(*obj*) → *int* or nil
arr.find_index { | item | ... } → *int* or nil
arr.find_index → *enumerator*

Returns the index of the first object in *arr* that is == to *obj* or for which the block returns a true value. Returns nil if no match is found. See also Enumerable#select and Array#rindex.

```
a = [ "a", "b", "c", "b" ]
a.find_index("b")          # => 1
a.find_index("z")          # => nil
a.find_index {|item| item > "a"} # => 1
```

flatten

arr.flatten(*level* = -1) → *an_array*

Returns a new array that is a flattening of this array (recursively). That is, for every element that is an array, extracts its elements into the new array. The level parameter controls how deeply the flattening occurs. If less than zero, all subarrays are expanded. If zero, no flattening takes place. If greater than zero, only that depth of subarray is expanded.

```
s = [ 1, 2, 3 ]       # => [1, 2, 3]
t = [ 4, 5, 6, [7, 8] ] # => [4, 5, 6, [7, 8]]
a = [ s, t, 9, 10 ]   # => [[1, 2, 3], [4, 5, 6, [7, 8]], 9, 10]
a.flatten(0)          # => [[1, 2, 3], [4, 5, 6, [7, 8]], 9, 10]
a.flatten             # => [1, 2, 3, 4, 5, 6, 7, 8, 9, 10]
a.flatten(1)          # => [1, 2, 3, 4, 5, 6, [7, 8], 9, 10]
a.flatten(2)          # => [1, 2, 3, 4, 5, 6, 7, 8, 9, 10]
```

flatten!

arr.flatten!(*level* = -1) → *arr* or nil

Same as Array#flatten but modifies the receiver in place. Returns nil if no modifications were made (i.e., *arr* contains no subarrays).

```
a = [ 1, 2, [3, [4, 5] ] ]
a.flatten! # => [1, 2, 3, 4, 5]
a.flatten! # => nil
a          # => [1, 2, 3, 4, 5]
```

frozen?

arr.frozen? → *true* or *false*

Returns true if *arr* is frozen or if it is in the middle of being sorted.

index

arr.index(*obj*) → *int* or nil
arr.index { | item | ... } → *int* or nil

Synonym for Array#find_index.

Directive	Meaning
@	Move to absolute position
A	Sequence of bytes (space padded, count is width)
a	Sequence of bytes (null padded, count is width)
B	Bit string (most significant first)
b	Bit string (least significant first)
C	Unsigned byte
c	Byte
D, d	Double-precision float, native format
E	Double-precision float, little-endian byte order
e	Single-precision float, little-endian byte order
F, f	Single-precision float, native format
G	Double-precision float, network (big-endian) byte order
g	Single-precision float, network (big-endian) byte order
H	Hex string (high nibble first)
h	Hex string (low nibble first)
I	Unsigned integer
i	Integer
L	Unsigned long
l	Long
M	Quoted printable, MIME encoding (see RFC2045)
m	Base64-encoded string; by default adds linefeeds every 60 characters; "m0" suppresses linefeeds
N	Long, network (big-endian) byte order
n	Short, network (big-endian) byte order
P	Pointer to a structure (fixed-length string)
p	Pointer to a null-terminated string
Q, q	64-bit number
S	Unsigned short
s	Short
U	UTF-8
u	UU-encoded string
V	Long, little-endian byte order
v	Short, little-endian byte order
w	BER-compressed integer°
X	Back up a byte
x	Null byte
Z	Same as "a," except a null byte is appended if the * modifier is given
	° The octets of a BER-compressed integer represent an unsigned integer in base 128, most significant digit first, with as few digits as possible. Bit eight (the high bit) is set on each byte except the last (*Self-Describing Binary Data Representation*, MacLeod).

Table 14—Template characters for Array.pack

insert

arr.insert(index, ‹ obj ›⁺}) → arr

If *index* is not negative, inserts the given values before the element with the given index. If *index* is negative, adds the values after the element with the given index (counting from the end).

```
a = %w{ a b c d }
a.insert(2, 99)       # => ["a", "b", 99, "c", "d"]
a.insert(-2, 1, 2, 3) # => ["a", "b", 99, "c", 1, 2, 3, "d"]
a.insert(-1, "e")     # => ["a", "b", 99, "c", 1, 2, 3, "d", "e"]
```

join

arr.join(separator=$,) → str

Returns a string created by converting each element of the array to a string and concatenating them, separated each by *separator*.

```
[ "a", "b", "c" ].join      # => "abc"
[ "a", "b", "c" ].join("-") # => "a-b-c"
```

keep_if

arr.keep_if { | obj | … } → array or enumerator

Modifies *arr* by removing all elements for which *block* is false (see also Enumerable#select and Array.select!). Returns an Enumerator object if no block is given.

```
a = [ 1, 2, 3, 4, 5, 6, 7, 8, 9 ]
a.keep_if {|element| element < 6 } # => [1, 2, 3, 4, 5]
a                                  # => [1, 2, 3, 4, 5]
a.keep_if(&:odd?)                  # => [1, 3, 5]
a                                  # => [1, 3, 5]
```

last

arr.last → obj or nil
arr.last(count) → an_array

Returns the last element, or last *count* elements, of *arr*. If the array is empty, the first form returns nil, and the second returns an empty array. (first is defined by Enumerable.)

```
[ "w", "x", "y", "z" ].last    # => "z"
[ "w", "x", "y", "z" ].last(1) # => ["z"]
[ "w", "x", "y", "z" ].last(3) # => ["x", "y", "z"]
```

length

arr.length → int

Returns the number of elements in *arr*.

```
[ 1, nil, 3, nil, 5 ].length # => 5
```

map!

arr.map! { | obj | … } → arr

Synonym for Array#collect!.

pack

arr.pack (*template*) → *binary_string*

Packs the contents of *arr* into a binary sequence according to the directives in *template* (see Table 14, *Template characters for Array.pack*, on page 430). Directives A, a, and Z may be followed by a count, which gives the width of the resulting field. The remaining directives also may take a count, indicating the number of array elements to convert. If the count is an asterisk (*), all remaining array elements will be converted. The directives s S i I l L may be followed by an underscore (_) or bang (!) to use the underlying platform's native size for the specified type; otherwise, they use a platform-independent size. The directives s S i I l L q Q may be followed by a less than sign to signify little endian or greater than sign for big endian. Spaces are ignored in the template string. Comments starting with # to the next newline or end of string are also ignored. See also String#unpack on page 690.

```
a = [ "a", "b", "c" ]
n = [ 65, 66, 67 ]
a.pack("A3A3A3") # => "a␣␣b␣␣c␣␣"
a.pack("a3a3a3") # => "a\0\0b\0\0c\0\0"
n.pack("ccc")    # => "ABC"
```

permutation

arr.permutation(*size=arr.size*) → *enumerator*
arr.permutation(*size=arr.size*) { | array | ... } → *arr*}

Constructs all permutations of the elements of *arr* of length *size*. If called with a block, passes each permutation to that block; otherwise, returns an enumerator object. An empty result is generated if no permutations of the given length exist. See also Array#combination.

```
words = {}
File.readlines("/usr/share/dict/words").map(&:chomp).each do |word|
  words[word.downcase] = 1
end


%w{ c a m e l }.permutation do |letters|
  anagram = letters.join
  puts anagram if words[anagram]
end
```

produces:

```
camel
clame
cleam
macle
```

pop

arr.pop(‹ n ›*) → *obj* or nil

Removes the last element (or the last *n* elements) from *arr*. Returns whatever is removed or nil if the array is empty.

```
a = %w{ f r a b j o u s }
a.pop    # => "s"
a        # => ["f", "r", "a", "b", "j", "o", "u"]
a.pop(3) # => ["j", "o", "u"]
a        # => ["f", "r", "a", "b"]
```

product

arr.product(‹ *arrays* ›*) → *result_array*
arr.product(‹ *arrays* ›*) ‹ { | combination | ... } › → *arr*

Generates all combinations of selecting an element each from *arr* and from any arrays passed as arguments. The number of elements in the result is the product of the lengths of *arr* and the lengths of the arguments (so if any of these arrays is empty, the result will be an empty array). Each element in the result is an array containing n+1 elements, where n is the number of arguments. If a block is present, it will be passed each combination, and *arr* will be returned.

```
suits = %w{ C D H S }
ranks = [ *2..10, *%w{ J Q K A } ]
card_deck = suits.product(ranks).shuffle
card_deck.first(13) # => [["S", 8], ["D", "K"], ["C", 9], ["S", "A"], ["H", "K"],
                    # .. ["S", 4], ["S", 7], ["D", 2], ["H", 6], ["S", "Q"],
                    # .. ["D", 3], ["D", 4], ["H", 10]]
```

push

arr.push(‹ *obj* ›*) → *arr*

Appends the given argument(s) to *arr*.

```
a = [ "a", "b", "c" ]
a.push("d", "e", "f") # => ["a", "b", "c", "d", "e", "f"]
```

rassoc

arr.rassoc(*key*) → *an_array* or nil

Searches through the array whose elements are also arrays. Compares *key* with the second element of each contained array using ==. Returns the first contained array that matches. See also Array#assoc.

```
a = [ [ 1, "one"], [2, "two"], [3, "three"], ["ii", "two"] ]
a.rassoc("two")  # => [2, "two"]
a.rassoc("four") # => nil
```

reject!

arr.reject! { | item | ... } → *arr* or nil

Equivalent to Array#delete_if but returns nil if *arr* is unchanged. Also see Enumerable#reject.

repeated_combination

arr.repeated_combination(*length*) { | comb | ... } → *arr*
arr.repeated_combination(*length*) → *enum*

Creates the set of combinations of length *length* of the elements of *arr*. If *length* is greater than arr.size, elements will be allowed to repeat. Passes each combination to the block, or returns an enumerator if no block is given.

```
a = [1, 2, 3]
a.repeated_combination(2).to_a # => [[1, 1], [1, 2], [1, 3], [2, 2], [2, 3], [3,
                               # .. 3]]
a.repeated_combination(3).to_a # => [[1, 1, 1], [1, 1, 2], [1, 1, 3], [1, 2, 2],
                               # .. [1, 2, 3], [1, 3, 3], [2, 2, 2], [2, 2, 3],
                               # .. [2, 3, 3], [3, 3, 3]]
```

repeated_permutation

arr.repeated_permutation(*length*) { | comb | ... } → *arr*
arr.repeated_permutation(*length*) → *enum*

Creates the set of permutations of length *length* of the elements of *arr*. If *length* is greater than arr.size elements will be allowed to repeat. Passes each permutation to the block, or returns an enumerator if no block given.

```
a = [:a, :b]
a.repeated_permutation(2).to_a # => [[:a, :a], [:a, :b], [:b, :a], [:b, :b]]
a.repeated_permutation(3).to_a # => [[:a, :a, :a], [:a, :a, :b], [:a, :b, :a],
                               # .. [:a, :b, :b], [:b, :a, :a], [:b, :a, :b],
                               # .. [:b, :b, :a], [:b, :b, :b]]
```

replace

arr.replace(*other_array*) → *arr*

Replaces the contents of *arr* with the contents of *other_array*, truncating or expanding *arr* if necessary.

```
a = [ "a", "b", "c", "d", "e" ]
a.replace([ "x", "y", "z" ]) # => ["x", "y", "z"]
a                            # => ["x", "y", "z"]
```

reverse

arr.reverse → *an_array*

Returns a new array using *arr*'s elements in reverse order.

```
[ "a", "b", "c" ].reverse # => ["c", "b", "a"]
[ 1 ].reverse            # => [1]
```

reverse!

arr.reverse! → *arr*

Reverses *arr* in place.

```
a = [ "a", "b", "c" ]
a.reverse!    # => ["c", "b", "a"]
a             # => ["c", "b", "a"]
[ 1 ].reverse! # => [1]
```

reverse_each

arr.reverse_each ‹ { | item | ... } › } → *arr*

Same as Array#each but traverses *arr* in reverse order.

```
a = [ "a", "b", "c" ]
a.reverse_each {|x| print x, " " }
```

produces:

```
c b a
```

rindex

Returns the index of the last object in *arr* that is == to *obj* or for which the block returns a true value. Returns nil if no match is found. See also Enumerable#select and Array#index.

```
a = [ "a", "b", "e", "b", "d" ]
a.rindex("b")                    # => 3
a.rindex("z")                    # => nil
a.rindex {|item| item =~ /[aeiou]/} # => 2
```

rotate

Returns a new array containing the elements of *arr* rotated *places* positions (so that the element that originally was at arr[places] is now at the front of the array. *places* may be negative.

```
a = [1, 2, 3, 4, 5]
a.rotate(2)  # => [3, 4, 5, 1, 2]
a.rotate(-2) # => [4, 5, 1, 2, 3]
```

rotate!

Rotate *arr* in place.

sample

Returns min(n, arr.size) random elements from *arr* or nil if *arr* is empty and *n* is not given.

```
a = [ "a", "b", "c", "d" ]
a.sample     # => "c"
a.sample(3)  # => ["b", "a", "c"]
a.sample(6)  # => ["b", "d", "a", "c"]
b = []
b.sample     # => nil
```

select!

Modifies *arr* by removing all elements for which *block* is false (see also Enumerable#select and Array#keep_if). Returns nil if no changes were made, returns an Enumerator object if no block is given, or returns *arr*.

```
a = [ 1, 2, 3, 4, 5, 6, 7, 8, 9 ]
a.select! {|element| element < 6 } # => [1, 2, 3, 4, 5]
a                                  # => [1, 2, 3, 4, 5]
a.select! {|element| element < 8 } # => nil
a                                  # => [1, 2, 3, 4, 5]
```

shift

Returns the first *n* elements (or the first element with no argument) of *arr* and removes it (shifting all other elements down by one). Returns nil if the array is empty.

```
args = [ "-m", "-q", "-v", "filename" ]
args.shift    # => "-m"
args.shift(2) # => ["-q", "-v"]
args          # => ["filename"]
```

shuffle

arr.shuffle → *an_array*
arr.shuffle(random: *rng*)→ *an_array*

Returns an array containing the elements of *arr* in random order. You can pass it a random number generator using the random: keyword parameter. Passing rngs with the same seed makes the shuffle deterministic.

New in 2.0

```
[ 1, 2, 3, 4, 5 ].shuffle                      # => [4, 5, 2, 1, 3]
[ 1, 2, 3, 4, 5 ].shuffle                      # => [5, 2, 1, 4, 3]
[ 1, 2, 3, 4, 5 ].shuffle(random: Random.new(123)) # => [2, 4, 5, 1, 3]
[ 1, 2, 3, 4, 5 ].shuffle(random: Random.new(123)) # => [2, 4, 5, 1, 3]
```

shuffle!

arr.shuffle! → *an_array*
arr.shuffle!(random: *rng*)→ *an_array*

Randomizes the order of the elements of *arr* in place.

size

arr.size → *int*

Synonym for Array#length.

slice

arr.slice(*int*) → *obj*
arr.slice(*start, length*) → *an_array*
arr.slice(*range*) → *an_array*

Synonym for Array#[ ].

```
a = [ "a", "b", "c", "d", "e" ]
a.slice(2) + a.slice(0) + a.slice(1) # => "cab"
a.slice(6)            # => nil
a.slice(1, 2)         # => ["b", "c"]
a.slice(1..3)         # => ["b", "c", "d"]
a.slice(4..7)         # => ["e"]
a.slice(6..10)        # => nil
a.slice(-3, 3)        # => ["c", "d", "e"]

# special cases
a.slice(5)     # => nil
a.slice(5, 1)  # => []
a.slice(5..10) # => []
```

slice!

arr.slice!(*int*) → *obj* or nil
arr.slice!(*start, length*) → *an_array* or nil
arr.slice!(*range*) → *an_array* or nil

Deletes the element(s) given by an index (optionally with a length) or by a range. Returns the deleted object, subarray, or nil if the index is out of range.

```
a = [ "a", "b", "c" ]
a.slice!(1)   # => "b"
a             # => ["a", "c"]
a.slice!(-1)  # => "c"
a             # => ["a"]
a.slice!(100) # => nil
a             # => ["a"]
```

sort!

arr.sort! → *arr*
arr.sort! { | a,b | ... } → *arr*

Sorts *arr* in place (see Enumerable#sort). *arr* is effectively frozen while a sort is in progress.

```
a = [ "d", "a", "e", "c", "b" ]
a.sort!  # => ["a", "b", "c", "d", "e"]
a        # => ["a", "b", "c", "d", "e"]
```

sort_by!

arr.sort_by! { | a | ... } → *arr*
arr.sort_by! → *enum*

Sorts *arr* in place (see Enumerable#sort_by). *arr* is effectively frozen while a sort is in progress.

```
a = [ 5, 2, 7, 4, 8, 9 ]
# Sort even numbers before odd, and then by rank
a.sort_by! {|e| [ e & 1, e ] } # => [2, 4, 8, 5, 7, 9]
a                              # => [2, 4, 8, 5, 7, 9]
```

to_a

arr.to_a → *arr*
array_subclass.to_a → *array*

If *arr* is an array, returns *arr*. If *arr* is a subclass of Array, invokes to_ary and uses the result to create a new array object.

to_ary

arr.to_ary → *arr*

Returns *arr*.

to_s

arr.to_s → *str*

Returns a string representation of *arr*. (In Ruby 1.9, the array as a literal.)

```
[ 1, 3, 5, 7, 9 ].to_s # => "[1, 3, 5, 7, 9]"
```

transpose

arr.transpose → *an_array*

Assumes that *arr* is an array of arrays and transposes the rows and columns.

```
a = [[1,2], [3,4], [5,6]]
a.transpose # => [[1, 3, 5], [2, 4, 6]]
```

uniq

arr.uniq ‹{ |element| ... }› → *an_array*

Returns a new array by removing duplicate values in *arr*, where duplicates are detected by comparing using eql? and hash. If the block is present, the comparisons are made based on the values returned by that block for each element in the array.

```
a = %w{ C a a b b A c a }
a.uniq                              # => ["C", "a", "b", "A", "c"]
a.uniq {|element| element.downcase } # => ["C", "a", "b"]
a.uniq(&:upcase)                    # => ["C", "a", "b"]
```

uniq!

arr.uniq! ‹{ |element| ... }› → *arr* or nil

Same as Array#uniq but modifies the receiver in place. Returns nil if no changes are made (that is, no duplicates are found).

```
a = [ "a", "a", "b", "b", "c" ]
a.uniq!   # => ["a", "b", "c"]
b = [ "a", "b", "c" ]
b.uniq!   # => nil
```

unshift

arr.unshift(‹ *obj* ›⁺}) → *arr*

Prepends object(s) to *arr*.

```
a = [ "b", "c", "d" ]
a.unshift("a")  # => ["a", "b", "c", "d"]
a.unshift(1, 2) # => [1, 2, "a", "b", "c", "d"]
```

values_at

arr.values_at(‹ *selector* ›*) → *an_array*

New in 2.0

Returns an array containing the elements in *arr* corresponding to the given selector(s). The selectors may be either integer indices or ranges. Returns nil for selectors beyond the bounds of the array.

```
a = %w{ a b c d e f }
a.values_at(1, 3, 5)          # => ["b", "d", "f"]
a.values_at(1, 3, 5, 7)       # => ["b", "d", "f", nil]
a.values_at(-1, -3, -5, -7)   # => ["f", "d", "b", nil]
a.values_at(1..3, 2...5)      # => ["b", "c", "d", "c", "d", "e"]
a.values_at(5..7, 1..2)       # => ["f", nil, nil, "b", "c"]
```

BasicObject

BasicObject is the root of Ruby's class hierarchy. It deliberately has just a few methods, allowing it to be conveniently used as the basis for a number of metaprogramming techniques.

If you write code in a direct descendent of BasicObject, you will not have unqualified access to the methods in Kernel, which normally get mixed in to Object. This example illustrates how to invoke Kernel methods explicitly:

```ruby
class SimpleBuilder < BasicObject
  def __puts_at_indent__(string)
    ::Kernel.puts " " * @indent + string
  end
  def method_missing(name, *args, &block)
    @indent ||= 0
    __puts_at_indent__("<#{name}>")
    @indent += 2
    __puts_at_indent__(args.join) unless args.empty?
    yield if ::Kernel.block_given?
    @indent -= 2
    __puts_at_indent__("</#{name}>")
  end
end


r = SimpleBuilder.new
r.person do
  r.name "Dave"
  r.address do
    r.street "123 Main"
    r.city   "Pleasantville"
  end
end
```

produces:

```
<person>
  <name>
    Dave
  </name>
  <address>
    <street>
      123 Main
    </street>
    <city>
      Pleasantville
    </city>
  </address>
</person>
```

Instance Methods

!   ! *obj* → *true* or *false*

Returns false unless *obj* is false. Because it's in BasicObject, ! is defined for all objects in Ruby.

==   *obj* == *other_obj* → *true* or *false*

Equality — At the BasicObject level, == returns true only if *obj* and *other_obj* are the same object. Typically, this method is overridden in descendent classes to provide class-specific meaning.

!=   *obj* != *other* → *true* or *false*

Returns the opposite of BasicObject#==.

__id__   *obj*.__id__ → *fixnum*

Synonym for Object#object_id. Prior to Ruby 1.9.3, this was an instance method of class Object.

---

equal?   *obj*.equal?(*other_obj*) → *true* or *false*

Alias for BasicObject#==.

---

instance_eval   *obj*.instance_eval(*string* ‹, *file* ‹, *line*››) → *other_obj*
                                        obj.instance_eval { | obj | ... } → *other_obj*}

Evaluates a string containing Ruby source code, or the given block, within the context of the receiver (*obj*). To set the context, the variable self is set to *obj* while the code is executing, giving the code access to *obj*'s instance variables. In the version of instance_eval that takes a String, the optional second and third parameters supply a filename and starting line number that are used when reporting compilation errors.

```ruby
class Klass
  def initialize
    @secret = 99
  end
end
k = Klass.new
k.instance_eval { @secret } # => 99
```

When metaprogramming, instance_eval is often used to execute the methods in a block in the context of the caller:

```ruby
class Recorder < BasicObject
  attr_reader :__calls__
  def method_missing(name, *args, &block)
    @__calls__ ||= []
    @__calls__ << [ name, args ]
  end
  def record(&block)
    instance_eval(&block)
  end
end
```

```
r = Recorder.new
r.record do
  disable "safety"
  pull    "control rod", dir: "out"
  run
end

p r.__calls__
```

produces:

```
[[:disable, ["safety"]], [:pull, ["control rod", {:dir=>"out"}]], [:run, []]]
```

instance_exec   *obj*.instance_exec(‹ *args* ›*) { | *args* | ... } → *other_obj*

Executes the block with self set to *obj*, passing *args* as parameters to the block.

```
class Dummy < BasicObject
  def initialize
    @iv = 33
  end
  def double_and_call(value, &block)
    instance_exec(value*2, &block)
  end
end

d = Dummy.new
d.double_and_call(22) do |param|
  ::Kernel::puts "Parameter = #{param}"
  ::Kernel::puts "@iv = #{@iv}"
end
```

produces:

```
Parameter = 44
@iv = 33
```

__send__   *obj*.__send__(*symbol* ‹, *args* ›*‹, *&block* ›) → *other_obj*

Invokes the method identified by *symbol*, passing it any arguments and block.

```
class Klass < BasicObject
  def hello(*args)
    "Hello " + args.join(' ')
  end
end
k = Klass.new
k.__send__ :hello, "gentle", "readers" # => "Hello gentle readers"
```

Private Instance Methods

method_missing   method_missing(*symbol* ‹ , **args* ›) → *other_obj*

Invoked by Ruby when *obj* is sent a message it cannot handle. *symbol* is the symbol for the method called, and *args* are any arguments that were passed to it. method_missing can be used to implement proxies, delegators, and forwarders. It can also be used to simulate the existence of methods in the receiver, as the example at the start of this section shows.

singleton_method_added   singleton_method_added(*symbol*)

Invoked as a callback whenever a singleton method is added to the receiver.

```ruby
module Chatty
  def Chatty.singleton_method_added(id)
    puts "Adding #{id} to #{self.name}"
  end
  def self.one()     end
  def two()          end
end
def Chatty.three() end
```

produces:

```
Adding singleton_method_added to Chatty
Adding one to Chatty
Adding three to Chatty
```

You can add the hook to any object:

```ruby
obj = "cat"

def obj.singleton_method_added(id)
  puts "Adding #{id} to #{self}"
end

def obj.speak
  puts "meow"
end
```

produces:

```
Adding singleton_method_added to cat
Adding speak to cat
```

singleton_method_removed   singleton_method_removed(*symbol*)

Invoked as a callback whenever a singleton method is removed from the receiver.

```ruby
module Chatty
  def Chatty.singleton_method_removed(id)
    puts "Removing #{id}"
  end
  def self.one()     end
  def two()          end
  def Chatty.three() end
```

```
  class <<self
    remove_method :three
    remove_method :one
  end
end
```

produces:

```
Removing three
Removing one
```

---

singleton_method_undefined   singleton_method_undefined(*symbol*)

Invoked as a callback whenever a singleton method is undefined in the receiver.

```
module Chatty
  def Chatty.singleton_method_undefined(id)
    puts "Undefining #{id}"
  end
  def Chatty.one()    end
  class << self
     undef_method(:one)
  end
end
```

produces:

```
Undefining one
```

Class **Bignum** < Integer

Bignum objects hold integers outside the range of Fixnum—Bignum objects are created automatically when integer calculations would otherwise overflow. When a calculation involving Bignum objects returns a result that will fit in a Fixnum, the result is automatically converted.

For the purposes of the bitwise operations and [ ], a Bignum is treated as if it were an infinite-length bitstring with 2's complement representation.

While Fixnum values are immediate, Bignum objects are not—assignment and parameter passing work with references to objects, not the objects themselves.

Instance Methods

Arithmetic operations

Performs various arithmetic operations on *big*.

big	+	*number*	Addition
big	–	*number*	Subtraction
big	*	*number*	Multiplication
big	/	*number*	Division
big	%	*number*	Modulo
big	**	*number*	Exponentiation
big	-@		Unary minus

Bit operations

Performs various operations on the binary representations of the Bignum.

~ *big*			Invert bits
big			*number*	Bitwise *or*
big	&	*number*	Bitwise *and*
big	^	*number*	Bitwise exclusive or
big	<<	*number*	Left-shift *number* bits
big	>>	*number*	Right-shift *number* bits (with sign extension)

<=>   *big* <=> *number* → -1, 0, +1, or nil

Comparison—Returns -1, 0, or +1 depending on whether *big* is less than, equal to, or greater than *number*. This is the basis for the tests in Comparable.

==   *big* == *obj* → *true* or *false*

Returns true only if *obj* has the same value as *big*. Contrast this with Bignum#eql?, which requires *obj* to be a Bignum.

```
68719476736 == 68719476736.0 # => true
```

[ ]   *big*[*n*] → 0, 1

Bit Reference—Returns the nth bit in the (assumed) binary representation of *big*, where *big*[0] is the least significant bit.

```
a = 9**15     # that's 9 raised to the 15th power

50.downto(0) do |n|
  print a[n]
end
```

produces:

```
000101110110100000111000011110010100111100010111001
```

---

abs   *big*.abs → *bignum*

Returns the absolute value of *big*.

```
1234567890987654321.abs  # => 1234567890987654321
-1234567890987654321.abs # => 1234567890987654321
```

---

div   *big*.div(*number*) → *other_number*

Synonym for Bignum#/.

```
-1234567890987654321.div(13731)      # => -89910996357706
-1234567890987654321.div(13731.0)    # => -89910996357706
-1234567890987654321.div(-987654321) # => 1249999989
```

---

divmod   *big*.divmod(*number*) → *array*

See Numeric#divmod on page 595.

---

eql?   *big*.eql?(*obj*) → *true* or *false*

Returns true only if *obj* is a Bignum with the same value as *big*. Contrast this with Bignum#==, which performs type conversions.

```
68719476736.eql? 68719476736   # => true
68719476736   ==  68719476736   # => true
68719476736.eql? 68719476736.0 # => false
68719476736   ==  68719476736.0 # => true
```

---

fdiv   *big*.fdiv(*number*) → *float*

Returns the floating-point result of dividing *big* by *number*. Alias for Bignum#quo.

```
-1234567890987654321.fdiv(13731)      # => -89910996357705.52
-1234567890987654321.fdiv(13731.0)    # => -89910996357705.52
-1234567890987654321.fdiv(-987654321) # => 1249999989.609375
```

magnitude

big.magnitude → bignum

Returns the magnitude of *big* (the distance of *big* from the origin of the number line). Synonym for Bignum#abs. See also Complex#magnitude.

modulo

big.modulo(number) → number

Synonym for Bignum#%.

remainder

big.remainder(number) → other_number

Returns the remainder after dividing *big* by *number*.

```
-1234567890987654321.remainder(13731)    # => -6966
-1234567890987654321.remainder(13731.24) # => -9906.22531493148
```

size

big.size → integer

Returns the number of bytes in the machine representation of *big*.

```
(256**10 - 1).size # => 12
(256**20 - 1).size # => 20
(256**40 - 1).size # => 40
```

to_f

big.to_f → float

Converts *big* to a Float. If *big* doesn't fit in a Float, the result is infinity.

to_s

big.to_s(base=10) → str

Returns a string containing the representation of *big* radix *base* (2 to 36).

```
12345654321.to_s       # => "12345654321"
12345654321.to_s(2)    # => "1011011111110110111011110000110001"
12345654321.to_s(8)    # => "133766736061"
12345654321.to_s(16)   # => "2dfdbbc31"
12345654321.to_s(26)   # => "1dp1pc6d"
78546939656932.to_s(36) # => "rubyrules"
```

Binding

Objects of class Binding encapsulate the execution context at some particular place in the code and retain this context for future use. Access to the variables, methods, value of self, and possibly an iterator block accessible in this context are all retained. Binding objects can be created using Object#binding and are made available to the callback of Object#set_trace_func and to the block passed to TracePoint.new.

New in 2.0

These binding objects can be passed as the second argument of the Object#eval method, establishing an environment for the evaluation.

```
class Demo
  def initialize(n)
    @secret = n
  end
  def get_binding
    return binding()
  end
end

k1 = Demo.new(99)
b1 = k1.get_binding
k2 = Demo.new(-3)
b2 = k2.get_binding

# Pass to eval...
eval("@secret", b1) # => 99
# Or eval via binding...
b2.eval("@secret")  # => -3

eval("@secret")     # => nil
```

Instance Methods

eval

bind.eval(*string* ‹ , *file* ‹ , *line* › ›) → *obj*

Evaluates the Ruby code in *string* using the context of *bind*. Equivalent to calling Object#eval with a second argument of *bind*. See the start of this section for an example.

Class   Class   <   Module

Classes in Ruby are first-class objects—each is an instance of class Class.

When a new class is defined (typically using class SomeName ... end), an object of type Class is created and assigned to a constant (SomeName, in this case). When Name.new is called to create a new object, the new instance method in Class is run by default, which in turn invokes allocate to allocate memory for the object, before finally calling the new object's initialize method.

Class Methods

new   Class.new(*super_class*=Object) ‹ { ... } › → *cls*

Creates a new anonymous (unnamed) class with the given superclass (or Object if no parameter is given). If called with a block, that block is used as the body of the class. Within the block, self is set to the class instance.

```ruby
name = "Dave"
FriendlyClass = Class.new do
  define_method :hello do
    "Hello, #{name}"
  end
end
f = FriendlyClass.new
f.hello    # => "Hello, Dave"
```

Instance Methods

allocate   *cls*.allocate → *obj*

Allocates space for a new object of *cls*'s class. The returned object must be an instance of *cls*. Calling new is basically the same as calling the class method allocate to create an object, followed by calling initialize on that new object. You cannot override allocate in normal programs; Ruby invokes it without going through conventional method dispatch.

```ruby
class MyClass
  def self.another_new(*args)
    o = allocate
    o.send(:initialize, *args)
    o
  end
  def initialize(a, b, c)
    @a, @b, @c = a, b, c
  end
end

mc = MyClass.another_new(4, 5, 6)
mc.inspect # => "#<MyClass:0x007fbdab10f430 @a=4, @b=5, @c=6>"
```

new   *cls*.new(‹ *args* ›*) → *obj*

Calls allocate to create a new object of *cls*'s class and then invokes the newly created object's initialize method, passing it *args*.

superclass

cls.superclass → super_class or nil

Returns the superclass of *cls* or returns nil.

```
Class.superclass        # => Module
Object.superclass       # => BasicObject
BasicObject.superclass  # => nil
```

Private Instance Methods

inherited

cls.inherited(sub_class)

Invoked by Ruby when a subclass of *cls* is created. The new subclass is passed as a parameter.

```
class Top
  def self.inherited(sub)
    puts "New subclass: #{sub}"
  end
end

class Middle < Top
end

class Bottom < Middle
end
```

produces:

```
New subclass: Middle
New subclass: Bottom
```

Comparable

The Comparable mixin is used by classes whose objects may be ordered. The class must define the <=> operator, which compares the receiver against another object, returning -1, 0, or +1 depending on whether the receiver is less than, equal to, or greater than the other object. Comparable uses <=> to implement the conventional comparison operators (<, <=, ==, >=, and >) and the method between?.

```ruby
class CompareOnSize
  include Comparable
  attr :str
  def <=>(other)
    str.length <=> other.str.length
  end
  def initialize(str)
    @str = str
  end
end

s1 = CompareOnSize.new("Z")
s2 = CompareOnSize.new([1,2])
s3 = CompareOnSize.new("XXX")

s1 < s2              # => true
s2.between?(s1, s3) # => true
s3.between?(s1, s2) # => false
[ s3, s2, s1 ].sort # => ["Z", [1, 2], "XXX"]
```

Instance Methods

Comparisons

$obj < other\_object \rightarrow$ *true* or *false*
$obj <= other\_object \rightarrow$ *true* or *false*
$obj == other\_object \rightarrow$ *true* or *false*
$obj >= other\_object \rightarrow$ *true* or *false*
$obj > other\_object \rightarrow$ *true* or *false*

Compares two objects based on the receiver's <=> method.

between?

obj.between?(*min, max*) $\rightarrow$ *true* or *false*

Returns false if *obj* <=> *min* is less than zero or if *obj* <=> *max* is greater than zero; returns true otherwise.

```ruby
3.between?(1, 5)            # => true
6.between?(1, 5)            # => false
'cat'.between?('ant', 'dog') # => true
'gnu'.between?('ant', 'dog') # => false
```

Complex < Numeric

Represents complex numbers, represented internally as numbers with a real part and an imaginary part, both of which can be any scalar number. Note that scalar comparison operations (<=>, <, and so on) are not defined on complex numbers (which would argue that Complex should not be a subclass of Numeric, but that ship has sailed). Also see the standard library named complex on page 738 for a way to add complex number support to standard math functions; also see the mathn library on page 768 for a way of integrating complex numbers into regular arithmetic (so that the square root of -1 returns Complex::I).

```
v1 = Complex(2,3)     # => (2+3i)
v2 = Complex("0+2i")  # => (0+2i)
v1 + v2               # => (2+5i)
v1 * v2               # => (-6+4i)
v2**2                 # => (-4+0i)
v2**2 == -4           # => true

# Euler's theorem
include Math
E**(PI*Complex::I) # => (-1.0+1.2246467991473532e-16i)
```

Class Constants

Complex::I   The imaginary unit.

Class Methods

polar
Complex.polar(*magnitude, angle*) → *complex*

Returns the complex number represented by the given polar coordinates.

```
Complex.polar(1.23, 0.5)    # => 1.0794265511251584+0.58969341248316696i
Complex.polar(1, Math::PI/2)  # => 6.123233995736766e-17+1.0i
```

rect
Complex.rect(*read, imag*) → *complex*

Returns the complex number represented by the given real and imaginary parts.

```
Complex.rect(1.23, 0.5)  # => 1.23+0.5i
```

rectangular
Complex.rectangular(*read, imag*) → *complex*

Synonym for Complex.rect.

Instance Methods

Arithmetic operations

Performs various arithmetic operations on *complex*.

complex	+	*numeric*	Addition
complex	–	*numeric*	Subtraction
complex	*	*numeric*	Multiplication
complex	/	*numeric*	Division
complex	**	*numeric*	Exponentiation
complex	-@		Unary minus
complex	-+		Unary plus

==

complex == *other* → *true* or *false*

Returns true if *complex* does equals *other*, converting *other* to a complex number if necessary.

```
Complex::I == Complex(0,1) # => true
Complex::I == Complex(1,0) # => false
Complex(1,0) == 1          # => true
Complex(1,0) == "1"        # => false
```

---

abs

complex.abs → *number*

Synonym for Complex#magnitude.

---

abs2

complex.abs2 → *number*

Returns the square of the absolute value (magnitude) of *complex*.

```
Complex::I.abs2   # => 1
Complex(1,1).abs2 # => 2
```

---

angle

complex.angle → *number*

Returns the angle between the x-axis and a line from the origin to *complex*. By convention, Complex(0,0).angl} is 0.

```
Complex(1, 0).angle # => 0.0
Complex(1, 1).angle # => 0.7853981633974483
Complex(0, 1).angle # => 1.5707963267948966
```

---

arg

complex.arg → *number*

Synonym for Complex#angle.

---

conj

complex.conj → *a_complex*

Synonym for Complex#conjugate.

conjugate

complex.conjugate → *a_complex*

Returns the conjugate of *complex* (the reflection of *complex* around the x-axis).

```
Complex::I.conjugate    # => (0-1i)
Complex(1,1).conjugate # => (1-1i)
```

denominator

complex.denominator → *number*

Returns the lowest common multiple of the denominators of the real and imaginary parts of *complex*.

```
Complex("1/3+1/4i").denominator # => 12
Complex(-2, 4).denominator      # => 1
```

eql?

complex.eql(*other*) → *true* or *false*

Returns true only if *other* is a complex number with real and imaginary parts eql? to *complex*'s.

```
Complex(1, 0).eql?(Complex(1,0))     # => true
Complex(1, 0).eql?(Complex(1.0, 0)) # => false
Complex(1, 0).eql?(1)                # => false
Complex(1, 0) == Complex(1,0)        # => true
Complex(1, 0) == Complex(1.0, 0)     # => true
Complex(1, 0) == 1                    # => true
```

fdiv

complex.fdiv(*other*) → *a_complex*

Returns *complex* / *other* after converting the real and imaginary parts of *complex* to floats. (Contrast with Complex#quo.)

```
c1 = Complex(1, 2)
c2 = Complex(2, 2)
c1 /c2      # => ((3/4)+(1/4)*i)
c1.fdiv(c2) # => (0.75+0.25i)
```

imag

complex.imag → *number*

Returns the imaginary part of *complex*.

```
Complex(2, -3).imag # => -3
```

imaginary

complex.imaginary → *number*

Synonym for Complex#imag.

magnitude

complex.magnitude → *int* or *float*

Returns the magnitude of *complex* (the distance of *complex* from the origin of the number line). The positive square root of $real^2 + imag^2$.

```
Complex(1, 1).magnitude # => 1.4142135623730951
Complex(3, 4).magnitude # => 5.0
Complex::I.magnitude    # => 1
```

numerator

complex.numerator → *a_complex*

Returns the numerator, treating the real and complex parts of *complex* as fractions to be combined over a common denominator.

```
c = Complex('2/3+3/4i')
c.numerator   # => (8+9i)
c.denominator # => 12
```

phase

complex.phase → [*magnitude, angle*]

Returns the phase angle of *complex* (the angle between the positive x-axis and the line from the origin to (*real, imag*)), measured in radians.

```
Complex(3, 4).phase  # => 0.9272952180016122
Complex(-3, 4).phase # => 2.214297435588181
```

polar

complex.polar → [*magnitude, angle*]

Returns *complex* as polar coordinates.

```
Complex(1,1).polar   # => [1.4142135623730951, 0.7853981633974483]
Complex(-2,-3).polar # => [3.605551275463989, -2.158798930342464]
```

quo

complex.quo(*other*) → *a_complex*

Returns *complex* / *other* after converting the real and imaginary parts of *complex* to rational numbers. (Contrast with Complex#fdiv.)

```
c1 = Complex(1, 2)
c2 = Complex(2, 2)
c1 /c2     # => ((3/4)+(1/4)*i)
c1.quo(c2) # => ((3/4)+(1/4)*i)
```

rationalize

complex.rationalize(*eps=nil*) → *rational*

Returns the real part of *complex* as a rational number, raising an exception if the imaginary part is not zero. The argument is always ignored. Effectively a synonym for Complex.to_r.

```
Complex(2.5, 0).rationalize # => (5/2)
```

rect

complex.rect → [*complex*.real, *complex*.imag]

Returns an array containing the real and imaginary components of *complex*.

```
Complex::I.rect # => [0, 1]
```

rectangular

complex.rectangular → [*complex*.real, *complex*.imag]

Synonym for Complex#rect.

real

complex.real → *number*

Returns the real part of *complex*.

```
Complex(2, 3).real # => 2
```

real?

complex.real? → *false*

Complex numbers are never real numbers (even if their imaginary part is zero).

```
Complex(1, 1).real? # => false
Complex(1, 0).real? # => false
```

to_f

complex.to_f → *float*

Returns the real part of *complex* as a float, raising an exception if the imaginary part is not zero.

```
Complex(2, 0).to_f # => 2.0
```

to_i

complex.to_i → *integer*

Returns the real part of *complex* as an integer, raising an exception if the imaginary part is not zero.

```
Complex(2.2, 0).to_i # => 2
```

to_r

complex.to_r → *rational*

Returns the real part of *complex* as a rational number, raising an exception if the imaginary part is not zero.

```
Complex(2.5, 0).to_r # => (5/2)
```

Dir

Objects of class Dir are directory streams representing directories in the underlying file system. They provide a variety of ways to list directories and their contents. See also File on page 488.

The directory used in these examples contains the two regular files (config.h and main.rb), the parent directory (..), and the directory itself (.).

Mixes In

Enumerable: all?, any?, chunk, collect, collect_concat, count, cycle, detect, drop, drop_while, each_cons, each_entry, each_slice, each_with_index, each_with_object, entries, find, find_all, find_index, first, flat_map, grep, group_by, include?, inject, lazy, map, max, max_by, member?, min, min_by, minmax, minmax_by, none?, one?, partition, reduce, reject, reverse_each, select, slice_before, sort, sort_by, take, take_while, to_a, zip

Class Methods

[ ]
Dir[glob_pattern] → array

Equivalent to calling Dir.glob(glob_pattern,0).

chdir
Dir.chdir(‹ dir ›) → 0
Dir.chdir(‹ dir ›) { | path | … } → obj

Changes the current working directory of the process to the given string. When called without an argument, changes the directory to the value of the environment variable HOME or LOGDIR. Raises a SystemCallError (probably Errno::ENOENT) if the target directory does not exist.

If a block is given, it is passed the name of the new current directory, and the block is executed with that as the current directory. The original working directory is restored when the block exits. The return value of chdir is the value of the block. chdir blocks can be nested, but in a multithreaded program an error will be raised if a thread attempts to open a chdir block while another thread has one open. This is because the underlying operating system only understands the concept of a single current working directory at any one time.

```
Dir.chdir("/private/var/log") # => 0
Dir.pwd                       # => "/private/var/log"
Dir.chdir("/private/tmp") do
  Dir.pwd                     # => "/private/tmp"
  Dir.chdir("/usr") do
    Dir.pwd                   # => "/usr"
  end
  Dir.pwd                     # => "/private/tmp"
end
Dir.pwd                       # => "/private/var/log"
```

chroot
Dir.chroot(dirname) → 0

Changes this process's idea of the file system root. Only a privileged process may make this call. Not available on all platforms. On Unix systems, see chroot(2) for more information.

```
Dir.chdir("/production/secure/root")
Dir.chroot("/production/secure/root")    #=> 0
Dir.pwd                                   #=> "/"
```

delete   Dir.delete(*dirname*) → 0

Deletes the named directory. Raises a subclass of SystemCallError if the directory isn't empty.

entries   Dir.entries(*dirname*) → *array*

Returns an array containing all of the filenames in the given directory. Will raise a System-CallError if the named directory doesn't exist.

```
Dir.entries("testdir") # => [".", "..", ".svn", "config.h", "main.rb"]
```

exist?   Dir.exist?(*path*) → *true* or *false*

Returns true if *path* exists and is a directory. Alias for File.directory?.

```
Dir.exist?("/tmp")  # => true
Dir.exist?("/temp") # => false
```

exists?   Dir.exists?(*path*) → *true* or *false*

Alias for Dir.exist?.

foreach   Dir.foreach(*dirname*) { | filename | ... } → nil

Calls the block once for each entry in the *dirname*, passing the filename as a parameter.

```
Dir.foreach("testdir") {|x| puts "Got #{x}" }
```

produces:

```
Got .
Got ..
Got .svn
Got config.h
Got main.rb
```

getwd   Dir.getwd → *dirname*

Returns a string containing the canonical path to the current working directory of this process. Note that on some operating systems this name may not be the name you gave to Dir.chdir. On OS X, for example, /tmp is a symlink.

```
Dir.chdir("/tmp") # => 0
Dir.getwd         # => "/private/tmp"
```

---

glob   Dir.glob(*glob_pattern*, ‹*flags*›) → *array*
                          Dir.glob(*glob_pattern*, ‹*flags*›) { | filename | ... } → false

---

Returns the filenames found by expanding the pattern given in *glob_pattern*, either as elements in *array* or as parameters to the block. Note that this pattern is not a regexp (it's closer to a shell glob). See File.fnmatch on page 491 for the meaning of the *flags* parameter. Case sensitivity depends on your system (so File::FNM_CASEFOLD is ignored). Metacharacters in the pattern are as follows:

---

*	Any sequence of characters in a filename: * will match all files, c* will match all files beginning with *c*, *c will match all files ending with *c*, and *c* will match all files that have *c* in their name.
**	Matches zero or more directories (so **/fred matches a file named *fred* in or below the current directory).
?	Matches any one character in a filename.
[chars]	Matches any one of *chars*. If the first character in *chars* is ^, matches any character not in the remaining set.
{patt,...}	Matches one of the patterns specified between braces. These patterns may contain other metacharacters.
\	Removes any special significance in the next character.

```
Dir.chdir("testdir")                    # => 0
Dir["config.?"]                         # => ["config.h"]
Dir.glob("config.?")                    # => ["config.h"]
Dir.glob("*.[a-z][a-z]")                # => ["main.rb"]
Dir.glob("*.[^r]*")                     # => ["config.h"]
Dir.glob("*.{rb,h}")                    # => ["main.rb", "config.h"]
Dir.glob("*")                           # => ["config.h", "main.rb"]
Dir.glob("*", File::FNM_DOTMATCH)       # => [".", "..", ".svn", "config.h", "main.rb"]

Dir.chdir("..")                         # => 0
Dir.glob("code/**/fib*.rb")             # => ["code/irb/fibonacci_sequence.rb",
                                        # .. "code/rdoc/fib_example.rb"]
Dir.glob("**/rdoc/fib*.rb")             # => ["code/rdoc/fib_example.rb"]
```

---

home   Dir.home(‹*user_name*›) → *string*

Returns the home directory of the given user (or the current user if no argument is given).

```
Dir.home               # => "/Users/dave"
Dir.home("nobody")     # => "/var/empty"
```

---

mkdir   Dir.mkdir(*dirname* ‹ , *permissions*›) → 0

Makes a new directory named *dirname*, with permissions specified by the optional parameter *permissions*. The permissions may be modified by the value of File.umask and are ignored on Windows. Raises a SystemCallError if the directory cannot be created. See also the discussion of permissions on page 488.

new

Dir.new(*dirname* ‹ , :encoding => *enc* ›) → *dir*

Returns a new directory object for the named directory. The optional hash parameter lets you specify the encoding used by filenames. If not given, it defaults to the file system local on the current machine.

open

Dir.open(*dirname* ‹ , :encoding => *enc* ›) → *dir*
Dir.open(*dirname* ‹ , :encoding => *enc* ›) { | dir | ... } → *obj*

With no block, open is a synonym for Dir.new. If a block is present, it is passed *dir* as a parameter. The directory is closed at the end of the block, and Dir.open returns the value of the block.

pwd

Dir.pwd → *dirname*

Synonym for Dir.getwd.

rmdir

Dir.rmdir(*dirname*) → 0

Synonym for Dir.delete.

unlink

Dir.unlink(*dirname*) → 0

Synonym for Dir.delete.

Instance Methods

close

dir.close → nil

Closes the directory stream. Any further attempts to access *dir* will raise an IOError.

```
d = Dir.new("testdir")
d.close   # => nil
```

each

dir.each { | filename | ... } → *dir*

Calls the block once for each entry in this directory, passing the filename of each entry as a parameter to the block.

```
d = Dir.new("testdir")
d.each  {|name| puts "Got #{name}" }
```

produces:

```
Got .
Got ..
Got .svn
Got config.h
Got main.rb
```

path

dir.path → dirname

Returns the path parameter passed to *dir*'s constructor.

```
d = Dir.new("..")
d.path    # => ".."
```

pos

dir.pos → int

Synonym for Dir#tell.

pos=

dir.pos(int) → int

Synonym for Dir#seek but returns the position parameter.

```
d = Dir.new("testdir") # => #<Dir:testdir>
d.read                  # => "."
i = d.pos               # => 1
d.read                  # => ".."
d.pos = i               # => 1
d.read                  # => ".."
```

read

dir.read → filename or nil

Reads the next entry from *dir* and returns it as a string. Returns nil at the end of the stream.

```
d = Dir.new("testdir")
d.read    # => "."
d.read    # => ".."
d.read    # => ".svn"
```

rewind

dir.rewind → dir

Repositions *dir* to the first entry.

```
d = Dir.new("testdir")
d.read    # => "."
d.rewind  # => #<Dir:testdir>
d.read    # => "."
```

seek

dir.seek(int) → dir

Seeks to a particular location in *dir*. *int* must be a value returned by Dir#tell (it is not necessarily a simple index into the entries).

```
d = Dir.new("testdir") # => #<Dir:testdir>
d.read                  # => "."
i = d.tell              # => 1
d.read                  # => ".."
d.seek(i)               # => #<Dir:testdir>
d.read                  # => ".."
```

tell

Returns the current position in *dir*. See also Dir#seek.

```
d = Dir.new("testdir")
d.tell    # => 0
d.read    # => "."
d.tell    # => 1
```

to_path

Synonym for Dir.path.

Encoding

An encoding describes how to map the binary data in the internal representation of strings into characters. Ruby has support for a large number of encodings built in—others can be loaded dynamically at runtime.

Encodings are identified by name (*UTF-8* or *ISO-8859-1*, for example). They are represented by encoding objects. The Encoding class contains predefined constants for these encoding objects. Often there are multiple objects for the same encoding. For example, the constants Encoding::IBM860 and Encoding::CP860 are both representations of the encoding named IBM860. In the two-part table Table 15, *Encoding names and class names*, on page 463, the first column shows the names of the encodings, and the second column lists the names on the constants in the Encoding class for the corresponding encoding object(s). An entry such as ISO-8859-1 -- 11 indicates that there are eleven separate encodings (with the obvious names).

Encodings are used when opening files, creating strings, and so on. The methods that accept an encoding as a parameter will take either an encoding name or an encoding object. Use of the object is marginally faster.

Chapter 17, *Character Encoding*, on page 239 is devoted to a discussion of encodings.

Class Methods

aliases

Encoding.aliases → *hash*

Returns a hash whose keys are aliases for encodings and whose values are the corresponding base encoding names.

```
Encoding.aliases["BINARY"] # => "ASCII-8BIT"
```

compatible?

Encoding.compatible?(*str1*, *str2*) → *enc* or nil

Determines whether two strings have compatible encodings (meaning, for example, that you could concatenate them). Returns the encoding of the string that would result from the concatenation or nil if the strings are not compatible.

```
# encoding: utf-8
ascii1 = "ant"
ascii2 = "bee"
iso    = "\xee"
iso.force_encoding(Encoding::ISO_8859_1)
utf    = "∂og"

Encoding.compatible?(ascii1, ascii2) # => #<Encoding:UTF-8>
Encoding.compatible?(ascii1, iso)    # => #<Encoding:ISO-8859-1>
Encoding.compatible?(ascii1, utf)    # => #<Encoding:UTF-8>
Encoding.compatible?(iso,    utf)    # => nil
```

Encoding	Class name(s)	Encoding	Class name(s)
ASCII-8BIT	ASCII_8BIT, BINARY	Big5	Big5, BIG5
Big5-HKSCS	Big5_HKSCS, BIG5_HKSCS, Big5_HKSCS_2008, BIG5_HKSCS_2008	Big5-UAO	Big5_UAO, BIG5_UAO
CP50220	CP50220	CP50221	CP50221
CP51932	CP51932	CP850	CP850, IBM850
CP852	CP852	CP855	CP855
CP949	CP949	CP950	CP950
CP951	CP951	Emacs-Mule	Emacs_Mule, EMACS_MULE
EUC-JP	EUC_JP, EucJP, EUCJP	EUC-JP-2004	EUC_JP_2004, EUC_JISX0213
EUC-KR	EUC_KR, EucKR, EUCKR	EUC-TW	EUC_TW, EucTW, EUCTW
eucJP-ms	EucJP_ms, EUCJP_MS, EUC_JP_MS	GB12345	GB12345
GB18030	GB18030	GB1988	GB1988
GB2312	EUC_CN, EucCN, EUCCN	GBK	GBK, CP936
IBM437	IBM437, CP437	IBM737	IBM737, CP737
IBM775	IBM775, CP775	IBM852	IBM852
IBM855	IBM855	IBM857	IBM857, CP857
IBM860 -- 6	IBM860 -- 6, CP8600 -- 6	IBM869	IBM869, CP869
ISO-2022-JP	ISO_2022_JP, ISO2022_JP	ISO-2022-JP-2	ISO_2022_JP_2, ISO2022_JP2
ISO-2022-JP-KDDI	ISO_2022_JP_KDDI	ISO-8859-1 -- 11	ISO8859_1 -- 11
ISO-8859-13 -- 16	ISO8859_13 -- 16	KOI8-R	KOI8_R, CP878
KOI8-U	KOI8_U	macCentEuro	MacCentEuro, MACCENTEURO
macCroatian	MacCroatian, MACCROATIAN	macCyrillic	MacCyrillic, MACCYRILLIC
macGreek	MacGreek, MACGREEK	macIceland	MacIceland, MACICELAND
MacJapanese	MacJapanese, MACJAPANESE, MacJapan, MACJAPAN	macRoman	MacRoman, MACROMAN
macRomania	MacRomania, MACROMANIA	macThai	MacThai, MACTHAI
macTurkish	MacTurkish, MACTURKISH	macUkraine	MacUkraine, MACUKRAINE
Shift_JIS	Shift_JIS, SHIFT_JIS	SJIS-DoCoMo	SJIS_DoCoMo, SJIS_DOCOMO
SJIS-KDDI	SJIS_KDDI	SJIS-SoftBank	SJIS_SoftBank, SJIS_SOFTBANK
stateless-ISO-2022-JP	Stateless_ISO_2022_JP, STATE-LESS_ISO_2022_JP	stateless-ISO-2022-JP-KDDI	Stateless_ISO_2022_JP_KDDI, STATE-LESS_ISO_2022_JP_KDDI
TIS-620	TIS_620	US-ASCII	US_ASCII, ASCII, ANSI_X3_4_1968
UTF-16	UTF_16	UTF-16BE	UTF_16BE, UCS_2BE
UTF-16LE	UTF_16LE	UTF-32	UTF_32
UTF-32BE	UTF_32BE, UCS_4BE	UTF-32LE	UTF_32LE, UCS_4LE
UTF-7	UTF_7, CP65000	UTF-8	UTF_8, CP65001
UTF8-DoCoMo	UTF8_DoCoMo, UTF8_DOCOMO	UTF8-KDDI	UTF8_KDDI
UTF8-MAC	UTF8_MAC, UTF_8_MAC, UTF_8_HFS	UTF8-SoftBank	UTF8_SoftBank, UTF8_SOFTBANK
Windows-1250 -- 1258	Windows_1250 -- 1258, WINDOWS_1250 -- 1258, CP1250 -- 1258	Windows-31J	Windows_31J, WINDOWS_31J, CP932, CsWindows31J, CSWINDOWS31J, SJIS, PCK
Windows-874	Windows_874, WINDOWS_874, CP874		

Table 15—Encoding names and class names

---

default_external
Encoding.default_external → enc

Returns the default external encoding, used when reading and writing data from I/O streams.

```
Encoding.default_external # => #<Encoding:UTF-8>
```

---

default_external=
Encoding.default_external = enc

Sets the default external encoding.

---

default_internal
Encoding.default_internal → enc or nil

Returns the default internal encoding, used when transcoding data read and written. Returns nil if no default encoding is set.

---

default_internal=
Encoding.default_internal = enc

Sets the default internal encoding.

```
Encoding.default_internal = 'utf-8'
Encoding.default_internal # => #<Encoding:UTF-8>
```

---

find
Encoding.find(name) → enc

Returns the encoding object for the given encoding name or throws an ArgumentError.

```
Encoding.find("Shift_JIS") # => #<Encoding:Shift_JIS>
```

---

list
Encoding.list → array

Returns a list of the encoding objects loaded into the current interpreter.

---

locale_charmap
Encoding.locale_charmap → name

Returns the name of the charmap of the current locale. This is normally set externally, often in an environment variable or other operating-system context.

```
ENV["LANG"]               # => "en_US.UTF-8"
Encoding.locale_charmap # => "UTF-8"
```

---

name_list
Encoding.name_list → array

Returns a list of the names of loaded encodings.

```
Encoding.name_list.sort.first(5) # => ["646", "ANSI_X3.4-1968", "ASCII",
                                 # .. "ASCII-8BIT", "BINARY"]
```

Instance Methods

ascii_compatible?   *enc*.ascii_compatible? → *true* or *false*

Returns true if the lower 127 codepoints in the encoding overlay the ASCII character set.

```
Encoding::UTF_8.ascii_compatible? # => true
Encoding::SJIS.ascii_compatible?  # => true
Encoding::UTF_7.ascii_compatible? # => false
```

dummy?   *enc*.dummy? → *true* or *false*

Dummy encodings are placeholders for encodings that cannot be handled properly by the current mechanism of Ruby multinationalization, often because they are stateful.

```
Encoding::UTF_7.dummy? # => true
Encoding::UTF_8.dummy? # => false
```

name   *enc*.name → *string*

Returns the name of *enc*.

```
Encoding::UTF_8.name   # => "UTF-8"
Encoding::CP65001.name # => "UTF-8"
```

names   *enc*.names → [‹ *string* ›⁺]

Returns the name of *enc*, along with the names of *enc*'s aliases.

```
Encoding::ISO8859_1.names # => ["ISO-8859-1", "ISO8859-1"]
Encoding::ASCII.names     # => ["US-ASCII", "ASCII", "ANSI_X3.4-1968", "646"]
```

replicate   *enc*.replicate(*name*) → *new_encoding*

Create a copy of the encoding *enc* with the given name (which must be unique).

Module	Enumerable	Relies on: each, <=>

The Enumerable mixin provides collection classes with traversal and searching methods and with the ability to sort. The class must provide a method each, which yields successive members of the collection. If Enumerable#max, min, sort, or sort_by is used, the objects in the collection must also implement a meaningful <=> operator, because these methods rely on an ordering between members of the collection.

Ruby 1.9 adds a substantial number of methods to this module, as well as changing the semantics of many others. Even experienced Ruby programmers should probably read this section carefully.

Instance Methods

all?
$enum$.all? ‹ { | obj | … } › → *true* or *false*

Passes each element of the collection to the given block. The method returns true if the block never returns false or nil. If the block is not given, Ruby adds an implicit block of {|obj| obj} (that is, all? will return true only if no collection member is false or nil).

```
[ nil, true, 99 ].all? # => false
```

any?
$enum$.any? ‹ { | obj | … } › → *true* or *false*

Passes elements of the collection in turn to the given block. The method returns true (and stops calling the block) if the block ever returns a value other than false or nil. If the block is not given, Ruby adds an implicit block of {|obj|~obj} (that is, any? will return true if at least one of the collection members is not false or nil). See also Enumerable#none? and Enumerable#one?.

```
[ nil, true, 99 ].any? # => true
```

chunk
$enum$.chunk { | element | … } → *enumerator*
$enum$.chunk(*state*) { | element, state | … } → *enumerator*

Passes each element of *enum* to the block. Use the value returned from the block as a key, and group successive elements with the same key together. The *enumerator* that is returned will yield the key and the successive values corresponding to that key. Here's a simple example that returns sequences of words that have the same length:

```
enum = %w{ ant bee coyote dophin elk }.chunk(&:size)
enum.next # => [3, ["ant", "bee"]]
enum.next # => [6, ["coyote", "dophin"]]
enum.next # => [3, ["elk"]]
```

If the block returns the values nil or :_separator, the corresponding value is not stored in the output enumerator, and a new output element is started.

```
enum = [ 1, 2, 3, 4, 5 ].chunk {|element| element.odd? ? :odd : :_separator}
enum.to_a # => [[:odd, [1]], [:odd, [3]], [:odd, [5]]]
```

The following example uses the fact that a failing pattern match returns nil:

```
# This code reads its own source and returns each comment block
File.foreach(__FILE__).chunk do |line|
  # A comment is a group of consecutive
  # lines starting with '#'
  line =~ /^\s*#/
end.each do |_, lines|
  p lines
end
```

produces:

```
["# This code reads its own source and returns each comment block\n"]
["  # A comment is a group of consecutive\n", "  # lines starting with '#'\n"]
```

If the block returns :_alone, this value is put into its own output element—it will not be grouped with the previous element even if that element's block also returned :_alone.

```
enum = [ 1, 2, 3 ].chunk { :_alone }
enum.to_a # => [[:_alone, [1]], [:_alone, [2]], [:_alone, [3]]]
```

If a *state* parameter is present, it is passed as the second parameter to every call to the block, permitting state to be maintained across calls.

See also Enumerable.slice_before.

collect

enum.collect { | obj | ... } → *array* or *enumerator*

Returns a new array containing the results of running *block* once for every element in *enum*. Returns an Enumerator object if no block is given.

```
(1..4).collect {|i| i*i } # => [1, 4, 9, 16]
(1..4).collect { "cat"  } # => ["cat", "cat", "cat", "cat"]
(1..4).collect(&:even?)   # => [false, true, false, true]
```

collect_concat

enum.collect_concat { | obj | ... } → *array*
enum.collect_concat → *enumerator*

Synonym for (the better named) Enumerable.flat_map.

count

enum.count(*obj*) → *int*
enum.count { | obj | ... } → *int*

Returns the count of objects in *enum* that equal *obj* or for which the block returns a true value. Returns the count of all elements in *enum* if neither a block nor an argument is given.

```
(1..4).count             # => 4
(1..4).count(3)          # => 1
(1..4).count {|obj| obj > 2 } # => 2
```

cycle

enum.cycle { | obj | ... } → nil or *enumerator*
enum.cycle(*times*) { | obj | ... } → nil or *enumerator*

Returns nil if *enum* has no elements; otherwise, passes the elements, one at a time, to the block, repeating when it reaches the end. The number of times it repeats is set by the parameter. If the parameter is missing, cycles forever. Equivalent to *enum*.to_a.cycle. See also Array#cycle. Returns an Enumerator object if no block is given.

```
('a'..'c').cycle(2)      # => #<Enumerator: "a".."c":cycle(2)>
('a'..'c').cycle(2).to_a # => ["a", "b", "c", "a", "b", "c"]
```

---

detect   *enum*.detect(*ifnone* = nil) { | obj | ... } → *obj* or nil or *enumerator*

Passes each entry in *enum* to *block*. Returns the first for which *block* is not false. Returns nil if no object matches unless the proc *ifnone* is given, in which case it is called and its result is returned. Returns an Enumerator object if no block is given.

```
(1..10).detect  {|i| i % 5 == 0 and i % 7 == 0 } # => nil
(1..100).detect {|i| i % 5 == 0 and i % 7 == 0 } # => 35
sorry = lambda { "not found" }
(1..10).detect(sorry) {|i| i > 50}                # => "not found"
```

---

drop   *enum*.drop(*n*) → *an_array*

Returns an array containing all but the first *n* elements of *enum*.

```
[ 1, 1, 2, 3, 5, 8, 13 ].drop(4)  # => [5, 8, 13]
[ 1, 1, 2, 3, 5, 8, 13 ].drop(99) # => []
```

---

drop_while   *enum*.drop_while { | item | ... } → *an_array* or *enumerator*

Passes elements in turn to the block until the block does not return a true value. Starting with that element, copies the remainder to an array and returns it. Returns an Enumerator object if no block is given.

```
[ 1, 1, 2, 3, 5, 8, 13 ].drop_while {|item| item < 6 } # => [8, 13]
```

---

each_cons   *enum*.each_cons(*length*) { | array | ... } → nil or *enumerator*

Passes to the block each consecutive subarray of size *length* from *enum*. Returns an Enumerator object if no block is given.

```
(1..4).each_cons(2) {|array| p array }
```

produces:

```
[1, 2]
[2, 3]
[3, 4]
```

---

each_entry   *enum*.each_entry { | element | ... } → *enum*
                                                   enum.each_entry → *enumerator*

Repeatedly calls enum.each, passing the result to the block. If each returns a single value, it is passed unchanged to the block. If a call to each returns multiple values, they are packaged into an array and passed to the block.

```
class Generator
  include Enumerable
  def each
    yield 1
    yield 2, 3
    yield 4
  end
end
g = Generator.new
g.each         {|entry| print entry, " : "}
puts
g.each_entry {|entry| print entry, " : "}
```

produces:

```
1 : 2 : 4 :
1 : [2, 3] : 4 :
```

---

each_slice

enum.each_slice(*length*) { | array | ... } → nil or *enumerator*

Divides *enum* into slices of size *length*, passing each in turn to the block. Returns an Enumerator object if no block is given.

```
(1..10).each_slice(4) {|array| p array }
```

produces:

```
[1, 2, 3, 4]
[5, 6, 7, 8]
[9, 10]
```

---

each_with_index

enum.each_with_index(‹ args ›*) { | obj, index | ... }
→ *enum* or *enumerator*

Calls *block*, passing in successive items from *enum* and the corresponding index. If any arguments are given, they are passed to each during the iteration. Returns an Enumerator object if no block is given.

```
%w(cat dog wombat).each_with_index do |item, index|
  puts "#{item} is at position #{index}"
end
```

produces:

```
cat is at position 0
dog is at position 1
wombat is at position 2
```

---

each_with_object

enum.each_with_object(*memo*) → *memo* or *enumerator*

Calls *block* with the item and the memo object, for each item in *enum*. Returns an Enumerator object if no block is given.

```
hash = %w(cat dog wombat).each_with_object({}) do |item, memo|
  memo[item] = item.upcase.reverse
end
hash      # => {"cat"=>"TAC", "dog"=>"GOD", "wombat"=>"TABMOW"}
```

entries

enum.entries → *array*

Synonym for Enumerable#to_a.

find

enum.find(*ifnone* = nil) { | obj | ... } → *obj* or nil

Synonym for Enumerable#detect.

find_all

enum.find_all { | obj | ... } → *array* or *enumerator*

Returns an array containing all elements of *enum* for which *block* is not false (see also Enumerable#reject). Returns an Enumerator object if no block is given.

```
(1..10).find_all {|i|  i % 3 == 0 } # => [3, 6, 9]
```

find_index

enum.find_index(*obj*) → *int* or nil
enum.find_index { | obj | ... } → *int* or nil or *enumerator*

Returns the index of the first object in *arr* that is == to *obj* or for which the block returns a true value. Returns nil otherwise. See also Enumerable#reject. Returns an Enumerator object if no block is given.

```
%w{ant bat cat dog}.find_index {|item|  item =~ /g/ } # => 3
%w{ant bat cat dog}.find_index {|item|  item =~ /h/ } # => nil
```

first

enum.first → *an_object* or nil
enum.first(*n*) → *an_array*

With no parameters, returns the first item of *enum* or nil. With a parameter, returns the first *n* items of *enum*.

```
%w{ant bat cat dog}.first    # => "ant"
%w{ant bat cat dog}.first(2) # => ["ant", "bat"]
```

flat_map

enum.flat_map { | obj | ... } → *array*
enum.flat_map → *enumerator*

Passes each element in *enum* to the block. If the returned value is an array (or is compatible with an array), append each element to the result; otherwise, append the block return value to the result. The effect is a single-level flattening of any returned value. If no block is given, return an enumerator.

```
[ 1, 2, 3 ].flat_map {|e| [ e, 100-e ]} # => [1, 99, 2, 98, 3, 97]
```

grep

enum.grep(*pattern*) → *array*
enum.grep(*pattern*) { | obj | ... } → *array*

Returns an array of every element in *enum* for which pattern === element. If the optional *block* is supplied, each matching element is passed to it, and the block's result is stored in the output array.

```
(1..100).grep 38..44                    # => [38, 39, 40, 41, 42, 43, 44]
c = IO.constants
c.grep(/SEEK/)                          # => [:SEEK_SET, :SEEK_CUR, :SEEK_END]
res = c.grep(/SEEK/) {|v| IO.const_get(v) }
res                                     # => [0, 1, 2]
[ 123, 9**11, 12.34 ].grep(Integer) # => [123, 31381059609]
```

group_by

enum.group_by { | item | ... } → *hash* or *enumerator*

Partitions *enum* by calling the block for each item and using the result returned by the block to group the items into buckets. Returns a hash where the keys are the objects returned by the block, and the values for a key are those items for which the block returned that object. Returns an Enumerator object if no block is given.

```
p (1..5).group_by {|item| item.even? ? "even" : "odd" }
```

produces:

```
{"odd"=>[1, 3, 5], "even"=>[2, 4]}
```

include?

enum.include?(*obj*) → *true* or *false*

Returns true if any member of *enum* equals *obj*. Equality is tested using ==.

```
IO.constants.include? :SEEK_SET        # => true
IO.constants.include? :SEEK_NO_FURTHER # => false
```

inject

enum.inject(*initial*) { | *memo, obj* | ... } → *obj*
enum.inject(*initial, sym*) → *obj*
enum.inject { | *memo, obj* | ... } → *obj*
enum.inject(*sym*) → *obj*

Combines the items in *enum* by iterating over them. For each item, passes an accumulator object (called *memo* in the examples) and the item itself to the block or invokes memo.send(sym, obj). At each step, *memo* is set to the value returned by the block on the previous step. The value returned by inject is the final value returned by the block. The first two forms let you supply an initial value for *memo*. The second two forms use the first element of the collection as the initial value (and skip that element while iterating). Some languages call this operation foldl or reduce. Ruby supports the latter as an alias for inject.

```
# Sum some numbers. These forms do the same thing
(5..10).inject(0) {|sum, n| sum + n }       # => 45
(5..10).inject {|sum, n| sum + n }          # => 45
(5..10).inject(0, :+)                       # => 45
(5..10).inject(:+)                          # => 45
# Multiply some numbers
(5..10).inject(1) {|product, n| product * n } # => 151200
(5..10).inject(&:*)                         # => 151200

# find the longest word
longest_word = %w{ cat sheep bear }.inject do |memo, word|
  memo.length > word.length ? memo : word
end
longest_word                                # => "sheep"
```

```
# find the length of the longest word
longest_length = %w{ cat sheep bear }.inject(0) do |memo, word|
  memo >= word.length ? memo : word.length
end
longest_length                          # => 5
```

lazy

enum.lazy → *lazy_enum*

New in 2.0

Returns a lazy enumerator for this enumerable object. See the description of lazy enumerators on page 61 for more details.

map

enum.map { | obj | ... } → *array*

Synonym for Enumerable#collect.

max

enum.max → *obj*
enum.max { | a,b | ... } → *obj*

Returns the object in *enum* with the maximum value. The first form assumes all objects implement <=>; the second uses the block to return a <=> b.

```
a = %w(albatross dog horse)
a.max                         # => "horse"
a.max {|a,b| a.length <=> b.length } # => "albatross"
```

max_by

enum.max_by { | item | ... } → *obj* or *enumerator*

Passes each item in the collection to the block. Returns the item corresponding to the largest value returned by the block. Returns an Enumerator object if no block is given.

```
a = %w(albatross dog horse fox)
a.max_by {|item| item.length }  # => "albatross"
a.max_by {|item| item.reverse } # => "fox"
```

member?

enum.member?(*obj*) → *true* or *false*

Synonym for Enumerable#include?.

min

enum.min → *obj*
enum.min { | a,b | ... } → *obj*

Returns the object in *enum* with the minimum value. The first form assumes all objects implement Comparable; the second uses the block to return a <=> b.

```
a = %w(albatross dog horse)
a.min                         # => "albatross"
a.min {|a,b| a.length <=> b.length } # => "dog"
```

min_by

enum.min_by { | item | ... } → *obj* or *enumerator*

Passes each item in the collection to the block. Returns the item corresponding to the smallest value returned by the block. Returns an Enumerator object if no block is given.

```
a = %w(albatross dog horse fox)
a.min_by {|item| item.length }  # => "dog"
a.min_by {|item| item.reverse } # => "horse"
```

minmax

enum.minmax → [*min, max*]
enum.minmax { | a,b | ... } → [*min, max*]

Compares the elements of *enum* using either <=> or the given block, returning the minimum and maximum values.

```
a = %w(albatross dog horse)
a.minmax                            # => ["albatross", "horse"]
a.minmax {|a,b| a.length <=> b.length } # => ["dog", "albatross"]
```

minmax_by

enum.minmax_by { | item | ... } → [*min, max*] or *enumerator*

Passes each item in *enum* to the block. Returns the items corresponding to the smallest and largest values returned by the block. Returns an Enumerator object if no block is given.

```
a = %w(albatross dog horse fox)
a.minmax_by {|item| item.length }  # => ["dog", "albatross"]
a.minmax_by {|item| item.reverse } # => ["horse", "fox"]
```

none?

enum.none? ‹ { | obj | ... } › → *true* or *false*

Passes each element of the collection to the given block. The method returns true if the block never returns a value other than false or nil. If the block is not given, Ruby adds an implicit block of {|obj| obj} (that is, none? will return false if any of the collection members is not false or nil). See also Enumerable#any? and Enumerable#one?.

```
[ nil, true, 99 ].none? # => false
```

one?

enum.one? ‹ { | obj | ... } › → *true* or *false*

Passes each element of the collection to the given block. The method returns true if the block returns true exactly one time. If the block is not given, Ruby adds an implicit block of {|obj| obj} (that is, one? will return true if at least one of the collection members is not false or nil). See also Enumerable#any? and Enumerable#none?.

```
[ nil, nil, 99 ].one? # => true
```

partition

enum.partition { | obj | ... } → [*true_array, false_array*] or *enumerator*

Returns two arrays, the first containing the elements of *enum* for which the block evaluates to true and the second containing the rest. Returns an Enumerator object if no block is given.

```
(1..6).partition {|i| (i&1).zero?} # => [[2, 4, 6], [1, 3, 5]]
```

---

reduce

enum.reduce(*initial*) { | *memo, obj* | ... } → *obj*
enum.reduce(*initial, sym*) → *obj*
enum.reduce { | *memo, obj* | ... } → *obj*
enum.reduce(*sym*) → *obj*

Synonym for Enumerable#inject.

---

reject

enum.reject { | obj | ... } → *array* or *enumerator*

Returns an array containing the elements of *enum* for which *block* is false (see also Enumerable#find_all). Returns an Enumerator object if no block is given.

```
(1..10).reject {|i|  i % 3 == 0 } # => [1, 2, 4, 5, 7, 8, 10]
```

---

reverse_each

enum.reverse_each { | obj | ... } → *enum*

Invokes the block with the elements of *enum* in reverse order. Creates an intermediate array internally, so this might be expensive on large collections. Returns an Enumerator object if no block is given.

```
(1..5).reverse_each {|i|  print i, " " }
```

produces:

```
5 4 3 2 1
```

---

select

enum.select { | obj | ... } → *array*

Synonym for Enumerable#find_all.

---

slice_before

enum.slice_before(*pattern*) → *enumerator*
enum.slice_before(‹ *state* ›) { | element, ‹ *state* › | ... } → *enumerator*

Chunks *enum* into a set of arrays and returns an enumerator of those arrays. A new array is started whenever the next element matches the pattern (using === when the block returns true). Think of this as a generalized String#split method.

```
p DATA.map(&:chomp).slice_before(/\w:/).to_a
__END__
colors
  red
  yellow
pitches
  high
  low
  middle
```

produces:

```
[["colors", "  red", "  yellow", "pitches", "  high", "  low", "  middle"]]
```

Collapse sequences of three or more consecutive things into first–last.

```
input = [ 1, 2, 3, 4, 5, 8, 9, 11, 12, 13, 15 ]

def returning(value)  # helper returns its parameter after calling the block
  yield
  value
end

State = Struct.new(:last_value)  # Need to box the value to make it mutable

# divide the input into runs of consecutive numbers
slices = input.slice_before(State.new(input.first)) do |value, state|
  returning(value != state.last_value.succ) do
    state.last_value  = value
  end
end

p(slices.map do |runs|    # replace runs of 3 or more with first–last
  runs.size < 3 ? runs : "#{ runs.first }-#{ runs.last }"
end.join(', '))
```

produces:

```
"1-5, 8, 9, 11-13, 15"
```

---

sort

enum.sort → array
enum.sort { | a, b | ... } → array

Returns an array containing the items in *enum* sorted, either according to their own <=> method or by using the results of the supplied block. The block should return -1, 0, or +1 depending on the comparison between *a* and *b*. See also Enumerable#sort_by.

```
(1..10).sort {|a,b| b <=> a} # => [10, 9, 8, 7, 6, 5, 4, 3, 2, 1]
```

---

sort_by

enum.sort_by { | obj | ... } → array

Sorts *enum* using keys generated by mapping the values in *enum* through the given block, using the result of that block for element comparison.

```
%w{ apple pear fig }.sort_by {|word| word.length} # => ["fig", "pear", "apple"]
```

Internally, sort_by generates an array of tuples containing the original collection element and the mapped value. This makes sort_by fairly expensive when the keysets are simple.

```
require 'benchmark'
a = (1..100000).map {rand(100000)}
Benchmark.bm(10) do |b|
  b.report("Sort")    { a.sort }
  b.report("Sort by") { a.sort_by {|val| val } }
end
```

produces:

```
                user     system      total        real
Sort        0.030000   0.000000   0.030000 (  0.026899)
Sort by     0.140000   0.000000   0.140000 (  0.145687)
```

However, in cases where comparing the keys is a nontrivial operation, the algorithm used by sort_by is considerably faster.

sort_by can also be useful for multilevel sorts. One trick, which relies on the fact that arrays are compared element by element, is to have the block return an array of each of the comparison keys. For example, to sort a list of words first on their length and then alphabetically, you could write the following:

```
words = %w{ puma cat bass ant aardvark gnu fish }
sorted = words.sort_by {|w| [w.length, w] }
sorted    # => ["ant", "cat", "gnu", "bass", "fish", "puma", "aardvark"]
```

Returns an Enumerator object if no block is given.

take   *enum*.take(*n*) → *array*

Returns an array containing the first *n* items from *enum*.

```
(1..7).take(3)                          # => [1, 2, 3]
{ 'a'=>1, 'b'=>2, 'c'=>3 }.take(2) # => [["a", 1], ["b", 2]]
```

take_while   *enum*.take_while { | item | ... } → *array* or *enumerator*

Passes successive items to the block, adding them to the result array until the block returns false or nil. Returns an Enumerator object if no block is given.

```
(1..7).take_while {|item| item < 3 }       # => [1, 2]
[ 2, 4, 6, 9, 11, 16 ].take_while(&:even?) # => [2, 4, 6]
```

to_a   *enum*.to_a(*args) → *array*

Returns an array containing the items in *enum*. This is done using the each method. Any arguments passed to to_a are passed to each.

```
(1..7).to_a                       # => [1, 2, 3, 4, 5, 6, 7]
{ 'a'=>1, 'b'=>2, 'c'=>3 }.to_a # => [["a", 1], ["b", 2], ["c", 3]]
```

zip   *enum*.zip(‹ *arg* ›⁺) → *array*
                                                     enum.zip(‹ *arg* ›⁺) { | arr | ... } → nil

Converts any arguments to arrays and then merges elements of *enum* with corresponding elements from each argument. The result is an array containing the same number of elements as *enum*. Each element is an *n*-element array, where *n* is one more than the count of arguments. If the size of any argument is less than the number of elements in *enum*, nil values are supplied. If a block given, it is invoked for each output array; otherwise, an array of arrays is returned.

```
a = [ 4, 5, 6 ]
b = [ 7, 8, 9 ]

(1..3).zip(a, b) # => [[1, 4, 7], [2, 5, 8], [3, 6, 9]]
[1, 2].zip([3])  # => [[1, 3], [2, nil]]
(1..3).zip       # => [[1], [2], [3]]
```

Enumerator

Enumerator allows you to capture the concept of an enumeration as an object. This allows you to store enumerations in variables, pass them as parameters, and so on.

You can also create enumerators with the method Object#to_enum (or via its alias, enum_for). By default, these methods look for an each method in the object you're enumerating, but this can be overridden by passing the name of a method (and possibly parameters to be used) that invokes a block for each item to be enumerated.

```ruby
str = "quick brown fox"
case what_to_process        # set elsewhere to :by_word
when :by_bytes
  enum = str.to_enum(:each_byte)
when :by_word
  enum = str.to_enum(:scan, /\w+/)
end
enum.each {|item| p item}
```

produces:

```
"quick"
"brown"
"fox"
```

Mixes In

Enumerable: all?, any?, chunk, collect, collect_concat, count, cycle, detect, drop, drop_while, each_cons, each_entry, each_slice, each_with_index, each_with_object, entries, find, find_all, find_index, first, flat_map, grep, group_by, include?, inject, lazy, map, max, max_by, member?, min, min_by, minmax, minmax_by, none?, one?, partition, reduce, reject, reverse_each, select, slice_before, sort, sort_by, take, take_while, to_a, zip

Class Methods

new   Enumerator.new(‹ *size*=nil ›) { | yielder | ... } → *enum*

Constructs an enumerator based on the block. The block is passed an object of class Enumerator::Yielder. You can use the << or yield methods of this *yielder* to supply values to be returned by the enumerator. This process is performed lazily (similar to the way that fibers can be used to generate sequences).

```ruby
def multiples_of(n)
  Enumerator.new do |yielder|
    number = 0
    loop do
      yielder.yield number
      number += n
    end
  end
end

twos = multiples_of(2)
threes = multiples_of(3)
```

```
5.times do
  puts "#{twos.next} #{threes.next}"
end
```

produces:

```
0 0
2 3
4 6
6 9
8 12
```

New in 2.0   The optional argument specifies the value that will be returned by the size method for this enumerator. If can be nil (meaning the size cannot be determined), a number, or a proc that returns a number.

Instance Methods

each   *enum*.each { | item, ... | ... } → *obj*

Calls the block for each item in the enumeration. This does not create an intermediate array. Instead, the original iterating method (the one used when creating the enumerator) is called, passing it the block passed to this method. The block receives as many parameters as the original method passes.

```
enum = (1..10).enum_for(:each_slice, 3)
enum.each { |item| p item }
```

produces:

```
[1, 2, 3]
[4, 5, 6]
[7, 8, 9]
[10]
```

Note that because Enumerator defines each and includes Enumerable, all the enumerable methods are available too.

```
enum = "quick brown fox".enum_for(:scan, /\w+/)
enum.minmax # => ["brown", "quick"]
```

each_with_index   *enum*.each_with_index { | item, ..., index | ... } → *obj*

Same as each but appends an index argument when calling the block. Returns a new Enumerator if no block is given.

```
enum = (1..10).enum_for(:each_slice, 3)
enum.each_with_index do |subarray, index|
  puts "#{index}: #{subarray}"
end
```

produces:

```
0: [1, 2, 3]
1: [4, 5, 6]
2: [7, 8, 9]
3: [10]
```

each_with_object

enum.each_with_object(*memo*) { | item, memo | ... } → *memo* or *enumerator*

Calls *block* for each item in *enum,* passing it the item and the parameter passed initially to each_with_object. Returns an Enumerator object if no block is given.

```
animals = %w(cat dog wombat).to_enum
hash = animals.each_with_object({}) do |item, memo|
  memo[item] = item.upcase.reverse
end
hash      # => {"cat"=>"TAC", "dog"=>"GOD", "wombat"=>"TABMOW"}
```

feed

enum.feed(*obj*) → nil

In a normal looping construct, the next keyword can take an optional parameter, which is returned to the code that is controlling the iteration as the value returned by yield. enum.feed does the same thing for enumerators, setting the value returned by yield in the underlying enumerable to *obj.*

next

enum.next → *obj*

Returns the next item in the enumeration. Raises StopIteration if you call it past the last item. Internally this is implemented using fibers and so cannot be called across threads. See also Enumerator.next_values.

```
array = [ 1, 2, 3, 4 ]
e1 = array.to_enum
e2 = array.to_enum
e1.next   # => 1
e1.next   # => 2
e2.next   # => 1
```

If the underlying method called by the enumerator has side effects (such as moving your position while reading a file), those side effects will be triggered. For this reason, next breaks the abstraction provided by Enumerator.

```
f = File.open("testfile")
enum1 = f.to_enum(:each_byte)
enum2 = f.to_enum
enum1.next # => 84
enum1.next # => 104
enum2.next # => "is is line one\n"
f.gets     # => "This is line two\n"
enum2.next # => "This is line three\n"
```

next_values

enum.next_values → *array*

Enumerator.next returns successive values yielded by *enum.* However, it effectively uses raw proc semantics and so is unable to distinguish the case when the iterator yields nil and the case where the yield is passed no parameter. Similarly, it cannot distinguish yield 1,2 from yield [1,2]—both are received as [1,2]. next_values overcomes this by always returning an array, and that array contains exactly what was passed to the yield.

```
def each
  yield 1
  yield nil
  yield 2, 3
  yield [4,5]
end
enum = to_enum
enum.next         # => 1
enum.next         # => nil
enum.next         # => [2, 3]
enum.next         # => [4, 5]

enum = to_enum
enum.next_values # => [1]
enum.next_values # => [nil]
enum.next_values # => [2, 3]
enum.next_values # => [[4, 5]]
```

peek   *enum*.peek → *obj*

Returns the value that would be returned by calling next but does not consume that value. Raises a StopIteration exception if called past the end of *enum*.

```
enum = %w{ ant bee cat }.to_enum
enum.peek # => "ant"
enum.peek # => "ant"
enum.next # => "ant"
enum.peek # => "bee"
```

peek_values   *enum*.peek_values → *array*

Returns the value that would be returned by calling next_values.

rewind   *enum*.rewind → *enum*

Resets the sequence of values to be returned by next.

```
array = [ 1, 2, 3, 4 ]
e1 = array.to_enum
e2 = array.to_enum
e1.next   # => 1
e1.next   # => 2
e2.next   # => 1
e1.rewind
e1.next   # => 1
e2.next   # => 2
```

Has no effect if the underlying method of the enumerator has side effects and therefore cannot be rewound.

size

enum.size → *int* or nil

Returns the size of this collection, or nil if the size cannot be calculated (this may or may not be the case with a lazy enumerator).

New in 2.0

```
File.open("/etc/passwd").to_enum.size # => nil
(1..Float::INFINITY).size             # => Infinity
loop.size                             # => Infinity
(1..10).find.size                     # => nil
```

with_index

enum.with_index { | item, ..., index | ... } → *obj*

Synonym for each_with_index.

with_object

enum.with_object(*memo*) { | item, memo | ... } → *memo* or *enumerator*

Synonym for each_with_object.

Module **Errno**

Ruby exception objects are subclasses of Exception. However, operating systems typically report errors using plain integers. Module Errno is created dynamically to map these operating system errors to Ruby classes, with each error number generating its own subclass of System-CallError. Because the subclass is created in module Errno, its name will start Errno::.

```
Exception
    StandardError
        SystemCallError
            Errno::XXX
```

The names of the Errno:: classes depend on the environment in which Ruby runs. On a typical Unix or Windows platform, you'll find Ruby has Errno classes such as Errno::EACCES, Errno::EAGAIN, Errno::EINTR, and so on.

The integer operating system error number corresponding to a particular error is available as the class constant Errno::error::Errno.

```
Errno::EACCES::Errno # => 13
Errno::EAGAIN::Errno # => 35
Errno::EINTR::Errno  # => 4
```

The full list of operating system errors on your particular platform is available as the constants of Errno. Any user-defined exceptions in this module (including subclasses of existing exceptions) must also define an Errno constant.

```
Errno.constants[0..4] # => [:NOERROR, :EPERM, :ENOENT, :ESRCH, :EINTR]
```

As of Ruby 1.8, exceptions are matched in rescue clauses using Module#===. The === method is overridden for class SystemCallError to compare based on the Errno value. Thus, if two distinct Errno classes have the same underlying Errno value, they will be treated as the same exception by a rescue clause.

Exception

Descendents of class Exception are used to communicate between raise methods and rescue statements in begin/end blocks. Exception objects carry information about the exception—its type (the exception's class name), an optional descriptive string, and optional traceback information.

The standard library defines the exceptions shown in Figure 1, *Standard exception hierarchy*, on page 146. Note that Ruby 1.9 has changed the hierarchy slightly. In particular, SecurityError is no longer a subclass of StandardError and so will not be rescued implicitly.

See also the description of Errno on page 482.

Class Methods

exception   Exception.exception(‹ *message* ›) → *exc*

Creates and returns a new exception object, optionally setting the message to *message*.

new   Exception.new(‹ *message* ›) → *exc*

Creates and returns a new exception object, optionally setting the message to *message*.

Instance Methods

==   *exc* == *other* → true or false

Returns true only if *other* shares the same message and backtrace as *exc*.

backtrace   *exc*.backtrace → *array*

Returns any backtrace associated with the exception. The backtrace is an array of strings, each containing either *filename:line: in 'method'* or *filename:line*.

```ruby
def a
  raise "boom"
end
def b
  a()
end
begin
  b()
rescue => detail
  print detail.backtrace.join("\n")
end
```

produces:

```
prog.rb:2:in `a'
prog.rb:5:in `b'
prog.rb:8:in `<main>'
```

exception

exc.exception(‹ *message* ›) → *exc* or *exception*

With no argument, returns the receiver. Otherwise, creates a new exception object of the same class as the receiver but with a different message.

message

exc.message → *msg*

Returns the message associated with this exception.

set_backtrace

exc.set_backtrace(*array*) → *array*

Sets the backtrace information associated with *exc*. The argument must be an array of String objects in the format described in Exception#backtrace.

status

exc.status → status

(SystemExit only.) Returns the exit status associated with this SystemExit exception. Normally this status is set using the Object#exit.

```
begin
  exit(99)
rescue SystemExit => e
  puts "Exit status is: #{e.status}"
end
```

produces:

```
Exit status is: 99
```

success?

exc.success? → true or false

(SystemExit only.) Returns true if the exit status is nil or zero.

```
begin
  exit(99)
rescue SystemExit => e
  print "This program "
  if e.success?
    print "did"
  else
    print "did not"
  end
  puts " succeed"
end
```

produces:

```
This program did not succeed
```

to_s

Returns the message associated with this exception (or the name of the exception if no message is set).

```
begin
  raise "The message"
rescue Exception => e
  puts e.to_s
  # This is the same as the previous puts
  puts e
end
```

produces:

```
The message
The message
```

FalseClass

The global value false is the only instance of class FalseClass and represents a logically false value in boolean expressions. The class provides operators allowing false to participate correctly in logical expressions.

Instance Methods

& false & *obj* → false

And—Returns false. *obj* is always evaluated because it is the argument to a method call—no short-circuit evaluation is performed in this case. In other words, the following code, which uses &&, will not invoke the lookup method.

```
def lookup(val)
  puts "Looking up #{val}"
  return true
end
false && lookup("cat")
```

However, this code, using &, will:

```
false & lookup("cat")
```

produces:

```
Looking up cat
```

^ false ^ *obj* → *true* or *false*

Exclusive Or—If *obj* is nil or false, returns false; otherwise, returns true.

| false | *obj* → *true* or *false*

Or—Returns false if *obj* is nil or false; true otherwise.

Class # Fiber

A fiber is a lightweight asymetrical coroutine. Code in a fiber is created in a suspended state. It runs when resumed and can suspend itself (passing a value back to the code that resumed it). There is a full description of fibers in Section 12.1, *Fibers*, on page 161.

```
fibonaccis = Fiber.new do
  n1 = n2 = 1
  loop do
    Fiber.yield n1
    n1, n2 = n2, n1+n2
  end
end
10.times { print fibonaccis.resume, ' ' }
```

produces:

```
1 1 2 3 5 8 13 21 34 55
```

Class Methods

new   Fiber.new { ... } → *fiber*

Uses the block as a new, suspended fiber.

yield   Fiber.yield(‹ val ›*) → *obj*

Suspends execution of the current fiber. Any parameters will be returned as the value of the resume call that awoke the fiber. Similarly, any values passed to resume will become the return value of the subsequent yield.

```
f = Fiber.new do |first|
  print first
  letter = "A"
  loop do
    print Fiber.yield(letter)
    letter = letter.succ
  end
end

10.times { |number|  print f.resume(number) }
```

produces:

```
0A1B2C3D4E5F6G7H8I9J
```

Instance Methods

resume   *fiber*.resume(‹ val ›*) → *obj*

Resumes *fiber*. See Fiber.yield for a discussion and example of parameter passing. It is an error to resume a fiber that is being used as a coroutine (one that calls transfer). See *Fiber*, on page 755.

New in 2.0

Class **File** < IO

A File is an abstraction of any file object accessible by the program and is closely associated with class IO, described later on page 536. File includes the methods of module FileTest as class methods, allowing you to write (for example) File.exist?("foo").

Files may be opened in binary mode (where the contents are transferred as 8-bit bytes in binary encoding) or text mode (where the contents are interpreted as codepoints in a particular encoding). These options are controlled by the mode parameter when a file is opened.

Each file has three associated times: *atime* is the time the file was last accessed, *ctime* is the time that the file status (not necessarily the file contents) were last changed, and *mtime* is the time the file's data was last modified. In Ruby, all these times are returned as Time objects.

In this section, *permission bits* are a platform-specific set of bits that indicate permissions of a file. On Unix-based systems, permissions are viewed as a set of three octets, for the owner, the group, and the rest of the world. For each of these entities, permissions may be set to read, write, or execute the file.

Owner			Group			Other		
r	w	x	r	w	x	r	w	x
400	200	100	40	20	10	4	2	1

The permission bits 0644 (in octal) would thus be interpreted as read/write for owner and read-only for group and other. Higher-order bits may also be used to indicate the type of file (plain, directory, pipe, socket, and so on) and various other special features. If the permissions are for a directory, the meaning of the execute bit changes; when set, the directory can be searched.

Non-POSIX operating systems may not support the full set of possible permissions. In this case, the remaining permission bits will be synthesized to resemble typical values. For instance, on Windows the default permission bits are 0644, which means read/write for owner and read-only for all others. The only change that can be made is to make the file read-only, which is reported as 0444.

The constant File::NULL is the name of your system's null device. Reading from it returns end-of-file, and writing to it is ignored.

See also Pathname on page 787 and IO on page 536.

Class Methods

absolute_path

File.absolute_path(*filename* ‹ , *dirstring* ›) → *filename*

Converts a path to an absolute path. Relative paths are referenced from the current working directory of the process unless *dirstring* is given, in which case it will be used as the starting point. Path names starting with ~ are not expanded, in contrast with File#expand_path.

```
puts File.absolute_path("bin")
puts File.absolute_path("../../bin", "/tmp/x")
```

produces:

```
/Users/dave/BS2/published/ruby4/Book/bin
/bin
```

atime

File.atime(filename) → time

Returns a Time object containing the last access time for the named file or returns epoch if the file has not been accessed.

```
File.atime("testfile") # => 2013-05-27 12:32:02 -0500
```

basename

File.basename(filename ‹, suffix ›) → string

Returns the last component of the filename given in *filename*. If *suffix* is given and is present at the end of *filename,* it is removed. Any extension can be removed by giving an extension of *.**.

```
File.basename("/home/gumby/work/ruby.rb")          # => "ruby.rb"
File.basename("/home/gumby/work/ruby.rb", ".rb")   # => "ruby"
File.basename("/home/gumby/work/ruby.rb", ".*")    # => "ruby"
```

blockdev?

File.blockdev?(filename) → true or false

Returns true if the named file is a block device and returns false if it isn't or if the operating system doesn't support this feature.

```
File.blockdev?("testfile") # => false
```

chardev?

File.chardev?(filename) → true or false

Returns true if the named file is a character device and returns false if it isn't or if the operating system doesn't support this feature.

```
File.chardev?("/dev/tty") # => true
```

chmod

File.chmod(permission ‹, filename ›+) → int

Changes permission bits on the named file(s) to the bit pattern represented by *permission*. Actual effects are operating system dependent (see the beginning of this section). On Unix systems, see chmod(2) for details. Returns the number of files processed.

```
File.chmod(0644, "testfile", "some_other_file") # => 2
```

chown

File.chown(owner, group ‹, filename ›+) → int

Changes the owner and/or group of the named file(s) to the given numeric owner and group IDs. Only a process with superuser privileges may change the owner of a file. The current owner of a file may change the file's group to any group to which the owner belongs. A nil or -1 owner or group ID is ignored. Returns the number of files processed.

```
File.chown(nil, 100, "testfile")
```

---

ctime   File.ctime(*filename*) → *time*

Returns a Time object containing the time that the file status associated with the named file
was changed.

```
File.ctime("testfile") # => 2013-05-27 12:32:04 -0500
```

---

delete   File.delete(‹*filename*›+) → *int*

Deletes the named file(s). Returns the number of files processed. See also Dir.rmdir.

```
File.open("testrm", "w+") {}
File.delete("testrm") # => 1
```

---

directory?   File.directory?(*path*) → *true* or *false*

Returns true if the named file is a directory; returns false otherwise.

```
File.directory?(".") # => true
```

---

dirname   File.dirname(*filename*) → *filename*

Returns all components of the filename given in *filename* except the last one.

```
File.dirname("/home/gumby/work/ruby.rb") # => "/home/gumby/work"
File.dirname("ruby.rb")                  # => "."
```

---

executable?   File.executable?(*filename*) → *true* or *false*

Returns true if the named file is executable. The tests are made using the effective owner of
the process.

```
File.executable?("testfile") # => false
```

---

executable_real?   File.executable_real?(*filename*) → *true* or *false*

Same as File#executable? but tests using the real owner of the process.

---

exist?   File.exist?(*filename*) → *true* or *false*

Returns true if the named file or directory exists.

```
File.exist?("testfile") # => true
```

---

exists?   File.exists? (*filename*) → *true* or *false*

Synonym for File.exist?.

expand_path

File.expand_path(*filename* ‹ , *dirstring* ›) → *filename*

Converts a path name to an absolute path name. Relative paths are referenced from the current working directory of the process unless *dirstring* is given, in which case it will be used as the starting point. The given path name may start with a ~, which expands to the process owner's home directory (the environment variable HOME must be set correctly). ~user expands to the named user's home directory. See also File#absolute_path.

```
File.expand_path("~/bin")                # => "/Users/dave/bin"
File.expand_path("../../bin", "/tmp/x")  # => "/bin"
```

extname

File.extname(*path*) → *string*

Returns the extension (the portion of filename in *path* after the period).

```
File.extname("test.rb")        # => ".rb"
File.extname("a/b/d/test.rb")  # => ".rb"
File.extname("test")           # => ""
```

file?

File.file?(*filename*) → *true* or *false*

Returns true if the named file is a regular file (not a device file, directory, pipe, socket, and so on).

```
File.file?("testfile")  # => true
File.file?(".")         # => false
```

fnmatch

File.fnmatch(*glob_pattern, path,* ‹ *flags* ›) → *true* or *false*

Returns true if *path* matches against *glob_pattern*. The pattern is not a regular expression; instead, it follows rules similar to shell filename globbing. A *glob_pattern* may contain the following metacharacters.

*	Matches zero or more characters in a file or directory name.
**	Matches zero or more characters, ignoring name boundaries. Most often used to scan subdirectories recursively.
?	Matches any single character.
[charset]	Matches any character from the given set of characters. A range of characters is written as from-to. The set may be negated with an initial caret (^).
\	Escapes any special meaning of the next character.

flags is a bitwise OR of the FNM_xxx constants.

FNM_EXTGLOB	Expand braces in the pattern. (new in 2.0)
FNM_NOESCAPE	A backslash does not escape special characters in globs, and a backslash in the pattern must match a backslash in the filename.
FNM_PATHNAME	Forward slashes in the filename are treated as separating parts of a path and so must be explicitly matched in the pattern.

FNM_DOTMATCH   If this option is not specified, filenames containing leading periods must be matched by an explicit period in the pattern. A leading period is one at the start of the filename or (if FNM_PATHNAME is specified) following a slash.

FNM_CASEFOLD   Filename matches are case insensitive.

See also Dir.glob on page 458.

```
File.fnmatch('cat',       'cat')       # => true
File.fnmatch('cat',       'category') # => false
File.fnmatch('c?t',       'cat')       # => true
File.fnmatch('c\?t',      'cat')       # => false

File.fnmatch('c??t',   'cat')                        # => false
File.fnmatch('c*',     'cats')                       # => true
File.fnmatch('c/**/t', 'c/a/b/c/t')                  # => true
File.fnmatch('c**t',   'c/a/b/c/t')                  # => true
File.fnmatch('c**t',   'cat')                        # => true
File.fnmatch('**.txt', 'some/dir/tree/notes.txt') # => true
File.fnmatch('c*t',    'cat')                        # => true
File.fnmatch('c\at',   'cat')                        # => true
File.fnmatch('c\at',   'cat', File::FNM_NOESCAPE) # => false
File.fnmatch('a?b',    'a/b')                        # => true
File.fnmatch('a?b',    'a/b', File::FNM_PATHNAME) # => false

File.fnmatch('*',   '.profile')                           # => false
File.fnmatch('*',   '.profile', File::FNM_DOTMATCH)       # => true
File.fnmatch('*',   'dave/.profile')                      # => true
File.fnmatch('*',   'dave/.profile', File::FNM_DOTMATCH) # => true
File.fnmatch('*',   'dave/.profile', File::FNM_PATHNAME) # => false
File.fnmatch('*/*', 'dave/.profile', File::FNM_PATHNAME) # => false
STRICT = File::FNM_PATHNAME | File::FNM_DOTMATCH
File.fnmatch('*/*', 'dave/.profile', STRICT)              # => true
```

---

fnmatch?   File.fnmatch?(glob_pattern, path, ‹flags›) → (true or false)

Synonym for File#fnmatch.

---

ftype   File.ftype(filename) → filetype

Identifies the type of the named file. The return string is one of file, directory, characterSpecial, blockSpecial, fifo, link, socket, or unknown.

```
File.ftype("testfile")  # => "file"
File.ftype("/dev/tty")  # => "characterSpecial"
system("mkfifo wibble") # => true
File.ftype("wibble")    # => "fifo"
```

---

grpowned?   File.grpowned?(filename) → true or false

Returns true if the effective group ID of the process is the same as the group ID of the named file. On Windows, returns false.

```
File.grpowned?("/etc/passwd") # => false
```

---

identical?   File.identical?(*name1, name2*) → *true* or *false*

Returns true only if *name1* and *name2* refer to the same file. Two separate files with the same content are not considered to be identical.

```
File.identical?("testfile", "./code/../testfile") # => true
File.symlink("testfile", "wibble")
File.identical?("testfile", "wibble")              # => true
File.link("testfile", "wobble")
File.identical?("testfile", "wobble")              # => true
File.identical?("wibble", "wobble")                # => true
```

---

join   File.join(‹ *string* ›+) → *filename*

Returns a new string formed by joining the strings using File::SEPARATOR. The various separators are as follows:

ALT_SEPARATOR	Alternate path separator (\ on Windows, nil otherwise)
PATH_SEPARATOR	Separator for filenames in a search path (such as : or ;)
SEPARATOR	Separator for directory components in a filename (such as \ or /)
Separator	Alias for SEPARATOR

```
File.join("usr", "mail", "gumby") # => "usr/mail/gumby"
```

---

lchmod   File.lchmod(*permission*, ‹ *filename* ›+) → 0

Equivalent to File.chmod but does not follow symbolic links (so it will change the permissions associated with the link, not the file referenced by the link). Often not available.

---

lchown   File.lchown(*owner*, *group*, ‹ *filename* ›+) → 0

Equivalent to File.chown but does not follow symbolic links (so it will change the owner associated with the link, not the file referenced by the link). Often not available.

---

link   File.link(*oldname*, *newname*) → 0

Creates a new name for an existing file using a hard link. Will not overwrite *newname* if it already exists (in which case link raises a subclass of SystemCallError). Not available on all platforms.

```
File.link("testfile", "testfile.2") # => 0
f = File.open("testfile.2")
f.gets                              # => "This is line one\n"
File.delete("testfile.2")
```

---

lstat   File.lstat(*filename*) → *stat*

Returns status information for *file* as an object of type File::Stat. Same as IO#stat on page 554 but does not follow the last symbolic link. Instead, reports on the link itself.

```
File.symlink("testfile", "link2test") # => 0
File.stat("testfile").size            # => 66
File.lstat("link2test").size          # => 8
File.stat("link2test").size           # => 66
```

---

mtime   File.mtime(*filename*) → *time*

Returns a Time object containing the modification time for the named file.

```
File.mtime("testfile") # => 2013-05-16 20:00:29 -0500
File.mtime("/tmp")     # => 2013-05-27 11:52:10 -0500
```

---

new   File.new(*filename, mode="r"* ‹ *, permission* › ‹ *options* ›) → *file*
                          File.new(*integer_fd* ‹ *, mode* ‹ *, options* › ›) → *file*

If the first parameter is an integer (or can be converted to an integer using to_int), it is the file descriptor or an already-open file. In that case, the call is passed to IO.new for processing.

More commonly, opens the file named by *filename* according to *mode* (the default is "r") and returns a new File object. The *mode* contains information on the way the file is to be opened and optionally on the encodings to be associated with the file data. Modes are most commonly represented as a string but can be expressed as an integer. Mode strings have the form file-mode[:external-encoding[:internal-encoding]]". The file-mode portion is one of the options listed in the following table. The two encodings are the names (or aliases) of encodings supported by your interpreter. See Chapter 17, *Character Encoding*, on page 239 for more information.

---

r	Read-only, starts at beginning of file (default mode).
r+	Read/write, starts at beginning of file.
w	Write-only, truncates an existing file to zero length or creates a new file for writing.
w+	Read/write, truncates existing file to zero length or creates a new file for reading and writing.
a	Write-only, starts at end of file if file exists; otherwise, creates a new file for writing.
a+	Read/write, starts at end of file if file exists; otherwise, creates a new file for reading and writing.
b	Binary file mode (may appear with any of the key letters listed earlier). As of Ruby 1.9, this modifier should be supplied on all ports opened in binary mode (on Unix as well as on DOS/Windows). To read a file in binary mode and receive the data as a stream of bytes, use the modestring "rb:ascii-8bit".

Table 16—Mode values

When expressed as an integer, the mode is specified by OR-ing together the values in the following table. If your system does not support the underlying functionality, the constants will not be defined. The descriptions below are just hints at the underlying functionality— see the man page for open(2) for the details.

File::APPEND	Opens the file in append mode; all writes will occur at end of file.
File::ASYNC	Generate a signal when input or output become possible.

File::BINARY	Use Ruby's binary mode.
File::CREAT	Creates the file on open if it does not exist.
File::DIRECT	Try to minimize the effects of caching.
File::DSYNC	Opens for synchronous I/O, blocking until buffered data (but not necessarily inode information) is written.
File::EXCL	When used with File::CREAT, opens will fail if the file exists.
File::NOATIME	Do not update the file's last access time on reading.
File::NOCTTY	When opening a terminal device (see IO#isatty on page 549), does not allow it to become the controlling terminal.
File::NOFOLLOW	Do not open the file if the name is a symbolic link.
File::NONBLOCK	Opens the file in nonblocking mode.
File::RDONLY	Opens for reading only.
File::RDWR	Opens for reading and writing.
File::SYNC	Opens for synchronous I/O, blocking until buffered data is written.
File::TRUNC	Opens the file and truncates it to zero length if the file exists.
File::WRONLY	Opens for writing only.

Optional permission bits may be given in *permission*. These bits are platform dependent; on Unix systems, see open(2) for details.

If the final parameter is a hash, it is used to control options, as described in the following table. The mode can be passed as one of the options of this hash.

autoclose:	If false, the underlying file will not be closed when this I/O object is finalized.
binmode:	Opens the IO object in binary mode if true (same as mode: "b").
encoding:	Specifies both external and internal encodings as "external:internal" (same format used in mode parameter.
external_encoding:	Specifies the external encoding.
internal_encoding:	Specifies the internal encoding.
mode:	Specifies what would have been the *mode* parameter (so File.open("xx", "r:utf-8") is the same as File.open("xx", mode: "r:utf-8").
perm:	Specifies what would have been the *permission* parameter.
textmode:	Open the file in text mode (the default).
	In addition, the options parameter can use the key/value pairs that are specified to String.encode to control the processing of text data. See Table 22, *Options to encode and encode!*, on page 675.

Table 17—File and I/O open options

See also IO.open on page 539 for a block form of File.new.

```
# open for reading, default external encoding
f = File.new("testfile", "r")

# open for reading, assume contents are utf-8
f = File.new("testfile", "r:utf-8")

# Same, using an options hash
f = File.new("testfile", mode: "r", external_encoding: "utf-8")

# Translate cr/lf to just lf (a String#encode option)
f = File.new("testfile", universal_newline: true)

# open for read/write. external utf-8 data will be converted to iso-8859-1
# when read, and converted from 8859-1 to utf-8 on writing
f = File.new("newfile",  "w+:utf-8:iso-8859-1")

# same as specifying "w+"
f = File.new("newfile", File::CREAT|File::TRUNC|File::RDWR, 0644)
```

owned?   File.owned?(*filename*) → *true* or *false*

Returns true if the effective user ID of the process is the same as the owner of the named file.

```
File.owned?("/etc/passwd") # => false
```

path   File.path(*obj*) → *string*

Returns the path of *obj*. If *obj* responds to to_path, its value is returned. Otherwise, attempt to convert *obj* to a string and return that value.

```
File.path("testfile")          # => "testfile"
File.path("/tmp/../tmp/xxx")    # => "/tmp/../tmp/xxx"
f = File.open("/tmp/../tmp/xxx")
File.path(f)                   # => "/tmp/../tmp/xxx"
```

pipe?   File.pipe?(*filename*) → *true* or *false*

Returns true if the OS supports pipes and the named file is one; false otherwise.

```
File.pipe?("testfile") # => false
```

readable?   File.readable?(*filename*) → *true* or *false*

Returns true if the named file is readable by the effective user ID of this process.

```
File.readable?("testfile") # => true
```

readable_real?   File.readable_real?(*filename*) → *true* or *false*

Returns true if the named file is readable by the real user ID of this process.

```
File.readable_real?("testfile") # => true
```

readlink

File.readlink(*filename*) → *filename*

Returns the given symbolic link as a string. Not available on all platforms.

```
File.symlink("testfile", "link2test") # => 0
File.readlink("link2test")            # => "testfile"
```

realdirpath

File.realdirpath(*path* ‹, *relative_to* ›) → *string*

Converts *path* to a full file path, with all symlinks resolved and relative paths made absolute. If a second parameter if present, it is used as the base for resolving leading relative path segments. The actual file (the past component of the path) need not exist.

```
puts File.realdirpath("/var/log/system.log")
puts File.realdirpath("../Common/xml")
puts File.realdirpath("Sites", "/Users/dave")
```

produces:

```
/private/var/log/system.log
/Users/dave/BS2/published/ruby4/Common/xml
/Users/dave/Sites
```

realpath

File.realpath(*path* ‹, *relative_to* ›) → *string*

Converts *path* to a full file path, with all symlinks resolved and relative paths made absolute. If a second parameter if present, it is used as the base for resolving leading relative path segments.

```
puts File.realpath("/var/log/system.log")
puts File.realpath("../PerBook/util/xml/ppbook.dtd")
puts File.realpath("Sites/index.html", "/Users/dave")
```

produces:

```
/private/var/log/system.log
/Users/dave/BS2/published/ruby4/PerBook/util/xml/ppbook.dtd
/Users/dave/Sites/index.html
```

rename

File.rename(*oldname, newname*) → 0

Renames the given file or directory to the new name. Raises a SystemCallError if the file cannot be renamed.

```
File.rename("afile", "afile.bak") # => 0
```

setgid?

File.setgid?(*filename*) → *true* or *false*

Returns true if the named file's set-group-id permission bit is set and returns false if it isn't or if the operating system doesn't support this feature.

```
File.setgid?("/usr/sbin/lpc") # => false
```

setuid?

File.setuid?(*filename*) → *true* or *false*

Returns true if the named file's set-user-id permission bit is set and returns false if it isn't or if the operating system doesn't support this feature.

```
File.setuid?("/bin/su") # => false
```

size

File.size(*filename*) → *int*

Returns the size of the file in bytes.

```
File.size("testfile") # => 66
```

size?

File.size?(*filename*) → *int* or nil

Returns nil if the named file is of zero length; otherwise, returns the size. Usable as a condition in tests.

```
File.size?("testfile")  # => 66
File.size?("/dev/zero") # => nil
```

socket?

File.socket?(*filename*) → *true* or *false*

Returns true if the named file is a socket and returns false if it isn't or if the operating system doesn't support this feature.

split

File.split(*filename*) → *array*

Splits the given string into a directory and a file component and returns them in a two-element array. See also File.dirname and File.basename.

```
File.split("/home/gumby/.profile") # => ["/home/gumby", ".profile"]
File.split("ruby.rb")              # => [".", "ruby.rb"]
```

stat

File.stat(*filename*) → *stat*

Returns a File::Stat object for the named file (see File::Stat on page 503).

```
stat = File.stat("testfile")
stat.mtime # => 2013-05-16 20:00:29 -0500
stat.ftype # => "file"
```

sticky?

File.sticky?(*filename*) → *true* or *false*

Returns true if the named file has its sticky bit set and returns false if it doesn't or if the operating system doesn't support this feature.

symlink

File.symlink(*oldname, newname*) → 0 or nil

Creates a symbolic link called *newname* for the file *oldname*. Returns nil on all platforms that do not support symbolic links.

```
File.symlink("testfile", "link2test") # => 0
```

symlink?

File.symlink?(*filename*) → *true* or *false*

Returns true if the named file is a symbolic link and returns false if it isn't or if the operating system doesn't support this feature.

```
File.symlink("testfile", "link2test") # => 0
File.symlink?("link2test")            # => true
```

truncate

File.truncate(*filename, int*) → 0

Truncates the file *filename* to be at most *int* bytes long. Not available on all platforms.

```
f = File.new("out", "w")
f.write("1234567890")   # => 10
f.close                 # => nil
File.truncate("out", 5) # => 0
File.size("out")        # => 5
```

umask

File.umask(‹ *int* ›) → *int*

Returns the current umask value for this process. If the optional argument is given, sets the umask to that value and returns the previous value. Umask values are *excluded* from the default permissions; so, a umask of 0222 would make a file read-only for everyone. See also the discussion of permissions on page 488.

```
File.umask(0006) # => 18
File.umask       # => 6
```

unlink

File.unlink(‹ *filename* ›+) → *int*

Synonym for File.delete. See also Dir.rmdir.

```
File.open("testrm", "w+") {} # => nil
File.unlink("testrm")        # => 1
```

utime

File.utime(*accesstime, modtime* ‹ *, filename* ›+) → *int*

Changes the access and modification times on a number of files. The times must be instances of class Time or integers representing the number of seconds since epoch. Returns the number of files processed. Not available on all platforms.

```
File.utime(0, 0, "testfile")         # => 1
File.mtime("testfile")               # => 1969-12-31 18:00:00 -0600
File.utime(0, Time.now, "testfile")  # => 1
File.mtime("testfile")               # => 2013-05-27 12:32:07 -0500
```

world_readable?

File.world_readable?(*filename*) → *perm_int* or nil

If *filename* is readable by others, returns an integer representing the file permission bits of *filename*. Returns nil otherwise. The meaning of the bits is platform dependent; on Unix systems, see stat(2).

```
File.world_readable?("/etc/passwd")           # => 420
File.world_readable?("/etc/passwd").to_s(8) # => "644"
```

world_writable?

File.world_writable?(*filename*) → *perm_int* or nil

If *filename* is writable by others, returns an integer representing the file permission bits of *filename*. Returns nil otherwise. The meaning of the bits is platform dependent; on Unix systems, see stat(2).

```
File.world_writable?("/etc/passwd")  # => nil
File.world_writable?("/tmp")         # => 511
File.world_writable?("/tmp").to_s(8) # => "777"
```

writable?

File.writable?(*filename*) → *true* or *false*

Returns true if the named file is writable by the effective user ID of this process.

```
File.writable?("/etc/passwd") # => false
File.writable?("testfile")    # => true
```

writable_real?

File.writable_real?(*filename*) → *true* or *false*

Returns true if the named file is writable by the real user ID of this process.

zero?

File.zero?(*filename*) → *true* or *false*

Returns true if the named file is of zero length and returns false otherwise.

```
File.zero?("testfile")  # => false
File.open("zerosize", "w") {}
File.zero?("zerosize")  # => true
```

Instance Methods

atime

file.atime → *time*

Returns a Time object containing the last access time for *file* or returns epoch if the file has not been accessed.

```
File.new("testfile").atime # => 1969-12-31 18:00:00 -0600
```

chmod

file.chmod(*permission*) → 0

Changes permission bits on *file* to the bit pattern represented by *permission*. Actual effects are platform dependent; on Unix systems, see chmod(2) for details. Follows symbolic links. See the discussion of permissions on page 488. Also see File.lchmod.

```
f = File.new("out", "w");
f.chmod(0644)        # => 0
```

chown

file.chown(*owner*, *group*) → 0

Changes the owner and group of *file* to the given numeric owner and group IDs. Only a process with superuser privileges may change the owner of a file. The current owner of a file may change the file's group to any group to which the owner belongs. A nil or -1 owner or group ID is ignored. Follows symbolic links. See also File.lchown.

```
File.new("testfile").chown(502, 400)
```

ctime

file.ctime → *time*

Returns a Time object containing the time that the file status associated with *file* was changed.

```
File.new("testfile").ctime # => 2013-05-27 12:32:07 -0500
```

flock

file.flock (*locking_constant*) → 0 or false

Locks or unlocks a file according to *locking_constant* (a logical *or* of the following values).

LOCK_EX	Exclusive lock. Only one process may hold an exclusive lock for a given file at a time.
LOCK_NB	Don't block when locking. May be combined with other lock options using | *(or)*
LOCK_SH	Shared lock. Multiple processes may each hold a shared lock for a given file at the same time.
LOCK_UN	Unlock.

Table 18—Lock-mode constants

Returns false if File::LOCK_NB is specified, and the operation would otherwise have blocked. Not available on all platforms.

```
File.new("testfile").flock(File::LOCK_UN) # => 0
```

lstat

file.lstat → *stat*

Same as IO#stat but does not follow the last symbolic link. Instead, reports on the link itself.

```
File.symlink("testfile", "link2test") # => 0
File.stat("testfile").size            # => 66
f = File.new("link2test")
f.lstat.size                          # => 8
f.stat.size                           # => 66
```

mtime

file.mtime → *time*

Returns a Time object containing the modification time for *file*.

```
File.new("testfile").mtime # => 2013-05-27 12:32:07 -0500
```

path   *file*.path → *filename*

Returns the path name used to create *file* as a string. Does not normalize the name.

```
File.new("testfile").path           # => "testfile"
File.new("/tmp/../tmp/xxx", "w").path # => "/tmp/../tmp/xxx"
```

size   *file*.size(*filename*) → *int*

Returns the size of *file* in bytes.

```
File.open("testfile").size # => 66
```

to_path   *file*.to_path → *filename*

Alias for File#path.

truncate   *file*.truncate(*int*) → 0

Truncates *file* to at most *int* bytes. The file must be opened for writing. Not available on all platforms.

```
f = File.new("out", "w")
f.syswrite("1234567890") # => 10
f.truncate(5)            # => 0
f.close()                # => nil
File.size("out")         # => 5
```

Class File::Stat

Objects of class File::Stat encapsulate common status information for File objects. The information is recorded at the moment the File::Stat object is created; changes made to the file after that point will not be reflected. File::Stat objects are returned by IO#stat, File.stat, File#lstat, and File.lstat. Many of these methods may return platform-specific values, and not all values are meaningful on all systems. See also Object#test on page 628.

Mixes In

Comparable: <, <=, ==, >, >=, between?

Instance Methods

<=>   *statfile <=> other_stat → -1, 0, 1*

Compares File::Stat objects by comparing their respective modification times.

```
f1 = File.new("f1", "w")
sleep 1
f2 = File.new("f2", "w")
f1.stat <=> f2.stat # => -1
# Methods in Comparable are also available
f1.stat > f2.stat    # => false
f1.stat < f2.stat    # => true
```

atime   *statfile.atime → time*

Returns a Time object containing the last access time for *statfile* or returns epoch if the file has not been accessed.

```
File.stat("testfile").atime      # => 1969-12-31 18:00:00 -0600
File.stat("testfile").atime.to_i # => 0
```

blksize   *statfile.blksize → int*

Returns the native file system's block size. Will return nil on platforms that don't support this information.

```
File.stat("testfile").blksize # => 4096
```

blockdev?   *statfile.blockdev? → true or false*

Returns true if the file is a block device and returns false if it isn't or if the operating system doesn't support this feature.

```
File.stat("testfile").blockdev?   # => false
File.stat("/dev/disk0").blockdev? # => true
```

blocks

statfile.blocks → *int*

Returns the number of native file system blocks allocated for this file or returns nil if the operating system doesn't support this feature.

```
File.stat("testfile").blocks # => 8
```

chardev?

statfile.chardev? → *true* or *false*

Returns true if the file is a character device and returns false if it isn't or if the operating system doesn't support this feature.

```
File.stat("/dev/tty").chardev? # => true
File.stat("testfile").chardev? # => false
```

ctime

statfile.ctime → *time*

Returns a Time object set to the time that the file status associated with *statfile* was changed.

```
File.stat("testfile").ctime # => 2013-05-27 12:32:07 -0500
```

dev

statfile.dev → *int*

Returns an integer representing the device on which *statfile* resides. The bits in the device integer will often encode major and minor device information.

```
File.stat("testfile").dev        # => 16777219
"%x" % File.stat("testfile").dev # => "1000003"
```

dev_major

statfile.dev_major → *int*

Returns the major part of File::Stat#dev or nil if the operating system doesn't support this feature.

```
File.stat("testfile").dev_major # => 1
```

dev_minor

statfile.dev_minor → *int*

Returns the minor part of File::Stat#dev or nil if the operating system doesn't support this feature.

```
File.stat("testfile").dev_minor # => 3
```

directory?

statfile.directory? → *true* or *false*

Returns true if *statfile* is a directory and returns false otherwise.

```
File.stat("testfile").directory? # => false
File.stat(".").directory?        # => true
```

executable?

statfile.executable? → *true or false*

Returns true if *statfile* is executable or if the operating system doesn't distinguish executable files from nonexecutable files. The tests are made using the effective owner of the process.

```
File.stat("testfile").executable? # => false
```

executable_real?

statfile.executable_real? → *true or false*

Same as executable? but tests using the real owner of the process.

file?

statfile.file? → *true or false*

Returns true if *statfile* is a regular file (not a device file, pipe, socket, and so on).

```
File.stat("testfile").file? # => true
```

ftype

statfile.ftype → *type_string*

Identifies the type of *statfile*. The return string is one of the following: file, directory, character-Special, blockSpecial, fifo, link, socket, or unknown.

```
File.stat("/dev/tty").ftype # => "characterSpecial"
```

gid

statfile.gid → *int*

Returns the numeric group ID of the owner of *statfile*.

```
File.stat("testfile").gid # => 20
```

grpowned?

statfile.grpowned? → *true or false*

Returns true if the effective group ID of the process is the same as the group ID of *statfile*. On Windows, returns false.

```
File.stat("testfile").grpowned?    # => true
File.stat("/etc/passwd").grpowned? # => false
```

ino

statfile.ino → *int*

Returns the inode number for *statfile*.

```
File.stat("testfile").ino # => 29399443
```

mode

statfile.mode → *int*

Returns an integer representing the permission bits of *statfile*. The meaning of the bits is platform dependent; on Unix systems, see stat(2).

```
File.chmod(0644, "testfile")       # => 1
File.stat("testfile").mode.to_s(8) # => "100644"
```

---

mtime
statfile.mtime → *time*

Returns a Time object containing the modification time for *statfile*.

```
File.stat("testfile").mtime # => 2013-05-27 12:32:07 -0500
```

---

nlink
statfile.nlink → *int*

Returns the number of hard links to *statfile*.

```
File.stat("testfile").nlink            # => 1
File.link("testfile", "testfile.bak") # => 0
File.stat("testfile").nlink            # => 2
```

---

owned?
statfile.owned? → *true* or *false*

Returns true if the effective user ID of the process is the same as the owner of *statfile*.

```
File.stat("testfile").owned?     # => true
File.stat("/etc/passwd").owned? # => false
```

---

pipe?
statfile.pipe? → *true* or *false*

Returns true if the operating system supports pipes and *statfile* is a pipe.

---

rdev
statfile.rdev → *int*

Returns an integer representing the device type on which *statfile* (which should be a special file) resides. Returns nil if the operating system doesn't support this feature.

```
File.stat("/dev/disk0s1").rdev # => 16777217
File.stat("/dev/tty").rdev      # => 33554432
```

---

rdev_major
statfile.rdev_major → *int*

Returns the major part of File::Stat#rdev or nil if the operating system doesn't support this feature.

```
File.stat("/dev/disk0s1").rdev_major # => 1
File.stat("/dev/tty").rdev_major      # => 2
```

---

rdev_minor
statfile.rdev_minor → *int*

Returns the minor part of File::Stat#rdev or nil if the operating system doesn't support this feature.

```
File.stat("/dev/disk0s1").rdev_minor # => 1
File.stat("/dev/tty").rdev_minor      # => 0
```

readable?   *statfile*.readable? → *true* or *false*

Returns true if *statfile* is readable by the effective user ID of this process.

```
File.stat("testfile").readable? # => true
```

readable_real?   *statfile*.readable_real? → *true* or *false*

Returns true if *statfile* is readable by the real user ID of this process.

```
File.stat("testfile").readable_real?    # => true
File.stat("/etc/passwd").readable_real? # => true
```

setgid?   *statfile*.setgid? → *true* or *false*

Returns true if *statfile* has the set-group-id permission bit set and returns false if it doesn't or if the operating system doesn't support this feature.

```
File.stat("testfile").setgid?            # => false
File.stat("/usr/sbin/postdrop").setgid? # => true
```

setuid?   *statfile*.setuid? → *true* or *false*

Returns true if *statfile* has the set-user-id permission bit set and returns false if it doesn't or if the operating system doesn't support this feature.

```
File.stat("testfile").setuid?    # => false
File.stat("/usr/bin/su").setuid? # => true
```

size   *statfile*.size → *int*

Returns the size of *statfile* in bytes.

```
File.stat("/dev/zero").size # => 0
File.stat("testfile").size  # => 66
```

size?   *statfile*.size? → *int* or nil

Returns nil if *statfile* is a zero-length file; otherwise, returns the file size. Usable as a condition in tests.

```
File.stat("/dev/zero").size? # => nil
File.stat("testfile").size?  # => 66
```

socket?   *statfile*.socket? → *true* or *false*

Returns true if *statfile* is a socket and returns false if it isn't or if the operating system doesn't support this feature.

```
File.stat("testfile").socket? # => false
```

sticky?

statfile.sticky? → *true* or *false*

Returns true if *statfile* has its sticky bit set and returns false if it doesn't or if the operating system doesn't support this feature.

```
File.stat("testfile").sticky? # => false
```

symlink?

statfile.symlink? → *true* or *false*

Returns true if *statfile* is a symbolic link; returns false if it isn't or if the operating system doesn't support this feature. Because File.stat automatically follows symbolic links, symlink? will always be false for an object returned by File.stat.

```
File.symlink("testfile", "alink") # => 0
File.stat("alink").symlink?       # => false
File.lstat("alink").symlink?      # => true
```

uid

statfile.uid → *int*

Returns the numeric user ID of the owner of *statfile*.

```
File.stat("testfile").uid # => 501
```

world_readable?

statfile.world_readable?(*filename*) → *perm_int* or nil

If *filename* is readable by others, returns an integer representing the file permission bits of *filename*. Returns nil otherwise. The meaning of the bits is platform dependent; on Unix systems, see stat(2).

```
File.stat("/etc/passwd").world_readable?         # => 420
File.stat("/etc/passwd").world_readable?.to_s(8) # => "644"
```

world_writable?

statfile.world_writable?(*filename*) → *perm_int* or nil

If *filename* is writable by others, returns an integer representing the file permission bits of *filename*. Returns nil otherwise. The meaning of the bits is platform dependent; on Unix systems, see stat(2).

```
File.stat("/etc/passwd").world_writable?  # => nil
File.stat("/tmp").world_writable?         # => 511
File.stat("/tmp").world_writable?.to_s(8) # => "777"
```

writable?

statfile.writable? → *true* or *false*

Returns true if *statfile* is writable by the effective user ID of this process.

```
File.stat("testfile").writable? # => true
```

writable_real? $\qquad$ *statfile*.writable_real? → *true* or *false*

Returns true if *statfile* is writable by the real user ID of this process.

```
File.stat("testfile").writable_real? # => true
```

zero? $\qquad$ *statfile*.zero? → *true* or *false*

Returns true if *statfile* is a zero-length file; returns false otherwise.

```
File.stat("testfile").zero? # => false
```

Module **FileTest**

FileTest implements file test operations similar to those used in File::Stat. The methods in FileTest are duplicated in class File. Rather than repeat the documentation here, we list the names of the methods and refer you to the documentation for File on page 488. FileTest appears to be a somewhat vestigial module.

The FileTest methods are: blockdev?, chardev?, directory?, executable?, executable_real?, exist?, exists?, file?, grpowned?, identical?, owned?, pipe?, readable?, readable_real?, setgid?, setuid?, size, size?, socket?, sticky?, symlink?, world_readable?, world_writable?, writable?, writable_real?, zero?

Class   **Fixnum**   <   Integer

A Fixnum holds integer values that can be represented in a native machine word (minus 1 bit). If any operation on a Fixnum exceeds this range, the value is converted to a Bignum.

Fixnum objects have immediate value. This means that when they are assigned or passed as parameters, the actual object is passed, rather than a reference to that object. Assignment does not alias Fixnum objects. Because there is effectively only one Fixnum object instance for any given integer value, you cannot, for example, add a singleton method to a Fixnum.

Instance Methods

Arithmetic operations

Performs various arithmetic operations on *fix*.

fix	+	*numeric*	Addition
fix	−	*numeric*	Subtraction
fix	*	*numeric*	Multiplication
fix	/	*numeric*	Division
fix	%	*numeric*	Modulo
fix	**	*numeric*	Exponentiation
fix	-@		Unary minus

Bit operations

Performs various operations on the binary representations of the Fixnum.

~ *fix*			Invert bits
fix	|	*numeric*	Bitwise *or*
fix	&	*numeric*	Bitwise *and*
fix	^	*numeric*	Bitwise *exclusive or*
fix	<<	*numeric*	Left-shift *numeric* bits
fix	>>	*numeric*	Right-shift *numeric* bits (with sign extension)

Comparisons

Compares *fix* to other numbers. Fixnum. <, <=, ==, >=, and >.

<=>   *fix* <=> *numeric* → -1, 0, +1, or nil

Comparison—Returns -1, 0, or +1 depending on whether *fix* is less than, equal to, or greater than *numeric*. Although Fixnum's grandparent mixes in Comparable, Fixnum does not use that module for performing comparisons, instead implementing the comparison operators explicitly.

```
42 <=> 13 # => 1
13 <=> 42 # => -1
-1 <=> -1 # => 0
```

[ ]

fix[*n*] → 0, 1

Bit Reference—Returns the *n*th bit in the binary representation of *fix*, where *fix*[0] is the least significant bit.

```
a = 0b11001100101010
30.downto(0) {|n| print a[n] }
```

produces:

```
00000000000000000011001100101010
```

abs

fix.abs → *int*

Returns the absolute value of *fix*.

```
-12345.abs # => 12345
12345.abs  # => 12345
```

div

fix.div(*numeric*) → *integer*

Division that always produces an integral result. Not affected by the mathn library (unlike Fixnum#/).

```
654321.div(13731)    # => 47
654321.div(13731.34) # => 47
```

even?

fix.even? → *true* or *false*

Returns true if *fix* is even.

```
1.even?  # => false
2.even?  # => true
```

divmod

fix.divmod(*numeric*) → *array*

See Numeric#divmod on page 595.

fdiv

fix.fdiv(*numeric*) → *float*

Returns the floating-point result of dividing *fix* by *numeric*.

```
63.fdiv(9)            # => 7.0
654321.fdiv(13731)    # => 47.652829364212366
654321.fdiv(13731.24) # => 47.65199646936475
```

magnitude

fix.magnitude → *int*

Returns the magnitude of *fix* (the distance of *fix* from the origin of the number line). Synonym for Fixnum#abs. See also Complex#magnitude.

modulo

fix.modulo(*numeric*) → *numeric*

Synonym for Fixnum#%.

```
654321.modulo(13731)    # => 8964
654321.modulo(13731.24) # => 8952.72000000001
```

odd?

fix.odd? → *true* or *false*

Returns true if *fix* is odd.

```
1.odd?    # => true
2.odd?    # => false
```

size

fix.size → *int*

Returns the number of *bytes* in the machine representation of a Fixnum.

```
1.size          # => 8
-1.size         # => 8
2147483647.size # => 8
```

succ

fix.succ → *int*

Returns *fix* + 1.

```
1.succ    # => 2
-1.succ   # => 0
```

to_f

fix.to_f → *float*

Converts *fix* to a Float.

to_s

fix.to_s(*base*=10) → *string*

Returns a string containing the representation of *fix* radix *base* (2 to 36).

```
12345.to_s                        # => "12345"
12345.to_s(2)                     # => "11000000111001"
12345.to_s(8)                     # => "30071"
12345.to_s(10)                    # => "12345"
12345.to_s(16)                    # => "3039"
12345.to_s(36)                    # => "9ix"
84823723233035811745497171.to_s(36) # => "anotherrubyhacker"
```

zero?

fix.zero? → *true* or *false*

Returns true if *fix* is zero.

```
42.zero?  # => false
0.zero?   # => true
```

Float < Numeric

Float objects hold real numbers using the native architecture's double-precision floating-point representation.

Class Constants

DIG	Precision of Float (in decimal digits).
EPSILON	The smallest Float such that 1.0+EPSILON != 1.0.
INFINITY	Positive infinity.
MANT_DIG	The number of mantissa digits (base RADIX).
MAX	The largest Float.
MAX_10_EXP	The maximum integer x such that 10^x is a finite Float.
MAX_EXP	The maximum integer x such that FLT_RADIX^{x-1} is a finite Float.
MIN	The smallest Float.
MIN_10_EXP	The minimum integer x such that 10^x is a finite Float.
MIN_EXP	The minimum integer x such that FLT_RADIX^{x-1} is a finite Float.
NAN	A value that is not a valid number.
RADIX	The radix of floating-point representations.
ROUNDS	The rounding mode for floating-point operations. Possible values include -1 if the mode is indeterminate, 0 if rounding is toward zero, 1 if rounding is to nearest representable value, 2 if rounding is toward infinity, and 3 if rounding is toward minus infinity.

Instance Methods

Arithmetic operations

Performs various arithmetic operations on *flt*.

flt	+	*numeric*	Addition
flt	–	*numeric*	Subtraction
flt	*	*numeric*	Multiplication
flt	/	*numeric*	Division
flt	%	*numeric*	Modulo
flt	**	*numeric*	Exponentiation
flt	-@		Unary minus

Comparisons

Compares *flt* to other numbers. <, <=, ==, >=, >.

<=>   *flt* <=> *numeric* → -1, 0, +1, or nil

Returns -1, 0, or +1 depending on whether *flt* is less than, equal to, or greater than *numeric*.

==   *flt* == *obj* → *true* or *false*

Returns true only if *obj* has the same value as *flt*. Contrast this with Float#eql?, which requires *obj* to be a Float.

```
1.0 == 1.0      # => true
(1.0).eql?(1.0) # => true
1.0 == 1        # => true
(1.0).eql?(1)   # => false
```

---

abs   *flt*.abs → *numeric*

Returns the absolute value of *flt*.

```
(-34.56).abs # => 34.56
-34.56.abs   # => 34.56
```

---

ceil   *flt*.ceil → *int*

Returns the smallest integer greater than or equal to *flt*.

```
1.2.ceil     # => 2
2.0.ceil     # => 2
(-1.2).ceil # => -1
(-2.0).ceil # => -2
```

---

divmod   *flt*.divmod(*numeric*) → *array*

See Numeric#divmod on page 595.

---

eql?   *flt*.eql?(*obj*) → *true* or *false*

Returns true only if *obj* is a Float with the same value as *flt*. Contrast this with Float#==, which performs type conversions.

```
1.0.eql?(1) # => false
1.0 == 1    # => true
```

---

fdiv   *flt*.fdiv(*number*) → *float*

Returns the floating-point result of dividing *flt* by *number*. Alias for Float#quo.

```
63.0.fdiv(9)       # => 7.0
1234.56.fdiv(3.45) # => 357.8434782608695
```

---

finite?   *flt*.finite? → *true* or *false*

Returns true if *flt* is a valid IEEE floating-point number (it is not infinite, and nan? is false).

```
(42.0).finite?    # => true
(1.0/0.0).finite? # => false
```

---

floor   *flt*.floor → *int*

Returns the largest integer less than or equal to *flt*.

```
1.2.floor      # => 1
2.0.floor      # => 2
(-1.2).floor   # => -2
(-2.0).floor   # => -2
```

infinite?   *flt*.infinite? → nil, -1, +1

Returns nil, -1, or +1 depending on whether *flt* is finite, -infinity, or +infinity.

```
(0.0).infinite?      # => nil
(-1.0/0.0).infinite? # => -1
(+1.0/0.0).infinite? # => 1
```

magnitude   *flt*.magnitude → *float*

Returns the magnitude of *flt* (the distance of *flt* from the origin of the number line). Synonym for Float#abs. See also Complex#magnitude.

modulo   *flt*.modulo(*numeric*) → *numeric*

Synonym for Float#%.

```
6543.21.modulo(137)    # => 104.21000000000004
6543.21.modulo(137.24) # => 92.92999999999961
```

nan?   *flt*.nan? → *true* or *false*

Returns true if *flt* is an invalid IEEE floating-point number.

```
(-1.0).nan?     # => false
(0.0/0.0).nan? # => true
```

quo   *flt*.quo(*number*) → *float*

Returns the floating-point result of dividing *flt* by *number*.

```
63.0.quo(9)        # => 7.0
1234.56.quo(3.45) # => 357.8434782608695
```

rationalize   *flt*.rationalize(‹ *epsilon* ›) → *rational*

Converts *flt* to a rational number with an approximate precision of *epsilon*. If *epsilon* is not given, a value will be chosen that preserves as many significant digits of the mantissa as possible.

```
1.3.rationalize                     # => (13/10)
1.333.rationalize                   # => (1333/1000)
1.33333333333333333.rationalize # => (4/3)
1.3333.rationalize(0.001)           # => (4/3)
1.3333.rationalize(1)               # => (1/1)
Math::PI.rationalize(0.01)          # => (22/7)
```

---

round
flt.round(digits=0) → numeric

Rounds *flt* to the nearest integer if the parameter is omitted or zero or rounds to the given number of digits.

```
1.5.round         # => 2
(-1.5).round      # => -2
3.14159.round     # => 3
3.14159.round(4)  # => 3.1416
3.14159.round(2)  # => 3.14
```

---

to_f
flt.to_f → flt

Returns *flt*.

---

to_i
flt.to_i → int

Returns *flt* truncated to an integer.

```
1.5.to_i    # => 1
(-1.5).to_i # => -1
```

---

to_int
flt.to_int → int

Synonym for Float#to_i.

---

to_r
flt.to_r → number

Converts *flt* to a rational number.

```
1.5.to_r      # => 3/2
(1.0/3).to_r  # => 6004799503160661/18014398509481984
```

---

to_s
flt.to_s → string

Returns a string containing a representation of *flt*. As well as a fixed or exponential form of the number, the call may return NaN, Infinity, and -Infinity.

---

truncate
flt.truncate → int

Synonym for Float#to_i.

---

zero?
flt.zero? → true or false

Returns true if *flt* is 0.0.

Module **GC**

The GC module provides an interface to Ruby's mark and sweep garbage collection mechanism. Some of the underlying methods are also available via the ObjectSpace module, described later on page 631.

Class Methods

count
GC.count → int

Returns a count of the number of times GC has run in the current process.

```
GC.count  # => 4
res = ""
10_000.times { res += "wibble" }
GC.count  # => 42
```

disable
GC.disable → true or false

Disables garbage collection, returning true if garbage collection was already disabled.

```
GC.disable # => false
GC.disable # => true
```

enable
GC.enable → true or false

Enables garbage collection, returning true if garbage collection was disabled.

```
GC.disable # => false
GC.enable  # => true
GC.enable  # => false
```

start
GC.start → nil

Initiates garbage collection, unless manually disabled.

```
GC.start  # => nil
```

stat
GC.stat → stats_hash

Returns a hash containing GC statistics. The contents of this hash are implementation dependend. The method may not be present in all Ruby implementations.

```
GC.stat  # => {:count=>4, :heap_used=>43, :heap_length=>43, :heap_increment=>0,
         # .. :heap_live_num=>13938, :heap_free_num=>8659, :heap_final_num=>41,
         # .. :total_allocated_object=>36625, :total_freed_object=>22687}
```

stress
GC.stress → true or false

Returns the current value of the stress flag (see GC.stress=).

stress=   GC.stress = *true* or *false* → *true* or *false*

Ruby will normally run garbage collection periodically. Setting the stress flag to true forces garbage collection to occur every time Ruby allocates a new object. This is typically used only for testing extensions (and Ruby itself).

```
GC.stress = true
```

Instance Methods

garbage_collect   garbage_collect → nil

Equivalent to GC.start.

```
include GC
garbage_collect # => nil
```

Module GC::Profiler

Provides low-level information on the state of garbage collection.

```
GC::Profiler.enable
animal = "cat"
22.times { animal *= 2 }
printf "Took %0.4fs in GC\n", GC::Profiler.total_time
GC::Profiler.report
GC::Profiler.disable
```

produces:

```
Took 0.0040s in GC
GC 8 invokes.
Index  Invoke     Use Size   Total        Total  GC Time(ms)
       Time(sec)  (byte)     Size(byte)   Object
    1   0.034     334160     700040       17501  1.286000
    2   0.039     329320     700040       17501  1.358000
    3   0.045     329320     700040       17501  1.351000
    4   0.056     329320     700040       17501  1.347000
```

Class Methods

clear   GC::Profiler.clear → nil

Clears existing profile data.

disable   GC::Profiler.disable → nil

Disables the collection of profile data.

enable   GC::Profiler.enable → nil

Enables the collection of profile data.

enabled?   GC::Profiler.enabled? → true or false

Returns true if profile collection is enabled.

raw_data   GC::Profiler.raw_data → array of hashes

Return raw profiling data, in time order, as an array of hashes, where each hash contains a data sample.   *New in 2.0*

```
GC::Profiler.enable

animal = "cat"
22.times { animal *= 2 }

p GC::Profiler.raw_data.size
p GC::Profiler.raw_data[0, 2]
```

produces:

```
5
[{:GC_TIME=>1.0999999999997123e-05, :GC_INVOKE_TIME=>0.03359,
 :HEAP_USE_SIZE=>691000, :HEAP_TOTAL_SIZE=>700040, :HEAP_TOTAL_OBJECTS=>17501,
 :GC_IS_MARKED=>false}, {:GC_TIME=>0.0014199999999999977,
 :GC_INVOKE_TIME=>0.033891, :HEAP_USE_SIZE=>331080, :HEAP_TOTAL_SIZE=>700040,
 :HEAP_TOTAL_OBJECTS=>17501, :GC_IS_MARKED=>0}]
```

report   GC::Profiler.report(*to*=STDOUT) → nil

Writes the profile result to the given stream.

result   GC::Profiler.result → string

Returns a string containing a summary of the profile data.

total_time   GC::Profiler.total_time → float

Returns the total time spend in garbage collection during this profile run.

Hash

A Hash is a collection of key/value pairs. It is similar to an Array, except that indexing is done via arbitrary keys of any object type, not an integer index. The order in which keys and/or values are returned by the various iterators over hash contents will generally be the order that those entries were initially inserted into the hash.

Hashes have a *default value*. This value is returned when an attempt is made to access keys that do not exist in the hash. By default, this value is nil.

Mixes In

Enumerable: all?, any?, chunk, collect, collect_concat, count, cycle, detect, drop, drop_while, each_cons, each_entry, each_slice, each_with_index, each_with_object, entries, find, find_all, find_index, first, flat_map, grep, group_by, include?, inject, lazy, map, max, max_by, member?, min, min_by, minmax, minmax_by, none?, one?, partition, reduce, reject, reverse_each, select, slice_before, sort, sort_by, take, take_while, to_a, zip

Class Methods

[ ]

Hash[‹ *key => value* ›*] → *hsh*
Hash[*obj*] → *hsh*

Creates a new hash populated with the given objects. Equivalent to creating a hash using the literal { key => value, ...}. Keys and values occur in pairs, so there must be an even number of arguments. In the second form, *obj* must respond to to_hash.

```
Hash["a", 100, "b", 200]      # => {"a"=>100, "b"=>200}
Hash["a" => 100, "b" => 200]  # => {"a"=>100, "b"=>200}
{ "a" => 100, "b" => 200 }    # => {"a"=>100, "b"=>200}
```

new

Hash.new → *hsh*
Hash.new(*obj*) → *hsh*
Hash.new { | hash, key | ... } → *hsh*

Returns a new, empty hash. If this hash is subsequently accessed by a key that doesn't correspond to a hash entry, the value returned depends on the style of new used to create the hash. In the first form, the access returns nil. If *obj* is specified, this single object will be used for all *default values*. If a block is specified, it will be called with the hash object and the key, and it should return the default value. It is the block's responsibility to store the value in the hash if required.

```
h = Hash.new("Go Fish")
h["a"] = 100
h["b"] = 200
h["a"]          # => 100
h["c"]          # => "Go Fish"
# The following alters the single default object
h["c"].upcase! # => "GO FISH"
h["d"]          # => "GO FISH"
h.keys          # => ["a", "b"]
```

```
# While this creates a new default object each time
h = Hash.new {|hash, key| hash[key] = "Go Fish: #{key}" }
h["c"]           # => "Go Fish: c"
h["c"].upcase! # => "GO FISH: C"
h["d"]           # => "Go Fish: d"
h.keys           # => ["c", "d"]
```

try_convert   Hash.try_convert(*obj*) → *a_hash* or nil

If *obj* is not already a hash, attempts to convert it to one by calling its to_hash method. Returns nil if no conversion could be made.

```
class ConfigFile
  def initialize(name)
    @content = File.read(name)
  end
  def to_hash
    result = {}
    @content.scan(/^(\w+):\s*(.*)/) do |name, value|
      result[name] = value
    end
    result
  end
end
config = ConfigFile.new("some_config")
Hash.try_convert(config) # => {"user_name"=>"dave", "password"=>"wibble"}
```

Instance Methods

==   *hsh* == *obj* → *true* or *false*

Equality—Two hashes are equal if they contain the same number of keys and the value corresponding to each key in the first hash is equal (using ==) to the value for the same key in the second. If *obj* is not a hash, attempts to convert it using to_hash and returns *obj* == *hsh*.

```
h1 = { "a" => 1, "c" => 2 }
h2 = { 7 => 35, "c" => 2, "a" => 1 }
h3 = { "a" => 1, "c" => 2, 7 => 35 }
h4 = { "a" => 1, "d" => 2, "f" => 35 }
h1 == h2  # => false
h2 == h3  # => true
h3 == h4  # => false
```

[]   *hsh*[*key*] → *value*

Element Reference—Retrieves the *value* stored for *key*. If not found, returns the default value (see Hash.new for details).

```
h = { "a" => 100, "b" => 200 }
h["a"]    # => 100
h["c"]    # => nil
```

[ ]=

hsh[*key*] = *value* → *value*

Element Assignment—Associates the value given by *value* with the key given by *key*. *key* should not have its value changed while it is in use as a key (a String passed as a key will be duplicated and frozen).

```
h = { "a" => 100, "b" => 200 }
h["a"] = 9
h["c"] = 4
h            # => {"a"=>9, "b"=>200, "c"=>4}
```

assoc

hsh.assoc(*key*) → [*key, val]* or nil

Returns the two element array [key, hsh[key]] or nil if *key* does not reference an entry in the hash.

```
h = { "a" => 100, "b" => 200 } # => {"a"=>100, "b"=>200}
h.assoc("a")                    # => ["a", 100]
h.assoc("c")                    # => nil
```

clear

hsh.clear → *hsh*

Removes all key/value pairs from *hsh*.

```
h = { "a" => 100, "b" => 200 } # => {"a"=>100, "b"=>200}
h.clear                        # => {}
```

compare_by_identity

hsh.compare_by_identity → *hsh*

Hashes normally compare key values using eql?, which returns true if two objects have the same *value*. If you call compare_by_identity, keys will instead be considered to be equal only if they are the same object. Note that when strings are used as keys, they are automatically duplicated, so you will never be able to retrieve a string-keyed entry if keys are compared using identity.

```
key = "key"
h = { key => 100, 99 => "ninety nine" }
h[key]      # => 100
h["key"]    # => 100
h[99]       # => "ninety nine"
h.compare_by_identity
h[key]      # => nil
h["key"]    # => nil
h[99]       # => "ninety nine"
```

compare_by_identity?

hsh.compare_by_identity? → *true* or *false*

Returns true if *hsh* compares keys by identity.

default

$hsh.\text{default}(\ key=\text{nil}\ ) \rightarrow obj$

Returns the default value, the value that would be returned by *hsh*[*key*] if *key* did not exist in *hsh*. See also Hash.new and Hash#default=.

```
h = Hash.new                        # => {}
h.default                           # => nil
h.default(2)                        # => nil

h = Hash.new("cat")                 # => {}
h.default                           # => "cat"
h.default(2)                        # => "cat"

h = Hash.new {|h,k| h[k] = k.to_i*10} # => {}
h.default                           # => nil
h.default(2)                        # => 20
```

default=

$hsh.\text{default} = obj \rightarrow hsh$

Sets the value returned for a key that does not exist in the hash. Use Hash#default_proc= to set the proc to be called to calculate a default.

```
h = { "a" => 100, "b" => 200 }
h.default = "Go fish"
h["a"]    # => 100
h["z"]    # => "Go fish"
# This doesn't do what you might hope... (but see default_proc=)
h.default = lambda { |hash, key| hash[key] = key + key }
h[2]      # => #<Proc:0x007fd91290e870@prog.rb:6 (lambda)>
h["cat"]  # => #<Proc:0x007fd91290e870@prog.rb:6 (lambda)>
```

default_proc

$hsh.\text{default\_proc} \rightarrow obj$ or nil

If Hash.new was invoked with a block, returns that block; otherwise, returns nil.

```
h = Hash.new {|h,k| h[k] = k*k } # => {}
p = h.default_proc                  # => #<Proc:0x007fbfe2847a20@prog.rb:1>
a = []                              # => []
p.call(a, 2)
a                                   # => [nil, nil, 4]
```

default_proc=

$hsh.\text{default\_proc} = proc \rightarrow proc$ or nil

Sets the proc to be called to calculate values to be returned when a hash is accessed with a key it does not contain. Removes the default proc if passed nil.

New in 2.0

```
h = { "a" => 100, "b" => 200 }
h.default = "Go fish"
h["a"]    # => 100
h["z"]    # => "Go fish"
h.default_proc = lambda { |hash, key| hash[key] = key + key }
h[2]      # => 4
h["cat"]  # => "catcat"
```

delete

hsh.delete(key) → value
hsh.delete(key) { | key | ... } → value

Deletes from *hsh* the entry whose key is to *key*, returning the corresponding value. If the key is not found, returns nil. If the optional code block is given and the key is not found, passes it the key and returns the result of *block*.

```ruby
h = { "a" => 100, "b" => 200 }
h.delete("a")                       # => 100
h.delete("z")                       # => nil
h.delete("z") {|el| "#{el} not found" } # => "z not found"
```

delete_if

hsh.delete_if ‹{ | key, value | ... }› → hsh or enumerator

Deletes every key/value pair from *hsh* for which *block* is true. Returns an Enumerator object if no block is given.

```ruby
h = { "a" => 100, "b" => 200, "c" => 300 }
h.delete_if {|key, value| key >= "b" } # => {"a"=>100}
```

each

hsh.each { | key, value | ... } → hsh

Calls *block* once for each key in *hsh*, passing the key and value as parameters.

```ruby
h = { "a" => 100, "b" => 200 }
h.each {|key, value| puts "#{key} is #{value}" }
```

produces:

```
a is 100
b is 200
```

each_key

hsh.each_key { | key | ... } → hsh

Calls *block* once for each key in *hsh*, passing the key as a parameter.

```ruby
h = { "a" => 100, "b" => 200 }
h.each_key {|key| puts key }
```

produces:

```
a
b
```

each_pair

hsh.each_pair { | key, value | ... } → hsh

Synonym for Hash#each.

each_value

hsh.each_value { | value | ... } → hsh

Calls *block* once for each key in *hsh*, passing the value as a parameter.

```ruby
h = { "a" => 100, "b" => 200 }
h.each_value {|value| puts value }
```

produces:
```
100
200
```

---

empty?   *hsh*.empty? → *true* or *false*

Returns true if *hsh* contains no key/value pairs.

```
{}.empty? # => true
```

---

fetch   *hsh*.fetch(*key* ‹ , *default* ›) → *obj*
                                                        hsh.fetch(*key*) { | key | ... } → *obj*}

Returns a value from the hash for the given key. If the key can't be found, several options
exist. With no other arguments, it will raise an IndexError exception; if *default* is given, then
that will be returned; if the optional code block is specified, then that will be run and its
result returned. fetch does not evaluate any default values supplied when the hash was created—it looks only for keys in the hash.

```
h = { "a" => 100, "b" => 200 }
h.fetch("a")                      # => 100
h.fetch("z", "go fish")           # => "go fish"
h.fetch("z") {|el| "go fish, #{el}"} # => "go fish, z"
```

The following example shows that an exception is raised if the key is not found and a default
value is not supplied.

```
h = { "a" => 100, "b" => 200 }
h.fetch("z")
```

produces:
```
        from prog.rb:2:in `<main>'
prog.rb:2:in `fetch': key not found: "z" (KeyError)
```

---

flatten   *hsh*.flatten(*depth* = 1) → *an_array*

Converts *hsh* to an array and then invokes Array#flatten! on the result.

```
h = { feline: [ "felix", "tom" ], equine: "ed" }
h.flatten    # => [:feline, ["felix", "tom"], :equine, "ed"]
h.flatten(1) # => [:feline, ["felix", "tom"], :equine, "ed"]
h.flatten(2) # => [:feline, "felix", "tom", :equine, "ed"]
```

---

has_key?   *hsh*.has_key?(*key*) → *true* or *false*

Returns true if the given key is present in *hsh*.

```
h = { "a" => 100, "b" => 200 }
h.has_key?("a") # => true
h.has_key?("z") # => false
```

has_value?
hsh.has_value?(value) → true or false

Returns true if the given value is present for some key in *hsh*.

```
h = { "a" => 100, "b" => 200 }
h.has_value?(100) # => true
h.has_value?(999) # => false
```

include?
hsh.include?(key) → true or false

Synonym for Hash#has_key?.

index
hsh.index(value) → key

Deprecated—use Hash#key instead.

invert
hsh.invert → other_hash

Returns a new hash created by using *hsh*'s values as keys and using the keys as values. If *hsh* has duplicate values, the result will contain only one of them as a key—which one is not predictable.

```
h = { "n" => 100, "m" => 100, "y" => 300, "d" => 200, "a" => 0 }
h.invert  # => {100=>"m", 300=>"y", 200=>"d", 0=>"a"}
```

keep_if
hsh.keep_if { | key, value | ... } → hsh or enumerator

Modifies *hsh* by removing all elements for which *block* is false (see also Enumerable#select and Hash.select!.) Returns an Enumerator object if no block is given.

```
a = { a: 1, b: 2, c: 3}
a.keep_if {|key, value| key =~ /[bc]/ } # => {:b=>2, :c=>3}
a                                       # => {:b=>2, :c=>3}
a.keep_if {|key, value| value.odd? }    # => {:c=>3}
a                                       # => {:c=>3}
```

key
hsh.key(value) → key or nil

Returns the key of the first hash entry whose value is *value*.

```
h = { a: 100, b: 200, c: 100 }
h.key(100) # => :a
h.key(200) # => :b
h.key(300) # => nil
```

key?
hsh.key?(key) → true or false

Synonym for Hash#has_key?.

keys

hsh.keys → *array*

Returns a new array populated with the keys from this hash. See also Hash#values.

```
h = { "a" => 100, "b" => 200, "c" => 300, "d" => 400 }
h.keys    # => ["a", "b", "c", "d"]
```

length

hsh.length → *fixnum*

Returns the number of key/value pairs in the hash.

```
h = { "d" => 100, "a" => 200, "v" => 300, "e" => 400 }
h.length        # => 4
h.delete("a")   # => 200
h.length        # => 3
```

member?

hsh.member?(*key*) → *true* or *false*

Synonym for Hash#has_key?.

merge

hsh.merge(*other_hash*) → *result_hash*
hsh.merge(*other_hash*) { | *key, old_val, new_val* | ... } → *result_hash*

Returns a new hash containing the contents of *other_hash* and the contents of *hsh*. With no block parameter, overwrites entries in *hsh* with duplicate keys with those from *other_hash*. If a block is specified, it is called with each duplicate key and the values from the two hashes. The value returned by the block is stored in the new hash.

```
h1 = { "a" => 100, "b" => 200 }
h2 = { "b" => 254, "c" => 300 }
h1.merge(h2)              # => {"a"=>100, "b"=>254, "c"=>300}
h1.merge(h2) {|k,o,n| o}  # => {"a"=>100, "b"=>200, "c"=>300}
h1                        # => {"a"=>100, "b"=>200}
```

merge!

hsh.merge!(*other_hash*) → *hsh*
hsh.merge!(*other_hash*) { | *key, old_val, new_val* | ... } → *hsh*

Like Hash#merge but changes the contents of *hsh*.

```
h1 = { "a" => 100, "b" => 200 }
h2 = { "b" => 254, "c" => 300 }
h1.merge!(h2)  # => {"a"=>100, "b"=>254, "c"=>300}
h1             # => {"a"=>100, "b"=>254, "c"=>300}
```

rassoc

hsh.rassoc(*val*) → *[key, val]* or *nil*

Searches *hsh* for the first element whose value is *val*, returning the key and value as a two-element array. Returns nil if the value does not occur in the hash.

```
h = { "a" => 100, "b" => 200, "c" => 100 }
h.rassoc(100) # => ["a", 100]
h.rassoc(200) # => ["b", 200]
```

rehash

hsh.rehash → hsh

Rebuilds the hash based on the current hash values for each key. If values of key objects have changed since they were inserted, this method will reindex *hsh*. If Hash#rehash is called while an iterator is traversing the hash, an IndexError will be raised in the iterator.

```
a = [ "a", "b" ]
c = [ "c", "d" ]
h = { a => 100, c => 300 }
h[a]        # => 100
a[0] = "z"
h[a]        # => nil
h.rehash    # => {["z", "b"]=>100, ["c", "d"]=>300}
h[a]        # => 100
```

reject

hsh.reject { | key, value | ... } → hash

Same as Hash#delete_if but uses (and returns) a copy of *hsh*. Equivalent to hsh.dup.delete_if.

reject!

hsh.reject! ‹ { | key, value | ... } › → hsh or enumerator

Equivalent to Hash#delete_if but returns nil if no changes were made. Returns an Enumerator object if no block is given.

replace

hsh.replace(other_hash) → hsh

Replaces the contents of *hsh* with the contents of *other_hash*.

```
h = { "a" => 100, "b" => 200 }
h.replace({ "c" => 300, "d" => 400 }) # => {"c"=>300, "d"=>400}
```

select

hsh.select { | key, value | ... } → hash

Returns a new hash consisting of [key, value] pairs for which the block returns true. Also see Hash#values_at. (This behavior differs from Ruby 1.8, which returns an array of arrays.)

```
h = { "a" => 100, "b" => 200, "c" => 300 }
h.select {|k,v| k > "a"} # => {"b"=>200, "c"=>300}
h.select {|k,v| v < 200} # => {"a"=>100}
```

select!

hsh.select! { | key, value | ... } → hsh, nil, or enumerator

Modifies *hsh* by removing all elements for which *block* is false (see also Enumerable#select and Hash#keep_if). Returns nil if no changes were made or returns an Enumerator object if no block is given. Otherwise, returns *hsh*.

```
a = { a: 1, b:2, c: 3}
a.select! {|key, value| value < 2 } # => {:a=>1}
a                                   # => {:a=>1}
a.select! {|key, value| value < 3 } # => nil
a                                   # => {:a=>1}
```

---

shift   *hsh*.shift → *array* or nil

Removes a key/value pair from *hsh* and returns it as the two-item array [key, value]. If the hash is empty, returns the default value, calls the default proc (with a key value of nil), or returns nil.

```
h = { 1 => "a", 2 => "b", 3 => "c" }
h.shift   # => [1, "a"]
h         # => {2=>"b", 3=>"c"}
```

---

size   *hsh*.size → *fixnum*

Synonym for Hash#length.

---

sort   *hsh*.sort → *array*
                                        hsh.sort { | a, b | ... } → *array*

Converts *hsh* to a nested array of [key, value] arrays and sorts it, using Array#sort. (Technically this is just the sort method of Enumerable. It's documented here because it's unusual for sort to return a different type.)

```
h = { "a" => 20, "b" => 30, "c" => 10 }
h.sort                     # => [["a", 20], ["b", 30], ["c", 10]]
h.sort {|a,b| a[1]<=>b[1] } # => [["c", 10], ["a", 20], ["b", 30]]
```

---

store   *hsh*.store(*key, value*) → *value*

Synonym for Element Assignment (Hash#[]=).

---

to_a   *hsh*.to_a → *array*

Converts *hsh* to a nested array of [key, value] arrays.

```
h = { "c" => 300, "a" => 100, "d" => 400, "c" => 300  }
h.to_a   # => [["c", 300], ["a", 100], ["d", 400]]
```

---

to_h   *hsh*.to_h → *hsh*

New in 2.0   Returns the hash. Converts the receiver to a hash if send to a subclass of Hash.

---

to_hash   *hsh*.to_hash → *hsh*

See the discussion in the ducktyping chapter on page 351.

---

to_s   *hsh*.to_s → *string*

Converts *hsh* to a string by converting the hash to an array of [key, value] pairs and then converting that array to a string using Array#join with the default separator.

```
h = { "c" => 300, "a" => 100, "d" => 400, "c" => 300  }
h.to_s   # => "{\"c\"=>300, \"a"=>100, \"d\"=>400}"
```

update   *hsh*.update(*other_hash*) → *hsh*
hsh.update(*other_hash*) { | *key, old_val,new_val* | ... } → *hsh*

Synonym for Hash#merge!.

value?   *hsh*.value?(*value*) → *true* or *false*

Synonym for Hash#has_value?.

values   *hsh*.values → *array*

Returns an array populated with the values from *hsh*. See also Hash#keys.

```
h = { "a" => 100, "b" => 200, "c" => 300 }
h.values  # => [100, 200, 300]
```

values_at   *hsh*.values_at(‹ *key* ›⁺) → *array*

Returns an array consisting of values for the given key(s). Will insert the *default value* for keys that are not found.

```
h = { "a" => 100, "b" => 200, "c" => 300 }
h.values_at("a", "c")      # => [100, 300]
h.values_at("a", "c", "z") # => [100, 300, nil]
h.default = "cat"
h.values_at("a", "c", "z") # => [100, 300, "cat"]
```

Class **Integer** < Numeric

Subclasses: Bignum, Fixnum

Integer is the basis for the two concrete classes that hold whole numbers, Bignum and Fixnum.

Instance Methods

ceil

int.ceil → *integer*

Synonym for Integer#to_i.

chr

int.chr → *string*
int.chr(*encoding*) → *string*

Returns a string containing the character represented by the receiver's value. Values less that 128 are always returned as ASCII. The encoding of strings representing higher values can be set using the optional parameter.

```
65.chr                   # => "A"
?a.chr                   # => "a"
233.chr                  # => "\xE9"
233.chr(Encoding::UTF_8) # => "é"
```

denominator

int.denominator → *integer*

Converts the denominator of the rational representation of *int*.

```
1.denominator   # => 1
1.5.denominator # => 2
num = 1.0/3
num.to_r        # => (6004799503160661/18014398509481984)
num.denominator # => 18014398509481984
```

downto

int.downto(*integer*) { |i| ... } → *int*

Iterates *block*, passing decreasing values from *int* down to and including *integer*.

```
5.downto(1) {|n| print n, ".. " }
print "  Liftoff!\n"
```

produces:

```
5.. 4.. 3.. 2.. 1..   Liftoff!
```

even?

int.even? → *true* or *false*

Returns true if *int* is even.

```
1.even?   # => false
2.even?   # => true
```

floor

int.floor → integer

Returns the largest integer less than or equal to *int*. Equivalent to Integer#to_i.

```
1.floor    # => 1
(-1).floor # => -1
```

gcd

int.gcd(*other_integer*) → integer

Returns the greatest common denominator of *int* and *other_integer*.

```
10.gcd(15) # => 5
10.gcd(16) # => 2
10.gcd(17) # => 1
```

gcdlcm

int.gcdlcm(*other_integer*) → [*gcd, lcm*]

Returns both the GCD and the LCM of *int* and *other_integer*.

```
10.gcdlcm(15) # => [5, 30]
10.gcdlcm(16) # => [2, 80]
10.gcdlcm(17) # => [1, 170]
```

integer?

int.integer? → true

Always returns true.

lcm

int.lcm(*other_integer*) → integer

Returns the lowest common multiple of *int* and *other_integer*.

```
10.lcm(15) # => 30
10.lcm(20) # => 20
10.lcm(-2) # => 10
```

next

int.next → integer

Returns the Integer equal to *int*+1.

```
1.next    # => 2
(-1).next # => 0
```

numerator

int.numerator → integer

Converts the numerator of the rational representation of *int*.

```
1.numerator   # => 1
1.5.numerator # => 3
num = 1.0/3
num.to_r      # => (6004799503160661/18014398509481984)
num.numerator # => 6004799503160661
```

odd?

int.odd? → *true* or *false*

Returns true if *int* is odd.

```
1.odd?    # => true
2.odd?    # => false
```

ord

int.ord → *int*

The ord method was added to assist in the migration from Ruby 1.8 to 1.9. It allows ?A.ord to return 65. If ?A returns a string, ord will be called on that string and return 65; if ?A returns an integer, then Numeric#ord is called, which is basically a no-op.

pred

int.pred → *integer*

Returns *int* - 1.

rationalize

int.rationalize(*eps*=nil) → *rational*

Returns the rational number int/1. The argument is always ignored. Effectively a synonym for Integer.to_r.

```
99.rationalize            # => (99/1)
-12345678.rationalize(99) # => (-12345678/1)
```

round

int.round → *integer*

Synonym for Integer#to_i.

succ

int.succ → *integer*

Synonym for Integer#next.

times

int.times { |i| ... } → *int*

Iterates block *int* times, passing in values from zero to *int* - 1.

```
5.times do |i|
  print i, " "
end
```

produces:

```
0 1 2 3 4
```

to_i

int.to_i → *int*

Returns *int*.

to_int

Synonym for Integer#to_i.

to_r

Converts *int* to a rational number.

```
1.to_r    # => 1/1
-1.to_r   # => -1/1
```

truncate

Synonym for Integer#to_i.

upto

Iterates *block*, passing in integer values from *int* up to and including *integer*.

```
5.upto(10) {|i| print i, " " }
```

produces:

```
5 6 7 8 9 10
```

Class IO

Subclasses: File

Class IO is the basis for all input and output in Ruby. An I/O stream may be *duplexed* (that is, bidirectional) and so may use more than one native operating system stream.

Many of the examples in this section use class File, the only standard subclass of IO. The two classes are closely associated.

As used in this section, *portname* may take any of the following forms:

- A plain string represents a filename suitable for the underlying operating system.

- A string starting with | indicates a subprocess. The remainder of the string following | is invoked as a process with appropriate input/output channels connected to it.

- A string equal to |- will create another Ruby instance as a subprocess.

The IO class uses the Unix abstraction of *file descriptors* (fds), small integers that represent open files. Conventionally, standard input has an fd of 0, standard output has an fd of 1, and standard error has an fd of 2.

Ruby will convert path names between different operating system conventions if possible. For instance, on Windows the filename /gumby/ruby/test.rb will be opened as \gumby\ruby\test.rb. When specifying a Windows-style filename in a double-quoted Ruby string, remember to escape the backslashes.

```
"c:\\gumby\\ruby\\test.rb"
```

Our examples here will use the Unix-style forward slashes; File::SEPARATOR can be used to get the platform-specific separator character.

I/O ports may be opened in any one of several different modes, which are shown in this section as *mode*. This mode string must be one of the values listed in Table 16, *Mode values*, on page 494. As of Ruby 1.9, the mode may also contain information on the external and internal encoding of the data associated with the port. If an external encoding is specified, Ruby assumes that the data it received from the operating system uses that encoding. If no internal encoding is given, strings read from the port will have this encoding. If an internal encoding is given, data will be transcoded from the external to the internal encoding, and strings will have that encoding. The reverse happens on output.

Mixes In

Enumerable: all?, any?, chunk, collect, collect_concat, count, cycle, detect, drop, drop_while, each_cons, each_entry, each_slice, each_with_index, each_with_object, entries, find, find_all, find_index, first, flat_map, grep, group_by, include?, inject, lazy, map, max, max_by, member?, min, min_by, minmax, minmax_by, none?, one?, partition, reduce, reject, reverse_each, select, slice_before, sort, sort_by, take, take_while, to_a, zip

Class Methods

---

binread   IO.binread(*name* ‹ , *length* ‹ , offset › ›) → *string*

Opens *name* with mode rb:ASCII-8BIT, reads *length* bytes starting at *offset*, and then closes the file. The bytes are returned in a string with ASCII-8BIT encoding. *offset* defaults to 0, and *length* defaults to the number of bytes between *offset* and the end of the file.

```
IO.binread("testfile", 20)     # => "This is line one\nThi"
IO.binread("testfile", 20, 20) # => "s is line two\nThis i"
str = IO.binread("testfile")
str.encoding                   # => #<Encoding:ASCII-8BIT>
str1 = IO.read("testfile")
str1.encoding                  # => #<Encoding:UTF-8>
```

---

binwrite   IO.binwrite(*portname*, *string* ‹ , *offset* › ‹ , *options* ›) → *int*

Opens the file for writing with mode wb:ASCII-8BIT, optionally seeks to the given offset, and then writes *string*. Returns the number of bytes written. The file is truncated before writing if no offset is specified.

options is an optional hash used to pass parameters to the underlying open call used by write. See IO.foreach for details.

---

copy_stream   IO.copy_stream(*from*, *to* ‹ , *max_length* ‹ , offset › ›) → *integer*

Copies *from* to *to*. These may be specified either as filenames or as open I/O streams. You may optionally specify a maximum length to copy and a byte offset to start the copy from. Returns the number of bytes copied.

```
IO.copy_stream("testfile", "newfile", 10, 10)
ip = File.open("/etc/passwd")
op = File.open("extract", "w")
op.puts "First 20 characters of /etc/passwd"
IO.copy_stream(ip, op, 20)
op.puts "\nEnd of extract"
op.close
puts File.readlines("extract")
```

produces:

```
First 20 characters of /etc/passwd
##
# User Database
#
End of extract
```

---

for_fd   IO.for_fd(*int*, *mode*) → *io*

Synonym for IO.new.

foreach

IO.foreach(*portname*, *separator*=$/ ‹ , *options* ›) { | line | ... } → nil
IO.foreach(*portname*, *limit* ‹ , *options* ›) { | line | ... } → nil
IO.foreach(*portname*, *separator*, *limit* ‹ , *options* ›) { | line | ... } → nil

Executes the block for every line in the named I/O port, where lines are separated by *separator*. If *separator* is nil, the entire file is passed as a single string. If the *limit* argument is present and positive, at most that many characters will be returned in each iteration. If only the *limit* argument is given and that argument is negative, then encodings will be ignored while looking for the record separator, which increases performance.

```
IO.foreach("testfile") {|x| puts "GOT: #{x}" }
```

produces:

```
GOT: This is line one
GOT: This is line two
GOT: This is line three
GOT: And so on...
```

options is an optional hash used to pass parameters to the underlying open call used by read. It may contain one or more of the following:

encoding:	The encoding for the string, either as "external" or "external:internal"
mode:	The mode string to be passed to open
open_args:	An array containing the arguments to be passed to open; other options are ignored if this one is present

```
IO.foreach("testfile", nil, mode: "rb", encoding: "ascii-8bit") do |content|
  puts content.encoding
end
IO.foreach("testfile", nil, open_args: ["r:iso-8859-1"]) do |content|
  puts content.encoding
end
```

produces:

```
ASCII-8BIT
ISO-8859-1
```

new

IO.new(*integer_fd*, *mode*="r" ‹ , *options* ›) → *io*

Returns a new IO object (a stream) for the given integer file descriptor and mode. The mode and options may be given as for File.new (see Table 16, *Mode values*, on page 494, and see Table 17, *File and I/O open options*, on page 495). See also IO#fileno and IO.for_fd.

```
a = IO.new(2, "w")        # '2' is standard error
STDERR.puts "Hello"
a.puts "World"
```

produces:

```
Hello
World
```

```
# encoding: utf-8
b = IO.new(2, mode: "w", encoding: "utf-8", crlf_newline: true)
b.puts "olé"
```

produces:

```
olé
```

---

open

IO.open(‹args›⁺) → *io*
IO.open(‹args›⁺) { | io | ... } → *obj*

IO.open creates a new IO object, passing *args* to that object's initialize method. If no block is given, simply returns that object. If a block is given, passes the IO object to the block. When the block exits (even via exception or program termination), the *io* object will be closed. If the block is present, IO.open returns the value of the block. The rough implementation is as follows:

```
class IO
  def open(*args)
    file = return_value = self.new(*args)
    begin
      return_value = yield(file)
    ensure
      file.close
    end if block_given?
    return_value
  end
end
```

Note that subclasses of IO such as File can use open even though their constructors take different parameters. Calling File.open(...) will invoke File's constructor, not IO's.

```
IO.open(1, "w") do |io|
  io.puts "Writing to stdout"
end
```

produces:

```
Writing to stdout
```

```
File.open("testfile", mode: "r", encoding: "utf-8") do |f|
  puts f.read
end
```

produces:

```
This is line one
This is line two
This is line three
And so on...
```

pipe

IO.pipe → [*read_io, write_io*]
IO.pipe(*encoding_string* ‹ , *encoding_options* ›) → [*read_io, write_io*]
IO.pipe(*external, internal* ‹ , *encoding_options* ›) → [*read_io, write_io*]
IO.pipe(... as above ...) { | read_io, write_io | ... }

Creates a pair of pipe endpoints (connected to each other) and returns them as a two-element array of IO objects. *write_io* is automatically placed into sync mode. Not available on all platforms.

Encodings for the pipes can be specified as a string ("external" or "external:internal") or as two arguments specifying the external and internal encoding names (or encoding objects). If both external and internal encodings are present, the *encoding_options* parameter specifies conversion options (see Table 22, *Options to encode and encode!*, on page 675).

If a block is given, it is passed the two I/O objects. They will be closed at the end of the block if they are still open.

In the following example, the two processes close the ends of the pipe that they are not using. This is not just a cosmetic nicety. The read end of a pipe will not generate an end-of-file condition if any writers have the pipe still open. In the case of the parent process, the rd.read will never return if it does not first issue a wr.close.

```
IO.pipe do |rd, wr|
  if fork
    wr.close
    puts "Parent got: <#{rd.read}>"
    rd.close
    Process.wait
  else
    rd.close
    puts "Sending message to parent"
    wr.write "Hi Dad"
    wr.close
  end
end
```

produces:

```
Sending message to parent
Parent got: <Hi Dad>
```

popen

IO.popen(*cmd, mode*="r") → *io*
IO.popen(*cmd, mode*="r") { | io | ... } → *obj*

Runs the specified command string as a subprocess; the subprocess's standard input and output will be connected to the returned IO object. The parameter *cmd* may be a string or (in Ruby 1.9) an array of strings. In the latter case, the array is used as the argv parameter for the new process, and no special shell processing is performed on the strings. In addition, if the array starts with a hash, it will be used to set environment variables in the subprocess, and if it ends with a hash, the hash will be used to set execution options for the subprocess. See Object#spawn for details. If *cmd* is a string, it will be subject to shell expansion. If the *cmd* string starts with a minus sign (-) and the operating system supports fork(2), then the current Ruby process is forked. The default mode for the new file object is r, but *mode* may be set to any of the modes in Table 16, *Mode values*, on page 494.

If a block is given, Ruby will run the command as a child connected to Ruby with a pipe. Ruby's end of the pipe will be passed as a parameter to the block. In this case, IO.popen returns the value of the block.

If a block is given with a *cmd_string* of "-", the block will be run in two separate processes: once in the parent and once in a child. The parent process will be passed the pipe object as a parameter to the block, the child version of the block will be passed nil, and the child's standard in and standard out will be connected to the parent through the pipe. Not available on all platforms. Also see the Open3 library on page 782 and Object#exec on page 615.

```
pipe = IO.popen("uname")
p(pipe.readlines)
puts "Parent is #{Process.pid}"
IO.popen("date") {|pipe| puts pipe.gets }
IO.popen("-") {|pipe| STDERR.puts "#{Process.pid} is here, pipe=#{pipe}" }
Process.waitall
```

produces:

```
["Darwin\n"]
Parent is 23465
Mon May 27 12:32:20 CDT 2013
23465 is here, pipe=#<IO:0x007f935290e768>
23468 is here, pipe=
```

Here's an example that uses the Ruby 1.9 options to merge standard error and standard output into a single stream. Note that buffering means that the error output comes back ahead of the standard output.

```
pipe = IO.popen([ "bc", { STDERR => STDOUT }], "r+" )
pipe.puts '1 + 3; bad_function()'
pipe.close_write
puts pipe.readlines
```

produces:

```
Runtime error (func=(main), adr=8): Function bad_function not defined.
4
```

---

read   IO.read(*portname, ‹length=$/ ‹, offset › › ‹, options ›) → string*

Opens the file, optionally seeks to the given offset, and then returns *length* bytes (defaulting to the rest of the file). read ensures the file is closed before returning.

options is an optional hash used to pass parameters to the underlying open call used by read. See IO.foreach for details.

```
IO.read("testfile")      # => "This is line one\nThis is line two\nThis is
                         # .. line three\nAnd so on...\n"
IO.read("testfile", 20)  # => "This is line one\nThi"
IO.read("testfile", 20, 10) # => "ne one\nThis is line "
```

readlines   IO.readlines(*portname, separator=$/* ‹ *, options* ›) → *array*
IO.readlines(*portname, limit* ‹ *, options* ›) → *array*
IO.readlines(*portname, separator, limit* ‹ *, options* ›) → *array*

Reads the entire file specified by *portname* as individual lines and returns those lines in an array. Lines are separated by *separator*. If *separator* is nil, the entire file is passed as a single string. If the *limit* argument is present and positive, at most that many characters will be returned in each iteration. If only the *limit* argument is given and that argument is negative, then encodings will be ignored while looking for the record separator, which increases performance. *options* is an optional hash used to pass parameters to the underlying open call used by read. See IO.foreach for details.

```
a = IO.readlines("testfile")
a[0]      # => "This is line one\n"
```

select   IO.select(*read_array* ‹ *, write_array* ‹ *, error_array* ‹ *, timeout* › › ›) → *array* or nil

See Object#select on page 624.

sysopen   IO.sysopen(*path,* ‹ *mode* ‹ *, perm* › ›) → *int*

Opens the given path, returning the underlying file descriptor as a Fixnum.

```
IO.sysopen("testfile") # => 5
```

try_convert   IO.try_convert(*obj*) → *an_io* or nil

If *obj* is not already an I/O object, attempts to convert it to one by calling its to_io method. Returns nil if no conversion could be made.

```
class SillyIOobject
  def to_io
    STDOUT
  end
end
IO.try_convert(SillyIOobject.new) # => #<IO:<STDOUT>>
IO.try_convert("Shemp")           # => nil
```

write   IO.write(*portname, string* ‹ *, offset* › ‹ *, options* ›) → *int*

Opens the file for writing, optionally seeks to the given offset, and then writes *string*. Returns the number of bytes written. The file is truncated before writing if no offset is specified.

options is an optional hash used to pass parameters to the underlying open call used by read. See IO.foreach for details.

```
IO.write("somefile", "my string") # => 9
IO.read("somefile")               # => "my string"
IO.write("somefile", "adden", 1)  # => 5
IO.read("somefile")               # => "maddening"
```

Instance Methods

<<

$io << obj \rightarrow io$

String Output—Writes *obj* to *io*. *obj* will be converted to a string using to_s.

```
STDOUT << "Hello " << "world!\n"
```

produces:

```
Hello world!
```

advise

$io.\text{advise}(advice, offset=0, length=0) \rightarrow \text{nil}$

Help your operating system optimize I/O by telling it how you plan to access this I/O object. The first parameter is a symbol from this table:

:normal	No particular access pattern is being given.
:sequential	The portion will be read sequentially.
:random	The portion will be read in random order.
:willneed	The portion will be needed in the near future.
:dontneed	The portion will not be needed in the near future.
:noreuse	The portion will not be reused in the near future.

Table 19—*advice* parameter to advise

The second and third parameters denote the region of the file to be accessed. Their default values of zeroes mean the entire file. See the posix_fadvise(2) man page for details.

autoclose=

$io.\text{autoclose} = \text{true or false} \rightarrow io$

Normally when an I/O object is finalized, the corresponding fd is automatically closed. By setting autoclose=false, you prevent this behavior. This is useful if you're using an I/O object to access an fd that's open elsewhere in your program, and you don't want to affect that other object.

autoclose?

$io.\text{autoclose}? \rightarrow \text{true or false}$

Returns the state of the autoclose flag for *io*.

binmode

$io.\text{binmode} \rightarrow io$

Puts *io* into binary mode. It is more common to use the "b" modifier in the mode string to set binary mode when you open a file. Binary mode is required when reading or writing files containing bit sequences that are not valid in the encoding of the file. Once a stream is in binary mode, it cannot be reset to nonbinary mode.

---

binmode?

io.binmode? → true or false

Returns true if *io* is in binary mode.

```
f = File.open("/etc/passwd")
f.binmode? # => false
f = File.open("/etc/passwd", "rb:binary")
f.binmode? # => true
```

---

bytes

io.bytes → enumerator

Returns an enumerator that iterates over the bytes (not characters) in *io,* returning each as an integer. See also IO#getbyte. Deprecated in Ruby 2.0.

New in 2.0
```
enum = File.open("testfile").bytes # => prog.rb:1: warning: IO#bytes is
                                   # .. deprecated; use #each_byte instead
enum.first(10)                     # => [84, 104, 105, 115, 32, 105, 115, 32,
                                   # .. 108, 105]
```

---

chars

io.chars → enumerator

Returns an enumerator that allows iteration over the characters in *io.* Deprecated in Ruby 2.0.

New in 2.0
```
enum = File.open("testfile").chars # => prog.rb:1: warning: IO#chars is
                                   # .. deprecated; use #each_char instead
enum.first(7)                      # => ["T", "h", "i", "s", " ", "i", "s"]
```

---

close

io.close → nil

Closes *io* and flushes any pending writes to the operating system. The stream is unavailable for any further data operations; an IOError is raised if such an attempt is made. I/O streams are automatically closed when they are claimed by the garbage collector.

---

close_on_exec?

io.close_on_exec? → true or false

Returns the state of the *close on exec* flag for *io.* Raises NotImplemented if not available.

---

close_on_exec=

io.close_on_exec = true or false → nil

Sets the *close on exec* flag for *io.* Raises NotImplemented if not available. I/O objects with this flag set will be closed across exec() calls.

---

close_read

io.close_read → nil

Closes the read end of a duplex I/O stream (in other words, one that contains both a read and a write stream, such as a pipe). Raises IOError if the stream is not duplexed.

```
f = IO.popen("/bin/sh","r+")
f.close_read
f.readlines
```

produces:

```
        from prog.rb:3:in `<main>'
prog.rb:3:in `readlines': not opened for reading (IOError)
```

close_write

io.close_write → nil

Closes the write end of a duplex I/O stream (in other words, one that contains both a read and a write stream, such as a pipe). Will raise IOError if the stream is not duplexed.

closed?

io.closed? → true or false

Returns true if *io* is completely closed (for duplex streams, both reader and writer) and returns false otherwise.

```
f = File.new("testfile")
f.close        # => nil
f.closed?      # => true
f = IO.popen("/bin/sh","r+")
f.close_write # => nil
f.closed?      # => false
f.close_read  # => nil
f.closed?      # => true
```

codepoints

io.codepoints { | codepoint | ... } → io
io.codepoints → enumerator

Synonym for IO#each_codepoint. Deprecated in Ruby 2.0.

New in 2.0

each

io.each(separator=$/) { | line | ... } → io
io.each(limit) { | line | ... } → io
io.each(separator, limit) { | line | ... } → io
io.each(args..) → enum

Executes the block for every line in *io*, where lines are separated by *separator*. If *separator* is nil, the entire file is passed as a single string. If the *limit* argument is present and positive, at most that many characters will be returned in each iteration. If only the *limit* argument is given and that argument is negative, then encodings will be ignored while looking for the record separator, which increases performance. Returns an enumerator if no block is given.

```
f = File.new("testfile")
f.each {|line| puts "#{f.lineno}: #{line}" }
```

produces:

```
1: This is line one
2: This is line two
3: This is line three
4: And so on...
```

each_byte

io.each_byte { | byte | ... } → nil
io.each_byte → *enum*

Calls the given block once for each byte (a Fixnum in the range 0 to 255) in *io*, passing the byte as an argument. The stream must be opened for reading, or IOerror will be raised. Returns an enumerator if no block is given.

```
f = File.new("testfile")
checksum = 0
f.each_byte {|x| checksum ^= x } # => #<File:testfile>
checksum                         # => 12
```

each_char

io.each_char { | char | ... } → nil
io.each_char → *enum*

Calls the given block, passing it each character (a string of length 1) in *io*. The stream must be opened for reading, or an IOerror will be raised. Returns an enumerator if no block is given.

```
f = File.new("testfile")
result = []
f.each_char {|ch| result << ch} # => #<File:testfile>
result[0, 5]                     # => ["T", "h", "i", "s", " "]
```

each_codepoint

io.each_codepoint { | codepoint | ... } → *io*
io.each_codepoint → *enumerator*

Iterates over the codepoints in *io*, returning each as an integer. With no block, an enumerator is returned.

```
#encoding: utf-8
File.open("/tmp/testfile", "w:utf-8") { |f| f.puts "∂og" }
File.open("/tmp/testfile") do |f|
  f.each_codepoint { |codepoint| printf "%#X ", codepoint }
end
```

produces:

```
0X2202 0X6F 0X67 0XA
```

each_line

io.each_line(...) { | line | ... } → *io*

Synonym for IO#each.

eof

io.eof → *true* or *false*

Returns true if *io* is at the end of the file. The stream must be opened for reading, or an IOError will be raised.

```
f = File.open("testfile")
f.eof     # => false
dummy = f.readlines
f.eof     # => true
```

eof?

io.eof? → *true* or *false*

Synonym for IO#eof.

external_encoding

io.external_encoding → *encoding*

Returns the encoding object representing the external encoding of this I/O object.

```
io = File.open("testfile", "r:utf-8:iso-8859-1")
io.external_encoding # => #<Encoding:UTF-8>
io.internal_encoding # => #<Encoding:ISO-8859-1>
```

fcntl

io.fcntl(*cmd*, *arg*) → *int*

Provides a mechanism for issuing low-level commands to control or query file-oriented I/O streams. Commands (which are integers), arguments, and the result are platform dependent. If *arg* is a number, its value is passed directly. If it is a string, it is interpreted as a binary sequence of bytes. On Unix platforms, see fcntl(2) for details. See the Fcntl module on page 754 for symbolic names for the first argument. Not implemented on all platforms.

fdatasync

io.fdatasync → 0

Uses the operating system's fdatasync(2) call to write all buffered data associated with io. Raises an exception if the operating system does not support fdatasync(2).

fileno

io.fileno → *int*

Returns an integer representing the numeric file descriptor for io.

```
STDIN.fileno  # => 0
STDOUT.fileno # => 1
```

flush

io.flush → *io*

Flushes any buffered data within io to the underlying operating system (note that this is Ruby internal buffering only; the OS may buffer the data as well).

```
STDOUT.print "no newline"
STDOUT.flush
```

produces:
```
no newline
```

fsync

io.fsync → 0 or nil

Immediately writes all buffered data in io to disk. Returns nil if the underlying operating system does not support fsync(2). Note that fsync differs from using IO#sync=. The latter ensures that data is flushed from Ruby's buffers but does not guarantee that the underlying operating system actually writes it to disk.

getbyte

io.getbyte → *fixnum* or nil

Returns the next 8-bit byte (as opposed to an encoded character) from *io* or returns nil at the end of the file. See also IO#bytes.

```
file = File.open("testfile")
file.getbyte # => 84
file.getbyte # => 104
```

getc

io.getc → *string* or nil

Gets the next character from *io*. Returns nil if called at the end of the file.

```
f = File.new("testfile")
f.getc   # => "T"
f.getc   # => "h"
```

gets

io.gets(*separator*=$/) → *string* or nil
io.gets(*limit*) → *string* or nil
io.gets(*separator, limit*) → *string* or nil

Reads the next "line" from the I/O stream; lines are separated by *separator*. A separator of nil reads the entire contents, and a zero-length separator reads the input a paragraph at a time (two or more successive newlines in the input separate paragraphs). If the *limit* argument is present and positive, at most that many characters will be returned in each iteration. If only the *limit* argument is given and that argument is negative, then encodings will be ignored while looking for the record separator, which increases performance. The line read in will be returned and also assigned to $_ (although the setting of $_ is considered ugly—it may be removed in future). Returns nil if called at the end of the file.

```
file = File.new("testfile")
file.gets            # => "This is line one\n"
$_                   # => "This is line one\n"
file.gets(10)        # => "This is li"
file.gets("line")    # => "ne two\nThis is line"
file.gets("line", 4) # => " thr"
```

internal_encoding

io.internal_encoding → *encoding*

Returns the encoding object representing the internal encoding of this I/O object.

```
io = File.open("testfile", "r:utf-8:iso-8859-1")
io.external_encoding # => #<Encoding:UTF-8>
io.internal_encoding # => #<Encoding:ISO-8859-1>
```

ioctl

io.ioctl(*cmd, arg*) → *int*

Provides a mechanism for issuing low-level commands to control or query I/O devices. The command (which is an integer), arguments, and results are platform dependent. If *arg* is a number, its value is passed directly. If it is a string, it is interpreted as a binary sequence of bytes. On Unix platforms, see ioctl(2) for details. Not implemented on all platforms.

isatty

io.isatty → *true* or *false*

Returns true if *io* is associated with a terminal device (tty) and returns false otherwise.

```
File.new("testfile").isatty   # => false
File.new("/dev/tty").isatty   # => true
```

lineno

io.lineno → *int*

Returns the current line number in *io*, which must be opened for reading. lineno counts the number of times gets is called, rather than the number of newlines encountered. The two values will differ if gets is called with a separator other than newline. See also the $. variable.

```
f = File.new("testfile")
f.lineno   # => 0
f.gets     # => "This is line one\n"
f.lineno   # => 1
f.gets     # => "This is line two\n"
f.lineno   # => 2
```

lineno=

io.lineno = *int* → *int*

Manually sets the current line number to the given value. $. is updated only on the next read.

```
f = File.new("testfile")
f.gets       # => "This is line one\n"
$.           # => 1
f.lineno = 1000
f.lineno     # => 1000
$.           # => 1
f.gets       # => "This is line two\n"
$.           # => 1001
```

lines

io.lines(*separator=$/*) → *enumerator*
io.lines(*limit*) → *enumerator*
io.lines(*separator, limit*) → *enumerator*

Returns an enumerator that allows iteration over the lines in *io*, where lines are terminated by *separator*. If *separator* is nil, the entire file is passed as a single string. If the *limit* argument is present and positive, at most that many characters will be returned in each iteration. If only the *limit* argument is given and that argument is negative, then encodings will be ignored while looking for the record separator, which increases performance. Deprecated in Ruby 2.0.

New in 2.0

pid

io.pid → *int*

Returns the process ID of a child process associated with *io*. This will be set by IO.popen.

```
pipe = IO.popen("-")
if pipe
  STDERR.puts "In parent, child pid is #{pipe.pid}"
  pipe.close
else
  STDERR.puts "In child, pid is #{$$}"
end
```

produces:

```
In parent, child pid is 23528
In child, pid is 23528
```

---

pos   *io*.pos → *int*

Returns the current offset (in bytes) of *io*.

```
f = File.new("testfile")
f.pos       # => 0
f.gets      # => "This is line one\n"
f.pos       # => 17
```

---

pos=   *io*.pos = *int* → 0

Seeks to the given position (in bytes) in *io*.

```
f = File.new("testfile")
f.pos = 17
f.gets      # => "This is line two\n"
```

---

print   *io*.print(‹ *obj*=$_ ›*) → nil

Writes the given object(s) to *io*. The stream must be opened for writing. If the output record separator ($\) is not nil, it will be appended to the output. If no arguments are given, prints $_. Objects that aren't strings will be converted by calling their to_s method. Returns nil.

```
STDOUT.print("This is ", 100, " percent.\n")
```

produces:

```
This is 100 percent.
```

---

printf   *io*.printf(*format* ‹ , *obj* ›*) → nil

Formats and writes to *io*, converting parameters under control of the format string. See the description Object#sprintf on page 626 for details.

---

putc   *io*.putc(*obj*) → *obj*

If *obj* is a string, write its first character. Otherwise treat *obj* as a number, and write its low-order byte as a character. Note that this is not encoding safe, because the byte may be just part of a multibyte sequence.

```
#encoding: utf-8
STDOUT.putc "ABC"
STDOUT.putc "∂og"
STDOUT.putc 65
```

produces:

A∂A

puts

io.puts(‹ obj ›[*]) → nil

Writes the given objects to *io* as with IO#print. Writes a newline after any that do not already end with a newline sequence. If called with an array argument, writes each element on a new line. If called without arguments, outputs a single newline.

```
STDOUT.puts("this", "is", "a", "test")
```

produces:

```
this
is
a
test
```

read

io.read(‹ int ‹ , buffer › ›) → string or nil

Reads at most *int* bytes from the I/O stream or to the end of the file if *int* is omitted. Returns nil if called at the end of the file. If *buffer* (a string) is provided, it is resized accordingly, and input is read directly into it.

```
f = File.new("testfile")
f.read(16)        # => "This is line one"
str = "cat"
f.read(10, str) # => "\nThis is l"
str             # => "\nThis is l"
```

readbyte

io.readbyte → fixnum

Returns the next 8-bit byte (as opposed to an encoded character) from *io*, raising EOFError at end of file. See also IO#bytes.

readchar

io.readchar → string

Reads a character as with IO#getc but raises an EOFError on end of file.

readline

io.readline(separator=$/) → string or nil
io.readline(limit) → string or nil
io.readline(separator, limit) → string or nil

Reads a line as with IO#gets but raises an EOFError on end of file.

readlines

io.readlines(*separator=$/*) → *array*
io.readlines(*limit*) → *array*
io.readlines(*separator, limit*) → *array*

Returns all of the lines in *io* as an array. Lines are separated by the optional *separator*. If *separator* is nil, the entire file is passed as a single string. If the *limit* argument is present and positive, at most that many characters will be returned in each iteration. If only the *limit* argument is given and that argument is negative, then encodings will be ignored while looking for the record separator, which increases performance.

```
f = File.new("testfile")
f.readlines        # => ["This is line one\n", "This is line two\n", "This is
                   # .. line three\n", "And so on...\n"]
f = File.new("testfile")
f.readlines("line") # => ["This is line", " one\nThis is line", " two\nThis is
                   # .. line", " three\nAnd so on...\n"]
f = File.new("testfile")
f.readlines(10)    # => ["This is li", "ne one\n", "This is li", "ne two\n",
                   # .. "This is li", "ne three\n", "And so on.", "..\n"]
```

readpartial

io.readpartial(*limit, result=""*) → *result*

Data read from files and devices is normally buffered. When reading line by line (for example using IO#gets), Ruby will read many lines at a time into an internal buffer and then return lines from that buffer. This buffering is normally transparent—Ruby will refill the buffer automatically when required. However, when reading from a device or pipe (as opposed to a file), you sometimes want to read whatever is in the buffer, reading from the device or pipe only if the buffer is empty when the read starts. This is what readpartial does —it returns any data available in local buffers immediately, only reading from the device or pipe (potentially blocking) if the buffer is empty. Raises EOFError when it reached EOF. See also IO#read_nonblock.

The following example comes from the internal documentation, with thanks to the anonymous author:

```
r, w = IO.pipe        #                    buffer         pipe content
w << "abc"            #                     ""            "abc".
r.readpartial(4096)   #=> "abc"             ""             ""
r.readpartial(4096)   # blocks because buffer and pipe is empty.

r, w = IO.pipe        #                    buffer         pipe content
w << "abc"            #                     ""            "abc"
w.close               #                     ""            "abc" EOF
r.readpartial(4096)   #=> "abc"             ""            EOF
r.readpartial(4096)   # raises EOFError

r, w = IO.pipe        #                    buffer         pipe content
w << "abc\ndef\n"     #                     ""            "abc\ndef\n"
r.gets                #=> "abc\n"          "def\n"          ""
w << "ghi\n"          #                    "def\n"        "ghi\n"
r.readpartial(4096)   #=> "def\n"           ""            "ghi\n"
r.readpartial(4096)   #=> "ghi\n"           ""             ""
```

read_nonblock

io.readpartial(*limit, result=""*) → *result*

Effectively the same as IO#readpartial, except in cases where no buffered data is available. In this case, it puts *io* into nonblocking mode before attempting to read data. This means that the call may return EAGAIN and EINTR errors, which should be handled by the caller.

reopen

io.reopen(*other_io*) → *io*
io.reopen(*path, mode*) → *io*

Reassociates *io* with the I/O stream given in *other_io* or to a new stream opened on *path*. This may dynamically change the actual class of this stream.

```
f1 = File.new("testfile")
f2 = File.new("testfile")
f2.readlines[0] # => "This is line one\n"
f2.reopen(f1)   # => #<File:testfile>
f2.readlines[0] # => "This is line one\n"
```

rewind

io.rewind → 0

Positions *io* to the beginning of input, resetting lineno to zero.

```
f = File.new("testfile")
f.readline # => "This is line one\n"
f.rewind   # => 0
f.lineno   # => 0
f.readline # => "This is line one\n"
```

seek

io.seek(*int, whence=SEEK_SET*) → 0

Seeks to a given offset *int* in the stream according to the value of *whence*.

IO::SEEK_CUR	Seeks to *int* plus current position
IO::SEEK_END	Seeks to *int* plus end of stream (you probably want a negative value for *int*)
IO::SEEK_SET	Seeks to the absolute location given by *int*

```
f = File.new("testfile")
f.seek(-13, IO::SEEK_END) # => 0
f.readline                # => "And so on...\n"
```

set_encoding

io.set_encoding(*external, internal=external‹, options›*) → *io*
io.set_encoding(*"external-name:internal-name"‹, options›*) → *io*

Sets the external and internal encodings for *io*. In the first form, encodings can be specified by name (using strings) or as encoding objects. In the second form, the external and internal encoding names are separated by a colon in a string. If present, *options* specifies the conversion options.

```
f = File.new("testfile")
f.internal_encoding                 # => nil
```

```
f.external_encoding                        # => #<Encoding:UTF-8>
f.set_encoding("ascii-8bit:iso-8859-1") # => #<File:testfile>
f.internal_encoding                        # => #<Encoding:ISO-8859-1>
f.external_encoding                        # => #<Encoding:ASCII-8BIT>
```

---

stat   *io*.stat → *stat*

Returns status information for *io* as an object of type File::Stat.

```
f = File.new("testfile")
s = f.stat
"%o" % s.mode # => "100644"
s.blksize      # => 4096
s.atime        # => 2013-05-27 12:32:23 -0500
```

---

sync   *io*.sync → *true* or *false*

Returns the current sync mode of *io*. When sync mode is true, all output is immediately flushed to the underlying operating system and is not buffered by Ruby. See also IO#fsync.

---

sync=   *io*.sync = *true* or *false* → *true* or *false*

Sets the sync mode to true or false. When sync mode is true, all output is immediately flushed to the underlying operating system and is not buffered internally. Returns the new state. See also IO#fsync.

```
f = File.new("testfile")
f.sync = true
```

---

sysread   *io*.sysread(*int* ‹, *buffer*›) → *string*

Reads *int* bytes from *io* using a low-level read and returns them as a string. If *buffer* (a string) is provided, input is read directly in to it. Do not mix with other methods that read from *io*, or you may get unpredictable results. Raises SystemCallError on error and EOFError at the end of the file.

```
f = File.new("testfile")
f.sysread(16)       # => "This is line one"
str = "cat"
f.sysread(10, str) # => "\nThis is l"
str                 # => "\nThis is l"
```

---

sysseek   *io*.sysseek(*offset*, *whence*=SEEK_SET) → *int*

Seeks to a given *offset* in the stream according to the value of *whence* (see IO#seek for values of *whence*). Returns the new offset into the file.

```
f = File.new("testfile")
f.sysseek(-13, IO::SEEK_END) # => 53
f.sysread(10)                # => "And so on."
```

syswrite

io.syswrite(*string*) → *int*

Writes the given string to *io* using a low-level write. Returns the number of bytes written. Do not mix with other methods that write to *io*, or you may get unpredictable results. Raises SystemCallError on error.

```
f = File.new("out", "w")
f.syswrite("ABCDEF") # => 6
```

tell

io.tell → *int*

Synonym for IO#pos.

to_i

io.to_i → *int*

Synonym for IO#fileno.

to_io

io.to_io → *io*

Returns *io*.

tty?

io.tty? → *true* or *false*

Synonym for IO#isatty.

ungetbyte

io.ungetbyte(*string* or *int*) → nil

Pushes back one or more bytes onto *io*, such that a subsequent buffered read will return them. Has no effect with unbuffered reads (such as IO#sysread).

```
f = File.new("testfile") # => #<File:testfile>
c = f.getbyte           # => 84
f.ungetbyte(c)          # => nil
f.getbyte               # => 84
f.ungetbyte("cat")      # => nil
f.getbyte               # => 99
f.getbyte               # => 97
```

ungetc

io.ungetc(*string*) → nil

Pushes back one or more characters onto *io*, such that a subsequent buffered read will return them. Has no effect with unbuffered reads (such as IO#sysread).

```
# encoding: utf-8
f = File.new("testfile") # => #<File:testfile>
c = f.getc              # => "T"
f.ungetc(c)             # => nil
f.getc                  # => "T"
f.ungetc("∂og")         # => nil
f.getc                  # => "∂"
f.getc                  # => "o"
```

write

io.write(*string*) → *int*

Writes the given string to *io*. The stream must be opened for writing. If the argument is not a string, it will be converted to a string using to_s. Returns the number of bytes written.

```
count = STDOUT.write( "This is a test\n" )
puts "That was #{count} bytes of data"
```

produces:

```
This is a test
That was 15 bytes of data
```

write_nonblock

io.write_nonblock(*string*) → *int*

Writes the given string to *io* after setting *io* into nonblocking mode. The stream must be opened for writing. If the argument is not a string, it will be converted to a string using to_s. Returns the number of bytes written. Your application should expect to receive errors typical of nonblocking I/O (including EAGAIN and EINTR).

Module **Kernel**

The Kernel module is included by class Object, so its methods are available in every Ruby object. The Kernel methods are documented in class Object on page 599.

Marshal

The marshaling library converts collections of Ruby objects into a byte stream, allowing them to be stored outside the currently active script. This data may subsequently be read and the original objects reconstituted. Marshaling is described in Section 25.7, *Marshaling and Distributed Ruby*, on page 403. Also see the YAML library on page 827.

Marshaled data has major and minor version numbers stored along with the object information. In normal use, marshaling can load only data written with the same major version number and an equal or lower minor version number. If Ruby's "verbose" flag is set (normally using -d, -v, -w, or --verbose), the major and minor numbers must match exactly. Marshal versioning is independent of Ruby's version numbers. You can extract the version by reading the first two bytes of marshaled data.

Some objects cannot be dumped: if the objects to be dumped include bindings, procedure or method objects, instances of class IO, or singleton objects, or if you try to dump anonymous classes or modules, a TypeError will be raised.

If your class has special serialization needs (for example, if you want to serialize in some specific format) or if it contains objects that would otherwise not be serializable, you can implement your own serialization strategy using the instance methods marshal_dump and marshal_load. If an object to be marshaled responds to marshal_dump, that method is called instead of _dump. marshal_dump can return an object of any class (not just a string). A class that implements marshal_dump must also implement marshal_load, which is called as an instance method of a newly allocated object and passed the object originally created by marshal_dump.

The following code uses this to store a Time object in the serialized version of an object. When loaded, this object is passed to marshal_load, which converts this time to a printable form, storing the result in an instance variable.

```ruby
class TimedDump
  attr_reader :when_dumped
  attr_accessor :other_data

  def marshal_dump
    [ Time.now, @other_data ]
  end
  def marshal_load(marshal_data)
    @when_dumped = marshal_data[0].strftime("%I:%M%p")
    @other_data  = marshal_data[1]
  end
end

t = TimedDump.new
t.other_data = "wibble"
t.when_dumped    # => nil

str = Marshal.dump(t)

newt = Marshal.load(str)
newt.when_dumped # => "12:32PM"
newt.other_data  # => "wibble"
```

Module Constants

MAJOR_VERSION Major part of marshal format version number
MINOR_VERSION Minor part of marshal format version number

Class Methods

dump
dump(*obj* ‹ , *io* › , *limit*=-1) → *io*

Serializes *obj* and all descendent objects. If *io* is specified, the serialized data will be written to it; otherwise, the data will be returned as a String. If *limit* is specified, the traversal of sub-objects will be limited to that depth. If the *limit* is negative, no checking of depth will be performed.

```
class Klass
  def initialize(str)
    @str = str
  end
  def say_hello
    @str
  end
end

o = Klass.new("hello\n")
data = Marshal.dump(o)
obj = Marshal.load(data)
obj.say_hello # => "hello\n"
```

load
load(*from* ‹ , *proc* ›) → *obj*

Returns the result of converting the serialized data in *from* into a Ruby object (possibly with associated subordinate objects). *from* may be either an instance of IO or an object that responds to to_str. If *proc* is specified, it will be passed each object as it is deserialized.

restore
restore(*from* ‹ , *proc* ›) → *obj*

A synonym for Marshal.load.

^{Class} **MatchData**

All pattern matches set the special variable $~ to a MatchData object containing information about the match. The methods Regexp#match and Regexp.last_match also return a MatchData object. The object encapsulates all the results of a pattern match, results normally accessed through the special variables $&, $', $`, $1, $2, and so on—see the list on page 311 for details.

Instance Methods

[ ]

match[i] → string
match[name] → string
match[start, length] → array
match[range] → array

Match Reference—MatchData acts as an array and/or hash and may be accessed using the normal indexing techniques. Numeric indices return the captures at the corresponding position in the regular expression (starting at 1), and symbol indices return the corresponding named capture. *match*[0] is equivalent to the special variable $& and returns the entire matched string. See also MatchData#values_at.

```
m = /(.)(.)(\d+)(\d)/.match("THX1138.")
m[0]                 # => "HX1138"
m[1, 2]              # => ["H", "X"]
m[1..3]              # => ["H", "X", "113"]
m[-3, 2]             # => ["X", "113"]
m = /..(?<digit_prefix>\d+)\d/.match("THX1138.")
m[:digit_prefix] # => "113"
```

begin

match.begin(*n*) → *int*
match.begin(*name*) → *int*

Returns the offset in the original string of the start of the *n*th capture or the named capture.

```
m = /(.)(.)(\d+)(\d)/.match("THX1138.")
m.begin(0)              # => 1
m.begin(2)              # => 2
m = /..(?<digit_prefix>\d+)\d/.match("THX1138.")
m.begin(:digit_prefix) # => 3
```

captures

match.captures → *array*

Returns the array of all the matching groups. Compare to MatchData#to_a, which returns both the complete matched string and all the matching groups.

```
m = /(.)(.)(\d+)(\d)/.match("THX1138.")
m.captures # => ["H", "X", "113", "8"]
```

captures is useful when extracting parts of a match in an assignment.

```
f1, f2, f3 = /(.)(.)(\d+)(\d)/.match("THX1138.").captures
f1          # => "H"
f2          # => "X"
f3          # => "113"
```

end

match.end(*n*) → *int*
match.end(*name*) → *int*

Returns the offset in the original string of the end of the *n*th capture or the named capture.

```
m = /(.)(.)(\d+)(\d)/.match("THX1138.")
m.end(0)              # => 7
m.end(2)              # => 3
m = /..(?<digit_prefix>\d+)\d/.match("THX1138.")
m.end(:digit_prefix) # => 6
```

length

match.length → *int*

Returns the number of elements in the match array.

```
m = /(.)(.)(\d+)(\d)/.match("THX1138.")
m.length  # => 5
m.size    # => 5
```

names

match.names → *array*

Returns the list of named captures in the regular expression that created *match*.

```
m = /(?<prefix>[A-Z]+)(?<hyphen>-?)(?<digits>\d+)/.match("THX1138.")
m.names    # => ["prefix", "hyphen", "digits"]
m.captures # => ["THX", "", "1138"]
m[:prefix] # => "THX"
```

offset

match.offset(*n*) → *array*
match.offset(*name*) → *array*

Returns an array containing the beginning and ending offsets of the *n*th or named capture.

```
m = /(.)(.)(\d+)(\d)/.match("THX1138.")
m.offset(0)              # => [1, 7]
m.offset(4)              # => [6, 7]
m = /..(?<digit_prefix>\d+)\d/.match("THX1138.")
m.offset(:digit_prefix) # => [3, 6]
```

post_match

match.post_match → *string*

Returns the portion of the original string after the current match. (Same as the special variable $'.)

```
m = /(.)(.)(\d+)(\d)/.match("THX1138: The Movie")
m.post_match # => ": The Movie"
```

pre_match

match.pre_match → *string*

Returns the portion of the original string before the current match. (Same as $`.)

```
m = /(.)(.)(\d+)(\d)/.match("THX1138.")
m.pre_match # => "T"
```

regexp

*match.*regexp → *a_regexp*

Returns the regexp object for the regular expression that created *match*.

```
m = /(.)(.)(\d+)(\d)/.match("THX1138: The Movie")
m.regexp  # => /(.)(.)(\d+)(\d)/
```

size

*match.*size → *int*

A synonym for MatchData#length.

string

*match.*string → *string*

Returns a frozen copy of the string passed in to *match*.

```
m = /(.)(.)(\d+)(\d)/.match("THX1138.")
m.string  # => "THX1138."
```

to_a

*match.*to_a → *array*

Returns the array of matches. Unlike MatchData#captures, returns the full string matched.

```
m = /(.)(.)(\d+)(\d)/.match("THX1138.")
m.to_a    # => ["HX1138", "H", "X", "113", "8"]
```

to_s

*match.*to_s → *string*

Returns the entire matched string.

```
m = /(.)(.)(\d+)(\d)/.match("THX1138.")
m.to_s    # => "HX1138"
```

values_at

*match.*values_at(‹ *index* ›*) → *array*

Returns the matches corresponding to the given indices.

```
m = /(.)(.)(\d+)(\d)/.match("THX1138.")
m.values_at(3,1,2) # => ["113", "H", "X"]
m.values_at(0, 4)  # => ["HX1138", "8"]
```

Math

The Math module contains module methods for basic trigonometric and transcendental functions. See class Float on page 513 for a list of constants that define Ruby's floating-point accuracy.

Module Constants

E	An approximation of *e* (base of natural logarithms)
PI	An approximation of π

Class Methods

acos
$$Math.acos(\ x\ ) \rightarrow float$$

Computes the arc cosine of x. Returns $0..\pi$.

acosh
$$Math.acosh(\ x\ ) \rightarrow float$$

Computes the inverse hyperbolic cosine of x.

asin
$$Math.asin(\ x\ ) \rightarrow float$$

Computes the arc sine of x. Returns $-\frac{\pi}{2}..\frac{\pi}{2}$.

asinh
$$Math.asinh(\ x\ ) \rightarrow float$$

Computes the inverse hyperbolic sine of x.

atan
$$Math.atan(\ x\ ) \rightarrow float$$

Computes the arc tangent of x. Returns $-\frac{\pi}{2}..\frac{\pi}{2}$.

atanh
$$Math.atanh(\ x\ ) \rightarrow float$$

Computes the inverse hyperbolic tangent of x.

atan2
$$Math.atan2(\ y, x\ ) \rightarrow float$$

Computes the arc tangent given y and x. Returns $-\pi..\pi$.

cbrt
$$Math.cbrt(\ numeric\ ) \rightarrow float$$

Returns the cube root of *numeric*.

cos
$$Math.cos(\ x\ ) \rightarrow float$$

Computes the cosine of x (expressed in radians). Returns $-1..1$.

cosh

Math.cosh(x) → *float*

Computes the hyperbolic cosine of x (expressed in radians).

erf

Math.erf(x) → *float*

Returns the error function of x.

erfc

Math.erfc(x) → *float*

Returns the complementary error function of x.

exp

Math.exp(x) → *float*

Returns e^x.

frexp

Math.frexp(*numeric*) → [*fraction, exponent*]

Returns the normalized fraction (a Float) and exponent (a Fixnum) of *numeric*.

```
fraction, exponent = Math.frexp(1234) # => [0.6025390625, 11]
fraction * 2**exponent               # => 1234.0
```

gamma

Math.gamma(x) → *float*

Returns the gamma function. For integral x, gamma(x) approximates factorial(x-1).

```
Math.gamma(2)     # => 1.0
Math.gamma(3)     # => 2.0
Math.gamma(4)     # => 6.0
Math.gamma(10.34) # => 784993.6091493163
```

hypot

Math.hypot(x, y) → *float*

Returns $sqrt(x^2 + y^2)$, the hypotenuse of a right-angled triangle with sides x and y.

```
Math.hypot(3, 4) # => 5.0
```

ldexp

Math.ldexp(*float, n*) → *float*

Returns the value of $float \times 2^n$.

```
fraction, exponent = Math.frexp(1234)
Math.ldexp(fraction, exponent) # => 1234.0
```

lgamma

Math.lgamma(x) → [*float, sign*]

The first element of the returned array is the natural logarithm of the absolute value of the gamma function of x. The second value is -1 if the gamma function returned a negative number, +1 otherwise.

---

log   Math.log(*numeric* ‹ , *base=E* ›) → *float*

Returns logarithm of *numeric*. With no *base* parameter, returns the natural logarith.

---

log10   Math.log10(*numeric*) → *float*

Returns the base 10 logarithm of *numeric*.

---

log2   Math.log2(*numeric*) → *float*

Returns the base 2 logarithm of *numeric*.

---

sin   Math.sin(*numeric*) → *float*

Computes the sine of *numeric* (expressed in radians). Returns -1..1.

---

sinh   Math.sinh(*float*) → *float*

Computes the hyperbolic sine of *numeric* (expressed in radians).

---

sqrt   Math.sqrt(*float*) → *float*

Returns the non-negative square root of *numeric*. Raises ArgError if *numeric* is less than zero.

---

tan   Math.tan(*float*) → *float*

Returns the tangent of *numeric* (expressed in radians).

---

tanh   Math.tanh(*float*) → *float*

Computes the hyperbolic tangent of *numeric* (expressed in radians).

Class	Method

Method objects are created by Object#method. They are associated with a particular object (not just with a class). They may be used to invoke the method within the object and as a block associated with an iterator. They may also be unbound from one object (creating an UnboundMethod) and bound to another.

```ruby
def square(n)
  n*n
end

meth  = self.method(:square)

meth.call(9)               # => 81
[ 1, 2, 3 ].collect(&meth) # => [1, 4, 9]
```

Instance Methods

[ ]   *meth*[⟨ *args* ⟩*] → *object*

Synonym for Method#call.

==   *meth* == *other* → *true* or *false*

Returns true if *meth* is the same method as *other*.

```ruby
def fred()
  puts "Hello"
end

alias bert fred # => nil

m1 = method(:fred)
m2 = method(:bert)

m1 == m2        # => true
```

---

arity   *meth*.arity → *fixnum*

Returns a non-negative integer for methods that take a fixed number of arguments. For Ruby methods that take a variable number of arguments, returns -n-1, where n is the number of required arguments. For methods written in C, returns -1 if the call takes a variable number of arguments. See also Method#parameters.

```ruby
class C
  def one;            end
  def two(a);         end
  def three(*a);      end
  def four(a, b);     end
  def five(a, b, *c); end
  def six(a, b, *c, &d); end
end
```

```
c = C.new
c.method(:one).arity    # => 0
c.method(:two).arity    # => 1
c.method(:three).arity  # => -1
c.method(:four).arity   # => 2
c.method(:five).arity   # => -3
c.method(:six).arity    # => -3

"cat".method(:size).arity     # => 0
"cat".method(:replace).arity  # => 1
"cat".method(:squeeze).arity  # => -1
"cat".method(:count).arity    # => -1
```

call   *meth*.call(‹ *args* ›*) → *object*

Invokes the *meth* with the specified arguments, returning the method's return value.

```
m = 12.method("+")
m.call(3)   # => 15
m.call(20)  # => 32
```

eql?   *meth*.eql?(*other*) → *true* or *false*

Returns true if *meth* is the same method as *other*.

```
def fred()
  puts "Hello"
end

alias bert fred # => nil

m1 = method(:fred)
m2 = method(:bert)
m1.eql?(m2)     # => true
```

name   *meth*.name → *string*

Returns the name of the method *meth*.

```
method = "cat".method(:upcase)
method.name # => :upcase
```

owner   *meth*.owner → *module*

Returns the class or module in which *meth* is defined.

```
method = "cat".method(:upcase)
method.owner # => String
```

parameters   *meth*.parameters → *array*

Returns an array describing the parameters taken by the method. Each entry in the array is itself an array. The first entry of each subarray contains the role of the parameter (:req for required, :opt for optional, :rest for a splat parameter, and :block for a block). If the parameter has a name, it will be the second entry in the subarray.

```
def m(a, b=1, *c, &d)
end
method(:m).parameters # => [[:req, :a], [:opt, :b], [:rest, :c], [:block, :d]]
```

receiver   *meth*.receiver → *obj*

Returns the object on which *meth* is defined.

```
method = "cat".method(:upcase)
method.receiver # => "cat"
```

source_location   *meth*.source_location → [*filename, lineno*] or nil

Returns the source filename and line number where *meth* was defined or nil if self was not defined in Ruby source.

```
internal_method = "cat".method(:upcase)
internal_method.source_location # => nil

require 'set'
set = Set.new
ruby_method = set.method(:clear)
ruby_method.source_location[0]  # => "/Users/dave/.rvm/rubies/ruby-2.0.0-p0/lib/r
                                # .. uby/2.0.0/set.rb"
ruby_method.source_location[1]  # => 131
```

to_proc   *meth*.to_proc → *prc*

Returns a Proc object corresponding to this method. Because to_proc is called by the interpreter when passing block arguments, method objects may be used following an ampersand to pass a block to another method call. See the example at the start of this section.

unbind   *meth*.unbind → unbound_method

Dissociates *meth* from its current receiver. The resulting UnboundMethod can subsequently be bound to a new object of the same class (see UnboundMethod on page 726).

Module

Subclasses: Class

A Module is a collection of methods and constants. The methods in a module may be instance methods or module methods. Instance methods appear as methods in a class when the module is included; module methods do not. Conversely, module methods may be called without creating an encapsulating object, and instance methods may not. See also Module#module_function on page 584.

In the descriptions that follow, the parameter *symbol* refers to a name, which is either a quoted string or a symbol (such as :name).

```
module Mod
  include Math
  CONST = 1
  def meth
    #  ...
  end
end
Mod.class             # => Module
Mod.constants         # => [:CONST, :DomainError, :PI, :E]
Mod.instance_methods # => [:meth]
```

Class Methods

constants

Module.constants → *array*
Module.constants(*include_parents*) → *array*

With no argument, returns a list of the top-level constants in the interpreter. With one argument, returns the constants defined in class Module (and its parents if the argument is true). This somewhat obscure interface is because Module is a kind of Class, and Class is a subclass of Module. The first form of call is a true call to the class method constants, while the second form actually proxies to the instance method form (see Module#constants later in this section).

```
module Mixin
  CONST_MIXIN = 1
end
class Module
  include Mixin
  SPURIOUS_CONSTANT = 2
end
Module.constants.sort[1..3]          # => [:ARGV, :ArgumentError, :Array]
Module.constants.include? :CONST_MIXIN # => false
Module.constants(false)              # => [:SPURIOUS_CONSTANT]
Module.constants(true)               # => [:SPURIOUS_CONSTANT, :CONST_MIXIN]
```

nesting

Module.nesting → *array*

Returns the list of modules nested at the point of call.

```ruby
module M1
  module M2
    nest = Module.nesting
    p nest
    p nest[0].name
  end
end
```

produces:

```
[M1::M2, M1]
"M1::M2"
```

---

new

Module.new → *mod*
Module.new { |mod| ... } → *mod*

Creates a new anonymous module. If a block is given, it is passed the module object, and the block is evaluated in the context of this module using module_eval.

```ruby
Fred = Module.new do
  def meth1
    "hello"
  end
  def meth2
    "bye"
  end
end
a = "my string"
a.extend(Fred) # => "my string"
a.meth1        # => "hello"
a.meth2        # => "bye"
```

Instance Methods

<, <=, ==, >, >=

mod relop module → true, false or *nil*

Hierarchy Query—One module is considered greater than another if it is included in (or is a parent class of) the other module. The other operators are defined accordingly. If there is no relationship between the modules, all operators return nil.

```ruby
module Mixin
end

module Parent
  include Mixin
end

module Unrelated
end

Parent > Mixin     # => false
Parent < Mixin     # => true
Parent <= Parent   # => true
Parent < Unrelated # => nil
Parent > Unrelated # => nil
```

<=>   *mod <=> other_mod → -1, 0, +1*

Comparison—Returns -1 if *mod* includes *other_mod*, 0 if *mod* is the same module as *other_mod*, and +1 if *mod* is included by *other_mod* or if *mod* has no relationship with *other_mod*.

===   *mod === obj → true or false*

Case Equality—Returns true if *obj* is an instance of *mod* or one of *mod*'s descendents. Of limited use for modules but can be used in case statements to test objects by class.

---

ancestors   *mod.ancestors → array*

Returns a list of modules included in *mod* (including *mod* itself).

```
module Mod
  include Math
  include Comparable
end

Mod.ancestors  # => [Mod, Comparable, Math]
Math.ancestors # => [Math]
```

---

autoload   *mod.autoload(name, file_name) → nil*

Registers *file_name* to be loaded (using Object#require) the first time that module *name* (which may be a String or a Symbol) is accessed in the namespace of *mod*. Note that the autoloaded file is evaluated in the top-level context. In this example, module_b.rb contains the following:

```
module A::B    # in module_b.rb
  def doit
    puts "In Module A::B"
  end
  module_function :doit
end
```

Other code can then include this module automatically.

```
module A
  autoload(:B, "module_b")
end

A::B.doit              # autoloads "module_b"
```
produces:

```
In Module A::B
```

autoload?

mod.autoload?(*name*) → *file_name* or nil

Returns the name of the file that will be autoloaded when the string or symbol *name* is referenced in the context of *mod* or returns nil if there is no associated autoload.

```
module A
  autoload(:B, "module_b")
end
A.autoload?(:B) # => "module_b"
A.autoload?(:C) # => nil
```

class_eval

mod.class_eval(*string* ‹, *file_name* ‹, *line_number* ››) → *obj*
mod.class_eval { ... } → *obj*

Synonym for Module#module_eval.

class_exec

mod.class_exec(‹ args ›⁺) { | args | ... } → *obj*

Synonym for Module#module_exec.

class_variable_defined?

mod.class_variable_defined?(*name*) → *true* or *false*

Returns true if the named class variable is defined in *mod*. The two @ signs are a required part of the name.

```
class One
  @@var1 = "wibble"
end
One.class_variable_defined?(:@@var1) # => true
One.class_variable_defined?(:@@var2) # => false
```

class_variable_get

mod.class_variable_get(*name*) → *obj*

Returns the value of the named class variable. The two @ signs must appear in the name.

```
class One
  @@var1 = "wibble"
end
One.class_variable_get(:@@var1)  # => "wibble"
One.class_variable_get("@@var1") # => "wibble"
```

class_variable_set

mod.class_variable_set(*name*, *value*) → *value*

Sets the value of the named class variable. The two @ signs must appear in the name.

```
class One
  @@var1 = "wibble"
end
One.class_variable_set(:@@var1, 99) # => 99
One.class_variable_get("@@var1")    # => 99
```

class_variables

mod.class_variables → *array*

Returns an array of the names of class variables in *mod*. (As of Ruby 1.9, class variables are no longer shared with child classes, so this listing is restricted to the class variables defined in *mod*.)

```
class One
  @@var1 = 1
end
class Two < One
  @@var2 = 2
end
One.class_variables # => [:@@var1]
Two.class_variables # => [:@@var2, :@@var1]
```

const_defined?

mod.const_defined?(*symbol* ‹ *search_parents*=true ›) → *true* or *false*

Returns true if a constant with the given name is defined by *mod* or the parents of *mod* (if the second parameter is true).

```
Math.const_defined? "PI" # => true
```

const_get

mod.const_get(*symbol*) → *obj*

New in 2.0

Returns the value of the named constant in *mod*. Ruby 2.0 allows this name to be qualified by one or more module names.

```
Math.const_get :PI           # => 3.141592653589793
Object.const_get("Math::PI") # => 3.141592653589793
```

const_missing

mod.const_missing(*symbol*) → *obj*

Invoked when a reference is made to an undefined constant in *mod*. It is passed a symbol for the undefined constant and returns a value to be used for that constant. The following code is very poor style. If a reference is made to an undefined constant, it attempts to load a file whose name is the lowercase version of the constant (thus, class Fred is assumed to be in file fred.rb). If found, it returns the value of the loaded class. It therefore implements a perverse kind of autoload facility.

```
def Object.const_missing(name)
  @looked_for ||= {}
  str_name = name.to_s
  raise "Class not found: #{name}" if @looked_for[str_name]
  @looked_for[str_name] = 1
  file = str_name.downcase
  require file
  klass = const_get(name)
  return klass if klass
  raise "Class not found: #{name}"
end
```

const_set

mod.const_set(*symbol, obj*) → *obj*

Sets the named constant to the given object, returning that object. Creates a new constant if no constant with the given name previously existed.

```
Math.const_set("HIGH_SCHOOL_PI", 22.0/7.0) # => 3.142857142857143
Math::HIGH_SCHOOL_PI - Math::PI           # => 0.0012644892673496777
```

constants

mod.constants(*include_parents* = true) → *array*

Returns an array of the names of the constants accessible in *mod*. If the parameter is true, this includes the names of constants in any included modules.

```
IO.constants(false)    # => [:WaitReadable, :WaitWritable, :SEEK_SET, :SEEK_CUR,
                       # .. :SEEK_END]
# Now include stuff defined in module File::Constants
IO.constants(true)[1,6] # => [:WaitWritable, :SEEK_SET, :SEEK_CUR, :SEEK_END,
                       # .. :RDONLY, :WRONLY]
```

include?

mod.include?(*other_mod*) → *true* or *false*

Returns true if *other_mod* is included in *mod* or one of *mod*'s ancestors.

```
module A
end

class B
  include A
end

class C < B
end

B.include?(A) # => true
C.include?(A) # => true
A.include?(A) # => false
```

included_modules

mod.included_modules → *array*

Returns the list of modules included in *mod*.

```
module Mixin
end

module Outer
  include Mixin
end

Mixin.included_modules # => []
Outer.included_modules # => [Mixin]
```

instance_method

mod.instance_method(*symbol*) → *unbound_method*

Returns an UnboundMethod representing the given instance method in *mod*.

```ruby
class Interpreter
  def do_a() print "there, "; end
  def do_d() print "Hello ";  end
  def do_e() print "!\n";     end
  def do_v() print "Dave";    end

  Dispatcher = {
    'a' => instance_method(:do_a),
    'd' => instance_method(:do_d),
    'e' => instance_method(:do_e),
    'v' => instance_method(:do_v)
  }

  def interpret(string)
    string.each_char {|ch| Dispatcher[ch].bind(self).call }
  end
end

interpreter = Interpreter.new
interpreter.interpret('dave')
```

produces:

```
Hello there, Dave!
```

instance_methods

mod.instance_methods(*inc_super*=true) → *array*

Returns an array containing the names of public and protected instance methods in the receiver. For a module, these are the public methods; for a class, they are the instance (not singleton) methods. With no argument or with an argument that is true, the methods in *mod* and *mod*'s superclasses are returned. When called with a module as a receiver or with a parameter that is false, the instance methods in *mod* are returned.

```ruby
module A
  def method1
  end
end
class B
  def method2
  end
end
class C < B
  def method3
  end
end

A.instance_methods            # => [:method1]
B.instance_methods(false)     # => [:method2]
C.instance_methods(false)     # => [:method3]
C.instance_methods(true).length # => 56
```

method_defined?

mod.method_defined?(*symbol*) → *true* or *false*

Returns true if the named method is defined by *mod* (or its included modules and, if *mod* is a class, its ancestors). Public and protected methods are matched.

```
module A
  def method1;  end
end
class B
  def method2;  end
end
class C < B
  include A
  def method3;  end
end

A.method_defined? :method1  # => true
C.method_defined? "method1" # => true
C.method_defined? "method2" # => true
C.method_defined? "method3" # => true
C.method_defined? "method4" # => false
```

module_eval

mod.module_eval(*string* ‹, *file_name* ‹, *line_number*› ›) → *obj*
mod.module_eval { ... } → *obj*

Evaluates the string or block in the context of *mod*. This can be used to add methods to a class. module_eval returns the result of evaluating its argument. The optional *file_name* and *line_number* parameters set the text for error messages.

```
class Thing
end
a = %q{def hello() "Hello there!" end}
Thing.module_eval(a)
puts Thing.new.hello()
Thing.module_eval("invalid code", "dummy", 123)
```

produces:

```
Hello there!
dummy:123:in `<main>': undefined local variable
    or method `code' for Thing:Class
```

module_exec

mod.module_exec(‹args›⁺) { | args | ... } → *obj*

Behaves the same as the block form for Module#module_eval, except any parameters passed to the method are in turn passed to the block. This gives you a way of passing in values that would otherwise not be in scope in the block (because *self* is changed).

```
class Thing
end
name  = :new_instance_variable
Thing.module_exec(name) do |iv_name|
  attr_accessor iv_name
end
```

```
t = Thing.new
t.new_instance_variable = "wibble"
p t
```

produces:

```
#<Thing:0x007f9b01847fa8 @new_instance_variable="wibble">
```

name   *mod*.name → *string*

Returns the name of the module *mod*.

private_class_method   *mod*.private_class_method(‹ *symbol* ›⁺) → nil

Makes existing class methods private. Often used to hide the default constructor new.

```
class SimpleSingleton   # Not thread safe
  private_class_method :new
  def SimpleSingleton.create(*args, &block)
    @me = new(*args, &block) if ! @me
    @me
  end
end
```

private_constant   *mod*.private_constant(‹ *symbol* ›⁺) → *mod*

Makes the given constants (which must already have been defined) private to the module. A private constant cannot be referenced using the module name as a scope, so they effectively can only be accessed within the context of the module itself.

```
module A
  B = "my constant"
  private_constant :B
  puts "Inside A, B = #{B.inspect}"
end

puts "Outside A, A::B = #{A::B.inspect}"
```

produces:

```
Inside A, B = "my constant"
prog.rb:7:in `<main>': private constant A::B referenced (NameError)
```

private_instance_methods   *mod*.private_instance_methods(*inc_super*=true) → *array*

Returns a list of the private instance methods defined in *mod*. If the optional parameter is true, the methods of any ancestors are included.

```
module Mod
  def method1;   end
  private :method1
  def method2;   end
end
Mod.instance_methods          # => [:method2]
Mod.private_instance_methods # => [:method1]
```

private_method_defined?

mod.private_method_defined?(*symbol*) → *true* or *false*

Returns true if the named private method is defined by *mod* (or its included modules and, if *mod* is a class, its ancestors).

```ruby
module A
  def method1;  end
end
class B
  private
  def method2;  end
end
class C < B
  include A
  def method3;  end
end

A.method_defined? :method1          # => true
C.private_method_defined? "method1" # => false
C.private_method_defined? "method2" # => true
C.method_defined? "method2"         # => false
```

protected_instance_methods

mod.protected_instance_methods(*inc_super*=true) → *array*

Returns a list of the protected instance methods defined in *mod*. If the optional parameter is true, the methods of any ancestors are included.

protected_method_defined?

mod.protected_method_defined?(*symbol*) → *true* or *false*

Returns true if the named protected method is defined by *mod* (or its included modules and, if *mod* is a class, its ancestors).

```ruby
module A
  def method1;  end
end
class B
  protected
  def method2;  end
end
class C < B
  include A
  def method3;  end
end

A.method_defined? :method1            # => true
C.protected_method_defined? "method1" # => false
C.protected_method_defined? "method2" # => true
C.method_defined? "method2"           # => true
```

public_class_method

mod.public_class_method(‹ *symbol* ›⁺) → nil

Makes a list of existing class methods public.

public_constant

mod.public_constant(‹ *symbol* ›⁺) → *mod*

Makes the given constants (which must already have been defined) public, overriding the effect of a previous call to privante_constant.

```ruby
module A
  B = "my constant"
  private_constant :B
  puts "Inside A, B = #{B.inspect}"
  public_constant :B
end

puts "Outside A, A::B = #{A::B.inspect}"
```

produces:

```
Inside A, B = "my constant"
Outside A, A::B = "my constant"
```

public_instance_method

mod.public_instance_method(*symbol*) → *unbound_method*

Returns an UnboundMethod representing the given public instance method in *mod*. See also Module#instance_method, which ignores scope.

```ruby
class Test
  def method_a; end
private
  def method_b; end
end
puts "method_a is #{Test.public_instance_method(:method_a)}"
puts "method_b is #{Test.public_instance_method(:method_b)}"
```

produces:

```
        from prog.rb:7:in `<main>'
method_a is #<UnboundMethod: Test#method_a>
prog.rb:7:in `public_instance_method': method `method_b' for class `Test' is
private (NameError)
```

public_instance_methods

mod.public_instance_methods(*inc_super*=true) → *array*

Returns a list of the public instance methods defined in *mod*. If the optional parameter is true, the methods of any ancestors are included.

public_method_defined?

mod.public_method_defined?(*symbol*) → *true* or *false*

Returns true if the named public method is defined by *mod* (or its included modules and, if *mod* is a class, its ancestors).

```
module A
  def method1;  end
end
class B
  protected
  def method2;  end
end
class C < B
  include A
  def method3;  end
end

A.method_defined? :method1         # => true
C.public_method_defined? "method1" # => true
C.public_method_defined? "method2" # => false
C.method_defined? "method2"        # => true
```

---

remove_class_variable
<code>remove_class_variable(symbol) → obj</code>

Removes the definition of the *symbol*, returning that variable's value. Prior to Ruby 1.9, this method was private.

```
class Dummy
  @@var = 99
end
Dummy.class_eval { p defined? @@var }
puts Dummy.remove_class_variable(:@@var)
Dummy.class_eval { p defined? @@var }
```

produces:

```
prog.rb:4: warning: class variable access from toplevel
nil
prog.rb:6: warning: class variable access from toplevel
99
nil
```

Private Instance Methods

alias_method
<code>alias_method(new_id, old_id) → mod</code>

Makes *new_id* a new copy of the method *old_id*. This can be used to retain access to methods that are overridden.

```
module Mod
  alias_method :orig_exit, :exit
  def exit(code=0)
    puts "Exiting with code #{code}"
    orig_exit(code)
  end
end
include Mod
exit(99)
```

produces:

```
Exiting with code 99
```

append_features   append_features(*other_mod*) → *mod*

When this module is included in another, Ruby calls append_features in this module, passing it the receiving module in *other_mod*. Ruby's default implementation is to add the constants, methods, and module variables of this module to *other_mod* if this module has not already been added to *other_mod* or one of its ancestors. Prior to Ruby 1.8, user code often redefined append_features, added its own functionality, and then invoked super to handle the real include. Now you should instead implement the method Module#included on page 582.

attr   attr(‹ symbol ›⁺) → nil

An alias for Module#attr_reader (as of Ruby 1.9).

attr_accessor   attr_accessor(‹ *symbol* ›⁺) → nil

Creates a reader and a writer method for each symbol passed as an argument. These methods provide access to the underlying instance variables of the name name (with a leading @ sign).

```ruby
class Test
  attr_accessor :name, :likes
  def initialize(name, likes)
    @name = name
    @likes = likes
  end
end
d = Test.new("Dave", "Ruby")
d.name = "Chad"
d.name    # => "Chad"
d.likes   # => "Ruby"
```

attr_reader   attr_reader(‹ *symbol* ›⁺) → nil

Creates instance variables and corresponding methods that return their values.

```ruby
class Test
  attr_reader :name, :likes
  def initialize(name, likes)
    @name = name
    @likes = likes
  end
end

d = Test.new("Dave", "Ruby")
d.name    # => "Dave"
d.likes   # => "Ruby"
```

attr_writer

attr_writer(‹*symbol*›⁺) → nil

Creates an accessor method to allow assignment to the attribute *symbol*.id2name.

```ruby
class Test
  attr_writer :name, :likes
  def initialize(name, likes)
    @name = name
    @likes = likes
  end
end
d = Test.new("Dave", "Ruby")
d.name = "Chad"
d          # => #<Test:0x007fc52210f8a8 @name="Chad", @likes="Ruby">
```

define_method

define_method(*symbol, method*) → *method*
define_method(*symbol*) { ... } → *proc*

Defines an instance method in the receiver. The *method* parameter can be a Proc, a Method, or an UnboundMethod object. If a block is specified, it is used as the method body. This block is evaluated using instance_eval. This is tricky to demonstrate because define_method is private. (This is why we resort to the send hack in this example.) See also Object#define_singleton_method.

```ruby
class A
  def fred
    puts "In Fred"
  end
  def create_method(name, &block)
    self.class.send(:define_method, name, &block)
  end
  define_method(:wilma) { puts "Charge it!" }
end
class B < A
  define_method(:barney, instance_method(:fred))
end
b = B.new
b.barney
b.wilma
b.create_method(:betty) { p self }
b.betty
```

produces:

```
In Fred
Charge it!
#<B:0x007fb6bb846600>
```

Note that it is possible to define methods with names that are not valid if you were to use the def keyword. These methods cannot be invoked directly.

```ruby
class Silly
  define_method("Oh !@!#^!") { "As Snoopy says" }
end
Silly.new.send("Oh !@!#^!") # => "As Snoopy says"
```

---

extend_object
extend_object(*obj*) → *obj*

Extends the specified object by adding this module's constants and methods (which are added as singleton methods). This is the callback method used by Object#extend.

```ruby
module Picky
  def Picky.extend_object(o)
    if String === o
      puts "Can't add Picky to a String"
    else
      puts "Picky added to #{o.class}"
      super
    end
  end
end
(s = Array.new).extend Picky   # Call Object.extend
(s = "quick brown fox").extend Picky
```

produces:

```
Picky added to Array
Can't add Picky to a String
```

---

extended
extended(*other_mod*)

Callback invoked whenever the receiver is used to extend an object. The object is passed as a parameter. This should be used in preference to Module#extend_object if your code wants to perform some action when a module is used to extend an object.

```ruby
module A
  def A.extended(obj)
    puts "#{self} extending '#{obj}'"
  end
end
"cat".extend(A)
```

produces:

```
A extending 'cat'
```

---

include
include(‹ *other_mod* ›+) → *mod*

Includes the listed modules in *self*. Typically used to make the instance methods in the included modules available in the receiver. Equivalent to the following code:

```ruby
def include(*modules)
  modules.reverse_each do |mod|
    mod.append_features(self)   # make the methods available
    mod.included(self)          # invoke a callback
  end
end
```

New in 2.0   See also Module#prepend.

included

included(other_mod)

Callback invoked whenever the receiver is included in another module or class. This should be used in preference to Module#append_features if your code wants to perform some action when a module is included in another.

```ruby
module A
  def A.included(mod)
    puts "#{self} included in #{mod}"
  end
end
module Enumerable
  include A
end
```

produces:

```
A included in Enumerable
```

method_added

method_added(symbol)

Invoked as a callback whenever a method is added to the receiver.

```ruby
module Chatty
  def Chatty.method_added(id)
    puts "Adding #{id.id2name}"
  end
  def one; end
end
module Chatty
  def two; end
end
```

produces:

```
Adding one
Adding two
```

method_removed

method_removed(symbol)

Invoked as a callback whenever a method is removed from the receiver.

```ruby
module Chatty
  def Chatty.method_removed(id)
    puts "Removing #{id.id2name}"
  end
  def one
  end
end
module Chatty
  remove_method(:one)
end
```

produces:

```
Removing one
```

---

method_undefined   method_undefined(*symbol*)

Invoked as a callback whenever a method is undefined in the receiver.

```ruby
module Chatty
  def Chatty.method_undefined(id)
    puts "Undefining #{id.id2name}"
  end
  def one
  end
end
module Chatty
  undef_method(:one)
end
```

produces:

```
Undefining one
```

---

module_function   module_function(‹*symbol*›*) → *mod*

Creates module functions for the named methods. These functions may be called with the module as a receiver. Module functions are copies of the original and so may be changed independently. The instance-method versions are made private. If used with no arguments, subsequently defined methods become module functions.

```ruby
module Mod
  def one
    "This is one"
  end
  module_function :one
end

class Cls
  include Mod
  def call_one
    one
  end
end

Mod.one     # => "This is one"
c = Cls.new
c.call_one # => "This is one"
module Mod
  def one
    "This is the new one"
  end
end
Mod.one     # => "This is one"
c.call_one # => "This is the new one"
```

prepend
prepend(‹ other_mod ›⁺) → mod

Includes the listed modules in *self*. Unlike Module#include. if the module contains methods with the same names as those in the including module, the included modules methods take precedence.

New in 2.0

```ruby
module Mod
  def meth; "In module Mod"; end
end
class Cls1
  def meth; "In class Cls1"; end
  include Mod
end
class Cls2
  def meth; "In class Cls2"; end
  prepend Mod
end
```

See also Module#include.

New in 2.0

private
private(‹ symbol ›[*]) → mod

With no arguments, sets the default visibility for subsequently defined methods to private. With arguments, sets the named methods to have private visibility. See "Access Control" on page 335.

```ruby
module Mod
  def a;  end
  def b;  end

  private

  def c;  end

  private :a
end
Mod.private_instance_methods # => [:a, :c]
```

protected
protected(‹ symbol ›[*]) → mod

With no arguments, sets the default visibility for subsequently defined methods to protected. With arguments, sets the named methods to have protected visibility. See "Access Control" on page 335.

public
public(‹ symbol ›[*]) → mod

With no arguments, sets the default visibility for subsequently defined methods to public. With arguments, sets the named methods to have public visibility. See "Access Control" on page 335.

refine

refine(*class*) { … } → *refmod*

New in 2.0 Defines a refinement for the given class. This is activated from the top-level of a source file with the Object#using method, which applies the methods defined in the block to the given class for the remainder of that source file. The tutorial on page 369 has more information. refine returns a special kind of module object that represents the change to be made to the host class.

```ruby
module SuperUpcase
  refine String do
    def upcase
      "!#{super}!"
    end
  end
end


puts "wombat".upcase
using SuperUpcase
puts "wombat".upcase
```

produces:

```
WOMBAT
!WOMBAT!
```

remove_const

remove_const(*symbol*) → *obj*

Removes the definition of the given constant, returning that constant's value. Predefined classes and singleton objects (such as *true*) cannot be removed.

remove_method

remove_method(*symbol*) → *mod*

Removes the method identified by *symbol* from the current class. For an example, see Module#undef_method.

undef_method

undef_method(‹ *symbol* ›⁺) → *mod*

Prevents the current class from responding to calls to the named method(s). Contrast this with remove_method, which deletes the method from the particular class; Ruby will still search superclasses and mixed-in modules for a possible receiver.

```ruby
class Parent
  def hello
    puts "In parent"
  end
end

class Child < Parent
  def hello
    puts "In child"
  end
end
```

```ruby
c = Child.new
c.hello

class Child
  remove_method :hello  # remove from child, still in parent
end
c.hello

class Child
  undef_method :hello   # prevent any calls to 'hello'
end
c.hello
```

produces:

```
In child
In parent
prog.rb:24:in `<main>': undefined method `hello' for #<Child:0x007fcfa4042ee8>
(NoMethodError)
```

Mutex

A mutex is a semaphore object that can be used to synchronize access to resources shared across threads. We discussed mutexes (and other synchronization mechanisms) in Section 12.4, *Mutual Exclusion*, on page 167. Because the code examples tend to be long, we haven't duplicated them in this library description.

Instance Methods

lock

mutex.lock → *mutex*

Takes a lock on *mutex*. Suspends if *mutex* is already locked by another thread and raises a ThreadError if the mutex is already locked by the calling thread or if called from a trap handler.

New in 2.0

locked?

mutex.locked? → *true* or *false*

Returns the current locked state of *mutex*.

owned?

mutex.owned? → *true* or *false*

New in 2.0   Returns true if the mutex is held by the current thread. Experimental in Ruby 2.0.

sleep

mutex.sleep(*time* | nil) → *seconds_slept*

Releases the current thread's lock on *mutex*, sleeps for *time* seconds (or forever if nil is passed), and then regains the lock. Returns the number of seconds actually slept. This may be less New in 2.0   than the number requested, so it is wise to check. May not be called from a trap handler.

synchronize

mutex.synchronize { … } → *obj*

Locks *mutex*, executes the block, and then unlocks *mutex*. Returns the value returned by the block. May not be called from a trap handler.

New in 2.0

try_lock

mutex.try_lock → *true* or *false*

If *mutex* is not currently locked, locks it and returns true. Otherwise, returns false. (That is, try_lock is like lock, but it will never wait for a mutex to become available.) May not be called New in 2.0   from a trap handler.

unlock

mutex.unlock → *mutex*

Unlock *mutex*, which must be locked by the current thread. May not be called from a trap New in 2.0   handler.

NilClass

The class of the singleton object nil.

Instance Methods

&   nil & *obj* → false

And—Returns false. Because *obj* is an argument to a method call, it is always evaluated; there is no short-circuit evaluation in this case.

```
nil && puts("logical and")
nil &  puts("and")
```

produces:

```
and
```

^   nil ^ *obj* → *true* or *false*

Exclusive Or—Returns false if *obj* is nil or false and returns true otherwise.

| nil | *obj* → *true* or *false*

Or—Returns false if *obj* is nil or false and returns true otherwise.

```
nil | false # => false
nil | 99    # => true
```

nil?   nil.nil? → true

Always returns true.

rationalize   *int*.rationalize(*eps*=nil) → Rational(0)

Returns Rational("0"). The argument is always ignored.

```
nil.rationalize # => (0/1)
```

to_a   nil.to_a → []

Always returns an empty array.

```
nil.to_a  # => []
```

to_c   nil.to_c → Complex(0,0)

Always returns the origin of the complex plane.

```
nil.to_c  # => (0+0i)
```

to_f

nil.to_f → 0.0

Always returns zero.

```
nil.to_f  # => 0.0
```

to_h

nil.to_h → {}

New in 2.0   Always returns an empty hash.

```
nil.to_h  # => {}
```

to_i

nil.to_i → 0

Always returns zero.

```
nil.to_i  # => 0
```

to_r

nil.to_r → Rational(0,1)

Always returns zero as a rational number.

```
nil.to_r  # => (0/1)
```

to_s

nil.to_s → ""

Always returns the empty string.

```
nil.to_s  # => ""
```

Class | **Numeric**

Subclasses: Float, Integer

Numeric is the fundamental base type for the abstract class Integer and the concrete number classes Bignum, Complex, Float, Fixnum, and Rational. Many methods in Numeric are overridden in child classes, and Numeric takes some liberties by calling methods in these child classes. Here's a complete list of the methods defined in all five classes:

	Numeric	Integer	Fixnum	Bignum	Float	Rational	Complex
%	✓	–	✓	✓	✓	–	–
&	–	–	✓	✓	–	–	–
*	–	–	✓	✓	✓	✓	✓
**	–	–	✓	✓	✓	✓	✓
+	–	–	✓	✓	✓	✓	✓
+@	✓	–	–	–	–	–	–
-	–	–	✓	✓	✓	✓	✓
-@	✓	–	✓	✓	✓	–	✓
/	–	–	✓	✓	✓	✓	✓
<	–	–	✓	✓	✓	–	–
<<	–	–	✓	✓	–	–	–
<=	–	–	✓	✓	✓	–	–
<=>	✓	–	✓	✓	✓	✓	–
==	–	–	✓	✓	✓	✓	✓
===	–	–	✓	✓	✓	–	–
>	–	–	✓	✓	✓	–	–
>=	–	–	✓	✓	✓	–	–
>>	–	–	✓	✓	–	–	–
[]	–	–	✓	✓	–	–	–
^	–	–	✓	✓	–	–	–
abs	✓	–	✓	✓	✓	–	✓
abs2	✓	–	–	–	–	–	✓
angle	✓	–	–	–	✓	–	✓
arg	✓	–	–	–	✓	–	✓
ceil	✓	✓	–	–	✓	✓	–
chr	–	✓	–	–	–	–	–
coerce	✓	–	–	✓	✓	✓	✓
conj	✓	–	–	–	–	–	✓
conjugate	✓	–	–	–	–	–	✓
denominator	✓	✓	–	–	✓	✓	✓
div	✓	–	✓	✓	–	–	–
divmod	✓	–	✓	✓	✓	–	–
downto	–	✓	–	–	–	–	–
eql?	✓	–	–	✓	✓	–	✓
even?	–	✓	✓	✓	–	–	–
fdiv	✓	–	✓	✓	✓	✓	✓
finite?	–	–	–	–	✓	–	–
floor	✓	✓	–	–	✓	✓	–
gcd	–	✓	–	–	–	–	–
gcdlcm	–	✓	–	–	–	–	–
i	✓	–	–	–	–	–	–
imag	✓	–	–	–	–	–	✓

	Numeric	Integer	Fixnum	Bignum	Float	Rational	Complex
imaginary	✓	–	–	–	–	–	✓
infinite?	–	–	–	–	✓	–	–
integer?	✓	✓	–	–	–	–	–
lcm	–	✓	–	–	–	–	–
magnitude	✓	–	✓	✓	✓	–	✓
modulo	✓	–	✓	✓	✓	–	–
nan?	–	–	–	–	✓	–	–
next	–	✓	–	–	–	–	–
nonzero?	✓	–	–	–	–	–	–
numerator	✓	✓	–	–	✓	✓	✓
odd?	–	✓	✓	✓	–	–	–
ord	–	✓	–	–	–	–	–
phase	✓	–	–	–	✓	–	✓
polar	✓	–	–	–	–	–	✓
pred	–	✓	–	–	–	–	–
quo	✓	–	–	–	✓	✓	✓
rationalize	–	✓	–	–	✓	✓	✓
real	✓	–	–	–	–	–	✓
real?	✓	–	–	–	–	–	✓
rect	✓	–	–	–	–	–	✓
rectangular	✓	–	–	–	–	–	✓
remainder	✓	–	–	✓	–	–	–
round	✓	✓	–	–	✓	✓	–
size	–	–	✓	✓	–	–	–
step	✓	–	–	–	–	–	–
succ	–	✓	✓	–	–	–	–
times	–	✓	–	–	–	–	–
to_c	✓	–	–	–	–	–	✓
to_f	–	–	✓	✓	✓	✓	✓
to_i	–	✓	–	–	✓	✓	✓
to_int	✓	✓	–	–	✓	–	–
to_r	–	✓	–	–	✓	✓	✓
to_s	–	–	✓	✓	✓	✓	✓
truncate	✓	✓	–	–	✓	✓	–
upto	–	✓	–	–	–	–	–
zero?	✓	–	✓	–	✓	–	–
|	–	–	✓	✓	–	–	–
~	–	–	✓	✓	–	–	–

Table 20—Methods in the numeric classes

Mixes In

Comparable: <, <=, ==, >, >=, between?

Instance Methods

+@

$+num \rightarrow num$

Unary Plus—Returns the receiver's value.

-@   *−num → numeric*

Unary Minus—Returns the receiver's value, negated.

<=>   *num <=> other → 0* or nil

Returns zero if *num* equals *other* and returns nil otherwise.

%   *num % numeric → numeric*

Synonym for Numeric#module. Equivalent to num.divmod(numeric)[1].

---

abs   *num.abs → numeric*

Returns the absolute value of *num*.

```
12.abs        # => 12
(-34.56).abs  # => 34.56
-34.56.abs    # => 34.56
```

---

abs2   *num.abs2 → numeric*

Returns the square of (the absolute value of) *num*.

```
12.abs2        # => 144
(-34.56).abs2  # => 1194.3936
-34.56.abs2    # => 1194.3936
```

---

angle   *num.angle → numeric*

For noncomplex numbers, returns π for negative numbers, 0 otherwise. See Complex for more details.

---

arg   *num.arg → numeric*

Synonym for Numeric#angle.

---

ceil   *num.ceil → int*

Returns the smallest integer greater than or equal to *num*. Class Numeric achieves this by converting itself to a Float and then invoking Float#ceil.

```
1.ceil       # => 1
1.2.ceil     # => 2
(-1.2).ceil  # => -1
(-1.0).ceil  # => -1
```

coerce

coerce is both an instance method of Numeric and part of a type conversion protocol. When a number is asked to perform an operation and it is passed a parameter of a class different from its own, it must first coerce both itself and that parameter into a common class so that the operation makes sense. For example, in the expression 1 + 2.5, the Fixnum 1 must be converted to a Float to make it compatible with 2.5. This conversion is performed by coerce. For all numeric objects, coerce is straightforward: if *numeric* is the same type as *num*, returns an array containing *numeric* and *num*. Otherwise, returns an array with both *numeric* and *num* represented as Float objects.

```
1.coerce(2.5) # => [2.5, 1.0]
1.2.coerce(3) # => [3.0, 1.2]
1.coerce(2)   # => [2, 1]
```

If a numeric object is asked to operate on a non-numeric, it tries to invoke coerce on that other object. For example, if you write this:

```
1 + "2"
```

then Ruby will effectively execute the code as follows:

```
n1, n2 = "2".coerce(1)
n2 + n1
```

In the more general case, this won't work, because most non-numerics don't define a coerce method. However, you can use this (if you feel so inclined) to implement part of Perl's automatic conversion of strings to numbers in expressions.

```
class String
  def coerce(other)
    case other
    when Integer
      begin
        return other, Integer(self)
      rescue
        return Float(other), Float(self)
      end
    when Float
      return other, Float(self)
    else super
    end
  end
end


1   + "2"   # => 3
1   - "2.3" # => -1.2999999999999998
1.2 + "2.3" # => 3.5
1.5 - "2"   # => -0.5
```

coerce is discussed in the tutorial on page 352.

conj

num.conj → *num*

Synonym for Numeric#conjugate.

conjugate

num.conjugate → *num*

Returns the complex conjugate of *num*. For noncomplex numbers, returns *num*.

denominator

num.denominator → *integer*

Returns the denominator of the rational representation of *num*.

```
1.denominator    # => 1
1.5.denominator  # => 2
num = 1.0/3
num.to_r         # => (6004799503160661/18014398509481984)
num.denominator  # => 18014398509481984
```

div

num.div(*numeric*) → *int*

Uses / to perform division and then converts the result to an integer. Numeric does not define the / operator; this is left to subclasses.

divmod

num.divmod(*numeric*) → *array*

Returns an array containing the quotient and modulus obtained by dividing *num* by *numeric*. If q,r = x.divmod(y), then q = *floor(float(x) / float(y))* and *x = q * y + r*. The quotient is rounded toward -infinity.

a	b	a.divmod(b)	a/b	a.modulo(b)	(a.remainder(b)
The modulo operator % always has the sign of the divisor, whereas remainder has the sign of the dividend.					
13	4	[3, 1]	3	1	1
13	-4	[-4, -3]	-4	-3	1
-13	4	[-4, 3]	-4	3	-1
-13	-4	[3, -1]	3	-1	-1
11.5	4	[2, 3.5]	2.875	3.5	3.5
11.5	-4	[-3, -0.5]	-2.875	-0.5	3.5
-11.5	4	[-3, 0.5]	-2.875	0.5	-3.5
-11.5	-4	[2, -3.5]	2.875	-3.5	-3.5

Table 21—Division, modulo, and remainder

eql?

num.eql?(*numeric*) → *true* or *false*

Returns true if *num* and *numeric* are the same type and have equal values.

```
1 == 1.0        # => true
1.eql?(1.0)     # => false
(1.0).eql?(1.0) # => true
```

---

fdiv   *num*.fdiv(*numeric*) → *numeric*

Synonym for Numeric#quo.

---

floor   *num*.floor → *int*

Returns the largest integer less than or equal to *num*. Numeric implements this by converting *int* to a Float and invoking Float#floor.

```
1.floor    # => 1
(-1).floor # => -1
```

---

i   *num*.i → Complex(0, *num*)

Returns the complex number whose imaginary part is *num*.

---

imag   *num*.imag → 0

Synonym for Numeric#imaginary.

---

imaginary   *num*.image → 0

Returns the imaginary part of *num*. Always 0 unless *num* is a complex number.

```
1.imaginary # => 0
```

---

integer?   *num*.integer? → *true* or *false*

Returns true if *num* is an Integer (including Fixnum and Bignum).

---

magnitude   *num*.magnitude → *int* or *float*

Returns the magnitude of *num* (the distance of *num* from the origin of the number line). See also Complex#magnitude.

```
3.magnitude    # => 3
-3.0.magnitude # => 3.0
```

---

modulo   *num*.modulo(*numeric*) → *numeric*

Equivalent to num.divmod(numeric)[1].

---

nonzero?   *num*.nonzero? → *num* or nil

Returns *num* if *num* is not zero and returns nil otherwise. This behavior is useful when chaining comparisons.

```
a = %w( z Bb bB bb BB a aA Aa AA A )
b = a.sort {|a,b| (a.downcase <=> b.downcase).nonzero? || a <=> b }
b          # => ["A", "a", "AA", "Aa", "aA", "BB", "Bb", "bB", "bb", "z"]
```

---

numerator   *num*.numerator → *integer*

Returns the numerator of the rational representation of *num*.

```
1.numerator    # => 1
1.5.numerator  # => 3
num = 1.0/3
num.to_r       # => (6004799503160661/18014398509481984)
num.numerator  # => 6004799503160661
```

---

phase   *num*.phase → [*magnitude, angle*]

Returns the phase angle of *num*. See Complex for more information. For noncomplex numbers, returns 0 if *num* is nonnegative, π otherwise.

```
123.phase # => 0
```

---

polar   *num*.polar → [*magnitude, angle*]

Returns *num* in polar form. See Complex for more information. For noncomplex numbers, returns [num,0].

```
123.polar # => [123, 0]
```

---

quo   *num*.quo(*numeric*) → *numeric*

Equivalent to Numeric#/ but overridden in subclasses. The intent of quo is to return the most accurate result of division (in context). Thus, 1.quo(2) will equal the rational number $\frac{1}{2}$, while 1/2 equals 0.

---

real   *num*.real → *num*

Returns the real part of *num*. Always *num* unless *num* is a complex number.

```
1.real    # => 1
1.5.real  # => 1.5
```

---

real?   *num*.real? → true

All the built-in numeric classes except Complex represent scalar types and hence respond true to real?.

```
1.real?           # => true
1.0.real?         # => true
Complex(1,0).real? # => false
```

---

rect   *num*.rect → [*num*, 0]

Returns an array containing the real and imaginary components of *num*. See also Complex#rect.

```
1.5.rect  # => [1.5, 0]
```

---

rectangular

num.rectangular → [*num*, 0]

Synonym for Numeric#rect.

---

remainder

num.remainder(*numeric*) → *another_numeric*

Returns num - (num/numeric).truncate. See Table 21, *Division, modulo, and remainder,* on page 595.

---

round

num.round → *int*

Rounds *num* to the nearest integer.

---

step

num.step(*end_num, step*) { | i | ... } → *num*
num.step(*end_num, step*) → *enumerator*

Invokes *block* with the sequence of numbers starting at *num*, incremented by *step* on each call. The loop finishes when the value to be passed to the block is greater than *end_num* (if *step* is positive) or less than *end_num* (if *step* is negative). If all the arguments are integers, the loop operates using an integer counter. If any of the arguments are floating-point numbers, all are converted to floats, and the loop is executed floor(n + n*Float::EPSILON)+1 times, where n = (end_num - num)/step. Otherwise, the loop starts at *num*, uses either the < or > operator to compare the counter against *end_num*, and increments itself using the + operator. Returns an enumerator if no block is given.

```
1.step(10, 2) {|i| print i, " " }
```

produces:

```
1 3 5 7 9
```

```
Math::E.step(Math::PI, 0.2) {|f| print f, " " }
```

produces:

```
2.718281828459045 2.9182818284590453 3.118281828459045
```

---

to_c

num.to_c → *complex*

Returns *num* as a complex number.

```
123.to_c  # => 123+0i
```

---

to_int

num.to_int → *int*

Invokes the child class's to_i method to convert *num* to an integer.

---

truncate

num.truncate → *int*

Returns *num* truncated to an integer.

---

zero?

num.zero? → *true* or *false*

Returns true if *num* has a zero value.

Class **Object** < BasicObject

Subclasses:

Object is the parent class of (almost) all classes in Ruby. Its methods are therefore available to all objects unless explicitly overridden.

Object mixes in the Kernel module, making the built-in kernel functions globally accessible. Although the instance methods of Object are defined by the Kernel module, we have chosen to document them here for clarity.

In the descriptions that follow, the parameter *symbol* refers to a name, which is either a quoted string or a symbol (such as :name).

Instance Methods

===   *obj* === *other_obj* → *true* or *false*

Case Equality—A synonym for Object#== but typically overridden by descendents to provide meaningful semantics in case statements.

<=>   *obj* <=> *other_obj* → 0 or nil

Comparison—For objects, returns 0 if *other_obj* is the same object as, or is equal to, *obj*. Otherwise, returns nil (which should be interpreted to mean that there's no meaning to the comparison). Overridden by subclasses that have comparison semantics.

=~   *obj* =~ *other_obj* → nil

Pattern Match—Overridden by descendents (notably Regexp and String) to provide meaningful pattern-match semantics.

!~   *obj* !~ *other_obj* → !(*obj* =~ *other_obj*)

Opposite of =~.

class   *obj*.class → *klass*

Returns the class object of *obj*. This method must always be called with an explicit receiver, because class is also a reserved word in Ruby.

```
1.class    # => Fixnum
self.class # => Object
```

clone   *obj*.clone → *other_obj*

Produces a shallow copy of *obj*—the instance variables of *obj* are copied, but not the objects they reference. Copies the frozen and tainted state of *obj*, along with any associated singleton class. See also the discussion under Object#dup.

```ruby
class Klass
  attr_accessor :str
end
s1 = Klass.new     # => #<Klass:0x007fc1bb10ee90>
s1.str = "Hello"   # => "Hello"
s2 = s1.clone      # => #<Klass:0x007fc1bb10e940 @str="Hello">
s2.str[1,4] = "i"  # => "i"
s1.inspect         # => "#<Klass:0x007fc1bb10ee90 @str=\"Hi\">"
s2.inspect         # => "#<Klass:0x007fc1bb10e940 @str=\"Hi\">"
```

define_singleton_method

obj.define_singleton_method(*symbol, method*) → *method*
obj.define_singleton_method(*symbol*) { … } → *proc*

Defines a singleton method in the receiver. The *method* parameter can be a Proc, Method, or UnboundMethod object. If a block is specified, it is used as the method body. This block is evaluated using instance_eval. See also Module#define_method.

```ruby
a = "cat"
a.define_singleton_method(:speak) do
  "#{self} says miaow"
end
a.speak   # => "cat says miaow"
```

define_singleton_method is also useful with Module#class_eval:

```ruby
class Test
  class_eval do
    define_method(:one)              { puts "instance method" }
    define_singleton_method(:two) { puts "class method" }
  end
end
t = Test.new
t.one
Test.two
```

produces:

```
instance method
class method
```

display

obj.display(*port=$>*) → nil

Prints *obj* on the given port (default $>). Equivalent to the following:

```ruby
def display(port=$>)
  port.write self
end
```

For example:

```ruby
1.display
"cat".display
[ 4, 5, 6 ].display
```

produces:

```
1cat[4, 5, 6]
```

dup

obj.dup → other_obj

Produces a shallow copy of *obj*—the instance variables of *obj* are copied, but not the objects they reference. dup copies the tainted state of *obj*. See also the discussion under Object#clone. In general, dup duplicates just the state of an object, while clone also copies the state, any associated singleton class, and any internal flags (such as whether the object is frozen). The taint status is copied by both dup and clone.

enum_for

obj.enum_for(using=:each, ‹ args ›⁺ → enumerator
obj.enum_for(using=:each, ‹ args ›⁺ { | *args | ... } → enumerator

Synonym for Object#to_enum.

eql?

obj.eql?(other_obj) → true or false

Returns true if *obj* and *other_obj* have the same value. Used by Hash to test members for equality. For objects of class Object, eql? is synonymous with ==. Subclasses normally continue this tradition, but there are exceptions. Numeric types, for example, perform type conversion across ==, but not across eql?. This means the following:

```
1 == 1.0   # => true
1.eql? 1.0 # => false
```

extend

obj.extend(‹ mod ›⁺) → obj

Mix the instance methods from each of the given modules in to *obj*. See Chapter 24, *Metaprogramming*, on page 357 for information on how this works. See also Module#extend_object.

```
module Mod
  def hello
    "Hello from Mod.\n"
  end
end

class Klass
  def hello
    "Hello from Klass.\n"
  end
end

k = Klass.new
k.hello        # => "Hello from Klass.\n"
k.extend(Mod)  # => #<Klass:0x007f9fe190f208>
k.hello        # => "Hello from Mod.\n"
```

Writing obj.extend(Mod) is basically the same as the following:

```
class <<obj
  include Mod
end
```

---

freeze
obj.freeze → *obj*

Prevents further modifications to *obj*. A RuntimeError will be raised if modification is attempted. You cannot unfreeze a frozen object. See also Object#frozen?.

```
a = [ "a", "b", "c" ]
a.freeze
a << "z"
```

produces:

```
prog.rb:3:in `<main>': can't modify frozen Array (RuntimeError)
```

---

frozen?
obj.frozen? → *true* or *false*

Returns the freeze status of *obj*.

```
a = [ "a", "b", "c" ]
a.freeze  # => ["a", "b", "c"]
a.frozen? # => true
```

---

hash
obj.hash → *fixnum*

Generates a Fixnum hash value for *obj*. This function must have the property that a.eql?(b) implies a.hash == b.hash. The hash value is used by class Hash. Any hash value that exceeds the capacity of a Fixnum will be truncated before being used. For instances of class Object, the hash is also the object_id. This will not always be the case for subclasses.

---

initialize_clone
obj.initialize_clone(*other*) → *other_obj* or *obj*

Invoked as a callback by Object#clone to initialize the cloned object. The default implementation is to call initialize_copy.

---

initialize_copy
obj.initialize_copy(*other*) → *other_obj* or *obj*

Part of the protocol used by Object#dup and #clone, initialize_copy is the fallback method invoked by Object#initialize_clone and #initialize_dup. If you need specialized copy semantics depending on whether clone or dup is called, override those more specific callbacks. If you want common behavior, override initialize_copy.

These methods should copy across any state information that dup and clone cannot copy themselves. For example, in the following code, a and b reference two instances of the container class, but each instance shares a single string object:

```
class Container
  attr_accessor :content
end
a = Container.new
a.content = "cat"
b = a.dup
a.content[1..-1] = "anary"
a.content # => "canary"
b.content # => "canary"
```

The next example uses initialize_copy to create a new string in the duplicated object.

```ruby
class Container
  attr_accessor :content
  def initialize_copy(other)
    @content = String.new(other.content)
  end
end
a = Container.new
a.content = "cat"
b = a.dup
a.content[1..-1] = "anary"
a.content # => "canary"
b.content # => "cat"
```

initialize_dup

obj.initialize_dup(*other*) → *other_obj* or *obj*

Invoked as a callback by Object#dup to initialize the duplicated object. The default implementation is to call initialize_copy.

inspect

obj.inspect → *string*

Returns a string containing a human-readable representation of *obj*. For objects of classes written in Ruby, displays the values of instance variables along with the class name if any instance variables exist. Override this in subclasses to change their behavior when inspected.

New in 2.0

```ruby
[ 1, 2, 3..4, 'five' ].inspect   # => [1, 2, 3..4, "five"]
Time.new.inspect                 # => 2013-05-27 12:32:34 -0500
class Demo
  def initialize; @a, @b = 1, 2; end
end
Demo.new.inspect                 # => #<Demo:0x007fb6d190f1e8 @a=1, @b=2>
```

instance_of?

obj.instance_of?(*klass*) → *true* or *false*

Returns true if *obj* is an instance of the given class. See also Object#kind_of?.

instance_variable_defined?

obj.instance_variable_defined?(*name*) → *true* or *false*

Returns true if the named variable is defined. Note that a common idiom, testing to see whether @fred is nil, is incorrect in two ways: first the variable could be defined but set to nil, and second it will generate a warning if debug mode is enabled.

```ruby
class Fred
  def initialize(p1, p2)
    @a, @b = p1, p2
  end
end
fred = Fred.new('cat', 99)
fred.instance_variable_defined?(:@a)  # => true
fred.instance_variable_defined?("@b") # => true
fred.instance_variable_defined?(:@c)  # => false
```

instance_variable_get

obj.instance_variable_get(*symbol*) → *other_obj*

Returns the value of the given instance variable (or throws a NameError exception). The @ part of the variable name should be included for regular instance variables.

```
class Fred
  def initialize(p1, p2)
    @a, @b = p1, p2
  end
end
fred = Fred.new('cat', 99)
fred.instance_variable_get(:@a)  # => "cat"
fred.instance_variable_get("@b") # => 99
```

instance_variable_set

obj.instance_variable_set(*symbol, other_obj*) → *other_obj*

Sets the instance variable names by *symbol* to *other_obj*, thereby frustrating the efforts of the class's author to attempt to provide proper encapsulation.

```
class Fred
  def initialize(p1, p2)
    @a, @b = p1, p2
  end
end
fred = Fred.new('cat', 99)
fred.instance_variable_set(:@a, 'dog')
fred.inspect # => #<Fred:0x007fcd9b047d40 @a="dog", @b=99>
```

instance_variables

obj.instance_variables → *array*

Returns an array of instance variable names for the receiver. Note that simply defining an accessor does not create the corresponding instance variable.

```
class Fred
  attr_accessor :a1
  def initialize
    @iv = 3
  end
end
Fred.new.instance_variables # => [:@iv]
```

is_a?

obj.is_a?(*klass*) → *true* or *false*

Synonym for Object#kind_of?.

kind_of?

obj.kind_of?(*klass*) → *true* or *false*

Returns true if *klass* is the class of *obj* or if *klass* is one of the superclasses of *obj* or modules included in *obj*.

```
module M
end
class A
  include M
end
class B < A; end
class C < B; end

b = B.new
b.instance_of? A # => false
b.instance_of? B # => true
b.instance_of? C # => false
b.instance_of? M # => false
b.kind_of? A      # => true
b.kind_of? B      # => true
b.kind_of? C      # => false
b.kind_of? M      # => true
```

method

obj.method(*symbol*) → *meth*

Looks up the named method in *obj*, returning a Method object (or raising NameError). The Method object is a closure, so instance variables and the value of self remain available.

```
class Demo
  def initialize(n)
    @iv = n
  end
  def hello()
    "Hello, @iv = #{@iv}"
  end
end

k = Demo.new(99)
m = k.method(:hello)
m.call    # => "Hello, @iv = 99"

l = Demo.new('Fred')
m = l.method("hello")
m.call    # => "Hello, @iv = Fred"
```

methods

obj.methods(*regular*=true) → *array*

If *regular* is true, returns a list of the names of methods publicly accessible in *obj* and *obj*'s ancestors. Otherwise, returns a list of *obj*'s singleton methods.

```
class Klass
  def my_method; end
end
k = Klass.new
def k.single; end
k.methods[0..6]  # => [:single, :my_method, :nil?, :===, :=~, :!~, :eql?]
k.methods.length # => 56
k.methods(false) # => [:single]
```

---

nil?   *obj*.nil? → *true* or *false*

All objects except nil return false.

---

object_id   *obj*.object_id → *fixnum*

Returns an integer identifier for *obj*. The same number will be returned on all calls to object_id for a given object, and no two active objects will share an ID. Object#object_id is a different concept from the :name notation, which returns the symbol ID of name. Replaces the deprecated Object#id.

---

private_methods   *obj*.private_methods → *array*

Returns a list of private methods accessible within *obj*. This will include the private methods in *obj*'s ancestors, along with any mixed-in module functions.

---

protected_methods   *obj*.protected_methods → *array*

Returns the list of protected methods accessible to *obj*.

---

public_method   *obj*.public_method(*symbol*) → *meth*

Looks up the named public method in *obj*, returning a Method object (or raising NameError if the method is not found or if it is found but not public).

```ruby
class Demo
  def initialize(n)
    @iv = n
  end
  def hello()
    puts "Hello, @iv = #{@iv}"
  end
end

k = Demo.new(99)
m = k.public_method(:hello)
m.call

l = Demo.new('Fred')
m = l.public_method(:initialize)
m.call
```

produces:

```
        from prog.rb:15:in `<main>'
Hello, @iv = 99
prog.rb:15:in `public_method': method `initialize' for class `Demo' is private
(NameError)
```

---

public_methods   *obj*.public_methods → *array*

Synonym for Object#methods.

---

public_send
obj.public_send(name, ‹args›⁺) → obj

Invokes *obj*'s public method *name*, passing in any arguments. Returns the value returned by the method. See also send, which will also call private and protected methods.

---

respond_to?
obj.respond_to?(symbol, include_priv=false) → true or false

Returns true if *obj* responds to the given method. Private and protected methods are included in the search only if the optional second parameter evaluates to true.

New in 2.0

---

respond_to_missing?
obj.respond_to_missing?(symbol, include_priv=false) → true or false

A callback invoked by the interpreter if respond_to? is called and does not find a method. This allows classes to indicate that they implement methods via method_missing.

```ruby
class Example
  def regular
  end
  def method_missing(name, *args, &block)
    if name == :dynamic
      # do something
    else
      super
    end
  end
  def respond_to_missing?(name, include_priv)
    name == :dynamic
  end
end

ex = Example.new
ex.respond_to?(:regular) # => true
ex.respond_to?(:dynamic) # => true
ex.respond_to?(:other)   # => false
```

---

send
obj.send(symbol ‹, args›*‹, &block›) → other_obj

Invokes the method identified by *symbol*, passing it any arguments and block. You can use BasicObject#__send__ if the name send clashes with an existing method in *obj*.

```ruby
class Klass
  def hello(*args)
    "Hello " + args.join(' ')
  end
end
k = Klass.new
k.send :hello, "gentle", "readers" # => "Hello gentle readers"
```

---

singleton_class
obj.singleton_class → klass

Returns the singleton class of *obj*, creating one if necessary. TrueClass, FalseClass, and NilClass are their own singleton classes. Fixnum has no singleton class.

```
obj = "cat"
old_way = class << obj; self; end
new_way = obj.singleton_class

old_way          # => #<Class:#<String:0x007fa2b1864060>>
new_way          # => #<Class:#<String:0x007fa2b1864060>>
new_way == old_way # => true
```

singleton_methods   *obj*.singleton_methods(*all*=true) → *array*

Returns an array of the names of singleton methods for *obj*. If the optional *all* parameter is true, the list will include methods in modules included in *obj*. (The parameter defaults to false in versions of Ruby prior to January 2004.)

```
module Other
  def three(); end
end

class Single
  def Single.four(); end
end

a = Single.new

def a.one(); end

class << a
  include Other
  def two(); end
end

Single.singleton_methods    # => [:four]
a.singleton_methods(false)  # => [:one, :two]
a.singleton_methods(true)   # => [:one, :two, :three]
a.singleton_methods         # => [:one, :two, :three]
```

taint   *obj*.taint → *obj*

Marks *obj* as tainted. If the $SAFE level is greater than zero, some objects will be tainted on creation. See Chapter 26, *Locking Ruby in the Safe*, on page 409.

tainted?   *obj*.tainted? → *true* or *false*

Returns true if the object is tainted.

```
a = "cat"
a.tainted? # => false
a.taint    # => "cat"
a.tainted? # => true
a.untaint  # => "cat"
a.tainted? # => false
```

---

tap obj.tap { | val | ... } → obj

Invokes the block, passing obj as a parameter. Returns obj. Allows you to write code that takes part in a method chain but that does not affect the overall value of the chain.

```
puts "dog"
    .reverse
        .tap {|o| puts "Reversed: #{o}"}
    .capitalize
```

produces:

```
Reversed: god
God
```

---

to_enum obj.to_enum(*using*=:each, ‹ args ›⁺) → *enumerator*
obj.to_enum(*using*=:each, ‹ args ›⁺ { | *args | ... } → *enumerator*

Returns an Enumerator object that will traverse the content of obj. By default, this enumerator will invoke the each method of self, but this can be overridden by passing a different method name as the first parameter. Any additional arguments passed to to_enum will be passed to the enumerator method.

```
by_bytes = "∂og".to_enum(:each_byte)
by_bytes.next # => 226
by_bytes.next # => 136
by_bytes.next # => 130
by_bytes.next # => 111

by_chars = "∂og".to_enum(:each_char)
by_chars.next # => "∂"
by_chars.next # => "o"
by_chars.next # => "g"
```

If the block is present, it is called to return the size of the collection without actually iterating over each element. This facilitates calculating the size of lazily evaluated enumerations. **New in 2.0**

---

to_s obj.to_s → *string*

Returns a string representing obj. The default to_s prints the object's class and an encoding of the object ID. As a special case, the top-level object that is the initial execution context of Ruby programs returns "main."

---

trust obj.trust → obj

Marks obj as trusted. (See the section on trust on page 411.)

---

untaint obj.untaint → obj

Removes the taint from obj.

---

untrust   *obj*.untrust → *obj*

Marks *obj* as untrusted. (See the section on trust on page 411.)

---

untrusted?   *obj*.untrusted? → *true* or *false*

Returns true if *obj* is untrusted, false otherwise.

Private Instance Methods

__callee__   __callee__ → *symbol* or nil

New in 2.0
Returns the name of the current method or nil outside the context of a method. If a method is called by an aliased name, that alias is returned, and not the original name.

```ruby
def fred
  puts "I'm in #{__callee__.inspect}"
end
fred
puts "Then in #{__callee__.inspect}"
```

produces:

```
I'm in :fred
Then in nil
```

__dir__   __dir__ → *string*

New in 2.0   The absolute path to the directory of the file containing the call to this method.

__method__   __method__ → *symbol* or nil

Synonym for __callee__.

' (backquote)   'cmd' → *string*

Returns the standard output of running *cmd* in a subshell. The built-in syntax %x{...} described in the tutorial on page 128 uses this method. Sets $? to the process status.

```ruby
`date`                  # => "Mon May 27 12:32:35 CDT 2013\n"
`ls testdir`.split[1]   # => "main.rb"
`echo oops && exit 99`  # => "oops\n"
$?.exitstatus           # => 99
```

Array   Array(*arg*) → *array*

Returns *arg* as an Array. First tries to call *arg*.to_ary and then *arg*.to_a. If both fail, creates a single element array containing *arg* (or an empty array if *arg* is nil).

```ruby
Array(1..5) # => [1, 2, 3, 4, 5]
```

Complex

Complex(*real, imag*=0) → *complex*

Returns the complex number with the given real and imaginary parts.

```
Complex(1)             # => 1+0i
Complex("1")           # => 1+0i
Complex("1", "3/2")    # => 1+3/2i
Complex("3+2i")        # => 3+2i
```

Float

Float(*arg*) → *float*

Returns *arg* converted to a float. Numeric types are converted directly; strings are converted by interpreting their content as either a decimal or (with a loading 0x) a hexadecimal floating-point constant—see the %a field specifier to sprintf; the rest are converted using *arg*.to_f. Converting nil generates a TypeError.

```
Float(1)                     # => 1.0
Float("123.456")             # => 123.456
Float("0x1.921fb54442d18p+1") # => 3.141592653589793
```

Hash

Hash(*arg*) → *hash*

Convert *arg* to a hash by calling its to_hash method.

New in 2.0

```
Hash(nil)         # => {}
Hash(x: 23, y: 67) # => {:x=>23, :y=>67}
h1 = { a:1, c:3 }
h2 = { b:2, d:4 }
Hash(**h1, **h2)  # => {:a=>1, :c=>3, :b=>2, :d=>4}
```

Integer

Integer(*arg*) → *int*

Converts *arg* to a Fixnum or Bignum. Numeric types are converted directly (floating-point numbers are truncated). If *arg* is a String, leading radix indicators (0, 0b, and 0x) are honored. Others are converted using to_int and to_i. This behavior is different from that of String#to_i. Converting nil generates a TypeError.

```
Integer(123.999) # => 123
Integer("0x1a")  # => 26
```

Rational

Rational(*numerator, denominator*=1) → *rational*

Returns the rational number with the given representation.

```
Rational(1)            # => 1/1
Rational("1")          # => 1/1
Rational("1", "2")     # => 1/2
Rational(1, 0.5)       # => 2/1
Rational("3/2")        # => 3/2
Rational("3/2", "4/5") # => 15/8
```

String

String(*arg*) → *string*

Converts *arg* to a String by calling its to_s method.

```
String(self)       # => "main"
String(self.class) # => "Object"
String(123456)     # => "123456"
```

---

abort

abort
abort(*msg*)

Terminates execution immediately with an exit code of 1. The optional String parameter is written to standard error before the program terminates.

---

at_exit

at_exit { ... } → *proc*

Converts *block* to a Proc object and registers it for execution when the program exits. If multiple handlers are registered, they are executed in reverse order of registration.

```
def do_at_exit(str1)
  at_exit { print str1 }
end
at_exit { puts "cruel world" }
do_at_exit("goodbye ")
exit
```

produces:

```
goodbye cruel world
```

---

autoload

autoload(*name, file_name*) → nil

Registers *file_name* to be loaded (using Object#require) the first time that the module *name* (which may be a String or a symbol) is accessed.

```
autoload(:MyModule, "/usr/local/lib/modules/my_module.rb")
```

Module.autoload lets you define namespace-specific autoload hooks:

```
module X
  autoload :XXX, "xxx.rb"
end
```

Note that xxx.rb should define a class in the correct namespace. That is, in this example, xxx.rb should contain the following:

```
class X::XXX
  # ...
end
```

---

autoload?

autoload?(*name*) → *file_name* or nil

Returns the name of the file that will be autoloaded when the string or symbol *name* is referenced in the top-level context or returns nil if there is no associated autoload.

```
autoload(:Fred, "module_fred") # => nil
autoload?(:Fred)               # => "module_fred"
autoload?(:Wilma)              # => nil
```

binding

binding → a_binding

Returns a Binding object, describing the variable and method bindings at the point of call. This object can be used when calling eval to execute the evaluated command in this environment. Also see the description of class Binding on page 447.

```
def get_binding(param)
  return binding
end
b = get_binding("hello")
eval("param", b) # => "hello"
```

block_given?

block_given? → true or false

Returns true if yield executes a block in the current context.

```
def try
  if block_given?
    yield
  else
    "no block"
  end
end

try             # => "no block"
try { "hello" } # => "hello"
block = lambda { "proc object" }
try(&block)     # => "proc object"
```

caller

caller(‹start‹, max_size››) → array
caller(‹range›) → array

Returns the current execution stack—an array containing strings in the form *file:line* or *file:line: in 'method'*. The optional *start* parameter determines the number of initial stack entries to omit from the result. The optional *max_size* parameter sets the maximum size of the returned array. Alternatively, passing a range parameter retrieves the given stack entries.

New in 2.0

```
def a(skip)
  caller(skip)
end
def b(skip)
  a(skip)
end
def c(skip)
  b(skip)
end
c(0)      # => ["prog.rb:2:in `a'", "/tmp/prog.rb:5:in `b'", "/tmp/prog.rb:8:in
          # .. `c'", "/tmp/prog.rb:10:in `<main>'"]
c(1)      # => ["prog.rb:5:in `b'", "/tmp/prog.rb:8:in `c'", "/tmp/prog.rb:11:in
```

```
            # ..  `<main>'"]
c(2)        # => ["prog.rb:8:in `c'", "/tmp/prog.rb:12:in `<main>'"]
c(3)        # => ["prog.rb:13:in `<main>'"]
```

---

caller_locations   caller_locations → array of caller sites

New in 2.0   Returns an array containing the call stack.

```
def outer
  inner
end

def inner
  p caller_locations
end

puts outer
```

produces:

```
["prog.rb:2:in `outer'", "/tmp/prog.rb:9:in `<main>'"]
prog.rb:2:in `outer'
prog.rb:9:in `<main>'
```

---

catch   catch(*object*=Object.new) { … } → obj

catch executes its block. If a throw is encountered, Ruby searches up its stack for a catch block with a parameter identical to the throw's parameter. If found, that block is terminated, and catch returns the value given as the second parameter to throw. If throw is not called, the block terminates normally, and the value of catch is the value of the last expression evaluated. catch expressions may be nested, and the throw call need not be in lexical scope. Prior to Ruby 1.9, the parameters to catch and throw had to be symbols—they can now be any object. When using literals, it probably makes sense to use only immediate objects.

```
def routine(n)
  print n, ' '
  throw :done if n <= 0
  routine(n-1)
end
catch(:done) { routine(4) }
```

produces:

```
4 3 2 1 0
```

---

chomp   chomp(‹rs›) → $_ or ‹string›

Equivalent to $_ = $_.chomp(rs), except no assignment is made if chomp doesn't change $_. See String#chomp on page 672. Available only if the -n or -p command-line options are present.

---

chop   chop → *string*

(Almost) equivalent to $_.dup.chop!, except that if chop performs no action, $_ is unchanged and nil is not returned. See String#chop! on page 672. Available only if the -n or -p command-line option is present.

define_method

define_method(*symbol, method*) → *method*
define_method(*symbol*) { ... } → *proc*

Defines a global method. The behavior is analogous to Module#define_method.

New in 2.0

```ruby
define_method(:adder, -> (a, b) { a+b })

adder(1, 2)          # => 3
adder("cat", "dog") # => "catdog"
```

Note that it is possible to define methods with names that are not valid if you were to use the def keyword. These methods cannot be invoked directly.

```ruby
class Silly
  define_method("Oh !@!#^!") { "As Snoopy says" }
end
Silly.new.send("Oh !@!#^!") # => "As Snoopy says"
```

eval

eval(*string* ‹, *binding* ‹, *file* ‹, *line*›››) → *obj*

Evaluates the Ruby expression(s) in *string*. If *binding* is given, the evaluation is performed in its context. The binding must be a Binding object. If the optional *file* and *line* parameters are present, they will be used when reporting syntax errors.

```ruby
def get_binding(str)
  return binding
end
str = "hello"
eval "str + ' Fred'"                    # => "hello Fred"
eval "str + ' Fred'", get_binding("bye") # => "bye Fred"
```

Local variables assigned within an eval are available after the eval only if they were defined at the outer scope before the eval executed. In this way, eval has the same scoping rules as blocks.

```ruby
a = 1
eval "a = 98; b = 99"
puts a
puts b
```

produces:

```
98
prog.rb:4:in `<main>': undefined local variable or method `b' for main:Object
(NameError)
```

exec

exec(‹ env, › *command* ‹, *args*›*, ‹options›)

Replaces the current process by running the given external command. If exec is given a single argument, that argument is taken as a line that is subject to shell expansion before being executed. If *command* contains a newline or any of the characters ?*?{}[]<>()~&|$;'`", or under Windows if *command* looks like a shell-internal command (for example dir), *command* is run under a shell. On Unix system, Ruby does this by prepending sh -c. Under Windows, it uses the name of a shell in either RUBYSHELL or COMSPEC.

If multiple arguments are given, the second and subsequent arguments are passed as parameters to *command* with no shell expansion. If the first argument is a two-element array, the first element is the command to be executed, and the second argument is used as the argv[0] value, which may show up in process listings. In MSDOS environments, the command is executed in a subshell; otherwise, one of the exec(2) system calls is used, so the running command may inherit some of the environment of the original program (including open file descriptors). Raises SystemCallError if the *command* couldn't execute (typically Errno::ENOENT).

```
exec "echo *"        # echoes list of files in current directory
# never get here

exec "echo", "*"     # echoes an asterisk
# never get here
```

env, if present, is a hash that adds to the environment variables in the subshell. An entry with a nil value clears the corresponding environment variable. The keys must be strings. *options*, if present, is a hash that controls the setup of the subshell. The possible keys and their meanings are listed under #spawn. See also Object#spawn and Object#system.

---

exit   exit(true | false | *status*=1)

Initiates the termination of the Ruby script. If called in the scope of an exception handler, raises a SystemExit exception. This exception may be caught. Otherwise, exits the process using exit(2). The optional parameter is used to return a status code to the invoking environment. With an argument of true, exits with a status of zero. With an argument that is false (or no argument), exits with a status of 1; otherwise, exits with the given status. The default exit value is 1.

```
fork { exit 99 }
Process.wait
puts "Child exits with status: #{$?.exitstatus}"
 begin
   exit
   puts "never get here"
 rescue SystemExit
   puts "rescued a SystemExit exception"
 end
 puts "after begin block"
```

produces:

```
Child exits with status: 99
rescued a SystemExit exception
after begin block
```

Just prior to termination, Ruby executes any at_exit functions and runs any object finalizers (see ObjectSpace on page 631).

```
at_exit { puts "at_exit function" }
ObjectSpace.define_finalizer("xxx",  lambda { |obj| puts "in finalizer" })
exit
```

produces:

```
at_exit function
in finalizer
```

---

exit!   exit!(true | false | *status*=1)

Similar to Object#exit, but exception handling, at_exit functions, and finalizers are bypassed.

---

fail   fail
                                                                          fail(*message*)
                                                      fail(*exception* ‹, *message* ‹, *array*››)}

Synonym for Object#raise.

---

fork   fork ‹{ … }› → *int* or nil

Creates a subprocess. If a block is specified, that block is run in the subprocess, and the subprocess terminates with a status of zero. Otherwise, the fork call returns twice, once in the parent, returning the process ID of the child, and once in the child, returning nil. The child process can exit using Object#exit! to avoid running any at_exit functions. The parent process should use Process.wait to collect the termination statuses of its children or it should call Process.detach to register disinterest in their status; otherwise, the operating system may accumulate zombie processes.

```
fork do
  3.times {|i| puts "Child: #{i}" }
end
3.times {|i| puts "Parent: #{i}" }
Process.wait
```

produces:

```
Parent: 0
Child: 0
Parent: 1
Child: 1
Parent: 2
Child: 2
```

---

format   format(*format_string* ‹, *arg*›*) → *string*

Synonym for Object#sprintf.

---

gem   gem(*gem_name* ‹, *version*›) → *true* or *false*

Adds the given gem to the applications include path so that subsequent requires will search. Defaults to the latest version of the gem if no version information is given. See *Gems and Versions*, on page 220 for more information and examples.

---

gem_original_require   gem_original_require ‹*filename*›⁺

The version of Object#require that does not know about RubyGems.

---

gets

gets(*separator=$/*) → *string* or nil

Returns (and assigns to $_) the next line from the list of files in ARGV (or $*) or from standard•
input if no files are present on the command line. Returns nil at end of file. The optional
argument specifies the record separator. The separator is included with the contents of each
record. A separator of nil reads the entire contents, and a zero-length separator reads the
input one paragraph at a time, where paragraphs are divided by two consecutive newlines.
If multiple filenames are present in ARGV, gets(nil) reads the contents one file at a time. Programming using $_ as an implicit parameter is losing favor in the Ruby community.

```
ARGV << "testfile"
print while gets
```

produces:

```
This is line one
This is line two
This is line three
And so on...
```

---

global_variables

global_variables → *array*

Returns an array of the names of global variables.

```
global_variables.grep /std/ # => [:$stdin, :$stdout, :$stderr]
```

---

gsub

gsub(*pattern, replacement*) → *string*
gsub(*pattern*) { ... } → *string*

Equivalent to $_.gsub(...), except that $_ will be updated if substitution occurs. Available only
when the -n or -p command-line option is present.

---

initialize

initialize(‹ *arg* ›⁺)

Called as the third and final step in object construction, initialize is responsible for setting up
the initial state of the new object. You use the initialize method the same way you'd use
constructors in other languages. If you subclass classes other than Object, you will probably
want to call super to invoke the parent's initializer.

```
class A
  def initialize(p1)
    puts "Initializing A: p1 = #{p1}"
    @var1 = p1
  end
end
class B < A
  attr_reader :var1, :var2
  def initialize(p1, p2)
    super(p1)
    puts "Initializing B: p2 = #{p2}"
    @var2 = p2
  end
end
```

```
b = B.new("cat", "dog")
puts b.inspect
```

produces:

```
Initializing A: p1 = cat
Initializing B: p2 = dog
#<B:0x007f817990eaa0 @var1="cat", @var2="dog">
```

iterator?

iterator? → *true* or *false*

Deprecated synonym for Object#block_given?.

lambda

lambda { ... } → *proc*

Creates a new procedure object from the given block. See the discussion in the tutorial on page 336 for an explanation of the difference between procedure objects created using lambda and those created using Proc.new. Note that lambda is now preferred over proc.

```
prc = lambda { "hello" }
prc.call  # => "hello"
```

load

load(*file_name*, *wrap*=false) → true

Loads and executes the Ruby program in the file *file_name*. If the filename does not resolve to an absolute path, the file is searched for in the library directories listed in $:. If the optional *wrap* parameter is true, the loaded script will be executed under an anonymous module, protecting the calling program's global namespace. In no circumstance will any local variables in the loaded file be propagated to the loading environment.

local_variables

local_variables → *array*

Returns the names of the current local variables.

```
fred = 1
for i in 1..10
  # ...
end
local_variables # => [:fred, :i]
```

Note that local variables are associated with bindings.

```
def fred
  a = 1
  b = 2
  binding
end
freds_binding = fred
eval("local_variables", freds_binding) # => [:a, :b]
```

loop

loop ‹ { ... } ›

Repeatedly executes the block.

```
loop do
  print "Type something: "
  line = gets
  break if line.nil?  || line =~ /^[qQ]/
  # ...
end
```

loop silently rescues the StopIteration exception, which works well with external iterators.

```
enum1 = [1, 2, 3].to_enum
enum2 = [10, 20].to_enum
loop do
  puts enum1.next + enum2.next
  end
```

produces:

```
11
22
```

---

open   open(*name* ‹ , *mode* ‹ , *permission* › ›) → *io* or nil
                                 open(*name* ‹ , *mode* ‹ , *permission* › ›) { | io | ... } → *obj*

Creates an IO object connected to the given stream, file, or subprocess.

If *name* does not start with a pipe character (|), treats it as the name of a file to open using the specified mode defaulting to "r" (see Table 16, *Mode values*, on page 494). If a file is being created, its initial permissions may be set using the third parameter, which is an integer. If this third parameter is present, the file will be opened using the low-level open(2) call rather than the fopen(3) call.

If a block is specified, it will be invoked with the IO object as a parameter, which will be closed when the block terminates. The call returns the value of the block in this case.

If *name* starts with a pipe character, a subprocess is created, connected to the caller by a pair of pipes. The returned IO object may be used to write to the standard input and read from the standard output of this subprocess. If the command following | is a single minus sign, Ruby forks, and this subprocess is connected to the parent. In the subprocess, the open call returns nil. If the command is not "--", the subprocess runs the command. If a block is associated with an open("|--") call, that block will be run twice—once in the parent and once in the child. The block parameter will be an IO object in the parent and nil in the child. The parent's IO object will be connected to the child's STDIN and STDOUT. The subprocess will be terminated at the end of the block.

```
open("testfile", "r:iso-8859-1") do |f|
  print f.gets
end
```

produces:

```
This is line one
```

Open a subprocess, and read its output:

```
cmd = open("|date")
print cmd.gets
cmd.close
```

produces:

```
Mon May 27 12:32:39 CDT 2013
```

Open a subprocess running the same Ruby program:

```
f = open("|-", "w+")
if f.nil?
  puts "in Child"
  exit
else
  puts "Got: #{f.gets}"
end
```

produces:

```
Got: in Child
```

Open a subprocess using a block to receive the I/O object:

```
open("|-") do |f|
  if f.nil?
    puts "in Child"
  else
    puts "Got: #{f.gets}"
  end
end
```

produces:

```
Got: in Child
```

---

p $p(\langle obj \rangle^+) \rightarrow obj$

For each object, writes *obj*.inspect followed by the current output record separator to the program's standard output. Also see the PrettyPrint library on page 789. Returns *obj*.

```
Info = Struct.new(:name, :state)
p Info['dave', 'TX']
```

produces:

```
#<struct Info name="dave", state="TX">
```

---

print $print(\langle obj \rangle^*) \rightarrow nil$

Prints each object in turn to STDOUT. If the output field separator ($,) is not nil, its contents will appear between each field. If the output record separator ($\) is not nil, it will be appended to the output. If no arguments are given, prints $_. Objects that aren't strings will be converted by calling their to_s print method.

```
print "cat", [1,2,3], 99, "\n"
$, = ", "
$\ = "\n"
print "cat", [1,2,3], 99
```

produces:

```
cat[1, 2, 3]99
cat, [1, 2, 3], 99
```

---

printf
$printf(\ io,\ format\ \langle,\ obj\rangle^*\ ) \rightarrow nil$
$printf(\ format\ \langle,\ obj\rangle^*\ ) \rightarrow nil$

Equivalent to the following:

```
  io.write(sprintf(format, obj, ...))
# or
  write(sprintf(format, obj, ...))
```

---

proc
$proc\ \{\ ...\ \} \rightarrow a\_proc$

Creates a new procedure object from the given block. Use Object#lambda instead.

```
prc = proc {|name| "Goodbye, #{name}" }
prc.call('Dave') # => "Goodbye, Dave"
```

---

putc
$putc(\ obj\ ) \rightarrow obj$

Equivalent to STDOUT.putc(obj). If *obj* is a string, output its first character; otherwise, attempts to convert *obj* to an integer and outputs the corresponding character code.

```
putc 65
putc 66.123
putc "CAT"
putc 12        # newline
```

produces:

ABC

---

puts
$puts(\ \langle arg\rangle^*\ ) \rightarrow nil$

Equivalent to STDOUT.puts(arg...).

---

raise
raise
$raise(\ message\ )$
$raise(\ exception\ \langle,\ message\ \langle,\ array\rangle\rangle\ )$

With no arguments, raises the exception in $! or raises a RuntimeError if $! is nil. With a single String argument (or an argument that responds to to_str), raises a RuntimeError with the string as a message. Otherwise, the first parameter should be the name of an Exception class (or an object that returns an Exception when its exception method is called). The optional second parameter sets the message associated with the exception, and the third parameter is an array of callback information. Exceptions are caught by the rescue clause of begin...end blocks.

```
raise "Failed to create socket"
raise ArgumentError, "No parameters", caller
```

---

rand
$rand(\ max=0\ ) \rightarrow number$
$rand(\ range\ ) \rightarrow number$

Converts *max* to an integer using $max_1 = max.to\_i.abs$. If the result is zero or nil, returns a pseudorandom floating-point number greater than or equal to 0.0 and less than 1.0. Otherwise, returns a pseudorandom integer greater than or equal to zero and less than max_1. If a range is passed, return a random number in that range. Object#srand may be used to ensure repeatable sequences of random numbers between different runs of the program. See also class Random on page 655.

```
srand 1234                 # => 27212588021548574773990619030416710243
[ rand,  rand ]            # => [0.1915194503788923, 0.6221087710398319]
[ rand(10), rand(1000) ] # => [4, 664]
srand 1234                 # => 1234
[ rand,  rand ]            # => [0.1915194503788923, 0.6221087710398319]
rand(5..10)                # => 9
rand(1.1..1.2)             # => 1.1612111893665362
```

readline   readline(‹ *separator=$/* ›) → *string*

Equivalent to Object#gets, except readline raises EOFError at end of file.

readlines   readlines(‹ *separator=$/* ›) → *array*

Returns an array containing each of the lines returned by calling gets(separator).

remove_instance_variable   remove_instance_variable(*symbol*) → *other_obj*

Removes the named instance variable from *obj*, returning that variable's value.

```
class Dummy
  def initialize
    @var = 99
  end
  def remove
    remove_instance_variable(:@var)
  end
  def var_defined?
    defined? @var
  end
end
d = Dummy.new
d.var_defined? # => "instance-variable"
d.remove       # => 99
d.var_defined? # => nil
```

require   require(*library_name*) → *true* or *false*

Ruby tries to load *library_name*, returning true if successful. If the filename is not an absolute path, it will be searched for in the directories listed in $:. If the file has the extension .rb, it is loaded as a source file; if the extension is .so, ..o, or ..dll,[1] Ruby loads the shared library as a Ruby extension. Otherwise, Ruby tries adding .rb, ..so, and so on, to the name. The name of the loaded feature is added to the array in $". A feature will not be loaded if its name already appears in $".[2] require returns true if the feature was successfully loaded.

---

1. Or whatever the default shared library extension is on the current platform
2. As of Ruby 1.9, this name is converted to an absolute path, so require 'a';require './a' will load a.rb once.

```
require 'my-library.rb'
require 'db-driver'
```

require_relative

require_relative(*library_path*) → *true* or *false*

Requires a library whose path is relative to the file containing the call. Thus, if the directory /usr/local/mylib/bin contains the file myprog.rb and that program contains the following line:

```
require_relative "../lib/mylib"
```

then Ruby will look for mylib in /usr/local/mylib/lib.

require_relative cannot be called interactively in irb.

select

select(*read_array* ‹ , *write_array* ‹ , *error_array* ‹ , *timeout* › › ›) → *array* or nil

Performs a low-level select call, which waits for data to become available from input/output devices. The first three parameters are arrays of IO objects or nil. The last is a timeout in seconds, which should be an Integer or a Float. The call waits for data to become available for any of the IO objects in *read_array*, for buffers to have cleared sufficiently to enable writing to any of the devices in *write_array*, or for an error to occur on the devices in *error_array*. If one or more of these conditions are met, the call returns a three-element array containing arrays of the IO objects that were ready. Otherwise, if there is no change in status for *timeout* seconds, the call returns nil. If all parameters are nil, the current thread sleeps forever.

```
select( [STDIN], nil, nil, 1.5 ) # => nil
```

set_trace_func

set_trace_func(*proc*) → *proc*
set_trace_func(nil) → nil

New in 2.0   (This method has been replaced by the TracePoint class in Ruby 2.0.) Establishes *proc* as the handler for tracing or disables tracing if the parameter is nil. *proc* takes up to six parameters: an event name, a filename, a line number, an object ID, a binding, and the name of a class. *proc* is invoked whenever an event occurs. Events are call (calls a Ruby method), c-call (calls a C-language routine), c-return (returns from a C-language routine), class (starts a class or module definition), end (finishes a class or module definition), line (executes code on a new line), raise (raises an exception), and return (returns from a Ruby method). Tracing is disabled within the context of *proc*. See the example in the tutorial on page 400 for more information.

sleep

sleep(*numeric=0*) → *fixnum*

Suspends the current thread for *numeric* seconds (which may be a Float with fractional seconds). Returns the actual number of seconds slept (rounded), which may be less than that asked for if the thread was interrupted by a SIGALRM or if another thread calls Thread#run. An argument of zero causes sleep to return immediately.

```
Time.now  # => 2013-05-27 12:32:41 -0500
sleep 1.9 # => 2
Time.now  # => 2013-05-27 12:32:43 -0500
```

spawn	spawn(‹ env,› *command* ‹ , *args* ›*, ‹ options ›) → *pid*

Executes *command* in a subshell, returning immediately. (Compare with Object#system, which waits for the command to complete before returning to the caller.) Returns the process ID for the subprocess running the command.

The *command* can be a string, which is passed to the system shell for interpretation or a command name followed by zero or more arguments. In this case, the command is executed and passed the given arguments—the shell is not involved. The command name may be a string or a two-element array, where the first element is the command itself and the second is the argv[0] value to be passed to exec(2). The latter may be used to change the process name on systems that support it.

```
pid = spawn("echo hello")
puts "Back in main program"
STDOUT.flush
rc, status = Process::waitpid2(pid)
puts "Status = #{status}"
```

produces:

```
Back in main program
hello
Status = pid 23941 exit 0
```

env, if present, is a hash that adds to the environment variables in the subshell. An entry with a nil value clears the corresponding environment variable. The keys must be strings.

```
pid = spawn({"FRED" => "caveman"}, "echo FRED = $FRED")
Process::waitpid2(pid)
```

produces:

```
FRED = caveman
```

The *options* hash controls the setup of the subshell. Keys and their meanings are:

Option	Effect on new process
:pgroup => true | 0 | *int*	If true or 0, the new process will be a process group leader. Otherwise, the process will belong to group *int*.
:rlimit_*xxx* => val | [cur, max]	Sets a resource limit. See Process.getrlimit for more information.
:unsetenv_others => true	Clears all environment variables; then sets only those passed in the *env* parameter.
:chdir => *dir*	Changes to directory *dir* before running the process.
:umask => *int*	Specifies the umask for the process.
fd_desc => *stream*	Sets the process's standard input, output, or error to *stream*. See the description that follows this table for information.
:close_others => true | false	By default, all file descriptors apart from 0, 1, and 2 are closed. You can specify false to leave them open.
io_obj => :close	Explicitly closes the file descriptor corresponding to *io_obj* in the child process.

The *fd_desc* parameter identifies an I/O stream to be opened or assigned in the child process. It can be one of :in, STDIN, or 0 to represent standard input; :out, STDOUT, or 1 for standard output; or :err, STDERR, or 2 for standard error. It can also be an array containing one or more of these, in which case all fds in the array will be opened on the same stream.

The *stream* parameter can be the following:

- One of :in, STDIN, or 0 to represent the current standard input; :out, STDOUT, or 1 for the current standard output; or :err, STDERR, or 2 for the current standard error.

- A string representing the name of a file or device.

- An array. If it contains [:child, fd], redirects to the fd of the child process. Otherwise, the first element is the name of a file or device, the optional second element is the mode, and the optional third element the permission. See the description of File#new on page 494 for details.

This example shows the options in action:

```
reader, writer = IO.pipe
pid = spawn("echo '4*a(1)' | bc -l", [ STDERR, STDOUT ] => writer)
writer.close
Process::waitpid2(pid)
reader.gets # => "3.14159265358979323844\n"
```

---

sprintf   sprintf(*format_string* ‹, *arguments*›*) → *string*

Returns the string resulting from applying *format_string* to any additional arguments. Within the format string, any characters other than format sequences are copied to the result.

A format sequence consists of a percent sign; followed by optional flags, width, and precision indicators; an optional name; and then terminated with a field type character. The field type controls how the corresponding sprintf argument is to be interpreted, and the flags modify that interpretation.

The flag characters are:

Flag	Applies To	Meaning
␣ (space)	bdEefGgiouXx	Leaves a space at the start of positive numbers.
digit$	all	Specifies the absolute argument number for this field. Absolute and relative argument numbers cannot be mixed in a sprintf string.
#	beEfgGoxX	Uses an alternative format. For the conversions b, o, X, and x, prefixes the result with b, 0, 0X, 0x, respectively. For E, e, f, G, and g, forces a decimal point to be added, even if no digits follow. For G and g, does not remove trailing zeros.
+	bdEefGgiouXx	Adds a leading plus sign to positive numbers.
-	all	Left-justifies the result of this conversion.
0 (zero)	bdEefGgiouXx	Pads with zeros, not spaces.
*	all	Uses the next argument as the field width. If negative, left-justifies the result. If the asterisk is followed by a number and a dollar sign, uses the indicated argument as the width.

The field width is an optional integer, followed optionally by a period and a precision. The width specifies the minimum number of characters that will be written to the result for this field. For numeric fields, the precision controls the number of decimal places displayed. As of Ruby 1.9, the number zero is converted to a zero-length string if a precision of 0 is given. For string fields, the precision determines the maximum number of characters to be copied from the string. (Thus, the format sequence %10.10s will always contribute exactly ten characters to the result.)

The field type characters are:

☞ Layout

Field	Conversion
A	Same as %a, but uses uppercase X and P.
a	Converts a float into hexadecimal representation 0x*significand*p*decimal-exp*.
B	Converts argument as a binary number (0B0101 if # modifier used).
b	Converts argument as a binary number (0b0101 if # modifier used).
c	Argument is the numeric code for a single character.
d	Converts argument as a decimal number.
E	Equivalent to e but uses an uppercase E to indicate the exponent.
e	Converts floating point-argument into exponential notation with one digit before the decimal point. The precision determines the number of fractional digits (default six).
f	Converts floating-point argument as [|-]ddd.ddd, where the precision determines the number of digits after the decimal point.
G	Equivalent to g but uses an uppercase E in exponent form.
g	Converts a floating-point number using exponential form if the exponent is less than -4 or greater than or equal to the precision, or in d.dddd form otherwise.
i	Identical to d.
o	Converts argument as an octal number.
p	The value of argument.inspect.
s	Argument is a string to be substituted. If the format sequence contains a precision, at most that many characters will be copied.
u	Treats argument as an unsigned decimal number.
X	Converts argument to hexadecimal with uppercase letters. Negative numbers will be displayed with two leading periods (representing an infinite string of leading FFs).
x	Converts argument to hexadecimal. Negative numbers will be displayed with two leading periods (representing an infinite string of leading FFs).

Here are some examples of sprintf in action:

```
sprintf("%d %04x", 123, 123)               # => "123 007b"
sprintf("%08b '%4s'", 123, 123)            # => "01111011 ' 123'"
sprintf("%1$*2$s %2$d %1$s", "hello", 8)   # => "   hello 8 hello"
sprintf("%1$*2$s %2$d", "hello", -8)       # => "hello    -8"
sprintf("%+g:% g:%-g", 1.23, 1.23, 1.23)   # => "+1.23: 1.23:1.23"
```

In Ruby 1.9, you can pass a hash as the second argument and insert values from this hash into the string. The notation <name> can be used between a percent sign and a field-type character, in which case the name will be used to look up a value in the hash, and that value will be formatted according to the field specification. The notation {name} is equivalent to <name>s, substituting the corresponding value as a string. You can use width and other flag characters between the opening percent sign and the {.

```
sprintf("%<number>d %04<number>x", number: 123)   # => "123␣007b"
sprintf("%08<number>b '%5{number}'", number: 123) # => "01111011␣'␣␣123'"
sprintf("%6<k>s: %<v>s", k: "Dave", v: "Ruby")    # => "␣␣Dave:␣Ruby"
sprintf("%6{k}: %{v}", k: "Dave", v: "Ruby")      # => "␣␣Dave:␣Ruby"
```

srand   srand(‹ number ›) → old_seed

Seeds the pseudorandom number generator to the value of *number*.to_i. If *number* is omitted or zero, uses Random.new_seed. (This is also the behavior if Object#rand is called without previously calling srand but without the sequence.) By setting the seed to a known value, scripts that use rand can be made deterministic during testing. The previous seed value is returned. Also see Object#rand on page 622 and class Random on page 655.

sub   sub(*pattern, replacement*) → $_
                                                    sub(*pattern*) { *block* } → $_

Equivalent to $_.sub(args), except that $_ will be updated if substitution occurs. Available only if the -n or -p command-line option is present.

syscall   syscall(*fixnum* ‹ , *args* ›*) → *int*

Calls the operating system function identified by *fixnum*. The arguments must be either String objects or Integer objects that fit within a native long. Up to nine parameters may be passed. The function identified by *fixnum* is system dependent. On some Unix systems, the numbers may be obtained from a header file called syscall.h. System is not always available.

```
syscall 4, 1, "hello\n", 6   # '4' is write(2) on our system
```

system   system(‹ env, › *command* ‹ , *args* ›*, ‹ options ›) → *true* or *false*~or nil

Executes *command* in a subshell, returning true if the command was found and ran successfully, false if the command exited with a nonzero exit status, and nil if the command failed to execute. An error status is available in $?. The arguments are processed in the same way as for Object#exec on page 615. *env*, if present, is a hash that adds to the environment variables in the subshell. An entry with a nil value clears the corresponding environment variable. The keys must be strings. *options*, if present, is a hash that controls the setup of the subshell. The possible keys and their meanings are listed under the spawn method.

```
system("echo *")
system("echo", "*")
system({"WILMA" => "shopper"}, "echo $WILMA")
```

produces:

```
config.h main.rb
*
shopper
```

test   test(*cmd, file1* ‹ , *file2* ›) → *obj*

Uses *cmd* to perform various tests on *file1* (see the first table that follows) or on *file1* and *file2* (see the second table).

Flag	Description	Returns
?A	Last access time for *file1*	Time
?b	True if *file1* is a block device	true or false
?c	True if *file1* is a character device	true or false
?C	Last change time for *file1*	Time
?d	True if *file1* exists and is a directory	true or false
?e	True if *file1* exists	true or false
?f	True if *file1* exists and is a regular file	true or false
?g	True if *file1* has the setgid bit set (false under NT)	true or false
?G	True if *file1* exists and has a group ownership equal to the caller's group	true or false
?k	True if *file1* exists and has the sticky bit set	true or false
?l	True if *file1* exists and is a symbolic link	true or false
?M	Last modification time for *file1*	Time
?o	True if *file1* exists and is owned by the caller's effective UID	true or false
?O	True if *file1* exists and is owned by the caller's real UID	true or false
?p	True if *file1* exists and is a fifo	true or false
?r	True if *file1* is readable by the effective UID/GID of the caller	true or false
?R	True if *file1* is readable by the real UID/GID of the caller	true or false
?s	If *file1* has nonzero size, returns the size; otherwise, returns nil	Integer or nil
?S	True if *file1* exists and is a socket	true or false
?u	True if *file1* has the setuid bit set	true or false
?w	True if *file1* exists and is writable by the effective UID/ GID	true or false
?W	True if *file1* exists and is writable by the real UID/GID	true or false
?x	True if *file1* exists and is executable by the effective UID/GID	true or false
?X	True if *file1* exists and is executable by the real UID/GID	true or false
?z	True if *file1* exists and has a zero length	true or false

Flag	Description
?-	True if *file1* is a hard link to *file2*
?=	True if the modification times of *file1* and *file2* are equal
?<	True if the modification time of *file1* is prior to that of *file2*
?>	True if the modification time of *file1* is after that of *file2*

throw   throw(*symbol* ‹ , *obj* ›)

Transfers control to the end of the active catch block waiting for *symbol*. Raises NameError if there is no catch block for the symbol. The optional second parameter supplies a return value for the catch block, which otherwise defaults to nil. For examples, see Object#catch on page 614.

trace_var

trace_var(*symbol, cmd*) → nil
trace_var(*symbol*) { | val | ... } → nil

Controls tracing of assignments to global variables. The parameter *symbol* identifies the variable (as either a string name or a symbol identifier). *cmd* (which may be a string or a Proc object) or the block is executed whenever the variable is assigned and receives the variable's new value as a parameter. Only explicit assignments are traced. Also see Object#untrace_var.

```
trace_var :$dave, lambda {|v| puts "$dave is now '#{v}'" }
$dave = "hello"
$dave.sub!(/ello/, "i")
$dave += " Dave"
```

produces:

```
$dave is now 'hello'
$dave is now 'hi Dave'
```

trap

trap(*signal, proc*) → *obj*
trap(*signal*) { ... } → *obj*

See the Signal module on page 664.

untrace_var

untrace_var(*symbol* ‹ , *cmd* ›) → *array* or nil

Removes tracing for the specified command on the given global variable and returns nil. If no command is specified, removes all tracing for that variable.

using

using *mod*

New in 2.0

Applies the refinements defined in the given module. The refinements apply to the current file (or string if eval is being used) from the point where using is called.

```
module SuperUpcase
  refine String do
    def upcase
      "!WOW! #{super} !WOW!"
    end
  end
end

"wombat".upcase # => "WOMBAT"
using SuperUpcase
"wombat".upcase # => "!WOW! WOMBAT !WOW!"
```

warn

warn ‹ msgs ›⁺

Writes the given message to STDERR (unless $VERBOSE is nil, perhaps because the -W0 command-line option was given). If multiple messages are given, writes each on a new line.

New in 2.0

```
warn "Danger, Will Robinson!"
```

produces:

```
Danger, Will Robinson!
```

ObjectSpace

The ObjectSpace module contains a number of routines that interact with the garbage collection facility and allow you to traverse all living objects with an iterator.

ObjectSpace also provides support for object finalizers. These are procs that will be called when a specific object is about to be destroyed by garbage collection.

```ruby
include ObjectSpace

a, b, c = "A", "B", "C"
puts "a's id is #{a.object_id}"
puts "b's id is #{b.object_id}"
puts "c's id is #{c.object_id}"

define_finalizer(a, lambda {|id| puts "Finalizer one on #{id}" })
define_finalizer(b, lambda {|id| puts "Finalizer two on #{id}" })
define_finalizer(c, lambda {|id| puts "Finalizer three on #{id}" })
```

produces:

```
a's id is 70124883293000
b's id is 70124883292960
c's id is 70124883292880
Finalizer three on 70124883292880
Finalizer two on 70124883292960
Finalizer one on 70124883293000
```

Class Methods

_id2ref ObjectSpace._id2ref(*object_id*) → *obj*

Converts an object ID to a reference to the object. May not be called on an object ID passed as a parameter to a finalizer.

```ruby
s = "I am a string"         # => "I am a string"
oid = s.object_id           # => 70207029149080
r = ObjectSpace._id2ref(oid) # => "I am a string"
r                           # => "I am a string"
r.equal?(s)                 # => true
```

---

count_objects ObjectSpace.count_objects → *histogram_hash*

Returns a hash where the keys are the interpreter-specific internal object types and the values are the number of objects of each type.

```ruby
ObjectSpace.count_objects # => {:TOTAL=>17493, :FREE=>60, :T_OBJECT=>49,
                          # .. :T_CLASS=>471, :T_MODULE=>21, :T_FLOAT=>4,
                          # .. :T_STRING=>7748, :T_REGEXP=>64, :T_ARRAY=>1464,
                          # .. :T_HASH=>57, :T_BIGNUM=>3, :T_FILE=>17,
                          # .. :T_DATA=>701, :T_MATCH=>20, :T_COMPLEX=>1,
                          # .. :T_RATIONAL=>2, :T_NODE=>6790, :T_ICLASS=>21}
```

---

define_finalizer

ObjectSpace.define_finalizer(*obj*, *a_proc*=proc())

Adds *a_proc* as a finalizer, called when *obj* is about to be destroyed. Note that if you use lambda to create the proc object, you must remember to include a parameter with the block. If you don't, the invocation of the lambda will silently fail when the finalizer is called because of a mismatch in the expected and actual parameter count.

---

each_object

ObjectSpace.each_object(‹ *class_or_mod* ›) { | obj | ... } → *fixnum*

Calls the block once for each living, nonimmediate object in this Ruby process. If *class_or_mod* is specified, calls the block for only those classes or modules that match (or are a subclass of) *class_or_mod*. Returns the number of objects found. Immediate objects (Fixnums, Symbols true, false, and nil) are never returned. In the following example, each_object returns both the numbers we defined and several constants defined in the Math module:

```
a = 102.7
b = 95        # Fixnum: won't be returned
c = 12345678987654321
count = ObjectSpace.each_object(Numeric) {|x| p x }
puts "Total count: #{count}"
```

produces:

```
(0+1i)
9223372036854775807
3
NaN
Infinity
1.7976931348623157e+308
2.2250738585072014e-308
274193223623034780067407936393989039126
12345678987654321
Total count: 9
```

---

garbage_collect

ObjectSpace.garbage_collect → nil

Initiates garbage collection (see module GC on page 517).

---

undefine_finalizer

ObjectSpace.undefine_finalizer(*obj*)

Removes all finalizers for *obj*.

Class	**Proc**

Proc objects are blocks of code that have been bound to a set of local variables. Once bound, the code may be called in different contexts and still access those variables.

```ruby
def gen_times(factor)
  return Proc.new {|n| n*factor }
end

times3 = gen_times(3)
times5 = gen_times(5)

times3.call(12)             # => 36
times5.call(5)              # => 25
times3.call(times5.call(4)) # => 60
```

Class Methods

new

Proc.new { ... } → *a_proc*
Proc.new → *a_proc*

Creates a new Proc object, bound to the current context. Proc.new may be called without a block only within a method with an attached block, in which case that block is converted to the Proc object.

```ruby
def proc_from
  Proc.new
end
proc = proc_from { "hello" }
proc.call # => "hello"
```

Instance Methods

[ ]

prc[‹ *params* ›*] → *obj*

Synonym for Proc#call.

==

Removed in Ruby 2.0.
New in 2.0

===

prc === *other* → *obj*

Equivalent to prc.call(other). Allows you to use procs in when clauses of case expressions, so you can write stuff such as:

```ruby
even = lambda {|num| num.even? }

(0..3).each do |num|
  case num
  when even then puts "#{num} is even"
  else           puts "#{num} is not even"
  end
end
```

produces:

```
0 is even
1 is not even
2 is even
3 is not even
```

---

arity   *prc*.arity → *integer*

Returns the number of arguments required by the block. If the block is declared to take no arguments, returns 0. If the block is known to take exactly n arguments, returns n. If the block has optional arguments, returns -(n+1), where n is the number of mandatory arguments. A proc with no argument declarations also returns -1, because it can accept (and ignore) an arbitrary number of parameters.

```
Proc.new {}.arity        # => 0
Proc.new {||}.arity      # => 0
Proc.new {|a|}.arity     # => 1
Proc.new {|a,b|}.arity   # => 2
Proc.new {|a,b,c|}.arity # => 3
Proc.new {|*a|}.arity    # => -1
Proc.new {|a,*b|}.arity  # => -2
```

In Ruby 1.9, arity is defined as the number of parameters that would not be ignored. In 1.8, Proc.new {}.arity returns -1, and in 1.9 it returns 0.

---

binding   *prc*.binding → *binding*

Returns the binding associated with *prc*.

```
def some_method
  a = "wibble"
  lambda {}
end

prc = some_method
eval "a", prc.binding # => "wibble"
```

---

call   *prc*.call(‹ *params* ›*) → *obj*

Invokes the block, setting the block's parameters to the values in *params* using something close to method-calling semantics. Returns the value of the last expression evaluated in the block.

```
a_proc = Proc.new {|a, *b| b.collect {|i| i*a }}
a_proc.call(9, 1, 2, 3) # => [9, 18, 27]
a_proc[9, 1, 2, 3]      # => [9, 18, 27]
```

If the block being called accepts a single parameter and you give call more than one parameter, only the first will be passed to the block. This is a change from Ruby 1.8.

```
a_proc = Proc.new {|a| puts a}
a_proc.call(1,2,3)
```

produces:

```
1
```

If you want a block to receive an arbitrary number of arguments, define it to accept *args.

```
a_proc = Proc.new {|*a| p a}
a_proc.call(1,2,3)
```

produces:

```
[1, 2, 3]
```

Blocks created using Object#lambda check that they are called with exactly the right number of parameters.

```
p_proc = Proc.new {|a,b| puts "Sum is: #{a + b}" }
p_proc.call(1,2,3)
p_proc = lambda {|a,b| puts "Sum is: #{a + b}" }
p_proc.call(1,2,3)
```

produces:

```
        from prog.rb:4:in `call'
        from prog.rb:4:in `<main>'
Sum is: 3
prog.rb:3:in `block in <main>': wrong number of arguments (3 for 2)
(ArgumentError)
```

---

curry

prc.curry → *curried_proc*

If you have a proc that takes arguments, you normally have to supply all of those arguments if you want the proc to execute successfully. However, it is also possible to consider an *n* argument proc to be the same as a single-argument proc that returns a new proc that has this first argument fixed and that takes *n-1* arguments. If you repeat this process recursively for each of these subprocs, you end up with a proc that will take from zero to *n* arguments. If you pass it all *n*, it simply executes the proc with those arguments. If you pass it *m* arguments (where *m < n*), it returns a new proc that has those arguments prebaked in and that takes *m-n* arguments. In this way, it is possible to partially apply arguments to a proc.

```
add_three_numbers = lambda {|a,b,c| a + b + c}
add_10_to_two_numbers = add_three_numbers.curry[10]
add_33_to_one_number  = add_10_to_two_numbers[23]

add_three_numbers[1,2,3]    # => 6
add_10_to_two_numbers[1,2]  # => 13
add_33_to_one_number[1]     # => 34
```

---

lambda?

prc.lambda? → *true* or *false*

Returns true if *prc* has lambda semantics (that is, if argument passing acts as it does with method calls). See the discussion in Section 22.13, *Blocks, Closures, and Proc Objects*, on page 335.

parameters

prc.parameters → *array*

Returns a description of the method's parameter list. See Method#parameters for details.

```
lambda {|a, b=1, *c, &d| }.parameters # => [[:req, :a], [:opt, :b], [:rest, :c],
                                       # .. [:block, :d]]
```

source_location

prc.source_location → [*filename, lineno*] or nil

Returns the source filename and line number where *prc* was defined or nil if *proc* was not defined in Ruby source.

```
variable = 123
prc = lambda { "some proc" }
prc.source_location # => ["prog.rb", 2]
```

to_proc

prc.to_proc → *prc*

Part of the protocol for converting objects to Proc objects. Instances of class Proc simply return themselves.

to_s

prc.to_s → *string*

Returns a description of *prc,* including information on where it was defined.

```
def create_proc
  Proc.new
end

my_proc = create_proc { "hello" }
my_proc.to_s # => "#<Proc:0x007fc7f4864318@prog.rb:5>"
```

yield

prc.yield(‹ *params* ›*) → *obj*

Synonym for Proc#call.

Module | **Process**

The Process module is a collection of methods used to manipulate processes. Programs that want to manipulate real and effective user and group IDs should also look at the Process::GID and Process::UID modules. Much of the functionality here is duplicated in the Process::Sys module.

Module Constants

PRIO_PGRP	Process group priority.
PRIO_PROCESS	Process priority.
PRIO_USER	User priority.
WNOHANG	Does not block if no child has exited. Not available on all platforms.
WUNTRACED	Returns stopped children as well. Not available on all platforms.
RLIM[IT]_*xxx*	Used by getrlimit and setrlimit.

Class Methods

abort   abort
                                                                          abort(*msg*)

Synonym for Object#abort.

daemon   Process.daemon(*stay_in_dir* = false, *keep_stdio_open* = false) → 0 or -1

Puts the current process into the background (either by forking and calling Process.setsid or by using the daemon(3) call if available). Sets the current working directory to / unless *stay_in_dir* is true. Redirects standard input, output, and error to /dev/null unless *keep_stdio_open* is true. Not available on all platforms.

detach   Process.detach(*pid*) → *thread*

Some operating systems retain the status of terminated child processes until the parent collects that status (normally using some variant of wait()). If the parent never collects this status, the child stays around as a *zombie* process. Process.detach prevents this by setting up a separate Ruby thread whose sole job is to reap the status of the process *pid* when it terminates. Use detach only when you do not intend to explicitly wait for the child to terminate. detach checks the status only periodically (currently once each second).

In this first example, we don't reap the first child process, so it appears as a zombie in the process status display.

```
pid = fork { sleep 0.1 }
sleep 1
system("ps -o pid,state -p #{pid}")
```

produces:

```
dyld: DYLD_ environment variables being ignored because main executable (/bin/ps)
is setuid or setgid
  PID STAT
24002 Z+
```

In the next example, Process.detach is used to reap the child automatically—no child processes are left running.

```
pid = fork { sleep 0.1 }
Process.detach(pid)
sleep 1
system("ps -o pid,state -p #{pid}")
```

produces:

```
dyld: DYLD_ environment variables being ignored because main executable (/bin/ps)
is setuid or setgid
  PID STAT
```

---

egid   Process.egid → *int*

Returns the effective group ID for this process.

```
Process.egid # => 20
```

---

egid=   Process.egid= *int* → *int*

Sets the effective group ID for this process.

---

euid   Process.euid → *int*

Returns the effective user ID for this process.

```
Process.euid # => 501
```

---

euid=   Process.euid= *int*

Sets the effective user ID for this process. Not available on all platforms.

---

exec   Process.exec(‹ env, › *command* ‹ , args ›*, ‹ options ›)

Synonym for Object#exec.

---

exit   Process.exit(*int*=0)

Synonym for Object#exit.

---

exit!   Process.exit!(true | false | *status*=1)

Synonym for Object#exit!. No exit handlers are run. 0, 1, or *status* is returned to the underlying system as the exit status.

```
Process.exit!(0)
```

---

fork   Process.fork ‹ { ... } › → *int* or nil

See Object#fork on page 617.

getpgid
Process.getpgid(*int*) → *int*

Returns the process group ID for the given process ID. Not available on all platforms.

```
Process.getpgid(Process.ppid()) # => 21366
```

getpgrp
Process.getpgrp → *int*

Returns the process group ID for this process. Not available on all platforms.

```
Process.getpgid(0) # => 21366
Process.getpgrp    # => 21366
```

getpriority
Process.getpriority(*kind, int*) → *int*

Gets the scheduling priority for specified process, process group, or user. The *kind* parameter indicates the kind of entity to find: Process::PRIO_PGRP, Process::PRIO_USER, or Process::PRIO_PRO-CESS. *int* is an ID indicating the particular process, process group, or user (an ID of 0 means *current*). Lower priorities are more favorable for scheduling. Not available on all platforms.

```
Process.getpriority(Process::PRIO_USER, 0)    # => 0
Process.getpriority(Process::PRIO_PROCESS, 0) # => 0
```

getrlimit
Process.getrlimit(*name*) → [*current, max*]

Returns the current and maximum resource limit for the named resource. The name may be a symbol or a string from the following list. It may also be an operating-specific integer constant. The Process module defines constants corresponding to these integers: the constants are named RLIMIT_ followed by one of the following: AS, CORE, CPU, DATA, FSIZE, MEMLOCK, NOFILE, NPROC, RSS, or STACK. Consult your system's getrlimit(2) man page for details. The return array may contain actual values or one of the constants RLIM_INFINITY, RLIM_SAVED_CUR, or RLIM_SAVED_MAX. Not available on all platforms. See also Process.setrlimit.

```
Process.getrlimit(:STACK)                   # => [8388608, 67104768]
Process.getrlimit("STACK")                  # => [8388608, 67104768]
Process.getrlimit(Process::RLIMIT_STACK)    # => [8388608, 67104768]
```

getsid
Process.getsid → *int*

Returns the session id (if supported).

New in 2.0

gid
Process.gid → *int*

Returns the group ID for this process.

```
Process.gid # => 20
```

gid=
Process.gid= *int* → *int*

Sets the group ID for this process.

---

groups

Process.groups → *groups*

Returns an array of integer supplementary group IDs. Not available on all platforms. See also Process.maxgroups.

```
Process.groups # => [20, 405, 402, 401, 403, 12, 33, 61, 79, 80, 81, 98, 100,
               # .. 204, 404]
```

---

groups=

Process.groups = *array* → *groups*

Sets the supplementary group IDs from the given array, which may contain either numbers or group names (as strings). Not available on all platforms. Available only to superusers. See also Process.maxgroups.

---

initgroups

Process.initgroups(*user, base_group*) → *groups*

Initializes the group access list using the operating system's initgroups call. Not available on all platforms. May require superuser privilege.

```
Process.initgroups("dave", 500)
```

---

kill

Process.kill(*signal, ‹pid›⁺*) → *int*

Sends the given signal to the specified process ID(s) or to the current process if *pid* is zero. *signal* may be an integer signal number or a string or symbol representing a POSIX signal name (either with or without a SIG prefix). If *signal* is negative (or starts with a - sign), kills process groups instead of processes. Not all signals are available on all platforms.

```
pid = fork do
  Signal.trap(:USR1) { puts "Ouch!"; exit }
  # ... do some work ...
end
# ...
Process.kill(:USR1, pid)
Process.wait
```

produces:

```
Ouch!
```

---

maxgroups

Process.maxgroups → *count*

The Process module has a limit on the number of supplementary groups it supports in the calls Process.groups and Process.groups=. The maxgroups call returns that limit, and the maxgroups= call sets it.

```
Process.maxgroups # => 16
```

---

maxgroups=

Process.maxgroups= *limit* → *count*

Sets the maximum number of supplementary group IDs that can be processed by the groups and groups= methods. If a number larger than 4096 is given, 4096 will be used.

---

pid   Process.pid → *int*

Returns the process ID of this process. Not available on all platforms.

```
Process.pid # => 24032
```

---

ppid   Process.ppid → *int*

Returns the process ID of the parent of this process. Always returns 0 on Windows. Not available on all platforms.

```
puts "I am #{Process.pid}"
Process.fork { puts "Parent is #{Process.ppid}" }
```

produces:

```
I am 24034
Parent is 24034
```

---

setpgid   Process.setpgid(*pid, int*) → 0

Sets the process group ID of *pid* (0 indicates this process) to *int*. Not available on all platforms.

---

setpgrp   Process.setpgrp → 0

Equivalent to setpgid(0,0). Not available on all platforms.

---

setpriority   Process.setpriority(*kind, int, int_priority*) → 0

See Process#getpriority.

```
Process.setpriority(Process::PRIO_USER, 0, 19)    # => 0
Process.setpriority(Process::PRIO_PROCESS, 0, 19) # => 0
Process.getpriority(Process::PRIO_USER, 0)        # => 19
Process.getpriority(Process::PRIO_PROCESS, 0)     # => 19
```

---

setrlimit   Process.setrlimit(*name, soft_limit, hard_limit=soft_limit*) → nil

---

Sets the limit for the named resource. See Process.getrlimit for a description of resource naming. Your system's setrlimit(2) man page will have a description of the limits. Not available on all platforms.

---

setsid   Process.setsid → *int*

Establishes this process as a new session and process group leader, with no controlling tty. Returns the session ID. Not available on all platforms.

```
Process.setsid # => 24039
```

---

spawn   Process.spawn(‹ env, › *command* ‹ , *args* ›*, ‹ options ›) → *pid*

Synonym for Object#spawn.

---

times   Process.times → *struct_tms*

Returns a Tms structure (see Struct::Tms on page 697) that contains user and system CPU times for this process.

```
t = Process.times
[ t.utime, t.stime ] # => [0.03, 0.01]
```

---

uid   Process.uid → *int*

Returns the user ID of this process.

```
Process.uid # => 501
```

---

uid=   Process.uid= *int* → *numeric*

Sets the (integer) user ID for this process. Not available on all platforms.

---

wait   Process.wait → *int*

Waits for any child process to exit and returns the process ID of that child. Also sets $? to the Process::Status object containing information on that process. Raises a SystemError if there are no child processes. Not available on all platforms.

```
Process.fork { exit 99 } # => 24046
Process.wait             # => 24046
$?.exitstatus            # => 99
```

---

waitall   Process.waitall → [[*pid1,status*], ...]

Waits for all children, returning an array of *pid/status* pairs (where *status* is an object of class Process::Status).

```
fork { sleep 0.2; exit 2 } # => 24049
fork { sleep 0.1; exit 1 } # => 24050
fork {          exit 0 } # => 24051
Process.waitall            # => [[24051, #<Process::Status: pid 24051 exit 0>],
                           # .. [24050, #<Process::Status: pid 24050 exit 1>],
                           # .. [24049, #<Process::Status: pid 24049 exit 2>]]
```

---

wait2   Process.wait2 → [*pid, status*]

Waits for any child process to exit and returns an array containing the process ID and the exit status (a Process::Status object) of that child. Raises a SystemError if no child processes exist.

```
Process.fork { exit 99 } # => 24054
pid, status = Process.wait2
pid                      # => 24054
status.exitstatus        # => 99
```

waitpid

Process.waitpid(*pid, int=0*) → *pid*

Waits for a child process to exit depending on the value of *pid*:

< -1	Any child whose progress group ID equals the absolute value of *pid*
-1	Any child (equivalent to wait)
0	Any child whose process group ID equals that of the current process
> 0	The child with the given PID

int may be a logical or of the flag values Process::WNOHANG (do not block if no child available) or Process::WUNTRACED (return stopped children that haven't been reported). Not all flags are available on all platforms, but a flag value of zero will work on all platforms.

```
include Process
pid = fork { sleep 2 }       # => 24057
Time.now                     # => 2013-05-27 12:32:49 -0500
waitpid(pid, Process::WNOHANG) # => nil
Time.now                     # => 2013-05-27 12:32:49 -0500
waitpid(pid, 0)              # => 24057
Time.now                     # => 2013-05-27 12:32:51 -0500
```

waitpid2

Process.waitpid2(*pid, int=0*) → [*pid, status*]

Waits for the given child process to exit, returning that child's process ID and exit status (a Process::Status object). *int* may be a logical or of the values Process::WNOHANG (do not block if no child available) or Process::WUNTRACED (return stopped children that haven't been reported). Not all flags are available on all platforms, but a flag value of zero will work on all platforms.

Module Process::GID

Provides a higher-level (and more portable) interface to the underlying operating system's concepts of real, effective, and saved group IDs. Discussing the semantics of these IDs is well beyond the scope of this book; readers who want to know more should consult POSIX documentation or read the intro(2) man pages on a recent Unix platform. All these methods throw NotImplementedError if the host operating does not support a sufficient set of calls. The descriptions that follow are based on notes in ruby-talk:76218 by Hidetoshi Nagai.

Class Methods

change_privilege

Process::GID.change_privilege(*gid*) → *gid*

Sets the real, effective, and saved group IDs to *gid*, raising an exception on failure (in which case the state of the IDs is not known). This method is not compatible with Process.gid=.

eid

Process::GID.eid → *egid*

Returns the effective group ID for this process. Synonym for Process.egid.

---

eid=   Process::GID.eid = *egid*

Synonym for Process::GID.grant_privilege.

---

grant_privilege   Process::GID.grant_privilege(*egid*) → *egid*

Sets the effective group ID to *egid*, raising an exception on failure. On some environments this may also change the saved group ID (see re_exchangeable?).

---

re_exchange   Process::GID.re_exchange → *egid*

Exchanges the real and effective group IDs, setting the saved group ID to the new effective group ID. Returns the new effective group ID.

---

re_exchangeable?   Process::GID.re_exchangeable → *true* or *false*

Returns true if real and effective group IDs can be exchanged on the host operating system and returns false otherwise.

---

rid   Process::GID.rid → *gid*

Returns the real group ID for this process. Synonym for Process.gid.

---

sid_available?   Process::GID.sid_available? → *true* or *false*

Returns true if the underlying platform supports saved group IDs and returns false otherwise. Currently, Ruby assumes support if the operating system has setresgid(2) or setegid(2) calls or if the configuration includes the POSIX_SAVED_IDS flag.

---

switch   Process::GID.switch → *egid*
                                                            Process::GID.switch { ... } → *obj*

Handles the toggling of group privilege. In the block form, automatically toggles the IDs back when the block terminates (but only if the block doesn't use other calls into Process::GID calls, which would interfere). Without a block, returns the original effective group ID.

Class **Process::Status**

Process::Status encapsulates the information on the status of a running or terminated system process. The built-in variable $? is either nil or a Process::Status object.

```
fork { exit 99 } # => 24060
Process.wait     # => 24060
$?.class         # => Process::Status
$?.to_i          # => 25344
$? >> 8          # => 99
$?.stopped?      # => false
$?.exited?       # => true
$?.exitstatus    # => 99
```

POSIX systems record information on processes using a 16-bit integer. The lower bits record the process status (stopped, exited, signaled), and the upper bits possibly contain additional information (for example, the program's return code in the case of exited processes). Before Ruby 1.8, these bits were exposed directly to the Ruby program. Ruby now encapsulates these in a Process::Status object. To maximize compatibility, however, these objects retain a bit-oriented interface. In the descriptions that follow, when we talk about the integer value of *stat*, we're referring to this 16-bit value.

Instance Methods

==	*stat* == *other* → *true* or *false*

Returns true if the integer value of *stat* equals *other*.

&	*stat* & *num* → *fixnum*

Logical AND of the bits in *stat* with *num*.

```
fork { exit 0x37 }
Process.wait
sprintf('%04x', $?.to_i)     # => "3700"
sprintf('%04x', $? & 0x1e00) # => "1600"
```

>>	*stat* >> *num* → *fixnum*

Shifts the bits in *stat* right *num* places.

```
fork { exit 99 } # => 24066
Process.wait     # => 24066
$?.to_i          # => 25344
$? >> 8          # => 99
```

coredump?	*stat*.coredump → *true* or *false*

Returns true if *stat* generated a core dump when it terminated. Not available on all platforms.

exited?	*stat*.exited? → *true* or *false*

Returns true if *stat* exited normally (for example using an exit call or finishing the program).

exitstatus	*stat*.exitstatus → *fixnum* or nil

Returns the least significant 8 bits of the return code of *stat*. Available only if exited? is true.

```
fork { }          # => 24069
Process.wait      # => 24069
$?.exited?        # => true
$?.exitstatus     # => 0

fork { exit 99 }  # => 24070
Process.wait      # => 24070
$?.exited?        # => true
$?.exitstatus     # => 99
```

---

pid

stat.pid → *fixnum*

Returns the ID of the process associated with this status object.

```
fork { exit } # => 24073
Process.wait  # => 24073
$?.pid        # => 24073
```

---

signaled?

stat.signaled? → *true* or *false*

Returns true if *stat* terminated because of an uncaught signal.

```
pid = fork { sleep 100 }
Process.kill(9, pid) # => 1
Process.wait         # => 24076
$?.signaled?         # => true
```

---

stopped?

stat.stopped? → *true* or *false*

Returns true if this process is stopped. This is returned only if the corresponding wait call had the WUNTRACED flag set.

---

success?

stat.success? → nil, or *true* or *false*

Returns true if *stat* refers to a process that exited successfully, returns false if it exited with a failure, and returns nil if *stat* does not refer to a process that has exited.

---

stopsig

stat.stopsig → *fixnum* or nil

Returns the number of the signal that caused *stat* to stop (or nil if self{} is not stopped).

---

termsig

stat.termsig → *fixnum* or nil

Returns the number of the signal that caused *stat* to terminate (or nil if self{} was not terminated by an uncaught signal).

---

to_i

stat.to_i → *fixnum*

Returns the bits in *stat* as a Fixnum. Poking around in these bits is platform dependent.

```
fork { exit 0xab }        # => 24079
Process.wait              # => 24079
sprintf('%04x', $?.to_i) # => "ab00"
```

---

to_s

stat.to_s → *string*

Equivalent to stat.to_i.to_s.

Process::Sys

Process::Sys provides system call–level access to the process user and group environment. Many of the calls are aliases of those in the Process module and are packaged here for completeness. See also Process::GID and Process::UID for a higher-level (and more portable) interface.

Class Methods

getegid
Process::Sys.getegid → gid

Returns the effective group ID for this process. Synonym for Process.egid.

geteuid
Process::Sys.getugid → uid

Returns the effective user ID for this process. Synonym for Process.euid.

getgid
Process::Sys.getgid → gid

Returns the group ID for this process. Synonym for Process.gid.

getuid
Process::Sys.getuid → uid

Returns the user ID for this process. Synonym for Process.uid.

issetugid
Process::Sys.issetugid → true or false

Returns true if this process was made setuid or setgid as a result of the last execve() system call and returns false if not. Raises NotImplementedError on systems that don't support issetugid(2).

setegid
Process::Sys.setegid(gid)

Sets the effective group ID to gid, failing if the underlying system call fails. Raises NotImplementedError on systems that don't support setegid(2).

seteuid
Process::Sys.seteuid(uid)

Sets the effective user ID to uid, failing if the underlying system call fails. Raises NotImplementedError on systems that don't support seteuid(2).

setgid
Process::Sys.setgid(gid)

Sets the group ID to gid, failing if the underlying system call fails. Raises NotImplementedError on systems that don't support setgid(2).

setregid
Process::Sys.setregid(rgid, egid)

Sets the real and effective group IDs to rgid and egid, failing if the underlying system call fails. Raises NotImplementedError on systems that don't support setregid(2).

---

setresgid   Process::Sys.setresgid(*rgid, egid, sgid*)

Sets the real, effective, and saved group IDs to *rgid*, *egid*, and *sgid*, failing if the underlying system call fails. Raises NotImplementedError on systems that don't support setresgid(2).

---

setresuid   Process::Sys.setresuid(*ruid, euid, suid*)

Sets the real, effective, and saved user IDs to *ruid*, *euid*, and *suid*, failing if the underlying system call fails. Raises NotImplementedError on systems that don't support setresuid(2).

---

setreuid   Process::Sys.setreuid(*ruid, euid*)

Sets the real and effective user IDs to *ruid* and *euid*, failing if the underlying system call fails. Raises NotImplementedError on systems that don't support setreuid(2).

---

setrgid   Process::Sys.setrgid(*rgid*)

Sets the real group ID to *rgid*, failing if the underlying system call fails. Raises NotImplementedError on systems that don't support setrgid(2).

---

setruid   Process::Sys.setruid(*ruid*)

Sets the real user ID to *ruid*, failing if the underlying system call fails. Raises NotImplementedError on systems that don't support setruid(2).

---

setuid   Process::Sys.setuid(*uid*)

Sets the user ID to *uid*, failing if the underlying system call fails. Raises NotImplementedError on systems that don't support setuid(2).

Module **Process::UID**

Provides a higher-level (and more portable) interface to the underlying operating system's concepts of real, effective, and saved user IDs. For more information, see the introduction to Process::GID on page 648.

Class Methods

change_privilege   Process::UID.change_privilege(*uid*) → *uid*

Sets the real, effective, and saved user IDs to *uid*, raising an exception on failure (in which case the state of the IDs is not known). Not compatible with Process.uid=.

---

eid   Process::UID.eid → *euid*

Returns the effective user ID for this process. Synonym for Process.euid.

eid=	Process::UID.eid = *euid*

Synonym for Process::UID.grant_privilege.

grant_privilege	Process::UID.grant_privilege(*euid*) → *euid*

Sets the effective user ID to *euid*, raising an exception on failure. On some environments this may also change the saved user ID.

re_exchange	Process::UID.re_exchange → *euid*

Exchanges the real and effective user IDs, setting the saved user ID to the new effective user ID. Returns the new effective user ID.

re_exchangeable?	Process::UID.re_exchangeable → *true* or *false*

Returns true if real and effective user IDs can be exchanged on the host operating system and returns false otherwise.

rid	Process::UID.rid → *uid*

Returns the real user ID for this process. Synonym for Process.uid.

sid_available?	Process::UID.sid_available? → *true* or *false*

Returns true if the underlying platform supports saved user IDs and returns false otherwise. Currently, Ruby assumes support if the operating system has setresuid(2) or seteuid(2) calls or if the configuration includes the POSIX_SAVED_IDS flag.

switch	Process::UID.switch → *euid*
	Process::UID.switch { ... } → *obj*

Handles the toggling of user privilege. In the block form, automatically toggles the IDs back when the block terminates (as long as the block doesn't use other Process::UID calls to interfere). Without a block, returns the original effective user ID.

Range

A Range represents an interval—a set of values with a start and an end. Ranges may be constructed using the s..e and s...e literals or using Range.new. Ranges constructed using .. run from the start to the end inclusively. Those created using ... exclude the end value. When used as an iterator, ranges return each value in the sequence.

```
(-1..-5).to_a   # => []
(-5..-1).to_a   # => [-5, -4, -3, -2, -1]
('a'..'e').to_a  # => ["a", "b", "c", "d", "e"]
('a'...'e').to_a # => ["a", "b", "c", "d"]
```

Ranges can be constructed using objects of any type, as long as the objects can be compared using their <=> operator and they support the succ method to return the next object in sequence.

```
class Xs                 # represent a string of 'x's
  include Comparable
  attr :length
  def initialize(n)
    @length = n
  end
  def succ
    Xs.new(@length + 1)
  end
  def <=>(other)
    @length <=> other.length
  end
  def inspect
    'x' * @length
  end
end

r = Xs.new(3)..Xs.new(6) # => xxx..xxxxxx
r.to_a                   # => [xxx, xxxx, xxxxx, xxxxxx]
r.member?(Xs.new(5))     # => true
```

In the previous code example, class Xs includes the Comparable module. This is because Enumerable#member? checks for equality using ==. Including Comparable ensures that the == method is defined in terms of the <=> method implemented in Xs.

Mixes In

Enumerable: all?, any?, chunk, collect, collect_concat, count, cycle, detect, drop, drop_while, each_cons, each_entry, each_slice, each_with_index, each_with_object, entries, find, find_all, find_index, first, flat_map, grep, group_by, include?, inject, lazy, map, max, max_by, member?, min, min_by, minmax, minmax_by, none?, one?, partition, reduce, reject, reverse_each, select, slice_before, sort, sort_by, take, take_while, to_a, zip

Class Methods

new   Range.new(*start, end, exclusive*=false) → *rng*

> Constructs a range using the given *start* and *end*. If the third parameter is omitted or is false, the range will include the end object; otherwise, it will be excluded.

Instance Methods

==   *rng* == *obj* → *true* or *false*

> Returns true if *obj* is a range whose beginning and end are the same as those in *rng* (compared using ==) and whose *exclusive* flag is the same as *rng*.

===   *rng* === *val* → *true* or *false*

> If *rng* excludes its end, returns *rng.start* ≤ *val* < *rng.end*. If *rng* is inclusive, returns *rng.start* ≤ *val* ≤ *rng.end*. Note that this implies that *val* need not be a member of the range itself (for example, a float could fall between the start and end values of a range of integers). Implemented by calling include?. Conveniently, the === operator is used by case statements.

```
case 74.95
when  1...50   then    puts "low"
when 50...75   then    puts "medium"
when 75...100 then    puts "high"
end
```

produces:

```
medium
```

begin   *rng*.begin → *obj*

> Returns the first object of *rng*.

bsearch   *rng*.bsearch { | val | ... } → *obj* or nil>

> The same basic functionality as Array#bsearch. However, the range variant is typically used to search for something outside the range itself. For example, the range values could be used as a parameter to a function, or to index into some other collection. Remember though that the value returned by that function or collection must increase as its parameter increases.

New in 2.0

> Here's a (poor) method that finds the number of binary digits required to represent a number:

```
def bit_size(n)
  (0...(8*n.size)).bsearch { |bitno| (1 << bitno) > n }
end

[ 0x05, 0x50, 0x5a010000 ].each do |n|
  printf "Bitsize of %b is %d\n", n, bit_size(n)
end
```

produces:

```
Bitsize of 101 is 3
Bitsize of 1010000 is 7
Bitsize of 1011010000000010000000000000000 is 31
```

And here's a somewhat surprising example that finds *x* for which *sin(x)* equals 0.5.

```
(0.0..Math::PI/2).bsearch {|x| Math.sin(x) >= 0.5} # => 0.5235987755982989
```

On my box, it has the answer correct to 1% within 14 iterations, and takes 62 iterations to find it to the limit of Float precision.

cover?   rng.cover?(*obj*) → *true* or *false*

Returns true if *obj* lies between the start and end of the range. For ranges defined with min..max, this means *min* ≤ *obj* ≤ *max*. For ranges defined with min...max, it means *min* ≤ *obj* < *max*.

```
(1..10).cover?(0)   # => false
(1..10).cover?(5)   # => true
(1..10).cover?(9.5) # => true
(1..10).cover?(10)  # => true
(1...10).cover?(10) # => false
```

each   rng.each { |i| ... } → *rng*

Iterates over the elements *rng*, passing each in turn to the block. Successive elements are generated using the succ method.

```
(10..15).each do |n|
  print n, ' '
end
```

produces:

```
10 11 12 13 14 15
```

end   rng.end → *obj*

Returns the object that defines the end of *rng*.

```
(1..10).end  # => 10
(1...10).end # => 10
```

eql?   rng.eql?(*obj*) → *true* or *false*

Returns true if *obj* is a range whose beginning and end are the same as those in *rng* (compared using eql?) and whose *exclusive* flag is the same as *rng*.

exclude_end?   rng.exclude_end? → *true* or *false*

Returns true if *rng* excludes its end value.

first   rng.first(*n* = 1) → *obj* or *array*

Returns the first (or first *n*) elements of *rng*.

```
('aa'..'bb').first    # => "aa"
('aa'..'bb').first(5) # => ["aa", "ab", "ac", "ad", "ae"]
```

include?

rng.include?(val) → true or false

Returns true if *val* is one of the values in *rng* (that is, if Range#each would return *val* at some point). If the range is defined to span numbers, this method returns true if the value lies between the start and end of the range, even if it is not actually a member (that is, it has the same behavior as Range#cover?). Otherwise, the parameter must be a member of the range.

```
r = 1..10
r.include?(5)       # => true
r.include?(5.5)     # => true
r.include?(10)      # => true
r = 1...10
r.include?(10)      # => false
r = 'a'..'z'
r.include?('b')     # => true
r.include?('ruby')  # => false
```

last

rng.last(n = 1) → obj or array

Returns the last (or last *n*) elements of *rng*.

```
('aa'..'bb').last    # => "bb"
('aa'..'bb').last(5) # => ["ax", "ay", "az", "ba", "bb"]
```

max

rng.max → obj
rng.max { | a,b | ... } → obj

Returns the maximum value in the range. The block is used to compare values if present.

```
(-3..2).max                       # => 2
(-3..2).max {|a,b| a*a <=> b*b }  # => -3
```

member?

rng.member?(val) → true or false

Synonym for Range#include?.

min

rng.min → obj
rng.min { | a,b | ... } → obj

Returns the minimum value in the range. The block is used to compare values if present.

```
(-3..2).min                       # => -3
(-3..2).min {|a,b| a*a <=> b*b }  # => 0
```

size

rng.size → int or nil

Returns the number of elements in *rng*. In Ruby 2.0, only works for ranges of integers.

New in 2.0

```
(1..26).size    # => 26
('a'..'z').size # => nil
```

step

rng.step(*n*=1) ‹{ | obj | ... }› → *rng* or *enum*

Iterates over *rng*, passing each nth element to the block. If the range contains numbers, addition by one is used to generate successive elements. Otherwise, step invokes succ to iterate through range elements. If no block is given, an enumerator is returned. The following code uses class Xs defined at the start of this section:

```
range = Xs.new(1)..Xs.new(10)
range.step(2) {|x| p x}
enum = range.step(3)
p enum.to_a
```

produces:

```
x
xxx
xxxxx
xxxxxxx
xxxxxxxxx
[x, xxxx, xxxxxxx, xxxxxxxxx]
```

Here's step with numbers:

```
(1..5).step(1).to_a        # => [1, 2, 3, 4, 5]
(1..5).step(2).to_a        # => [1, 3, 5]
(1..5).step(1.5).to_a      # => [1.0, 2.5, 4.0]
(1.0..5.0).step(1).to_a    # => [1.0, 2.0, 3.0, 4.0, 5.0]
(1.0..5.0).step(2).to_a    # => [1.0, 3.0, 5.0]
(1.0..5.0).step(1.5).to_a # => [1.0, 2.5, 4.0]
```

Class · Random

A random number generator, based on the Mersenne Twister MT19937 (the period is $2^{19937}-1$). The global rand and srand methods are wrappers for this class.

Class Methods

new   Random.new(‹ *seed*=Random.new_seed ›) → *rand*

Creates a new random random number generator with the given seed. The seed will be converted to an integer.

new_seed   Random.new_seed → *bignum*

Returns a number that can be used as a seed. The value is derived from a system random number generator if available; otherwise, it combines the time, the process ID, and a sequence number.

```
Random.new_seed # => 205460400778463129775182461758071944669
```

rand   Random.rand(*max*=0) → *number*
                                                 Random.rand(*range*) → *number*

Synonym for Object#rand on page 622.

srand   Random.rand(*seed*) → *old_seed*

Synonym for Object#srand on page 628.

Instance Methods

bytes   *rand*.bytes(*length*) → *string*

Returns a binary-encoded string, *length* bytes long, containing random bits.

```
rand = Random.new
rand.bytes(10) # => "T\xAEP\xD5\0\xAD\x7F\x84b\xC9"
```

rand   *rand*.rand(*max*=0) → *number*
                                                 rand.rand(*range*) → *number*

Converts *max* to an integer using max_1 = max.to_i.abs. If the result is zero or nil, returns a pseudorandom floating-point number greater than or equal to 0.0 and less than 1.0. Otherwise, returns a pseudorandom integer greater than or equal to zero and less than max_1. If a range is passed, return a random number in that range.

seed   *rand*.seed → *bignum*

Returns the seed for this random number generator.

Rational < Numeric

Rational numbers are expressed as the ratio of two integers. When the denominator exactly divides the numerator, a rational number is effectively an integer. Rationals allow exact representation of fractional numbers, but some real values cannot be expressed exactly and so cannot be represented as rationals.

Class Rational is normally relatively independent of the other numeric classes, in that the result of dividing two integers with the / operator will normally be a (truncated) integer (the quo method will always return a rational result). However, if the mathn library is loaded into a program, integer division may generate a Rational result. Also see the rational library on page 794 for additional methods on rational numbers.

```
r1 = Rational("1/2")    # => 1/2
r2 = 4.quo(5)           # => 4/5
r1 * r2                 # => 2/5
```

Instance Methods

Arithmetic operations

Performs various arithmetic operations on *rat*.

rat	+	*numeric*	Addition
rat	-	*numeric*	Subtraction
rat	*	*numeric*	Multiplication
rat	/	*numeric*	Division
rat	%	*numeric*	Modulo
rat	**	*numeric*	Exponentiation
rat	-@		Unary minus

Comparisons

Compares *rat* to other numbers: <, <=, ==, >=, and >.

<=>   *rat* <=> *numeric* → -1, 0, +1, or nil

Comparison—Returns -1, 0, or +1 depending on whether *rat* is less than, equal to, or greater than *numeric*. Although Rational's grandparent mixes in Comparable, Rational does not use that module for performing comparisons, instead implementing the comparison operators explicitly.

```
Rational("4/2") <=> Rational("98/49") # => 0
Rational("3/4") <=> 41                # => -1
Rational("0") <=> 0.0                 # => 0
```

==   *rat* == *numeric*

Returns true if *rat* has the same value as *numeric*. Comparisons against integers and rational numbers are exact; comparisons against floats first convert *rat* to a float.

ceil

rat.ceil → *numeric*

Returns the smallest integer greater than or equal to *rat*.

```
Rational("22/7").ceil   # => 4
Rational("-22/7").ceil  # => -3
```

denominator

rat.denominator → *a_number*

Returns the denominator of *rat*.

```
Rational("2/3").denominator  # => 3
```

fdiv

rat.fdiv(*numeric*) → *float*

Returns the floating-point result of dividing *rat* by *numeric*.

```
Rational("11/2") / 2      # => 11/4
Rational("11/2").fdiv 2   # => 2.75
```

floor

rat.floor → *numeric*

Returns the largest integer less than or equal to *rat*.

```
Rational("22/7").floor   # => 3
Rational("-22/7").floor  # => -4
```

numerator

rat.numerator → *a_number*

Returns the numerator of *rat*.

```
Rational("2/3").numerator  # => 2
```

quo

rat.quo(*numeric*) → *numeric*

Synonym for Rational#/.

rationalize

rat.rationalize → *rat*
rat.rationalize(*epsilon*) → *rational*

With no argument, returns *rat*; otherwise, returns a new Rational with the given precision.

```
r = Math::PI.to_r    # => (884279719003555/281474976710656)
r.rationalize        # => (884279719003555/281474976710656)
r.rationalize(0.01)  # => (22/7)
```

round

rat.round → *numeric*

Rounds *rat* to the nearest integer.

```
Rational("22/7").round   # => 3
Rational("-22/7").round  # => -3
```

---

to_f   *rat*.to_f → *float*

Returns the floating-point representation of *rat*.

```
Rational("37/4").to_f # => 9.25
```

---

to_i   *rat*.to_i → *integer*

Returns the truncated integer value of *rat*.

```
Rational("19/10").to_i  # => 1
Rational("-19/10").to_i # => -1
```

---

to_r   *rat*.to_r → *rat*

Returns *rat*.

---

truncate   *rat*.truncate → *numeric*

Returns *rat* truncated to an integer.

```
Rational("22/7").truncate  # => 3
Rational("-22/7").truncate # => -3
```

Regexp

A Regexp holds a regular expression, used to match a pattern against strings. Regexps are created using the /.../ and %r{...} literals and using the Regexp.new constructor. See the reference on in *Regular Expressions*, on page 303 for more details.

Class Constants

EXTENDED	Ignores spaces and newlines in regexp
IGNORECASE	Matches are case insensitive
MULTILINE	Newlines treated as any other character

Class Methods

compile

Regexp.compile(*pattern* ‹, *options* ‹, *lang* › ›) → *rxp*

Synonym for Regexp.new.

escape

Regexp.escape(*string*) → *escaped_string*

Escapes any characters that would have special meaning in a regular expression. For any string, Regexp.new(Regexp.escape(str)) =~ str will be true.

```
Regexp.escape('\\[]*?{}.')    # => \\\[\]\*\?\{\}\.
```

last_match

Regexp.last_match → *match*
Regexp.last_match(*int*) → *string*

The first form returns the MatchData object generated by the last successful pattern match. This is equivalent to reading the global variable $~. MatchData has its own reference on page 559.

The second form returns the nth field in this MatchData object.

```
/c(.)t/ =~ 'cat'      # => 0
Regexp.last_match     # => #<MatchData "cat" 1:"a">
Regexp.last_match(0)  # => "cat"
Regexp.last_match(1)  # => "a"
Regexp.last_match(2)  # => nil
```

new

Regexp.new(*string* ‹, *options* ‹, *lang* › ›) → *rxp*
Regexp.new(*regexp*) → *new_regexp*

Constructs a new regular expression from the *string* or the *regexp*. In the latter case, that regexp's options are propagated, and new options may not be specified. If *options* is a number, it should be one or more of Regexp::EXTENDED, Regexp::IGNORECASE, or Regexp::MULTILINE, *or*-ed together. Otherwise, if the *options* parameter is not nil, the regexp will be case insensitive. The *lang* can be set to "N" or "n" to force the regular expression to have ASCII-8BIT encoding;[3] otherwise, the encoding of the string determines the encoding of the regular expression.

---

3. No other values are accepted as of Ruby 1.9.

```
# encoding: utf-8
r1 = Regexp.new('^[a-z]+:\\s+\w+')      # => /^[a-z]+:\s+\w+/
r2 = Regexp.new('cat', true)            # => /cat/i
r3 = Regexp.new('dog', Regexp::EXTENDED) # => /dog/x
r4 = Regexp.new(r2)                     # => /cat/i
r5 = Regexp.new("∂elta")                # => /∂elta/
r1.encoding                             # => #<Encoding:US-ASCII>
r5.encoding                             # => #<Encoding:UTF-8>
```

---

quote   Regexp.quote(*string*) → *escaped_string*

Synonym for Regexp.escape.

---

try_convert   Regexp.try_convert(*obj*) → *a_regexp* or nil

If *obj* is not already a regular expression, attempts to convert it to one by calling its to_regexp method. Returns nil if no conversion could be made.

```
Regexp.try_convert("cat") # => nil
class String
  def to_regexp
    Regexp.new(self)
  end
end
Regexp.try_convert("cat") # => /cat/
```

---

union   Regexp.union(‹ pattern ›*) → *a_regexp*

Returns a regular expression that will match any of the given patterns. With no patterns, produces a regular expression that will never match. If a pattern is a string, it will be given the default regular expression options. If a pattern is a regular expression, its options will be honored in the final pattern. The patterns may also be passed in a single array.

```
Regexp.union("cat")        # => /cat/
Regexp.union("cat", "dog") # => /cat|dog/
Regexp.union(%w{ cat dog }) # => /cat|dog/
Regexp.union("cat", /dog/i) # => /cat|(?i-mx:dog)/
```

Instance Methods

==   *rxp* == *other_regexp* → *true* or *false*

Equality—Two regexps are equal if their patterns are identical, they have the same character set code, and their casefold? values are the same.

```
/abc/  == /abc/x # => false
/abc/  == /abc/i # => false
/abc/u == /abc/n # => false
```

=== $rxp === string \rightarrow true$ or $false$

Case Equality—Like Regexp#=~ but accepts nonstring arguments (returning false). Used in case statements.

```
a = "HELLO"
case a
when /\A[a-z]*\z/; print "Lower case\n"
when /\A[A-Z]*\z/; print "Upper case\n"
else               print "Mixed case\n"
end
```

produces:

```
Upper case
```

=~ $rxp =~ string \rightarrow int$ or nil

Match—Matches *rxp* against *string*, returning the offset of the start of the match or nil if the match failed. Sets $~ to the corresponding MatchData or nil.

```
/SIT/  =~ "insensitive" # => nil
/SIT/i =~ "insensitive" # => 5
```

~ $\sim rxp \rightarrow int$ or nil

Match—Matches *rxp* against the contents of $_. Equivalent to rxp =~ $_. You should be ashamed if you use this:

```
$_ = "input data"
~ /at/    # => 7
```

---

casefold? rxp.casefold? $\rightarrow true$ or $false$

Returns the value of the case-insensitive flag. Merely setting the i option inside *rxp* does not set this flag.

```
/cat/.casefold?      # => false
/cat/i.casefold?     # => true
/(?i:cat)/.casefold? # => false
```

---

encoding rxp.encoding $\rightarrow an\_encoding$

Returns the character encoding for the regexp.

```
/cat/.encoding  # => #<Encoding:US-ASCII>
/cat/s.encoding # => #<Encoding:Windows-31J>
/cat/u.encoding # => #<Encoding:UTF-8>
```

---

fixed_encoding? rxp.fixed_encoding? $\rightarrow true$ or $false$

A regular expression containing only 7-bit characters can be matched against a string in any encoding. In this case, fixed_encoding? returns false. Otherwise, it returns true.

```
/cat/.fixed_encoding?  # => false
/cat/s.fixed_encoding? # => true
/cat/u.fixed_encoding? # => true
```

---

match   *rxp*.match(*string, offset=0*) → *match* or nil

rxp.match(*string, offset=0*) { | match | ... } → *obj*

Returns a MatchData object describing the match or nil if there was no match. This is equivalent to retrieving the value of the special variable $~ following a normal match. The match process will start at *offset* into *string*. If a block is given and the match is successful, the block will be invoked with the MatchData object, and the value returned by the block will be the value returned by match.

```
md = /(.)(d)(.)/.match("abcdefabcdef")
md          # => #<MatchData "cde" 1:"c" 2:"d" 3:"e">
md[1]       # => "c"
md.begin(1) # => 2
md = /(.)(d)(.)/.match("abcdedcba", 4)
md          # => #<MatchData "edc" 1:"e" 2:"d" 3:"c">
md.begin(1) # => 4

result = /(...)...(...)/.match("catanddog") do |md|
  md[1] + "&" + md[2]
end
result      # => "cat&dog"
```

---

named_captures   *rxp*.named_captures → *hash*

Returns a hash whose keys are the names of captures and whose values are each an array containing the number of the capture in *rxp*.

```
/(?<a>.).(?<b>.)/.named_captures         # => {"a"=>[1], "b"=>[2]}
/(?<a>.)(.)(?<b>.)/.named_captures       # => {"a"=>[1], "b"=>[2]}
/(?<a>.)(?<b>.)(?<a>.)/.named_captures # => {"a"=>[1, 3], "b"=>[2]}
```

---

names   *rxp*.names → *array*

Returns an array containing the names of captures in *rxp*.

```
/(.)(.)(.)/.names                 # => []
/(?<first>.).(?<last>.)/.names # => ["first", "last"]
```

---

options   *rxp*.options → *int*

Returns the set of bits corresponding to the options used when creating this regexp (see Regexp.new for details). Note that additional bits may be set in the returned options; these are used internally by the regular expression code. These extra bits are ignored if the options are passed to Regexp.new.

```
# Let's see what the values are...
Regexp::IGNORECASE                # => 1
Regexp::EXTENDED                  # => 2
Regexp::MULTILINE                 # => 4
```

```
/cat/.options                  # => 0
/cat/ix.options                # => 3
Regexp.new('cat', true).options   # => 1
Regexp.new('cat', 0, 'n').options # => 32

r = /cat/ix
Regexp.new(r.source, r.options)   # => /cat/ix
```

---

source   *rxp*.source → *string*

Returns the original string of the pattern.

```
/ab+c/ix.source # => "ab+c"
```

---

to_s   *rxp*.to_s → *string*

Returns a string containing the regular expression and its options (using the (?xx:yyy) notation). This string can be fed back into Regexp.new to a regular expression with the same semantics as the original. (However, Regexp#== may not return true when comparing the two, because the source of the regular expression itself may differ, as the example shows.) Regexp#inspect produces a generally more readable version of *rxp*.

```
r1 = /ab+c/ix       # => /ab+c/ix
s1 = r1.to_s        # => "(?ix-m:ab+c)"
r2 = Regexp.new(s1) # => /(?ix-m:ab+c)/
r1 == r2            # => false
r1.source           # => "ab+c"
r2.source           # => "(?ix-m:ab+c)"
```

Module **Signal**

Many operating systems allow signals to be sent to running processes. Some signals have a defined effect on the process, and others may be trapped at the code level and acted upon. For example, your process may trap the USR1 signal and use it to toggle debugging, and it may use TERM to initiate a controlled shutdown.

```
pid = fork do
  Signal.trap("USR1") do
    $debug = !$debug
    puts "Debug now: #$debug"
  end
  Signal.trap(:TERM) do    # symbols work too...
    puts "Terminating..."
    exit
  end
  # . . . do some work . . .
end

Process.detach(pid)

# Controlling program:
Process.kill("USR1", pid)
# ...
Process.kill(:USR1, pid)
# ...
Process.kill("TERM", pid)
```

produces:

```
Debug now: true
Debug now: false
Terminating...
```

The list of available signal names and their interpretation is system dependent. Signal delivery semantics may also vary between systems; in particular, signal delivery may not always be reliable.

Class Methods

list   Signal.list → *hash*

Returns a list of signal names mapped to the corresponding underlying signal numbers.

```
Signal.list # => {"ABRT"=>6, "ALRM"=>14, "BUS"=>10, "CHLD"=>20, "CLD"=>20,
            # .. "CONT"=>19, "EMT"=>7, "EXIT"=>0, "FPE"=>8, "HUP"=>1, "ILL"=>4,
            # .. "INFO"=>29, "INT"=>2, "IO"=>23, "IOT"=>6, "KILL"=>9, "PIPE"=>13,
            # .. "PROF"=>27, "QUIT"=>3, "SEGV"=>11, "STOP"=>17, "SYS"=>12,
            # .. "TERM"=>15, "TRAP"=>5, "TSTP"=>18, "TTIN"=>21, "TTOU"=>22,
            # .. "URG"=>16, "USR1"=>30, "USR2"=>31, "VTALRM"=>26, "WINCH"=>28,
            # .. "XCPU"=>24, "XFSZ"=>25}
```

signame

Signal.signame(num) → string

Return the (abbreviated) name of the signal with the given number. An ArgumentError is raised if the number does not correspond to a signal.

New in 2.0

```
Signal.signame(1)  # => "HUP"
Signal.signame(15) # => "TERM"
```

trap

Signal.trap(signal, command) → obj
Signal.trap(signal) { … } → obj

Specifies the handling of signals. The first parameter is a signal name (a string or symbol such as SIGALRM, SIGUSR1, and so on) or a signal number. The characters SIG may be omitted from the signal name. The command or block specifies code to be run when the signal is raised. If the command is nil, the string IGNORE or SIG_IGN, or the empty string, the signal will be ignored. If the command is DEFAULT or SIG_DFL, the operating system's default handler will be invoked. If the command is EXIT, the script will be terminated by the signal. Otherwise, the given command or block will be run.

The special signal name EXIT or signal number zero will be invoked just prior to program termination.

Trap cannot be used with the signals BUS, FPE, ILL, SEGV, or VTALRM.

New in 2.0

trap returns the previous handler for the given signal.

```
Signal.trap(0, lambda { |signo| puts "exit pid #{$$} with #{signo}" })
Signal.trap("CLD")    { |signo| puts "Child died (#{signo})" }
if fork   # parent
  do_something # ...
else
  puts "In child, PID=#{$$}"
end
```

produces:

```
In child, PID=24189
exit pid 24189 with 0
Child died (20)
exit pid 24188 with 0
```

Note that you must specify a block taking a parameter if you use lambda to create the proc object.

String

A String object holds and manipulates a sequence of characters. String objects may be created using String.new or as literals (see *Strings*, on page 300).

Because of aliasing issues, users of strings should be aware of the methods that modify the contents of a String object. Typically, methods with names ending in ! modify their receiver, while those without a ! return a new String. However, exceptions exist, such as String#[]=.

In this description, I try to differentiate between the bytes in a string and the characters in a string. Internally, a string is a sequence of 8-bit bytes. These are represented externally as small Fixnums. At the same time, these byte sequences are interpreted as a sequence of characters. This interpretation is controlled by the encoding of the string. In some encodings (such as US-ASCII and ISO-8859), each byte corresponds to a single character. In other encodings (such as UTF-8), a varying number of bytes comprise each character.

As of Ruby 1.9, String no longer mixes in Enumerable.

Mixes In

Comparable: <, <=, ==, >, >=, between?

Class Methods

new   String.new(*val=""*) → *str*

Returns a new string object containing a copy of *val* (which should be a String or implement to_str). Note that the new string object is created only when one of the strings is modified.

```ruby
str1 = "wibble"
str2 = String.new(str1)
str1.object_id # => 70198849846720
str2.object_id # => 70198849846680
str1[1] = "o"
str1           # => "wobble"
str2           # => "wibble"
```

try_convert   String.try_convert(*obj*) → *a_string* or nil

If *obj* is not already a string, attempts to convert it to one by calling its to_str method. Returns nil if no conversion could be made.

```ruby
String.try_convert("cat") # => "cat"
String.try_convert(0xbee) # => nil
```

Instance Methods

%   *str* % *arg* → *string*

Format—Uses *str* as a format specification and returns the result of applying it to *arg*. If the format specification contains more than one substitution, then *arg* must be an Array containing the values to be substituted. See Object#sprintf on page 626 for details of the format string.

```
puts "%05d" % 123
puts "%-5s: %08x" % [ "ID", self.object_id ]
puts "%-5<name>s: %08<value>x" % { name: "ID", value: self.object_id }
```

produces:

```
00123
ID    : 3ff795471248
ID    : 3ff795471248
```

---

*   *str * int → string*

Copies—Returns a new String containing *int* copies of the receiver.

```
"Ho! " * 3 # => "Ho! Ho! Ho! "
```

+   *str + string → string*

Concatenation—Returns a new String containing *string* concatenated to *str*. If both strings contain non-7-bit characters, their encodings must be compatible.

```
"Hello from " + "RubyLand" # => "Hello from RubyLand"
```

<<   *str << fixnum → str*
                                                                              str << obj → str

Append—Concatenates the given object to *str*. If the object is a Fixnum, it is considered to be a codepoint in the encoding of *str* and converted to the appropriate character before being appended.

```
a = "hello world"
a.force_encoding("utf-8")
a << 33         # => "hello world!"
a << " Says the " # => "hello world! Says the "
a << 8706        # => "hello world! Says the ∂"
a << "og"        # => "hello world! Says the ∂og"
```

<=>   *str <=> other_string → -1, 0, +1, or nil*

Comparison—Returns -1 if *str* is less than, 0 if *str* is equal to, and +1 if *str* is greater than *other_string*. If the strings are of different lengths and the strings are equal when compared to the shortest length, then the longer string is considered greater than the shorter one. In older versions of Ruby, setting $= allowed case-insensitive comparisons; you must now use String#casecmp.

<=> is the basis for the methods <, <=, >, >=, and between?, included from module Comparable. The method String#== does not use Comparable#==.

```
"abcdef" <=> "abcde"   # => 1
"abcdef" <=> "abcdef"  # => 0
"abcdef" <=> "abcdefg" # => -1
"abcdef" <=> "ABCDEF"  # => 1
```

== *str == obj → true* or *false*

Equality—If *obj* is a String, returns true if *str* has the same encoding, length, and content as *obj*; returns false otherwise. If *obj* is not a String but responds to to_str, returns *obj == str*; otherwise, returns false.

```
"abcdef" == "abcde"  # => false
"abcdef" == "abcdef" # => true
```

=~ *str =~ regexp → int* or *nil*

Match—Equivalent to regexp =~ str. Prior versions of Ruby permitted an arbitrary operand to =~; this is now deprecated. Returns the position where the match starts or returns nil if there is no match or if *regexp* is not a regular expression.[4]

```
"cat o' 9 tails" =~ /\d/ # => 7
"cat o' 9 tails" =~ 9    # => nil

"cat o' 9 tails" =~ "\d"
```

produces:

```
        from prog.rb:1:in `<main>'
prog.rb:1:in `=~': type mismatch: String given (TypeError)
```

[ ]
str[int] → string or *nil*
str[int, int] → string or *nil*
str[range] → string or *nil*
str[regexp] → string or *nil*
str[regexp, int] → string or *nil*
str[regexp, name] → string or *nil*
str[string] → string or *nil*

Element Reference—If passed a single *int*, returns the character at that position. (Prior to Ruby 1.9, an integer character code was returned.) If passed two *ints*, returns a substring starting at the offset given by the first, and a length given by the second. If given a range, a substring containing characters at offsets given by the range is returned. In all three cases, if an offset is negative, it is counted from the end of *str*. Returns nil if the initial offset falls outside the string and the length is not given, the length is negative, or the beginning of the range is greater than the end.

If *regexp* is supplied, the matching portion of *str* is returned. If a numeric parameter follows the regular expression, that component of the MatchData is returned instead. If a String is given, that string is returned if it occurs in *str*. If a name follows the regular expression, the corresponding named match is returned. In all cases, nil is returned if there is no match.

```
a = "hello there"
a[1]                        # => "e"
a[1,3]                      # => "ell"
a[1..3]                     # => "ell"
a[1...3]                    # => "el"
```

---

4. Except for a strange corner case. If *regexp* is a string or can be coerced into a string, a TypeError exception is raised.

```
a[-3,2]                         # => "er"
a[-4..-2]                       # => "her"
a[-2..-4]                       # => ""
a[/[aeiou](.)\1/]               # => "ell"
a[/[aeiou](.)\1/, 0]            # => "ell"
a[/[aeiou](.)\1/, 1]            # => "l"
a[/[aeiou](.)\1/, 2]            # => nil
a[/(..)e/]                      # => "the"
a[/(..)e/, 1]                   # => "th"
a[/(?<vowel>[aeiou])/, :vowel]  # => "e"
a["lo"]                         # => "lo"
a["bye"]                        # => nil
```

[ ]=

str[int] = string
str[int, int] = string
str[range] = string
str[regexp] = string
str[regexp, int] = string
str[string] = string}

Element Assignment—Replaces some or all of the content of *str*. The portion of the string affected is determined using the same criteria as String#[ ]. If the replacement string is not the same length as the text it is replacing, the string will be adjusted accordingly. If the regular expression or string is used because the index doesn't match a position in the string, IndexError is raised. If the regular expression form is used, the optional second *int* allows you to specify which portion of the match to replace (effectively using the MatchData indexing rules). The forms that take a Fixnum will raise an IndexError if the value is out of range; the Range form will raise a RangeError, and the Regexp and String forms will silently ignore the assignment.

```
a = "hello"
a[2] = "u"                      (a → "heulo")
a[2, 4] = "xyz"                 (a → "hexyz")
a[-4, 2] = "xyz"                (a → "hxyzlo")
a[2..4] = "xyz"                 (a → "hexyz")
a[-4..-2] = "xyz"               (a → "hxyzo")
a[/[aeiou](.)\1(.)/] = "xyz"    (a → "hxyz")
a[/[aeiou](.)\1(.)/, 1] = "xyz" (a → "hexyzlo")
a[/[aeiou](.)\1(.)/, 2] = "xyz" (a → "hellxyz")
a["l"] = "xyz"                  (a → "hexyzlo")
a["ll"] = "xyz"                 (a → "hexyzo")
a[2, 0] = "xyz"                 (a → "hexyzllo")
```

ascii_only?

str.ascii_only? → true or *false*

Returns true if the string contains no characters with a character code greater than 127 (that is, it contains only 7-bit ASCII characters).

```
# encoding: utf-8
"dog".ascii_only?          # => true
"∂og".ascii_only?          # => false
"\x00 to \x7f".ascii_only? # => true
```

---

b
str.b → *string*

New in 2.0

Returns a copy of the contents of *str* with ASCII-8BIT encoding. This is a convenient way to get to the byte values of any string.

```
str = "∂øg"
str.length  # => 3

bstr = str.b
bstr.length # => 6
```

---

bytes
str.bytes → *enum* | *array*
str.bytes { | byte | ... } → *str*

New in 2.0

Returns an enumerator (Ruby 1.9) or array (Ruby 2.0) for the bytes (integers in the range 0 to 255) in *str*. With a block, passes each byte to the block and returns the original string. See also String#codepoints and #chars.

```
# encoding: utf-8
"dog".bytes                     # => [100, 111, 103]
"∂og".bytes                     # => [226, 136, 130, 111, 103]
result = []
"∂og".bytes {|b| result << b } # => "∂og"
result                          # => [226, 136, 130, 111, 103]
```

---

bytesize
str.bytesize → *int*

Returns the number of bytes (not characters) in *str*. See also String#length.

```
# encoding: utf-8
"dog".length    # => 3
"dog".bytesize  # => 3
"∂og".length    # => 3
"∂og".bytesize # => 5
```

---

byteslice
str.byteslice(*offset, length*=1) → *string* or nil
str.byteslice(*range*) → *string* or nil

Returns the string consisting of *length* bytes starting at byte position *offset,* or between the offsets given by the range. A negative offset counts from the end of the string. The returned string retains the encoding of *str,* but may not be valid in that encoding.

```
# encoding: utf-8
a = "∂dog"
a.bytes.to_a        # => [226, 136, 130, 100, 111, 103]
a.byteslice(0)      # => "\xE2"
a.byteslice(0, 2)   # => "\xE2\x88"
```

```
a.byteslice(0, 3)    # => "∂"
a.byteslice(-2, 2)   # => "og"
a.byteslice(-2..-1)  # => "og"
```

capitalize

str.capitalize → *string*

Returns a copy of *str* with the first character converted to uppercase and the remainder to lowercase.

```
"hello world".capitalize # => "Hello world"
"HELLO WORLD".capitalize # => "Hello world"
"123ABC".capitalize      # => "123abc"
```

capitalize!

str.capitalize! → *str* or nil

Modifies *str* by converting the first character to uppercase and the remainder to lowercase. Returns nil if no changes are made.

```
a = "hello world"
a.capitalize! # => "Hello world"
a             # => "Hello world"
a.capitalize! # => nil
```

casecmp

str.casecmp(*string*) → -1, 0, +1

Case-insensitive version of String#<=>.

```
"abcdef".casecmp("abcde")   # => 1
"abcdef".casecmp("abcdef")  # => 0
"aBcDeF".casecmp("abcdef")  # => 0
"abcdef".casecmp("abcdefg") # => -1
"abcdef".casecmp("ABCDEF")  # => 0
```

center

str.center(*int*, *pad*=" ") → *string*

If *int* is greater than the length of *str*, returns a new String of length *int* with *str* centered between the given padding (defaults to spaces); otherwise, returns *str*.

```
"hello".center(4)          # => "hello"
"hello".center(20)         # => "       hello        "
"hello".center(4, "_-^-")  # => "hello"
"hello".center(20, "_-^-") # => "_-^_-^hello_-^_-^_-"
"hello".center(20, "-")    # => "-------hello--------"
```

chars

str.chars → *enum* | *array*
str.chars { | char | ... } → *str*

Returns an enumerator (Ruby 1.9) or array (Ruby 2.0) for the characters (single character strings) in *str*. With a block, passes each character to the block and returns the original string. See also String#bytes and String#codepoints.

New in 2.0

```
# encoding: utf-8
"dog".chars.to_a              # => ["d", "o", "g"]
"∂og".chars.to_a              # => ["∂", "o", "g"]
result = []
"∂og".chars {|b| result << b } # => "∂og"
result                        # => ["∂", "o", "g"]
```

---

chr   *str*.chr → *string*

Returns the first character of *str*.

```
# encoding: utf-8
"dog".chr   # => "d"
"∂og".chr # => "∂"
```

---

clear   *str*.clear → *str*

Removes the content (but not the associated encoding) of *str*.

```
# encoding: utf-8
str = "∂og"
str.clear     # => ""
str.length    # => 0
str.encoding # => #<Encoding:UTF-8>
```

---

chomp   *str*.chomp(*rs=$/*) → *string*

Returns a new String with the given record separator removed from the end of *str* (if present). If $/ has not been changed from the default Ruby record separator, then chomp also removes carriage return characters (that is, it will remove \n, \r, and \r\n).

```
"hello".chomp             # => "hello"
"hello\n".chomp           # => "hello"
"hello\r\n".chomp         # => "hello"
"hello\n\r".chomp         # => "hello\n"
"hello\r".chomp           # => "hello"
"hello \n there".chomp # => "hello \n there"
"hello".chomp("llo")      # => "he"
```

---

chomp!   *str*.chomp!(*rs=$/*) → *str* or nil

Modifies *str* in place as described for String#chomp, returning *str* or returning nil if no modifications were made.

---

chop   *str*.chop → *string*

Returns a new String with the last character removed. If the string ends with \r\n, both characters are removed. Applying chop to an empty string returns an empty string. String#chomp is often a safer alternative, because it leaves the string unchanged if it doesn't end in a record separator.

```
"string\r\n".chop  # => "string"
"string\n\r".chop  # => "string\n"
"string\n".chop    # => "string"
"string".chop      # => "strin"
"x".chop.chop      # => ""
```

chop!

str.chop! → str or nil

Processes *str* as for String#chop, returning *str* or returning nil if *str* is the empty string. See also String#chomp!.

codepoints

str.codepoints → enum | array
str.codepoints { | integer | ... } → str

Returns an enumerator (Ruby 1.9) or array (Ruby 2.0) for the codepoints (integers representation of the characters) in *str*. With a block, passes each integer to the block and returns the original string. See also String#bytes and String#chars.

New in 2.0

```
# encoding: utf-8
"dog".codepoints.to_a              # => [100, 111, 103]
"∂og".codepoints.to_a              # => [8706, 111, 103]
result = []
"∂og".codepoints {|b| result << b } # => "∂og"
result                             # => [8706, 111, 103]
```

concat

str.concat(int) → str
str.concat(obj) → str

Synonym for String#<<.

count

str.count(‹ string ›[+]) → int

Each *string* parameter defines a set of characters to count. The intersection of these sets defines the characters to count in *str*. Any parameter that starts with a caret ($\wedge$) is negated. The sequence c_1-c_2 means all characters between c_1 and c_2.

```
a = "hello world"
a.count "lo"          # => 5
a.count "lo", "o"     # => 2
a.count "hello", "^l" # => 4
a.count "ej-m"        # => 4
```

crypt

str.crypt(settings) → string

Applies a one-way cryptographic hash to *str* by invoking the standard library function crypt. The argument is to some extent system dependent. On traditional Unix boxes, it is often a two-character *salt* string. On more modern boxes, it may also control things such as DES encryption parameters. See the man page for crypt(3) for details.

```
# standard salt
"secret".crypt("sh")        # => "shRK3aVg8FsI2"
# On OSX: DES, 2 interactions, 24-bit salt
"secret".crypt("_...0abcd") # => "_...0abcdROn65JNDj12"
```

delete   *str*.delete(‹ *string* ›⁺) → *new_string*

Returns a copy of *str* with all characters in the intersection of its arguments deleted. Uses
the same rules for building the set of characters as String#count.

```
"hello".delete("l","lo")      # => "heo"
"hello".delete("lo")          # => "he"
"hello".delete("aeiou", "^e") # => "hell"
"hello".delete("ej-m")        # => "ho"
```

delete!   *str*.delete!(‹ *string* ›⁺) → *str* or nil

Performs a delete operation in place, returning *str* or returning nil if *str* was not modified.

```
a = "hello"
a.delete!("l","lo") # => "heo"
a                   # => "heo"
a.delete!("l")      # => nil
```

downcase   *str*.downcase → *string*

Returns a copy of *str* with all uppercase letters replaced with their lowercase counterparts.
The operation is locale insensitive — only characters *A* to *Z* are affected. Multibyte characters
are skipped.

```
"hEllO".downcase # => "hello"
```

downcase!   *str*.downcase! → *str* or nil

Replaces uppercase letters in *str* with their lowercase counterparts. Returns nil if no changes
were made.

dump   *str*.dump → *string*

Produces a version of *str* with all nonprinting characters replaced by \nnn notation and all
special characters escaped.

each_byte   *str*.each_byte → *enum*
                                               str.each_byte { | byte | ... } → *str*

Synonym for String#bytes. The each_byte form is falling out of favor.

each_char   *str*.each_char → *enum*
                                               str.each_char { | char | ... } → *str*

Synonym for String#chars. The each_char form is falling out of favor.

each_codepoint

str.each_codepoint → *enum*
str.each_codepoint { | integer | ... } → *str*

Synonym for String#codepoints.

each_line

str.each_line(*sep=$/*) → *enum*
str.each_line(*sep=$/*) { | substr | ... } → *str*}

Synonym for String#lines. The each_line form is falling out of favor.

empty?

str.empty? → *true* or *false*

Returns true if *str* has a length of zero.

```
"hello".empty? # => false
"".empty?      # => true
```

encode

str.encode → *a_string*
str.encode(*to_encoding* ‹, options›) → *a_string*
str.encode(*to_encoding, from_encoding,* ‹, options›) → *a_string*

Transcodes *str*, returning a new string encoded with *to_encoding*. If no encoding is given, transcodes using default_internal encoding. The source encoding is either the current encoding of the string or *from_encoding*. May raise a RuntimeError if characters in the original string cannot be represented in the target encoding. The *options* parameter defines the behavior for invalid transcodings and other boundary conditions. It can be a hash (recommended) or an *or*-ing of integer values. Encodings can be passed as Encoding objects or as names.

Option	Meaning
:replace => *string*	Specifies the string to use if :invalid or :undef options are present. If not specified, uFFFD is used for Unicode encodings and ? for others.
:invalid => :replace	Replaces invalid characters in the source string with the replacement string. If :invalid is not specified or nil, raises an exception.
:undef => :replace	Replaces characters that are not available in the destination encoding with the replacement string. If :undef not specified or nil, raises an exception.
:universal_newline => true	Converts crlf and cr line endings to lf.
:crlf_newline => true	Converts lf to crlf.
:cr_newline => true	Converts lf to cr.
:xml => :text	:attr	After encoding, escape characters that would otherwise have special meaning in XML PCDATA or attributes. In all cases, converts & to &, < to <, > to >, and undefined characters to a hexadecimal entity (&#xhh;). For :attr, also converts " to ".

Table 22—Options to encode and encode!

```
# encoding: utf-8
ole_in_utf = "olé"
ole_in_utf.encoding  # => #<Encoding:UTF-8>
ole_in_utf.dump      # => "ol\u{e9}"

ole_in_8859 = ole_in_utf.encode("iso-8859-1")
ole_in_8859.encoding # => #<Encoding:ISO-8859-1>
ole_in_8859.dump     # => "ol\xE9"
```

Using a default internal encoding of ISO-8859-1 and a source file encoding of UTF-8:

```
#!/usr/local/rubybook/bin/ruby -E:ISO-8859-1
# encoding: utf-8
utf_string = "olé"
utf_string.encoding # => #<Encoding:UTF-8>
iso_string = utf_string.encode
iso_string.encoding # => #<Encoding:ISO-8859-1>
```

Attempt to transcode a string with characters not available in the destination encoding:

```
# encoding: utf-8
utf = "∂og"
utf.encode("iso-8859-1")
```

produces:

```
        from prog.rb:3:in `<main>'
prog.rb:3:in `encode': U+2202 from UTF-8 to ISO-8859-1
(Encoding::UndefinedConversionError)
```

You can replace the character in error with something else:

```
# encoding: utf-8
utf = "∂og"
utf.encode("iso-8859-1", undef: :replace)                    # => "?og"
utf.encode("iso-8859-1", undef: :replace, replace: "X" ) # => "Xog"
```

---

encode!

str.encode! → str
str.encode!($to\_encoding$ ‹, $options$›) → str
str.encode!($to\_encoding, from\_encoding,$ ‹, $options$›) → str

Transcodes str in place.

---

encoding

str.encoding → $an\_encoding$

Returns the encoding of str.

```
# encoding: utf-8
"cat".encoding # => #<Encoding:UTF-8>
```

---

end_with?

str.end_with?(‹ suffix ›⁺) → *true* or *false*

Returns true if str ends with any of the given suffixes.

```
"Apache".end_with?("ache")                   # => true
"ruby code".end_with?("python", "perl", "code") # => true
```

eql?

str.eql?(obj) → true or false

Returns true if *obj* is a String with identical contents to *str*.

```
"cat".eql?("cat") # => true
```

force_encoding

str.force_encoding(encoding) → str

Sets the encoding associated with *str* to *encoding*. Note that this does not change the underlying bytes in *str*—it simply tells Ruby how to interpret those bytes as characters.

```
# encoding: utf-8
∂og_in_bytes = [226, 136, 130, 111, 103]  # utf-8 byte sequence
str = ∂og_in_bytes.pack("C*")
str.encoding # => #<Encoding:ASCII-8BIT>
str.length   # => 5
str.force_encoding("utf-8")
str.encoding # => #<Encoding:UTF-8>
str.length   # => 3
str          # => "∂og"
```

getbyte

str.getbyte(offset) → int or nil

Returns the byte at *offset* (starting from the end of the string if the offset is negative). Returns nil if the offset lies outside the string.

```
# encoding: utf-8
str = "∂og"
str.bytes.to_a  # => [226, 136, 130, 111, 103]
str.getbyte(0)  # => 226
str.getbyte(1)  # => 136
str.getbyte(-1) # => 103
str.getbyte(99) # => nil
```

gsub

str.gsub(pattern, replacement) → string
str.gsub(pattern) { | match | ... } → string
str.gsub(pattern) → enum

Returns a copy of *str* with *all* occurrences of *pattern* replaced with either *replacement* or the value of the block. The *pattern* will typically be a Regexp; if it is a String, then no regular expression metacharacters will be interpreted (that is, /\d/ will match a digit, but '\d' will match a backslash followed by a *d*).

If a string is used as the replacement, special variables from the match (such as $& and $1) cannot be substituted into it, because substitution into the string occurs before the pattern match starts. However, the sequences \1, \2, and so on, may be used to interpolate successive numbered groups in the match, and \k<name> will substitute the corresponding named captures. These sequences are shown in the following table.

Sequence	Text That Is Substituted
\1, \2, ... \9	The value matched by the *n*th grouped subexpression
\&	The last match
\`	The part of the string before the match
\'	The part of the string after the match
\+	The highest-numbered group matched
\k<name>	The named capture

Table 23—Backslash sequences in substitution

In the block form, the current match is passed in as a parameter, and variables such as $1, $2, $`, $&, and $' will be set appropriately. The value returned by the block will be substituted for the match on each call.

The result inherits any tainting in the original string or any supplied replacement string.

```
"hello".gsub(/[aeiou]/, '*')                # => "h*ll*"
"hello".gsub(/([aeiou])/, '<\1>')           # => "h<e>ll<o>"
"hello".gsub(/./) {|s| s[0].to_s + ' '}     # => "h e l l o "
"hello".gsub(/(?<double>l)/, '-\k<double>-') # => "he-l--l-o"
```

If no block or replacement string is given, an enumerator is returned.

```
"hello".gsub(/../).to_a # => ["he", "ll"]
```

If a hash is given as the replacement, successive matched groups are looked up as keys, and the corresponding values are substituted into the string.

```
repl = Hash.new("?")
repl["a"] = "*"
repl["t"] = "T"
"cat".gsub(/(.)/, repl) # => "?*T"
```

gsub!

str.gsub!(*pattern, replacement*) → *string*
str.gsub!(*pattern*) { | match | ... } → *string*
str.gsub!(*pattern*) → *enum*

Performs the substitutions of String#gsub in place, returning *str*, or returning nil if no substitutions were performed. If no block or replacement string is given, an enumerator is returned.

hex

str.hex → *int*

Treats leading characters from *str* as a string of hexadecimal digits (with an optional sign and an optional 0x) and returns the corresponding number. Zero is returned on error.

```
"0x0a".hex    # => 10
"-1234".hex   # => -4660
"0".hex       # => 0
"wombat".hex  # => 0
```

include?

str.include?(*string*) → *true* or *false*

Returns true if *str* contains the given string.

```
"hello".include? "lo" # => true
"hello".include? "ol" # => false
"hello".include? ?h   # => true
```

index

str.index(*string* ‹ , *offset* ›) → *int* or nil
str.index(*regexp* ‹ , *offset* ›) → *int* or nil

Returns the index of the first occurrence of the given substring or pattern in *str*. Returns nil if not found. If the second parameter is present, it specifies the position in the string to begin the search.

```
"hello".index('e')          # => 1
"hello".index('lo')         # => 3
"hello".index('a')          # => nil
"hello".index(/[aeiou]/, -3) # => 4
```

insert

str.insert(*index, string*) → *str*

Inserts *string* before the character at the given *index*, modifying *str*. Negative indices count from the end of the string and insert after the given character. After the insertion, *str* will contain *string* starting at *index*.

```
"abcd".insert(0, 'X')  # => "Xabcd"
"abcd".insert(3, 'X')  # => "abcXd"
"abcd".insert(4, 'X')  # => "abcdX"
"abcd".insert(-3, 'X') # => "abXcd"
"abcd".insert(-1, 'X') # => "abcdX"
```

intern

str.intern → *symbol*

Returns the Symbol corresponding to *str*, creating the symbol if it did not previously exist. Can intern any string, not just identifiers. See Symbol#id2name on page 700.

```
"Koala".intern # => :Koala
sym = "$1.50 for a soda!?!?".intern
sym.to_s       # => "$1.50 for a soda!?!?"
```

length

str.length → *int*

Returns the number of characters in *str*. See also String#bytesize.

lines

str.lines(*sep=$/*) → *enum* | *array*
str.lines(*sep=$/*) { | substr | ... } → *str*}

Splits *str* using the supplied parameter as the record separator ($/ by default) and passing each substring in turn to the supplied block. If a zero-length record separator is supplied, the string is split into paragraphs, each terminated by multiple \n characters. With no block, returns a enumerator (Ruby 1.9) or an array (Ruby 2.0).

New in 2.0

```
print "Example one\n"
"hello\nworld".lines {|s| p s}
print "Example two\n"
"hello\nworld".lines('l') {|s| p s}
print "Example three\n"
"hello\n\n\nworld".lines('') {|s| p s}
```

produces:

```
Example one
"hello\n"
"world"
Example two
"hel"
"l"
"o\nworl"
"d"
Example three
"hello\n\n\n"
"world"
```

---

ljust   *str*.ljust(*width, padding=" "*) → *string*

If *width* is greater than the length of *str*, returns a new String of length *width* with *str* left justified and padded with copies of *padding*; otherwise, returns a copy of *str*.

```
"hello".ljust(4)          # => "hello"
"hello".ljust(20)         # => "hello␣␣␣␣␣␣␣␣␣␣␣␣␣␣␣
                          # .. ␣"
"hello".ljust(20, "*")    # => "hello***************"
"hello".ljust(20, " dolly") # => "hello␣dolly␣dolly␣do"
```

---

lstrip   *str*.lstrip → *string*

Returns a copy of *str* with leading whitespace characters removed. Also see String#rstrip and String#strip.

```
"  hello  ".lstrip     # => "hello␣␣"
"\000 hello  ".lstrip  # => "\0␣hello␣␣"
"hello".lstrip         # => "hello"
```

---

lstrip!   *str*.lstrip! → *str* or nil

Removes leading whitespace characters from *str*, returning nil if no change was made. See also String#rstrip! and String#strip!.

```
"  hello  ".lstrip! # => "hello␣␣"
"hello".lstrip!     # => nil
```

match

str.match(*pattern*) → *match_data* or nil
str.match(*pattern*) { | matchdata | ... } → *obj*

Converts *pattern* to a Regexp (if it isn't already one) and then invokes its match method on *str*. If a block is given, the block is passed the MatchData object, and the match method returns the value of the block.

```
'seed'.match('(.)\1')                    # => #<MatchData "ee" 1:"e">
'seed'.match('(.)\1')[0]                  # => "ee"
'seed'.match(/(.)\1/)[0]                  # => "ee"
'seed'.match('ll')                        # => nil
'seed'.match('ll') {|md| md[0].upcase }   # => nil
'seed'.match('xx')                        # => nil
```

next

str.next → *string*

Synonym for String#succ.

next!

str.next! → *str*

Synonym for String#succ!.

oct

str.oct → *int*

Treats leading characters of *str* as a string of octal digits (with an optional sign) and returns the corresponding number. Returns 0 if the conversion fails.

```
"123".oct      # => 83
"-377".oct     # => -255
"bad".oct      # => 0
"0377bad".oct  # => 255
```

ord

str.ord → *int*

Returns the integer code point of the first character of *str*.

```
# encoding: utf-8
"d".ord   # => 100
"dog".ord # => 100
"∂".ord # => 8706
```

partition

str.partition(*pattern*) → [*before, match, after*]

Searches *str* for *pattern* (which may be a string or a regular expression). Returns a three-element array containing the part of the string before the pattern, the part that matched the pattern, and the part after the match. If the pattern does not match, the entire string will be returned as the first element of the array, and the other two entries will be empty strings.

```
"THX1138".partition("11")    # => ["THX", "11", "38"]
"THX1138".partition(/\d\d/)  # => ["THX", "11", "38"]
"THX1138".partition("99")    # => ["THX1138", "", ""]
```

prepend

str.prepend(*other*) → *str*

Inserts *other* at the beginning of *str*.

```
str = "1138"
str.prepend("THX") # => "THX1138"
str               # => "THX1138"
```

replace

str.replace(*string*) → *str*

Replaces the contents, encoding, and taintedness of *str* with the corresponding values in *string*.

```
s = "hello"        # => "hello"
s.replace "world" # => "world"
```

reverse

str.reverse → *string*

Returns a new string with the characters from *str* in reverse order.

```
# Every problem contains its own solution...
"stressed".reverse # => "desserts"
```

reverse!

str.reverse! → *str*

Reverses *str* in place.

rindex

str.rindex(*string* ‹ , *int* ›) → *int* or nil
str.rindex(*regexp* ‹ , *int* ›) → *int* or nil

Returns the index of the last occurrence of the given substring, character, or pattern in *str*. Returns nil if not found. If the second parameter is present, it specifies the position in the string to end the search—characters beyond this point will not be considered.

```
"hello".rindex('e')         # => 1
"hello".rindex('l')         # => 3
"hello".rindex('a')         # => nil
"hello".rindex(/[aeiou]/, -2) # => 1
```

rjust

str.rjust(*width*, *padding*=" ") → *string*

If *width* is greater than the length of *str*, returns a new String of length *width* with *str* right justified and padded with copies of *padding*; otherwise, returns a copy of *str*.

```
"hello".rjust(4)             # => "hello"
"hello".rjust(20)            # => "␣␣␣␣␣␣␣␣␣␣␣␣␣␣␣h
                             # .. ello"
"hello".rjust(20, "-")       # => "---------------hello"
"hello".rjust(20, "padding") # => "paddingpaddingphello"
```

---

rpartition   *str*.rpartition(*pattern*) → [*before, match, after*]

Searches *str* for *pattern* (which may be a string or a regular expression), starting at the end of the string. Returns a three-element array containing the part of the string before the pattern, the part that matched the pattern, and the part after the match. If the pattern does not match, the entire string will be returned as the last element of the array, and the other two entries will be empty strings.

```
"THX1138".rpartition("1")   # => ["THX1", "1", "38"]
"THX1138".rpartition(/1\d/) # => ["THX1", "13", "8"]
"THX1138".rpartition("99")  # => ["", "", "THX1138"]
```

---

rstrip   *str*.rstrip → *string*

Returns a copy of *str*, stripping first trailing null characters and then stripping trailing whitespace characters. See also String#lstrip and String#strip.

```
"  hello  ".rstrip      # => "␣␣hello"
"  hello \000 ".rstrip # => "␣␣hello"
"  hello \000".rstrip  # => "␣␣hello"
"hello".rstrip          # => "hello"
```

---

rstrip!   *str*.rstrip! → *str* or *nil*

Removes trailing null characters and then removes trailing whitespace characters from *str*. Returns nil if no change was made. See also String#lstrip! and #strip!.

```
"  hello  ".rstrip! # => "␣␣hello"
"hello".rstrip!      # => nil
```

---

scan   *str*.scan(*pattern*) → *array*
                                        str.scan(*pattern*) { | match, ... | ... } → *str*}

Both forms iterate through *str*, matching the pattern (which may be a Regexp or a String). For each match, a result is generated and either added to the result array or passed to the block. If the pattern contains no groups, each individual result consists of the matched string, $&. If the pattern contains groups, each individual result is itself an array containing one entry per group. If the pattern is a String, it is interpreted literally (in other words, it is not taken to be a regular expression pattern).

```
a = "cruel world"
a.scan(/\w+/)      # => ["cruel", "world"]
a.scan(/.../)      # => ["cru", "el ", "wor"]
a.scan(/(...)/)    # => [["cru"], ["el "], ["wor"]]
a.scan(/(..)(..)/) # => [["cr", "ue"], ["l ", "wo"]]
```

And the block form:

```
a.scan(/\w+/) {|w| print "<<#{w}>> " }
puts
a.scan(/(.)(.)/) {|a,b| print b, a }
puts
```

produces:

```
<<cruel>> <<world>>
rceu lowlr
```

setbyte   *str*.setbyte(*offset, byte*) → *byte*

Sets the byte at *offset* (starting from the end of the string if the offset is negative) to *byte*.
Cannot be used to change the length of the string. Does not change the encoding of the string.

```
str = "defog"
# a utf-8 delta character
str.setbyte(0, 226) # => 226
str.setbyte(1, 136) # => 136
str.setbyte(2, 130) # => 130
str                 # => "∂og"
str.length          # => 3
str.force_encoding("utf-8")
str.length          # => 3
str                 # => "∂og"
```

size   *str*.size → *int*

Synonym for String#length.

slice   *str*.slice(*int*) → *string* or nil
                                           str.slice(*int, int*) → *string* or nil
                                          str.slice(*range*) → *string* or nil
                                         str.slice(*regexp*) → *string* or nil
                                   str.slice(*match_string*) → *string* or nil

Synonym for String#[ ].

```
a = "hello there"
a.slice(1)          # => "e"
a.slice(1,3)        # => "ell"
a.slice(1..3)       # => "ell"
a.slice(-3,2)       # => "er"
a.slice(-4..-2)     # => "her"
a.slice(-2..-4)     # => ""
a.slice(/th[aeiou]/) # => "the"
a.slice("lo")       # => "lo"
a.slice("bye")      # => nil
```

slice!   *str*.slice!(*int*) → *string* or nil
                                           str.slice!(*int, int*) → *string* or nil
                                          str.slice!(*range*) → *string* or nil
                                         str.slice!(*regexp*) → *string* or nil
                                   str.slice!(*match_string*) → *string* or nil

Deletes the specified portion from *str* and returns the portion deleted. The forms that take
a Fixnum will raise an IndexError if the value is out of range; the Range form will raise a
RangeError, and the Regexp and String forms will silently not change the string.

```
string = "this is a string"
string.slice!(2)      # => "i"
string.slice!(3..6)   # => " is "
string.slice!(/s.*t/) # => "sa st"
string.slice!("r")    # => "r"
string                # => "thing"
```

split
str.split(pattern=$;, ‹limit›) → array

Divides *str* into substrings based on a delimiter, returning an array of these substrings.

If *pattern* is a String, then its contents are used as the delimiter when splitting *str*. If *pattern* is a single space, *str* is split on whitespace, with leading whitespace and runs of contiguous whitespace characters ignored.

If *pattern* is a Regexp, *str* is divided where the pattern matches. Whenever the pattern matches a zero-length string, *str* is split into individual characters. If pattern includes groups, these groups will be included in the returned values.

If *pattern* is omitted, the value of $; is used. If $; is nil (which is the default), *str* is split on whitespace as if "␣" were specified.

If the *limit* parameter is omitted, trailing empty fields are suppressed. If *limit* is a positive number, at most that number of fields will be returned (if *limit* is 1, the entire string is returned as the only entry in an array). If negative, there is no limit to the number of fields returned, and trailing null fields are not suppressed.

```
" now's   the time".split       # => ["now's", "the", "time"]
" now's   the time".split(' ')  # => ["now's", "the", "time"]
" now's   the time".split(/ /)  # => ["", "now's", "", "", "the", "time"]
"a@1bb@2ccc".split(/@\d/)       # => ["a", "bb", "ccc"]
"a@1bb@2ccc".split(/@(\d)/)     # => ["a", "1", "bb", "2", "ccc"]
"1, 2.34,56, 7".split(/,\s*/)   # => ["1", "2.34", "56", "7"]
"hello".split(//)               # => ["h", "e", "l", "l", "o"]
"hello".split(//, 3)            # => ["h", "e", "llo"]
"hi mom".split(/\s*/)           # => ["h", "i", "m", "o", "m"]
"".split                        # => []
"mellow yellow".split("ello")   # => ["m", "w y", "w"]
"1,2,,3,4,,".split(',')         # => ["1", "2", "", "3", "4"]
"1,2,,3,4,,".split(',', 4)      # => ["1", "2", "", "3,4,,"]
"1,2,,3,4,,".split(',', -4)     # => ["1", "2", "", "3", "4", "", ""]
```

squeeze
str.squeeze(‹string›*) → squeezed_string

The parameter(s) specify a set of characters using the procedure described for String#count on page 673. Returns a new string where runs of the same character that occur in this set are replaced by a single character. If no arguments are given, all runs of identical characters are replaced by a single character.

```
"yellow moon".squeeze             # => "yelow mon"
"  now   is   the".squeeze(" ")   # => " now is the"
"putters putt balls".squeeze("m-z") # => "puters put balls"
```

---

squeeze!   *str*.squeeze!(‹ *string* ›*) → *str* or nil

Squeezes *str* in place, returning *str*. Returns nil if no changes were made.

---

start_with?   *str*.start_with?(‹ prefix ›+) → *true* or *false*

Returns true if *str* starts with any of the given prefixes.

```
"Apache".start_with?("Apa")                      # => true
"ruby code".start_with?("python", "perl", "ruby") # => true
```

---

strip   *str*.strip → *string*

Returns a new string, stripping leading whitespace and trailing null and whitespace characters from *str*.

```
"    hello    ".strip # => "hello"
"\tgoodbye\r\n".strip # => "goodbye"
"goodbye  \000".strip # => "goodbye"
"goodbye \000 ".strip # => "goodbye"
```

---

strip!   *str*.strip! → *str* or nil

Removes leading whitespace and trailing null and whitespace characters from *str*. Returns nil if *str* was not altered.

---

sub   *str*.sub(*pattern, replacement*) → *string*
                                 str.sub(*pattern*) { | match | ... } → *string*

Returns a copy of *str* with the first occurrence of *pattern* replaced with either *replacement* or the value of the block. See the description of String#gsub on page 677 for a description of the parameters.

```
"hello".sub(/[aeiou]/, '*')               # => "h*llo"
"hello".sub(/([aeiou])/, '<\1>')          # => "h<e>llo"
"hello".sub(/./) {|s| s[0].to_s + ' '}    # => "h ello"
"hello".sub(/(?<double>l)/, '-\k<double>-') # => "he-l-lo"
```

---

sub!   *str*.sub!(*pattern, replacement*) → *str* or nil
                                  str.sub!(*pattern*) { | match | ... } → *str* or nil

---

Performs the substitutions of String#sub in place, returning *str*. Returns nil if no substitutions were performed.

---

succ   *str*.succ → *string*

Returns the successor to *str*. The successor is calculated by incrementing characters starting from the rightmost alphanumeric (or the rightmost character if there are no alphanumerics) in the string. Incrementing a digit always results in another digit, and incrementing a letter results in another letter of the same case. Incrementing nonalphanumerics uses the underlying character set's collating sequence.

If the increment generates a "carry," the character to the left of it is incremented. This process repeats until there is no carry, adding a character if necessary. An exception is when the carry is generated by a sequence of digits in a string containing digits, nonalpha characters, and more digits, in which case the carry applies to the digits. This allows for incrementing (for example) numbers with decimal places.

```
"abcd".succ       # => "abce"
"THX1138".succ    # => "THX1139"
"<<koala>>".succ  # => "<<koalb>>"
"1999zzz".succ    # => "2000aaa"
"ZZZ9999".succ    # => "AAAA0000"
"***".succ        # => "**+"
"1.9".succ        # => "2.0"
"1//9".succ       # => "2//0"
"1/9/9/9".succ    # => "2/0/0/0"
"1x9".succ        # => "1y0"
```

---

succ!

str.succ! → str

Equivalent to String#succ but modifies the receiver in place.

---

sum

str.sum(n=16) → int

Returns a basic n-bit checksum of the characters in str, where n is the optional parameter, defaulting to 16. The result is simply the sum of the binary value of each character in str modulo 2^n-1. This is not a particularly good checksum—see the digest libraries on page 747 for better alternatives.

```
"now is the time".sum    # => 1408
"now is the time".sum(8) # => 128
```

---

swapcase

str.swapcase → string

Returns a copy of str with uppercase alphabetic characters converted to lowercase and lowercase characters converted to uppercase. The mapping depends on the string encoding, but not all encodings produce expected results.

```
# encoding: utf-8
"Hello".swapcase          # => "hELLO"
"cYbEr_PuNk11".swapcase   # => "CyBeR_pUnK11"
"∂0g".swapcase            # => "∂0G"
```

---

swapcase!

str.swapcase! → str or nil

Equivalent to String#swapcase but modifies str in place, returning str. Returns nil if no changes were made.

to_c
str.to_c → *complex*

Returns the result of interpreting leading characters in *str* as a complex number. Extraneous characters past the end of a valid number are ignored. If there is not a valid number at the start of *str*, Complex(0,0) is returned. The method never raises an exception.

```
"123".to_c       # => 123+0i
"4+5/6i".to_c    # => 4+5/6i
"thx1138".to_c   # => 0+0i
```

to_f
str.to_f → *float*

Returns the result of interpreting leading characters in *str* as a floating-point number. Extraneous characters past the end of a valid number are ignored. If there is not a valid number at the start of *str*, 0.0 is returned. The method never raises an exception (use Object#Float to validate numbers).

```
"123.45e1".to_f    # => 1234.5
"45.67 degrees".to_f # => 45.67
"thx1138".to_f     # => 0.0
```

to_i
str.to_i(*base*=10) → *int*

Returns the result of interpreting leading characters in *str* as an integer base *base* (2 to 36). Given a base of zero, to_i looks for leading 0, 0b, 0o, 0d, or 0x and sets the base accordingly. Leading spaces are ignored, and leading plus or minus signs are honored. Extraneous characters past the end of a valid number are ignored. If there is not a valid number at the start of *str*, 0 is returned. The method never raises an exception.

```
"12345".to_i           # => 12345
"99 red balloons".to_i # => 99
"0a".to_i              # => 0
"0a".to_i(16)          # => 10
"0x10".to_i            # => 0
"0x10".to_i(0)         # => 16
"-0x10".to_i(0)        # => -16
"hello".to_i(30)       # => 14167554
"1100101".to_i(2)      # => 101
"1100101".to_i(8)      # => 294977
"1100101".to_i(10)     # => 1100101
"1100101".to_i(16)     # => 17826049
```

to_r
str.to_r → *rational*

Returns the result of interpreting leading characters in *str* as a rational number. Extraneous characters past the end of a valid number are ignored. If there is not a valid number at the start of *str*, Rational(0,1) is returned. The method never raises an exception.

```
"123".to_r       # => 123/1
"5/6".to_r       # => 5/6
"5/six".to_r     # => 5/1
"thx1138".to_r   # => (0/1)
```

---

to_s   *str*.to_s → *str*

Returns the receiver.

---

to_str   *str*.to_str → *str*

Synonym for String#to_s. to_str is used by methods such as String#concat to convert their arguments to a string. Unlike to_s, which is supported by almost all classes, to_str is normally implemented only by those classes that act like strings. Of the built-in classes, only Exception and String implement to_str.

---

to_sym   *str*.to_s → *symbol*

Returns the symbol for *str*. This can create symbols that cannot be represented using the :xxx notation. A synonym for String#intern.

```
s = 'cat'.to_sym       # => :cat
s == :cat              # => true
'cat and dog'.to_sym   # => :"cat and dog"
s == :'cat and dog'    # => false
```

---

tr   *str*.tr(*from_string*, *to_string*) → *string*

Returns a copy of *str* with the characters in *from_string* replaced by the corresponding characters in *to_string*. If *to_string* is shorter than *from_string*, it is padded with its last character. Both strings may use the c_1–c_2 notation to denote ranges of characters, and *from_string* may start with a ^, which denotes all characters except those listed.

```
"hello".tr('aeiou', '*')   # => "h*ll*"
"hello".tr('^aeiou', '*')  # => "*e**o"
"hello".tr('el', 'ip')     # => "hippo"
"hello".tr('a-y', 'b-z')   # => "ifmmp"
```

---

tr!   *str*.tr!(*from_string*, *to_string*) → *str* or nil

Translates *str* in place, using the same rules as String#tr. Returns *str* or returns nil if no changes were made.

---

tr_s   *str*.tr_s(*from_string*, *to_string*) → *string*

Processes a copy of *str* as described under String#tr and then removes duplicate characters in regions that were affected by the translation.

```
"hello".tr_s('l', 'r')    # => "hero"
"hello".tr_s('el', '*')   # => "h*o"
"hello".tr_s('el', 'hx')  # => "hhxo"
```

tr_s!

> *str*.tr_s!(*from_string, to_string*) → *str* or nil

Performs String#tr_s processing on *str* in place, returning *str*. Returns nil if no changes were made.

unpack

> *str*.unpack(*format*) → *array*

Decodes *str* (which may contain binary data) according to the format string, returning an array of the extracted values. The format string consists of a sequence of single-character directives, summarized in Table 24, *Directives for unpack,* on page 692. Each directive may be followed by a number, indicating the number of times to repeat this directive. An asterisk (*) will use up all remaining elements. The directives sSiIlL may each be followed by an underscore (_) or bang (!} to use the underlying platform's native size for the specified type; otherwise, it uses a platform-independent consistent size. The directives s S i I l L q Q may be followed by a less than sign to signify little endian or greater than sign for big endian. Spaces are ignored in the format string. Comments starting with # to the next newline or end of string are also ignored. The encoding of the string is ignored; unpack treats the string as a sequence of bytes. See also Array#pack on page 432.

```
"abc \0\0abc \0\0".unpack('A6Z6') # => ["abc", "abc "]
"abc \0\0".unpack('a3a3')         # => ["abc", " \0\0"]
"aa".unpack('b8B8')               # => ["10000110", "01100001"]
"aaa".unpack('h2H2c')             # => ["16", "61", 97]
"\xfe\xff\xfe\xff".unpack('sS')   # => [-2, 65534]
"now=20is".unpack('M*')           # => ["now is"]
"whole".unpack('xax2aX2aX1aX2a')  # => ["h", "e", "l", "l", "o"]
```

upcase

> *str*.upcase → *string*

Returns a copy of *str* with all lowercase letters replaced with their uppercase counterparts. The mapping depends on the string encoding, but not all encodings produce expected results.

```
# encoding: utf-8
"hEllO".upcase # => "HELLO"
"∂og".upcase # => "∂OG"
```

upcase!

> *str*.upcase! → *str* or nil

Upcases the contents of *str*, returning nil if no changes were made.

upto

> *str*.upto(*string, exclude_end*=false) { |s| ... } → *str* or *enumerator*

Iterates through successive values, starting at *str* and ending at *string* inclusive (or omitting *string* if the second parameter is true). Passes each value in turn to the block. The String#succ method is used to generate each value. Returns an Enumerator object if no block is given.

```
"a8".upto("b6") {|s| print s, ' ' }
puts
for s in "a8".."b6"
  print s, ' '
end
```

produces:

```
a8 a9 b0 b1 b2 b3 b4 b5 b6
a8 a9 b0 b1 b2 b3 b4 b5 b6
```

```ruby
"a8".upto("b6", true).to_a # => ["a8", "a9", "b0", "b1", "b2", "b3", "b4", "b5"]
```

If the two strings contain just the digits 0 to 9, then successive numeric values (as strings) are generated. Leading zeros are handled appropriately.

```ruby
"99".upto("103").to_a      # => ["99", "100", "101", "102", "103"]
"00008".upto("00012").to_a # => ["00008", "00009", "00010", "00011", "00012"]
```

valid_encoding?

str.valid_encoding? → *true* or *false*

Returns true if *str* contains a valid byte sequence in its current encoding.

```ruby
# encoding: binary
str = "\xE2"
str.force_encoding("utf-8")
str.valid_encoding? # => false
str = "\xE2\x88\x82"
str.force_encoding("utf-8")
str.valid_encoding? # => true
```

Format	Function	Returns
A	Sequence of bytes with trailing nulls and ASCII spaces removed.	String
a	Sequence of bytes.	String
B	Extracts bits from each byte (MSB first).	String
b	Extracts bits from each byte (LSB first).	String
C	Extracts a byte as an unsigned integer.	Fixnum
c	Extracts a byte as an integer.	Fixnum
d,D	Treat sizeof(double) bytes as a native double.	Float
E	Treats sizeof(double) bytes as a double in little-endian byte order.	Float
e	Treats sizeof(float) bytes as a float in little-endian byte order.	Float
f,F	Treats sizeof(float) bytes as a native float.	Float
G	Treats sizeof(double) bytes as a double in network byte order.	Float
g	Treats sizeof(float) bytes as a float in network byte order.	Float
H	Extracts hex nibbles from each byte (most significant first).	String
h	Extracts hex nibbles from each byte (least significant first).	String
I	Treats sizeof(int)° successive bytes as an unsigned native integer.	Integer
i	Treats sizeof(int)° successive bytes as a signed native integer.	Integer
L	Treats four° successive bytes as an unsigned native long integer.	Integer
l	Treats four° successive characters as a signed native long integer.	Integer
M	Extracts a quoted-printable string.	String
m	Extracts a Base64-encoded string. By default, accepts \n and \r. "m0" rejects these.	String
N	Treats four bytes as an unsigned long in network byte order.	Fixnum
n	Treats two bytes as an unsigned short in network byte order.	Fixnum
P	Treats sizeof(char *) bytes as a pointer and returns *len* bytes from the referenced location.	String
p	Treats sizeof(char *) bytes as a pointer to a null-terminated string.	String
Q	Treats eight bytes as an unsigned quad word (64 bits).	Integer
q	Treats eight bytes as a signed quad word (64 bits).	Integer
S	Treats two° bytes characters as an unsigned short in native byte order.	Fixnum
s	Treats two° successive bytes as a signed short in native byte order.	Fixnum
U	Extracts UTF-8 characters as unsigned integers.	Integer
u	Extracts a UU-encoded string.	String
V	Treats four bytes as an unsigned long in little-endian byte order.	Fixnum
v	Treats two bytes as an unsigned short in little-endian byte order.	Fixnum
w	BER-compressed integer (see Array#pack for more information).	Integer
X	Skips backward one byte.	—
x	Skips forward one byte.	—
Z	String with trailing nulls removed.	String
@	Skips to the byte offset given by the length argument.	—

° *May be modified by appending _ or ! to the directive.*

Table 24—Directives for String#unpack

| Class | **Struct** |

Subclasses: Struct::Tms

A Struct is a convenient way to bundle a number of attributes together, using accessor methods, without having to write an explicit class.

The Struct class is a generator of specific classes, each one of which is defined to hold a set of variables and their accessors. In these examples, we'll call the generated class *Customer*, and we'll show an example instance of that class as *joe*.

Also see OpenStruct on page 786.

In the descriptions that follow, the parameter *symbol* refers to a name, which is either a quoted string or a Symbol (such as :name).

Mixes In

Enumerable: all?, any?, chunk, collect, collect_concat, count, cycle, detect, drop, drop_while, each_cons, each_entry, each_slice, each_with_index, each_with_object, entries, find, find_all, find_index, first, flat_map, grep, group_by, include?, inject, lazy, map, max, max_by, member?, min, min_by, minmax, minmax_by, none?, one?, partition, reduce, reject, reverse_each, select, slice_before, sort, sort_by, take, take_while, to_a, zip

Class Methods

new
$$\text{Struct.new(‹ string › ‹ , symbol ›}^+) \rightarrow Customer$$
$$\text{Struct.new(‹ string › ‹ , symbol ›}^+) \{ ... \} \rightarrow Customer$$

Creates a new class, named by *string*, containing accessor methods for the given symbols. If the name *string* is omitted, an anonymous structure class will be created. Otherwise, the name of this struct will appear as a constant in class Struct, so it must be unique for all Structs in the system and should start with a capital letter. Assigning a structure class to a constant effectively gives the class the name of the constant.

Struct.new returns a new Class object, which can then be used to create specific instances of the new structure. The remaining methods listed next (class and instance) are defined for this generated class. See the description that follows for an example.

```
# Create a structure with a name in Struct
Struct.new("Customer", :name, :address)  # => Struct::Customer
Struct::Customer.new("Dave", "123 Main") # => #<struct Struct::Customer
                                         # .. name="Dave", address="123 Main">

# Create a structure named by its constant
Customer = Struct.new(:name, :address) # => Customer
Customer.new("Dave", "123 Main")       # => #<struct Customer name="Dave",
                                       # .. address="123 Main">
```

A block passed to the constructor is evaluated in the context of the new struct's class and hence allows you conveniently to add instance methods to the new struct.

```ruby
Customer = Struct.new(:name, :address) do
  def to_s
    "#{self.name} lives at #{self.address}"
  end
end
Customer.new("Dave", "123 Main").to_s # => "Dave lives at 123 Main"
```

---

new   *Customer*.new(‹ *obj* ›⁺) → *joe*

Creates a new instance of a structure (the class created by Struct.new). The number of actual parameters must be less than or equal to the number of attributes defined for this class; unset parameters default to nil. Passing too many parameters will raise an ArgumentError.

```ruby
Customer = Struct.new(:name, :address, :zip)

joe = Customer.new("Joe Smith", "123 Maple, Anytown NC", 12345)
joe.name  # => "Joe Smith"
joe.zip   # => 12345
```

[ ]   *Customer*[‹ *obj* ›⁺] → *joe*

Synonym for new (for the generated structure).

```ruby
Customer = Struct.new(:name, :address, :zip)

joe = Customer["Joe Smith", "123 Maple, Anytown NC", 12345]
joe.name  # => "Joe Smith"
joe.zip   # => 12345
```

---

members   *Customer*.members → *array*

Returns an array of symbols representing the names of the instance variables.

```ruby
Customer = Struct.new("Customer", :name, :address, :zip)
Customer.members # => [:name, :address, :zip]
```

Instance Methods

==   *joe* == *other_struct* → *true* or *false*

Equality—Returns true if *other_struct* is equal to this one: they must be of the same class as generated by Struct.new, and the values of all instance variables must be equal (according to Object#==).

```ruby
Customer = Struct.new(:name, :address, :zip)

joe   = Customer.new("Joe Smith", "123 Maple, Anytown NC", 12345)
joejr = Customer.new("Joe Smith", "123 Maple, Anytown NC", 12345)
jane  = Customer.new("Jane Doe", "456 Elm, Anytown NC", 12345)

joe == joejr # => true
joe == jane  # => false
```

[ ]

joe[symbol] → obj
joe[integer] → obj

Attribute Reference—Returns the value of the instance variable named by *symbol* or indexed (0..length-1) by *int*. Raises NameError if the named variable does not exist or raises IndexError if the index is out of range.

```
Customer = Struct.new(:name, :address, :zip)
joe = Customer.new("Joe Smith", "123 Maple, Anytown NC", 12345)
joe["name"] # => "Joe Smith"
joe[:name]  # => "Joe Smith"
joe[0]      # => "Joe Smith"
```

[ ]=

joe[symbol] = obj → obj
joe[int] = obj → obj

Attribute Assignment—Assigns to the instance variable named by *symbol* or *int* the value *obj* and returns it. Raises a NameError if the named variable does not exist or raises an IndexError if the index is out of range.

```
Customer = Struct.new(:name, :address, :zip)
joe = Customer.new("Joe Smith", "123 Maple, Anytown NC", 12345)
joe["name"] = "Luke"
joe[:zip]   = "90210"
joe.name  # => "Luke"
joe.zip   # => "90210"
```

each

joe.each { | obj | ... } → joe

Calls *block* once for each instance variable, passing the value as a parameter.

```
Customer = Struct.new(:name, :address, :zip)
joe = Customer.new("Joe Smith", "123 Maple, Anytown NC", 12345)
joe.each {|x| puts(x) }
```

produces:

```
Joe Smith
123 Maple, Anytown NC
12345
```

each_pair

joe.each_pair { | symbol, obj | ... } → joe

Calls *block* once for each instance variable, passing the name (as a symbol) and the value as parameters.

```
Customer = Struct.new(:name, :address, :zip)
joe = Customer.new("Joe Smith", "123 Maple, Anytown NC", 12345)
joe.each_pair {|name, value| puts("#{name} => #{value}") }
```

produces:

```
name => Joe Smith
address => 123 Maple, Anytown NC
zip => 12345
```

---

length
joe.length → *int*

Returns the number of attributes.

```
Customer = Struct.new(:name, :address, :zip)
joe = Customer.new("Joe Smith", "123 Maple, Anytown NC", 12345)
joe.length # => 3
```

---

members
joe.members → *array*

Returns the names of the instance variables as an array of symbols.

```
Customer = Struct.new(:name, :address, :zip)
joe = Customer.new("Joe Smith", "123 Maple, Anytown NC", 12345)
joe.members # => [:name, :address, :zip]
```

---

size
joe.size → *int*

Synonym for Struct#length.

---

to_a
joe.to_a → *array*

Returns the values for this instance as an array.

```
Customer = Struct.new(:name, :address, :zip)
joe = Customer.new("Joe Smith", "123 Maple, Anytown NC", 12345)
joe.to_a[1] # => "123 Maple, Anytown NC"
```

---

to_h
joe.to_h → *hash*

Returns a hash of key/values pairs in this struct.

```
Customer = Struct.new(:name, :address, :zip)
joe = Customer.new("Joe Smith", "123 Maple, Anytown NC", 12345)
joe.to_h  # => {:name=>"Joe Smith", :address=>"123 Maple, Anytown NC",
          # .. :zip=>12345}
```

---

values
joe.values → *array*

Synonym for to_a.

---

values_at
joe.values_at(‹*selector*›*) → *array*

Returns an array containing the elements in *joe* corresponding to the given indices. The selectors may be integer indices or ranges.

```
Lots = Struct.new(:a, :b, :c, :d, :e, :f)
l = Lots.new(11, 22, 33, 44, 55, 66)
l.values_at(1, 3, 5)    # => [22, 44, 66]
l.values_at(0, 2, 4)    # => [11, 33, 55]
l.values_at(-1, -3, -5) # => [66, 44, 22]
```

Struct::Tms < Struct

This structure is returned by Process.times. It holds information on process times on those platforms that support it. Not all values are valid on all platforms. This structure contains the following instance variables and the corresponding accessors:

utime	Amount of user CPU time, in seconds
stime	Amount of system CPU time, in seconds
cutime	Total of completed child processes' user CPU time, in seconds (always 0 on Windows)
cstime	Total of completed child processes' system CPU time, in seconds (always 0 on Windows)

See also Struct on page 693 and Process.times on page 642.

```ruby
def eat_cpu
  10_000.times { File.open("/etc/passwd").close  }
end
3.times { fork { eat_cpu } }
eat_cpu
Process.waitall
t = Process::times
[ t.utime, t.stime]    # => [0.13, 0.24]
[ t.cutime, t.cstime ] # => [0.27, 0.68]
```

Symbol

Symbol objects represent names inside the Ruby interpreter. They are generated using the :name or :"arbitrary text" literal syntax and by using the various to_sym methods. The same Symbol object will be created for a given name string for the duration of a program's execution, regardless of the context or meaning of that name. Symbols can be arbitrary sequences of characters. Like strings, a symbol literal containing any characters with the top bit set will have an encoding determined by the encoding of the source file containing the definition.

Ruby 1.9 added string-like functionality to symbols.

Mixes In

Comparable: <, <=, ==, >, >=, between?

Class Methods

all_symbols   Symbol.all_symbols → *array*

Returns an array of all the symbols currently in Ruby's symbol table.

```
list = Symbol.all_symbols
list.size          # => 2240
list.grep(/attr_/) # => [:attr_reader, :attr_writer, :attr_accessor, :attr_name]
```

Instance Methods

<=>   *sym* <=> *other_sym* → -1, 0, +1, or nil

Compares *sym* to *other_sym* after converting each to strings. <=> is the basis for the methods <, <=, >, >=, and between?, included from module Comparable. The method Symbol#== does not use Comparable#==.

```
:abcdef <=> :abcde   # => 1
:abcdef <=> :abcdef  # => 0
:abcdef <=> :abcdefg # => -1
:abcdef <=> :ABCDEF  # => 1
```

==   *sym* == *obj* → *true* or *false*

Returns true only if *sym* and *obj* are symbols with the same object_id.

```
:abcdef == :abcde  # => false
:abcdef == :abcdef # => true
```

=~   *sym* =~ *obj* → *int* or nil

Converts *sym* to a string and matches it against *obj*.

```
:abcdef =~ /.[aeiou]/ # => 3
:abcdef =~ /xx/       # => nil
```

[ ]

$$sym[\ int\ ] \rightarrow string \text{ or nil}$$
$$sym[\ int,\ int\ ] \rightarrow string \text{ or nil}$$
$$sym[\ range\ ] \rightarrow string \text{ or nil}$$
$$sym[\ regexp\ ] \rightarrow string \text{ or nil}$$
$$sym[\ regexp,\ int\ ] \rightarrow string \text{ or nil}$$
$$sym[\ string\ ] \rightarrow string \text{ or nil}$$

Converts *sym* to a string and then indexes it using the same parameters as String#[].

```
:"hello there"[1]              # => "e"
:"hello there"[1,3]            # => "ell"
:"hello there"[1..3]           # => "ell"
:"hello there"[-3,2]           # => "er"
:"hello there"[-4..-2]         # => "her"
:"hello there"[-2..-4]         # => ""
:"hello there"[/[aeiou](.)\1/]     # => "ell"
:"hello there"[/[aeiou](.)\1/, 1]  # => "l"
```

capitalize

$sym.\text{capitalize} \rightarrow symbol$

Returns a symbol with the first character of *sym* converted to uppercase and the remainder to lowercase.

```
:hello.capitalize           # => :Hello
:"HELLO WORLD".capitalize   # => :"Hello world"
:"123ABC".capitalize        # => :"123abc"
```

casecmp

$sym.\text{casecmp}(\ other\ ) \rightarrow \text{-1, 0, +1, or nil}$

Case-insensitive version of Symbol#<=>. Returns nil if *other* is not a symbol.

```
:abcdef.casecmp(:abcde)    # => 1
:abcdef.casecmp(:abcdef)   # => 0
:abcdef.casecmp(:ABCDEF)   # => 0
:aBcDeF.casecmp(:abcdef)   # => 0
:abcdef.casecmp(:abcdefg)  # => -1
:abcdef.casecmp("abcdef")  # => nil
```

downcase

$sym.\text{downcase} \rightarrow symbol$

Returns a symbol with all the characters of *sym* converted to lowercase.

```
:Hello.downcase           # => :hello
:"HELLO WORLD".downcase   # => :"hello world"
:"123ABC".downcase        # => :"123abc"
```

empty?

$sym.\text{empty} \rightarrow true \text{ or } false$

Returns true if the string representation of *sym* is empty.

```
:hello.empty? # => false
:"".empty?    # => true
```

encoding

sym.encoding → enc

Returns the encoding of *sym*.

```
# encoding: utf-8
:hello.encoding   # => #<Encoding:US-ASCII>
:"∂og".encoding # => #<Encoding:UTF-8>
```

id2name

sym.id2name → string

Returns the string representation of *sym*.

```
:fred.id2name                # => "fred"
:"99 red balloons!".id2name # => "99 red balloons!"
```

inspect

sym.inspect → string

Returns the representation of *sym* as a symbol literal.

```
:fred.inspect                # => :fred
:"99 red balloons!".inspect # => :"99 red balloons!"
```

intern

sym.intern → sym

Synonym for Symbol#to_sym.

length

sym.length → int

Returns the number of characters in the string representation *sym*.

```
# encoding: utf-8
:dog.length   # => 3
:∂og.length # => 3
```

match

sym.match(regexp) → int or nil

Converts *self* to a string and then matches it against *regexp*. Unlike String#match, does not support blocks or non-regexp parameters.

```
:hello.match(/(.)\1/) # => 2
:hello.match(/ll/)    # => 2
```

next

sym.next → symbol

Synonym for Symbol#succ.

size

sym.size → int

Synonym for Symbol#length.

slice

$$sym.\text{slice}(\ int\ ) \rightarrow string \text{ or nil}$$
$$sym.\text{slice}(\ int, int\ ) \rightarrow string \text{ or nil}$$
$$sym.\text{slice}(\ range\ ) \rightarrow string \text{ or nil}$$
$$sym.\text{slice}(\ regexp\ ) \rightarrow string \text{ or nil}$$
$$sym.\text{slice}(\ match\_string\ ) \rightarrow string \text{ or nil}$$

Synonym for Symbol#[ ].

succ

$$sym.\text{succ} \rightarrow symbol$$

Returns the successor to *sym* using the same rules as String#succ.

```
:abcd.succ      # => :abce
:THX1138.succ   # => :THX1139
:"1999zzz".succ # => :"2000aaa"
```

swapcase

$$sym.\text{swapcase} \rightarrow symbol$$

Returns a symbol with the case of all the characters of *sym* swapped.

```
:Hello.swapcase    # => :hELLO
:"123ABC".swapcase # => :"123abc"
```

to_proc

$$sym.\text{to\_proc} \rightarrow proc$$

Allows a symbol to be used when a block is expected. The symbol acts as a method invoked on each parameter to the block. See *The Symbol.to_proc Trick,* on page 352 for more information.

```
%w{ant bee cat}.map(&:reverse) # => ["tna", "eeb", "tac"]
```

to_s

$$sym.\text{to\_s} \rightarrow string$$

Synonym for Symbol#id2name.

to_sym

$$sym.\text{to\_sym} \rightarrow sym$$

Symbols are symbol-like!

upcase

$$sym.\text{upcase} \rightarrow symbol$$

Returns a symbol with all the characters of *sym* in uppercase.

```
:Hello.upcase    # => :HELLO
:"123Abc".upcase # => :"123ABC"
```

Thread

Thread encapsulates the behavior of a thread of execution, including the main thread of the Ruby script. See the tutorial beginning Chapter 12, *Fibers, Threads, and Processes*, on page 161.

In the descriptions that follow, the parameter *symbol* refers to a name that is either a quoted string or a symbol (such as :name).

Class Methods

abort_on_exception   Thread.abort_on_exception → *true* or *false*

Returns the status of the global *abort on exception* condition. The default is false. When set to true or if the global $DEBUG flag is true (perhaps because the command-line option -d was specified), all threads will abort (the process will exit(0)) if an exception is raised in any thread. See also Thread.abort_on_exception=.

abort_on_exception=   Thread.abort_on_exception= *true* or *false*→ *true* or *false*

When set to true, all threads will abort if an exception is raised. Returns the new state.

```
Thread.abort_on_exception = true
t1 = Thread.new do
  puts  "In new thread"
  raise "Exception from thread"
end
sleep(0.1)
puts "not reached"
```

produces:

```
In new thread
prog.rb:4:in `block in <main>': Exception from thread (RuntimeError)
```

current   Thread.current → *thread*

Returns the currently executing thread.

```
Thread.current # => #<Thread:0x007fb2340c0ce0 run>
```

exclusive   Thread.exclusive { ... } → *obj*

Executes the block and returns whatever the block returns. Internally uses a Mutex so that only one thread can be executing code under the control of Thread.exclusive at a time.

exit   Thread.exit

Terminates the currently running thread and schedules another thread to be run. If this thread is already marked to be killed, exit returns the Thread. If this is the main thread, or the last thread, exits the process.

---

fork   Thread.fork { ... } → *thread*

Synonym for Thread.start.

---

kill   Thread.kill(*thread*)

Causes the given thread to exit (see Thread.exit).

```
count = 0
a = Thread.new { loop { count += 1 } }
sleep(0.1)     # => 0
Thread.kill(a) # => #<Thread:0x007fefc210f400 run>
count          # => 910465
# give it time to die...
sleep 0.01
a.alive?       # => false
```

---

list   Thread.list → *array*

Returns an array of Thread objects for all threads that are either runnable or stopped.

```
Thread.new { sleep(200) }
Thread.new { 1000000.times {|i| i*i } }
Thread.new { Thread.stop }
Thread.list.each {|thr| p thr }
```

produces:

```
#<Thread:0x007fa3b90c0cd8 run>
#<Thread:0x007fa3b910f810 sleep>
#<Thread:0x007fa3b910f630 run>
#<Thread:0x007fa3b902b728 sleep>
```

---

main   Thread.main → *thread*

Returns the main thread for the process.

```
Thread.main # => #<Thread:0x007ffc9b8c0ce0 run>
```

---

new   Thread.new(‹*arg*›*) { |args| ... } → *thread*

Creates and runs a new thread to execute the instructions given in *block*. Any arguments passed to Thread.new are passed into the block.

```
x = Thread.new { sleep 0.1; print "x"; print "y"; print "z" }
a = Thread.new { print "a"; print "b"; sleep 0.2; print "c" }
x.join; a.join # wait for threads to finish
```

produces:

```
abxyzc
```

---

pass   Thread.pass

Invokes the thread scheduler to pass execution to another thread.

```
a = Thread.new { print "a"; Thread.pass; print "b" }
b = Thread.new { print "x"; Thread.pass; print "y" }
a.join; b.join
```

produces:

```
axby
```

---

start

Thread.start(‹ *args* ›*) { | args | ... } → *thread*

Basically the same as Thread.new. However, if class Thread is subclassed, then calling start in that subclass will not invoke the subclass's initialize method.

---

stop

Thread.stop

Stops execution of the current thread, putting it into a *sleep* state, and schedules execution of another thread. Resets the *critical* condition to false.

```
a = Thread.new { print "a"; Thread.stop; print "c" }
sleep 0.01
print "b"
a.wakeup
a.join
```

produces:

```
abc
```

Instance Methods

[ ]

thr[*symbol*] → *obj* or nil

New in 2.0

Attribute Reference—Returns the value of a fiber-local variable, using either a symbol or a string name. If the specified variable does not exist, returns nil. Every thread has an implicit root fiber, so this method is always available. See also Thread#thread_variable_get.

```
a = Thread.new { Thread.current["name"] = "A"; Thread.stop }
b = Thread.new { Thread.current[:name]  = "B"; Thread.stop }
c = Thread.new { Thread.current["name"] = "C"; Thread.stop }
sleep 0.01  # let them all run
Thread.list.each {|x| puts "#{x.inspect}: #{x[:name]}" }
```

produces:

```
#<Thread:0x007fd5fc0c0ce0 run>:
#<Thread:0x007fd5fc10eda0 sleep>: A
#<Thread:0x007fd5fc10ebc0 sleep>: B
#<Thread:0x007fd5fc02b898 sleep>: C
```

[ ]=

thr[*symbol*] = *obj* → *obj*

Attribute Assignment—Sets or creates the value of a fiber-local variable, using either a symbol or a string. See also Thread#thread_variable_set.

abort_on_exception

thr.abort_on_exception → *true* or *false*

Returns the status of the thread-local *abort on exception* condition for *thr*. The default is false. See also Thread.abort_on_exception=.

abort_on_exception=

thr.abort_on_exception= *true* or *false*→ *true* or *false*

When set to true, causes all threads (including the main program) to abort if an exception is raised in *thr*. The process will effectively exit(0).

add_trace_func

thr.add_trace_func(*proc*) → *proc*
thr.add_trace_func(nil) → nil

Adds a trace function to *thr* (see Thread#set_trace_func). (This method has been replaced by the TracePoint class in Ruby 2.0.)

New in 2.0

alive?

thr.alive? → *true* or *false*

Returns true if *thr* is running or sleeping.

```
thr = Thread.new { }
thr.join              # => #<Thread:0x007fd26312c248 dead>
Thread.current.alive? # => true
thr.alive?            # => false
```

backtrace

thr.backtrace → *array*

Returns the backtrace of *thr*.

```
thr = Thread.new do
  print "starting\n"
  def sleeper(n)
    print "sleeping\n"
    sleep n
  end
  sleeper(10)
end
p thr.status
p thr.backtrace
Thread.pass
p thr.status
p thr.backtrace
```

produces:

```
"run"
starting
sleeping
["prog.rb:5:in `sleep'", "/tmp/prog.rb:5:in `sleeper'", "/tmp/prog.rb:7:in `block
in <main>'"]
"sleep"
["prog.rb:5:in `sleep'", "/tmp/prog.rb:5:in `sleeper'", "/tmp/prog.rb:7:in `block
in <main>'"]
```

backtrace_locations

thr.backtrace → *array*

New in 2.0   Analog of the global caller_locations method.

```
thr = Thread.new do
  print "starting\n"
  def sleeper(n)
    print "sleeping\n"
    sleep n
  end
  sleeper(10)
end
p thr.backtrace_locations
```

produces:

```
[]
starting
sleeping
```

exit

thr.exit → *thr* or nil

Terminates *thr* and schedules another thread to be run. If this thread is already marked to be killed, exit returns the Thread. If this is the main thread, or the last thread, exits the process.

group

thr.group → *thread_group*

Returns the ThreadGroup owning *thr*, or nil.

```
thread = Thread.new { sleep 99 }
Thread.current.group.list # => [#<Thread:0x007f836a0c0ce8 run>,
                          # .. #<Thread:0x007f836a83f820 run>]
new_group = ThreadGroup.new
thread.group.list         # => [#<Thread:0x007f836a0c0ce8 run>,
                          # .. #<Thread:0x007f836a83f820 run>]
new_group.add(thread)
thread.group.list         # => [#<Thread:0x007f836a83f820 run>]
Thread.current.group.list # => [#<Thread:0x007f836a0c0ce8 run>]
```

join

thr.join → *thr*
thr.join(*limit*) → *thr*

The calling thread will suspend execution and run *thr*. Does not return until *thr* exits or until *limit* seconds have passed. If the time limit expires, nil will be returned; otherwise, *thr* is returned.

Any threads not joined will be killed when the main program exits. If *thr* had previously raised an exception and the abort_on_exception and $DEBUG flags are not set (so the exception has not yet been processed), it will be processed at this time.

New in 2.0   You cannot join to the current or main thread.

```
a = Thread.new { print "a"; sleep(10); print "b"; print "c" }
x = Thread.new { print "x"; Thread.pass; print "y"; print "z" }
x.join # Let x thread finish, a will be killed on exit.
```

produces:

```
axyz
```

The following example illustrates the *limit* parameter:

```
y = Thread.new { loop { sleep 0.1; print "tick...\n" }}
y.join(0.25)
puts "Gave up waiting..."
```

produces:

```
tick...
tick...
Gave up waiting...
```

---

keys   *thr*.keys → *array*

Returns an array of the names of the fiber-local variables (as symbols).

New in 2.0

```
thr = Thread.new do
  Thread.current[:cat] = 'meow'
  Thread.current["dog"] = 'woof'
end
thr.join  # => #<Thread:0x007feeb312c0d8 dead>
thr.keys  # => [:cat, :dog]
```

---

key?   *thr*.key?(*symbol*) → *true* or *false*

Returns true if the given string (or symbol) exists as a thread-local variable.

```
me = Thread.current
me[:oliver] = "a"
me.key?(:oliver)  # => true
me.key?(:stanley) # => false
```

---

kill   *thr*.kill

Synonym for Thread#exit.

---

priority   *thr*.priority → *int*

Returns the priority of *thr*. The default is zero; higher-priority threads will run before lower-priority threads.

```
Thread.current.priority # => 0
```

---

priority=   *thr*.priority= *int* → *thr*

Sets the priority of *thr* to *integer*. Higher-priority threads will run before lower-priority threads. If you find yourself messing with thread priorities to get things to work, you're doing something wrong.

```
count_high = count_low = 0
Thread.new do
  Thread.current.priority = 1
  loop { count_high += 1 }
end
Thread.new do
  Thread.current.priority = -1
  loop { count_low += 1 }
end

sleep 0.1
count_high # => 3651144
count_low  # => 1829723
```

raise

thr.raise
thr.raise(*message*)
thr.raise(*exception* ‹, *message* ‹, *array*››)

Raises an exception (see Object#raise on page 622 for details) from *thr*. The caller does not have to be *thr*.

```
Thread.abort_on_exception = true
a = Thread.new { sleep(200) }
a.raise("Gotcha")
a.join
```

produces:

```
        from prog.rb:2:in `block in <main>'
prog.rb:2:in `sleep': Gotcha (RuntimeError)
```

run

thr.run → *thr*

Wakes up *thr*, making it eligible for scheduling. If not in a critical section, then invokes the scheduler.

safe_level

thr.safe_level → *int*

Returns the safe level in effect for *thr*. Setting thread-local safe levels can help when implementing sandboxes that run insecure code.

```
thr = Thread.new { $SAFE = 3; sleep }
Thread.current.safe_level # => 0
thr.safe_level            # => 0
```

set_trace_func

thr.set_trace_func(*proc*) → *proc*
thr.set_trace_func(nil) → nil

Analog to the global set_trace_func method, but for a particular thread.

---

status
thr.status → string, false or nil

Returns the status of *thr*: sleep if *thr* is sleeping or waiting on I/O, run if *thr* is executing, aborting if *thr* will raise an exception when joined, false if *thr* terminated normally, and nil if *thr* terminated with an exception.

```ruby
a = Thread.new { raise("die now") }
b = Thread.new { Thread.stop }
c = Thread.new { Thread.exit }
c.join                   # => #<Thread:0x007fc28082b6e0 dead>
sleep 0.1                # => 0
a.status                 # => nil
b.status                 # => "sleep"
c.status                 # => false
Thread.current.status    # => "run"
```

---

stop?
thr.stop? → true or false

Returns true if *thr* is dead or sleeping.

```ruby
a = Thread.new { Thread.stop }
b = Thread.current
Thread.pass
a.stop?   # => false
b.stop?   # => false
```

---

terminate
thr.terminate

Synonym for Thread#exit.

---

thread_variable?
thr.thread_variable?(name) → true or false

Determines if there is a thread-local (as opposed to fiber local) variable with the given name.

New in 2.0

---

thread_variables
thr.thread_variables → array

Returns the names of current thread local variables.

New in 2.0

```ruby
thr = Thread.current
thr.thread_variables                      # => []
thr.thread_variable_set(:option, "X12")   # => "X12"
thr.thread_variable_set(:speed,   123)    # => 123
thr[:fiber_not_thread] = :other
thr.thread_variables                      # => [:option, :speed]

# fiber variables are in a different bucket
thr.keys                                  # => [:__recursive_key__,
                                          # .. :fiber_not_thread]
```

---

thread_variable_get
thr.thread_variable_get(name) → obj or nil

Return the value of the thread-local variable with the given name.

New in 2.0

thread_variable_set   *thr*.thread_variable_get(*name, val*) → *val*

New in 2.0   Set the value of the thread-local variable with the given name to the given value.

value   *thr*.value → *obj*

New in 2.0   Waits for *thr* to complete (via Thread#join) and returns its value. Because value uses join, you cannot get the value of the current or main thread.

```
a = Thread.new { 2 + 2 }
a.value   # => 4
```

wakeup   *thr*.wakeup → *thr*

Marks *thr* as eligible for scheduling (it may still remain blocked on I/O, however). Does not invoke the scheduler (see Thread#run).

Class   ThreadGroup

A ThreadGroup keeps track of a number of threads. A Thread can belong to only one ThreadGroup at a time; adding a thread to a group will remove it from its current group. Newly created threads belong to the group of the thread that created them.

Class Constants

Default   Default thread group.

Class Methods

new   ThreadGroup.new → *thgrp*

Returns a newly created ThreadGroup. The group is initially empty.

Instance Methods

add   *thgrp*.add(*thread*) → *thgrp*

Adds the given thread to this group, removing it from any other group.

```
puts "Default group is #{ThreadGroup::Default.list}"
tg = ThreadGroup.new
t1 = Thread.new { sleep }
t2 = Thread.new { sleep }
puts "t1 is #{t1}, t2 is #{t2}"
tg.add(t1)
puts "Default group now #{ThreadGroup::Default.list}"
puts "tg group now #{tg.list}"
```

produces:

```
Default group is [#<Thread:0x007fee488c0cd8 run>]
t1 is #<Thread:0x007fee4890f1d0>, t2 is #<Thread:0x007fee4890eff0>
Default group now [#<Thread:0x007fee488c0cd8 run>, #<Thread:0x007fee4890eff0
sleep>]
tg group now [#<Thread:0x007fee4890f1d0 sleep>]
```

---

enclose

thgrp.enclose → *thgrp*

Prevents threads being added to and removed from *thgrp*. New threads may still be started.

```
thread = Thread.new { sleep 99 }
group = ThreadGroup.new
group.add(thread)
group.enclose
ThreadGroup::Default.add(thread)   # This will raise an exception
```

produces:

```
        from prog.rb:5:in `<main>'
prog.rb:5:in `add': can't move from the enclosed thread group (ThreadError)
```

---

enclosed?

thgrp.enclose → *true* or *false*

Returns true if this thread group has been enclosed.

---

list

thgrp.list → *array*

Returns an array of all existing Thread objects that belong to this group.

```
ThreadGroup::Default.list # => [#<Thread:0x007f82e98c0cd0 run>]
```

Time

Time is an abstraction of dates and times. Time is stored internally as the number of seconds and microseconds since the *epoch*, January 1, 1970 00:00 UTC. On some operating systems, this offset is allowed to be negative. Also see the Date library module on page 744. The Time class treats Greenwich mean time (GMT) and Coordinated Universal Time (UTC)[5] as equivalent. GMT is the older way of referring to these baseline times but persists in the names of calls on POSIX systems.

All times are stored with some number of microseconds, so times that are apparently equal when displayed may be different when compared.

As of Ruby 1.9.2, the range of dates that can be represented is no longer limited by the underlying operating system's time representation (so there's no year 2038 problem). As a result, the year passed to the methods gm, local, new, mktime, and utc must now include the century—a year of 90 now represents 90 and not 1990.

Mixes In

Comparable: <, <=, ==, >, >=, between?

Class Methods

at
$$\text{Time.at(\textit{time})} \rightarrow \textit{time}$$
$$\text{Time.at(\textit{seconds} ‹, \textit{microseconds}›)} \rightarrow \textit{time}$$

Creates a new Time object with the value given by *time* or the given number of *seconds* (and optional *microseconds*) from epoch. Microseconds may be a float—this allows setting times with nanosecond granularity on systems that support it. A nonportable feature allows the offset to be negative on some systems.

```
Time.at(0)           # => 1969-12-31 18:00:00 -0600
Time.at(946702800)   # => 1999-12-31 23:00:00 -0600
Time.at(-284061600)  # => 1960-12-31 00:00:00 -0600
t = Time.at(946702800, 123.456)
t.usec               # => 123
t.nsec               # => 123456
```

gm
$$\text{Time.gm(\textit{year} ‹, \textit{month} ‹, \textit{day} ‹, \textit{hour} ‹, \textit{min} ‹, \textit{sec} ‹, \textit{usec}››››››)} \rightarrow \textit{time}$$
$$\text{Time.gm(\textit{sec, min, hour, day, month, year, wday, yday, isdst, tz})} \rightarrow \textit{time}$$

Creates a time based on given values, interpreted as UTC. The year must be specified. Other values default to the minimum value for that field (and may be nil or omitted). Months may be specified by numbers from 1 to 12 or by the three-letter English month names. Hours are specified on a 24-hour clock (0..23). Raises an ArgumentError if any values are out of range. Will also accept ten arguments in the order output by Time#to_a.

```
Time.gm(2000,"jan",1,20,15,1) # => 2000-01-01 20:15:01 UTC
```

---

5. Yes, UTC really does stand for Coordinated Universal Time. There was a committee involved.

local
Time.local(*sec, min, hour, day, month, year, wday, yday, isdst, tz*) → *time*
Time.local(*year ‹, month ‹, day ‹, hour ‹, min ‹, sec ‹, usec › › › › › › ›)* → *time*

Same as Time.gm but interprets the values in the local time zone. The first form accepts ten arguments in the order output by Time#to_a.

```
Time.local(2000,"jan",1,20,15,1) # => 2000-01-01 20:15:01 -0600
```

mktime
Time.mktime(*year ‹, month ‹, day ‹, hour ‹, min ‹, sec ‹, usec › › › › › › ›)* → *time*
Time.mktime(*sec, min, hour, day, month, year, wday, yday, isdst, tz*) → *time*

Synonym for Time.local.

new
Time.new → *time*
Time.new(*year ‹, month ‹, day ‹, hour ‹, min ‹, sec ‹, utc_offset › › › › › ›)*

The first form returns a Time object initialized to the current system time. The object created will be created using the resolution available on your system clock and so may include fractional seconds.

```
a = Time.new       # => 2013-05-27 12:33:12 -0500
b = Time.new       # => 2013-05-27 12:33:12 -0500
a == b             # => false
"%.6f" % a.to_f # => "1369675992.686567"
"%.6f" % b.to_f # => "1369675992.686600"
```

The second form creates a Time object for the given date and time. The optional *utc_offset* may be a number representing seconds or a string such as "+06:00".

```
Time.new(2010, 12, 25, 8, 0, 0, "-06:00") # => 2010-12-25 08:00:00 -0600
```

now
Time.now → *time*

Synonym for Time.new.

utc
Time.utc(*year ‹, month ‹, day ‹, hour ‹, min ‹, sec ‹, usec › › › › › › ›)* → *time*
Time.utc(*sec, min, hour, day, month, year, wday, yday, isdst, tz*) → *time*

Synonym for Time.gm.

```
Time.utc(2000,"jan",1,20,15,1) # => 2000-01-01 20:15:01 UTC
```

Instance Methods

+
time + numeric → *time*

Addition—Adds some number of seconds (possibly fractional) to *time* and returns that value as a new time.

```
t = Time.now       # => 2013-05-27 12:33:12 -0500
t + (60 * 60 * 24) # => 2013-05-28 12:33:12 -0500
```

-

$$time - time \rightarrow float$$
$$time - numeric \rightarrow time$$

Difference—Returns a new time that represents the difference between two times or subtracts the given number of seconds in *numeric* from *time*.

```
t = Time.now        # => 2013-05-27 12:33:12 -0500
t2 = t + 2592000 # => 2013-06-26 12:33:12 -0500
t2 - t              # => 2592000.0
t2 - 2592000        # => 2013-05-27 12:33:12 -0500
```

<=>

$$time <=> other\_time \rightarrow -1, 0, +1$$
$$time <=> other \rightarrow nil\}$$

Comparison—Compares *time* with *other_time* or with *numeric*, which is the number of seconds (possibly fractional) since epoch. As of Ruby 1.9, nil is returned for comparison against anything other than a Time object.

```
t = Time.now        # => 2013-05-27 12:33:13 -0500
t2 = t + 2592000 # => 2013-06-26 12:33:13 -0500
t <=> t2            # => -1
t2 <=> t            # => 1
t <=> t             # => 0
```

---

day-name?

$$time.monday? \rightarrow true \text{ or } false$$
$$time.tuesday? \rightarrow true \text{ or } false$$
$$time.wednesday? \rightarrow true \text{ or } false$$
$$time.thursday? \rightarrow true \text{ or } false$$
$$time.friday? \rightarrow true \text{ or } false$$
$$time.saturday? \rightarrow true \text{ or } false$$
$$time.sunday? \rightarrow true \text{ or } false$$

Returns true if the time is on the given day.

---

asctime

$$time.asctime \rightarrow string$$

Returns a canonical string representation of *time*.

```
Time.now.asctime # => "Mon May 27 12:33:13 2013"
```

---

ctime

$$time.ctime \rightarrow string$$

Synonym for Time#asctime.

---

day

$$time.day \rightarrow int$$

Returns the day of the month (1..n) for *time*.

```
t = Time.now # => 2013-05-27 12:33:13 -0500
t.day          # => 27
```

---

dst?   *time*.dst? → *true* or *false*

Synonym for Time#isdst.

```
Time.local(2000, 7, 1).dst? # => true
Time.local(2000, 1, 1).dst? # => false
```

---

getgm   *time*.getgm → *time*

Returns a new Time object representing *time* in UTC.

```
t = Time.local(2000,1,1,20,15,1) # => 2000-01-01 20:15:01 -0600
t.gmt?                           # => false
y = t.getgm                      # => 2000-01-02 02:15:01 UTC
y.gmt?                           # => true
t == y                           # => true
```

---

getlocal   *time*.getlocal → *time*
                                                                     time.getlocal(*utc_offset*) → *time*

Returns a new Time object representing *time* in local time (using the local time zone in effect
for this process) or with the given offset from UTC.

```
t = Time.gm(2000,1,1,20,15,1) # => 2000-01-01 20:15:01 UTC
t.gmt?                        # => true
l = t.getlocal                # => 2000-01-01 14:15:01 -0600
l.gmt?                        # => false
t == l                        # => true
t.getlocal("-06:00")          # => 2000-01-01 14:15:01 -0600
t.getlocal(-21600)            # => 2000-01-01 14:15:01 -0600
```

---

getutc   *time*.getutc → *time*

Synonym for Time#getgm.

---

gmt?   *time*.gmt? → *true* or *false*

Returns true if *time* represents a time in UTC.

```
t = Time.now                  # => 2013-05-27 12:33:13 -0500
t.gmt?                        # => false
t = Time.gm(2000,1,1,20,15,1) # => 2000-01-01 20:15:01 UTC
t.gmt?                        # => true
```

---

gmtime   *time*.gmtime → *time*

Converts *time* to UTC, modifying the receiver.

```
t = Time.now # => 2013-05-27 12:33:13 -0500
t.gmt?       # => false
t.gmtime     # => 2013-05-27 17:33:13 UTC
t.gmt?       # => true
```

gmt_offset

time.gmt_offset → int

Returns the offset in seconds between the time zone of *time* and UTC.

```
t = Time.gm(2000,1,1,20,15,1) # => 2000-01-01 20:15:01 UTC
t.gmt_offset                   # => 0
l = t.getlocal                 # => 2000-01-01 14:15:01 -0600
l.gmt_offset                   # => -21600
```

gmtoff

time.gmtoff → *int*

Synonym for Time#gmt_offset.

hour

time.hour → *int*

Returns the hour of the day (0..23) for *time*.

```
t = Time.now # => 2013-05-27 12:33:13 -0500
t.hour       # => 12
```

isdst

time.isdst → *true* or *false*

Returns true if *time* occurs during daylight saving time in its time zone.

```
Time.local(2000, 7, 1).isdst # => true
Time.local(2000, 1, 1).isdst # => false
```

localtime

time.localtime → *time*
time.localtime(*utc_offset*) → *time*

Converts *time* to local time (using the local time zone in effect for this process or the given offset from UTC), modifying the receiver.

```
t = Time.gm(2000, "jan", 1, 20, 15, 1)
t.gmt?          # => true
t.localtime     # => 2000-01-01 14:15:01 -0600
t.gmt?          # => false
t = Time.gm(2000, "jan", 1, 20, 15, 1)
t.localtime(7200) # => 2000-01-01 22:15:01 +0200
```

mday

time.mday → *int*

Synonym for Time#day.

min

time.min → *int*

Returns the minute of the hour (0..59) for *time*.

```
t = Time.now # => 2013-05-27 12:33:13 -0500
t.min        # => 33
```

---

mon   *time*.mon → *int*

Returns the month of the year (1..12) for *time*.

```
t = Time.now # => 2013-05-27 12:33:14 -0500
t.mon          # => 5
```

---

month   *time*.month → *int*

Synonym for Time#mon.

---

nsec   *time*.nsec → *int*

Returns just the number of nanoseconds for *time*.

```
t = Time.now       # => 2013-05-27 12:33:14 -0500
"%10.6f" % t.to_f # => "1369675994.128473"
t.nsec             # => 128473000
t.usec             # => 128473
```

---

round   *time*.round(*digits*=0) → *new_time*

Returns a new time with the fractional seconds rounded to the specified number of decimal
digits. (This may affect the rest of the time fields if the rounding causes the number of seconds
to increment.)

```
require 'time'
t = Time.utc(2010, 10, 11, 12, 13, 59.75)

t.iso8601(3)           # => "2010-10-11T12:13:59.750Z"
t.round(2).iso8601(3) # => "2010-10-11T12:13:59.750Z"
t.round(1).iso8601(3) # => "2010-10-11T12:13:59.800Z"
t.round.iso8601(3)     # => "2010-10-11T12:14:00.000Z"
```

---

sec   *time*.sec → *int*

Returns the second of the minute (0..60)[6] for *time*.

```
t = Time.now # => 2013-05-27 12:33:14 -0500
t.sec          # => 14
```

---

6. Yes, seconds really can range from zero to 60. This allows the system to inject leap seconds every now
    and then to correct for the fact time measured by atomic clocks differs from time measured by a spinning
    earth.

strftime

time.strftime(*format*) → *string*

Formats *time* according to the directives in the given format string. Directives look like:

%‹flags›‹width› conversion

The optional flags may be one or more of:

-	Don't pad numbers with spaces
_	Pad numbers with spaces
0	Pad numbers with zeroes
^	Convert field to uppercase
#	Reverse the case of the field
:	Use colons for the %z conversion. One colon in the flag puts a colon between hours and minutes. Two colons in the flag adds a seconds field.

The *width* specifies the minimum result width for the field.

The available conversions are:

Format	Meaning
%%	Literal %
%a	The abbreviated weekday name ("Sun")
%A	The full weekday name ("Sunday")
%b	The abbreviated month name ("Jan")
%B	The full month name ("January")
%c	The preferred local date and time representation
%C	The two digit century (currently 20)
%d	Day of the month (01..31)
%D	Date (%m/%d/%y)
%e	Day of the month, blank padded (␣1..31)
%F	ISO8601 date (%Y-%m-%d)
%g	Last 2 digits of ISO8601 week-based year
%G	ISO8601 week-based year
%h	The abbreviated month name ("Jan")
%H	Hour of the day, 24-hour clock (00..23)
%I	Hour of the day, 12-hour clock (01..12)
%j	Day of the year (001..366)
%k	Hour of the day, 24-hour clock, blank padded (␣0..23)
%l	Hour of the day, 12-hour clock, blank padded (␣1..12)
%L	Milliseconds of the second
%m	Month of the year (01..12)
%M	Minute of the hour (00..59)
%n	Newline
%N	Fractional seconds
%p	Meridian indicator ("AM" or "PM")
%P	Meridian indicator ("am" or "pm")
%r	12 hour time (%I:%M:%S %p)

Format	Meaning
%R	24 hour time (%H:%M)
%s	Number of seconds since 1970-01-01 00:00:00 UTC
%S	Second of the minute (00..60)
%t	Tab
%T	24 hour time (%H:%M:%S)
%u	Day of the week (Monday is 1, 1..7)
%U	Week number of the current year, starting with the first Sunday as the first day of the first week (00..53)
%w	Day of the week (Sunday is 0, 0..6)
%v	VMS date (%e-%^b-%4Y)
%V	ISO8601 week number (01..53)
%W	Week number of the current year, starting with the first Monday as the first day of the first week (00..53)
%x	Preferred representation for the date alone, no time
%X	Preferred representation for the time alone, no date
%y	Year without a century (00..99)
%Y	Year with century
%z	Time zone offset (+/-hhmm). Use %:z or %::z to format with colons
%Z	Time zone name
%%	Literal % character

Table 25—Time#strftime directives

Any text not listed as a directive will be passed through to the output string.

```
t = Time.now
t.strftime("Printed on %m/%d/%Y") # => "Printed on 05/27/2013"
t.strftime("at %I:%M%P")          # => "at 12:33pm"
# force the am/pm flag to upper case
t.strftime("at %I:%M%^P")         # => "at 12:33PM"
```

subsec
time.subsec → *rational*

Return just the fractional number of seconds in *time* as a rational. (Compare with Time#usec, which returns an integer.)

```
t = Time.now
t.usec   # => 436218
t.subsec # => (218109/500000)
```

succ
time.succ → *later_time*

Deprecated. Use time + 1.

to_a
time.to_a → *array*

Returns a ten-element *array* of values for *time*: {[sec, min, hour, day, month, year, wday, yday, isdst, zone]}. See the individual methods for an explanation of the valid ranges of each value. The ten elements can be passed directly to the methods Time.utc or Time.local to create a new Time.

```
Time.now.to_a # => [14, 33, 12, 27, 5, 2013, 1, 147, true, "CDT"]
```

to_f

time.to_f → *float*

Returns the value of *time* as a floating-point number of seconds since epoch. Consider using Time#to_r if accuracy is required.

```
Time.now.to_f # => 1369675994.585341
```

to_i

time.to_i → *int*

Returns the value of *time* as an integer number of seconds since epoch.

```
Time.now.to_i # => 1369675994
```

to_r

time.to_r → *rational*

Returns a rational number containing time as a number of seconds since epoch (including fractional seconds).

```
Time.now.to_r # => (54787039789213/40000)
```

to_s

time.to_s → *string*

Returns a string representing *time*. Equivalent to calling Time#strftime with a format string of "%Y-%m-%d %H:%M:%S %z" (with UTC replacing the time zone for a UTC time).

```
Time.now.to_s                    # => "2013-05-27 12:33:14 -0500"
Time.utc(2011, 12, 25, 1, 2, 3).to_s # => "2011-12-25 01:02:03 UTC"
```

tv_nsec

time.tv_nsec → *int*

Synonym for Time#nsec.

tv_sec

time.tv_sec → *int*

Synonym for Time#to_i.

tv_usec

time.tv_usec → *int*

Synonym for Time#usec.

usec

time.usec → *int*

Returns just the number of microseconds for *time*. (Compare with Time#subsec, which returns a rational.)

```
t = Time.now        # => 2013-05-27 12:33:14 -0500
"%10.6f" % t.to_f # => "1369675994.878664"
t.nsec            # => 878664000
t.usec            # => 878664
```

utc

time.utc → *time*

Synonym for Time#gmtime.

```
t = Time.now # => 2013-05-27 12:33:14 -0500
t.utc?        # => false
t.utc         # => 2013-05-27 17:33:14 UTC
t.utc?        # => true
```

utc?

time.utc? → *true* or *false*

Returns true if *time* represents a time in UTC.

```
t = Time.now                      # => 2013-05-27 12:33:15 -0500
t.utc?                            # => false
t = Time.gm(2000,"jan",1,20,15,1) # => 2000-01-01 20:15:01 UTC
t.utc?                            # => true
```

utc_offset

time.utc_offset → *int*

Synonym for Time#gmt_offset.

wday

time.wday → *int*

Returns an integer representing the day of the week, 0..6, with Sunday == 0.

```
t = Time.now # => 2013-05-27 12:33:15 -0500
t.wday        # => 1
```

yday

time.yday → *int*

Returns an integer representing the day of the year, 1..366.

```
t = Time.now # => 2013-05-27 12:33:15 -0500
t.yday        # => 147
```

year

time.year → *int*

Returns the year for *time* (including the century).

```
t = Time.now # => 2013-05-27 12:33:15 -0500
t.year        # => 2013
```

zone

time.zone → *string*

Returns the name of the time zone used for *time*.

```
t = Time.gm(2000, "jan", 1, 20, 15, 1)
t.zone     # => "UTC"
t = Time.local(2000, "jan", 1, 20, 15, 1)
t.zone     # => "CST"
```

TracePoint

Using tracepoints you can trace the execution of certain events in your running program. The TracePoint class obsoletes the prior set_trace_func method.

When you create a trace point object, you give it the names of one or more events that you want to monitor. You also pass it a block. Whenever a monitored event fires, the block is invoked, passing in the trace point object, which now contains a description of that particular event event. Trace point objects are initially disabled—you need to enable them before they start firing.

```
tp = TracePoint.new(:line, :call, :return) do |tp|
  p tp
end

tp.enable

def add(a,b)
  a + b
end

p add(1,2)

tp.disable
```
produces:
```
#<TracePoint:line@prog.rb:7>
#<TracePoint:line@prog.rb:11>
#<TracePoint:call `add'@prog.rb:7>
#<TracePoint:line@prog.rb:8 in `add'>
#<TracePoint:return `add'@prog.rb:9>
3
#<TracePoint:line@prog.rb:13>
```

The events you can capture are:

:b_call	block entry
:b_return	block exit
:c_call	call a C-language routine
:c_return	return from a C-language routine
:call	call a Ruby method
:class	start class/module definition
:end	end a class/module definition
:line	execute a ne source code line
:raise	raise an exception
:return	return from a Ruby method
:thread_begin	start a thread
:thread_end	end a thread

Class Methods

new   TracePoint.new(‹ event_names ›*) { | tp | ... } → *tp*

Creates a new tracer for the given event names (or all events if no list is given). The returned object is both used to enable and disable this tracer and as the object thatis passed to the block when the events trigger. See the sample code at the start of this section to see this in action, and the table that follows it for a list of event names.

trace   TracePoint.trace(‹ event_names ›*) { | tp | ... } → *tp*

Sets up a trace point handler an immediately enables it.

```
tp = TracePoint.trace do |tp|
  p tp
end
a = 1
b = 2
tp.disable
```

produces:

```
#<TracePoint:c_return `trace'@prog.rb:1>
#<TracePoint:line@prog.rb:4>
#<TracePoint:line@prog.rb:5>
#<TracePoint:line@prog.rb:6>
#<TracePoint:c_call `disable'@prog.rb:6>
```

Instance Methods

binding   *tp.binding → binding_of_event*

The binding at the time of the event.

defined_class   *tp.defined_class → singleton class*

The class or module in which the event occurred.

disable   *tp.disable → true or false*

Disable this tracer, returning true if the tracer was enabled at the time.

enable   *tp.enable → true or false*

Enable this tracer, returning true if the tracer was already enabled.

enabled?   *tp.enabled? → true or false*

Returns true if the tracer is enabled.

event   *tp.event → symbol*

Returns the name of the event. See the table at the start of this section.

lineno

tp.lineno → fixnum

The source line number where the event occurred.

method_id

tp.method_id → symbol

The name of the method in which the event occurred.

path

tp.path → string

The full path to the Ruby source file in which the event occurred.

raised_exception

tp.raised_exception → Exception

The exception raised for a :raise event.

return_value

tp.return_value → obj

The value returned by a :return event.

self

tp.self → obj

The value of *self* at the time the event occurred.

Class **TrueClass**

The global value true is the only instance of class TrueClass and represents a logically true value in boolean expressions. The class provides operators allowing true to be used in logical expressions.

Instance Methods

&   true & *obj* → *true* or *false*

And—Returns false if *obj* is nil or false and returns true otherwise.

---

^   true ^ *obj* → *true* or *false*

Exclusive Or—Returns true if *obj* is nil or false and returns false otherwise.

| true | *obj* → true

Or—Returns true. Because *obj* is an argument to a method call, it is always evaluated; short-circuit evaluation is not performed in this case.

```
true |  puts("or")
true || puts("logical or")
```

produces:

```
or
```

Class · **UnboundMethod**

Ruby supports two forms of objectified methods. Class Method is used to represent methods that are associated with a particular object: these method objects are bound to that object. Bound method objects for an object can be created using Object#method.

Ruby also supports unbound methods, which are method objects that are not associated with a particular object. These can be created either by calling unbind on a bound method object or by calling Module#instance_method.

Unbound methods can be called only after they are bound to an object. That object must be a kind_of? the method's original class.

```ruby
class Square
  def area
    @side * @side
  end
  def initialize(side)
    @side = side
  end
end

area_unbound = Square.instance_method(:area)

s = Square.new(12)
area = area_unbound.bind(s)
area.call # => 144
```

Unbound methods are a reference to the method at the time it was objectified: subsequent changes to the underlying class will not affect the unbound method.

```ruby
class Test
  def test
    :original
  end
end
um = Test.instance_method(:test)
class Test
  def test
    :modified
  end
end
t = Test.new
t.test          # => :modified
um.bind(t).call # => :original
```

Instance Methods

arity   *umeth*.arity → *fixnum*

See Method#arity on page 565.

bind

umeth.bind(*obj*) → *method*

Bind *umeth* to *obj*. The class of *obj* must be the same as or a descendent of the class from which *umeth* was originally obtained.

```
Line 1 class A
         def test
           puts "In test, class = #{self.class}"
         end
     5 end
       class B < A
       end
       class C < B
       end
     10
       um = B.instance_method(:test)
       bm = um.bind(C.new)
       bm.call
       bm = um.bind(B.new)
     15 bm.call
       bm = um.bind(A.new)
       bm.call
```

produces:

```
            from prog.rb:16:in `<main>'
In test, class = C
In test, class = B
prog.rb:16:in `bind': bind argument must be an instance of B (TypeError)
```

name

umeth.name → *string*

Returns the name of the method *umeth*.

```
um = String.instance_method(:upcase)
um.name    # => :upcase
```

owner

umeth.owner → *module*

Returns the class or module in which *umeth* is defined.

```
um = String.instance_method(:upcase)
um.owner   # => String
```

parameters

umeth.parameters → *array*

Returns a description of the method's parameter list. See Method#parameters for details.

source_location

umeth.source_location → [*filename, lineno*] or nil

Returns the source filename and line number where *umeth* was defined or nil if self was not defined in Ruby source. See Method#source_location for an example.

CHAPTER 28

Standard Library

The Ruby interpreter comes with a large number of classes, modules, and methods built in —they are available as part of the running program. When you need a facility that isn't part of the built-in repertoire, you'll often find it in a library that you can require into your program. Sometimes you'll need to download one of these libraries (perhaps as a Ruby gem).

However, Ruby also ships as standard with a large number of libraries. Some of these are written in pure Ruby and will be available on all Ruby platforms. Others are Ruby extensions, and some of these will be present only if your system supports the resources that they need. All can be included into your Ruby program using require. And, unlike libraries you may find on the Internet, you can pretty much guarantee that all Ruby users will have these libraries already installed on their machines.

Ruby 1.9 has more than 100 standard libraries included in the distribution. For each of these libraries, this section shows a one- or a two-page summary. For each library, we give some introductory notes and typically an example or two of use. You won't find detailed method descriptions here; for that, consult the library's own documentation.

It's all very well suggesting that you "consult the library's own documentation," but where can you find it? The answer is that it depends. Some libraries have already been documented using RDoc (see Chapter 19, *Documenting Ruby*, on page 263). That means you can use the ri command to get the documentation.

If there's no RDoc documentation available, the next place to look is the library. If you have a source distribution of Ruby, these library files are in the ext/ and lib/ subdirectories. If instead you have a binary-only installation, you can still find the source of pure-Ruby library modules (normally in the lib/ruby/1.9/ directory under your Ruby installation). Often, library source directories contain documentation that the author has not yet converted to RDoc format.

If you still can't find documentation, turn to your search engine of choice. Many of the Ruby standard libraries are also hosted as external projects. The authors develop them stand-alone and then periodically integrate the code into the standard Ruby distribution. For example, if you want detailed information on the API for the YAML library, Try searching for *yaml ruby*—you'll probably end up at http://www.yaml.org/YAML_for_ruby.html.

The next port of call is the ruby-talk mailing list. Ask a (polite) question there, and chances are that you'll get a knowledgeable response within hours. See the tips in Section A1.3, *Mailing Lists*, on page 830 for pointers on how to subscribe.

And if you *still* can't find documentation, you can always follow Obi Wan's advice and do what we did when documenting Ruby—use the source. You'd be surprised at how easy it is to read the actual source of Ruby libraries and work out the details of usage.

There are some libraries that we don't document, either because they are pretty low level or because we cover them extensively elsewhere in the book. These libraries include:

New in 2.0

- debug—the Ruby debugger, covered in Section 14.1, *Ruby Debugger*, on page 195.
- iconv—has been removed from Ruby 2.0. Use String#encode.
- mkmf—covered in the online guide to extending Ruby.
- objspace—extensions to the ObjectSpace class designed to be used by the Ruby core team.
- psych—an interface to libyaml. You'll probably just use the YAML library.
- racc—this is the runtime used by the Racc parser generator. If you need this library, you'll also need the external Racc system.
- rake—see Section 15.6, *The Rake Build Tool*, on page 222.
- rdoc—see Chapter 19, *Documenting Ruby*, on page 263.
- rubygems—covered in Section 15.5, *RubyGems Integration*, on page 217 and in *Using RubyGems*, on page 234.

28.1 Library Changes in Ruby 1.9

These are the library changes in Ruby 1.9:

- Much of the Complex and Rational libraries are now built in to the interpreter. However, requiring the external libraries adds some functionally. In the case of Rational, this functionality is minimal.
- The CMath library has been added.
- The Enumerator library is now built in.
- The Fiber library has been added (it adds coroutine support to fibers).
- The Fiddle library (an interface to libffi, which supports calling functions in shared librries) is documented as a replacement for DL.
- ftools has been removed (and replaced by fileutils).
- The Generator library has been removed (use fibers).
- Notes on using irb from inside applications have been added.
- jcode has been removed in favor of built-in encoding support.
- The json library has been added.
- The matrix library no longer requires that you include mathn.
- The mutex library is now built in.
- parsedate has been removed. The Date class handles most of its functionality.
- readbytes has been removed. Class IO now supports the method directly.
- A description of Ripper has been added.
- A description of SecureRandom has been added.
- The shell library has been omitted, because it seems more like a curiosity than something folks would use (and it's broken under 1.9).
- The soap library has been removed.
- I've omitted the sync library. It is broken under 1.9, and the monitor library seems to be cleaner.
- Win32API is now deprecated in favor of using the DL library.

Abbrev

Given a set of strings, calculates the set of unambiguous abbreviations for those strings and returns a hash where the keys are all the possible abbreviations and the values are the full strings. Thus, given input of "car" and "cone," the keys pointing to "car" would be "ca" and "car," and those pointing to "cone" would be "co," "con," and "cone."

An optional pattern or a string may be specified—only those input strings matching the pattern, or beginning with the string, are considered for inclusion in the output hash.

Including the Abbrev library also adds an abbrev method to class Array.

- Shows the abbreviation set of some words:

```ruby
require 'abbrev'

Abbrev::abbrev(%w{ruby rune}) # => {"ruby"=>"ruby", "rub"=>"ruby",
                              # .. "rune"=>"rune", "run"=>"rune"}
```

- A trivial command loop using abbreviations:

```ruby
require 'abbrev'

COMMANDS = %w{ sample send start status stop }.abbrev

while line = gets
  line = line.chomp

  case COMMANDS[line]
  when "sample" then    # ...
  when "send"   then    # ...
  # ...
  else
    STDERR.puts "Unknown command: #{line}"
  end
end
```

Performs encoding and decoding of binary data using a Base64 representation. This allows you to represent any binary data in purely printable characters. The encoding is specified in RFC 2045 and RFC 4648.[1]

- Encodes and decodes strings. Note the newlines inserted into the Base64 string.

```
require 'base64'
str = "Now is the time for all good coders\nto learn Ruby"
converted = Base64.encode64(str)
puts converted
puts Base64.decode64(converted)
```

produces:

```
Tm93IGlzIHRoZSB0aW1lIGZvciBhbGwgZ29vZCBjb2RlcnMKdG8gbGVhcm4g
UnVieQ==
Now is the time for all good coders
to learn Ruby
```

- Now uses RFC 4648 variants:

```
require 'base64'
str = "Now is the time for all good coders\nto learn Ruby"
converted = Base64.strict_encode64(str)
puts converted
puts Base64.strict_decode64(converted)
```

produces:

```
Tm93IGlzIHRoZSB0aW1lIGZvciBhbGwgZ29vZCBjb2RlcnMKdG8gbGVhcm4gUnVieQ==
Now is the time for all good coders
to learn Ruby
```

---

1. http://www.faqs.org/rfcs/rfc2045.html and http://www.faqs.org/rfcs/rfc4648.html

Allows code execution to be timed and the results tabulated. The Benchmark module is easier to use if you include it in your top-level environment.

See also: Profile (page 791)

- Compares the costs of four kinds of method dispatch:

```ruby
require 'benchmark'
include Benchmark
string = "Stormy Weather"
m = string.method(:length)
bm(6) do |x|
  x.report("direct") { 100_000.times { string.length } }
  x.report("call")   { 100_000.times { m.call } }
  x.report("send")   { 100_000.times { string.send(:length) } }
  x.report("eval")   { 100_000.times { eval "string.length" } }
end
```

produces:

```
              user      system      total         real
direct    0.010000    0.000000    0.010000 (   0.012705)
call      0.020000    0.000000    0.020000 (   0.022576)
send      0.020000    0.000000    0.020000 (   0.020664)
eval      1.220000    0.000000    1.220000 (   1.224656)
```

- Which is better: reading all of a dictionary and splitting it or splitting it line by line? Use bmbm to run a rehearsal before doing the timing:

```ruby
require 'benchmark'
include Benchmark
bmbm(6) do |x|
  x.report("all") do
    str = File.read("/usr/share/dict/words")
    words = str.scan(/[-\w']+/)
  end
  x.report("lines") do
    words = []
    File.foreach("/usr/share/dict/words") do |line|
      words << line.chomp
    end
  end
end
```

produces:

```
Rehearsal -------------------------------------------
all     0.200000    0.010000    0.210000 (   0.218034)
lines   0.150000    0.020000    0.170000 (   0.165469)
---------------------------------- total: 0.380000sec

              user      system      total         real
all     0.180000    0.010000    0.190000 (   0.185983)
lines   0.290000    0.010000    0.300000 (   0.302548)
```

| Library | **BigDecimal** | Large-Precision Decimal Numbers |

Ruby's standard Bignum class supports integers with large numbers of digits. The BigDecimal class supports decimal numbers with large numbers of decimal places. The standard library supports all the normal arithmetic operations. BigDecimal also comes with some extension libraries.

bigdecimal/ludcmp
> Performs an LU decomposition of a matrix.

bigdecimal/math
> Provides the transcendental functions *sqrt, sin, cos, atan, exp,* and *log,* along with functions for computing *PI* and *E.* All functions take an arbitrary precision argument.

bigdecimal/jacobian
> Constructs the Jacobian (a matrix enumerating the partial derivatives) of a given function. Not dependent on BigDecimal.

bigdecimal/newton
> Solves the roots of nonlinear function using Newton's method. Not dependent on BigDecimal.

bigdecimal/nlsolve
> Wraps the bigdecimal/newton library for equations of big decimals.

You can find English-language documentation in the file ext/bigdecimal/bigdecimal_en.html in the Ruby source distribution.

- ```
  # Calculate the area of a circle using BigDecimal numbers

  require 'bigdecimal'
  require 'bigdecimal/math'
  include BigMath

  pi = BigMath::PI(20)    # 20 is the number of decimal digits

  radius = BigDecimal("2.14156987652974674392")

  area = pi * radius**2

  area.to_s # => "0.14408354044685604417672003380667956168859984 6410
            # .. 4450325832158247587804055458617809099301 90528E2"
  ```

- ```
  # The same with regular floats

  radius = 2.14156987652974674392

  Math::PI * radius**2 # => 14.408354044685602
  ```

The CGI class provides support for programs used as Common Gateway Interface (CGI) scripts in a web server. CGI objects are initialized with data from the environment and from the HTTP request, and they provide convenient accessors to form data and cookies. They can also manage sessions using a variety of storage mechanisms. Class CGI also provides basic facilities for HTML generation and class methods to escape and unescape requests and HTML.

See also: CGI::Session (page 737)

- Escapes and unescapes special characters in URLs and HTML. Numeric entities less than 256 will be encoded based on the encoding of the input string. Other numeric entities will be left unchanged.

```
require 'cgi'
CGI.escape('c:\My Files')                   # => c%3A%5CMy+Files
CGI.unescape('c%3a%5cMy+Files')             # => c:\My Files
CGI::escapeHTML('"a"<b & c')                 # => &quot;a&quot;&lt;b &amp; c
CGI.unescapeHTML('&quot;a&quot;&lt;=&gt;b') # => "a"<=>b
CGI.unescapeHTML('&#65;&#x41;')              # => AA
str = '2&#x3c0;r'
str.force_encoding("utf-8")
CGI.unescapeHTML(str)                        # => 2πr
```

- Access information from the incoming request:

```
require 'cgi'
c = CGI.new
c.auth_type                    # => "basic"
c.user_agent                   # => "Mozscape Explorari V5.6"
```

- Access form fields from an incoming request. Assume that the following script, installed as test.cgi, was linked to using http://mydomain.com/test.cgi?fred=10&barney=cat:

```
require 'cgi'
c = CGI.new
c['fred'] # => "10"
c.keys    # => ["fred", "barney"]
c.params  # => {"fred"=>["10"], "barney"=>["cat"]}
```

- If a form contains multiple fields with the same name, the corresponding values will be returned to the script as an array. The [] accessor returns just the first of these—index the result of the params method to get them all.

In this example, assume the form has three fields called "name":

```
require 'cgi'
c = CGI.new
c['name']            # => "fred"
c.params['name']     # => ["fred", "wilma", "barney"]
c.keys               # => ["name"]
c.params             # => {"name"=>["fred", "wilma", "barney"]}
```

- Sends a response to the browser. (Not many folks use this form of HTML generation—use one of the templating libraries described in Section 20.3, *Templating Systems*, on page 280.

```ruby
require 'cgi'
cgi = CGI.new("html5")
cgi.http_header("type" => "text/html", "expires" => Time.now + 30)
cgi.out do
  cgi.html do
    cgi.head{ cgi.title{"Hello World!"} } +
    cgi.body do
      cgi.pre do
        CGI::escapeHTML(
          "params: " + cgi.params.inspect + "\n" +
          "cookies: " + cgi.cookies.inspect + "\n")
      end
    end
  end
end
```

- Stores a cookie in the client browser:

```ruby
require 'cgi'
cgi = CGI.new("html5")
cookie = CGI::Cookie.new('name' => 'mycookie',
                         'value' => 'chocolate chip',
                         'expires' => Time.now + 3600)

cgi.out('cookie' => cookie) do
  cgi.head + cgi.body { "Cookie stored" }
end
```

- Retrieves a previously stored cookie:

```ruby
require 'cgi'
cgi = CGI.new("html5")
cookie = cgi.cookies['mycookie']

cgi.out('cookie' => cookie) do
  cgi.head + cgi.body { "Flavor: " + cookie[0] }
end
```

CGI::Session

A CGI::Session maintains a persistent state for web users in a CGI environment. Sessions may be memory resident or may be stored on disk. See the discussion in *Sessions,* on page 285 for details.

See also: CGI (page 735)

```
sl_cgi_session/session.rb
# Store the timestamp of last access, along with the access count
# using a session object

require 'cgi'
require 'cgi/session'

cgi = CGI.new("html3")
sess = CGI::Session.new(cgi,
                        "session_key" => "rubyweb",
                        "prefix" => "web-session.")

if sess['lastaccess']
  msg = "<p>You were last here #{sess['lastaccess']}.</p>"
else
  msg = "<p>Looks like you haven't been here for a while</p>"
end

count = (sess["accesscount"] || 0).to_i
count += 1

msg << "<p>Number of visits: #{count}</p>"

sess["accesscount"] = count
sess["lastaccess"]  = Time.now.to_s
sess.close

cgi.out {
  cgi.html {
    cgi.body {
      msg
    }
  }
}
```

CMath

As of Ruby 1.9, the Complex class is built in to the interpreter. There is no need to require the complex library to create and manipulate complex numbers. However, if you want the transcendental functions defined by Math to work with complex numbers, you must also require the cmath library. The functions affected are as follows: acosh, acos, asinh, asin, atan2, atanh, atan, cosh, cos, exp, log10, log, sinh, sin, sqrt, tanh, and tan.

The complex library makes these complex functions the default (so, if you require 'complex', you can use Math::sin and not CMath::sin).

- ```
  require 'cmath'
  point = Complex(2, 3)
  CMath::sin(point) # => (9.15449914691143-4.1689069559665565i)
  CMath::cos(point) # => (-4.189625690968807-9.109227893755337i)
  ```

Complex

Loads the cmath library, which defines the transcendental functions for complex numbers. It then arranges things so that these complex-aware functions are the ones invoked when you use Math::. The net effect is that, after requiring complex, you can use functions such as Math::sin on any numeric value, including complex numbers.

- Using transcendental numbers with complex arguments will, by default, cause an error:

```
point = Complex(2, 3)
Math::sin(point)
```

produces:

```
        from prog.rb:2:in `sin'
        from prog.rb:2:in `<main>'
prog.rb:2:in `to_f': can't convert 2+3i into Float (RangeError)
```

- However...

```
require 'complex'
point = Complex(2, 3)
Math::sin(point) # => (9.15449914691143-4.1689069559665565i)
```
```

Continuation

Continuation objects are generated by the Object#callcc method, which becomes available only when the continuation library is loaded. They hold a return address and execution context, allowing a nonlocal return to the end of the callcc block from anywhere within a program. Continuations are somewhat analogous to a structured version of C's setjmp/longjmp (although they contain more state, so you may consider them closer to threads). This (somewhat contrived) example allows the inner loop to abandon processing early.

- Does a nonlocal exit when a condition is met:

```ruby
require 'continuation'
callcc do |cont|
  for i in 0..4
    print "\n#{i}: "
    for j in i*5...(i+1)*5
      cont.call() if j == 7
      printf "%3d", j
    end
  end
end
print "\n"
```

produces:

```
0:   0  1  2  3  4
1:   5  6
```

- The call stack for methods is preserved in continuations:

```ruby
require 'continuation'
def strange
  callcc {|continuation| return continuation}
  print "Back in method, "
end
print "Before method. "
continuation = strange()
print "After method. "
continuation.call if continuation
```

produces:

```
Before method. After method. Back in method, After method.
```

| Library
coverage | Experimental Code Coverage Analysis |

The coverage module counts the number of times each line of Ruby code is executed in one or more source files and provides a summary as a hash. The keys of the hash are the names of files that were analyzed, and the values are each an array containing counts (on a per-line basis).

Here's a simple implementation of the Fizz Buzz program:

sl_coverage/fizzbuzz.rb
```ruby
1.upto(100).with_object('') do |i, x|
  if i % 3 == 0
    x += 'Fizz'
  end
  if i % 5 == 0
    x += 'Buzz'
  end
  if x.empty?
    puts i
  else
    puts x
  end
end
```

And here's a program that loads and runs that program, using the coverage library to report on execution counts. (Note that it discards the output of the FizzBuzz program, simply to save space on this page.)

```ruby
require 'coverage'
Coverage.start
STDOUT.reopen("/dev/null")
require_relative 'fizzbuzz.rb'
Coverage.result.each do |file_name, counts|
  File.readlines(file_name).each.with_index do |code_line, line_number|
    count = counts[line_number] || "--"
    STDERR.printf "%3s: %s", count, code_line
  end
end
```

produces:
```
  1: 1.upto(100).with_object('') do |i, x|
100:   if i % 3 == 0
 33:     x += 'Fizz'
--:   end
100:   if i % 5 == 0
 20:     x += 'Buzz'
--:   end
100:   if x.empty?
 53:     puts i
--:   else
 47:     puts x
--:   end
--: end
```

| Library | **CSV** | Comma-Separated Values |

Comma-separated data files are often used to transfer tabular information (and are a *lingua franca* for importing and exporting spreadsheet and database information). As of Ruby 1.9, the old library has been replaced by James Edward Gray II's FasterCSV version. It has a few incompatibilities with the original. In particular, CSV.open now works like File.open, not File.foreach, and options are passed as a hash and not positional parameters.

Ruby's CSV library deals with arrays (corresponding to the rows in the CSV file) and strings (corresponding to the elements in a row). If an element in a row is missing, it will be represented as a nil in Ruby.

The files used in these examples are as follows:

sl_csv/csvfile
```
12,eggs,2.89,
2,"shirt, blue",21.45,special
1,"""Hello Kitty"" bag",13.99
```

sl_csv/csvfile_hdr
```
Count,Description,Price
12,eggs,2.89,
2,"shirt, blue",21.45,special
1,"""Hello Kitty"" bag",13.99
```

- Reads a file containing CSV data and processes line by line:

```ruby
require 'csv'
CSV.foreach("csvfile") do |row|
  qty = row[0].to_i
  price = row[2].to_f
  printf "%20s: $%5.2f %s\n", row[1], qty*price, row[3] || " ---"
end
```

produces:

```
              eggs: $34.68   ---
       shirt, blue: $42.90 special
 "Hello Kitty" bag: $13.99   ---
```

- Processes a CSV file that contains a header line. Automatically converts fields that look like numbers.

```ruby
require 'csv'
total_cost = 0
CSV.foreach("csvfile_hdr", headers: true, converters: :numeric) do |data|
  total_cost += data["Count"] * data["Price"]
end
puts "Total cost is #{total_cost}"
```

produces:

```
Total cost is 91.57
```

- Writes CSV data to an existing open stream (STDOUT in this case). Uses | as the column separator.

```
require 'csv'
CSV(STDOUT, col_sep: "|") do |csv|
  csv << [ 1, "line 1", 27 ]
  csv << [ 2, nil, 123 ]
  csv << [ 3, "|bar|", 32.5]
end
```

produces:

```
1|line 1|27
2||123
3|"|bar|"|32.5
```

- Accesses a CSV file as a two-dimensional table:

```
require 'csv'

table = CSV.read("csvfile_hdr",
                  headers: true,
                  header_converters: :symbol)
puts "Row count = #{table.count}"
puts "First row = #{table[0].fields}"
puts "Count of eggs = #{table[0][:count]}"
table << [99, "red balloons", 1.23]
table[:in_stock] = [10, 5, 10, 10]
puts "\nAfter adding a row and a column, the new table is:"
puts table
```

produces:

```
Row count = 3
First row = ["12", "eggs", "2.89", nil]
Count of eggs = 12

After adding a row and a column, the new table is:
count,description,price,,in_stock
12,eggs,2.89,,10
2,"shirt, blue",21.45,special,5
1,"""Hello Kitty"" bag",13.99,10
99,red balloons,1.23,,10
```

The Curses library is a thin wrapper around the C curses or ncurses libraries, giving applications a device-independent way to draw on consoles and other terminal-like devices. As a nod toward object-orientation, curses windows and mouse events are represented as Ruby objects. Otherwise, the standard curses calls and constants are simply defined in the Curses module.

Only if: curses or ncurses installed in target environment

sl_curses/pong_paddle.rb

```ruby
# Draw the paddle for game of 'pong' that moves in response to up and down keys
require 'curses'
include Curses

class Paddle
  HEIGHT = 4
  PADDLE = " \n" + "||\n"*HEIGHT + " "
  def initialize
    @top = (Curses::lines - HEIGHT)/2
    draw
  end
  def up
    @top -= 1 if @top > 1
  end
  def down
    @top += 1 if (@top + HEIGHT + 1) < lines
  end
  def draw
    setpos(@top-1, 0)
    addstr(PADDLE)
    refresh
  end
end

init_screen
begin
  cbreak
  noecho
  stdscr.keypad(true)
  paddle = Paddle.new

  loop do
    case ch = getch
    when "Q", "q"                 then  break
    when Key::UP, 'U', 'u'        then  paddle.up
    when Key::DOWN, 'D', 'd'      then  paddle.down
    else
      beep
    end
    paddle.draw
  end
ensure
  close_screen
end
```

The date library implements classes Date and DateTime, which provide a comprehensive set of facilities for storing, manipulating, and converting dates with or without time components. The classes can represent and manipulate civil, ordinal, commercial, Julian, and standard dates, starting January 1, 4713 BCE. The DateTime class extends Date with hours, minutes, seconds, and fractional seconds, and it provides some support for time zones. The classes also provide support for parsing and formatting date and datetime strings. The classes have a rich interface—consult the ri documentation for details. The introductory notes in the file lib/date.rb in the Ruby source tree are also well worth reading.

- Experiment with various representations:

```ruby
require 'date'

d = Date.new(2000, 3, 31)
[d.year, d.yday, d.wday]       # => [2000, 91, 5]
[d.month, d.mday]              # => [3, 31]
[d.cwyear, d.cweek, d.cwday]   # => [2000, 13, 5]
[d.jd, d.mjd]                  # => [2451635, 51634]
d1 = Date.commercial(2000, 13, 7)
d1.to_s                        # => "2000-04-02"
[d1.cwday, d1.wday]            # => [7, 0]
```

- Essential information about Christmas:

```ruby
require 'date'

now = DateTime.now
year = now.year
year += 1 if now.month == 12 && now.day > 25
xmas = DateTime.new(year, 12, 25)

diff = xmas - now

puts "It's #{diff.to_i} days to Christmas"
puts "Christmas #{year} falls on a #{xmas.strftime('%A')}"
```

produces:

```
It's 211 days to Christmas
Christmas 2013 falls on a Wednesday
```

DBM files implement simple, hashlike persistent stores. Many DBM implementations exist: the Ruby library can be configured to use one of the DBM libraries db, dbm (ndbm), gdbm, and qdbm. The interface to DBM files is similar to class Hash, except that DBM keys and values will be strings. This can cause confusion, as the conversion to a string is performed silently when the data is written. The DBM library is a wrapper around the lower-level access method. For true low-level access, see also the GDBM and SDBM libraries.

Only if: a DBM library is installed in target environment

See also: gdbm (page 760) sdbm (page 803)

The following creates a simple DBM file and then reopens it read-only and reads some data. Note the conversion of a date object to its string form.

sl_dbm/dbm1.rb
```ruby
require 'dbm'
require 'date'

DBM.open("data.dbm") do |dbm|
  dbm['name'] = "Walter Wombat"
  dbm['dob']  = Date.new(1997, 12,25)
end

DBM.open("data.dbm", nil, DBM::READER) do |dbm|
  p dbm.keys
  p dbm['dob']
  p dbm['dob'].class
end
```

Produces:
```
["name", "dob"]
"1997-12-25"
String
```

Delegator   Delegate Calls to Other Object

Object delegation is a way of *composing* objects—extending an object with the capabilities of another—at runtime. The Ruby Delegator class implements a simple but powerful delegation scheme, where requests are automatically forwarded from a master class to delegates or their ancestors and where the delegate can be changed at runtime with a single method call.

See also: Forwardable (page 759)

- For simple cases where the class of the delegate is fixed, make the master class a subclass of DelegateClass, passing the name of the class to be delegated as a parameter. In the master class's initialize method, pass the object to be delegated to the superclass.

```ruby
require 'delegate'

class Words < DelegateClass(Array)
  def initialize(list = "/usr/share/dict/words")
    words = File.read(list).split
    super(words)
  end
end

words = Words.new
words[9999]        # => "anticontagionist"
words.size         # => 235886
words.grep(/matz/) # => ["matzo", "matzoon", "matzos", "matzoth"]
```

- Use SimpleDelegator to delegate to a particular object (which can be changed):

```ruby
require 'delegate'

words = File.read("/usr/share/dict/words").split
names = File.read("/usr/share/dict/propernames").split

stats = SimpleDelegator.new(words)
stats.size # => 235886
stats[226] # => "abidingly"
stats.__setobj__(names)
stats.size # => 1308
stats[226] # => "Deirdre"
```

The Digest module is the home for a number of classes that implement message digest algorithms: MD5, RIPEMD-160, SHA1, and SHA2 (256, 384, and 512 bit). The interface to all these classes is identical.

- You can create a binary or hex digest for a given string by calling the class method digest or hexdigest.

- You can also create an object (optionally passing in an initial string) and determine the object's hash by calling the digest or hexdigest instance methods. You can then append to the string using the update method and then recover an updated hash value.

- Calculates some MD5 and SHA1 hashes:

```ruby
require 'digest/md5'
require 'digest/sha1'

for hash_class in [ Digest::MD5, Digest::SHA1 ]

  puts "Using #{hash_class.name}"

  # Calculate directly
  puts hash_class.hexdigest("hello world")

  # Or by accumulating
  digest = hash_class.new
  digest << "hello"
  digest << " "
  digest << "world"
  puts digest.hexdigest
  puts digest.base64digest    # new in 1.9.2
  puts
end
```

produces:

```
Using Digest::MD5
5eb63bbbe01eeed093cb22bb8f5acdc3
5eb63bbbe01eeed093cb22bb8f5acdc3
XrY7u+Ae7tCTyyK7j1rNww==

Using Digest::SHA1
2aae6c35c94fcfb415dbe95f408b9ce91ee846ed
2aae6c35c94fcfb415dbe95f408b9ce91ee846ed
Kq5sNclPz7QV2+lfQIuc6R7oRu0=
```

dRuby allows Ruby objects to be distributed across a network connection. Although expressed in terms of clients and servers, once the initial connection is established, the protocol is effectively symmetrical: either side can invoke methods in objects on the other side. Normally, objects passed and returned by remote calls are passed by value; including the DRbUndumped module in an object forces it to be passed by reference (useful when implementing callbacks).

See also: Rinda (page 798) XMLRPC (page 826)

- This server program is *observable*—it notifies all registered listeners of changes to a count value:

sl_drb/drb_server1.rb
```
require 'drb'
require 'drb/observer'

class Counter
  include DRb::DRbObservable

  def run
    5.times do |count|
      changed
      notify_observers(count)
    end
  end
end

counter = Counter.new
DRb.start_service('druby://localhost:9001', counter)
DRb.thread.join
```

- This client program interacts with the server, registering a listener object to receive callbacks before invoking the server's run method:

sl_drb/drb_client1.rb
```
require 'drb'

class Listener
  include DRbUndumped

  def update(value)
    puts value
  end
end

DRb.start_service
counter = DRbObject.new(nil, "druby://localhost:9001")

listener = Listener.new
counter.add_observer(listener)
counter.run
```

Includes the English library file in a Ruby script, and you can reference the global variables such as $_ using less-cryptic names, listed in the following table. Prior to Ruby 1.9, the name $PROGRAM_NAME was declared using English. It is now predefined in the Ruby interpreter.

\toprule $*	$ARGV	$_	$LAST_READ_LINE
$?	$CHILD_STATUS	$"	$LOADED_FEATURES
$<	$DEFAULT_INPUT	$&	$MATCH
$>	$DEFAULT_OUTPUT	$.	$NR
$!	$ERROR_INFO	$,	$OFS
$@	$ERROR_POSITION	$\	$ORS
$;	$FIELD_SEPARATOR	$,	$OUTPUT_FIELD_SEPARATOR
$;	$FS	$\	$OUTPUT_RECORD_SEPARATOR
$=	$IGNORECASE	$$	$PID
$.	$INPUT_LINE_NUMBER	$'	$POSTMATCH
$/	$INPUT_RECORD_SEPARATOR	$`	$PREMATCH
$~	$LAST_MATCH_INFO	$$	$PROCESS_ID
$+	$LAST_PAREN_MATCH	$/	$RS

The following code shows some regular variable names along with their English counterparts.

```
require 'English'

$OUTPUT_FIELD_SEPARATOR = ' -- '
"waterbuffalo" =~ /buff/
print $., $INPUT_LINE_NUMBER, "\n"
print $', $POSTMATCH, "\n"
print $$, $PID
```

produces:

```
0 -- 0 --
alo -- alo --
24658 -- 24658
```

ERb is a lightweight templating system, allowing you to intermix Ruby code and plain text. This is sometimes a convenient way to create HTML documents but also is usable in other plain-text situations. See Section 20.3, *Templating Systems*, on page 280 for other templating solutions.

ERB breaks its input text into chunks of regular text and program fragments. It then builds a Ruby program that, when run, outputs the result text and executes the program fragments. Program fragments are enclosed between <% and %> markers. The exact interpretation of these fragments depends on the character following the opening <%:

Sequence	Action
<% *ruby code* %>	Inserts the given Ruby code at this point in the generated program. If it outputs anything, include this output in the result.
<%= *ruby expression* %>	Evaluate expression and insert its value in the output of the generated program.
<%# ... %>	Comment (ignored).
<%% and %%>	Replaced in the output by <% and%> respectively.

Table 26—Directives for ERB

The following code uses <%...%> blocks to execute a Ruby loop, and <%=...%> to substitute a value into the output.

```
require 'erb'
input = %{<% high.downto(low) do |n|    # set high, low externally %>
  <%= n %> green bottles, hanging on the wall
  <%= n %> green bottles, hanging on the wall
  And if one green bottle should accidentally fall
  There'd be <%= n-1 %> green bottles, hanging on the wall
<% end %>}
high,low = 10, 8
erb = ERB.new(input)
erb.run(binding)
```

produces:

```
10 green bottles, hanging on the wall
  10 green bottles, hanging on the wall
  And if one green bottle should accidentally fall
  There'd be 9 green bottles, hanging on the wall

    . . .
```

An optional second parameter to ERB.new sets the safe level for evaluating expressions. If nil, expressions are evaluated in the current thread; otherwise, a new thread is created, and its $SAFE level is set to the parameter value.

The optional third parameter to ERB.new allows some control of the interpretation of the input and of the way whitespace is added to the output. If the third parameter is a string and that string contains a percent sign, then ERb treats lines starting with a percent sign specially. Lines starting with a single percent sign are treated as if they were enclosed in <%...%>. Lines starting with a double percent sign are copied to the output with a single leading percent sign.

```
require 'erb'
str = %{\
% 2.times do |i|
  This is line <%= i %>
%end
%%%done}
ERB.new(str, 0, '%').run
```

produces:

```
  This is line 0
  This is line 1
%%done
```

If the third parameter contains the string <>, then a newline will not be written if an input line starts with an ERB directive and ends with %>. If the trim parameter contains >>, then a newline will not be written if an input line ends %>.

```
require 'erb'
str1 = %{\
* <%= "cat" %>
<%= "dog" %>
}
ERB.new(str1, 0, ">").run
ERB.new(str1, 0, "<>").run
```

produces:

```
* catdog* cat
dog
```

The erb library also defines the helper module ERB::Util that contains two methods: html_escape (aliased as h) and url_encode (aliased as u). These are equivalent to the CGI methods escapeHTML and escape, respectively (except escape encodes spaces as plus signs, and url_encode uses %20).

```
require 'erb'
include ERB::Util
str1 = %{\
h(a) = <%= h(a) %>
u(a) = <%= u(a) %>
}
a = "< a & b >"
ERB.new(str1).run(binding)
```

produces:

```
h(a) = &lt; a &amp; b &gt;
u(a) = %3C%20a%20%26%20b%20%3E
```

You may find the command-line utility erb is supplied with your Ruby distribution. This allows you to run erb substitutions on an input file; see erb --help for details.

The Etc module provides a number of methods for querying the passwd and group facilities
Only if: Unix or Cygwin   on Unix systems.

- Finds out information about the currently logged-in user:

```
require 'etc'

name = Etc.getlogin
info = Etc.getpwnam(name)
info.name  # => "dave"
info.uid   # => 501
info.dir   # => "/Users/dave"
info.shell # => "/bin/zsh"

group = Etc.getgrgid(info.gid)
group.name # => "staff"
```

- Returns the names of users on the system used to create this book:

```
require 'etc'

users = []
Etc.passwd {|passwd| users << passwd.name }
users[1,5].join(", ") # => "_appleevents, _appowner, _appserver, _ard,
                      #  .. _assetcache"
```

- Returns the IDs of groups on the system used to create this book:

```
require 'etc'

ids = []
Etc.group {|entry| ids << entry.gid }
ids[1,5].join(", ") # => "55, 87, 81, 79, 33"
```

The expect library adds the method expect to all IO objects. This allows you to write code that waits for a particular string or pattern to be available from the I/O stream. The expect method is particularly useful with pty objects (see the Pty library on page 794) and with network connections to remote servers, where it can be used to coordinate the use of external interactive processes.

If the global variable $expect_verbose is true, the expect method writes all characters read from the I/O stream to STDOUT.

See also: pty (page 794)

- Connects to the local FTP server, logs in, and prints out the name of the user's directory. (Note that it would be a lot easier to do this using the net/ftp library.)

```
# This code might be specific to the particular ftp daemon.

require 'expect'
require 'socket'

$expect_verbose = true

socket = TCPSocket.new('localhost', 'ftp')

socket.expect("ready")
socket.puts("user testuser")
socket.expect("331 User testuser accepted, provide password.")
socket.puts("pass wibble")
socket.expect("logged in.\r\n")
socket.puts("pwd")
puts(socket.gets)
socket.puts "quit"
```

produces:

```
220 ::1 FTP server (tnftpd 20100324+GSSAPI) ready.
331 User testuser accepted, provide password.
230 User testuser logged in.
257 "/Users/testuser" is the current directory.
```

The Fcntl module provides symbolic names for each of the host system's available fcntl(2) constants (defined in fcntl.h). That is, if the host system has a constant named F_GETLK defined in fcntl.h, then the Fcntl module will have a corresponding constant Fcntl::F_GETLK with the same value as the header file's #define.

- Different operating system will have different Fcntl constants available. The value associated with a constant of a given name may also differ across platforms. Here are the values on our Mac OS X system:

```
require 'fcntl'

Fcntl.constants.sort.each do |name|
  printf "%10s: 0x%06x\n", name, Fcntl.const_get(name)
end
```

produces:

```
FD_CLOEXEC: 0x000001
    F_DUPFD: 0x000000
    F_GETFD: 0x000001
    F_GETFL: 0x000003
    F_GETLK: 0x000007
    F_RDLCK: 0x000001
    F_SETFD: 0x000002
    F_SETFL: 0x000004
    F_SETLK: 0x000008
   F_SETLKW: 0x000009
    F_UNLCK: 0x000002
    F_WRLCK: 0x000003
  O_ACCMODE: 0x000003
    O_CREAT: 0x000200
     O_EXCL: 0x000800
   O_NDELAY: 0x000004
   O_NOCTTY: 0x020000
 O_NONBLOCK: 0x000004
   O_RDONLY: 0x000000
     O_RDWR: 0x000002
    O_TRUNC: 0x000400
   O_WRONLY: 0x000001
```

The Fiber class that is built into Ruby provides a generator-like capability—fibers may be created and resumed from some controlling program. If you want to extend the Fiber class to provide full, symmetrical coroutines, you need first to require the fiber library. This adds two instance methods, transfer and alive?, to Fiber objects and adds the singleton method current to the Fiber class.

- It is difficult to come up with a meaningful, concise example of symmetric coroutines that can't more easily be coded with asymetric (plain old) fibers. So, here's an artificial example:

```ruby
require 'fiber'

# take items two at a time off a queue, calling the producer
# if not enough are available
consumer = Fiber.new do |producer, queue|
  5.times do
    while queue.size < 2
      queue = producer.transfer(consumer, queue)
    end
    puts "Consume #{queue.shift} and #{queue.shift}"
  end
end

# add items three at a time to the queue
producer = Fiber.new do |consumer, queue|
  value = 1
  loop do
    puts "Producing more stuff"
    3.times { queue << value; value += 1}
    puts "Queue size is #{queue.size}"
    consumer.transfer queue
  end
end

consumer.transfer(producer, [])
```

produces:

```
Producing more stuff
Queue size is 3
Consume 1 and 2
Producing more stuff
Queue size is 4
Consume 3 and 4
Consume 5 and 6
Producing more stuff
Queue size is 3
Consume 7 and 8
Producing more stuff
Queue size is 4
Consume 9 and 10
```

Fiddle Access Dynamically Loaded Libraries (.dll and .so)

The Fiddle module is a wrapper around libffi, a library that provides access to shared libraries. On Windows boxes, it can be used to interface with functions in DLLs. Under Unix it can load shared libraries. Because Ruby does not have typed method parameters or return values, you must define the types expected by the methods you call by specifying their signatures.

- Here's a trivial C program that we'll build as a shared library:

sl_fiddle/lib.c
```c
#include <stdio.h>
int print_msg(char *text, int number) {
  int count = printf("Text: %s (%d)\n", text, number);
  fflush(stdout);
  return count;
}
```

- Generates a proxy to access the print_msg method in the shared library. The way this book is built, the shared library is in the same directory as the Ruby code; this directory must be added to the directories searched when looking for dynamic objects. You can do this by setting the DYLD_LIBRARY_PATH environment variable.

```ruby
require 'fiddle'
include Fiddle
lib       = Fiddle.dlopen("lib.so")
print_msg = Fiddle::Function.new(lib['print_msg'],        # entry point
                                 [TYPE_VOIDP, TYPE_INT],   # parameter types
                                 TYPE_INT)                 # return type
msg_size  = print_msg.call("Answer", 42)
puts "Just wrote #{msg_size} bytes"
```

produces:

```
Text: Answer (42)
Just wrote 18 bytes
```

FileUtils is a collection of methods for manipulating files and directories. Although generally applicable, the model is particularly useful when writing installation scripts and Rake tasks.

Many methods take a *src* parameter and a *dest* parameter. If *dest* is a directory, *src* may be a single filename or an array of filenames. For example, the following copies the files a, b, and c to /tmp:

```
cp( %w{ a b c }, "/tmp")
```

Most functions take a set of options. These may be zero or more of the following:

Option	Meaning
:verbose	Traces execution of each function (by default to STDERR, although this can be overridden by setting the class variable @fileutils_output.
:noop	Does not perform the action of the function (useful for testing scripts).
:force	Overrides some default conservative behavior of the method (for example, over-writing an existing file).
:preserve	Attempts to preserve atime, mtime, and mode information from *src* in *dest*. (Setuid and setgid flags are always cleared.)

For maximum portability, use forward slashes to separate the directory components of file-names, even on Windows.

FileUtils contains three submodules that duplicate the top-level methods but that have different default options: module FileUtils::Verbose sets the verbose option, module FileUtils::NoWrite sets noop, and FileUtils::DryRun sets verbose and noop.

See also: un (page 821)

```
require 'fileutils'
include FileUtils::Verbose
cd("/tmp") do
  cp("/etc/passwd", "tmp_passwd")
  chmod(0666, "tmp_passwd")
  cp_r("/usr/include/net/", "headers")
  rm("tmp_passwd")      # Tidy up
  rm_rf("headers")
end
```

produces:

```
cd /tmp
cp /etc/passwd tmp_passwd
chmod 666 tmp_passwd
cp -r /usr/include/net/ headers
rm tmp_passwd
rm -rf headers
cd -
```

The Find module supports the top-down traversal of a set of file paths, given as arguments to the find method. If an argument is a file, its name is passed to the block associated with the call. If it's a directory, then its name and the name of all its files and subdirectories will be passed in. If no block is associated with the call, an Enumerator is returned.

Within the block, the method prune may be called, which skips the current file or directory, restarting the loop with the next directory. If the current file is a directory, that directory will not be recursively entered. In the following example, we don't list the contents of the local Subversion cache directories:

```ruby
require 'find'
Find.find("/etc/passwd", "code/ducktyping") do |f|
  type = case
         when File.file?(f)      then "File: "
         when File.directory?(f) then "Dir:  "
         else "?"
         end
  puts "#{type} #{f}"
  Find.prune if f =~ /.svn/
end
```

produces:

```
File:  /etc/passwd
Dir:   code/ducktyping
Dir:   code/ducktyping/.svn
File:  code/ducktyping/addcust.rb
File:  code/ducktyping/roman3.rb
File:  code/ducktyping/testaddcust1.rb
File:  code/ducktyping/testaddcust2.rb
File:  code/ducktyping/testaddcust3.rb
```

Forwardable

Forwardable provides a mechanism to allow classes to delegate named method calls to other objects.

See also: Delegator (page 746)

- This simple symbol table uses a hash, exposing a subset of the hash's methods:

```ruby
require 'forwardable'

class SymbolTable
  extend Forwardable
  def_delegator(:@hash, :[],  :lookup)
  def_delegator(:@hash, :[]=, :add)
  def_delegators(:@hash, :size, :has_key?)
  def initialize
    @hash = Hash.new
  end
end

st = SymbolTable.new
st.add('cat', 'feline animal') # => "feline animal"
st.add('dog', 'canine animal') # => "canine animal"
st.add('cow', 'bovine animal') # => "bovine animal"

st.has_key?('cow')             # => true
st.lookup('dog')              # => "canine animal"
```

- Forwards can also be defined for individual objects by extending them with the Single-Forwardable module. It's hard to think of a good reason to use this feature, so here's a silly one:

```ruby
require 'forwardable'

TRICKS = [ "roll over", "play dead" ]

dog = "rover"
dog.extend SingleForwardable
dog.def_delegator(:TRICKS, :each, :can)

dog.can do |trick|
  puts trick
end
```

produces:

```
roll over
play dead
```

Only if: gdbm library
available

Interfaces to the gdbm database library.[2] Although the DBM library provides generic access to gdbm databases, it doesn't expose some features of the full gdbm interface, such as the cache size, synchronization mode, reorganization, and locking. Only one process may have a GDBM database open for writing (unless locking is disabled).

See also: DBM (page 745) SDBM (page 803)

- Stores some values into a database and then reads them back. The second parameter to the open method specifies the file mode, and the next parameter uses two flags that (1) create the database if it doesn't exist and (2) force all writes to be synced to disk. Create on open is the default Ruby gdbm behavior.

```ruby
require 'gdbm'

GDBM.open("data.dbm", 0644, GDBM::WRCREAT | GDBM::SYNC) do |dbm|
  dbm['name'] = "Walter Wombat"
  dbm['dob']  = "1969-12-25"
  dbm['uses'] = "Ruby"
end

GDBM.open("data.dbm") do |dbm|
  p dbm.keys
  p dbm['dob']
  dbm.delete('dob')
  p dbm.keys
end
```

- Opens a database read-only. The attempt to delete a key would fail.

```ruby
require 'gdbm'

GDBM.open("data.dbm", 0, GDBM::READER) do |dbm|
  p dbm.keys
  dbm.delete('name')   # !! fails !!
end
```

---

2.   http://www.gnu.org/software/gdbm/gdbm.html

Class GetoptLong supports GNU-style command-line option parsing. Options may be a minus sign (-) followed by a single character or may be two minus signs (–) followed by a name (a long option). Long options may be abbreviated to their shortest unambiguous lengths.

A single internal option may have multiple external representations. For example, the option to control verbose output could be any of -v, --verbose, or --details. Some options may also take an associated value.

Each internal option is passed to GetoptLong as an array, containing strings representing the option's external forms and a flag. The flag specifies how GetoptLong is to associate an argument with the option (NO_ARGUMENT, REQUIRED_ARGUMENT, or OPTIONAL_ARGUMENT).

If the environment variable POSIXLY_CORRECT is set, all options must precede nonoptions on the command line. Otherwise, the default behavior of GetoptLong is to reorganize the command line to put the options at the front. This behavior may be changed by setting the attribute GetoptLong#ordering= to one of PERMUTE, REQUIRE_ORDER, or RETURN_IN_ORDER. The environment variable POSIXLY_CORRECT may not be overridden.

See also: OptionParser (page 784)

```ruby
# Call using "ruby example.rb --size 10k -v -q a.txt b.doc"

require 'getoptlong'

# Fake out an initial command line
ARGV.clear.push  *%w(--size 10k -v -q a.txt b.doc)

# specify the options we accept and initialize
# the option parser

opts = GetoptLong.new(
  [ "--size",    "-s",             GetoptLong::REQUIRED_ARGUMENT ],
  [ "--verbose", "-v",             GetoptLong::NO_ARGUMENT ],
  [ "--query",   "-q",             GetoptLong::NO_ARGUMENT ],
  [ "--check",   "--valid", "-c",  GetoptLong::NO_ARGUMENT ]
)

# process the parsed options

opts.each do |opt, arg|
  puts "Option: #{opt}, arg #{arg.inspect}"
end

puts "Remaining args: #{ARGV.join(', ')}"
```
produces:
```
Option: --size, arg "10k"
Option: --verbose, arg ""
Option: --query, arg ""
Remaining args: a.txt, b.doc
```

GServer

This is a simple framework for writing TCP servers. To use it, subclass the GServer class, set the port (and potentially other parameters) in the constructor, and then implement a serve method to handle incoming requests.

GServer manages a thread pool for incoming connections, so your serve method may be running in multiple threads in parallel.

You can run multiple GServer copies on different ports in the same application.

- When a connection is made on port 2000, responds with the current time as a string. Terminates after handling three requests.

```ruby
require 'gserver'
class TimeServer < GServer
  def initialize
    super(2000)
    @count = 3
  end
  def serve(client)
    client.puts Time.now
    @count -= 1
    stop if @count.zero?
  end
end
server = TimeServer.new
server.start.join
```

- You can test this server by reading from localhost on port 2000. We use curl to do this—you could also use telnet:

```
$ curl -s localhost:2000
2013-05-27 12:33:22 -0500
```

IO/console

Require io/console, and I/O objects associated with terminals gain the methods IO#raw, IO#raw!, IO#getch, IO#echo=, IO#echo?, IO#noecho, IO#winsize, IO#winsize=, IO#iflush, IO#oflush, and IO#ioflush. The IO class also gains a singleton method, IO.console, which returns an I/O object connected to the controlling terminal of the process.

- Prompt for a password with no echo.

```ruby
require 'io/console'
password = STDIN.noecho do
  print "Your password: "
  gets
end
```

- What's the size of the controlling terminal?

```ruby
require "io/console"
IO.console.winsize # => [22, 137]
```

| Library | **IO/nonblock** | Turn blocking I/O on and off |

If a program requires io/nonblock, I/O objects gain the methods IO#nonblock, IO#nonblock?, and IO#nonblock=. The first takes a block, and runs that block with the given file description in nonblocking mode. The second lets you query the blocking status of a file descriptor, and the last lets you turn blocking on and off. You'll probably want to investigate IO.select, as you'll need it to tell when the file cn be read or written.

| Library | **IO/Wait** | Check for Pending Data to Be Read |

Including the library io/wait adds the methods IO#nread, IO#ready?, and IO#wait to the standard IO class. These allow an IO object opened on a stream (not a file) to be queried to see whether data is available to be read without reading it and to wait for a given number of bytes to become available.

Only if: FIONREAD feature in ioctl(2)

- Sets up a pipe between two processes and writes 10 bytes at a time into it. Periodically sees how much data is available.

```
require 'io/wait'

reader, writer = IO.pipe

if (pid = fork)
  writer.close
  8.times do
    sleep 0.03
    if reader.ready?
      len = reader.nread
      puts "#{len} bytes available: #{reader.sysread(len)}"
    else
      puts "No data available"
    end
  end
  Process.waitpid(pid)
else
  reader.close
  5.times do |n|
    sleep 0.04
    writer.write n.to_s * 10
  end
  writer.close
end
```

produces:

```
No data available
10 bytes available: 0000000000
10 bytes available: 1111111111
10 bytes available: 2222222222
No data available
10 bytes available: 3333333333
10 bytes available: 4444444444
No data available
```

IPAddr

Class IPAddr holds and manipulates Internet Protocol (IP) addresses. Each address contains three parts: an address, a mask, and an address family. The family will typically be AF_INET for IPv4 and IPv6 addresses. The class contains methods for extracting parts of an address, checking for IPv4-compatible addresses (and IPv4-mapped IPv6 addresses), testing whether an address falls within a subnet, and performing many other functions. It is also interesting in that it contains as data its own unit tests.

```
require 'ipaddr'

v4 = IPAddr.new('192.168.23.0/24')
v4                 # => #<IPAddr: IPv4:192.168.23.0/ 255.255.255.0>
v4.mask(16)        # => #<IPAddr: IPv4:192.168.0.0/ 255.255.0.0>
v4.reverse         # => "0.23.168.192.in-addr.arpa"
v6 = IPAddr.new('3ffe:505:2::1')
v6                 # => #<IPAddr: IPv6:3ffe:0505:0002:0000:0000:0000:0000:0001/
                   # .. ffff:ffff:ffff:ffff:ffff:ffff:ffff:ffff>
v6.mask(48)        # => #<IPAddr: IPv6:3ffe:0505:0002:0000:0000:0000:0000:0000/
                   # .. ffff:ffff:ffff:0000:0000:0000:0000:0000>

# the value for 'family' is OS dependent. This
# value is for OS X
v6.family          # => 30

other = IPAddr.new("192.168.23.56")
v4.include?(other) # => true
```

The irb library is most commonly associated with the console command irb. However, you can also start an irb session from within your running application. A common technique is to trap a signal and start irb in the handler.

The following program sets up a signal handler that runs irb when the user hits ^C. The user can change the value of the instance variable @value. When they exit from irb, the original program continues to run with that new value.

sl_irb/run_irb.rb
```ruby
require 'irb'

trap "INT" do
  IRB.start
end

count = 0
loop do
  count += 1
  puts count
  puts "Value = #{@value}" if defined? @value
  sleep 1
end
```

Here's a simple session using it:

```
$ ruby code/sl_irb/run_irb.rb
1
2
3
^Cruby-1.9.2-p0 > @value = "wibble"
 => "wibble"
ruby-1.9.2-p0 > exit
4
Value = wibble
5
Value = wibble
. . .
```

JSON is a language-independent data interchange format based on key/value pairs (hashes in Ruby) and sequences of values (arrays in Ruby).[3] JSON is frequently used to exchange data between JavaScript running in browsers and server-based applications. JSON is not a general-purpose object marshaling format. Although you can add to_json methods to your own classes, you will lose interoperability.

See also: yaml (page 827)

- Serializes a data structure into a string and writes that to a file:

```
require 'json'
data = { name: 'dave', address: [ 'tx', 'usa' ], age: 17 }
serialized = data.to_json
serialized  # => {"name":"dave","address":["tx","usa"],"age":17}
File.open("data", "w") {|f| f.puts serialized}
```

- Reads the serialized data from the file and reconstitutes it:

```
require 'json'
serialized = File.read("data")
data = JSON.parse(serialized)
data       # => {"name"=>"dave", "address"=>["tx", "usa"], "age"=>17}
```

- The methods j and jj convert their argument to JSON and write the result to STDOUT (jj prettyprints). This can be useful in irb.

```
require 'json'
data = { name: 'dave', address: [ 'tx', 'usa' ], age: 17 }
puts "Regular"
j data
puts "Pretty"
jj data
```

produces:

```
Regular
{"name":"dave","address":["tx","usa"],"age":17}
Pretty
{
  "name": "dave",
  "address": [
    "tx",
    "usa"
  ],
  "age": 17
}
```

---

3.   http://www.ietf.org/rfc/rfc4627.txt

Logger

Writes log messages to a file or stream. Supports automatic time- or size-based rolling of log files. Messages can be assigned severities, and only those messages at or above the logger's current reporting level will be logged.

- During development, you may want to see all messages:

```ruby
require 'logger'
log = Logger.new(STDOUT)
log.level = Logger::DEBUG
log.datetime_format = "%H:%M:%S"
log.info("Application starting")
3.times do |i|
  log.debug("Executing loop, i = #{i}")
  temperature = some_calculation(i)  # defined externally
  if temperature > 50
    log.warn("Possible overheat. i = #{i}")
  end
end

log.info("Application terminating")
```

produces:

```
I, [12:33:23#24712]  INFO -- : Application starting
D, [12:33:23#24712] DEBUG -- : Executing loop, i = 0
D, [12:33:23#24712] DEBUG -- : Executing loop, i = 1
D, [12:33:23#24712] DEBUG -- : Executing loop, i = 2
W, [12:33:23#24712]  WARN -- : Possible overheat. i = 2
I, [12:33:23#24712]  INFO -- : Application terminating
```

- In deployment, you can turn off anything below INFO:

```ruby
require 'logger'
log = Logger.new(STDOUT)
log.level = Logger::INFO
log.datetime_format = "%H:%M:%S"

# as above...
```

produces:

```
I, [12:33:23#24714]  INFO -- : Application starting
W, [12:33:23#24714]  WARN -- : Possible overheat. i = 2
I, [12:33:23#24714]  INFO -- : Application terminating
```

- Logs to a file, which is rotated when it gets to about 10KB. Keeps up to five old files.

```ruby
require 'logger'
log = Logger.new("application.log", 5, 10*1024)

log.info("Application starting")
# ...
```

The mathn library attempts to bring some unity to numbers under Ruby, making classes Bignum, Complex, Fixnum, Integer, and Rational work and play better together. It automatically includes the libraries complex, rational, matrix, and prime.

- Types will tend to convert between themselves in a more natural way (so, for example, Complex::I squared will evaluate to -1, rather than Complex[-1,0]).

- Division will tend to produce more accurate results. The conventional division operator (/) is redefined to use quo, which doesn't round.

- Related to the previous point, rational numbers will be used in preference to floats when possible. Dividing one by two results in the rational number $\frac{1}{2}$, rather than 0.5 (or 0, the result of normal integer division).

See also: Matrix (page 769) Rational (page 794) Complex (page 738) Prime (page 790)

- Without mathn:

```
require 'matrix'
36/16                     # => 2
Math.sqrt(36/16)          # => 1.4142135623730951

Complex::I * Complex::I  # => (-1+0i)

(36/16)**-2               # => 1/4
(-36/16)**-2              # => 1/9

(36/16)**(1/2)            # => 1
(-36/16)**(1/2)           # => 1

(36/16)**(-1/2)           # => 1/2
(-36/16)**(-1/2)          # => -1/3

Matrix.diagonal(6,7,8)/3 # => Matrix[[2, 0, 0], [0, 2, 0], [0, 0, 2]]
```

- With mathn:

```
36/16                     # => 9/4
Math.sqrt(36/16)          # => 3/2

Complex::I * Complex::I  # => -1

(36/16)**-2               # => 16/81
(-36/16)**-2              # => 16/81

(36/16)**(1/2)            # => 3/2
(-36/16)**(1/2)           # => (9.184850993605148e-17+1.5i)

(36/16)**(-1/2)           # => 2/3
(-36/16)**(-1/2)          # => (4.082155997157844e-17-0.6666666666666666i)

Matrix.diagonal(6,7,8)/3 # => Matrix[[2, 0, 0], [0, 7/3, 0], [0, 0, 8/3]]
```

Matrix

The matrix library defines classes Matrix and Vector, representing rectangular matrices and vectors. As well as the normal arithmetic operations, they provide methods for matrix-specific functions (such as rank, inverse, and determinants) and a number of constructor methods (for creating special-case matrices—zero, identity, diagonal, singular, and vector).

As of Ruby 1.9, matrices use quo internally for division, so rational numbers may be returned as a result of integer division. In prior versions of Ruby, you'd need to include the mathn library to achieve this.

```ruby
require 'matrix'

m1 = Matrix[ [2, 1], [-1, 1] ]

m1[0,1]            # => 1

m1.inv             # => Matrix[[1/3, -1/3], [1/3, 2/3]]

m1 * m1.inv        # => Matrix[[1/1, 0/1], [0/1, 1/1]]

m1.determinant     # => 3

m1.singular?       # => false

v1 = Vector[3, 4]  # => Vector[3, 4]

v1.covector        # => Matrix[[3, 4]]

m1 * v1            # => Vector[10, 1]

m2 = Matrix[ [1,2,3], [4,5,6], [7,8,9] ]

m2.minor(1, 2, 1, 2) # => Matrix[[5, 6], [8, 9]]
```

MiniTest

New in Ruby 1.9, MiniTest is now the standard unit testing framework supplied with Ruby. The minitest library contains classes for unit tests, mock objects, and a (trivial) subset of RSpec-style testing syntax.

The unit testing framework is similar to the original Test::Unit framework. However, if you want functionality that is the same as Test::Unit, use the Test::Unit wrappers for MiniTest—simply require "test/unit" as normal.

Chapter 13, *Unit Testing*, on page 175 contains a tutorial on unit testing with Ruby.

Monitors are a mutual-exclusion mechanism. They allow separate threads to define shared resources that will be accessed exclusively, and they provide a mechanism for a thread to wait for resources to become available in a controlled way.

The monitor library actually defines three separate ways of using monitors: by subclassing, as a mixin, and as a extension to a particular object. In this section, we show the mixin form of Monitor. The subclassing form is effectively identical. In both it and when including MonitorMixin in an existing class, it is essential to invoke super in the class's initialize method.

See also: Thread (page 702)

```ruby
# This example would be better written using fibers.
require 'monitor'
require 'mathn'

numbers = []
numbers.extend(MonitorMixin)
number_added = numbers.new_cond

consumer = Thread.new do              # Reporter thread
  5.times do
    numbers.synchronize do
      number_added.wait_while { numbers.empty? }
      puts numbers.shift
    end
  end
end

generator = Thread.new do             # Prime number generator thread
  primes = Prime.each
  5.times do
    numbers.synchronize do
      numbers << primes.next
      number_added.signal
    end
  end
end

generator.join
consumer.join
```

produces:

```
2
3
5
7
11
```

Mutex_m

mutex_m is a variant of class Mutex on page 588 that allows mutex facilities to be mixed into any object.

The Mutex_m module defines methods that correspond to those in Mutex but with the prefix mu_ (so that lock is defined as mu_lock and so on). These are then aliased to the original Mutex names.

See also: Mutex (page 588) Thread (page 702)

```ruby
require 'mutex_m'

class Counter
  include Mutex_m
  attr_reader :count
  def initialize
    @count = 0
    super
  end
  def tick
    lock
    @count += 1
    unlock
  end
end

c = Counter.new

t1 = Thread.new { 100_000.times {  c.tick } }
t2 = Thread.new { 100_000.times {  c.tick } }

t1.join
t2.join

c.count   # => 200000
```

Net::FTP

The net/ftp library implements a File Transfer Protocol (FTP) client. As well as data transfer commands (getbinaryfile, gettextfile, list, putbinaryfile, and puttextfile), the library supports the full complement of server commands (acct, chdir, delete, mdtm, mkdir, nlst, rename, rmdir, pwd, size, status, and system). Anonymous and password-authenticated sessions are supported. Connections may be active or passive.

See also: open-uri (page 781)

```ruby
require 'net/ftp'

ftp = Net::FTP.new('ftp.ruby-lang.org')
ftp.login
ftp.chdir('pub/ruby/doc')
puts ftp.list('*txt')
ftp.getbinaryfile('MD5SUM.txt', 'md5sum.txt', 1024)
ftp.close
puts File.read('md5sum.txt')
```

produces:

```
-rw-rw-r--   1 1027     100          12149 Sep 10 06:02 MD5SUM.txt
-rw-rw-r--   1 1027     100          13565 Sep 10 06:03 SHA1SUM.txt
d529768c828c930c49b3766d13dc1f2c  ruby-man-1.4.6-jp.tar.gz
8eed63fec14a719df26247fb8384db5e  ruby-man-1.4.6.tar.gz
623b5d889c1f15b8a50fe0b3b8ba4b0f  ruby-man-ja-1.6.6-20011225-rd.tar.gz
5f37ef2d67ab1932881cd713989af6bf  ruby-man-ja-html-20050214.tar.bz2
e9949b2023a63b6259b02bed4fb13064  ruby-man-ja-html-20050214.tar.gz

. . .
```

The net/http library provides a simple client to fetch headers and web page contents using the HTTP and HTTPS protocols.

The get post and head methods return a response object, with the content of the response accessible through the response's body method.

See also: OpenSSL (page 783) open-uri (page 781) URI (page 822)

- Opens a connection and fetches a page, displaying the response code and message, header information, and some of the body:

```ruby
require 'net/http'

Net::HTTP.start('www.pragprog.com') do |http|
  response = http.get('/categories/new')
  puts "Code = #{response.code}"
  puts "Message = #{response.message}"
  response.each {|key, val| printf "%-14s = %-40.40s\n", key, val }
  p response.body[0, 55]
end
```

produces:

```
Code = 302
Message = Found
content-type    = text/html; charset=utf-8
date            = Mon, 27 May 2013 17:36:21 GMT
location        = http://pragprog.com/categories/new
server          = nginx/1.2.6
status          = 302 Found
x-request-id    = 1c76c5446f0a1dd001ceb768f2611364
x-runtime       = 0.004833
x-ua-compatible = IE=Edge,chrome=1
content-length  = 100
connection      = keep-alive
"<html><body>You are being <a href=\"http://pragprog.com/"
```

- Fetches a single page, displaying the response code and message, header information, and some of the body:

```ruby
require 'net/http'

response = Net::HTTP.get_response('www.pragprog.com',
                                  '/categories/new')
puts "Code = #{response.code}"
puts "Message = #{response.message}"
response.each {|key, val| printf "%-14s = %-40.40s\n", key, val }
p response.body[0, 55]
```

produces:

```
Code = 302
Message = Found
content-type    = text/html; charset=utf-8
date            = Mon, 27 May 2013 17:36:21 GMT
```

```
location        = http://pragprog.com/categories/new
server          = nginx/1.2.6
status          = 302 Found
x-request-id    = ab9de753032bb022cbd33fefbe030f56
x-runtime       = 0.005468
x-ua-compatible = IE=Edge,chrome=1
content-length  = 100
connection      = keep-alive
"<html><body>You are being <a href=\"http://pragprog.com/"
```

- Follows redirections (the open-uri library does this automatically). This code comes from the RDoc documentation.

```ruby
require 'net/http'
require 'uri'

 def fetch(uri_str, limit=10)
   fail 'http redirect too deep' if limit.zero?
   puts "Trying: #{uri_str}"
   response = Net::HTTP.get_response(URI.parse(uri_str))
   case response
   when Net::HTTPSuccess      then response
   when Net::HTTPRedirection then fetch(response['location'], limit-1)
   else response.error!
   end
 end

 response = fetch('http://www.ruby-lang.org')
 p response.body[0, 50]
```

produces:

```
Trying: http://www.ruby-lang.org
"<html>\n  <head>\n     <script type=\"text/javascript\""
```

- Searches our site for things about Ruby and lists the authors. (This would be tidier using Hpricot.)

```ruby
require 'net/http'

uri = URI.parse('http://pragprog.com/search')
response = Net::HTTP.post_form(uri, "q" => "ruby")
puts response.body.scan(%r{<p class="by-line">by (.*?)</p>})[0,3]
```

produces:

```
Caleb Tennis
Maik Schmidt
Bruce Tate
```

The Internet Mail Access Protocol (IMAP) is used to allow mail clients to access mail servers. It supports plain-text login and the IMAP login and CRAM-MD5 authentication mechanisms. Once connected, the library supports threading, so multiple interactions with the server may take place at the same time.

The examples that follow are taken with minor modifications from the RDoc documentation in the library source file.

The TMail gem provides an interface for creating and parsing email messages.

See also: Net::POP (page 776)

- Lists senders and subjects of messages to "dave" in the inbox:

```
require 'net/imap'

imap = Net::IMAP.new('my.mailserver.com')
imap.authenticate('LOGIN', 'dave', 'secret')
imap.examine('INBOX')
puts "Message count: #{ imap.responses["EXISTS"]}"
imap.search(["TO", "dave"]).each do |message_id|
  envelope = imap.fetch(message_id, "ENVELOPE")[0].attr["ENVELOPE"]
    puts "#{envelope.from[0].name}: \t#{envelope.subject}"
end
```

- Moves all email messages with a date in April 2008 from the folder Mail/sent-mail to Mail/sent-apr08:

```
require 'net/imap'
imap = Net::IMAP.new('my.mailserver.com')
imap.authenticate('LOGIN', 'dave', 'secret')
imap.select('Mail/sent-mail')
if not imap.list('Mail/', 'sent-apr08')
  imap.create('Mail/sent-apr08')
end
imap.search(["BEFORE", "01-May-2008",
             "SINCE",  "1-Apr-2008"]).each do |message_id|
  imap.copy(message_id, "Mail/sent-apr08")
  imap.store(message_id, "+FLAGS", [:Deleted])
end
imap.expunge
```

Net::POP

The net/pop library provides a simple client to fetch and delete mail on a Post Office Protocol (POP) server.

The class Net::POP3 is used to access a POP server, returning a list of Net::POPMail objects, one per message stored on the server. These POPMail objects are then used to fetch and/or delete individual messages.

The library also provides class APOP, an alternative to the POP3 class that performs encrypted authentication.

```ruby
require 'net/pop'
pop = Net::POP3.new('server.ruby-stuff.com')
pop.start('joe', 'secret') do |server|
  msg = server.mails[0]

  # Print the 'From:' header line
  from = msg.header.split("\r\n").grep(/^From: /)[0]
  puts from
  puts
  puts "Full message:"
  text = msg.pop
  puts text
end
```

produces:

```
From: dave@facet.ruby-stuff.com (Dave Thomas)

Full message:
Return-Path: <dave@facet.ruby-stuff.com>
Received: from facet.ruby-stuff.com (facet.ruby-stuff.com [10.96.0.122])
        by pragprog.com (8.11.6/8.11.6) with ESMTP id i2PJMW701809
        for <joe@carat.ruby-stuff.com>; Thu, 25 Mar 2008 13:22:32 -0600
Received: by facet.ruby-stuff.com (Postfix, from userid 502)
        id 4AF228B1BD; Thu, 25 Mar 2008 13:22:36 -0600 (CST)
To: joe@carat.ruby-stuff.com
Subject: Try out the new features!
Message-Id: <20080325192236.4AF228B1BD@facet.ruby-stuff.com>
Date: Thu, 25 Mar 2008 13:22:36 -0600 (CST)
From: dave@facet.ruby-stuff.com (Dave Thomas)
Status: RO

Ruby 1.9 has even more new features, both in
the core language and in the supplied libraries.

Try it out!
```

Net::SMTP   Simple SMTP Client

The net/smtp library provides a simple client to send electronic mail using the Simple Mail Transfer Protocol (SMTP). It does not assist in the creation of the message payload—it simply delivers messages once an RFC 822 message has been constructed. The TMail gem provides an interface for creating and parsing email messages.

- Sends an e-mail from a string:

```ruby
require 'net/smtp'

msg = "Subject: Test\n\nNow is the time\n"
Net::SMTP.start('pragprog.com') do |smtp|
  smtp.send_message(msg, 'dave@pragprog.com', ['dave'])
end
```

- Sends an e-mail using an SMTP object and an adapter:

```ruby
require 'net/smtp'

Net::SMTP::start('pragprog.com', 25, "pragprog.com") do |smtp|
  smtp.open_message_stream('dave@pragprog.com', # from
                           [ 'dave' ]           # to
                          ) do |stream|
    stream.puts "Subject: Test1"
    stream.puts
    stream.puts "And so is this"
  end
end
```

- Sends an e-mail to a server requiring CRAM-MD5 authentication:

```ruby
require 'net/smtp'

msg = "Subject: Test\n\nNow is the time\n"
Net::SMTP.start('pragprog.com', 25, 'pragprog.com',
                'user', 'password', :cram_md5) do |smtp|
  smtp.send_message(msg, 'dave@pragprog.com', ['dave'])
end
```

Net::Telnet

The net/telnet library provides a complete implementation of a telnet client and includes features that make it a convenient mechanism for interacting with nontelnet services.

- Connects to localhost, runs the date command, and disconnects:

```
require 'net/telnet'
tn = Net::Telnet.new({})
tn.login "testuser", "wibble"
tn.cmd "date" # => "date\nMon May 27 12:33:29 CDT 2013\nlight-boy:~ testuser$ "
```

- The methods new, cmd, login, and waitfor take an optional block. If present, the block is passed output from the server as it is received by the routine. This can be used to provide real-time output, rather than waiting (for example) for a login to complete before displaying the server's response.

```
require 'net/telnet'
tn = Net::Telnet.new({})           {|str| print str }
tn.login("testuser", "wibble")     {|str| print str }
tn.cmd("date")                     {|str| print str }
```

produces:

```
Trying localhost...
Connected to localhost.

Darwin/BSD (light-boy.local) (ttys007)

login: testuser
Password:
Last login: Mon May 27 12:33:29 on ttys007
light-boy:~ testuser$ date
Mon May 27 12:33:29 CDT 2013
light-boy:~ testuser$
```

- Query a WHOIS server on port 43.

```
require 'net/telnet'
tn = Net::Telnet.new('Host'        => 'whois.domain.com',
                     'Port'        => '43',
                     'Timeout'     => 5,
                     'Telnetmode' => false)
tn.write("pragprog.com\r\n")
puts tn.sock.grep(/ on /)
```

produces:

```
Record last updated on 15-Oct-2012.
Record expires on 19-Jan-2016.
Record created on 19-Jan-1999.
```

The NKF module is a wrapper around Itaru Ichikawa's Network Kanji Filter (NKF) library (version 1.7). It provides functions to guess at the encoding of JIS, EUC, and SJIS streams and to convert from one encoding to another. Even though Ruby 1.9 now supports these encodings natively, this library is still useful for guessing encodings.

- As of Ruby 1.9, NFK uses the built-in encoding objects:

```
require 'nkf'
NKF::AUTO # => nil
NKF::JIS  # => #<Encoding:ISO-2022-JP (dummy)>
NKF::EUC  # => #<Encoding:EUC-JP>
NKF::SJIS # => #<Encoding:Shift_JIS>
```

- Guesses at the encoding of a string. (Thanks to Nobu Nakada for the examples on this page.)

```
require 'nkf'
p NKF.guess("Yukihiro Matsumoto")
p NKF.guess("\e$B$^$D$b$H$f$-$R$m\e(B")
p NKF.guess("\244\336\244\304\244\342\244\310\244\346\244\255\244\322\244\355")
p NKF.guess("\202\334\202\302\202\340\202\306\202\344\202\253\202\320\202\353")
```

produces:

```
#<Encoding:US-ASCII>
#<Encoding:ISO-2022-JP (dummy)>
#<Encoding:EUC-JP>
#<Encoding:Shift_JIS>
```

- The NFK.nkf method takes two parameters. The first is a set of options, passed on to the NKF library. The second is the string to translate. The following examples assume that your console is set up to accommodate Japanese characters. The text at the end of the three ruby commands is Yukihiro Matsumoto in Hiragana.

```
$ ruby -e 'p *ARGV' まっもと ゆきひろ
"\244\336\244\304\244\342\244\310\244\346\244\255\244\322\244\355"

$ ruby -rnkf -e 'p NKF.nkf(*ARGV)' -- -Es まっもと ゆきひろ
"\202\334\202\302\202\340\202\306\202\344\202\253\202\320\202\353"

$ ruby -rnkf -e 'p NKF.nkf(*ARGV)' -- -Ej まっもと ゆきひろ
"\e$B$^$D$b$H$f$-$R$m\e(B"
```

Observable

The Observer pattern, also known as Publish/Subscribe, provides a simple mechanism for one object (the source) to inform a set of interested third-party objects when its state changes (see *Design Patterns [GHJV95]*). In the Ruby implementation, the notifying class mixes in the module Observable, which provides the methods for managing the associated observer objects. The observers must implement the update method to receive notifications.

```ruby
require 'observer'

class CheckWaterTemperature # Periodically check the water
  include Observable

  def run
    last_temp = nil
    loop do
      temp = Temperature.fetch   # external class...
      puts "Current temperature: #{temp}"
      if temp != last_temp
        changed                  # notify observers
        notify_observers(Time.now, temp)
        last_temp = temp
      end
    end
  end
end

class Warner
  def initialize(&limit)
    @limit = limit
  end
  def update(time, temp)         # callback for observer
    if @limit.call(temp)
      puts "--- #{time.to_s}: Temperature outside range: #{temp}"
    end
  end
end

checker = CheckWaterTemperature.new
checker.add_observer(Warner.new {|t| t < 80})
checker.add_observer(Warner.new {|t| t > 120})
checker.run
```

produces:

```
Current temperature: 83
Current temperature: 75
--- 2013-05-27 12:33:30 -0500: Temperature outside range: 75
Current temperature: 90
Current temperature: 134
--- 2013-05-27 12:33:30 -0500: Temperature outside range: 134
Current temperature: 134
Current temperature: 112
Current temperature: 79
--- 2013-05-27 12:33:30 -0500: Temperature outside range: 79
```

The open-uri library extends Object#open, allowing it to accept URIs for FTP and HTTP as well as local filenames. Once opened, these resources can be treated as if they were local files, accessed using conventional IO methods. The URI passed to open is either a string containing an HTTP or FTP URL or a URI object (see the URI library on page 822). When opening an HTTP resource, the method automatically handles redirection and proxies. When using an FTP resource, the method logs in as an anonymous user.

The IO object returned by open in these cases is extended to support methods that return metainformation from the request: content_type, charset, content_encoding, last_modified, status, base_uri, meta.

See also: URI (page 822)

```ruby
require 'open-uri'
require 'pp'

open('http://ruby-lang.org') do |f|
  puts "URI: #{f.base_uri}"
  puts "Content-type: #{f.content_type}, charset: #{f.charset}"
  puts "Encoding: #{f.content_encoding}"
  puts "Last modified: #{f.last_modified}"
  puts "Status: #{f.status.inspect}"
  pp f.meta
  puts "----"
  3.times {|i| puts "#{i}: #{f.gets}" }
end
```

produces:

```
URI: http://www.ruby-lang.org/
Content-type: text/html, charset: iso-8859-1
Encoding: []
Last modified: 2013-05-22 16:31:36 -0500
Status: ["200", "OK"]
{"date"=>"Mon, 27 May 2013 17:33:23 GMT",
 "server"=>"nginx/0.7.67",
 "content-type"=>"text/html",
 "content-length"=>"748",
 "last-modified"=>"Wed, 22 May 2013 21:31:36 GMT",
 "accept-ranges"=>"bytes",
 "via"=>"1.1 www.ruby-lang.org"}
----
0: <html>
1:   <head>
2:     <script type="text/javascript">
```

| Library | Open3 | Run Subprocess and Connect to All Streams |

Runs a command in a subprocess. Data written to *stdin* can be read by the subprocess, and data written to standard output and standard error in the subprocess will be available on the *stdout* and *stderr* streams. The subprocess is actually run as a grandchild, and as a result, Process#waitall cannot be used to wait for its termination (hence the sleep in the following example). Note also that you probably cannot assume that the application's output and error streams will not be buffered, so output may not arrive when you expect it to arrive.

```ruby
require 'open3'

def read_from(label, stream)
  while line = stream.gets
    puts "#{label}: #{line}"
  end
end

Open3.popen3('bc') do | stdin, stdout, stderr |
  t1 = Thread.new { read_from('STDOUT', stdout) }
  t2 = Thread.new { read_from('STDERR', stderr) }
  stdin.puts "3 * 4"
  stdin.puts "1 / 0"
  stdin.puts "2 ^ 5"
  stdin.close
  t1.join
  t2.join
end
```

produces:

```
STDOUT: 12
STDERR: Runtime error (func=(main), adr=3): Divide by zero
STDOUT: 32
```

OpenSSL

The Ruby OpenSSL extension wraps the freely available OpenSSL library.[4] It provides the Secure Sockets Layer and Transport Layer Security (SSL and TLS) protocols, allowing for secure communications over networks. The library provides functions for certificate creation and management, message signing, and encryption/decryption. It also provides wrappers to simplify access to HTTPS servers, along with secure FTP. The interface to the library is large (roughly 330 methods), but the average Ruby user will probably use only a small subset of the library's capabilities.

Only if: OpenSSL library available

See also: Net::FTP (page 772) Net::HTTP (page 773) Socket (page 807)

- Accesses a secure website using HTTPS. Note that SSL is used to tunnel to the site, but the requested page also requires standard HTTP basic authorization.

```ruby
require 'net/https'

USER = "xxx"
PW   = "yyy"

site = Net::HTTP.new("www.securestuff.com", 443)
site.use_ssl = true
response = site.get2("/cgi-bin/cokerecipe.cgi",
                     'Authorization' => 'Basic ' +
                     ["#{USER}:#{PW}"].pack('m').strip)
```

- Creates a socket that uses SSL. This isn't a good example of accessing a website. However, it illustrates how a socket can be encrypted.

```ruby
require 'socket'
require 'openssl'

socket = TCPSocket.new("www.secure-stuff.com", 443)

ssl_context = OpenSSL::SSL::SSLContext.new()

unless ssl_context.verify_mode
  warn "warning: peer certificate won't be verified this session."
  ssl_context.verify_mode = OpenSSL::SSL::VERIFY_NONE
end
sslsocket = OpenSSL::SSL::SSLSocket.new(socket, ssl_context)
sslsocket.sync_close = true
sslsocket.connect

sslsocket.puts("GET /secret-info.shtml")
while line =  sslsocket.gets
  p line
end
```

---

4.   http://www.openssl.org

OptionParser

OptionParser is a flexible and extensible way to parse command-line arguments. It has a particularly rich abstraction of the concept of an option.

- An option can have multiple short names (options preceded by a single hyphen) and multiple long names (options preceded by two hyphens). Thus, an option that displays help may be available as -h, -?, --help, and --about. Users may abbreviate long option names to the shortest nonambiguous prefix.

- An option may be specified as having no argument, an optional argument, or a required argument. Arguments can be validated against patterns or lists of valid values.

- Arguments may be returned as objects of any type (not just strings). The argument type system is extensible (we add Date handling in the example).

- Arguments can have one or more lines of descriptive text, used when generating usage information.

Options are specified using the on and def methods. These methods take a variable number of arguments that cumulatively build a definition of each option. The arguments accepted by these methods are:

"-x" "-xARG" "-x=ARG" "-x[OPT]" "-x[=OPT]" "-x PLACE"

Option has short name x. First form has no argument, next two have mandatory argument, next two have optional argument, last specifies argument follows option. The short names may also be specified as a range (such as "-[a-c]").

"--switch" "--switch=ARG" "--switch=[OPT]" "--switch PLACE"

Option has long name switch. First form has no argument, next has a mandatory argument, the next has an optional argument, and the last specifies the argument follows the switch.

"--no-switch"

Defines a option whose default value is false.

"=ARG" "=[OPT]"

Argument for this option is mandatory or optional. For example, the following code says there's an option known by the aliases -x, -y, and -z that takes a mandatory argument, shown in the usage as N:

```
opt.on("-x", "-y", "-z", "=N")
```

"description"

Any string that doesn't start - or = is used as a description for this option in the summary. Multiple descriptions may be given; they'll be shown on additional lines.

/pattern/

Any argument must match the given pattern.

array

Argument must be one of the values from array.

proc or method

Argument type conversion is performed by the given proc or method (rather than using the block associated with the on or def method call).

ClassName

Argument must match that defined for ClassName, which may be predefined or added using OptionParser.accept. Built-in argument classes are

Object: Any string. No conversion. This is the default.

String: Any nonempty string. No conversion.

Integer: Ruby/C-like integer with optional sign (0ddd is octal, 0bddd binary, 0xddd hexadecimal). Converts to Integer.

Float: Float number format. Converts to Float.

Numeric: Generic numeric format. Converts to Integer for integers, Float for floats.

Array: Argument must be of list of strings separated by a comma.

OptionParser::DecimalInteger: Decimal integer. Converted to Integer.

OptionParser::OctalInteger: Ruby/C-like octal/hexadecimal/binary integer.

OptionParser::DecimalNumeric: Decimal integer/float number. Integers converted to Integer, floats to Float.

TrueClass, FalseClass: Boolean switch.

See also: GetoptLong (page 761)

```ruby
require 'optparse'
require 'date'

# Add Dates as a new option type
OptionParser.accept(Date, /(\d+)-(\d+)-(\d+)/) do |d, mon, day, year|
  Date.new(year.to_i, mon.to_i, day.to_i)
end

opts = OptionParser.new
opts.on("-x")                          {|val| puts "-x seen" }
opts.on("-s", "--size VAL", Integer) {|val| puts "-s #{val}" }
opts.on("-a", "--at DATE",  Date)    {|val| puts "-a #{val}" }

my_argv = [ "--size", "1234", "-x", "-a", "12-25-2008", "fred", "wilma" ]

rest = opts.parse(*my_argv)
puts "Remainder = #{rest.join(', ')}"
puts opts.to_s
```

produces:

```
-s 1234
-x seen
-a 2008-12-25
Remainder = fred, wilma
Usage: prog [options]
    -x
    -s, --size VAL
    -a, --at DATE
```

OpenStruct Open (dynamic) Structure

An open structure is an object whose attributes are created dynamically when first assigned. In other words, if *obj* is an instance of an OpenStruct, then the statement obj.abc=1 will create the attribute *abc* in *obj* and then assign the value 1 to it.

```
require 'ostruct'

os = OpenStruct.new( "f1" => "one", :f2 => "two" )
os.f3 = "cat"
os.f4 = 99
os.f1      # => "one"
os.f2      # => "two"
os.f3      # => "cat"
os.f4      # => 99
```

OpenStruct uses method_missing to intercept calls. This might cause a problem, because calls to a method defined in class Object will not invoke method_missing—they'll simply call the method in Object. In practice, this isn't a problem, because you typically call a setter before calling a getting, and when you do call the setter method, ostruct will defined getter and setter methods, overriding those in Object. Here's a typical example; because we call ice.freeze= first, the freeze= and freeze methods will be dynamically created in the ostruct, and the getter will work as expected.

```
require 'ostruct'

ice = OpenStruct.new
ice.freeze = "yes"
ice.freeze # => #<OpenStruct freeze="yes">
```

However, if you don't first call the setter, the freeze getter will not invoke method_missing— it'll simply call the underlying freeze method in Object.

```
require 'ostruct'

ice = OpenStruct.new
p ice.freeze
ice.freeze = "yes"
```

produces:

```
#<OpenStruct>
prog.rb:5:in `<main>': can't modify frozen OpenStruct (TypeError)
```

Pathname

A Pathname represents the absolute or relative name of a file. It has two distinct uses. First, it allows manipulation of the parts of a file path (extracting components, building new paths, and so on). Second (and somewhat confusingly), it acts as a façade for some methods in classes Dir, File, and module FileTest, forwarding on calls for the file named by the Pathname object.

See also: File (page 488)

- Path name manipulation:

```
require 'pathname'

p1 = Pathname.new("/usr/bin")
p2 = Pathname.new("ruby")
p3 = p1 + p2
p4 = p2 + p1
p3.parent          # => #<Pathname:/usr/bin>
p3.parent.parent # => #<Pathname:/usr>
p1.absolute?       # => true
p2.absolute?       # => false
p3.split           # => [#<Pathname:/usr/bin>, #<Pathname:ruby>]

p5 = Pathname.new("testdir")
puts p5.realpath
puts p5.children
```

produces:

```
/Users/dave/BS2/published/ruby4/Book/testdir
testdir/.svn
testdir/config.h
testdir/main.rb
```

- Path name as proxy for file and directory status requests:

```
require 'pathname'

p1 = Pathname.new("/usr/bin/ruby")
p1.file?                  # => true
p1.directory?             # => false
p1.executable?            # => true
p1.size                   # => 34752

p2 = Pathname.new("testfile") # => #<Pathname:testfile>

p2.read                   # => "This is line one\nThis is line two\nThis is
                          # .. line three\nAnd so on...\n"
p2.readlines              # => ["This is line one\n", "This is line two\n",
                          # .. "This is line three\n", "And so on...\n"]
```

PP uses the PrettyPrint library to format the results of inspecting Ruby objects. As well as the methods in the class, it defines a global function, pp, which works like the existing p method but formats its output.

PP has a default layout for all Ruby objects. However, you can override the way it handles a class by defining the method pretty_print, which takes a PP object as a parameter. It should use that PP object's methods text, breakable, nest, group, and pp to format its output (see PrettyPrint for details).

See also: JSON (page 766) PrettyPrint (page 789) YAML (page 827)

- Compares "p" and "pp":

  ```
  require 'pp'

  Customer = Struct.new(:name, :sex, :dob, :country)
  cust = Customer.new("Walter Wall", "Male", "12/25/1960", "Niue")

  puts "Regular print"
  p cust

  puts "\nPretty print"
  pp cust
  ```

  produces:

  ```
  Regular print
  #<struct Customer name="Walter Wall", sex="Male", dob="12/25/1960",
  country="Niue">

  Pretty print
  #<struct Customer
   name="Walter Wall",
   sex="Male",
   dob="12/25/1960",
   country="Niue">
  ```

- You can tell PP not to display an object if it has already displayed it:

  ```
  require 'pp'

  a = "string"
  b = [ a ]
  c = [ b, b ]
  PP.sharing_detection = false
  pp c

  PP.sharing_detection = true
  pp c
  ```

  produces:

  ```
  [["string"], ["string"]]
  [["string"], [...]]
  ```

PrettyPrint implements a pretty printer for structured text. It handles details of wrapping, grouping, and indentation. The PP library uses PrettyPrint to generate more legible dumps of Ruby objects.

See also: PP (page 788)

The following program prints a chart of Ruby's classes, showing subclasses as a bracketed list following the parent. To save some space, we show just the classes in the Numeric branch of the tree.

```ruby
require 'prettyprint'

@children = Hash.new { |h,k| h[k] = Array.new }
ObjectSpace.each_object(Class) do |cls|
  @children[cls.superclass] << cls if cls <= Numeric
end
def print_children_of(printer, cls)
  printer.text(cls.name)
  kids = @children[cls].sort_by(&:name)
  unless kids.empty?
    printer.group(0, " [", "]") do
      printer.nest(3) do
        printer.breakable
        kids.each_with_index do |k, i|
          printer.breakable unless i.zero?
          print_children_of(printer, k)
        end
      end
      printer.breakable
    end
  end
end
printer = PrettyPrint.new(STDOUT, 30)
print_children_of(printer, Object)
printer.flush
```

produces:

```
Object [
   Numeric [
      Complex
      Float
      Integer [
         Bignum
         Fixnum
      ]
      Rational
   ]
]
```

prime

Provides facilities for generating prime numbers, as well as factoring numbers. Note that the Prime class is a singleton.

See also: mathn (page 768)

- The prime library extends the number classes to include new functionality and adds a new class Prime:

```ruby
require 'prime'
# 60 = 2**2 * 3 * 5
60.prime?         # => false
60.prime_division # => [[2, 2], [3, 1], [5, 1]]
```

- You can also use it to generate sequences of primes:

```ruby
require 'prime'
Prime.each {|p| break if p > 20; print p, " " }
```

produces:

```
2 3 5 7 11 13 17 19
```

- Because Prime.each returns an enumerator if no block is present, we can write the previous example more concisely.

```ruby
require 'prime'
puts Prime.each.take_while {|p| p <= 20 }.join(" ")
```

produces:

```
2 3 5 7 11 13 17 19
```

Profile   Profile Execution of a Ruby Program

The profile library is a trivial wrapper around the Profiler module, making it easy to profile the execution of an entire program. Profiling can be enabled from the command line using the -r profile option or from within a source program by requiring the profile module.

Unlike Ruby 1.8, Ruby 1.9 does not profile primitive methods such as Fixnum#== and Fixnum#+. This helps boost Ruby's performance.

See also: Benchmark (page 733) Profiler__ (page 792)

```ruby
require 'profile'
def ackerman(m, n)
  if m == 0 then  n+1
  elsif n == 0 and m > 0 then ackerman(m-1, 1)
  else ackerman(m-1, ackerman(m, n-1))
  end
end
ackerman(3, 3)
```

produces:

```
  %   cumulative   self              self     total
 time   seconds   seconds    calls  ms/call  ms/call  name
100.00     0.04      0.04   . 2432     0.02     0.64  Object#ackerman
  0.00     0.04      0.00       1      0.00     0.00  TracePoint#enable
  0.00     0.04      0.00       1      0.00     0.00  Module#method_added
  0.00     0.04      0.00       1      0.00     0.00  TracePoint#disable
  0.00     0.04      0.00       1      0.00    40.00  #toplevel
```

The Profiler__ module can be used to collect a summary of the number of calls to, and the time spent in, methods in a Ruby program. The output is sorted by the total time spent in each method. The profile library is a convenience wrapper that profiles an entire program.

See also: Benchmark (page 733) profile (page 791)

```ruby
require 'profiler'

# ...Omit definition of connection and fetching methods...

def calc_discount(qty, price)
  case qty
  when 0..10 then 0.0
  when 11..99 then price * 0.05
  else price * 0.1
  end
end

def calc_sales_totals(rows)
  total_qty =  total_price = total_disc = 0
  rows.each do |row|
    total_qty   += row.qty
    total_price += row.price
    total_disc  += calc_discount(row.qty, row.price)
  end
end

connect_to_database
rows = read_sales_data

Profiler__::start_profile
calc_sales_totals(rows)
Profiler__::stop_profile
Profiler__::print_profile(STDOUT)
```

produces:

%	cumulative	self		self	total	
time	seconds	seconds	calls	ms/call	ms/call	name
28.57	0.02	0.02	648	0.03	0.03	Range#include?
28.57	0.04	0.02	1	20.00	70.00	Array#each
14.29	0.05	0.01	325	0.03	0.37	Object#calc_sales_totals
14.29	0.06	0.01	324	0.03	0.12	Object#calc_discount
14.29	0.07	0.01	648	0.02	0.05	Range#===
0.00	0.07	0.00	1	0.00	0.00	TracePoint#enable
0.00	0.07	0.00	648	0.00	0.00	Float#<=>
0.00	0.07	0.00	648	0.00	0.00	Fixnum#<=>
0.00	0.07	0.00	648	0.00	0.00	SalesData#price
0.00	0.07	0.00	3	0.00	0.00	Fixnum#+
0.00	0.07	0.00	648	0.00	0.00	SalesData#qty
0.00	0.07	0.00	1	0.00	0.00	TracePoint#disable
0.00	0.07	0.00	1	0.00	70.00	#toplevel

The PStore class provides transactional, file-based, persistent storage of Ruby objects. Each PStore can store several object hierarchies. Each hierarchy has a root, identified by a key (often a string). At the start of a PStore transaction, these hierarchies are read from a disk file and made available to the Ruby program. At the end of the transaction, the hierarchies are written back to the file. Any changes made to objects in these hierarchies are therefore saved on disk, to be read at the start of next transaction that uses that file.

In normal use, a PStore object is created and then is used one or more times to control a transaction. Within the body of the transaction, any object hierarchies that had previously been saved are made available, and any changes to object hierarchies, and any new hierarchies, are written back to the file at the end.

The following example stores two hierarchies in a PStore. The first, identified by the key "names", is an array of strings. The second, identified by "tree", is a simple binary tree.

```ruby
require 'pstore'
require 'pp'
class T
  def initialize(val, left=nil, right=nil)
    @val, @left, @right = val, left, right
  end
  def to_a
    [ @val, @left.to_a, @right.to_a ]
  end
end

def T(*args)
  T.new(*args)
end

store = PStore.new("/tmp/store")
store.transaction do
  store['names'] = [ 'Douglas', 'Barenberg', 'Meyer' ]
  store['tree']  = T('top',
                     T('A', T('B')),
                     T('C', T('D', nil, T('E'))))
end

# now read it back in
store.transaction do
  puts "Roots: #{store.roots.join(', ')}"
  puts store['names'].join(', ')
  pp store['tree'].to_a
end
```

produces:

```
Roots: names, tree
Douglas, Barenberg, Meyer
["top",
 ["A", ["B", [], []], []],
 ["C", ["D", [], ["E", [], []]], []]]
```

| Library | **PTY** | Pseudo-Terminal Interface: Interact with External Processes |

Only if: Unix with pty support

Many Unix platforms support a *pseudo-terminal*—a device pair where one end emulates a process running on a conventional terminal, and the other end can read and write that terminal as if it were a user looking at a screen and typing on a keyboard.

The PTY library provides the method spawn, which starts the given command (by default a shell), connecting it to one end of a pseudo-terminal. It then returns the reader and writer streams connected to that terminal, allowing your process to interact with the running process.

Working with pseudo-terminals can be tricky. See IO#expect on page 753 for a convenience method that makes life easier. You might also want to track down Ara T. Howard's Session module for an even simpler approach to driving subprocesses.[5]

See also: expect (page 753)

This example runs irb in a subshell and asks it to convert the string "cat" to uppercase:

```
require 'pty'
require 'expect'

$expect_verbose = true

PTY.spawn("irb") do |reader, writer, pid|
  reader.expect(/> /)
  writer.puts "'cat'.upcase"
  reader.expect("=> ")
  answer = reader.gets
  puts "Answer = #{answer}"
end
```

produces:

```
2.0.0p0 :001 > 'cat'.upcase
 => Answer = "CAT"
```

| Library | **Rational** | Rational Numbers |

The Rational class is now built in to Ruby. The vestigial Rational library simply defines a few aliases for backward compatibility. For the classes Fixnum and Bignum, the following aliases are defined:

Floating-point division
    quof is an alias for fdiv.

Rational division
    rdiv is an alias for quo.

Exponentiation
    power! and rpower are aliases for **.

---

5.   Currently found at http://www.codeforpeople.com/lib/ruby/session/

Readline

The Readline module allows programs to prompt for and receive lines of user input. The module allows lines to be edited during entry, and command history allows previous commands to be recalled and edited. The history can be searched, allowing the user to (for example) recall a previous command containing the text *ruby*. Command completion allows context-sensitive shortcuts: tokens can be expanded in the command line under control of the invoking application. In typical GNU fashion, the underlying readline library supports more options than any user could need and emulates both vi and emacs key bindings.

Only if: GNU readline present

This meaningless program implements a trivial interpreter that can increment and decrement a value. It uses the Abbrev on page 731 module to expand abbreviated commands when the Tab key is pressed.

sl_readline/readline.rb
```ruby
require 'abbrev'
require 'readline'
include Readline

ABBREV = %w{ exit inc dec }.abbrev
Readline.completion_proc = -> string { ABBREV[string] }

value = 0
loop do
  cmd = readline("wibble [#{value}]: ", true) || "exit"
  case cmd.strip
  when "exit"    then break
  when "inc"     then value += 1
  when "dec"     then value -= 1
  else                puts "Invalid command #{cmd}"
  end
end
```

```
wibble [0]: inc
wibble [1]: <up-arrow>      => inc
wibble [2]: d<tab>          => dec
wibble [1]: in<esc><p>      => inc
wibble [2]: exit
```

Resolv

The resolv library is a pure-Ruby implementation of a DNS client—it can be used to convert domain names into corresponding IP addresses. It also supports reverse lookups and the resolution of names in the local hosts file.

Loading the additional library resolv-replace insinuates the resolv library into Ruby's socket library on page 807.

Basic name lookups are already built-in to the standard socket libraries. The resolv library exists because, prior to Ruby 1.9, calling the operating system to do a name lookup would suspend all interpreter threads. That is no longer the case.

| Library | **REXML** | XML Processing Library |

REXML is a pure-Ruby XML processing library, including DTD-compliant document parsing, XPath querying, and document generation. It supports both tree-based and stream-based document processing. Because it is written in Ruby, it is available on all platforms supporting Ruby. REXML has a full and complex interface—this section contains a few small examples.

- Assume the file demo.xml contains this:

```xml
<classes language="ruby">
  <class name="Numeric">
    Numeric represents all numbers.
    <class name="Float">
      Floating point numbers have a fraction and a mantissa.
    </class>
    <class name="Integer">
      Integers contain exact integral values.
      <class name="Fixnum">
        Fixnums are stored as machine ints.
      </class>
      <class name="Bignum">
        Bignums store arbitraty-sized integers.
      </class>
    </class>
  </class>
</classes>
```

- Reads and processes the XML:

```ruby
require 'rexml/document'

xml = REXML::Document.new(File.open("code/sl_rexml/demo.xml"))

puts "Root element: #{xml.root.name}"
print "The names of all classes: "
xml.elements.each("//class") {|c| print c.attributes["name"], " " }

print "\nDescription of Fixnum: "
p xml.elements["//class[@name='Fixnum']"].text
```

produces:

```
Root element: classes
The names of all classes: Numeric Float Integer Fixnum Bignum
Description of Fixnum: "\n        Fixnums are stored as machine ints.\n        "
```

- Reads in a document, adds and deletes elements, and manipulates attributes before writing it back out:

```ruby
require 'rexml/document'
include REXML

xml = Document.new(File.open("code/sl_rexml/demo.xml"))

cls = Element.new("class")
cls.attributes["name"] = "Rational"
```

```
cls.text = "Represents complex numbers"

# Remove Integer's children, and add our new node as
# the one after Integer
int = xml.elements["//class[@name='Integer']"]
int.delete_at(1)
int.delete_at(2)
int.next_sibling = cls

# Change all the 'name' attributes to class_name
xml.elements.each("//class") do |c|
  c.attributes['class_name'] = c.attributes['name']
  c.attributes.delete('name')
end

# and write it out with a XML declaration at the front
xml << XMLDecl.new
xml.write(STDOUT, 2)
```

produces:

```
<?xml version='1.0'?>
<classes language='ruby'>
  <class class_name='Numeric'>
     Numeric represents all numbers.
    <class class_name='Float'>
       Floating point numbers have a fraction and a mantissa.
    </class>
    <class class_name='Integer'>
       Integers contain exact integral values.
    </class>
    <class class_name='Rational'>
      Represents complex numbers
    </class>
  </class>
</classes>
```

Tuplespaces are a distributed blackboard system. Processes may add tuples to the blackboard, and other processes may remove tuples from the blackboard that match a certain pattern. Originally presented by David Gelernter, tuplespaces offer an interesting scheme for distributed cooperation among heterogeneous processes.

Rinda, the Ruby implementation of tuplespaces, offers some interesting additions to the concept. In particular, the Rinda implementation uses the === operator to match tuples. This means that tuples may be matched using regular expressions, the classes of their elements, and the element values.

See also: DRb (page 748)

- The blackboard is a DRb server that offers a shared tuplespace:

```
require 'rinda/tuplespace'
MY_URI = "druby://127.0.0.1:12131"
DRb.start_service(MY_URI, Rinda::TupleSpace.new)
DRb.thread.join
```

- The arithmetic agent accepts messages containing an arithmetic operator and two numbers. It stores the result back on the blackboard.

```
require 'rinda/rinda'
MY_URI = "druby://127.0.0.1:12131"
DRb.start_service
ts = Rinda::TupleSpaceProxy.new(DRbObject.new(nil, MY_URI))
loop do
  op, v1, v2 = ts.take([ %r{^[-+/*]$}, Numeric, Numeric])
  ts.write(["result", v1.send(op, v2)])
end
```

- The client places tuples on the blackboard and reads back the result of each:

```
require 'rinda/rinda'
MY_URI = "druby://127.0.0.1:12131"
DRb.start_service
ts = Rinda::TupleSpaceProxy.new(DRbObject.new(nil, MY_URI))

queries = [[ "+", 1, 2 ], [ "*", 3, 4 ], [ "/", 8, 2 ]]
queries.each do |q|
  ts.write(q)
  ans = ts.take(["result", nil])
  puts "#{q[1]} #{q[0]} #{q[2]} = #{ans[1]}"
end
```

produces:

```
1 + 2 = 3
3 * 4 = 12
8 / 2 = 4
```

The ripper library gives you access to Ruby's parser. It can tokenize input, return lexical tokens, and return a nested S-expression. It also supports event-based parsing.

- Tokenize a line of Ruby code:

```ruby
require "ripper"
content = "a=1;b=2;puts a+b"
p Ripper.tokenize(content)
```

produces:

```
["a", "=", "1", ";", "b", "=", "2", ";", "puts", " ", "a", "+", "b"]
```

- Does a lexical analysis, returning token types, values, and line and column numbers:

```ruby
require "ripper"
require "pp"
content = "a=1;b=2;puts a+b"
pp Ripper.lex(content)[0,5]
```

produces:

```
[[[1, 0], :on_ident, "a"],
 [[1, 1], :on_op, "="],
 [[1, 2], :on_int, "1"],
 [[1, 3], :on_semicolon, ";"],
 [[1, 4], :on_ident, "b"]]
```

- Returns the sexp representing a chunk of code:

```ruby
require "ripper"
require "pp"
content = "a=1;b=2;puts a+b"
pp Ripper.sexp(content)
```

produces:

```
[:program,
 [[:assign, [:var_field, [:@ident, "a", [1, 0]]], [:@int, "1", [1, 2]]],
  [:assign, [:var_field, [:@ident, "b", [1, 4]]], [:@int, "2", [1, 6]]],
  [:command,
   [:@ident, "puts", [1, 8]],
   [:args_add_block,
    [[:binary,
      [:var_ref, [:@ident, "a", [1, 13]]],
      :+,
      [:var_ref, [:@ident, "b", [1, 15]]]]],
    false]]]]
```

- As a (silly) example of event-based lexical analysis, here's a program that finds class definitions and their associated comment blocks. For each, it outputs the class name and the comment. It might be considered the zeroth iteration of an RDoc-like program.

  The parameter to parse is an accumulator—it is passed between event handlers and can be used to construct the result.

```ruby
require 'ripper'

# This class handles parser events, extracting
# comments and attaching them to class definitions
class BabyRDoc < Ripper::Filter
  def initialize(*)
    super
    reset_state
  end

  def on_default(event, token, output)
    reset_state
    output
  end

  def on_sp(token, output)
    output
  end
  alias on_nil on_sp

  def on_comment(comment, output)
    @comment << comment.sub(/^\s*#\s*/, "      ")
    output
  end

  def on_kw(name, output)
    @expecting_class_name = (name == 'class')
    output
  end

  def on_const(name, output)
    if @expecting_class_name
      output << "#{name}:\n"
      output <<  @comment
    end
    reset_state
    output
  end

  private

  def reset_state
    @comment = ""
    @expecting_class_name = false
  end
end

BabyRDoc.new(File.read(__FILE__)).parse(STDOUT)
```

produces:

```
BabyRDoc:
    This class handles parser events, extracting
    comments and attaching them to class definitions
```

Rich Site Summary or RDF Site Summary or Really Simple Syndication—take your pick.
RSS is the protocol of choice for disseminating news on the Internet. The Ruby RSS library
supports creating and parsing streams compliant with RSS 0.9, RSS 1.0, and RSS 2.0.

- Reads and summarizes the latest stories from http://ruby-lang.org:

```ruby
require 'rss/2.0'
require 'open-uri'

open('http://ruby-lang.org/en/feeds/news.rss') do |http|
  response = http.read
  result = RSS::Parser.parse(response, false)
  puts "Channel: " + result.channel.title
  result.items.each_with_index do |item, i|
    puts "#{i+1}. #{item.title}" if i < 3
  end
end
```

produces:

```
Channel: Ruby News
1. Ruby 1.9.3-p429 is released
2. Ruby 2.0.0-p195 is released
3. Object taint bypassing in DL and Fiddle in Ruby (CVE-2013-2065)
```

- Generates some RSS information:

```ruby
require 'rss/0.9'

rss  = RSS::Rss.new("0.9")
chan = RSS::Rss::Channel.new
chan.title       = "The Daily Dave"
chan.description = "Dave's Feed"
chan.language    = "en-US"
chan.link        = "http://pragdave.pragprog.com"
rss.channel      = chan

image = RSS::Rss::Channel::Image.new
image.url   = "http://pragprog.com/pragdave.gif"
image.title = "PragDave"
image.link  = chan.link
chan.image  = image

3.times do |i|
  item = RSS::Rss::Channel::Item.new
  item.title       = "My News Number #{i}"
  item.link        = "http://pragprog.com/pragdave/story_#{i}"
  item.description = "This is a story about number #{i}"
  chan.items << item
end

puts rss.to_s
```

Scanf

Implements a version of the C library scanf function, which extracts values from a string under the control of a format specifier.

The Ruby version of the library adds a scanf method to both class IO and class String. The version in IO applies the format string to the next line read from the receiver. The version in String applies the format string to the receiver. The library also adds the global method Object#scanf, which uses as its source the next line of standard input.

Scanf has one main advantage over using regular expressions to break apart a string: a regular expression extracts strings, whereas scanf will return objects converted to the correct type.

- Splits a date string into its constituents:

```
require 'scanf'

date = "2010-12-15"
year, month, day = date.scanf("%4d-%2d-%2d")
year       # => 2010
month      # => 12
day        # => 15
year.class # => Fixnum
```

- The block form of scanf applies the format multiple times to the input string, returning each set of results to the block. The numbers are returned as integers, not strings:

```
require 'scanf'

data = "cat:7 dog:9 cow:17 walrus:31"

data.scanf("%[^:]:%d ") do |animal, value|
  puts "A #{animal.strip} has #{value}"
end
```

produces:

```
A cat has 7
A dog has 9
A cow has 17
A walrus has 31
```

- Extracts hex numbers:

```
require 'scanf'

data = "decaf bad"
data.scanf("%3x%2x%x") # => [3564, 175, 2989]
```

SDBM

The SDBM database implements a simple key/value persistence mechanism. Because the underlying SDBM library itself is provided with Ruby, there are no external dependencies, and SDBM should be available on all platforms supported by Ruby. SDBM database keys and values must be strings. SDBM databases are effectively hashlike.

See also: DBM (page 745) GDBM (page 760)

The example that follows stores a record in a new database and then fetches it back. Unlike the DBM library, all values to SDBM must be strings (or implement to_str).

```ruby
require 'sdbm'
require 'date'

SDBM.open("data.dbm") do |dbm|
  dbm['name'] = "Walter Wombat"
  dbm['dob']  = Date.new(1997, 12,25).to_s
  dbm['uses'] = "Ruby"
end

SDBM.open("data.dbm", nil) do |dbm|
  p dbm.keys
  p dbm['dob']
end
```

produces:

```
["name", "dob", "uses"]
"1997-12-25"
```

SecureRandom

Provides access to one of your operating system's secure random number generators. If the OpenSSL library is installed, the module uses its random_bytes method. Otherwise, the module looks for and uses /dev/urandom or the CryptGenRandom method in the Windows API.

- Generates some random numbers:

```ruby
require 'securerandom'
# Random floats such that 0.0 <= rand < 1.0
SecureRandom.random_number(0)    # => 0.26256698786247024
SecureRandom.random_number(0)    # => 0.6885743213737645

# Random integers such that 0 <= rand < 1000
SecureRandom.random_number(1000) # => 112
SecureRandom.random_number(1000) # => 273
```

- Generates ten random bytes, returning the result as a hex string, a Base64 string, and a string of binary data. A different random string is returned for each call.

```ruby
require 'securerandom'
SecureRandom.hex(10)          # => "bf4262e94d093ffbb4a7"
SecureRandom.base64(10)       # => "X/8YpCbCEyO2zA=="
SecureRandom.random_bytes(10) # => "\x7FO\0r\r\xC1?\xB7b#"
```

A Set is a collection of unique values (where uniqueness is determined using eql? and hash). Convenience methods let you build sets from enumerable objects.

- Basic set operations:

```ruby
require 'set'

set1 = Set.new([:bear, :cat, :deer])

set1.include?(:bat)  # => false
set1.add(:fox)       # => #<Set: {:bear, :cat, :deer, :fox}>

partition = set1.classify {|element| element.to_s.length }

partition            # => {4=>#<Set: {:bear, :deer}>, 3=>#<Set: {:cat, :fox}>}

set2 = [ :cat, :dog, :cow ].to_set
set1 | set2          # => #<Set: {:bear, :cat, :deer, :fox, :dog, :cow}>
set1 & set2          # => #<Set: {:cat}>
set1 - set2          # => #<Set: {:bear, :deer, :fox}>
set1 ^ set2          # => #<Set: {:dog, :cow, :bear, :deer, :fox}>
```

- Partitions the users in our /etc/passwd file into subsets where members of each subset have adjacent user IDs:

```ruby
require 'etc'
require 'set'

users = []
Etc.passwd {|u| users << u }

related_users = users.to_set.divide do |u1, u2|
  (u1.uid - u2.uid).abs <= 1
end

related_users.each do |relatives|
  relatives.each {|u| print "#{u.uid}/#{u.name} " }
  puts "\n======="
end
```

produces:

```
235/_assetcache 234/_krb_anonymous 233/_krb_kerberos 232/_krb_changepw
231/_krb_kadmin 230/_krb_krbtgt 229/_avbdeviced 228/_netstatistics 227/_dovenull

=======
93/_calendar 92/_securityagent 91/_tokend
=======
202/_coreaudiod 203/_screensaver 201/Guest 200/_softwareupdate
=======
. . .
```

Shellwords   Manipulate Shell Lines Using POSIX Semantics

Given a string representative of a shell command line, splits it into word tokens according to POSIX semantics. Also allows you to create properly escaped shell lines from individual words.

- Spaces between double or single quotes are treated as part of a word.

- Double quotes may be escaped using a backslash.

- Spaces escaped by a backslash are not used to separate words.

- Otherwise, tokens separated by whitespace are treated as words.

```ruby
require 'shellwords'
include Shellwords

line = %{Code Ruby Be Happy!}
shellwords(line)                    # => ["Code", "Ruby", "Be", "Happy!"]

line = %{"Code Ruby" 'Be Happy'!}
shellwords(line)                    # => ["Code Ruby", "Be Happy!"]

line = %q{Code\ Ruby "Be Happy"!}
shellwords(line)                    # => ["Code Ruby", "Be Happy!"]

shelljoin(["Code Ruby", "Be Happy"])  # => Code\ Ruby Be\ Happy
```

In addition, the library adds shellsplit and shelljoin methods to classes String and Array, respectively:

```ruby
require 'shellwords'
include Shellwords
%{Code\\ Ruby Be Happy!}.shellsplit # => ["Code Ruby", "Be", "Happy!"]
["Code Ruby", "Be Happy"].shelljoin # => "Code\\ Ruby Be\\ Happy"
```

The Singleton design pattern ensures that only one instance of a particular class may be created for the lifetime of a program (see *Design Patterns [GHJV95]*).

The singleton library makes this simple to implement. Mix the Singleton module into each class that is to be a singleton, and that class's new method will be made private. In its place, users of the class call the method instance, which returns a singleton instance of that class.

In this example, the two instances of MyClass are the same object:

```ruby
require 'singleton'

class MyClass

  attr_accessor :data
  include Singleton
end

a = MyClass.instance # => #<MyClass:0x007feb190604d0>
b = MyClass.instance # => #<MyClass:0x007feb190604d0>
a.data = 123         # => 123
b.data               # => 123
a.object_id          # => 70323856933480
b.object_id          # => 70323856933480
```

The socket extension defines nine classes for accessing the socket-level communications of the underlying system. All of these classes are (indirect) subclasses of class IO, meaning that IO's methods can be used with socket connections.

The hierarchy of socket classes reflects the reality of network programming and hence is somewhat confusing. The BasicSocket class largely contains methods common to data transfer for all socket-based connections. It is subclassed to provide protocol-specific implementations: IPSocket and UNIXSocket (for domain sockets). These in turn are subclassed by TCPSocket, UDP-Socket, and SOCKSSocket.

BasicSocket is also subclassed by class Socket, which is a more generic interface to socket-oriented networking. Although classes such as TCPSocket are specific to a protocol, Socket objects can, with some work, be used regardless of protocol.

TCPSocket, SOCKSSocket, and UNIXSocket are each connection oriented. Each has a corresponding xxxxServer class, which implements the server end of a connection.

The socket libraries are something that you may never use directly. However, if you do use them, you'll need to know the details. For that reason, we've put a reference section online at http://pragprog.com/book/ruby3/programming-ruby-1-9?tab=tab-contents.

The following code shows a trivial UDP server and client:

```ruby
# Simple logger prints messages received on UDP port 12121
require 'socket'
socket = UDPSocket.new
socket.bind("127.0.0.1", 12121)
loop do
  msg, sender  = socket.recvfrom(100)
  host = sender[3]
  puts "#{Time.now}: #{host} '#{msg}'"
  STDOUT.flush
end

# Exercise the logger
require 'socket'
log = UDPSocket.new
log.connect("127.0.0.1", 12121)
log.print "Up and Running!"
# process ... process ..
log.print "Done!"
```

produces:

```
2013-05-27 12:33:39 -0500: 127.0.0.1 'Up and Running!'
2013-05-27 12:33:39 -0500: 127.0.0.1 'Done!'
```

In some ways, the distinction between strings and file contents is artificial: the contents of a file are basically a string that happens to live on disk, not in memory. The StringIO library aims to unify the two concepts, making strings act as if they were opened IO objects. Once a string is wrapped in a StringIO object, it can be read from and written to as if it were an open file. This can make unit testing a lot easier. It also lets you pass strings into classes and methods that were originally written to work with files. StringIO objects take their encoding from the string you pass in or the default external encoding is that no string is passed.

- Reads and writes from a string:

```
require 'stringio'

sio = StringIO.new("time flies like an arrow")
sio.read(5)           # => "time "
sio.read(5)           # => "flies"
sio.pos = 19
sio.read(5)           # => "arrow"
sio.rewind            # => 0
sio.write("fruit")    # => 5
sio.pos = 16
sio.write("a banana") # => 8
sio.rewind            # => 0
sio.read              # => "fruitflies like a banana"
```

- Uses StringIO as a testing aid:

```
require 'stringio'
require 'csv'
require 'test/unit'

class TestCSV < Test::Unit::TestCase
  def test_simple
    StringIO.open do |op|
      CSV(op) do |csv|
        csv << [ 1, "line 1", 27 ]
        csv << [ 2, nil, 123 ]
      end
      assert_equal("1,line 1,27\n2,,123\n", op.string)
    end
  end
end
```

produces:

```
Run options:
# Running tests:

.
Finished tests in 0.004047s, 247.0966 tests/s, 247.0966 assertions/s.
1 tests, 1 assertions, 0 failures, 0 errors, 0 skips

ruby -v: ruby 2.0.0p0 (2013-02-24 revision 39474) [x86_64-darwin12.2.0]
```

StringScanner

StringScanner objects progress through a string, matching (and optionally returning) tokens that match a given pattern. Unlike the built-in scan methods, StringScanner objects maintain a current position pointer in the string being examined, so each call resumes from the position in the string where the previous call left off. Pattern matches are anchored to this previous point.

- Implements a simple language:

```ruby
require 'strscan'

# Handle the language:
#   set <var> = <value>
#   get <var>

values = {}

while line = gets

  scanner = StringScanner.new(line.chomp)

  scanner.scan(/(get|set)\s+/) or fail "Missing command"
  cmd = scanner[1]

  var_name = scanner.scan(/\w+/) or fail "Missing variable"

  case cmd
  when "get"
    puts "#{var_name} => #{values[var_name].inspect}"

  when "set"
    scanner.skip(/\s+=\s+/) or fail "Missing '='"
    value = scanner.rest
    values[var_name] = value
  else
    fail cmd
  end
end
```

Run this from the command line, typing in phrases from the language:

```
$ ruby strscan.rb
set a = dave
set b = hello
get b
b => "hello"
get a
a => "dave"
```

Syslog

Only if: Unix system with syslog

New in 2.0

The Syslog class is a simple wrapper around the Unix syslog(3) library. It allows messages to be written at various severity levels to the logging daemon, where they are disseminated according to the configuration in syslog.conf. Ruby 2.0 adds support for Syslog::Logger, which is compatible with the Logger API.

The following examples assume the log file is /var/log/system.log.

- Adds to our local system log. We'll log all the levels configured for the user facility for our system (which is every level except debug and info messages).

```ruby
require 'syslog'
log = Syslog.open("test")   # "test" is the app name
log.debug("Warm and fuzzy greetings from your program")
log.info("Program starting")
log.notice("I said 'Hello!'")
log.warning("If you don't respond soon, I'm quitting")
log.err("You haven't responded after %d milliseconds", 7)
log.alert("I'm telling your mother...")
log.emerg("I'm feeling totally crushed")
log.crit("Aarrgh....")
  system("tail -6 /var/log/system.log")
```

produces:

```
Sep 16 12:48:44 dave-4 test[35121]: Warm and fuzzy greetings from your program
Sep 16 12:48:44 dave-4 test[35121]: Program starting
Sep 16 12:48:44 dave-4 test[35121]: I said 'Hello!'
Sep 16 12:48:44 dave-4 test[35121]: If you don't respond soon, I'm quitting
Sep 16 12:48:44 dave-4 test[35121]: You haven't responded after 7 milliseconds
Sep 16 12:48:44 dave-4 test[35121]: I'm telling your mother...
Sep 16 12:48:44 dave-4 test[35121]: I'm feeling totally crushed
Sep 16 12:48:44 dave-4 test[35121]: Aarrgh....
```

- Logs only errors and above:

```ruby
require 'syslog'
log = Syslog.open("test")
log.mask = Syslog::LOG_UPTO(Syslog::LOG_ERR)
log.debug("Warm and fuzzy greetings from your program")
log.info("Program starting")
log.notice("I said 'Hello!'")
log.warning("If you don't respond soon, I'm quitting")
log.err("You haven't responded after %d milliseconds", 7)
log.alert("I'm telling your mother...")
log.emerg("I'm feeling totally crushed")
log.crit("Aarrgh....")

system("tail -4 /var/log/system.log")
```

produces:

```
Sep 16 12:48:44 dave-4 test[35124]: You haven't responded after 7 milliseconds
Sep 16 12:48:44 dave-4 test[35124]: I'm telling your mother...
Sep 16 12:48:44 dave-4 test[35124]: I'm feeling totally crushed
Sep 16 12:48:44 dave-4 test[35124]: Aarrgh....
```

Tempfile   Temporary File Support

Class Tempfile creates managed temporary files. Although they behave the same as any other IO objects, temporary files are automatically deleted when the Ruby program terminates. Once a Tempfile object has been created, the underlying file may be opened and closed a number of times in succession.

Tempfile does not directly inherit from IO. Instead, it delegates calls to a File object. From the programmer's perspective, apart from the unusual new, open, and close semantics, a Tempfile object behaves as if it were an IO object.

If you don't specify a directory to hold temporary files when you create them, the tmpdir library will be used to find a system-dependent location.

See also: tmpdir (page 818)

```ruby
require 'tempfile'
tf = Tempfile.new("afile")
tf.path    # => "/var/folders/44/j19_ml3n3dx7bwrb_qmbcjyc0000gn/T/afile20130527-24
           # .. 867-1greefy"
tf.puts("Cosi Fan Tutte")
tf.close
tf.open
tf.gets    # => "Cosi Fan Tutte\n"
tf.close(true)
```

Test::Unit is a unit testing framework based on the original SUnit Smalltalk framework. It provides a structure in which unit tests may be organized, selected, and run. Tests can be run from the command line or using one of several GUI-based interfaces.

Chapter 13, *Unit Testing*, on page 175 contains a tutorial on Test::Unit.

Maybe we have a simple playlist class, designed to store and retrieve songs:

```ruby
require_relative 'song.rb'
require 'forwardable'

class Playlist
  extend Forwardable
  def_delegator(:@list, :<<, :add_song)
  def_delegators(:@list, :size, :empty?)
  def initialize
    @list = []
  end
  def find(title)
    @list.find {|song| song.title == title}
  end
end
```

We can write unit tests to exercise this class. The Test::Unit framework is smart enough to run the tests in a test class if no main program is supplied.

```ruby
require 'test/unit'
require_relative 'playlist.rb'

class TestPlaylist < Test::Unit::TestCase
  def test_adding
    pl = Playlist.new
    assert_empty(pl)
    assert_nil(pl.find("My Way"))
    pl.add_song(Song.new("My Way", "Sinatra"))
    assert_equal(1, pl.size)
    s = pl.find("My Way")
    refute_nil(s)
    assert_equal("Sinatra", s.artist)
    assert_nil(pl.find("Chicago"))
    # .. and so on
  end
end
```

produces:

```
Run options:
# Running tests:

.
Finished tests in 0.004140s, 241.5459 tests/s, 1690.8213 assertions/s.
1 tests, 7 assertions, 0 failures, 0 errors, 0 skips

ruby -v: ruby 2.0.0p0 (2013-02-24 revision 39474) [x86_64-darwin12.2.0]
```

The thread library adds some utility functions and classes for supporting threads. Much of this has been superseded by the Monitor class, but the thread library contains two classes, Queue and SizedQueue, that are still useful. Both classes implement a thread-safe queue that can be used to pass objects between producers and consumers in multiple threads. The Queue object implements a unbounded queue. A SizedQueue is told its capacity; any producer that tries to add an object when the queue is at that capacity will block until a consumer has removed an object.

The following example was provided by Robert Kellner. It has three consumers taking objects from an unsized queue. Those objects are provided by two producers, which each add three items.

```ruby
require 'thread'
queue = Queue.new

consumers = (1..3).map do |i|
  Thread.new("consumer #{i}") do |name|
    begin
      obj = queue.deq
      print "#{name}: consumed #{obj.inspect}\n"
    end until obj == :END_OF_WORK
  end
end

producers = (1..2).map do |i|
  Thread.new("producer #{i}") do |name|
    3.times do |j|
      queue.enq("Item #{j} from #{name}")
    end
  end
end

producers.each(&:join)
consumers.size.times { queue.enq(:END_OF_WORK) }
consumers.each(&:join)
```

produces:

```
consumer 1: consumed "Item 0 from producer 1"
consumer 1: consumed "Item 1 from producer 1"
consumer 1: consumed "Item 2 from producer 1"
consumer 1: consumed "Item 0 from producer 2"
consumer 2: consumed "Item 1 from producer 2"
consumer 3: consumed "Item 2 from producer 2"
consumer 1: consumed :END_OF_WORK
consumer 3: consumed :END_OF_WORK
consumer 2: consumed :END_OF_WORK
```

ThreadsWait   Wait for Multiple Threads to Terminate

Class ThreadsWait handles the termination of a group of thread objects. It provides methods to allow you to check for termination of any managed thread and to wait for all managed threads to terminate.

The following example kicks off a number of threads that each wait for a slightly shorter length of time before terminating and returning their thread number. Using ThreadsWait, we can capture these threads as they terminate, either individually or as a group.

```ruby
require 'thwait'

group = ThreadsWait.new

# construct threads that wait for 1 second, .9 second, etc.
# add each to the group

9.times do |i|
  thread = Thread.new(i) {|index| sleep 1.0 - index/10.0; index }
  group.join_nowait(thread)
end

# any threads finished?
group.finished?             # => false

# wait for one to finish
group.next_wait.value       # => 8

# wait for 5 more to finish
5.times { group.next_wait } # => 5

# wait for next one to finish
group.next_wait.value       # => 2

# and then wait for all the rest
group.all_waits             # => nil
```

The time library adds functionality to the built-in class Time, supporting date and/or time formats used by RFC 2822 (e-mail), RFC 2616 (HTTP), and ISO 8601 (the subset used by XML schema).

```ruby
require 'time'

# Convert external formats into Time objects

Time.rfc2822("Thu, 1 Apr 2010 16:32:45 CST")     # => 2010-04-01 17:32:45 -0500
Time.rfc2822("Thu, 1 Apr 2010 16:32:45 -0600")   # => 2010-04-01 17:32:45 -0500

Time.httpdate("Thu, 01 Apr 2010 16:32:45 GMT")    # => 2010-04-01 11:32:45 -0500
Time.httpdate("Thursday, 01-Apr-04 16:32:45 GMT") # => 2004-04-01 16:32:45 UTC
Time.httpdate("Thu Apr  1 16:32:45 2010")         # => 2010-04-01 16:32:45 UTC

Time.xmlschema("2010-04-01T16:32:45")             # => 2010-04-01 16:32:45 -0500
Time.xmlschema("2010-04-01T16:32:45.12-06:00")    # => 2010-04-01 22:32:45 UTC

# Convert time objects into external formats

Time.now.rfc2822   # => "Mon, 27 May 2013 12:33:41 -0500"
Time.now.httpdate  # => "Mon, 27 May 2013 17:33:41 GMT"
Time.now.xmlschema # => "2013-05-27T12:33:41-05:00"
```

Timeout   Run a Block with Timeout

The Timeout.timeout method takes a parameter representing a timeout period in seconds, an optional exception parameter, and a block. The block is executed, and a timer is run concurrently. If the block terminates before the timeout, timeout returns the value of the block. Otherwise, the exception (default Timeout::Error) is raised.

```ruby
require 'timeout'

for snooze in 1..2
  puts "About to sleep for #{snooze}"
  begin
    Timeout::timeout(1.5) do |timeout_length|
      puts "Timeout period is #{timeout_length}"
      sleep(snooze)
      puts "That was refreshing"
    end
  rescue Timeout::Error
    puts "Woken up early!!"
  end
end
```

produces:

```
About to sleep for 1
Timeout period is 1.5
That was refreshing
About to sleep for 2
Timeout period is 1.5
Woken up early!!
```

Be careful when using timeouts—you may find them interrupting system calls that you cannot reliably restart, resulting in possible data loss.

Tk

Of all the Ruby options for creating GUIs, the Tk library is probably the most widely supported, running on Windows, Linux, Mac OS X, and other Unix-like platforms.[6] Although it doesn't produce the prettiest interfaces, Tk is functional and relatively simple to program.

Only if: Tk library installed

sl_tk/curves.rb
```ruby
# encoding: utf-8
require 'tk'
include Math

def plot(val)
  Integer(val * 180 + 200)
end

TkRoot.new do |root|
  title "Curves"
  geometry "400x400"

  TkCanvas.new(root) do |canvas|
    width 400
    height 400
    pack('side'=>'top', 'fill'=>'both', 'expand'=>'yes')

    points = [ ]
    a = 2
    b = 3
    0.0.step(8, 0.1) do |t|
      x = Math.sin(a*t)
      y = Math.cos(b*t)
      points << plot(x) << plot(y)
    end
    TkcLine.new(canvas, *(points), smooth: 'on', width: 10, fill: 'blue')
  end
end
Tk.mainloop
```

produces:

---

6.   All these environments require that the Tcl/Tk libraries are installed before the Ruby Tk extension can be used.

The tmpdir library adds the tmpdir method to class Dir. This method returns the path to a temporary directory that *should* be writable by the current process. (This will not be true if none of the well-known temporary directories is writable and if the current working directory is also not writable.) Candidate directories include those referenced by the environment variables TMPDIR, TMP, TEMP, and USERPROFILE; the directory /tmp; and (on Windows boxes) the temp subdirectory of the Windows or System directory.

```ruby
require 'tmpdir'

Dir.tmpdir # => "/var/folders/44/j19_ml3n3dx7bwrb_qmbcjyc0000gn/T"

ENV['TMPDIR'] = "/wibble"        # doesn't exist
ENV['TMP']    = "/sbin"          # not writable
ENV['TEMP']   = "/Users/dave/tmp" # just right

Dir.tmpdir # => "/Users/dave/tmp"
```

The mktmpdir method can be used to create a new temporary directory:

```ruby
require 'tmpdir'

name = Dir.mktmpdir

# .. process, process, process ..

Dir.rmdir(name)
```

The tracer library uses Object#set_trace_func to trace all or part of a Ruby program's execution. The traced lines show the thread number, file, line number, class, event, and source line. The events shown are - for a change of line, < for a call, > for a return, C for a class definition, and E for the end of a definition.

- You can trace an entire program by including the tracer library from the command line:

```ruby
class Account
  def initialize(balance)
    @balance = balance
  end
  def debit(amt)
    if @balance < amt
      fail "Insufficient funds"
    else
      @balance -= amt
    end
  end
end
acct = Account.new(100)
acct.debit(40)
```

```
$ ruby -r tracer account.rb
#0:prog.rb:15::-:    acct = Account.new(100)
#0:prog.rb:3:Account:>:  def initialize(balance)
#0:prog.rb:4:Account:-:     @balance = balance
#0:prog.rb:5:Account:<:   end
#0:prog.rb:16::-:. acct.debit(40)
#0:prog.rb:6:Account:>:  def debit(amt)
#0:prog.rb:7:Account:-:    if @balance < amt
#0:prog.rb:10:Account:-:      @balance -= amt
#0:prog.rb:12:Account:<:   end
```

- You can also use tracer objects to trace just a portion of your code and use filters to select what to trace:

```ruby
require 'tracer'
tracer = Tracer.new
tracer.add_filter lambda {|event, *rest| event == "line" }
acct = Account.new(100)
tracer.on { acct.debit(40) }
```

produces:

```
#0:prog.rb:18::-: tracer.on { acct.debit(40) }
#0:prog.rb:6:Account:-:    if @balance < amt
#0:prog.rb:9:Account:-:       @balance -= amt
```

Given a set of dependencies between nodes (where each node depends on zero or more other nodes and there are no cycles in the graph of dependencies), a topological sort will return a list of the nodes ordered such that no node follows a node that depends on it. One use for this is scheduling tasks, where the order means that you complete the dependencies before you start any task that depends on them. The make program uses a topological sort to order its execution.

In the Ruby implementation, you mix in the TSort module and define two methods: tsort_each_node, which yields each node in turn, and tsort_each_child, which, given a node, yields each of that node's dependencies.

- Given the set of dependencies among the steps for making a piña colada, what is the optimum order for undertaking the steps?

```ruby
require 'tsort'

class Tasks
  include TSort
  def initialize
    @dependencies = {}
  end
  def add_dependency(task, *relies_on)
    @dependencies[task] = relies_on
  end
  def tsort_each_node(&block)
    @dependencies.each_key(&block)
  end
  def tsort_each_child(node, &block)
    deps = @dependencies[node]
    deps.each(&block) if deps
  end
end

tasks = Tasks.new
tasks.add_dependency(:add_rum,       :open_blender)
tasks.add_dependency(:add_pc_mix,    :open_blender)
tasks.add_dependency(:add_ice,       :open_blender)
tasks.add_dependency(:close_blender, :add_rum, :add_pc_mix, :add_ice)
tasks.add_dependency(:blend_mix,     :close_blender)
tasks.add_dependency(:pour_drink,    :blend_mix)
tasks.add_dependency(:pour_drink,    :open_blender)
puts tasks.tsort
```

produces:

```
open_blender
add_rum
add_pc_mix
add_ice
close_blender
blend_mix
pour_drink
```

Why un? When you invoke it from the command line with the -r option to Ruby, it spells -run. This pun gives a hint as to the intent of the library: it lets you run commands (in this case, a subset of the methods in FileUtils) from the command line. In theory this gives you an operating system–independent set of file manipulation commands, possibly useful when writing portable Makefiles.

See also: FileUtils (page 757)

- The available commands are as follows:

```
$ ruby -run -e cp – ‹options›* source dest
$ ruby -run -e ln – ‹options›* target linkname
$ ruby -run -e mv – ‹options›* source dest
$ ruby -run -e rm – ‹options›* file
$ ruby -run -e mkdir – ‹options›* dirs
$ ruby -run -e rmdir – ‹options›* dirs
$ ruby -run -e install – ‹options›* source dest
$ ruby -run -e chmod – ‹options›* octal_mode file
$ ruby -run -e touch – ‹options›* file
```

  Note the use of -- to tell the Ruby interpreter that options to the program follow.

  You can get a list of all available commands with this:

```
$ ruby -run -e help
```

  For help on a particular command, append the command's name:

```
$ ruby -run -e help mkdir
```

URI encapsulates the concept of a Uniform Resource Identifier (URI), a way of specifying some kind of (potentially networked) resource. URIs are a superset of URLs: URLs (such as the addresses of web pages) allow specification of addresses by location, and URIs also allow specification by name.

URIs consist of a scheme (such as http, mailto, ftp, and so on), followed by structured data identifying the resource within the scheme.

URI has factory methods that take a URI string and return a subclass of URI specific to the scheme. The library explicitly supports the ftp, http, https, ldap, and mailto schemes; others will be treated as generic URIs. The module also has convenience methods to escape and unescape URIs. The class Net::HTTP accepts URI objects where a URL parameter is expected.

See also: open-uri (page 781) Net::HTTP (page 773)

```ruby
require 'uri'

uri = URI.parse("http://pragprog.com:1234/mypage.cgi?q=ruby")
uri.class    # => URI::HTTP
uri.scheme   # => "http"
uri.host     # => "pragprog.com"
uri.port     # => 1234
uri.path     # => "/mypage.cgi"
uri.query    # => "q=ruby"

uri = URI.parse("mailto:ruby@pragprog.com?Subject=help&body=info")
uri.class    # => URI::MailTo
uri.scheme   # => "mailto"
uri.to       # => "ruby@pragprog.com"
uri.headers  # => [["Subject", "help"], ["body", "info"]]

uri = URI.parse("ftp://dave@anon.com:/pub/ruby;type=i")
uri.class    # => URI::FTP
uri.scheme   # => "ftp"
uri.host     # => "anon.com"
uri.port     # => 21
uri.path     # => "pub/ruby"
uri.typecode # => "i"
```

In Ruby, objects are not eligible for garbage collection if references still exist to them. Normally, this is a Good Thing—it would be disconcerting to have an object simply evaporate while you were using it. However, sometimes you may need more flexibility. For example, you might want to implement an in-memory cache of commonly used file contents. As you read more files, the cache grows. At some point, you may run low on memory. The garbage collector will be invoked, but the objects in the cache are all referenced by the cache data structures and so will not be deleted.

A weak reference behaves like any normal object reference with one important exception—the referenced object may be garbage collected, even while references to it exist. In the cache example, if the cached files were accessed using weak references, once memory runs low, they will be garbage collected, freeing memory for the rest of the application.

- Weak references introduce a slight complexity. Because the object referenced can be deleted by garbage collection at any time, code that accesses these objects must take care to ensure that the references are valid. Two techniques can be used. First, the code can reference the objects normally. Any attempt to reference an object that has been garbage collected will raise a WeakRef::RefError exception.

```ruby
require 'weakref'
# Generate lots of small strings. Hopefully the early ones will have
# been garbage collected...
refs = (1..10000).map {|i| WeakRef.new("#{i}") }
puts "Last element is #{refs.last}"
puts "First element is #{refs.first}"
```

produces:

```
Last element is 10000
prog.rb:6:in `<main>': Invalid Reference - probably recycled (WeakRef::RefError)
```

- Alternatively, use the WeakRef#weakref_alive? method to check that a reference is valid before using it. Garbage collection must be disabled during the test and subsequent reference to the object. In a single-threaded program, you could use something like this:

```ruby
ref = WeakRef.new(some_object)

# .. some time later

gc_was_disabled = GC.disable
if ref.weakref_alive?
  # do stuff with 'ref'
end
GC.enable unless gc_was_disabled
```

WEBrick

WEBrick is a pure-Ruby framework for implementing HTTP-based servers. The Ruby standard library includes WEBrick services that implement a standard web server (serving files and directory listings) and servlets supporting CGI, erb, file download, and the mounting of Ruby lambdas.

The Web programming chapter has more examples of WEBrick on page 286.

- The following code mounts two Ruby procs on a web server.

  Requests to http://localhost:2000/hello run one proc, and the other proc is invoked by requests to http://localhost:2000/bye.

```ruby
#!/usr/bin/ruby

require 'webrick'
include WEBrick

hello_proc = lambda do |req, resp|
  resp['Content-Type'] = "text/html"
  resp.body = %{
      <html><body>
        Hello. You're calling from a #{req['User-Agent']}
       <p>
        I see parameters: #{req.query.keys.join(', ')}
      </body></html>
  }
end

bye_proc = lambda do |req, resp|
  resp['Content-Type'] = "text/html"
  resp.body = %{
      <html><body>
        <h3>Goodbye!</h3>
      </body></html>
  }
end


hello =  HTTPServlet::ProcHandler.new(hello_proc)
bye   =  HTTPServlet::ProcHandler.new(bye_proc)

s = HTTPServer.new(:Port => 2000)
s.mount("/hello", hello)
s.mount("/bye",    bye)

trap("INT"){ s.shutdown }
s.start
```

This is an interface to Windows automation, allowing Ruby code to interact with Windows applications. The Ruby interface to Windows is discussed in more detail in Chapter 21, *Ruby and Microsoft Windows*, on page 289.

Only if: Windows

- Opens Internet Explorer and asks it to display our home page:

```
require 'win32ole'

ie = WIN32OLE.new('InternetExplorer.Application')
ie.visible = true
ie.navigate("http://www.pragprog.com")
```

- Creates a new chart in Microsoft Excel and then rotates it. This code is one of the samples that comes with the library.

```
require 'win32ole'

#    -4100 is the value for the Excel constant xl3DColumn.
ChartTypeVal = -4100;

#    Creates OLE object to Excel
#excel = WIN32OLE.new("excel.application.5")
excel = WIN32OLE.new("excel.application")

# Create and rotate the chart

excel.visible = TRUE;
excel.Workbooks.Add();
excel.Range("a1").value = 3;
excel.Range("a2").value = 2;
excel.Range("a3").value = 1;
excel.Range("a1:a3").Select();
excelchart = excel.Charts.Add();
excelchart.type = ChartTypeVal;

i = 30
i.step(180, 10) do |rot|
#    excelchart['Rotation'] = rot;
    excelchart.rotation=rot;
end
# Done, bye

excel.ActiveWorkbook.Close(0);
excel.Quit();
```

XMLRPC allows clients to invoke methods on networked servers using the XML-RPC protocol. Communications take place over HTTP. The server may run in the context of a web server, in which case ports 80 or 443 (for SSL) will typically be used. The server may also be run stand-alone. The Ruby XML-RPC server implementation supports operation as a CGI script, as a mod_ruby script, as a WEBrick handler, and as a stand-alone server. Basic authentication is supported, and clients can communicate with servers via proxies. Servers may throw FaultException errors—these generate the corresponding exception on the client (or optionally may be flagged as a status return to the call).

See also: dRuby (page 748) WEBrick (page 824)

- The following simple server accepts a temperature in Celsius and converts it to Fahrenheit. It runs within the context of the WEBrick web server.

sl_xmlrpc/xmlserver.rb
```ruby
require 'webrick'
require 'xmlrpc/server'
xml_servlet = XMLRPC::WEBrickServlet.new
xml_servlet.add_handler("convert_celcius") do |celcius|
  celcius*1.8 + 32
end
xml_servlet.add_multicall # Add support for multicall
server = WEBrick::HTTPServer.new(:Port => 2000)
server.mount("/RPC2", xml_servlet)
trap("INT"){ server.shutdown }
server.start
```

- This client makes calls to the temperature conversion server. Note that in the output we show both the server's logging and the client program's output.

```ruby
require 'xmlrpc/client'
server = XMLRPC::Client.new("localhost", "/RPC2", 2000)
puts server.call("convert_celcius", 0)
puts server.call("convert_celcius", 100)
puts server.multicall(['convert_celcius', -10], ['convert_celcius', 200])
```

produces:
```
[2013-05-27 12:33:44] INFO  WEBrick 1.3.1
[2013-05-27 12:33:44] INFO  ruby 2.0.0 (2013-02-24) [x86_64-darwin12.2.0]
[2013-05-27 12:33:44] INFO  WEBrick::HTTPServer#start: pid=24895 port=2000
localhost - - [27/May/2013:12:33:45 CDT] "POST /RPC2 HTTP/1.1" 200 124
- -> /RPC2
localhost - - [27/May/2013:12:33:45 CDT] "POST /RPC2 HTTP/1.1" 200 125
- -> /RPC2
localhost - - [27/May/2013:12:33:45 CDT] "POST /RPC2 HTTP/1.1" 200 290
- -> /RPC2
32.0
212.0
14.0
392.0
```

The YAML library (also described in the tutorial on page 405) serializes and deserializes Ruby object trees to and from an external, readable, plain-text format. YAML can be used as a portable object marshaling scheme, allowing objects to be passed in plain text between separate Ruby processes. In some cases, objects may also be exchanged between Ruby programs and programs in other languages that also have YAML support. While Ruby 1.9.2 can use libyaml if it is available, Ruby 2.0 makes it a requirement, and bundles it with the interpreter.

See also: json (page 766)

New in 2.0

- YAML can be used to store an object tree in a flat file:

```ruby
require 'yaml'
tree = { name: 'ruby',
         uses: [ 'scripting', 'web', 'testing', 'etc' ]
       }

File.open("tree.yml", "w") {|f| YAML.dump(tree, f)}
```

- Once stored, it can be read by another program:

```ruby
require 'yaml'
tree = YAML.load_file("tree.yml")
tree[:uses][1]           # => "web"
```

- The YAML format is also a convenient way to store configuration information for programs. Because it is readable, it can be maintained by hand using a normal editor and then read as objects by programs. For example, a configuration file may contain the following:

sl_yaml/config.yml
```
---
username: dave
prefs:
  background: dark
  foreground: cyan
  timeout: 30
```

We can use this in a program:

```ruby
require 'yaml'

config = YAML.load_file("code/sl_yaml/config.yml")
config["username"]               # => "dave"
config["prefs"]["timeout"] * 10 # => 300
```

Only if: zlib library
available

The Zlib module is home to a number of classes for compressing and decompressing streams and for working with gzip-format compressed files. They also calculate zip checksums.

• Compresses /etc/passwd as a gzip file and then reads the result back:

```ruby
require 'zlib'

# These methods can take a filename
Zlib::GzipWriter.open("passwd.gz") do |gz|
  gz.write(File.read("/etc/passwd"))
end

system("ls -l /etc/passwd passwd.gz")
puts

# or a stream
File.open("passwd.gz") do |f|
  gzip = Zlib::GzipReader.new(f)
  data = gzip.read.split(/\n/)
  puts data[15,3]
end
```

produces:

```
-rw-r--r--  1 root   wheel  5086 Jul 20  2011 /etc/passwd
-rw-rw-r--  1 dave   staff  1621 May 27 12:33 passwd.gz

_installassistant:*:25:25:Install Assistant:/var/empty:/usr/bin/false
_lp:*:26:26:Printing Services:/var/spool/cups:/usr/bin/false
_postfix:*:27:27:Postfix Mail Server:/var/spool/postfix:/usr/bin/false
```

• Compresses data sent between two processes:

```ruby
require 'zlib'

rd, wr = IO.pipe

if fork
  rd.close
  zipper = Zlib::Deflate.new
  zipper << "This is a string "
  data = zipper.deflate("to compress", Zlib::FINISH)
  wr.write(data)
  wr.close
  Process.wait
else
  wr.close
  text = Zlib.inflate(rd.read)
  puts "We got: #{text}"
end
```

produces:

```
We got: This is a string to compress
```

Support

One of the major features of open source projects is the technical support. Articles in the media often criticize open source efforts for not having the same tech support that a commercial product has. And boy is that a good thing! Instead of dialing up some overworked and understaffed help desk and being treated to music for an hour or so *without* ever getting the answer you need, we have a better solution: the Ruby community. The author of Ruby, the authors of this book, and many other Ruby users are willing and able to lend you a hand, should you need it.

The syntax of Ruby remains fairly stable, but as with all evolving software, new features are added every now and again. As a result, both printed books and the online documentation can fall behind. All software has bugs, and Ruby is no exception. There aren't many, but they do crop up.

If you experience a problem with Ruby, feel free to ask in the mailing lists. Generally you'll get timely answers from knowledgeable folks. However, as with all large communities, you may also find people with a less-than-perfect understanding of Ruby responding. As with all things on the Internet, use your judgment.

Before posting, do the right thing and search the Web for similar questions—by now most common questions have already been answered in the mailing lists or on someone's blog. But if you can't find the answer you need, ask, and a correct answer will usually show up with remarkable speed and precision.

A1.1 Web Sites

Because the Web changes too fast, we've kept this list short. Visit one of the sites here, and you'll find a wealth of links to other online Ruby resources.

The official Ruby home page is http://www.ruby-lang.org.

You'll find many open source Ruby projects on Github (http://github.com) and RubyForge (http://www.rubyforge.org). http://rubygems.org is the official RubyGems repository.[1] (GitHub used to be another source of RubyGems—this is no longer the case.)

http://www.ruby-doc.org is a portal to various sources of Ruby documentation. Much of it comes from previous editions of this book.

---

1. In March 2010, RubyGems.org, GemCutter.org, and RubyForge.org became a single, unified server of gems.

While you're surfing, drop in on http://www.pragprog.com and see what we're up to.

A1.2 Usenet Newsgroup

Ruby has its own newsgroup, comp.lang.ruby. Traffic on this group is archived and mirrored to the ruby-talk mailing list. It can be read via Google Groups.

A1.3 Mailing Lists

You'll find many mailing lists talking about Ruby. The first three here are in English, and the remainder are mostly Japanese but with some English-language posts.

ruby-talk@ruby-lang.org	English-language discussion of Ruby (mirrored to comp.lang.ruby)
ruby-doc@ruby-lang.org	Documentation standards and tools
ruby-core@ruby-lang.org	English discussion of core implementation topics
ruby-list@ruby-lang.org	Japanese language discussion of Ruby
ruby-dev@ruby-lang.org	List for Ruby developers
ruby-ext@ruby-lang.org	List for people writing extensions for or with Ruby
ruby-math@ruby-lang.org	Ruby in mathematics

See the "Mailing Lists" topic under http://www.ruby-lang.org/ for details on joining a list.

The mailing lists are archived and can be searched here: http://blade.nagaokaut.ac.jp/ruby/ruby-talk/index.shtml or here: http://www.ruby-talk.org

A1.4 Bug Reporting

If you think you've spotted a bug in Ruby, you may want to browse the Ruby Issue Tracking system at http://redmine.ruby-lang.org/. You may also want to check to see whether a new version of Ruby is available—perhaps the bug you've found has already been fixed.

Before submitting a bug, it might be a good idea to post a question about it to the ruby-talk mailing list. Often, one person's bug is another person's language feature. Also, Ruby can be complicated, and sometimes its behavior can be subtle.

Once you've decided you have a genuine bug, submit a bug report via the Ruby Issue Tracking site mentioned previosuly. When reporting a suspected bug, it's a good idea to include the output of running ruby -v along with any problematic source code. People will also need to know the operating system you're running. If you compiled your own version of Ruby, it may be a good idea to attach your rbconfig.rb file as well.

If you have a problem using irb, be aware of its limitations (see the reference section on page 253. See what happens using just Ruby itself.

Bibliography

[Fri97]   Jeffrey E. F. Friedl. *Mastering Regular Expressions*. O'Reilly & Associates, Inc., Sebastopol, CA, 1997.

[GHJV95]   Erich Gamma, Richard Helm, Ralph Johnson, and John Vlissides. *Design Patterns: Elements of Reusable Object-Oriented Software*. Addison-Wesley, Reading, MA, 1995.

[Mey97]   Bertrand Meyer. *Object-Oriented Software Construction*. Prentice Hall, Englewood Cliffs, NJ, Second, 1997.

Index

J

K

L

U

Put Fun in Functional Programming

Looking for functional programming that's closer to Ruby, but with a battle-proven environment that's unrivaled for massive scalability, concurrency, distribution and fault tolerance? Maybe the time is right for the Next Big Thing. Maybe it's *Elixir*, running on the Erlang VM.

You want to explore functional programming, but are put off by the academic feel (tell me about monads just one more time). You know you need concurrent applications, but also know these are almost impossible to get right. Meet Elixir, a functional, concurrent language built on the rock-solid Erlang VM. Elixir's pragmatic syntax and built-in support for metaprogramming will make you productive and keep you interested for the long haul. This book is *the* introduction to Elixir for experienced programmers.

Maybe you need something that's closer to Ruby, but with a battle-proven environment that's unrivaled for massive scalability, concurrency, distribution, and fault tolerance. Maybe the time is right for the Next Big Thing. Maybe it's *Elixir*.

Check out the short video on Elixir at youtu.be/hht9s6nAAx8, or the 30 minute, more detailed video at youtu.be/a-off4Vznjs and enjoy.

Dave Thomas
(240 pages) ISBN: 9781937785581. $36
http://pragprog.com/book/elixir

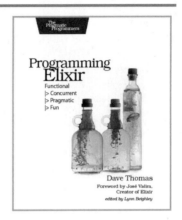

A multi-user game, web site, cloud application, or networked database can have thousands of users all interacting at the same time. You need a powerful, industrial-strength tool to handle the really hard problems inherent in parallel, concurrent environments. You need Erlang. In this second edition of the best-selling *Programming Erlang*, you'll learn how to write parallel programs that scale effortlessly on multicore systems.

Joe Armstrong
(510 pages) ISBN: 9781937785536. $42
http://pragprog.com/book/jaerlang2

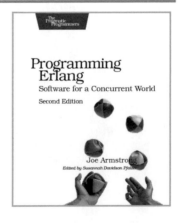